# DEVELOPMENTAL PSYCHOLOGY

## A READER

**Edited by**
**David Messer**
Professor of Developmental Psychology,
University of Hertfordshire

and

**Julie Dockrell**
Professor of Psychology, South Bank University

**ARNOLD**

A member of the Hodder Headline Group
LONDON • NEW YORK • SYDNEY • AUCKLAND

First published in Great Britain in 1998 by
Arnold, a member of the Hodder Headline Group,
338 Euston Road, London NW1 3BH

**http://www.arnoldpublishers.com**

Co-published in the United States of America by
Oxford University Press Inc.,
198 Madison Avenue, New York, NY10016

The advice and information in this book are believed to be true and accurate at the date of
going to press, but neither the editors nor the publisher can accept any legal responsibility or liability for any errors or omissions.

*British Library Cataloguing in Publication Data*
A catalogue entry for this book is available from the British Library

*Library of Congress Cataloging-in-Publication Data*
Developmental psychology: a reader/edited by David Messer and Julie Dockrell.
    p.       cm.
  Includes bibliographical references and index.
  1. Developmental psychology. I. Messer, David J., 1952–
  II. Dockrell, Julie.
BF713.D4644    1998      98–16494
155–dc21      CIP

ISBN 0 340 70562 0 (pb)
     0 340 70561 2 (hb)

1 2 3 4 5 6 7 8 9 10

Production Editor: Rada Radojicic
Production Controller: Helen Whitehorn

Typeset by J&L Composition Ltd, Filey, North Yorkshire
Printed and bound in Great Britain by MPG Books, Bodmin, Cornwall

# CONTENTS

# ACKNOWLEDGEMENTS

The editors and publishers would like to thank the following for permission to use copyright material in this book.

Ablex Publishing Corporation for Landsmann, L. T., 'Early Literacy Development: Evidence from Different Orthographic Systems', in M. Spoolders (ed.) *Literacy Acquisition* (1990); Academic Press for Geary, D., 'A componential analysis of early learning deficit in mathematics', *Journal of Experimental Child Psychology* 49, 363–83; and Markman, E. and Hutchinson, J. E., 'Children's sensitivity to constraints on word meaning: taxonomic versus thematic relations', *Cognitive Psychology* 16, 1–27. © 1984 Academic Press, Inc.; the American Psychological Association for Brice Heath, S., 'Oral and Literate Traditions Among Black Americans Living in Poverty', *American Psychologist* Volume 44 (2) 367–373 (1989). © 1996 by the American Psychological Association. Reprinted with permission; and Rogoff, B. and Morelli, G., 'Perspectives on children's development from cultural psychology', *American Psychologist* 44, 343–48. Copyright © 1989 by the American Psychological Association. Reprinted with permission; Blackwell Publishers Ltd for McShane, J., 'The origins of representations' from *Cognitive Development*; Oakhill, J. and Yuill, N., 'Learning to read: psychology in the classroom', in K. Furnell and M. Stuart (1995); and Schaffer, H. R., 'When do children first form attachments to other people?' from *Making Decisions About Children* (2nd edition, 1998); Cambridge University Press for Arnett, J. 'The Young and the Reckless: Adolescent Reckless Behaviour', *Current Directions in Psychological Science* 4 (3) (1995), 67–71. © 1995 American Psychological Society; Berndt, T. J., 'Friendship and Friends' Influence in Adolescence', *Current Directions in Psychological Science* 1 (3): 156–159 (1992). © 1992 American Psychological Society; Dunn, J., 'Siblings and Development', *Current Directions in Psychological Science* 1 (1) (1992), 6–9. © 1992 American Psychological Society; Johnson, M., 'Imprinting and the Development of face recognition', *Current Directions in Psychological Science* 1 (2): 52–55 (1992). © 1992 American Psychological Society; Karmiloff-Smith, A., 'A Precis of Beyond Modularity: A developmental perspective on cognitive science', *Behavioral and Brain Sciences* 17: 693–745 (1994). © 1994 Cambridge University Press; Marcus, G. F., 'Why do children say "breaked"?'. *Current Directions in Psychological Science* 5 (3), 81–85. © 1996 American Psychological Society; McClintock, M. K. and Gilbert, H., 'Rethinking Puberty: the development of sexual attraction', *Current Directions in Psychological Science*

5 (6): 178–183 (1996). © 1996 American Psychological Society; and Melhuish, E., 'Behaviour Measures. A Measure of Love? An Overview of the Assessment of Attachment', *Association of Child Psychology and Psychiatry Review and Newsletter* 15 (6), 269–275 (1993). © 1993 Association for Child Psychology and Psychiatry; Carfax Publishing Ltd for Hughes, M. and Donaldson, M. (1979) 'The use of hiding games for studying the coordination of viewpoints', *Educational Review* Volume 31; and Wood, D. and Wood, H., 'Vygotsky, tutoring and learning', *Oxford Review of Education* Volume 22 (1): 5–16 (1996); Elsevier Science B. V. for Frith, U. and Happe, F. (1994) 'Autism: Beyond "Theory of Mind"', *Cognition*, Volume 50; European Journal of Psychology of Education for Gathercole, S. and Baddeley, A. D., 'Phonological working memory: a critical building block for reading development and vocabulary acquisition', *European Journal of Psychology* 8, 259–272, (1993); Lawrence Erlbaum Associates, Inc., for Joiner, R., Messer, D., Light, P. and Littleton, K., 'Peer presence and peer interaction in computer based problem solving: a brief report', *Cognition and Instruction* 13, 583–4 (1995); Macmillan Magazines Ltd for Bradley, L. and Bryant, P. E., 'Categorising sounds and learning to read – a casual connection'. Reprinted by permission from *Nature* Volume 301, pp 419–520. Copyright © 1983 Macmillan Magazines Ltd; Psychology Press for Skuse, D. 'Extreme deprivation in early childhood' in D. Bishop and K. Mogford (eds) *Language Development in Exceptional Circumstances* (1993). Reprinted with permission of Psychology Press; The Royal Society of Medicine Press Ltd for Farrington, D. P., 'Childhood origins of teenage antisocial behaviour and adult social dysfunction', *Journal of Royal Society of Medicine* 86, 13–17. © 1993 Journal of the Royal Society of Medicine; the Society for Research in Child Development for Tomasello, M. and Farrar, M. J., 'Joint Attention and Early Language', *Child Development* 57, 1454–1463 (1986). © Society for Research in Child Development, Inc.; and Walker, L. J., 'A Longitudinal Study of Moral Reasoning', *Child Development* 60, 157–166 (1989). © Society for Research in Child Development, Inc.

To the best of our knowledge all copyright holders of material reproduced in this book have been traced. Any rights not acknowledged here will be noted in subsequent printings if notice is given to the publisher.

We would like to thank our colleagues who suggested readings to us and Assimina Ralli for her support in collating the material.

# INTRODUCTION

## Using the reader

The aim of this chapter is to assist your study of child development and help you to make best use of this book. We do this in two ways. In the first place we outline the history of child development and consider the key questions that concern researchers in the field. These key questions should help structure the ways in which you consider the evidence and arguments presented in the subsequent readings. In the second place we provide guidelines for reading the articles and preparing your own study of the topic. The chapter concludes by outlining the structure of the book.

## Historical context

The aim of this reader is to provide a set of key theoretical and empirical articles which will be relevant to your studies. Developmental Psychology is a well established subject in Psychology and it has a long history which as we shall see can be traced back to the observations of children in the late 19th century and to even earlier work which involves case studies, philosophical musings and pronouncements about child rearing. Views of children have varied widely over the course of history. The Ancient Greeks and Romans acknowledged the importance of the childhood years, yet the status of children in these societies was atrocious. It has been argued that strong concern and affection for children, and a belief that childhood is an intrinsically valuable period, are associated with the rise of affluent households in the 16th and 17th century (Aries, 1962). It is important to realize that even today views of childhood will vary across cultures and political regimes.

Debate about the mechanisms of development began in earnest in the 17th century. At this point several very different views of development emerged. The famous English philosopher John Locke (1632–1704) saw children as a *tabula rasa*. [Tabula rasa is a Latin phrase meaning blank slate.] This blank slate was thought to be capable of developing in any direction depending on the environment that the child encountered. Locke argued that knowledge came to the child through experience and learning and so children were seen to be the products of their environment. In contrast the French philosopher Rousseau (1712–1778) saw children as inherently good and urged parents and educators to allow their natural tendencies to flower. In many ways the notions that we now hold about maturation can be traced back to some of Rousseau's ideas. He believed development went through a set of predictable stages which are guided by an innate timetable. Today all theories of learning assume some innate capabilities. The pivotal issue is what kind of processes or information is assumed to be innate. The innate learning mechanism for behaviourist theories involves a process of association. In Piaget's theory of development, processes such as accommodation and assimilation are regarded as innate (see Bremner, in press). More recently psychologists have used the term 'cognitive constraints' to refer to the inherited limits placed on cognitive processes. Effectively, a constraint means that we are programmed to prioritize certain types of information and not others, that is, the cognitive system makes certain types of information more salient and more likely to be processed or learnt. This can be put more technically as 'factors intrinsic to the learner which result in non-random selection among the logically possible characteristics of an informational pattern' (Keil, 1990: 137).

It was not until the second half of the 19th century that the scientific study of child development began [see McShane, 1991:1–11]. The American G. Stanley Hall (1844–1924) is credited with founding the field of developmental psychology. He introduced a systematic and scientific approach to the study of children. Although neither his research nor his theories have stood the test of time, his lasting contribution was his promotion of child development as a field of scientific endeavour. At the same time in Europe, Binet (1857–1911) was pioneering experimental studies with children. These studies culminated in the development of the first intelligence test for children (Binet and Simon, 1905). This early test was designed to meet the needs of educational selection. The aim was to identify those children who might not benefit from public education; the hope was that an unbiased evaluation of scholastic aptitude could be made. Similar tests to that developed by Binet are used by child psychologists today.

In addition to the influence provided by these specific individuals, child development has been influenced by ideas from other fields. Consequently, it is useful to outline briefly the ways in which different beliefs about human nature have impinged on the way we study and understand children today.

*Evolutionary thinking*: this emphasizes the way change occurs to meet the demands of environment. Biological factors are seen as fundamentally important and the model implies that many of the present day behaviours of humans had their origins a long time ago. Ethological approaches to the study of child development originate from this frame of thought and were evident very early in the history of developmental psychology. Recently evolutionary psychology has played a major role in an understanding of the origins and nature of human intelligence (Cosmides and Tooby, 1994; Baron-Cohen, 1991).

*Psychoanalysis*: Freud (1856–1939) played a pivotal position in forcing psychologists to consider the unconscious and the critical role that early experience may play in later development. Freud's model was developed from his clinical work with adults, rather than working with children directly. The central theme of Freudian developmental theory is that we are born with sexual energy (libido). During development different areas are the focus of this physical pleasure. Four stages were identified – oral, anal, phallic and latent, the first three reflecting the loci of this pleasure. Freud concluded that infants and young children were sexual beings and the way they were allowed to express these feelings was at the heart of their emotional development. Children's experiences at each of these stages was believed to strongly affect their later development. However, many psychologists have felt that there is insufficient empirical evidence to support this model, and some work has not supported predictions derived from the theory (Caldwell, 1964).

*Behaviourism* [sometimes referred to as learning theory]: John B. Watson (1878–1958) was the founding father of behaviourism. The major focus of study for behaviourists is how the individual behaves rather than the way the individual thinks or feels. Attempts to explain behaviour in terms of mental processes were replaced by explanations (in terms of laws of learning) that concentrated exclusively on the functional relations between environmental stimuli and behavioural responses. (To understand behavioural and learning accounts of child development you must understand the various types of conditioning that operate on the child such as respondent conditioning, operant conditioning and discrimination learning.) The major influence of this approach is thus on observable behaviour and this led to a whole structuring of the child's world to influence subsequent behaviour. Watson, for example, was convinced that the conditioning methods of behaviourism could be applied successfully to induce children's learning. One of the most famous examples of this approach is the case of little Albert. To test the validity of their ideas Watson and Rayner (1920) attempted to condition a fear response in Albert, a 9-month-old baby, to a previously neutral stimulus – a white rat. It is unclear now how successful the experiment was (Harris, 1979) but it became a focal point for the claim by Watson and others that conditioning was the key to understanding development.

*Cognitive Psychology*: The rise of cognitive psychology in the 1950s produced a range of impressive data which enhanced our understanding of the workings of the adult mind. To some extent this could be seen as a reaction to the behavourist approach which avoided discussion of thoughts or states which could not be directly observed. There has been particular emphasis on memory processes and more recently on an analogy between information processing by humans and by computers. Developmentalists drew on adult studies of the human mind to help structure the way they studied children's thought processes. Basically two approaches to studying the mind can be derived from these early studies. The first approach emphasizes processing. The second approach focused on information.

*Genetic and Biological Influences*: Interest in cognitive psychology was also accompanied in the 1950s and 1960s by a reawakening of interest in the way that biological processes influence behaviour. Many investigations have been conducted to show that the newborn is not be a *tabula rasa*, but has reflex behaviours, attentional preferences, and is adapted for the type of care that parents provide. The interest in genetic and biological processes has continued (Pike and Plomin, in press) and recently has been stimulated by the development of DNA mapping and by new techniques which allow the mapping of activity in the brain.

*Systems theory*: Many of the influences discussed above view the child in isolation from the wider context in which she develops. From a systemic view children are understood as part of a wider social network. This needs to be considered when investigating development of their cognitive skills and social behaviour. From this viewpoint the child's development is influenced very much by what happens around her. Bronfenbrenner (1979) has tried to specify more precisely what the nature of environmental influences might be. In Bronfenbrenner's theory of the ecology of human development the environment is envisioned as a series of nested structures that extend beyond the immediate setting. Each level is thought greatly to affect the child – (see Dockrell, 1997 as an example).

## The key development questions – what and how

Developmental Psychology has grown dramatically in size over the last 20 or 30 years. It is usual for developmental psychology to form an important and popular component of Psychology degrees and it is central to other courses in other areas such as linguistics, social work and courses for health professionals. However, the expansion of knowledge has had the consequence that it would be perfectly possible to have a whole degree devoted to this subject. It has been, therefore, important for us to select articles that either describe key developmental processes or address key developmental questions.

Child development is a field of study which focuses on the changes that occur from birth to adolescence. It attempts in the first instance to identify a child's repertoire of behaviours at a particular age. Secondly, the discipline aims to identify the factors that influence particular development processes, that is to specify the way that development occurs. Consider the case of learning to talk. Studying children's language has allowed us to identify a series of stages children progress through in learning a language – infants babble, toddlers use single words, then words are combined two at a time and finally children use complex sentences which reflect the rules of their language. Thus, we can describe the patterns of development. It is less clear what factors determine this pattern of development. Is it the way the child's caretaker talks? Is it the child's genetic endowment?

The quest to identify the mechanism(s) of development is long standing. Studies investigating child language can be traced back to

Ancient Egypt (Psamtik I). These early isolation studies aimed to discover whether infants have a natural tendency to create language and if so what sort of language. While the authenticity and veracity of these early experiments is suspect (Campbell and Grieve, 1982) the central concern with what causes development remains in present day investigations. The role of nature or nurture underlies many developmental questions. That is, to what extent is development determined by the child's genetic endowment (nature) or the environment (nurture)? Of course, developmental questions rarely result in simple answers which fit neatly into this dichotomy. Development is often a complex interplay between what the child brings to the process and the context in which development occurs. Elman et al. (1996) argue that the view of development as an interactive process is indeed the correct one.

The task of identifying a behaviour and monitoring its changes over time can be a very complex problem. Three important issues have to be considered

- what behaviour is being studied?
- the way the behaviour changes over time
- the extent to which there is continuity between the child's early behaviours and skills in relation to later ones

These are important topics so we will spend a little time exploring their meaning.

## What behaviour?

Some of you may find this a surprising question. Obviously, you may think, if we are interested in moral development, we study children's morals or if we are interested in their thinking we study thought processes. Even if we ignore the fact that young children cannot talk to us about complex issues (and of course infants cannot talk at all) a moment's reflection will highlight some difficulties involved in assessing children's beliefs and knowledge. When you are inferring the presence or absence of a set of beliefs or behaviours you must be sure you are tapping the right phenomenon. The question we must always ask ourselves is 'are we measuring what we are intending to measure'?

As an example let us consider one of the most frequently used methods of assessing children's knowledge, that is asking them questions. Normally we assume that children's responses will be based on what they know or believe. Children may be correct, incorrect or say they 'don't know'. Whichever way they respond we assume we are assessing their true abilities. Hughes and Grieve (1983) have shown that this is not always the case. In their study they asked children bizarre questions such as 'Is milk bigger than water?'. As presented the questions were meaningless. Children had no way of answering these questions without clarification of meaning or the provision of further information. However, children invariably answered these questions without asking for more information. What this study shows is that children try to make sense of the situations presented to them. Developmentalists cannot assume that the children's responses simply reflect their knowledge about the problems that are the primary interest of the investigation.

As you read the papers in this collection you should consider how the children make sense of the tasks that are presented to them.

## Changes over time?

It is a truism to say that children develop. The question for developmentalists is to find the best way of describing the changes that happen over time. A distinction that is often drawn in developmental work is between quantitative and qualitative changes. Quantitative changes occur when the older child has more of a given skill, characteristic or ability than a younger child. For example, the numbers of digits that a child can repeat back (digit span) increases incrementally as they get older (Case, Kurland, and Goldberg, 1982). On the other hand children at different stages of development may have unique ways of thinking or feeling. Stages are seen as qualitative shifts in the way the child understands or processes information. However, many argue that the developmental picture is unlikely to be so neat. Large gaps between observational periods may provide data which appears stage like in transition whereas intensive local observation may appear quite different (cf. Siegler, 1988).

## Continuity of behaviour through the lifespan

How much continuity is there between childhood and adulthood? This again is not a straightforward question and there are no ways of simply measuring continuity. Behaviours that reflect a certain tendency in childhood may not occur in adults, e.g. temper tantrums or thumb sucking. Alternatively, particular states or emotions may be manifested in different ways across the lifespan. Children who are anxious may manifest this anxiety in completely different ways from adults who are anxious. There has, for example, been much concern to identify measures of cognition which predict (suggest) continuity throughout development. Of course if continuity in information processing from infancy could be identified it would provide an important 'window on the nature and underpinnings of mature cognitive function' (Columbo, 1993: 3).

The discovery of continuity is an issue about which developmental psychologists have different feelings. Some seem to suggest that the discovery of continuity gives justification for the study of development as it can answer questions about what behaviours or characteristics are related across time (e.g. Sigman and Bornstein, 1986). Such an approach carries with it the assumption that despite the changes across ages some capacities are related to earlier ones. Other developmentalists stress the unpredictability of development. This fits in with a view that we do change and that our development is not predetermined by earlier experiences (Clarke and Clarke, in press).

**Using the reader and reading the chapters**

The aim of this reader is to provide in one place a set of articles which are relevant to the study of Developmental Psychology. Some of these articles will be ones that are discussed on your course – these have an obvious relevance. Others may not be mentioned by your lecturer, but still may be relevant. An increasingly common complaint from both lecturers and external examiners is that exam essays do not show enough evidence of reading beyond the core references, and it also seems to be true that examiners suggest that more credit is given for examples of critical reading beyond the core references. Thus, there are good reasons to read the articles even if they do not appear on a course list.

As a discipline Child Development focuses on specific questions [the what and the how] yet it covers a wide range of topics. The vast number of publications in Developmental Psychology has meant that there are very many suitable publications which could be included in this volume. An illustration of this range can be given from a recent CD rom search on Psychological Abstracts using the keywords, psychology, children and 1997, which produced over 2000 references for this single year! To try and deal with this 'excess of riches' we have aimed to provide a balance between papers which are classics in the field and more recent publications which already have had an impact and which we suspect will continue to increase in importance. We have also tried to achieve a balance between theoretical, empirical and review papers. Examples of all three types are included. A balance has also been attempted between the many different subtopics in Developmental Psychology. It is probably true to say that in the past the amount of research on children of different ages declined in quantity as age of the sample increased; this probably reflected a fascination with infancy as the beginning of life and the beginning of psychological processes. However, this seems to be changing with there being a growing interest in developmental processes in school aged children and in adolescents. The large range of subtopics makes it a challenging task to select a set of reasonably representative papers. In trying to do this we have taken account of the type of research that is the current focus of interest together with a consideration of the topics which are typically covered in undergraduate psychology degrees. Regretfully we have decided to restrict the coverage to work on infants, children and adolescents.

When reading the articles we have chosen it is important to bear in mind the following issues.

*Terminology*

Disciplines often use terms in very specialized ways. Even words that we use in day to day conversation can have special meanings. The study of Child Development is no exception. As an example consider the term 'stage'. In child development it has a specialized meaning – specifically 'A developmental period, usually part of a regular sequence'.

As you read the chapters make sure you are clear about the terms' intended meanings. You can find specialists' terms defined in a dictionary of psychology and you can always use an encyclopaedia of psychology if you want further information on certain topics.

## Style and general issues

Academic writing is formal. There is a set style for referencing the work of researchers. This is detailed in the American Psychological Association manual. In general you should use your own wording to answer questions and explain concepts. If you include short extracts from another writer's work you must say where it originates otherwise it is plagiarism. If you use more than a few lines you should reference page numbers as well as the source you are citing, e.g. 'Philosophers and scientists, as well as parents of course, have been pondering the roots of infant love for centuries' (Sylva and Lunt, 1982: 27).

Academic writing is nonsexist and professional. Generally children should be referred to as a generic group unless you have something special to say about boys or girls. You will find that some studies in child development refer to the individuals taking part in the studies as subjects. Recently psychologists have moved away from the use of the term 'subjects' for reporting results of studies involving humans. The preferred term is 'participants'. There is no scientific difference between these terms, rather it reflects a growing concern for appropriate use of language and an appreciation of ethical dilemmas in research.

Whenever we involve humans and animals in our attempts to answer scientific questions ethical questions arise. Guidelines to protect the participants of developmental work have been developed by the American Psychological Association and the British Psychological Association. The issue of Ethics and Child Research is addressed in Harris (1993: 20)

## Advice on using the reader

The following provides a set of tips which we hope will help you make the most of the chapters in the reader. These tips reflect things that most of us do when reading an article for the first time. As with many aspects of learning and education there is no right or wrong way to go about this process, and every individual needs to consider what aspects of our recommendations will suit them best. Consequently, we hope to provide a useful set of suggestions rather than a prescription for action. There are three key stages which will help you. Firstly, plan what you want to do. Monitor your reading as you proceed and finally self-evaluate – have you achieved what you planned?

## Your aims

One of the first things to do before reading an article is to ask yourself the question, 'Why am I going to read this?'. There are many possible answers – the article may be a core reference for the course, you may need to write an essay, you may want to gain a better understanding of a topic, you may not understand something or you may just be interested in the subject matter. The important point is that whatever the reasons for reading the chapter it is useful to consider what are your aims and how best to achieve them. For example, if you are reading a core reference will it be useful to take notes for revision, but will you need to make notes if you are writing an essay, do you need to think about the way the chapter related to your course material, or are you happy simply to read the material and let the knowledge sit relatively unanalysed in your mind?

Our message is that the more you structure reading and any associated note taking, and the more effort that you give to integrating the content of the chapter with your other knowledge, then the more you will achieve from the reading. Bear in mind that achieving good marks in assessments involves more than knowing the content of articles. It is equally if not more important to understand why an article is important, what message it provides and how it is positioned in relation to other findings and theories. Some students find it useful to work in pairs where both of you read the article and then discuss it together. Learning becomes a collaborative exercise. Remember always to write down the source of your notes. It is very easy to forget where the information comes from.

### The context of the article

Having thought about what you want to achieve by reading an article, it is then very useful to try to work out the author's purpose in writing the article and why it is considered important. To try to deal with such issues we would recommend that before starting to read a chapter you first read the summary we provide at the start of each section of the book. This will give a context for the article and explain why we think it is an important one for you to read. It may also be helpful to look at the section on the key developmental questions and consider how the article you are reading addresses these issues.

### Date of publication

The date of publication and the type of publication provide you with useful clues. The date of publication is important for at least two reasons. One reason is the convention that essays or reports in Psychology, like any academic work, need to contain pointers to the source of particular claims. Providing the name of the author together with the date of publication is helpful as it indicates which article, out of a number of possibilities, you are discussing. It is usually considered essential for such information to be included in course work. In exams expectations are not as high, but it would be very strange for a top level script not to contain some reference to authors' names and dates of publication. The date of publication is also important in indicating whether the ideas are still likely to be accepted. The older the work the more likely it is that there have been challenges to the views expressed in the article.

## The type of publication

The source of the publication can tell you something about the type of article that you are reading. Articles published in Journals usually (but not always) have the main purpose of reporting findings. This enables investigators to provide information about their research to a wider audience, and for them to have some sort of stamp of approval placed on their work. Most Journal articles are reviewed by other investigators who are knowledgeable about the field of the research. The reviewers make recommendations to Journal editors about whether the article is worthy of publication in the Journal. It should be recognized that the process of reviewing is an imperfect one. Sometimes there are defects in Journal articles which the reviewers do not spot, and authors often argue that the strengths of articles which are rejected by the Journal are not appreciated (some Journals will reject around three-quarters of the manuscripts submitted to them). In the majority of cases, to minimize bias, the reviewers are not told the identity of the author. However, in many cases the reviewers can work this out from the content of the article and the way authors tend often to cite their own work!

Not all Journals are devoted solely to the reporting of research investigation. There are some Journals which only include review articles (e.g. Psychological Review, Developmental Review) and other Journals publish the occasional review article or make it a limited but regular feature of their format. There is generally considered to be a hierarchy in the prestige and requirements demanded by Journals. As a result, articles published in some Journals generally are accorded more respect, and perhaps are read by more people than articles published in less prestigious Journals.

Chapters in edited books often are written to provide a summary of a series of experiments, or a review of a particular topic. The placing of a number of contributions on the same theme in an edited book can increase the impact of the chapters, and they can be as well known as Journal articles. Articles published in edited books usually do not go through the same process of independent review. It is the responsibility of the editor to provide feedback to the author and in most cases the editor will also have asked the author to contribute to the book. Because of this chapters from edited books are sometimes criticized for not reaching as exacting standards as Journal publications. However, it can be the case that without the constraints of meeting the criticism of independent reviewers authors may be more innovative and speculative in their chapter of an edited book.

## Getting an overview

The next most obvious step is to try to obtain a better idea of what is the main message to be taken away from the article. There are a variety of ways of achieving this, one of which is to read through the summary, if one is provided, at the beginning of the article (not all of the articles have an abstract in this reader). Another way is to read the final discussion section, while a third possibility is to skim the whole article and then re-read it more carefully. Depending on your reasons for reading the article, it would be sensible to use one or even all of these techniques to get an overview of the important points that need to be carefully thought through with a more careful reading.

## *The structure of articles*

Most contributions to the book begin with an introduction which provides the background to the research or theory being presented by the author(s) and gives reasons for why we should be interested in the rest of the article. These sections can be very useful, particularly in recent publications. The review of previous work invariably gives a good summary of previous findings and relevant theories. This can be used to supplement your lecture notes – it may provide a different perspective from that given by your lecturer, and there may be new references which are worth reading. In older publications it is important to bear in mind that the review is likely to be out of date, with the more recent and subsequent work not being cited. For this reason there may be less of a need to read in detail this part of such articles. In Journal articles about research investigations, the introduction usually ends with a description of the aims or hypotheses. Paying attention to this can be of great help in trying to understand why the investigator conducted the study and what he or she was trying to achieve.

The introduction to Journal articles is usually followed by a methods section. The precise format of methods sections varies. Below we outline the key components of these sections. There is often a tendency to ignore methods sections or only skim read them. This can be a mistake if you are interested in being able to criticize the study. Ignoring the methods section can result in confusion about what the findings tell you. The results section is often treated by students in the same way as the methods section, skim read or ignored. Similar arguments, as before, can be advanced for reading the results section in detail. Often the subtleties and inconsistencies of the data are only evident here. The final section is the discussion. The discussion should provide you with the important implications of the study. Comparisons with previous findings are often discussed and theoretical arguments may be advanced. This is often a good place to get ideas for future research. Academic articles invariably end with a list of those publications which have been mentioned in the text. This is not necessarily a comprehensive list, but it can provide a useful source if more detailed reading of a topic is required.

## Writing your own research paper or essay

The reader provides examples of research articles and what might be considered 'essays'. For this reason it is worth looking at the Journal articles if you have to write up an experiment or project. There is a customary form in which research reports are written, with particular types of information being placed in particular sections of the report. This conventional organization is of great assistance to the reader. You will see this format being used in articles in psychological Journals. One thing to notice is that there are minor differences between Journals in the exact format that is used. Different Journals make different requirements for contributors, even to the extent of there being different ways of providing a reference list. You need to be aware of this and of the need to follow the requirements provided by your department.

We have already discussed the purpose of the main sections of a Journal 'report'. However, it is perhaps worth emphasizing a number of points: the title should be a concise statement of the main topic and should refer either to the major variables or to the theoretical issues that you have investigated. The abstract should be brief and should be fully intelligible without the reader having to refer to the body of the report. It should briefly mention: the problem under investigation; the major variables which were manipulated and measured; the main results obtained; the principal conclusions and main discussion points. Although the abstract is placed at the beginning of the report for the reader's convenience, it is often easier for the writer to produce the abstract after writing the rest of the report.

Make sure your introduction shows that you understand why the study has been conducted. Often you will be asked to run a study that someone else has designed. This can make for difficulties, but you should try to understand what are the reasons for running the study, particularly in relation to previous work that has been conducted. The introduction should mainly consist of a review of the background theories and findings which are directly relevant to the problem under investigation. It should usually proceed from *the general to the specific*, giving the aim of the study in a few paragraphs, showing its relationship to previous work in the area, the possible theoretical implications of the study and the rationale or logical link between the problem being investigated.

Give a clear account of the what was done (i.e. the methods). You should not assume that the person reading the report knows all the details of the investigation. Often this is quite difficult, as it is very easy to assume that the person reading the report has the same knowledge about the methods as you have. It is conventional and convenient to subdivide the Method section into the following four separately labelled subsections: Design, Participants, Materials and Procedure.

The Results section should only be used to describe, in a summary form, the collected data and the statistical treatment of these data. In the results section think about the order in which you present the findings. Try to fit them together in a logical sequence. When describing your data, choose the medium that presents them clearly and economically. It may be helpful to summarize your results and analyses in tables or graphs, but do not repeat the same data in several places and do not include tables with data that can be presented as well in a few sentences in the text. Graphs are generally easier to understand than tables. Tables are useful for large bodies of data when accuracy is important. Computer software gives the possibility of providing much more interesting ways of presenting data, but do not use it simply because it is available.

You should not attempt to discuss the implications of these data until the next section. Individual scores, raw data and details of your statistical calculations should also not usually be included in the Results, but should instead appear in the Appendix at the end of the Report. Qualitative introspective reports by the subjects during and after the study should be recorded as a matter of course, but should normally only be described in the Results or Discussion sections.

When reporting the results of statistical tests in the Results section, you can assume that your reader has a professional knowledge of statistics. Thus, you should only include the essential details of the tests unless you are told to the contrary it is better to leave out basic assumptions (such as rejecting the null hypothesis) and non-essential details. There are conventional styles for reporting the results of statistical tests. As a general guide, the figures (the obtained value of the statistic, the degrees of freedom and the significance level) are given in parentheses after a verbal statement as to whether or not the results were significant. For example: ' . . . This difference was analysed using the Wilcoxon test (one-tailed) and was found to be significant (T = 8, p < 0.025). '' . . . The association between these two variables was tested using the $2 \times 2$ chi-square test (two-tailed) and was found not to be insignificant ($\chi 2 = 2.96$, df = 1, p > 0.05)'.

In the discussion section you should interpret your results and evaluate the study. Thus, the Discussion section should contain:

i)   an interpretation of the results obtained, especially with respect to the theories and predictions which were outlined in the introduction. It is often useful to make sure that the introduction and discussion fit together,
ii)  a discussion of the individual results and introspective reports which support this interpretation,
iii) a discussion of any negative results and inconsistencies in data or introspective reports,
iv)  critical evaluation of the design or the procedure that was used,
v)   tentative suggestions for further research,
vi)  finally, a brief statement of the general conclusions which can be drawn from the study, especially with respect to the overall aim of the research which was outlined in the Introduction.

## Reviews

The reviews and theoretical papers in this reader also provide examples of the way that psychologists write 'essays'. Here the format is even more varied than that of Journal articles. However, you will probably notice that articles which are easier to understand and follow usually set up what the issues are and what the author is trying to do at the beginning of the publication. Often psychology essays call for the marshalling of information to support the argument that you are making, rather than large sections where you put forward your own opinion without supporting evidence from research. This is not to say that your opinion is not important, but you should develop your opinion in an argument which uses established findings and theories, rather than give arguments simply based on your own feelings and experience.

A useful technique for planning an essay is to look at the question and decide whether you want to agree with the answer, disagree, or answer 'don't know'. Such initial feelings can then be used to work out a structure to the essay. At the most simple (and often most effective) this could be a list of evidence which supports an argument, and a list which provides counter-evidence to the argument. The important part of the essay writing is to think how each study you discuss is relevant to answering the question. All too often, especially in exam answers, students will simply list back the content of their lectures, with little or no thought about whether the information is relevant to answering the question. The attitude sometimes seems to be 'I had better write about all I know' or 'well it might be relevant so to be on the safe side I'll include the study'. It must be admitted that such techniques will usually enable a person to achieve pass marks and or marks in the bottom half of the range. However, to achieve better marks a very different technique is needed. This requires thought about why the studies you quote are relevant to the answer you are giving. It might also require you to leave out material you have learnt or know, because it is not relevant to the argument.

In some cases you might genuinely be uncertain about what a question means, or whether a certain body of research is relevant to the answer. It is important to think through these uncertainties and make it clear, in as brief a statement as possible, why you have chosen to follow a particular line of reasoning. Such statements show the marker that you have thought about these issues, and provide a defence against criticism for including irrelevant material or excluding relevant material.

Attention should be paid to what you are being asked to do 'evaluate', 'compare', with the most difficult being 'consider' and 'discuss'. The last two titles make it relatively easy to obtain an average mark, but often it is more difficult to obtain a good or very good mark. The reason for this is that almost anything that is written is appropriate for 'discuss', but this in itself does not make a very good or inspired answer. It is usually worth considering whether you can make a 'discussion' question more interesting by setting a more specific question within the remit of the subject of your essay. For example, if you were asked to 'Discuss mother–infant attachment', it would be worth considering whether you could make the question more specific so that the discussion is of whether 'attachment predicts later characteristics', or 'what features predict secure attachment'. In this way it would be possible to provide a more focused discussion of the research evidence rather than an essay which could degenerate into a list of everything you know about attachment.

An issue which often worries students, is what to include. In the second or third year of your degree it usually is no longer necessary to have to assume that the marker of your essay (particularly exam essays) does not know anything about the subject, something that is sometimes told to students at lower levels. As a result, it is usually appropriate to leave out descriptions of well known procedures, unless this is a particular concern of the essay title. Consequently, it may not be necessary to describe Ainsworth's strange situtation (see Chapter IV), or the procedure used to assess children's theory of mind. Such descriptions can take up valuable space and time, and because they are relatively easy to learn and write about they do not usually impress the person marking the essay. It is also worth bearing in mind that although quoting the names and dates of research publications can seem like a requirement for mindless rote learning, the use of references reduces the need for a full description of the study (after all this is why authors of academic publications use the name and date of publications). Giving the name and the date of publication not only shows that you know who conducted the research and when, but it also allows you to assume that the marker also knows this study and as a result you can concentrate on the interpretation of the findings rather than a description of them.

If you are in your second or third year you should already recognize that most psychology essays are more concerned with the way that you marshal research evidence to argue a particular point of view. As you will see from the articles in this volume, the authors have viewpoints about psychological theories and data, and what they do is put this together to make a new point or develop an existing argument. They do not simply make a list of issues or 'facts', but put forward the information towards a particular conclusion with which they want the reader to agree.

Lastly, it is worth acknowledging that writing is a skill that can develop over a lifetime. We suspect that most if not all of the articles in this reader were redrafted at least several times. Often it is the ability to see what can be improved that is the skill which is needed to increase the effectiveness of one's writing. A problem that all of us face is a form of egocentrism in taking the viewpoint of the other person for granted. As a result we often do not fully explain our own ideas or we leave out parts of the argument. Rereading an essay several weeks or months after writing it can be an instructive process as you can then be more objective about the material that you read with a fresh eye. Over the short term it is always worthwhile rereading your essay when it is part of course work.

## Revision

### Using the reader for revision

Even the most experienced of us find examinations threatening and worrying. Yet most of us survive them. The key is good preparation and planning. The first step is to prepare and understand what is required of you. Use course descriptions and course aims to identify the structure of what you have been taught and what it is you should know. Second, try and identify how many topics you should thoroughly revise to pass the exam successfully. Work out how many questions you need to answer and then work out the relation between the number of questions and number of topics. Never assume that you can 'get away' with the minimum number of topics or be confident that a certain topic will come up. Usually external examiners see the examination papers and they can make changes.

After checking course descriptions it helps to look at past exam questions. This is useful as it gives you an idea of what type of essay titles are provided and what level of detail is expected. Looking at past exam question papers can provide a basis for 'question spotting', but several words of caution are needed about this. One is that courses change so do not be unduly alarmed if an unfamiliar topic appears on a past paper, but do check this with the appropriate lecturer if you are at all worried about the topic appearing in your examination. Another word of caution is that rumours often abound about what is the usual format of an exam – usually there are no constraints to make a 'usual format', so it is best not to gamble on the fact that as a question was asked last year it will or will not appear this year.

It is always useful to begin revision by looking through your lecture notes. After all, it would be perverse of the lecturer to ask a question about material that was not covered on the course. The detail of the lecture notes varies a lot between people, but at the minimum they should give an indication of theories, investigations, and the controversies in an area. Lectures also provide another type of indirect information – an idea of what are the important questions and issues in an area which may well be related to the topics on the examination paper. Usually revision needs to go beyond lecture notes to include text books and original articles. This is important to gain a fuller understanding of a topic and to be able to show evidence of background reading. A useful strategy is to start with the most recently published articles and work backwards. As we have already mentioned this will mean you spend more time on current issues and obtain an up to date perspective about previous research which is also likely to save you time. In conducting revision it is also important to identify the way that a course is constructed – whether it is largely based on a text which will simplify the process of revision, or whether the lectures are prepared from a variety of sources. The integration of new material with a set of lecture notes can be a frustrating business because the new information does not necessarily slot into the structure provided by the lecture notes. One way to deal with this is simply to have the extra information attached to your lecture notes in the relevant place. However, the more that the new material can be integrated with your original notes, at least in your mind, the more successful the revision will be.

## Structure of book

The book contains six sections which are arranged according to an approximate chronological order. Each section starts with an overview and provides a context in which to consider the work. Not surprisingly the first section, 'Social Relationships at the Start of Life' is about infancy. The papers in this section deal with infant abilities and the process of attachment. The second section considers the important topic of Language and Communication, an area of research which has been for a long time a topic of debate and discussion. The study of Cognition and Representations continues to have a central place in Developmental Psychology and is the subject of the third section. Here key views about the process of change are discussed. This is followed by a section on Literacy and Numeracy, topics which are major concerns of education in middle childhood. All too easily the study of cognitive development can be divorced from the wider context of children's activities, and the fifth section about Others and their Influence has publications which seek to examine the broader context of learning, social and cultural processes. The final section looks Towards Adulthood, with a focus on processes occurring in adolescence that may influence later life.

## References

Aries, P. (1962). *Centuries of Childhood*. London: Jonathan Cape.

Baron-Cohen, S. (1991). Precursors to a theory of mind: understanding attention in others. In A. Whiten (Ed.) *Natural Theories of Mind Evolution, Development and Simulation of Everyday Mind Reading*. Oxford: Basil Blackwell.

Baron-Cohen, S., Allen, J., and Gillberg, C. (1992). Can autism be detected at 18 months? The needle, the haystack, and the C.H.A.T. *British Journal of Psychiatry, 161*, 839–843.

Binet, A. and Simon, T. (1905). Application des methodes nouvelles diagnostique de niveau intellectual chez des enfants normaux et anormaux d'hospice et d'ecole primaire. *L'annee psychologique, 11*, 245–336.

Bremner, G. (in press). In D. J. Messer and W. S. Millar. *Developmental Psychology*. London: Arnold.

Bronfenbrenner, U. (1979). *The Ecology of Human Development*. Cambridge: Harvard University Press.

Caldwell, B. M. (1964). The effects of infant care. In H. L. Hoffman and L. W. Hoffman (Eds.), *Review of Child Development Research*. New York: Russell Sage Foundation.

Campbell, R. N. and Grieve, R. (1982). Royal investigations of the origin of language. *Historiographica Linguistica 1X* (Nos.) 43–74.

Case, R., Kurland, M., and Goldberg, J. (1982). Operational efficiency and the growth of short term memory span. *Journal of Experimental Child Psychology, 33*, 386–404.

Clarke, M. and Clarke, A. (in press). The prediction of individual development. In D. J. Messer, and F. J. Jones, (Eds.), *Psychology for Social Workers*, Hemel Hempstead: Pretice Hall.

Columbo, J. (1993). *Infant Cognition: predicting later intellectual functioning*. Newbury Park Ca: Sage Publications.

Cosmides, L. and Tooby, J. (1994). Beyond Intuition and instinct blindness – towards an evolutionarily rigorous theory of mind. *Cognition, 50*, 41–77.

Dockrell, J. (1997), Children's developing value systems In G. A. Lindsay and D. Thompson (Eds), *Count me in – values into practice in special education*. London: David Fulton.

Elman, J. L., Bates, E., Johnson, M. *et al.* (1996). Rethinking Innateness: Connectionism in a Development Framework. Cambridge Mass: MIT Press.

Harris, A. C. (1993). *Child Development*. 2nd Edition. St Paul, MN: West Publishing Group.

Hughes, M. and Grieve, R. (1983). On asking children bizarre questions. In M. Donaldson, R. Grieve and C. Pratt (Eds.), *Early Childhood Development and Education*. Oxford: Basil Blackwell.

Karmiloff-Smith, A. (1992). *Beyond Modularity: A Developmental Perspective on Cognitive Science*. London: MIT Press.

Keil, F. C. (1990). Constraints on constraints: surveying the epigenetic landscape. *Cognitive Science, 14*, 135–168.

McShane, J. (1991). *Cognitive Development*. Oxford: Basil Blackwell.

Pike, A. and Plomin, R. (in press). Genetics and development. In D. Messer and S. Millar (Eds.) *Developmental Psychology*. London: Arnold.

Schaffer, H. R. (1990). *Making Decisions About Children: psychological questions and answers*. Basil Blackwell Ltd.

Siegler, R. S. (1988). Individual differences in strategy choices. *Child development, 59*, 833–851.

Sigman, M. and Bornstein, M. (1986). Continuity in mental development from infancy. *Child Development, 57*, 251–274.

Sylva, K. and Lunt, I. (1982). *Child Development: a first course*. Blackwell.

Watson, J. B. and Rayner, R. A. (1920). Conditional emotional reactions. *Journal of Experimental Psychology, 3*, 1–14.

# SECTION I
# *SOCIAL RELATIONSHIPS AT THE START OF LIFE*

## Editors' Introduction

Infancy is usually considered by psychologists as the period of life before language is used, before about 24 months of age. The lack of speech has provided an impetus to investigate whether processes occurring during infancy are responsible for the acquisition of language (see Section II), and there are links between early word use and later language (Bates et al., 1995). In addition, the lack of speech makes this both an especially interesting and a difficult period for investigators. It is not possible to ask infants what they are thinking or for them to comment on what they see. As a result, many of the important research papers in this area have involved technical innovations, and these technical innovations have led to a gradual erosion of the assumption that the infant's world is the 'booming, buzzing confusion' as described by William James. His description suggested that infants perceive their world as a chaotic array of stimuli, but that with experience cognitive processes gradually establish order from this chaos.

These assumptions about a lack of early innate cognitive capacities have been challenged by research in the last 30 or 40 years. A research paper which was part of this re-evaluation of infant capacities and which attracted considerable attention because of the nature of the findings was a study of newborn imitation by Meltzoff and Moore in 1977. This study reported that babies only a few hours old would respond to an adult who stuck their tongue out, or opened their mouth, by producing the same actions. This does not seem to be an exchange of insults but a form of imitation. The findings attracted interest because Piaget did not believe that this form of imitation occurs until later on in the first year because infants lacked this representational capacity (see the chapter by McShane in Section III). In addition, the findings raised intriguing questions about how infants are able to respond to faces, which are a class of stimuli which they have only seen for a limited amount of time, and questions about how they are able to produce imitative motor movements in part of their body which the infant cannot see. In addition, these early imitative abilities have provoked questions about their social origins. More recently, Meltzoff has argued that imitation is possible because young infants perceive adults as being like themselves, in that they are things with intentions and social purposes (Meltzoff and Gopnik, 1993).

It is self evident that social relationships and social interaction are key features of the first 2 years of life. Social relationships and attachment have been considered from a variety of perspectives. The first article in the reader discusses imprinting. This is a process whereby a newborn animal forms a special relation with another entity. Work on imprinting has been very influential in showing that early relationships need not be based on reinforcement such as food, but may be biologically determined as an aid to survival. If young animals learn to follow their parent, they should have a better chance of survival. This work has influenced the way that psychologists have thought about human attachment, even though few of them would claim that there is exactly the same type of process in humans as in other animals. However, there are findings which suggest that newborns have innate dispositions to respond to certain types of stimuli. These findings which are discussed by Mark Johnson indicate that newborn babies will prefer to follow a schematic representation of the human face rather than the same features scrambled with respect to their position; they seem to have a preference for human like stimuli. Such findings are controversial as others argue that infants are only responding to the light intensity that is present in a visual stimulus (Kleiner, 1987). According to this argument there is nothing special about the way infants respond to faces – they are merely responding to a class of stimuli that they find interesting. This view contrasts with other findings which suggest that newborns will respond to the mother's face in preference to that of another woman (Bushnell et al., 1989) and therefore suggests that there is not merely a preference for faces, but a preference for the face of their mother.

The next chapter by Rudolph Schaffer provides a very useful summary about the formation of attachments between infants and their mother (much less attention has been paid to other adults such as fathers). Central to this chapter is the way that children react in the short term to separations from particular people and the way that this changes with age. Schaffer summarizes some of the classic studies on this subject, studies which thankfully would be much more difficult to conduct today because of changes in child care practices. Today there is such a widely held assumption that young infants need to remain with their principal caregiver that it is difficult to appreciate the changes in attitudes that have occurred over the last 30 years. Furthermore, the way that child care arrangements have changed in hospitals and other institutions can be attributed to studies such as these which showed the short-term effects of separations on children in terms of protest, despair and detachment.

One important feature of research on attachment has been the use of the strange situation to assess the type of attachment between infants and adults (see IJzendoorn and Schuengel, in press). The strange situation was developed by Mary Ainsworth, and built on the ideas of John Bowlby. The strange situation has been important because it provided a way to assess the type of relationship between infant and mother. Early attempts to measure attachment had usually been based on the assumption that attachment could be measured in a similar way to temperature. For example, it might be thought that the more a child was distressed at separation then the stronger was her attachment to that person. This way of assessing attachment did not meet with much success. Ainsworth attempted a different and more successful approach by examining the overall organization of behaviour. In a strange situation children are classified according to whether they are securely attached to an adult, whether they tend to avoid the adult, or whether they are ambivalent in their behaviour with the adult. There has been a tremendous amount of research which has used the strange situation to investigate attachment. Edward Melhuish provides a brief, but comprehensive summary of this work. In the review he notes a particularly interesting recent development has been the finding that measures of maternal attachment with their own mother, predict the type of attachment a child has to the mother.

Behind this research on attachment is a debate about the origins of infant social abilities. One view about this is that newborn babies simply react to people as they would to an inanimate object – they do not differentiate between people and other things (e.g. Kleiner, 1987). It is only with time and experience that infants come to recognize people as something special in their environment. The opposite view is that babies are born with some understanding that people are special and that newborns can communicate and relate to people. Advocates of this viewpoint often use the term intersubjectivity to describe the way that two individuals can recognize each other as having the characteristics which are typical of a thinking organism, such as intentions, motivations, and communicative capacities. Colwyn Trevarthen's (1979) work did much to gain recognition for this idea. To understand this claim it is useful to think about any interactions you have had with a young infant and consider whether the child was relating to you as a person, or to you as an interesting set of stimuli. You might also ask yourself whether it would be possible to prove that infants are relating to people in a special way. This debate about infant capacities has been given added significance by interest in the origins of autism. Autism is a condition in which the children have difficulty in understanding that people can have different thoughts, interests and motivations from their own. Peter Hobson (1993) has argued that typical children directly perceive the emotions of people enabling them to respond to the emotions of others. He also argues that children with autism are unable to do this and fail to 'read' the signals which the rest of us automatically use. There are of course other explanations of autism and the chapter by Frith and Happe (this volume) provides a summary of such views (see also Powell, in press).

Infancy involves dramatic changes in cognitive and social abilities, a change from the vulnerability of the newborn to the competence of the toddler who has gained an understanding of so much in such a comparatively short time. As we have seen, infancy is an important period for the development of social abilities. Given all this it is not surprising that a long-standing and common assumption is that the early years are formative and predictive of an individual's development (see Bornstein and Sigman, 1986). Such an assumption has not gone without challenge and there has been an increasing recognition that a person's life path is not determined by early experiences (Clarke and Clarke, in press). Nevertheless there are still many findings which show that infancy is an important phase of life and these help to make it a period of life which receives considerable attention from both parents and psychologists.

## References

Bates, E., Dale, P., and Thal, D. (1995). Individual differences and their implications for theories of child language. In P. Fletcher and B. MacWhinney (Eds.), *Handbook of Child Language*. Oxford: Blackwell.

Bornstein, M. H. and Sigman, M. (1986). Continuity in mental development from infancy. *Child Development, 57*, 251–74.

Bushnell, I. W. R., Sai, F., and Mullin, J. T. (1989). Neonatal recognition of the mother's face. *British Journal of Developmental Psychology, 7*, 3–15.

Clarke, M. and Clarke, A. (in press). In D. Messer, and F. Jones (Eds.), *Psychology for Social Workers*. Prentice Hall: Hemel Hempstead.

Hobson, P. (1993). Perceiving attitudes, conceiving minds. In C. Lewis and P. Mitchell (Eds.), *Origins of an Understanding of Mind*. Hillsdale, NJ: Erlbaum.

IJzendoorn, M. H. van and Schuengel, C. (in press). The development of attachment relationships: infancy and beyond. In D. Messer and S. Millar (Eds.), *Developmental Psychology*. London: Arnold.

Kleiner, K. A. (1987). Amplitude and phase spectra as indices of infants' pattern of preferences. *Infant Behaviour and Development, 10*, 49–59.

Meltzoff, A. and Moore, K. (1977). Imitation of facial and manual gestures by human neonates. *Science, 198*, 75–78.

Meltzoff, A. and Gopnik, A. (1993). The role of imitation in understanding persons and developing a theory of mind. In S. Baron-Cohen and H. Tager-Flusberg (Eds.). Understanding Other Minds. Oxford: OUP.

Powell, S. (in press). In D. Messer and S. Millar (Eds.). *Developmental Psychology*. London: Arnold.

Trevarthen, C. (1979). Communication and co-operation in early infancy. In M. Bullowa (Ed.), *Before Speech*. Cambridge: CUP.

## Further Reading

Bremner, G. (in press). Making sense of the physical world in infancy. In D. Messer and S. Millar (Eds.). *Developmental Psychology*. London: Arnold.

Schaffer, H. (1996). *Social Development*. Oxford: Blackwell.

# 1 Mark H. Johnson
'Imprinting and the Development of Face Recognition: From Chick to Man'

Reprinted in full from: *Current Directions in Psychological Science* **1**, 52–55 (1992)

Filial imprinting is the process whereby young precocial birds learn to recognize the first conspicuous object that they see after hatching. The writings of the Austrian ethologist Konrad Lorenz on imprinting have given rise to half a century of active research on this process by ethologists and psychologists from a variety of different backgrounds.[1] Many of the original claims made by Lorenz have turned out to be only partially correct. For example, we now know that the process is not as rigidly irreversible as once believed. A prolonged period of exposure to a second object can sometimes result in a reversal of the original preference. Evidence for imprinting has also been reported in some mammalian species, such as spiny mice and guinea pigs, but the measure that yields this evidence (approach and following) cannot be used with species that are relatively immobile for some time after birth (such as humans).

Visual imprinting in the domestic chick can be studied easily in the laboratory in the following way. A chick is hatched and reared in darkness before being exposed to a conspicuous object, such as one of those shown in Figure 1.1. This period of exposure is called *training* and usually lasts for a period of several hours. Hours or days later, the chick is given a preference test in which it is released in the presence of two objects: the object to which it was exposed earlier and a novel object it has never seen before. The extent to which the chick attempts to approach the familiar object as opposed to the novel one is measured, and a *preference score* calculated. If the chick has imprinted strongly, it shows a high preference for the familiar object.

## The neural basis of imprinting

Using a variety of neuroanatomical, neurophysiological, and biochemical techniques, Gabriel Horn and Patrick Bateson, of the University of Cambridge, set out to investigate the brain mechanisms that underlie imprinting. These authors and their collaborators established over a number of years that a particular region of the chick forebrain called IMHV (the intermediate and medial part of the hyperstriatum ventrale) is essential for imprinting.[2] This region receives input from the main visual projection areas of the chick, and may be analogous to mammalian association cortex.

One of the techniques used to verify that IMHV is crucial for imprinting was to place small lesions in this region of the chick brain. Placed prior to training, these lesions reduced chicks' ability to learn about the object to which they were exposed; placed shortly after training, the lesions impaired

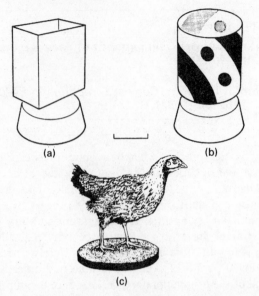

**Figure 1.1** Examples of objects that have been used as imprinting stimuli in various experiments: (a) a rotating colored box illuminated from within, (b) a rotating colored cylinder illuminated from within, and (c) a rotating stuffed jungle fowl (an ancestor of the farmyard chicken) illuminated from above. Scale bar = 10 cm. (See Horn[2] for further details.)

chicks' ability to recognize the 'familiar' object (i.e., the chicks no longer showed a preference for the object to which they were exposed). The lesions had no effect on a variety of other behaviors and learning tasks, such as learning to press a particular pedal to obtain a reward, but a group of lesioned chicks were unable to learn to recognize the other individual chickens with which they were raised.[2] Thus, the effect of the lesions seemed specific to the recognition of objects and conspecifics.

After a number of these lesion studies, a striking stimulus-dependent effect of IMHV lesions on imprinting became apparent: Although birds trained on a simple artificial object such as a rotating red box were severely impaired by the lesions, chicks trained by exposure to a stuffed hen were only mildly impaired. Subsequently, a variety of other stimulus-dependent neurophysiological effects were found. For example, administration of the hormone testosterone increased preference in birds exposed to the stuffed hen, but had no effect on birds trained on the red box. In contrast, administration of the drug DSP4 (which depletes forebrain levels of catecholamines) affected birds trained on the red box but had little effect on birds trained on the stuffed hen. These and other observations of stimulus-dependent neurophysiological effects caused my colleagues and me to inquire whether chicks might not have some spontaneous, or untrained, preferences that interact with learning. Although such an idea had been suggested by others for some time, no evidence had been offered to support it.

To investigate this question, we gave preference tests (in which chicks had a choice between the red box and the stuffed hen) to chicks that had been reared in darkness. Even though these chicks had never seen anything other than darkness, they showed a strong preference for the stuffed hen. This finding raised two further questions: What rearing conditions allow this spontaneous preference to develop? And what visual characteristics of the hen cause it to be preferred over the red box? The answer to the first question turned out to be that chicks require only an opportunity to run about a little between 12 and 36 hr after hatching. A brief period of motor activity at this age *enables* the subsequent emergence of the spontaneous preference. Interestingly, it is likely that chicks undergo such experience at around this age in their natural rearing environment. One hypothesis is that this enabling is mediated by the hormone testosterone.

To address the second question, we conducted a series of experiments in which we gave chicks a choice between the intact stuffed hen and a variety of three-dimensional objects created by cutting up and jumbling parts of a stuffed hen. The results of these studies indicated that the crucial characteristic was that the head region be intact.[3] That is, the whole, intact stuffed hen was preferred to any stimulus with the head and neck region dismembered or absent. In contrast, the chicks showed no clear preference between the normal stuffed hen and any stimulus in which the head and neck region was intact. Furthermore, when the chicks were given a choice between the intact stuffed hen and the head and neck region alone, they showed a slight preference for the latter, indicating that the rest of the hen's body may have acted as a distractor from this critical region. Finally, the intact head did not have to be the head of a chicken – heads of several other species were just as effective.

Considering all of these findings, my colleagues and I proposed that there are two comparatively independent processes underlying filial preference behavior in the chick: first, a predisposition to attend toward objects resembling conspecifics and, second, a learning system subserved by the neural structure IMHV. We further suggested that, in the natural environment, the first system ensures that the second leads the chick to learn about the characteristics of a particular mother hen.

In recent years, we have tested predictions from this two-process account of filial imprinting. One of these predictions was that although IMHV lesions impair the acquired portion of filial preference, they should not impair the predisposition. This prediction was confirmed: Chicks with IMHV lesions are unable to learn about the characteristics of a particular object to which they are exposed, but they show the same predisposition to approach henlike objects as dark-reared, untrained chicks do. A second prediction was that although normal, intact chicks should be able to learn about the characteristics of particular hens, IMHV-lesioned chicks should not. We tested this prediction by training chicks on one of two different stuffed hens. Although normal, intact chicks (and a control group of chicks with lesions placed elsewhere in the forebrain) subsequently showed a preference for the particular stuffed hen to which they were exposed, chicks with IMHV lesions had no such preference and approached the two stuffed hens equally. That is, they appeared to be unable to learn about the characteristics of an individual mother hen.

**Two systems in the development of face recognition**

The evidence favors the idea of two independent systems being involved in the chick's recognition of its mother. The first of these systems directs the attention of the young animal toward the appropriate class of object to learn about in the absence of any prior specific experience. The second system is concerned with learning about the characteristics of the objects to which attention has been directed by the first system. Despite the large differences between chick and human, John Morton and I have speculated that, given some fundamental similarities in the way that the vertebrate brain develops, two analogous processes might underlie the development of face recognition in the human infant.[4]

Until recently, it was commonly believed that human infants do not learn about the structure of the human face until 2 or 3 months of age. In a large number of studies, infants around 1 month of age showed no discrimination between a schematic face and a stimulus created from the features of a face that were jumbled up. In contrast, infants 2 to 3 months of age looked more toward the face.[5] Against this prevailing trend, one study reported that newborn infants (in the 1st hr of life) tracked a slowly, moving face stimulus further than they tracked a number of scrambled faces.[6] This study was largely ignored, partly because it conflicted with the majority of other studies, and partly because of a number of methodological problems. Very recently, the debate regarding whether newborns respond preferentially to faces has been reopened by a successful replication of the newborn tracking study:[7] In two independent experiments, newborns tracked a schematic face pattern further than they tracked a variety of scrambled faces and other nonface stimuli (see Figure 1.2).

These independent replications (performed in such a way as to avoid some of the methodological problems of the original study) have established that

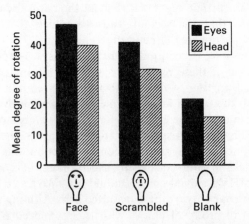

**Figure 1.2**  Data from Experiment 1 of Johnson, Dziurawiec, Ellis, and Morton,[7] showing the extent of newborns' eye and head turns in following a face, a scrambled face, and a blank (unpatterned) stimulus. The infants followed the face significantly further than the other stimuli.

infants in the 1st hr of life do indeed preferentially respond to some stimuli resembling faces. If this preference could be shown to be specific to the structure of faces, and not simply to some unidimensional psychophysical measure such as spatial frequency, then it would have one of the characteristics of the predisposition described earlier in the chick. Perhaps the most successful of the theories put forward to account for sensory preferences in human infants are those based on the filtered spatial frequency of stimuli.[8] Although some authors have suggested that newborns' preferences for faces may be accounted for solely in terms of these psychophysical characteristics, closer analysis indicates that face stimuli are usually more attractive relative to abstract stimuli than would be predicted by such a theory. Given that no simple unidimensional psychophysical measure proposed so far can account for the newborns' preferential tracking response, what are the characteristics of the schematic face that cause it to be preferred?

To date, the results of our experiments with newborns have indicated that the particular details of the features of a face may not be important. A stimulus composed of three 'blobs' corresponding to the eyes and mouth is almost as effective as a full schematic face, as long as it is presented with two 'eye blobs' at the top. Although much further experimentation must be done, it is likely that the newborns' response to facelike stimuli is not specific to human faces.

In the two-process model of filial imprinting in the chick, the predisposition is dissociable in terms of its neural substrate from the learning system responsible for imprinting. Is there any evidence that the face preference found in newborn infants has a different neural substrate from that involved in the preference that appears at 2 months of age?

There is widespread agreement among scientists who study the neuroanatomical and neurophysiological properties of the primate cortex that the cortical structures subserving vision are only partially developed at the time of birth. Indeed, it is well established that the primary visual cortex undergoes substantial maturational changes over the first few months of life in the human infant.[9] We might expect, therefore, that some of the transitions in visually guided behavior that occur over the first few months of life would be a result of the continuing maturation of cortical visual areas. With this in mind, it is interesting to note that several 'reflex-type' behaviors present in the newborn human infant drop out in the 2nd month of life: for example, the imitation of facial movements and orienting of the head toward a sound source.[10] Several authors have proposed that such declines are due to the inhibition of subcortical circuits by developing cortical circuitry.

Recently, we have traced the preferential tracking of facelike stimuli over the first 5 months of life and discovered that this behavior, too, drops out sharply between 4 and 6 weeks after birth, suggesting the possibility that it is mediated primarily by subcortical structures such as the superior colliculus. As mentioned earlier, it is during the 3rd month of life that standard infant testing techniques first reveal a preference for facelike stimuli over scrambled-face stimuli. One possibility is that the onset of this later developing preference is due to the further maturation of cortical circuitry. If these inferences are correct, they suggest that the preferential responding to faces found in the newborn is mediated by neural circuitry different from that mediating the later emerging, and more specific, preference to attend to faces.

I proposed earlier that the chick's predisposition serves to ensure the appropriate input for the learning system subserved by IMHV. That is, the information that the young animal possesses prior to experience of the external world ensures that the chick learns about particularly important classes of stimuli, such as the visual characteristics of its mother. The same may be true of the human infant. The information that the newborn human's brain has about faces may be sufficient to ensure that developing cortical circuitry is exposed more toward this vitally important class of stimuli than toward other objects of less importance.

## Notes

1  Bolhuis, J. J. (1991). Mechanisms of avian imprinting, *Biological Reviews, 66,* 303–345.
2  Horn, G. (1985). *Memory, Imprinting and the Brain.* Oxford: Oxford University.
3  Johnson, M. H., and Horn, G. (1988). Development of filial preferences in dark-reared chicks, *Animal Behavior, 36,* 675–683.
4  Morton, J., and Johnson, M. H. (1991). Conspec and Conlern: A two process theory of infant face recognition, *Psychological Review, 98,* 164–181.
5  Maurer, D. (1985). Infants' perception of facedness, in *Social Perception in Infants,* T. N. Field and N. Fox (Eds.), Norwood, NJ: Ablex.
6  Goren, C. C., Sarty, M., and Wu, P. Y. K. (1975). Visual following and pattern discrimination of facelike stimuli by newborn infants, *Pediatrics, 56,* 544–549.
7  Johnson, M. H., Dziuraweic, S., Ellis, H. D., and Morton, J. (1991). Newborns' preferential tracking of face-like stimuli and its subsequent decline, *Cognition, 40,* 1–21.
8  Banks, M., and Salapatek, P. (1981). Infant pattern vision: A new approach based on the contrast sensitivity function, *Journal of Experimental Child Psychology, 31,* 1–45.
9  Johnson, M. H. (1990). Cortical maturation and the development of visual attention in early infancy, *Journal of Cognitive Neuroscience, 2,* 81–95.
10 Johnson, M. H. (1990). Cortical maturation and perceptual development, in *Sensory-Motor Organizations and Development in Infancy and Early Childhood,* H. Bloch and B. Bertenthal (Eds.), Dordrecht, The Netherlands: Kluwer Academic.

## Further reading

Johnson, M. H., and Morton, J. (1991). *Biology and Cognitive Development: The Case of Face Recognition.* Oxford: Basil Blackwell.

# 2    H. R. Schaffer
## 'When do Children First Form Attachments to Other People?'

Reprinted in full from: *Making Decisions about Children*, 2nd edition (Blackwell, 1998), 20–29

## Background

The formation of a child's first emotional relationship (more often than not with the mother) is widely regarded as one of the most important achievements of childhood. It is from that relationship that the young child derives its confidence in the world; the sheer physical availability of the other person spells security. A major break in that relationship may be experienced as highly distressing and constitute a considerable trauma. It is therefore necessary to know something of its developmental course, including the age when one can first expect an attachment to another person to show itself.

The term 'attachment' has traditionally been used to refer to the child's part of the relationship – as opposed to the term 'bonding' which has come to be used for the parent's part. There has been a great deal of research in the last few decades on the nature of early attachments, and though most of it initially took a non-developmental form, being concerned more with its manifestation in children at one particular age (especially around one year) than with changes over time, we do have some indication as to when and how children's attachments to significant others first appear.

That an attachment has to be learned, in the sense that it is based on experience with the other person, cannot be doubted. The questions of interest are: how much experience it takes and at what age children become capable of benefiting from that experience.

Initially, a child's caretakers are interchangeable. At birth the child does not yet 'know' its mother; a familiarization process has to take place. There is, in fact, considerable evidence that such familiarization occurs very quickly and that infants by 2 or 3 months are already capable of distinguishing familiar from unfamiliar people. (There are even some intriguing findings that immediately after birth infants can distinguish the mother's voice from that of any other voice – something that can only be explained by learning in the womb!). However, being able to recognize the mother by, for instance, smiling at her more readily or being more easily comforted by her touch, does not in itself signify that an attachment has been formed to her. Such recognition is only a prerequisite to attachment formation; in all other respects infants remain quite indiscriminate. Thus they will accept care and attention from anyone, however unfamiliar, and show no sign of upset when separated from the parent or any orientation towards her during her absence.

The interchangeability of caretakers is best seen in separation situations. It is well known that young children (say between one and four years of age) tend to be extremely upset when removed from their parents, particularly when placed in such strange environments as hospitals or children's homes. The often quite intense and prolonged fretting that then occurs is an indication of the child's need for the parent's presence – a presence which normally provides the young child with comfort and security and a secure base from which it can explore the environment. Without it, security is shattered; the ministrations of strangers, however kindly offered, are rejected and indeed seem to add to the stress experienced. The separation situation thus highlights the fact that a meaningful, emotionally highly-charged, lasting relationship has been formed and that a break in that relationship will produce, in the short term at any rate, some highly distressing, undesirable consequences.

The question can therefore be asked: how early in infancy does separation from a mother (or other permanent caretaker) have an impact on children and cause them to be upset? Is it possible to indicate some age when people cease to be interchangeable, when the child's positive feelings have become focused on just one or two specific individuals while others are responded to more negatively? To establish such an age is clearly desirable; it means that we can determine when children become vulnerable to the loss of their mother-figure and what the limits of the earlier period are when changes in caretaker may take place relatively safely. This was indeed one of the first issues to which research workers addressed themselves when scientific investigation of children's attachments began in the late 1950s.

## Research findings

### Summaries

*H. R. Schaffer, and W. M. Callender (1959), 'Psychologic effects of hospitalisation in infancy', Pediatrics, 24, pp. 528–39.*
In this early study use was made of the separation situation to highlight the extent to which infants of different ages within the first year of life require their mother's presence and refuse to accept attention from other people. In particular the intention was to establish the age when the mother's absence becomes a cause for distress and strange caretakers are no longer acceptable.

The most frequent separation situation is, of course, hospitalization. Accordingly, 76 infants, aged between three and 51 weeks, were observed when admitted to a children's hospital. The length of their stay there varied from four to 49 days, though most remained for less than two weeks. Observation sessions took place on each of the first three days following admission and again on the last three days preceding discharge. Each session lasted two hours and included a feed and the visiting period. The observer kept a running record of the infants' behaviour, with particular reference to their responsiveness to other people, play with toys, feeding and amount of crying. In addition all infants were subsequently visited at home, first within a week of discharge and thereafter periodically until all overt effects of the separation experience had apparently subsided.

It emerged from the findings that the infants' reactions to hospitalization fell into two quite distinct syndromes, each associated with a particular age range and divided from each other at approximately seven months of age. Those above that age showed the classical separation upset: acute fretting following admission, negative behaviour to all strangers, often quite desperate clinging to the mother during her visits, disturbed feeding and sleeping patterns and, following return home, a period of insecurity shown especially by fear of being left alone by the mother. Infants below seven months old, on the other hand, showed minimal upset; in most cases admission to hospital evoked no observable disturbance: instead, an immediate adjustment to the new environment and the people in it was the typical reaction. On return home these younger infants showed some isolated symptoms but none of the clinging to the mother that was seen in older babies. In general, it appeared that the separation experience had very different meanings for those in the first and those in the second half-year of life: only at the older age were there responses suggesting that infants had formed a definite tie to the mother and that a break in that tie was experienced as upsetting.

*H. R. Schaffer and P. E. Emerson (1964), 'The development of social attachments in infancy', Monographs of the Society for Research in Child Development, 29, 3 (serial no. 94).*
The study described above was a cross-sectional one: that is, infants were seen only at one particular age when they happened to be admitted to hospital. To trace the way in which a particular function like attachment to the mother emerges in the course of development one really needs a longitudinal study, i.e., seeing the *same* infants at different ages. The present investigation accordingly took such a form.

A group of 60 infants was followed up at four-weekly intervals throughout the first year of life and then seen once again at 18 months old. In the course of home visits reports were obtained from the mothers about the infants' behaviour in a number of everyday separation situations such as being left alone in a room, left with a babysitter or put to bed at night; observational checks on the accuracy of the mothers' reports were built into the procedure. For each of the seven separation situations investigated information was obtained on every visit as to whether the infant protested or not, the intensity and regularity of the protest and whose departure elicited it. In addition the infant's reaction to the research worker was assessed by means of a standardized approach procedure held at the beginning of each visit in order to see how readily the child accepted the attention of a relatively unfamiliar person.

As in the previous study, the age when separation protest was first recorded was of particular interest. For the majority of infants this was at the beginning of the second half-year, i.e., in the same age range as had been pinpointed by the earlier research. Before that age, protest in separation situations sometimes occurred, but it was indiscriminate in nature in that the infant cried for attention from anyone, whether familiar or not. After that age it was focused on certain specific individuals: it was they and not others who were capable of stopping the child from crying. There were considerable differences in the precise age when infants first began to show such differential behaviour to other people, ranging from 22 weeks of age to the beginning of the second year. In the majority of cases, however, it was somewhere around the age of seven or eight months that it first became evident that these infants had now formed a very definite, lasting relationship with certain quite specific individuals.

*K. H. Tennes and E. E. Lampl (1966), 'Some aspects of mother–child relationship pertaining to infantile separation anxiety',* Journal of Nervous and Mental Diseases, *143, pp. 426–37.*

Replication of any research findings is essential, and this study provides a welcome confirmation that the third quarter of the first year is indeed the period when focused attachments first appear – again on the basis of using children's responses to separation as an indicator, and again by means of a longitudinal study.

27 infants were followed up from three to 23 months of age at monthly or bimonthly intervals. On each occasion the infants were observed under naturalistic conditions at home, and in semi-structured situations in a university observation room. Detailed descriptions of mother–child interactions were recorded by several observers simultaneously. Methods for assessing separation and stranger anxiety were built into the procedure, i.e., by asking the mother to leave the room and by the examiner approaching the infant on first arrival. The behavioural responses of the infants in these two situations were rated on six-point scales.

The majority of infants first developed separation anxiety during the third quarter of the first year. The average age of onset was around eight months. Here too, considerable individual differences were noted, however, ranging from four to 18 months old. According to an earlier report on this same study, negative responsiveness to strangers appeared somewhat earlier, usually preceding separation anxiety by a few weeks. The indices taken together show how indiscriminate sociability with others, as seen in the early months, gives way to highly discriminate behaviour and appears to do so relatively suddenly once an infant reaches the relevant age range.

*L. J. Yarrow (1967), 'The development of focused relationships', in J. Hellmuth (ed.),* Exceptional Infant: The Normal Infant, *vol. 1 (Seattle, WA: Special Child Publications).*

A rather different approach was taken in this study, in that it investigated infants' reactions to adoptive placements. In so far as a new mother-figure was immediately provided following the break with the previous mother, it was possible to study the effects of separation per se, uncontaminated by the effects of such other conditions as institutional deprivation.

The total sample involved 100 infants, though at any one age the number available was generally somewhat smaller. Observation sessions took place prior to and following the separation; they were conducted in the home-setting and were of one and a half hours duration. A series of simple situations were incorporated in each session, involving the presentation of various inanimate and social stimuli, including the mother's and the observer's face and voice. The latency, duration and intensity of a variety of behavioural responses were recorded. Information from the mother was also obtained regarding the infant's behaviour in various everyday social situations.

By the age of eight months, all of the infants showed strong overt disturbances to permanent separation from the mother. At three months old no infant showed such disturbance, at five months 20 per cent did so and at six months 59 per cent. According to comments in a subsequent paper the author believes that the upset found at some of the younger ages, i.e., in the first half-year, may have been elicited by changes in routine and in type of stimulation provided rather than by a change in the mother-figure as such.

*J. Kagan, R. B. Kearsley and P. R. Zelazzo (1978),* Infancy: Its Place in Human Development *(Cambridge, MA: Harvard University Press).*
The primary focus of this study is on the effects of daycare (a subject to which we shall return later), with reference, amongst other things, to the way in which children's relationships with their mothers is affected thereby. As one of the assessments a separation situation was arranged in order to see whether this highlighted any differences in the child–mother relationship of children with and children without daycare experience.

For this assessment 87 infants were available, including a daycare and a matched homecare control group. Included in the sample were children of both Caucasian and Chinese ethnic origin. Children between four and 29 months old were observed in a specially arranged separation situation, which involved the mother leaving the child alone in a relatively unfamiliar setting while playing happily. The occurrence and duration of crying were recorded by observers from behind a one-way screen. The sample included 59 children who participated on all six occasions that the procedure was administered between the ages of five and 20 months.

The incidence of crying in response to separation was found to be low up to seven months of age, after which it rose sharply, peaking at 13 months and then declining. Every one of the 59 children seen longitudinally cried on at least one occasion; most cried on several occasions. After seven months of age children reacted to the mother's departure with crying much more quickly, and especially so in the age range 13 to 20 months. There were no differences between the two ethnic groups, and there were also no differences between the daycare and the homecare children, suggesting that the onset and early course of separation upset is a general phenomenon that appears to be unaffected by the amount of daily contact with the mother.

*Comments on research*

There is a most welcome degree of agreement among the various research studies as to when children first become vulnerable to separation from a mother-figure: the third quarter of the first year seems to be the crucial time when this is likely to occur. It is then that separation becomes a psychologically meaningful and emotionally disturbing event, as a result of which changes in mother-figure are now no longer tolerated. Investigators concur that before this age any disturbances in behaviour appear to be related to changes in routine or in the general environment rather than to loss of the mother; the disturbances are moreover brief and do not involve the distress which is such a central feature of the child's reaction subsequently. There is some disagreement as to the age when that distress reaches its peak: according to some reports the intensity of upset is every bit as great at seven or eight months as it is in two- or three-year-old children, while others locate the peak at the end of the first or the beginning of the second year. The diversity may be due to the different kinds of measures and procedures used (amount of crying or intensity of crying, natural or arranged separations, and so forth), but suffice it to say that the longitudinal studies agree that the onset is relatively sudden – a step-wise development – and not a slow and gradual one. Thus, sometime after the beginning of the second half-year, infants reach an important milestone in their social development. From then on their positive responsiveness tends to become restricted to certain familiar individuals while other, unfamiliar individuals elicit mostly negative responses and wariness. The combined effect is to ensure that caretakers are no longer interchangeable; the child has become capable of forming 'proper' social attachments.

Relatively sudden, step-wise changes are by no means uncommon in behavioural development, so the rapid onset of the capacity for separation upset is hardly surprising. A lot of research has found the third quarter of the first year to be a time of considerable change: it heralds the onset of a large number of new achievements, including the development of recall memory. This is particularly relevant here: in earlier months infants may have been able to *recognize* persons or objects, i.e., show signs of remembering them when they were present, but in their absence they behaved on the basis of 'out of sight out of mind'. *Recall* involves memory of an absent person or thing, and it is this which is indicated by separation upset. Previously, however excited infants might be by the mother's presence they showed no orientation to her in her absence; once this particular milestone has been reached, however, they are capable of missing her.

Step-wise changes do not, of course, mean that the development comes totally out of the blue. It may be the culmination of various prior events without which this particular development could not have taken place. The ability to differentiate familiar from unfamiliar people is clearly one prerequisite; mother must first be known in order to be missed. Yet research has found few experiential variables that seem to have any bearings on when this development takes place. Thus it has not been found possible to relate variations in the age at onset of separation upset to variations in mothers' child-rearing practices; there are no differences according to whether a mother works or not; infants born blind and thus without visual experience of the mother also develop separation upset at the usual age; and finally the age at onset is very similar in a wide range of different cultures, despite the considerable diversity of child-rearing practices. It seems that the timing of this particular milestone is primarily determined by the child's inherent development programme; given reasonably normal prior experience the child is bound to reach this point.

## Implications for practice

Any break in a child's existing relationships is likely to cause distress. The nature and severity of that distress varies with age; it will be greatest in the early years when children still require frequent access to the physical presence of those individuals who are the objects of their attachment. Such individuals spell security for the infants; with that gone upset is likely to be intense and prolonged. That alone justifies preventive action, never mind any possible long-term consequences, and amongst such actions is the search for a 'safe period' at the beginning of life when social ties have not yet been established and when, from the child's point of view, there is nothing yet to sever.

Such a period, according to the research findings summarized above, extends over the first half-year of life or so. From then on children become vulnerable to separation. It follows that, wherever there is a choice, any measure involving the child's removal from home should be taken during the safe period. It is, for instance, always maintained that adoption placements ought to take place as early as possible; the findings we have quoted provide a rationale for such a belief and define more precisely what is meant by 'as early as possible'. Similarly hospitalizations – or at least those that involve elective procedures where there is a choice as to when the child is to be admitted – should also be timed according to our knowledge of children's emotional vulnerability. While there may, of course, be good medical reasons for wanting to delay admission till the child is somewhat older, these should be weighed against the psychological considerations spelled out above.

Two qualifications should, however, be added. First, as most of the research reports stress, there is a considerable range in the age at onset of separation upset. It is true that the majority of infants reach this point during the third quarter of the first year; some, however, show signs of distress several months before then while others appear not to do so until much later. This is, of course, not surprising; the same variation applies to any developmental milestone. It does mean, however, that one cannot precisely predict when any given child will become vulnerable to separation. There is some evidence that children who are developmentally ahead in other respects such as motor functioning are also likely to be ahead in this respect, but the association is not close enough to allow for accurate prediction. All one can do under the circumstances is to indicate the age range (i.e., the third quarter of the first year) when it is most probable that such a development will take place; for the majority of children this will be a justified assumption.

The other point refers to the fact that even in the first six months of life there may be some undesirable effects of separation. Feeding and sleeping disturbances have been reported, as well as bewilderment caused by changes in the physical environment. These symptoms are generally brief in duration, but they do indicate the need to prepare the infant's new caretakers for such reactions and, wherever possible, to attempt to preserve routines. If, of course, the child's new environment is unsatisfactory (lacking in stimulation or failing to provide consistent care), deleterious effects will ensue however young the child may be. The 'safe period' refers only to the child's vulnerability to separation from the mother-figure; it does not imply that children at that age are immune from everything. Care must clearly be taken with respect to the environment in which even the youngest infant is placed.

**Further reading**

Bowlby, J. (1982). *Attachment and Loss*, vol. 1, 2nd edn. London: Hogarth Press.

Crowell, J. A., and Waters, E. (1990). 'Separation anxiety', in M. Lewis and S. M. Miller (Eds.), *Handbook of Developmental Psychopathology*. New York: Plenum Press.

Schaffer, R. (1977). *Mothering*. London: Fontana; Cambridge, MA: Harvard University Press.

## 3    E. C. Melhuish
### 'Behaviour Measures: A Measure of Love? An Overview of the Assessment of Attachment'

Reprinted in full from: *Association of Child Psychology and Psychiatry Review & Newsletter* **15**, 269–275 (1993)

### A measure of love? An overview of the assessment of attachment

Love relationships have long interested psychologists, and a current manifestation is attachment theory. Bowlby (1958, 1969, 1973, 1980) produced a theoretical framework for the study of attachments through an integration of ideas from psychodynamic, ethological and systems theories. Within the theory the capacity of attachment derives from the child's initial attachment to the primary caregiver, and the theory further considers how the development of attachments may proceed across the lifespan. However, the initial focus was on infant–mother attachment.

### Assessment in infancy

Without empirical support the theory would have had little effect on the development of psychology. However, Ainsworth developed Bowlby's ideas and operationalized them in ways conducive to empirical research, and this has led to attachment theory becoming one of the most influential theories in psychology. Ainsworth and colleagues produced the most widely used method for assessing infant attachment to a caregiver; the Strange Situation (Ainsworth and Wittig, 1969).

The Strange Situation consists of eight 3-minute episodes involving two separations and reunions in an unfamiliar setting. The procedure is designed to place the infant in increasingly stressful situations producing increased arousal of the attachment system and elicitation of attachment-related behaviours. The infant's responses during reunion are particularly salient for assessment. Using this method a classification of infant attachments to mothers was developed. Securely attached infants (type B) show signs of missing mother upon separation and warmly greet her upon reunion. Insecurely attached infants might be insecure-avoidant (type A) and show little distress upon separation and avoid or ignore the mother at reunion, or insecure-ambivalent/resistant (type C) and show distress upon separation and while seeking contact upon reunion, may show some resistance. These three major categories reflect earlier descriptions of types of attachment by Bowlby, Ainsworth, Boston and Rosenblith (1956). There are several subcategories and for a full description of the procedure and classification the best source is Ainsworth, Blehar, Waters and Wall (1978). Around 65–70% of American infants show secure attachment (type B) and 30–35% show one of the insecure patterns (type A 20–25%; type C 10–15%).

Several studies, notably by Sroufe and colleagues, (Sroufe, Fox and Pancake 1983; Suess, Grossman and Sroufe 1992; Elicker and Sroufe, 1993) have documented the predictive validity of attachment assessment with regard to later socio-emotional development. However, such association over time may reflect stability in family characteristics rather than the developmental consequences of early experience.

The stability of attachment classification is important, and most studies of stability have focused on the 12–18 month age range and have found high levels of stability (73% to 85%) (Waters, 1978; Main and Weston, 1981). However, lower stability has been found. Vaughn, Egeland, Sroufe and Waters (1979) and Egeland and Farber (1984) report stability of 60% over 12–18 months for disadvantaged families. Thompson, Lamb and Estes (1982) found stability of only 53% between 12.5 and 19.5 months. There are indications that instability of attachment is associated with changes in care environments. The most striking evidence of stability comes from Main and Cassidy (1988) who found 84% stability between 1 and 6 years. The high stability may reflect selection procedures which excluded birth complications, major life changes, and separations from parents. Hence the sample was homogenous with a reduced likelihood of disruptions to attachment patterns.

Often researchers using the traditional A, B, C, attachment classifications reported difficulties in categorizing some children. In particular, clinically-oriented researchers working with abusing families and high risk samples found this a frequent problem (e.g. Egeland and Sroufe, 1981; Crittenden, 1988), suggesting the need for more categories. Main and Solomon (1990) have proposed a D classification, insecure-disorganized/disoriented. Children from such D dyads show inconsistent and contradictory behaviour, a lack of obvious goals, and signs of confusion, apprehension and indecision toward the parent. The majority of infants of abusing parents may have a D classification (Lyons-Ruth, Connell, Zoll and Stahl, 1987; Carlson, Cicchetti, Barnet and Braunwald 1989). Also the majority of children classified as D at 1 year are classified as controlling at 6 years (Main and Cassidy, 1988).

The Strange Situation has been primarily used in the USA. Does the method have cross-cultural validity? Research in several countries indicated that overall it does, but interpretation should reflect cross-cultural variations. Firstly, the distribution of classifications varies from the American, white, middle-class patterns of 70% B, 20% A and 10% C type infants. In Germany (Grossman, Grossman, Spangler, Suess and Unzer, 1985) there is a higher percentage of type A infants. While in Japan (Miyake, Chen and Campos, 1985) and in Israeli Kibbutzim (Sagi *et al*, 1985) the percentage of type C infants is higher. Van IJzendoorn and Kroonenberg (1988) analyzed data from 32 studies in 8 countries. They concluded that while considerable variation between cultures exists, that the secure classification (B) is modal for all cultures and that the method appears valid for all cultures currently studied. However, there are difficulties in transferring the procedure to very different cultures. Grossman, Fremmer-Bombik and Grossman (1990) report difficulties in classifying a substantial proportion of Japanese infants and there was a range of responses, e.g. particularly intense and persistent crying to separation, not conforming to behaviour observed in Western research.

As well as inter-cultural variability, the issue of intra-cultural applicability of the Strange Situation arises e.g. with regard to children who differ in their experience of non-parental care. Belsky (1988) has argued that more than 20 hours a week of non-parental care for much of the first year is a risk factor for insecure attachment. Clarke-Stewart (1988) points out that the Strange Situation does not have equivalent ecological validity for children reared at home as those with extensive non-parental care, in that separations are much more part of everyday life. Hence, it is not appropriate to interpret behaviour in the Strange Situation as equivalent for children with such different care histories. This issue remains unresolved and is currently the focus of several studies.

An issue that could be raised with regard to the Strange Situation is the ethics of the procedure. It relies essentially on inducing stress in infants, because it is under such conditions that attachment behaviours are activated. Is it ethical to do this? The justification is based on the notion that the procedure investigates a part of everyday life under controlled conditions. However, it is clear some infants become very upset, and is this justified to test a theoretical idea?

**Other assessment methods for infants/toddlers**

Amongst the most well-known of alternative approaches is the interview procedure of Schaffer and Emerson (1964) focusing on seven separation situations. For each situation, the presence, consistency, intensity and direction of infant distress is covered. Maternal bias is minimized by enquiring only about overt, easily observable behaviour and the age of onset, intensity and breadth of attachments is estimated.

Another procedure in the home setting has been described by Melhuish (1987). The procedure involves a set sequence of approach behaviours by a stranger, followed by a separation and reunion episode. Behaviour signifying emotional reactions were coded at each stage. This procedure differentiated between 18 month old children with differing day care histories.

An adaptation of Ainsworth's methods has been used by Aber and Baker (1990) with toddlers in a clinical setting to enable aspects of attachment behaviour to be measured. This approach is particularly designed for clinical use with 19–24 months old. Attachment measures are used as part of intervention and monitoring procedures with clinical populations and it is this area that currently offers the most scope for clinical use. An example is the assessment of child–parent relationships in the course of family therapy, but these approaches are still experimental.

**Assessment of attachment on older children**

Early research focused on infancy and the Strange Situation was dominant. Subsequently, interest shifted to attachment in later life. Measures consistent with attachment theory yet appropriate to the developing competencies of children were needed. One approach has been to adapt the Strange Situation for older children. Cassidy and Marvin with the McArthur Working Group on Attachment (1989) have produced the Preschool Attachment System, a procedure and coding system for classifying attachment in 3–4 year olds and Main and Cassidy (1988) have done a similar job for 6 year olds. Children's behaviour during separations and reunions with the attachment figure in familiar surroundings is videotaped and coded. Main and Cassidy (1988) report very high stability using such procedures for 1–6 year olds for children without major life changes.

· The characteristics of secure or insecure attachments differ with age but there are continuities. The following descriptions from a coding manual for 3–4 year olds give some colour to the attachment categories. The securely attached child often shows relaxed pleasure upon reunion, with little ambivalence, avoidance, or controlling behaviour. Children do not often seek proximity of contact immediately but 'gravitate' slowly to the parent. Insecurely attached (avoidant) children may show avoidance by minimal responses to parental overtures, with an absence of affection and anger, and no particular interest in the parent's presence. Essentially they are distant and cool. Insecurely attached (ambivalent) show dependency through the display of immature behaviours, such as sucking fingers, wriggling the body, and using 'baby talk'. Insecurely attached (controlling) may show rejection, hostility, or negative behaviour in an attempt to gain control of the interaction. If disorganized they may show incomplete sequences of behaviour, appear confused or disoriented. More important than the specifics of behaviour is the patterning of behaviour for what it reveals about the child's strategy of interaction.

The Strange Situation is a time-consuming procedure requiring specialized facilities and training. Researchers have sought ways of using the mother's experience to produce a more efficient assessment. One approach has been the use of Q-sort methodology (Block and Block, 1980). In a Q-sort, there are a large number of items (Q-set), one to a card, where each item is a behavioural description. The observer sorts the cards into piles, from 'most characteristic' to 'least characteristic of child'. Examples of items are:

- Child smiles and vocalizes spontaneously to mother on reunion.
- Child does not accept mother's assurances when wary.
- Child becomes easily angry with mother.
- Child's predominant mood is happy.

The number of items per pile is controlled to produce an approximately normal distribution. Waters and Deane (1985) produced a 100-item Q-set on attachment for 1–3 year olds, covering a wide range of attachment behaviour. The Q-sort produces a continuous security score from more to less secure. Waters and Deane report mothers' classifications on the Q-sort agree well ($r = 0.8$) with the classifications of trained observers. While Q-sorts can be used with infants, most applications have been with older children.

Vaughn (1985) compared the Strange Situation classification at 12–15 months of age with Q-sorts at 2 and 3 years. The Q-sorts distinguished between the secure and insecure groups of children, and several studies (e.g. Vaughn and Waters, 1990) show good agreement between Q-sorts and Strange Situation results. However, van Dam and van IJzendoorn (1988) tested the concurrent validity of the parent version of the Q-sort against Strange Situation classifications at 18 months old and did not find good evidence of concurrent validity. Hence the issue of the validity of Q-sort methodology is not entirely resolved.

Despite these problems, the Q-sort approach has been widely used and adaptations have been produced for mothers, caregivers, and observers and for children of various ages. Studies using Q-sorts support the predictions of attachment theory with regard to socio-emotional development in 3 and 4 year olds (e.g. Aber and Baker, 1990; Teti, Nakagawa, Das and Wirth, 1991).

The Q-sort does not involve stress upon the child but involves the report of behaviour as observed naturalistically. According to attachment theory, the attachment system becomes more strongly activated under stress, hence the Q-sort may not incorporate the appropriate observations for attachment classification if the observer has not seen appropriate stressful situations. In addition, the enforcement of an arbitrary distribution of items may produce a distortion of placement of items and hence assessment.

## Representational methods

Several researchers (e.g. Main, Kaplan and Cassidy, 1985) have considered the possibility of measuring attachment via representational methods rather than via behavioural analysis. These developments in attachment research take up themes elaborated in the second and third parts of the attachment trilogy (Bowlby, 1973, 1980). Examples are:

1  Child's reaction to family photographs (Main *et al.*, 1985)
2  Child's drawings of family members (Kaplan and Main, 1986)
3  Doll-story completion tasks (Cassidy, 1988)
4  Puppet interview with child (Cassidy, 1988)
5  Child's responses to pictures of separations, where children are asked about the feelings of a child undergoing a separation. (Klagsbrun and Bowlby, 1976; Main *et al.*, 1985 – the Separation Anxiety Test (SAT)).

An example of the use of representational methods is a study by Shouldice and Stevenson-Hinde (1992) comparing SAT results with behaviour in a separation-reunion situation for 4–5 year old children. Secure children (as judged by separation-reunion behaviour) showed less emotional reactions in the SAT responses, and gave more appropriate emotional responses than children classified as insecure. However, agreement between SAT results and reunion behaviour were not strong enough to indicate that the SAT could be used as an alternative to direct observation of attachment behaviour.

Representational techniques derive from the concept of the internal working model which is central to attachment theory. The internal working model mediates emotional and behavioural reactions to attachment figures, and potentially others. The internal working model is a hypothetical construct and constitutes the child's expectations regarding potential and actual attachment figures and the self. Insecurely attached children will have negative expectations, and reactions can be viewed as defence mechanisms or coping strategies for dealing with such expectations. Such reactions may involve avoidance, anger or incoherence/disorganization and if attachment figures are represented as rejecting, then the self will be considered as complementary, i.e. unworthy of affection. Securely attached children would not show such reactions as they have positive expectations of attachment figures and can cope with interactions which would be represented as warm and supportive and the self as worthy of affection. Presently these representational methods of assessment show much promise but have yet to be developed sufficiently to replace behavioural analysis. They might best be used as part of a multi-method assessment of attachment as used by Main *et al.* (1985).

## Attachment classification for adults

George, Kaplan and Main (1985) and Main (1985) report on the Adult Attachment Interview (AAI) which, based upon the adults' memories of childhood and present attachment orientations, produces an attachment classification for adults in terms of four categories of secure (F, autonomous), dismissing (D), preoccupied (E) and unresolved (U). Such procedures may be developed for clinical use (Dozier, 1990). This instrument has been used to relate infant's attachments to mother to mother's own attachment patterns (Main *et al.*, 1985; Grossman, Fremmer-Bombik, Rudolph and Grossman, 1988). These findings have also been replicated where the AAI has been given to mothers during pregnancy and subsequently related to infant–mother attachment (Fonagy, Steele and Steele, 1991; Ward *et al.*, 1991; Levine, Tuber, Slade and Ward, 1991).

The levels of association between mothers' AAI classification and children's Strange Situation classification are greater than might be expected given the measurement error in the methods and are such that the AAI classification appears almost as strongly associated with the Strange Situation classification as either measure is with itself. There are several possible interpretations. Here two are considered. Possibly researchers who classify infant behaviour come to know something about maternal characteristics and/or vice versa and hence there may be measurement contamination. Even when the AAI is scored blind, the Strange Situation rater would have considerable experience of the mother as she would be in videotapes being rated and probably interacted intensively with researchers. This knowledge of the mother may contaminate ratings of infant attachment behaviour. Alternatively, the mother's AAI results may be a better predictor of a child's socio-emotional development than the Strange Situation itself, thus eliminating the need for the Strange Situation.

Another perspective on the infant–parent attachment comes from Bretherton, Biringen, Ridgeway, Maslin and Sherman (1989) who developed an interview for evaluating the parental view of the parental–child attachment. They found strong associations between the results of this interview with the mothers of 2 year olds and results from the Strange Situation at 18 months old, a Q-sort at 2 years old, and a classification of attachment at 3 years old, based either on reunion behaviours or a story completion task (Bretherton, Ridgeway and Cassidy, 1990).

## Summary

Research derived from attachment theory is now concerned with relationships across the life span. The sudden expansion of the scope of research can be linked to the landmark publication edited by Bretherton and Waters (1985). Hence most methodologies are recent and likely to be modified. Developments in this field are currently exciting and fast-moving and attachment theory itself is expanding and changing. The theory has been found useful in applied situations. In developmental psychopathology the theory and methods have been applied to such areas as child abuse (Cicchetti and Carlson, 1989) and family therapy (Lieberman and Pawl, 1988). Such applied research is a major source of new ideas for the theory. There is nothing so practical as a good theory and putting the theory to practice improves the theory.

## References

Aber, J. S., and Baker, A. J. L. (1990). Security of attachment in toddlerhood: modifying assessment procedures for joint clinical and research purposes. In M. T. Greenberg, D. Cicchetti and E. M. Cummings (Eds.), *Attachment in the Pre-school Years*. Chicago: University of Chicago Press.

Ainsworth, M., and Wittig, B. A. (1969). Attachment and exploratory behaviour of 1-year-olds in a strange situation. In B. M. Foss (Ed.), *Determinants of Infant Behaviour*, Vol. 4. London: Methuen.

Ainsworth, M., Blehar, M. C., Waters, E., and Wall, S. (1978). *Patterns of Attachment*. Hillsdale, NJ: Lawrence Erlbaum Associates.

Belsky, J. (1988). The 'effects' of infant day care reconsidered. *Early Childhood Research Quarterly*, 235–272.

Block, J. H., and Block, J. (1980). The role of ego control and ego-resiliency in the organization of behaviour. In A. Collins (Ed.), *Minnesota Symposium of Child Psychology*, Vol. 13, 39–101. Hillsdale, NJ: Lawrence Erlbaum Associates.

Bowlby, J., Ainsworth, M., Boston, M., and Rosenblith, D. (1956). The effects of mother-child separation: a follow-up study. *British Journal of Medical Psychology*, 29, 211–247.

Bowlby, J. (1958). The nature of the child's tie to his mother. *International Journal of Psycho-Analysis*. Vol. 39.

Bowlby, J. (1969). Attachment: *Vol 1 of Attachment and Loss*. London: Hogarth.

Bowlby, J. (1973). Separation: *Vol 2 of Attachment and Loss*. London: Hogarth.

Bowlby, J. (1980). *Loss: Sadness and Depression: Vol 3 of Attachment and Loss*. London: Hogarth.

Bretherton, I., Biringen, Z., Ridgeway, D., Maslin, C., and Sherman, M. (1989). Attachment: The parental perspective. *Infant Mental Health Journal, 10*, 203–221.

Bretherton, I., Ridgeway, D., and Cassidy, J. (1990). Assessing internal working models in the attachment relationship: An attachment story completion task for 3 year-olds. In M. T. Greenburg, D. Cichetti, and E. M. Cummings (Eds.), *Attachment During the Preschool Years*. Chicago: University of Chicago Press.

Bretherton, I., and Waters, E. (1985). Growing points of attachment theory and research. *Monographs of the Society for Research in Child Development, 50*, (1–2, Serial No. 209).

Carlson, V., Cicchetti, D., Barnett, D., and Braunwald, K. (1989). Finding order in disorganization: Lessons from research on maltreated infants' attachments to their caregivers. In D. Cicchetti and V. Carlson (Eds.), *Child Maltreatment: Theory and Research on the Causes and Consequences of Child Abuse and Neglect*. New York: Cambridge University Press.

Cassidy, J., Marvin, R., and the MacArthur Working Group on attachment (1989). Attachment organization in three and four year-olds: Coding guidelines. Unpublished manuscript, University of Virginia and Pennsylvania State University.

Cassidy, J. (1988). Child-mother attachment and the self in six-year-olds. *Child Development, 59*, 121–134.

Cicchetti, D., and Carlson, V. (1989). *Child Maltreatment Theory and Research on the Causes and Consequences of Child Abuse and Neglect*. New York: Cambridge University Press.

Clarke-Stewart, K. A. (1988). The 'effects' of infant day care reconsidered: risks for parents, children and researchers. *Early Childhood Research Quarterly, 3*, 293–318.

Crittenden, P. M. (1988). Relationships at risk. In J. Belsky and T. Nezworski (Eds.), *Clinical Implications of Attachment*. Hillsdale, NJ: Erlbaum.

Dozier, M. (1990). Attachment organization and treatment use for adults with serious psychopathological disorders. *Development and Psychopathology, 2*, 47–60.

Egeland, B., and Sroufe, L. A. (1981). Attachment and early maltreatment. *Child Development, 52*, 44–52.

Egeland, B., and Farber, E. (1984). Infant-mother attachment: factors relating to its development and changes over time. *Child Development, 55*, 753–771.

Elicker, J., and Sroufe, L. A. (1993). Predicting peer competence and peer relationships in childhood from early parent-child relationships. In R. Parke and C. Ladd (Eds.), *Family-Peer Relationships: Modes of Linkage*. Hillsdale, NJ: Erlbaum.

Fonagy, P., Steele, M., and Steele, H. (1991). Intergenerational patterns of attachment: maternal representations during pregnancy and subsequent infant-mother attachments. *Child Development, 62*, 891–905.

George, C., Kaplan, N., and Main, M. (1985). The Berkeley *Adult Attachment Interview*. Berkeley, CA: University of California.

Grossman, K., Grossman, K. E., Spangler, G., Suess, G., and Unzer, L. (1985). In I. Bretherton and E. Waters (Eds.), Growing points in attachment theory and research. *Monographs of the Society for Research in Child Development*. Serial No. 209, Vol. 50, 3–35 monograph.

Grossman, K., Fremmer-Bombik, E., Rudolph, J., and Grossman, K. E. (1988). Maternal attachment representations as related to patterns of infant-mother attachment and maternal care during the first year. In R. A. Hinde and J. Stevenson-Hinde (Eds.), *Relationships within Families: Mutual Influences*. Clarendon: Oxford.

Grossman, K., Fremmer-Bombik, E., and Grossman, K. E. (1990). *Familiar and Unfamiliar Patterns of Attachment in Japanese Infants*. Research and Clinical Centre for Child Development, Faculty of Education, Hokkaido University, Sapporo, Japan. Annual Report; Occasional Paper No. 2.

Kaplan, N., and Main, M. (1986). Assessments of attachment organizations through children's family drawings. Unpublished classification system. Department of Psychology, University of California, Berkeley, CA: 94720, USA.

Klagsbrun, M., and Bowlby, J. (1976). Responses to separation from parents: a clinical test for young children. *Projective Psychology, 21*, 2, 7–26.

Lamb, M. E., Thompson, R. A., Gardner, W. P., Charnove, E. L., and Estes, D. (1984). Security of infantile attachment as assessed in the 'strange situation': its study and biological interpretation. *Behavioral and Brain Sciences, 7*, 127–171.

Levine, L. V., Tuber, S. B., Slade, A., and Ward, M. J. (1991). Mother's mental representations and their relationship to mother-infant interaction. *Bulletin of the Menninger Clinic, 55*, 454–469.

Lieberman, A. J., and Pawl, J. H. (1988). Clinical implications of attachment theory. In J. Belsky and T. Nezworkski (Eds.), *Clinical Implications of Attachment.* NJ: Erlbaum.

Lyons-Ruth, K., Connell, D., Zoll, D., and Stahl, J. (1987). Infants at social risk: relationships among infant maltreatment, maternal behaviour, and infant attachment behaviour. *Developmental Psychology, 23*, 223–232.

Main, M. (1985). An adult attachment classification system: Its relation to infant-parent attachment. Paper presented at the biennial meeting of the Society meeting of the Society for Research in Child Development, Toronto.

Main, M., and Weston, D. (1981). The quality of toddlers' relationship to mother and father. *Child Development, 52*, 932–940.

Main, M., and Cassidy, J. (1988). Categories of Response to reunion with the parent at age six: predicted from infant attachment classifications and stable over a one-month period. *Developmental Psychology, 24*, 415–426.

Main, M., Kaplan, N., and Cassidy, J. (1985). Security in infancy, childhood and adulthood: a move to a level of representation. In I. Bretherton and E. Waters (Eds.), *Growing points of attachment theory and research. Monographs of the Society for Research in Child Development, 50* (1–2 Serial No. 209).

Main, M., and Solomon, J. (1990). Procedure for identifying insecure-disorganized/disoriented infants within the Ainsworth Strange Situation. In M. T. Greenberg, D. Cichetti and E. M. Cummings (Eds.), *Attachment During the Preschool Years.* Chicago: University of Chicago Press.

Melhuish, E. C. (1987). Socio-emotional behaviour at 18 months as a function of day care experience, temperament and gender. *Infant Mental Health Journal, 4*, 364–373.

Miyake, K., Chen, S. J., Campos, J. J. (1985). Infant temperament, mother's mode of interaction, and attachment in Japan: an interim report. In I. Bretherton and E. Waters (Eds.), *Growing points of attachment theory and research.* (pp. 276–297). *Monographs of the Society for Research and Child Development, 50* (1–2, Serial No. 209).

Sagi, A., Lamb, M. E., Lewkowickz, K. S., Shoham, R., Dvir, R., and Estes, D. (1985). Security of infant-mother, father, and -metapelet among kibbutz reared Israeli children. In I. Bretherton and E. Waters (Eds.), *Growing points of attachment theory and research Monographs of the Society for Research in Child Development, 50* (1–2, Serial No. 209), 257–275.

Schaffer, H. R., and Emerson, P. E. (1964). The development of social attachments in infancy. *Monographs of the Society for Research in Child Development, 29*, No. 3 (whole No. 94)

Shouldice, A., and Stevenson-Hinde, J. (1992). Coping with security distress: The

Separation Anxiety Test and attachment classification at 4.5 years. *Journal of Child Psychology & Psychiatry, 33,* 331–348.

Sroufe, L. A., Fox, N., and Pancake, V. (1983). Attachment and dependency in developmental perspective. *Child Development, 54,* 1615–1627.

Suess, G. J., Grossman, K. E., and Sroufe, L. A. (1992). Effects of infant attachment to mother and father on quality of adaptation in preschool: from dyadic to individual organisation of self. *International Journal of Behavioural Development, 15,* 43–66.

Teti, D. M., Nakagawa, M., Das, R., and Wirth, O. (1991). Security of attachment between preschoolers and their mothers: Relations among social interaction, parenting stress and mothers' sorts of the attachment Q-set. *Developmental Psychology, 27,* 440–447.

Thompson, R., Lamb, M., and Estes, D. (1982). Stability of infant-mother attachment and its relationships to changing life circumstances in an unselected middle-class sample. *Child Development, 53,* 144–148.

van-Dam, M., and van IJzendoorn, M. H. (1988). Measuring attachment security: concurrent and predictive validity of the parental attachment Q-set. *Journal of Genetic Psychology, 149,* 447–457.

van IJzendoorn, M. H., and Kroonenberg, P. M. (1988). Cross-cultural patterns of attachment: a meta-analysis of the Strange Situation. *Child Development, 59,* 147–156.

Vaughn, B. (1985). Relations between scores on the Attachment Behaviour Q-set and Strange Situation Classifications. Conference of the International Society for the Study of Behavioural Development. Tours, France.

Vaughn, B., Egeland, B., Sroufe, L. A., and Waters, E. (1979). Individual differences in infant-mother attachment at twelve and eighteen months: Stability and change in families under stress. *Child Development, 50,* 971–975.

Vaughn, B. E., and Waters, E. (1990). Attachment behaviour at home and in the laboratory: Q-sort observations and Strange Situation classifications of one-year-olds. *Child Development, 61,* 1965–1973.

Ward, M. J., Carlson, E. A., Altmann, S., Levin, L., Greenberg, R. H., and Kessler, D. B. (1991). Predicting infant-mother attachment from adolescents' prenatal working models of relationships. 7th International Conference on Infant Studies, Montreal, Quebec, Canada.

Waters, E. (1978). The reliability and stability of individual differences in infant-mother attachment. *Child Development, 49,* 483–494.

Waters, E., and Deane, K. E. (1985). Defining and assessing individual differences in attachment relationships: Q-methodology and the organisation of behaviour in infancy and early childhood. In I. Bretherton and E. Waters (Eds.), *Growing points in attachment theory and research. Monographs of the Society for Research in Child Development, 50* (Serial No. 209), 3–35.

# SECTION II
# *LANGUAGE AND COMMUNICATION*

## Editors' Introduction

Philosophers, psychologists and linguists have struggled to describe the language system and explain its development. Language is a rule-governed symbol system capable of representing or coding one's understanding of the world. We can produce an infinite variety of sentences to describe an infinite variety of situations. Yet there are language specific restrictions about the ways in which the words can be combined in sentences. Language is a system composed of a number of levels or subcomponents. For example, there is the syntactic level that includes sentences, clauses and phrases. There is also the lexical or word level which is the vocabulary that we build up as we develop. Chapter 1 in Barrett (1998) provides an excellent description of these various levels and subsystems.

It is important to distinguish between communication, which is the transmission of information, and language, which is primarily a representational system. Infants communicate from the minute they are born, yet the ability to use language emerges as the child's cognitive skills enable him to understand and organize the world. Steven Pinker in his best-selling novel *The Language Instinct* argues that 'Language is so tightly woven into the human experience that it is scarcely possible to imagine life without it' (Pinker, 1994). Yet, as the final paper in this section illustrates there are children who have delays or difficulties in language. The study of atypical or exceptional language development has become very popular over the last 10 years. The basic argument is that by studying how the language system goes wrong we can have a better insight into how the system actually works.

When you look at the literature about language development, you will notice that there are two major research paradigms and two opposing theoretical paradigms. The research paradigm is split between experimental and observational research. Observational research often involves the use of a diary which records the child's utterances. Observational and diary data tend to be naturalistic, that is they are collected as the child moves through its normal daily routines with familiar people. Such methods are less frequently used with children above the age of about three. This is because of practical reasons and also because the child's language becomes so complex it is hard to collect adequate samples. By corollary in the past very little experimental language work was done with children who are less than 2 years of age. This trend is changing and as our first paper shows it is indeed possible to experiment with 1-year-olds. The second major division in the areas relates to explanation of how language develops (for a more detailed discussion of these issues see Messer, 1994, chapter 12). Nativists see language as an innately specified cognitive structure. This structure is viewed as specifically human and responsible for the universal aspects of language. It is argued that there are principles and rules common to languages in general – a universal grammar. Children's knowledge of universal grammar allows them to acquire the particular grammar of the language that they hear. In contrast social interactionists highlight the fact that children do not break into language in a vacuum, rather it occurs in the context of early social communication.

The first paper by Tomasello and Farrar focuses on the embryonic language system. They argue that one of the fundamental achievements of infancy, which is the development of joint visual attention, has a key role to play in explaining early comprehension and production of words. Their paper is important for a number of reasons. First, there is the successful use of combined investigative procedures. Through observational work the authors identify a number of correlations between the mother's and the infant's behaviour. Correlation does not, of course, explain causality. They clearly detail how their results could be interpreted as the mother influencing the infant's language but equally there is the possibility that the infant influences the mother. The second study uses experimentation, which is the only sure way of specifying causality, to clarify the situation. In this study the authors address the role of input on lexical acquisition in a clearly specified way, that is they specify what they term learning conditions in such a fashion that the work could be replicated. Finally, throughout the paper they highlight some of the pitfalls of this kind of research such as aggregating data across children when there is much variability in their scores. You might like to consider further whether you are convinced by their explanation of the low production scores in the second experiment. Do you think the children really were shy? What alternative explanations might there be and how would you test them?

The second paper by Markman and Hutchinson is also about lexical acquisition and is a classic of its kind. These authors take a very different stance from Tomasello and Farrar by arguing that there are constraints in the ways in which children interpret the meanings of new words. Like the Tomasello paper this one examines the acquisition of object words. It is important to remember that object words only account for a proportion of the child's vocabulary. Nonetheless their results appear to show that children consider words to be categorical in nature. When children encounter a new item and that item is given a name, such as *aardvark*, and they are instructed to 'Look for another aardvark that is the same as this aardvark' children tend to search for an item that is categorically related to the named item. Two possible explanations of this constraint are suggested: firstly that the constraint is innate and secondly, that it is induced early on in the acquisition process. As you read the paper examine the data in detail. You will see that if a constraint is at work it is not an absolute one, that is it does not always work. For example, in Experiment 2 the inclusion of the novel word raised taxonomic choices from 49% to 69%. Why are children not making taxonomic choices in 30% of the trials? Secondly, their explanation of the relationship between the justifications the children provide and their choice responses is open to alternative interpretations. Read this section carefully for experiment 2. Consider how you would replicate their coding system.

Error analysis has contributed to major developments in the study of language processes (see for example Cutler, 1988). In the third paper in this section Gary Marcus illustrates how analysing children's errors can help in our understanding of the cognitive system. Observational data has suggested that children pass through three phases when acquiring the past tense. Initially children produce the past tense correctly for a small group of regular verbs, such as dance/danced, and irregular verbs, such as go/went. Following this period of correct usage children over-regularize the 'ed' ending, e.g. go/goed and finally they reach a point where such errors no longer occur. There have been many attempts to explain why children over-regularize the 'ed' ending when forming the past tense, including a number of connectionist models (see Plunkett, 1995). Marcus' proposal is somewhat different. He argues for the existence of mental rules which govern the use of 'ed'. Errors occur because of retrieval failures. A number of different types of convergent evidence are used to make the argument. As you read the paper you should attempt to identify these different sources of evidence. Should similar weight be given to each data set or do some forms of data provide stronger evidence than others? In all analyses of syntactic and semantic aspects of language it is important to understand that language performance is influenced by a wide set of factors. An important demonstration of this is the work of Virginia Valian and her colleagues (1996). They have demonstrated that children's grammatical development is influenced by factors other than purely linguistic ones and that these factors need to be carefully evaluated when considering both typical and atypical development.

Explaining language development involves both considering different languages but also different contexts of development. Theories of language learning also need to consider social and contextual factors. The fourth paper in this section by Shirley Brice Heath forces us to broaden our views of language to consider patterns of socialization. In the past some psychologists believed that language differences should be explained in terms of linguistic deprivation and disadvantage – differences which, at times, were felt to require remediation. Interpretations of this kind are now routinely challenged. Brice Heath demonstrates how the oral skills of black Americans sustain adaptive and innovative strategies for problem solving – strategies, she argues, that are not taught in schools and whose fundamental contribution is denied. You might like to consider particular examples from your own experience where differences in socialization practices are considered in terms of the possible benefits that they might bring. Differences do not mean that the dominant practices are best. You should compare these arguments with those made by Rogoff and Morell in their paper in the section on Others and their Influence.

The final contribution to this section considers what Dorothy Bishop and Kay Mogford (1988) refer to as language development in exceptional circumstances. Variations in normal patterns of development have been described as experiments of nature. As defined by Bronfenbrenner (1979) an experiment of nature involves the use of naturally occurring situations to test our developmental ideas. This method of enquiry has a long history and has become a major methodological approach in the last decade. David Skuse uses examples of children who have suffered extreme forms of deprivation to highlight those factors that are robust and those that are deemed fragile in the developmental process. Robust features withstand such environmental deprivations while fragile features do not. An important factor brought out through Skuse's analysis is the need to clarify the extent to which the child is experiencing other difficulties. The rapid progress of most of these children is extremely satisfying. Yet, as with all retrospective studies, we need to be very careful in accepting the data at face value. If the child does not progress we can never be sure whether this should be explained by particular child-based factors which led to isolation in the first place or the isolation, per se. Recall Campbell and Grieve's (1982) distinction mentioned in the introduction between authenticity and veracity of the very early reports of isolation from language input. What other information would you wish to see about the language of these children?

## References

Bishop, D. and Mogford, K. (1988). *Language Development in Exceptional Circumstances*. London: Churchill Livingstone.

Bronfenbrenner, U. (1979). *The Ecology of Human Development: experiments by nature and design*. Cambridge, MA: Harvard University Press.

Cutler, A. (1988). The perfect speech error. In L. M. Hyman and C. S. Li (Eds.), *Language, Speech and Mind: Studies in honour of Victoria A. Fromkin*. London: Routledge.

Pinker, S. (1994). *The Language Instinct*. Penguin.

Plunkett, K. (1995). Connectionists approaches to language acquisition. In P. Fletcher and B. MacWhinney (Eds.), *The Handbook of Child Language*. Oxford: Blackwell.

Valian, V., Aubry, S., and Hoeffner, J. (1996). Young children's imitation of sentence subjects: Evidence of processing limitations. *Developmental Psychology*, *32*, 153–164.

## Further Reading

Barrett, M. (Ed.) (1998). *The Psychology of Language*. Sussex: Psychology Press.

Clark, E., and Grossman, J. (1998). Pragmatic directions and word learning. *Journal of Child Language*.

Dockrell, J. E. and Grove, N. (in press). Children with sensory impairments. In D. Messer and S. Millar (Eds.) *Developmental Psychology*. London: Arnold.

Elman, J., Bates, E., Johnson, M., Karmiloff-Smith, A., Parisi, D., and Plunkett, K. (1996). *Rethinking Innateness: A connectionist perspective*. Cambridge, MA: MIT Press.

Grove, N. and Dockrell, J. E. (in press). Children with learning disabilities. In D. Messer and S. Millar (Eds.) *Developmental Psychology*. London: Arnold.

Messer, D. (in press). Communication and language. In D. Messer and S. Millar (Eds.) *Developmental Psychology*. London: Arnold.

Messer, D. (1994). *The Development of Communication: From social interaction to language*. Chichester: Wiley.

Ochs, E. and Schiefflin, B. (1995). The impact of language socialization on grammatical development. In P. Fletcher and B. MacWhinney (Eds.), *The Handbook of Child Language*. Oxford: Blackwell.

Rice, M. (Ed.) (1996). *Towards a Genetics of Language*. Lawrence Erlbaum Associates.

# 4    Michael Tomasello and Michael J. Farrar
### 'Joint Attention and Early Language'

Reprinted in full from: *Child Development* 57, 1454–1463 (1986)

By the time children begin productive language use, they have already established with their caregivers a variety of social-communicative routines. Ninio and Bruner (1978) and Ratner and Bruner (1978) analyzed the structure of these routines and demonstrated how such nonlinguistic interactions 'scaffold' the child's early language. In effect, these interactions provide the young child with a predictable referential context that makes both her and her mother's language immediately meaningful. In his theoretical work, Bruner (e.g., 1981, 1983, 1985) has stressed that the underlying mechanism at work in these mother-child 'formats' is joint attention. Because young children do not possess adult devices – either linguistic or nonlinguistic – for establishing the joint attention necessary for communication, recurrent interactive episodes help the infant to determine adults' attentional focus and thus the intended referent of their language. In this way, formats support early communicative interactions and so facilitate the child's early language development (see also Bakeman and Adamson, 1984).

Tomasello and Todd (1983) provided the first direct evidence that individual differences in the ability of mother-child dyads to establish and maintain a joint attentional focus are related to the child's subsequent language growth. They videotaped mother-child dyads in their homes with a set of novel toys at monthly intervals for a period of 6 months, beginning with the child's first birthday. The amount of time dyads spent in joint attentional episodes during the 6 months was positively related to the child's vocabulary size at the end of this period. Several lines of evidence, including cross-lagged correlations, supported the argument that these episodes facilitated the child's early language development. This finding was replicated in a study comparing singleton and twin children (Tomasello, Mannle and Kruger, 1986), in which positive correlations were found between time in joint attention at 15 months of age and vocabulary size at 21 months of age for each group of children separately as well as for the sample as a whole.

A second finding of these studies was that directiveness on the part of mothers – either verbal or nonverbal attempts to direct the child's attention or behavior – was negatively related to the proportion of object labels in the child's vocabulary. Others have found a similar relationship (e.g., Della Corte, Benedict and Klein, 1983; Nelson, 1973). Nelson (1981) hypothesized that this relationship is due to the child's inferences about the functional significance of language based on the way people around him use it. If adults use language primarily to refer to and categorize the world (e.g., naming novel objects), the child will infer that this is its primary function and the acquisition of object labels will be very important. Conversely, if adults are constantly using language for social-regulative purposes (e.g., to greet, thank, exhort, prohibit), the child will infer that this is its primary function and the acquisition of object labels will be less important.

Tomasello and Todd (1983) offered a different interpretation. They argued that adult directiveness makes it more difficult for child and adult to establish a joint attentional focus. When the adult attempts to redirect the child's attention in referring to an object, if the child is to determine the intended referent she must shift her attention so as to coordinate with the adult's. On the other hand, when the adult's reference follows into the child's already established attentional focus, the child need not actively make such a determination; coordination of attention depends only on the adult's skill at determining the child's focus. These authors thus argue that adult directiveness has an effect not so much on the child's overall assessment of the function of language but rather on the learning conditions surrounding the acquisition of individual words.

In the current view, then, joint attention is important for early language both on the 'macro' level of extended periods of adult-child interaction and on the 'micro' level of adult-child attempts to coordinate a specific piece of language with a joint attentional focus on its intended referent. The current study was designed to investigate these two types of attentional process in more detail. Two studies were conducted. The first was based on naturalistic observation of children just beginning to learn language. In contrast to Tomasello and Todd (1983), who looked only at time spent in joint attentional episodes, the current study focused on the language that occurred in these episodes. On the macro level, it was hypothesized that mother-child linguistic interaction would be facilitated when the interactants were jointly focused on some aspect of the nonlinguistic context. It was thus expected that inside, as opposed to outside, episodes of joint attention mother-child dyads would talk more and carry on longer conversations. Further, it was expected that while children would be encouraged to use longer sentences, mothers would use shorter sentences in these episodes because the intensity of these interactions encourages mothers' best Child Directed Speech speech register. In addition, because joint focus on the nonlinguistic context provides a predetermined conversational topic, mothers were expected to use less directive language inside joint episodes. On the micro level, it was hypothesized that object labels presented in an attempt to follow into the child's attentional focus would facilitate the establishment of joint attention and thus be positively related to the child's use of object-names. Conversely, object labels presented in an attempt to redirect the child's attentional focus were expected to discourage joint attention and thus be negatively related to the child's lexical acquisition. These relationships were expected to be stronger inside than outside macro-level episodes of joint attention.

The second study was a lexical training study designed to provide experimental corroboration for the findings on the micro level, that is, for the relationship between directiveness and lexical acquisition. Children in their second year of life were presented with novel object words either in an attempt to redirect their attentional focus or, alternatively, in an attempt to follow into their current attentional focus. It was predicted that children would learn new words more easily when they were presented in the latter condition. If this were indeed the case, it would provide experimental corroboration that adult directiveness is associated with slower early lexical acquisition, and it would provide evidence for the operation of attentional factors in this process.

## Study 1

### Method

*Subjects.* Twenty-four white, middle-class children – equal numbers of firstborns and later-borns, males and females – were recruited by personal contact from local day-care facilities. Children were all between 12 and 18 months of age at recruitment (mean age = 14.6 months) and, according to maternal report, had begun productive language use.

*Observational procedure.* Each mother-child dyad was videotaped at home for a period of 15 min on two occasions, once when children were 15 months and once when they were 21 months of age. Dyads were provided with a set of novel toys and given no special instructions except to 'Do what you normally would do.' A research assistant and camera-person were present at each session. Mothers were told at recruitment that we were interested in their child's language development, and they were instructed at that time to begin noting the child's normal language practices. At each of the taping sessions, mothers were interviewed about their child's use of language.

*Coding procedure.* Each videotape was first coded for episodes of joint attentional focus. As defined by Tomasello and Todd (1983), these were episodes that met the following conditions: (1) they began with one member of the dyad initiating interaction with the other, (2) both members then visually focused on a single object or activity for a minimum of 3 sec (either member could look away briefly during an extended interaction), and (3) at some point during the joint focus (possibly at initiation) the child directed some overt behavior toward the mother (especially a look to the face) as evidence that he was aware of their interaction, thus excluding mere onlooking. An example might be: the child hands the mother a spoon, looking to her face; she places it in a cup; he takes it out, mouths it, and puts it back in the cup, looking to the mother; they continue this until someone (usually the child) shifts attention. Had the child played with these objects alone, this would not have been a joint attentional episode even if the mother was visually focused on the objects throughout.

The language inside and outside these episodes was of interest. It was coded in two ways. First, each videotape was transcribed by a team of two research assistants. An independent assistant coded the transcripts for specific language measures and then, using the joint attention coding, tabulated data on the language measures separately for inside and outside the episodes of joint attentional focus. Language measures for both mother and child were: number of utterances and Mean Length of Utterance (MLU). For mothers only, the proportional distribution of utterances into comments, questions, and directives was also determined. For children only, the total number of words and object-labels per minute was also determined. In addition, two measures of the dyad's conversational behavior were of interest: number of conversations (a conversation was defined as adjacent utterances on a common topic) and mean number of child turns per conversation (as an indication of conversation length).

The comparison of these measures inside and outside episodes of joint attentional focus constituted the macro level of analysis.

The second coding, on a more micro level, concerned attentional factors associated with maternal reference to objects. In a separate coding of the videotapes, an independent team of two coders established for each maternal reference to an object (in which the object word received some prosodic stress): (*a*) whether or not it was made in an attempt to follow into the child's ongoing attentional focus (i.e., visual), as opposed to an attempt to redirect her attention or behavior, (*b*) whether or not the mother gestured or provided some other nonverbal indication of her attentional focus while making the reference, and (*c*) whether or not the child actually visually focused on the object at the time of the object reference. In this way, each object reference was assigned one of eight unique patterns generated by a factorial combination of the three dichotomies. Each of these patterns was designated by a sequence of three '+' or '−' symbols, one for each of the three criteria used in their determination. For example, an object reference in which the adult followed into the child's attentional focus, gestured, and the child focused on the object successfully was designated by '+ + +'. These data were then tabulated separately for inside and outside periods of joint attentional focus.

It is important to note that these two levels of analysis are independent, not only in the methodological sense that they were were coded independently, but also conceptually. Though on the surface it would seem that a joint attentional focus on the macro level would automatically imply that the mother's object references would follow into the child's focus, this is not necessarily so. First, joint attentional episodes sometimes involve several objects (e.g., placing blocks in a bowl). If a mother directed the child's attention to one of these objects and the child was focused on another, then this was considered a directive inside a joint episode. Second, a mother could make an attempt within a joint episode to redirect her child's attention to outside objects. If the child did not attend, or attended only briefly and then returned to the object of joint focus, this also was counted as a directive within a joint episode. Conversely, it could also happen that a mother could follow into her child's focus when not in a joint attentional episode. If this did not result in an extended (3-sec) period of joint focus, this was counted as an attempt to follow into the child's attention outside a joint attentional episode.

The language interview used to assess the child's language development at 15 and 21 months of age was an adaptation of the Bates (1979) interview which, in addition to utilizing spontaneously generated information, prompts the mother to provide examples of the child's language use by asking her about specific contexts in which children talk. (For example: What does she do when she wants food? Any special foods? What about when she wants her bottle? When she's in the high chair? At the refrigerator? In the store?) From this interview, a vocabulary list (including pat phrases) was compiled. Vocabulary size was computed, as well as the proportion of the child's lexical items that were object labels (i.e., general nominals as defined by Nelson, 1973). This latter measure was used in an attempt to capture language-acquisition style independently of sheer size of vocabulary.

Reliability was computed for each of the measures by having a second team of assistants code 20% of the subjects and compute the percentage of their agreement with the original coders. Reliabilities were as follows: judgments of joint attentional episodes (durations had to be within 3 sec) agreed at 84%; child language measures (including conversation) agreed at 88%–100%; maternal language measures (including types of object reference) agreed at 82%–100%.

*Results*

At both time periods, mother-child dyads spent about two-thirds of their interaction time inside joint attentional episodes and about one-third of their time outside these episodes. Because of this difference, all measures of frequency were divided by the appropriate measure of time to yield a 'per-minute' frequency. All other measures were proportions of one language measure relative to another. Each mother and child language measure was analyzed with a $2 \times 2$ repeated-measures ANOVA, using joint attentional state (inside and outside) and child age (15 and 21 months) as independent variables.

*Child and dyad language.* Table 4.1 presents means and standard deviations for all child and dyad language measures. All of these measures were higher inside than outside the joint attentional episodes; for four of the six measures the difference was statistically significant. Inside, as opposed to outside, joint attentional episodes children produced more: utterances per minute, $F(1,23) = 11.72$, $p < .05$; words per minute, $F(1,23) = 10.02$, $p < .05$; and words referring to objects per minute, $F(1,23) = 17.16$, $p < .01$. The child's average number of turns per conversation was higher inside as opposed to outside joint attentional episodes, $F(1,18) = 16.01$, $p < .01$ (only 19 dyads had conversations). Child age produced several main effects and interacted with joint attentional state for several of these measures, as shown in Table 4.1. In each case of interaction, differences between the values inside and outside joint attentional episodes were greater when the child was 21 months of age.

**Table 4.1** Language measures inside and outside joint attentional episodes at both child ages

| Language measures | 15 Months | | | | 21 Months | | | |
|---|---|---|---|---|---|---|---|---|
| | Inside joint episodes | | Outside joint episodes | | Inside joint episodes | | Outside joint episodes | |
| Child: | | | | | | | | |
| Utterances (per min) | 1.0 | (1.4) | .6 | (.82) | 3.7 | (3.1) | 1.6 | (1.3)*ab |
| MLU | 1.2 | (.24) | .9 | (.83) | 1.3 | (.29) | 1.1 | (.42) |
| Words (per min) | 1.2 | (.17) | .8 | (1.0) | 4.9 | (4.7) | 2.0 | (1.1)*a |
| Object labels (per min) | .6 | (.10) | .5 | (.75) | 1.8 | (2.0) | .8 | (1.6)**a |
| Dyad: | | | | | | | | |
| Conversations (per min) | .5 | (.51) | .4 | (.41) | .9 | (.87) | .7 | (.69)a |
| Average child turns | 1.7 | (.73) | 1.0 | (.86) | 4.5 | (2.2) | 2.4 | (1.7)**a |
| Mother: | | | | | | | | |
| Utterances (per min) | 16.9 | (8.2) | 8.6 | (5.6) | 12.1 | (5.1) | 9.1 | (4.7)** |
| MLU | 3.9 | (.67) | 4.2 | (.65) | 4.4 | (.51) | 4.9 | (.10)*a |
| % Comment | .56 | (.11) | .46 | (.18) | .48 | (.09) | .41 | (.20)*a |
| % Question | .29 | (.12) | .32 | (.15) | .36 | (.11) | .46 | (.20)*a |
| % Directive | .15 | (.07) | .22 | (.15) | .16 | (.08) | .13 | (.10)b |

\* Inside and outside joint episodes different, $p < .05$.

\*\* Inside and outside joint episodes different, $p < .01$.

a 15 months different from 21 months, $p < .05$.

Because of the relatively high variability on some of the child and dyad measures, subjects were also assessed on an individual basis. The pattern of results remained the same. Out of 24 children, 20 had higher values inside joint attentional episodes on the utterances per minute and words per minute measures ($p < .01$, sign test), and 16 children had more object labels ($p < .08$). Seventeen of the 19 children who had conversations had higher values inside joint episodes on both the conversations per minute and the average length of conversation measures ($p < .01$, sign test).

*Maternal language.* Table 4.1 also presents means and standard deviations for maternal language measures. Like their children, mothers produced more utterances per minute inside as opposed to outside joint attentional episodes, $F(1,23) = 15.87$, $p < .001$. their MLUs, however, were *shorter* inside than outside the episodes, $F(1,23) = 3.90$, $p < .05$. Of the maternal utterances, a higher proportion were comments, $F(1,23) = 6.61$, $p < .05$, and a lower proportion were questions, $F(1,23) = 4.07$, $p < .05$, inside the joint attentional episodes. Proportion of directives showed a significant interaction of joint attentional state and child age, $F(1,22) = 6.06$, $p < .05$, such that mothers produced proportionally more directives outside joint episodes at the 15-month child age only (Newman-Keuls). As shown in Table 4.1, child age produced two main effects: comments became proportionally less frequent over child age, while questions became more frequent. There were no differences in the number of object references per minute made by mothers or in the distribution of these into the eight object reference types as a function of joint attention; these are therefore not presented in Table 4.1.

*Maternal language and child lexical development.* General measures of the mothers' language (utterances per minute; MLU; and proportion of comments, questions, and directives) did not correlate with the child's vocabulary size or proportion of nominals at 15 or at 21 months. What did correlate were the eight types of object references. Table 4.2 presents these correlations, controlling for child age in months. The overall pattern is quite striking and very clear-cut. Nothing the mothers did outside joint attentional episodes correlated, either positively or negatively, with either measure of the child's lexical development. Inside the joint attentional episodes, on the other hand, three of the object reference types in which the mother followed into the child's attentional focus (+ + +, + + −, + − −) correlated positively with either the child's vocabulary size, proportion of nominals, or both. For the most part, directive object references were negatively related to the child's language. Especially important was the finding that directives not accompanied by gestures and to which the child did not attend (− − −) were negatively associated with the child's vocabulary size at 21 months. Interestingly, the one positive correlation for directives was when the mother was gesturing to the object and the child focused on it successfully (− + +).

To help determine the direction of causality in these correlations, cross-lagged panel correlations were performed for each of the eight object reference types with both child language measures, both inside and outside joint attentional episodes. If the 'opposite' cross-lagged correlations – that is, maternal measures at 21 months with child language measures at 15 months

**Table 4.2**   Partial correlations of maternal object references at 15 months with child language measures at both child ages as a function of joint attentional episode

| | Inside joint episodes | | | | Outside joint episodes | | | |
|---|---|---|---|---|---|---|---|---|
| | Vocabulary size | | % Nominals | | Vocabulary size | | % Nominals | |
| Type of object reference | 15 Months | 21 Months | 15 Months | 21 Months | 15 Months | 21 Months | 15 Months | 21 Months |
| − − − | −.30 | −.46* | −.12 | −.17 | −.17 | −.06 | −.10 | −.07 |
| − − + | −.27 | −.23 | −.06 | −.13 | −.07 | −.09 | −.01 | −.34 |
| − + − | −.25 | −.14 | −.24 | −.03 | −.23 | −.08 | −.18 | .03 |
| − + + | .46* | .26 | .38 | .22 | −.06 | −.11 | .04 | .17 |
| + − − | .54* | .37 | .47* | .20 | .10 | −.17 | .18 | −.34 |
| + + − | .45* | .34 | .27 | .21 | .05 | .08 | .03 | .31 |
| + − + | .17 | .08 | .20 | .13 | .13 | .28 | .23 | −.04 |
| + + + | .50* | .62* | .44* | .61* | −.11 | −.04 | .14 | −.17 |

\* $p < .05$.

– are similar to those reported above, then it is likely that the child's language is influencing the object reference types as much as the reverse. However, of the 32 'opposite' cross-lagged correlations, only one was statistically significant: frequency of the + + + model inside joint episodes correlated with child vocabulary size at .55, $p < .05$.

*Discussion*

There were three main findings in this study. The first was that during periods of joint attentional focus both mothers and children talked more, the dyad engaged in longer conversations, and mothers used shorter sentences and more comments. It is tempting to conclude from this that, as hypothesized, periods of joint attentional focus in some way scaffold early mother-child linguistic interactions. However, another plausible hypothesis is that the causality is in the opposite direction: the dyad's ability to interact linguistically is a major factor in the establishment and maintenance of joint attentional episodes. There is undoubtedly some truth to this. However, it is not the case that language is a necessary condition for a joint attentional focus – virtually every dyad had some joint interactions with no language. Nor is it the case that language is sufficient for joint visual attention – all dyads had linguistic interactions outside of joint attentional episodes. Also, it is important to note that while the child's linguistic competence increased across the two observation sessions, the time in joint interaction did not. Thus, for all of these reasons the causality could not flow exclusively from language to joint attention. The most plausible interpretation, then, is that the direction of influence is 'transactive': joint attentional episodes scaffold the prelinguistic child into language, which helps the child establish and maintain these episodes, which facilitates further linguistic interactions.

The second finding was that the types of object references mothers made inside the episodes of joint attentional focus were related to the child's subsequent language development, whereas these same measures outside the joint episodes did not correlate. This is despite the fact that there was no systematic difference between the types of models given inside and outside joint attentional episodes. However, because periods of heightened linguistic activity for the child corresponded to joint attentional episodes, it may be that children are more tuned in to maternal language when they themselves are speaking or when they are engaged in conversations of a certain length. Thus, again, language may be part of the cause as well as the effect. Again, it is probably best to think in transactive terms. In this case, the causal factor may best be conceived as periods of joint attention, which involve linguistic as well as nonlinguistic elements.

The third main finding concerned the specific relationships between object reference types and the child's language. Inside the joint attentional episodes, three of the four object reference types that followed into the child's attentional focus correlated positively with the child's subsequent lexical development, whereas one of the directive types correlated negatively. It is interesting to note that the only directive type that correlated positively was the one in which the mother made her attentional focus clear by gesturing and in which the child focused successfully on the referent object $(- + +)$. It is puzzling at first glance that the $+ + -$ and the $+ [- -$ reference types correlated positively with the child's subsequent vocabulary since, in these, the child was not focused on the object at the precise moment the name was provided. However, by definition of follow-in, in both of these reference types the child was focused on the object when the mother began her utterance. These two types thus indicate situations in which the child looked away from the object before its name was uttered. Many times this simply meant that the child looked to the mother's face as she spoke and returned to a focus on the object soon thereafter. Though in some cases the child shifted his attention permanently, most often these reference types do represent an instance of joint attentional focus and thus should facilitate the child's word learning.

Once again in this third finding, however, either direction of influence is possible. In contrast to the current hypothesis that the object reference type affects the child's lexical acquisition, it is possible that the correlations are due to the child's influence on the mother: linguistically competent children induced mothers to provide certain types of object references. However, the cross-lagged correlations argue against this interpretation. Frequency of the $- - -$ object reference type at 15 months correlated negatively with child language at 21 months, but child language at 15 months did not correlate with object reference types at 21 months. This pattern indicates that the direction of influence is most likely from the object reference types to the child's language. In the case of the $+ + +$ type, the child vocabulary measure correlated with the object reference type both within and between time-points, and so the direction of influence is unclear. However, the same panel analysis of the '% Nominals' measure of child language produced the pattern favoring the interpretation that it was the object reference type that influenced the child's language and not vice versa; that is, there was no correlation between child language at 15 months and object reference type at 21 months. Overall, then, the most plausible interpretation of the pattern of correlations in the current study is that object references that follow into the child's attentional focus facilitate lexical acquisition, especially of object labels.

## Study 2

In an attempt to provide experimental corroboration for the third finding of the correlational study – the relationship between object reference type and the child's lexical acquisition – a lexical training study was designed. The focus was on the general finding that object labels given as the adult was following into the child's attentional focus were positively related to lexical acquisition, while those given as directives were negatively related.

### Method

*Subjects.* Ten middle-class children, six males and four females, were recruited by personal contact from local day-care facilities. Children were between 14 and 23 months of age at recruitment (mean age = 17.4) and attended day-care on a daily basis. As determined by a maternal interview, all children were producing at least several words.

*Procedure.* After some initial 'warm-up' visits to the classroom two research assistants saw children individually in a quiet room at the day-care facility. One researcher trained and tested the child, while the other observed and recorded her behavior. Each child participated in four training sessions, two per week for 2 weeks, as well as a follow-up testing session 2 weeks after the final training session. One session lasted 15–20 min.

Each child was assigned four objects from a set chosen to be unfamiliar to children of this age (e.g., gauge, clip, bow, wrench, etc.). The child was assigned objects so that they matched her phonological preferences, as determined by the maternal interview at recruitment. For each child, each of her four objects was then randomly assigned to one of two attentional strategy conditions (follow-in or direct), such that there were two objects in each condition. In the follow-in condition, the experimenter waited until the child was engaged with the target object (visual and tactile contact) and then addressed the child with a short sentence in which the object word was stressed. In the direct condition, the experimenter waited until the child was not engaged with any object and then held up the target object and addressed her with a short sentence in which the object word was stressed. Half of the sentences in each condition modeled the word in the middle of the sentence (e.g., 'The *clip* is here') and half modeled it at the end of the sentence (e.g., 'Here's the *clip*').

At the beginning of the first session the child was asked for the name of each of her four objects. None of the children produced the correct name of any object. In each session, children were given four trials for each object. Each name was modeled once (order was randomly selected for each child for each session from the list of 24 possible orders), and then the entire sequence was repeated three more times. Any language the child used during the session was recorded. Productions that were judged by both researchers to be instances of the modeled word (judged on phonological similarity and contextual appropriateness) were recorded and labeled as either imitative (if they occurred directly after a model) or spontaneous. All of these productions (including imitations) constituted the spontaneous production measure. After all models had been given in a session, two tests were administered. First, in the elicited production test the experimenter simply held up each object (in random order) and asked 'What is this?' If the child failed to respond, she was asked two times more. Second, in the comprehension task the experimenter placed the four objects side by side and asked for each object in turn (in random order with each object replaced after each trial) by instructing the child to 'Give me the —' and holding out his hand. Again, if the child failed to respond, he was given two trials more. Two weeks following the final training session, the elicited production and comprehension tasks were given again (and any spontaneous productions were noted) in a short follow-up session in which there was no training.

*Results*

Table 4.3 presents means and standard deviations for the three dependent measures as a function of attentional strategy training condition. Because there was no systematic effect of session, the values used for analysis and presented in Table 4.3 are the values obtained by summing across the four training sessions. There was no effect of the placement of the word in the sentence (middle or end) or of the order of conditions. These were therefore excluded from further analysis.

Children comprehended the modeled words better in the follow-in condition, $t(9) = 2.41$, $p < .05$. In this condition, the children averaged correct responses on 50% of the trials overall: the mean score was 4.0 out of eight trials per child per condition (two words for four sessions). This proportion was significantly above the chance performance of 25% (assuming children always picked an object, which they did not), $p < .05$, whereas the proportion of correct responses in the direct condition was not. There were no statistically reliable effects found for either of the production measures, which were both quite low in both conditions; of the 40 trained words (four per child, 10 children) there were only 14 productions, and these came from only five children.

Due to illnesses and absences, only seven of the 10 children could be given follow-up testing within a few days of the 2-week interval. Again, children spoke very little, and so neither production measure produced differences. (However, it should be noted that all of the three productions recorded in the

**Table 4.3** Means and standard deviations of child performance measures as a function of training condition (summed across all 4 sessions)

| Child performance measure | Follow-in | Direct |
|---|---|---|
| Frequency of spontaneous production | .40 (.50) | .40 (.50) |
| Frequency of elicited production | .10 (.30) | .50 (.50) |
| Percent comprehension | 50 (09) | 32 (10)* |
| Percent comprehension (follow-up) | 64 (13) | 36 (13)* |

* Conditions different, $p < .05$.

follow-up session were from the follow-in condition.) Analysis of the comprehension task produced a significant difference in favor of the follow-in condition: 64% to 36%, $t(6) = 4.58$ $p < .05$. Analysis of individual subjects confirmed this trend: six of the seven children had better comprehension scores in the follow-in condition, and the other child had equal scores in both conditions. The probability of this occurring by chance alone is less than .05, sign test.


*Discussion*

The main finding of the training study was that the follow-in strategy produced greater word learning, as measured by comprehension, than the direct condition. The very small amount of production does not permit firm conclusions. Though it is possible that more training would have produced more productions, other lexical training studies have obtained results with this amount of training (cf. Schwartz and Terrell, 1983). More likely, the small amount of production was probably due to the children's general shyness alone with strangers.

The results of this study help to explain those of Study 1. By themselves, the correlations of that study could be explained if it were the case that the child was (*a*) particularly attracted to some objects, (*b*) thus 'primed' to learn their names, and (*c*) played with these objects most often. If this were the case it would mean that when mothers followed in, it would most often be attractive objects the child was playing with, and thus conditions for word learning would be maximal. Objects named in a directive manner would be those of little or no interest (the child was not playing with them) and so learning conditions would be less favorable. The results of Study 2, however, cannot be explained in this way since in this study objects were randomly assigned to conditions. Together, then, the results of the two studies are most economically explained by positing a facilitative effect of joint attentional processes.

Another possible explanation for the correlations of Study 1 is Nelson's (1981) functional hypothesis. It is possible that children with more directive mothers were learning that the primary function of language is social-regulative, and thus they were less interested in learning object names. Children of mothers who more often followed-in to their attention attributed to language more cognitive significance and thus learned more object labels. This interpretation is not plausible in Study 2, however. In this study the same child learned words differentially depending on how they were presented. This could not be the product of one overall hypothesis about the functional significance of language. It is of course possible that Nelson's hypothesized mechanism is at work in the real world (and Study 1), while the current finding is a laboratory phenomenon; or it is possible that the two mechanisms are both operative, though on different levels. Once again, however, the most economical explanation of the two studies together is in terms of joint attentional processes.

**General discussion**

The current studies, in combination with findings of previous research, suggest that joint attention is important to early language acquisition in two ways. First, relatively extended episodes of joint attentional focus between adult and child provide important non-linguistic scaffolding for the young child's early linguistic interactions. This effect seems to extend well into the second half of the child's second year of life, beyond the very earliest stages of communicative development where most previous research has concentrated (e.g., that of Bruner and his colleagues). Further, what happens in these episodes seems to be of special importance for acquiring new language. Keith Nelson (e.g., 1982) has argued that, in general, when learning conditions are favorable the child's acquisition of novel linguistic structures may often be based on a single, or at most a very few, adult exemplars of that structure. The results of the current study suggest that for the initial phases of lexical development, relatively extended episodes of joint attentional focus between child and adult may constitute an important part of such conditions. This is presumably because such episodes are periods when the child is attentive, motivated, and best able to determine the meaning of her mother's language (cf. Ninio and Bruner, 1978; Ratner and Bruner, 1978).

Within joint attentional episodes, it would seem to be important that the adult talk about the object on which the child is focused, rather than constantly trying to redirect the child's attention. Roth (1985) has shown, in fact, that when mothers follow into their child's attentional focus, they are more likely to elaborate semantically on previous child utterances. In the current interpretation, the important factor in all cases is the relative ease with which the child is able to establish the attentional focus of the adult and thus the referential context of her language. It is interesting to note in this regard that something very similar to this also operates at the level of conversational interaction. Olsen-Fulero (1982) has demonstrated that directiveness has an adverse effect on early mother-child conversations. If conversational topic may be thought of as analogous to an object of joint visual attention, then these results parallel those of the current study.

One final point should be made. All of the measures in the current study were of visual, not auditory, attention. This is quite simply because visual attention is most easily observable. It is possible, for example, that the child was indeed attending aurally to an object when she was coded as not attending – for example, when the mother shook a rattle that the child recognized. It is also possible that the child was not attending aurally to the mother's language in some cases – a situation not dealt with in the current study. Undoubtedly, a systematic account of auditory attention is necessary for a thorough understanding of the role of attentional factors in the language acquisition process.

Individual differences in early language acquisition present a challenge and an opportunity for researchers. As Katherine Nelson (1981) has pointed out, explaining these differences may play a crucial role in discovering the basic cognitive and social process that underlie language development. Thus far explanations have centered on such factors as cognitive style differences among children (Bretherton, NcNew, Snyder and Bates, 1983), social-interactional differences among mother-child dyads (Nelson, 1973), and differences among the social environments of children (i.e., the amount of interaction with fathers, siblings, peers, strangers, etc.; see Mannle and Tomasello, in press). It is safe to assume that each of these has some role to play. In this study we have attempted to identify and explore another set of factors that, like the others, may be fundamental for language acquisition and at the same time contribute to individual differences. Joint attentional processes are clearly worthy of future research attention.

## References

Bakeman, R., and Adamson, L. (1984). Coordinating attention to people and objects in mother-infant and peer-infant interaction. *Child Development, 55,* 1278–1289.

Bates, E. (1979). *The emergence of symbols: Cognition and communication in infancy.* New York: Academic Press.

Bretherton, I., McNew, S., Snyder, L., and Bates, E. (1983). Individual differences at 20 months: Analytic and holistic strategies in language acquisition. *Journal of Child Language, 10,* 293–320.

Bruner, J. (1981). The pragmatics of acquisition. In W. Deutsch (Ed.), *The child's construction of language* (pp. 35–56). New York: Academic Press.

Bruner, J. (1983). The acquisition of pragmatic commitments. In R. Golinkoff (Ed.), *The transition from prelinguistic to linguistic communication* (pp. 27–42). Hillsdale, NJ: Erlbaum.

Bruner, J. (1985). *Child's talk: Learning to use language.* New York: Norton.

Della Corte, M., Benedict, H., and Klein, D. (1983). The relationship of pragmatic dimensions of mothers' speech to the referential-expressive distinction. *Journal of Child Language, 10,* 35–44.

Mannle, S., and Tomasello, M. (in press). Fathers, siblings, and the bridge hypothesis. To appear in K. E. Nelson and A. van Kleek (Eds.), *Children's language, Vol 6.* Hillsdale, NJ: Erlbaum.

Nelson, K. (1973). Structure and strategy in learning to talk. *Monographs of the Society for Research in Child Development, 38* (1–2, Serial No. 149).

Nelson, K. (1981). Individual differences in language development: Implications for development and language. *Developmental Psychology, 17,* 170–187.

Nelson, K. E. (1982). Theories of the child's acquisition of syntax. *Annals of the New York Academy of Sciences, 345,* 45–69.

Ninio, A., and Bruner, J. (1978). The achievement and antecedents of labelling. *Journal of Child Language, 5,* 1–16.

Olsen-Fulero, L. (1982). Style and stability in mother conversational behavior. *Journal of Child Language, 9,* 543–564.

Ratner, N., and Bruner, J. (1978). Games, social exchange, and the acquisition of language. *Journal of Child Language, 5,* 391–402.

Roth, P. (1985). *Timing and function of maternal speech to 12-month-olds.* Manuscript submitted for publication.

Schwartz, R., and Terrell, B. (1983). The role of input frequency in lexical acquisition. *Journal of Child Language, 10,* 57–66.

Tomasello, M., Mannle, S., and Kruger, A. (1986). The linguistic environment of one to two year old twins. *Development Psychology, 22,* 169–176.

Tomasello, M., and Todd, J. (1983). Joint attention and lexical acquisition style. *First Language, 4,* 197–212.

# 5    E. M. Markman and J. E. Hutchinson
## 'Children's Sensitivity to Constraints on Word Meaning: Taxonomic versus Thematic Relations'

Reprinted in full from: *Cognitive Psychology* **16**, 1–27 (1984)

One of the major problems confronting someone learning a language is to figure out the meaning of a word given the enormous number of possible meanings for any particular word. Children commonly learn their first words (category terms) through ostensive definition: a parent or other teacher points to an object and labels it. Especially in the early phases of language acquisition, when children cannot understand a description of a category, children's learning of new category terms must depend heavily on ostensive definition. Once an adult points to an object and labels it, how does the child settle on an interpretation? At first sight this would seem to be a simple problem, and in fact children make hundreds of such inferences correctly when acquiring new vocabulary. This apparent simplicity, however, belies a complex inferential problem that was formulated by Quine (1960) in his well-known argument about translation. Imagine that someone points to a dog and says 'chien,' and our job is to figure out what 'chien' means. An obvious hypothesis is that it means 'dog.' But this is not necessary. It could mean 'furry object,' or 'brown object,' or 'medium-sized object,' and so on. To decide if the new term refers to dogs, one might set up test situations by pointing to various objects and asking whether or not 'chien' applies. Quine's argument is that no matter how many test situations one constructs, there will always be more than one hypothesis for the meaning of a new term that is consistent with the existing evidence.

Young children beginning to acquire their native language continually face this problem of narrowing down the meaning of a term from an indefinite number of possibilities. Someone points in some direction and then utters a word. On what grounds is the child to conclude that a new unfamiliar word, e.g., 'dog', refers to dogs? What is to prevent a child from concluding that 'dog' is a proper name for that particular dog? What prevents the child from concluding that 'dog' means 'four-legged object' or 'black object' or any number of other characteristics that dogs share? And finally, what prevents the child from concluding that 'dog,' in addition to referring to that particular dog, also refers to the bone the dog is chewing on or to the tree the dog is lying under? These last examples of thematic relations pose a particular problem because children are very interested in such relations and may find them more salient than categorical relations. Before continuing to discuss how children narrow down the possible meanings of terms, we briefly review the work on classification showing children's fascination with thematic relations.

One widely used procedure for studying how children form categories of objects is to ask them to sort objects into groups. Typically children are presented with objects from several different categories, for example, vehicles, animals, clothing, and people. They are instructed to put together the objects that are alike or that go together or are given freedom to manipulate and group the objects as they like. Another variant of the sorting procedure is a match to sample task. In this case, children are shown a target object and two choices, one in the same category as the target and one in a different category. Children must choose which is most like the target. This task in particular is similar to the one that children face in ostensive definition, in that someone points to an object and the child must determine which other objects are like it.

Here is a somewhat oversimplified summary of what is often found in these studies. Children older than about 7 sort objects on the basis of the object's taxonomic category. For example, they place all and only the vehicles together, all and only the clothing together, and so on. They perceive the perceptual or functional properties that the objects share (perhaps in a family resemblance structure (Rosch and Mervis, 1975)) and so find the common taxonomic category to be a natural way of organizing objects. Younger children sort on some other basis. Sometimes, especially when geometric figures are used, young children create spatial configurations with the objects, arranging them into designs or patterns. When more meaningful objects are used, children represent causal and temporal relations among the objects as well as spatial relations. These thematic relations emphasize events rather than taxonomic similarity. For example, children might sort a man and a car together because the man is driving the car. Or they might place a boy, a coat, and a dog together because the boy will wear his coat when he takes the dog for a walk.

This attention to thematic relations between objects rather than to how objects are alike is a common finding replicated in many studies. In addition to sorting experiments, this thematic bias shows up in studies of memory clustering and word association (Inhelder and Piaget, 1964; Denney, 1974; Denney and Ziobrowski, 1972; Nelson, 1977). These findings indicate that children are more interested in the thematic relations among objects or that thematic relations are simpler or more readily constructed than categorical relations.

It is not surprising that children notice these thematic relations. They are obviously very important for making sense of the world for adults and children alike. As we move about in our daily life, we observe people inter-acting or using tools or other artifacts to accomplish goals. We view natural occurrences such as storms, and we admire scenery. Much of our perception is interpretive, trying to figure out what is happening and how. Even infants tend to place causal interpretations on events they perceive (cf. Gibson and Spelke, 1983). Thus, these event-like structures are a fundamentally important and natural way of organizing information. Moreover, there seem to be fewer developmental and cross-cultural differences in understanding this type of organization (Mandler, Scribner, Cole and DeForest, 1980). This is in marked contrast to the cross-cultural and developmental differences found in studies of taxonomic classification. In sum, interest in thematic relations is not limited to young children. Nor should attention to thematic relations be viewed as a useless or nonproductive bias. Noticing causal, spatial, and temporal relations between objects is essential for understanding the world. It is children's attention to categorical relations and not their attention to thematic relations that changes most with development.

When the procedures used in sorting tasks specifically guide children's attention toward categories and away from thematic relations, children do show some understanding of categorical organization (see Carey, in press; Gelman and Baillargeon, 1983; Markman and Callanan, 1983; Horton, Note 1, for reviews). To take one example, Smiley and Brown (1979) tested whether 5- and 6-year-old children could understand taxonomic relations even though they prefer thematic ones. They presented children with a target picture and two choice pictures. One of the choices was thematically related to the target, and one of the choices was taxonomically related to the target. For example, children were shown a spider (target), a spider web (thematic choice), and a grasshopper (taxonomic choice). The experimenter pointed to the spider and asked for 'the one that goes best with this one.' As usual, these young children tended to pick the spider web, rather than the grasshopper, thereby indicating a thematic relation. Nevertheless, when they were asked about the grasshopper, all of the children could explain the taxonomic relation. Thus, children have a rudimentary ability to organize objects taxonomically, but it is often obscured by their attention to thematic relations.

Although children are biased toward organizing objects thematically, single words, in particular count nouns, do not often encode thematic relations.[1] English does not have a single noun for thematically related objects such as a boy and his bike, a spider and its web, or a baby and its bottle. Thus to return to Quine's problem of induction, we are faced with a kind of paradox. Children seem to readily learn concrete nouns like 'ball' or 'dog' that refer to object categories. Yet they tend to notice and remember thematic relations between objects more readily than categorical relations. How is it that children readily learn labels for categories of objects if they are attending to these thematic relations between objects instead? To take a concrete example, imagine a mother pointing to a baby and saying 'baby.' Based on the sorting studies, we should assume that the child will be attending to the baby shaking a rattle or to the baby being diapered. Why, then, doesn't the child infer that 'baby' also refers to the rattle or to the diaper, in addition to the particular baby?

As a possible solution to this problem, we propose that children have implicit hypotheses about the possible meaning of words that help them acquire words for categories. Children may well prefer to construe the environment in a way that conflicts with the way that language is organized. But even very young children may be aware of the constraint on word meaning so that when they believe that they are learning a new *word*, they shift their attention from thematic to categorical organization.

This proposal has a strong and a weak form. The strong form is that sensitivity to the constraint on word meaning can help children discover and learn new categories. That is, on hearing an unfamiliar word, children will search for categorical relations. If no familiar, previously unlabeled category is available, children will analyze the environment to form a new categorical relation to label. In this way, the constraint on possible word meanings could help children acquire new categories. The weak form of the proposal is that children use the constraint to help them link a new word to a concept they already know. If a familiar categorical relation is not available, however, children will not attempt to search for a new one.

The four studies that follow test mainly the weak form of the hypothesis. Experiment 1 focuses on 2- and 3-year-old children's knowledge of the constraint on word meaning for basic level categorization. Experiments 2 and 3 focus on 4- and 5-year-olds' sensitivity to the constraint for superordinate level categories. And Experiment 4 tests the hypothesis for 4- and 5-year-olds who were taught new taxonomic and new thematic relations for unfamiliar objects.

All of the experiments use a match to sample procedure with a target picture, taxonomic choice, and thematic choice. In the No Word condition, children are shown the target and asked to simply 'find another one.' In the Novel Word condition, children hear a new label for the target (e.g., 'biv') and are asked to 'find another biv.' The Novel Word task is quite like ostensive definition: someone points to an object and labels it, and the child must figure out what else the label refers to. We predicted that the majority of choices in the Novel Word condition would be taxonomic. The No Word task also has much in common with ostensive definition, except that no label is given. We expected children in this condition to give many more thematic responses than children in the Novel Word condition.

## Experiment 1

This first study investigates whether hearing a novel word will cause 2- to 3-year-old children to shift their attention from thematic to categorical relations. Basic level categories (such as 'dog' or 'chair') were used with these young children rather than general superordinate level categories (such as 'animal' or 'furniture'). The basic level, according to Rosch and her colleagues, is the level of categorization at which category members have the most features in common without being confusable with members of contrasting categories (Rosch, 1978; Rosch, Mervis, Gray, Johnson and Boyes-Braem, 1976; Mervis and Rosch, 1981).[2]

### Methods

*Subjects.*  Forty-one children from nursery schools in Palo Alto, California, participated in the study. They ranged in age from 2 years 5 months to 3 years 11 months, with a mean age of 3 years 4 months. An additional two children failed to pass a pretest described below and were not included in the study. Children were randomly assigned to one of two conditions with the constraint that the conditions be roughly equated for age and sex.

### Procedure

*Pretest.*  A simple pretest was given to ensure that the children understood instructions to find an object that is the same as another. A target picture was propped up against a frame and the child's attention was drawn to the picture. Then another identical picture and a distractor were placed on the table in front of the child, and the child was asked to 'find one that is the same as this one' (the target picture). Three sets of pictures were used: two identical circles with a squiggle as the distractor, two rectangles with a *z* as the distractor, and two arrows with a U-shaped figure as the distractor. Children were scored as passing the pretest only if they answered all three items correctly.

*No word condition.* The procedure used in this condition was very similar to the pretest procedure. Children were first introduced to a hand puppet and were told to put the picture they chose in the puppet's mouth. On each trial, the experimenter propped the target picture against the frame and told the child, 'Look carefully now. See this?' as she pointed to the picture. Then the experimenter placed the two choice pictures on the table and told the child to 'find another one that is the same as this,' as she continued to point to the target picture. The instructions were designed to make it as clear as possible to these young children that we were looking for a taxonomic match.

One of the choice pictures was a member of the same basic level category as the target: for example, the target might be a poodle and the choice a German shepherd (both dogs). We attempted to make the two category exemplars fairly dissimilar yet still readily identifiable to these young children. The other choice picture was a strong thematic associate to the target – in this case, dog food. There were 10 such triads in all. They are listed in Table 5.1. The left–right placement of the thematic and category choices was randomly determined for each subject with the constraint that half of the thematic choices be on the left and half be on the right. The presentation order of the 10 items was also randomly determined for each subject.

*Novel word condition.* The materials and procedure for this condition were identical to those of the No Word condition, with one change. Children in this condition were told that the puppet could talk in puppet talk. They were instructed to listen carefully to find the right picture. The puppet gave the target picture an unfamiliar name and used the same name in the instructions for picking a choice picture. For example, the puppet might say, 'See this? It is a sud. Find another sud that is the same as this sud.' Ten meaningless one-syllable words were used and a different random assignment of words to pictures was made for each child.

**Table 5.1** Stimulus materials for experiment 1

| Standard object | Taxonomic choice | Thematic choice |
|---|---|---|
| Police car | Car | Policemen |
| Tennis shoe | High-heeled shoe | Foot |
| Dog | Dog | Dog food |
| Straight backed chair | Easy chair | Man in sitting position |
| Crib | Crib | Baby |
| Birthday cake | Chocolate cake | Birthday present |
| Blue jay | Duck | Nest |
| Outside door | Swinging door | Key |
| Male football player | Man | Football |
| Male child in swimsuit | Female child in overalls | Swimming pool |

*Results*

When children in the No Word condition had to select between another category member and a thematically related object, they chose the thematic relation almost half of the time. They selected other category members a mean of 5.95 times out of 10 (59%), $SD = 2.28$. This was not significantly different from chance. When the target picture was labeled with an unfamiliar word children were much more likely to select categorically. They now chose the other category member a mean of 8.29 times out of 10 (83%), $SD = 1.82$. This was significantly different from chance, $t(20) = 8.08$, $p < .01$, and was significantly different from the No Word condition, $t(39) = 3.63$, $p < .001$. The effect held up over every item and was significant when items rather than subjects were treated as a random factor, paired $t(9) = 8.40$, $p < .001$. As predicted, when children think they are learning a new word they look for categorical relationships between objects and pay less attention to thematic relations. These results support the hypothesis at least for very young children and basic level categories. The next three studies examine whether the effect holds up for familiar superordinate level categories and for newly learned object categories.

**Experiment 2**

This study tests the hypothesis that hearing a new word will induce older preschoolers to look for superordinate level taxonomic relations rather than thematic relations. The superordinate level of categorization, according to Rosch and her colleagues, is more abstract than the basic level. Members of superordinate level categories share fewer attributes, especially perceptual attributes, than members of basic level categories (Rosch, 1978; Rosch et al., 1976; Mervis and Rosch, 1981).

*Methods*

*Subjects*  Sixty children attending nursery schools in Palo Alto, California, and surrounding towns participated in the study. They ranged in age from 4 years 4 months to 5 years 3 months, with a mean age of 4 years 10 months. An additional two children were dropped from the study, one who did not cooperate with the experimenter and one who did not understand the task. The children were randomly assigned to four conditions, 15 per condition, with the constraint that the conditions be roughly equated for age and sex.

*Procedure*
  *No Word condition.* The procedure used in this condition was very similar to that used in the No Word condition of Experiment 1, except that superordinate level categories were used instead of basic level categories. The experimenter saw each child individually for one 15- to 20-min session. Subjects were shown 30 colorful pictures of common objects. Ten of the pictures served as targets. Associated with each of the target pictures were two choice pictures. One of the choice pictures was related in a thematic way to the target (e.g., milk/cow). The other choice picture was a member of

the same superordinate category as the target (e.g., pig/cow). An attempt was made to use a variety of thematic relations rather than just one, so as not to limit the generality of the results. A complete list of the stimulus materials appears in Table 5.2. As in Experiment 1, the instructions in the No Word condition were designed to make it as clear as possible that we were looking for a taxonomic match.

On each trial in the No Word condition, the experimenter, using a hand puppet, said, 'I'm going to show you a (new) picture. Then you'll have to find another one that is the same kind of thing.' The experimenter then placed the target picture face up on the table directly in front of the child, and said, 'See this?' She placed the two choice pictures to the left and right of the target, then said, 'Can you find another one that is the same kind of thing as this one? Find another one that is the same kind of thing as this one.' The left–right position of the choice pictures was randomized for each child in such a way that thematic and taxonomic choices each appeared half the time on the left and half the time on the right, across the 10 stimulus triads. The order of presentation of triads was also randomized for each subject. After children made a choice, they were asked to justify their response: 'How do you know these two are the same kind of thing?'

*Novel Word condition.* The materials and procedure for this condition were identical to those of the No Word condition, except that the target picture was now labeled with a novel word. Children were told that the puppet could talk in puppet talk, and that they were to listen carefully to what he said. The instructions now included an unfamiliar label for the target: 'I'm going to show you a kind of dax. Then you'll have to find another kind of dax. See this? It's a kind of dax. Can you find another kind of dax?' A different meaningless one-syllable word was used for each target picture. Children again were asked to justify their choices. Because they were given a label, we expected children in the Novel Word condition to choose the taxonomically related picture more often than children in the No Word condition.

Two additional control conditions were included to attempt to rule out one alternative explanation for increased taxonomic responding in the Novel Word condition. We are arguing that when children hear a word, they focus on categorical relationships because of general knowledge of what nouns encode, and not because of specific knowledge about the word's meaning. But children already knew real word names

**Table 5.2**  Stimulus materials for experiments 2 and 3

| Standard object | Taxonomic choice | Thematic choice |
| --- | --- | --- |
| Cow | Pig | Milk |
| Ring | Necklace | Hand |
| Door | Window | Key |
| Crib | Adult bed | Baby |
| Bee | Ant | Flower |
| Hanger | Hook | Dress |
| Cup | Glass | Kettle |
| Car | Bicycle | Car tire |
| Sprinkler[a] | Watering can | Grass |
| Paintbrush[a] | Crayons | Easel |
| Train[b] | Bus | Tracks |
| Dog[b] | Cat | Bone |

[a] This set was used only in Experiment 2.
[b] This set was used only in Experiment 3.

for the target pictures and they conceivably could have translated the unfamiliar labels. Translation of the unfamiliar words into known words might help children choose taxonomically. We could not control for the possibility that children were translating, but we did run one condition to determine what word children might translate into if they were translating, and another condition to determine what effect such translation would have.

*Translation condition.* Children might translate the unfamiliar word either into a basic level word or into a superordinate level word. For instance, given a cow as a target picture and told that it was a 'dax,' they might translate 'dax' into 'cow' (basic level) or they might translate 'dax' into 'animal' (superordinate level). In the Translation condition, we looked at the kinds of translations children make when they are explicitly asked to translate the unfamiliar word. The procedure was identical to that of the Novel Word condition except children were also asked 'What do you think dax means?' – once right after the target picture was introduced (but before children saw the choice pictures), and again after they made a choice.

When we analyzed the children's translations of these novel words, we found that on the first translation, before seeing the choice pictures, children almost never translated the unfamiliar labels into superordinate terms (only 6.7% of the time. Forty-seven percent of the first translations were basic level words. The rest of the translations were descriptive phrases. Even after making a choice, subjects still produced superordinates only 7.3% of the time, while the mean percentage of basic level translations decreased to 19%. Thus if children in the Novel Word condition spontaneously translated the unfamiliar word, they would be very unlikely to translate it into a superordinate level word.

*Basic Word condition.* If children are going to translate into a single known word, it will be into a basic level category term. The Basic Word condition tested whether translation into a basic level word would facilitate taxonomic responding.

The materials and procedure for this condition were identical to those in the Novel Word condition. The instructions simply substituted the basic level word for the target, in place of the unfamiliar label. For the example with the cow target, the experimenter said: 'I'm going to show you a picture of a cow. Then you'll have to find another picture that is the same kind of thing. See this? It's a cow. Can you find another one that is the same kind of thing as this one?' As in the other three conditions, children were asked to justify their choices.

*Results*

As is typical for children this age, when no word was present they made a number of thematic choices. When children in the No Word condition had to select between another member of the same superordinate category and a thematically related object, they chose the categorical relation only 4.93 times out of 10 (49%), $SD = 2.88$. This was not different from chance. As predicted, the presence of a new word caused children to focus more attention on taxonomic relations. When the target picture was labeled with an unfamiliar word, children now chose the other category member a mean of 6.87 times out of 10 (69%), $SD = 2.55$. This was more often than would be expected by chance, $t(14) = 2.75$, $p < .05$. The difference between the conditions was significant by a one-tailed $t$ test, $t(28) = 1.88$, $p < .05$.

Children who heard the target described with a basic level word chose the categorically related object 57% of the time. This was not significantly different from either the Novel Word or the No Word condition. It was also not significantly different from chance.

The results were more clear-cut when items were treated as a random factor and conditions as a within groups factor. Pictures labeled with unfamiliar words elicited significantly more taxonomic responses than the same pictures not labeled, paired $t(9) = 4.95$, $p < .002$. This effect held up for 9 out of the 10 stimulus triads. Pictures labeled with a basic object word elicited an intermediate number of taxonomic responses: significantly more than in the No Word condition, paired $t(9) = 4.14$, $p < .01$, but significantly fewer than in the Novel Word condition, paired $t(9) = 2.49$, $p < .05$.

Converging evidence for the hypothesis came from the justifications that children gave for their choices. Two raters coded the justifications as thematic, categorical, or irrelevant, and agreed on 90% of the classifications. Thematic justifications expressed an interactive relationship between the target and the object chosen. An example is 'The *cow* makes *milk*.' Children justified more of their choices thematically when they heard no word (51%) than when they heard an unfamiliar word (19%), $t(28) = 3.17$ $p < .005$. Likewise, they justified more of their choices thematically when they heard a familiar basic level word (38%) than when they heard an unfamiliar word, $t(28) = 1.92$, $p = .062$. There was no difference in the numbers of thematic justifications given in the No Word and Basic Word conditions.

Justifications and choices were not perfectly correlated, as the kind of justification children gave did not always match the kind of choice they made. Children seemed to explain their choices in terms of the task as they saw it. For example, when children chose thematically in the Novel Word condition, they seemed reluctant to justify the thematic choice with a thematic explanation. When they heard a novel word, they justified thematic choices with a thematic explanation an average of only 44% of the time. The children seemed to be in conflict between having chosen thematically but believing that the word implies a taxonomic relation. After choosing a cow and milk as being the same kind of thing, for example, many children did not justify their selection in the most natural way (stating that milk comes from a cow). They had to manufacture some justification to satisfy the experimenter, and so ended up on giving a relatively high proportion of irrelevant justifications for their thematic choices such as 'I don't know' (mean = 39%), compared to children in the No Word condition (mean = 6%), $t(24) = 2.52$, $p < .02$. When children in the No Word condition made a thematic choice they did not have the same conflict and were quite willing to give thematic justifications. These children, who did not hear a word, justified their thematic choices thematically the majority (a mean of 84%) of the time. The difference between the Novel and No Word conditions in propensity to justify thematic choices thematically was significant, $t(24) = 2.71$, $p < .02$. Children in the Basic Word condition justified thematic choices thematically an average of 67% of the time. This was not significantly different from either the Novel Word or No Word condition.

In sum, when an object was labeled with an unfamiliar word, children were more likely to look for another object from the same superordinate level category than when the object was not labeled. Children almost certainly were not translating the novel word into a superordinate level term, so that cannot account for the effect. If children were translating the term into a basic level word for the object, that would have helped them to choose a categorically related object. However, the justifications from children hearing a novel word differed from those of children hearing a basic level word, suggesting that translation into known terms was not accounting for the results.

**Experiment 3**

Experiment 3 is a modified replication of Experiment 2. In Experiment 2 the No Word instructions ('Find another one that is the same kind of thing') were designed to promote as much taxonomic responding as possible. The No Word condition was the baseline measure of taxonomic responding, and we hypothesized that the presence of a new word would elevate taxonomic responses above even this baseline. Thus, this was a conservative test of the hypothesis.

In Experiment 3 we attempted to make the No Word instructions more neutral. A neutral instruction is more like the natural language learning context since in both cases, children view objects and hear them labeled without instructions about what relations to attend to. In this study, children were asked to 'Find another one.' This is less explicit than the earlier instructions, but for adults still clearly implies that taxonomic similarity is called for. In this way we could compare what children naturally found salient to their choices when they heard a novel word. In Experiment 3 we also used slightly younger children, who would be expected to show a greater baseline preference for thematic relations.

*Methods*

*Subjects*  Sixty children attending nursery schools in Palo Alto, California, and surrounding towns participated in the study. They ranged in age from 4 years 0 months to 4 years 10 months, with a mean age of 4 years 5 months. An additional seven children were dropped from the study because they showed response bias, always choosing the picture on the same side. The children were randomly assigned to three conditions, 20 per condition, with the constraint that the conditions be roughly equated for age and sex.

*Procedure*

*No Word condition.* The procedure used in this condition was very similar to that used in the No Word condition of Experiment 2. Subjects were shown 30 colorful pictures of common objects. Ten of the pictures served as targets. Associated with each of the target pictures were two choice pictures, one thematically related to the target and one taxonomically related to the target. Eight out of ten of the picture sets were the same as those used in Experiment 2. The two new sets are noted in Table 5.2.

On each trial in the No Word condition, the experimenter said, 'I'm going to show you something. Then I want you to think carefully, and find another one. See this? Can you find another one?' After children selected a picture, the experimenter asked them to justify their choice: 'How did you know it was this one?' The left–right position of the choice pictures was again randomized for each child in such a way that thematic and taxonomic choices each appeared half the time on the left and half the time on the right. The order of presentation of triads for each subject was also randomized.

*Novel Word condition.* The materials and procedure for this condition were identical to those of the No Word condition, except that a novel word was used to describe the target picture. Children were told that the puppet could talk in puppet talk, and that they were to listen carefully to what he said. The instructions included an unfamiliar label for the target, which the child was asked to repeat, in order to ensure attention to the word: 'I'm going to show you a dax. Then I want you to think carefully, and find another dax. See this dax? Can you say dax? Can you find another dax?' Children were again asked to justify their choices.

*Basic Word condition.* The materials and procedure for this condition were identical to those in the Novel Word condition. The instructions simply substituted the basic level word for the target in place of the unfamiliar word. For the example with the cow target, the experimenter said: I'm going to show you a cow. Then I want you to think carefully, and find another cow. See this cow? Can you say cow? Can you find another cow?' Children seemed willing to make a choice, despite the fact that neither of the choice pictures was a cow (the two choices were pig and milk). As in the other two conditions, children were asked to justify their choices.

*Results*

As usual, when children in the No Word condition had to choose between another member of the same superordinate category and a thematically related object, they often chose the thematic relation. They selected the other category member a mean of only 2.50 times out of 10 (25%), $SD = 2.11$. This was less often than would be expected by chance, $t(19) = 5.17, p < .001$. When the target picture was labeled with an unfamiliar word, children were much more likely than children hearing no label to select categorically. They now chose the other category member a mean of 6.45 times out of 10 (65%), $SD = 1.60$. This was more often than would be expected by chance, $t(19) = 3.96, p < .001$. Children in the Novel Word condition selected the other category member significantly more often than children in the No Word condition, $t(38) = 6.50, p < .001$.

When the data were analyzed with items as a random factor and conditions as a within groups factor, we again found the predicted difference. Pictures labeled with novel words elicited significantly more taxonomic responses than the same pictures not labeled, paired $t(9) = 8.90, p < .001$, and the difference held up for every item.

As in Experiment 2, converging evidence for the hypothesis came from the justifications that children gave for their choices. Children who heard a novel word tended to give more justifications that referred to the categorical relations between the objects, while children who did not hear a label for the objects referred more to thematic relations. Children were credited wtih referring to a categorical relationship if they attempted to find a common property for the objects (e.g., 'They are both round') or a common function (e.g., 'You can wear both of them'), or if they gave the two objects a common label (e.g., 'They are both animals'). Children were scored as giving a thematic justification, if they described an interactive relationship between the two objects (e.g., 'The *cow* makes *milk*'). Two raters coded the justifications into categorical, thematic, and miscellaneous categories and agreed on 94% of the classifications.

Children who heard a novel label for the picture justified 34% of their choices by referring to a categorical relation while children who did not hear a label gave categorical justifications only 10% of the time, $t(38) = 2.99, p < .005$. Children justified fewer of their choices thematically when they heard an unfamiliar word (25%) than when they heard no word (67%), $t(38) = 4.34, p < .001$. Thus, children focused more on categorical relationships when they heard an unfamiliar word than when they heard no word. Moreover, as in Experiment 2, even when children chose thematically in the Novel Word condition, they seemed reluctant to justify the thematic choice with a thematic explanation. When they heard an unfamiliar label, they justified thematic choices with a thematic explanation only an average of 44% of the time. Children in the No Word condition who did not hear a label justified thematic choices thematically an average of 79% of the time, $t(38) = 2.02, p < .06$.

In sum, when young children are asked to classify things, they often classify them thematically. But simply hearing a new word induces children to focus more on categorical relationships. These results, although supporting the hypothesis, need to be interpreted in light of the results from the Basic Word condition. Children in the Basic Word condition gave just as many taxonomic responses as children in the Novel Word condition. The mean percentage of taxonomic responses in the Basic Word condition was 62%, as compared to 65% for the Novel Word condition. The percentage of choices justified thematically in the Basic Word condition (38%) also did not differ significantly from the percentage of choices justified thematically in the Novel Word condition (25%). The question is, were children in the Novel Word condition really translating into a basic level word?

A closer examination of the data suggests that translation into a basic level word is not accounting for the advantage of the novel word. That is, the Novel Word condition and Basic Word condition differ in several ways. One piece of evidence for a difference is a significant condition × item interaction, $F(18,513) = 2.34, p < .002$. The relative difficulty of different items, in terms of how many taxonomic responses they elicit, stays approximately the same for the Novel Word and No Word conditions, but changes for the Basic Word condition. Some items received a high number of taxonomic responses in the Basic Word condition and a low number of taxonomic responses in the Novel Word condition, or vice versa. For example, one target picture was a cup. The taxonomic choice was a glass. Children who heard the basic level word 'cup' chose the glass much more often (95% of the time) than children who heard the unfamiliar word 'biv' (40% of the time). It seems that children were very willing to overgeneralize the word 'cup' to mean 'glass,' too. Cup functioned almost as a superordinate term for both cup and glass. Children were probably not translating 'biv' into 'cup,' or they would have chosen the glass a high percentage of the time in the Novel Word condition as well.

It may be that the basic word can only help children to choose taxonomically when they can easily overgeneralize it. We examined the justifications children gave to see if there was evidence for overgeneralization of basic level terms. Children's justifications in the Novel Word and Basic Word conditions, and also their translations in the Translation condition of Experiment 2, were coded for the number of times children spontaneously called both the target and the taxonomic choice by the same basic level word. We had tried to choose the target pictures so that their basic word names could not function as names for both the target and the taxonomic choice. But apparently, we were not totally successful, as we found three items for which children naturally seemed willing to overgeneralize the basic word name: cup overgeneralized to glass, hanger overgeneralized to hook, and bee overgeneralized to ant.

The data were reanalyzed without these three ill-chosen items. When this was done the condition × item interaction disappeared. The new mean percentages of taxonomic responses for each condition were 64% for the Novel Word condition, 50% for the Basic Word condition, and 24% for the No Word condition. The difference between the Novel Word condition and the Basic Word condition in number of taxonomic responses now approached significance, $t(38) = 1.81, p = .075$. The Basic Word condition still had significantly more taxonomic responses than the No Word condition, $t(38) = 3.48, p < .002$. When the results were reanalyzed with items as a random factor and conditions as a within group factor, the differences were more striking. Items described by basic level words elicited significantly fewer taxonomic responses than items described by unfamiliar words, paired $t(6) = 2.46, p < .05$. More taxonomic responses were still given to items in the Basic Word condition than to the same items in the No Word condition, paired $t(6) = 3.90, p < .01$.

One argument that children were not translating the unfamiliar word, then, is that the pattern of responses to items in the Novel Word and Basic Word conditions was different. Moreover, the pattern for the Basic Word condition suggests that the basic word was more likely to lead to taxonomic responding when children could overgeneralize it.

Other evidence that children in the Novel Word condition were not simply translating the word into a basic level term comes from the justifications for thematic choices. Children who heard a basic level word did not seem as reluctant to justify thematic responses thematically as children who heard an unfamiliar word. The proportion of thematic responses justified thematically was 70% in the Basic Word condition, as opposed to 44% in the Novel Word condition, $t(38) = 2.28, p < .05$. Thus the justification data show that the basic level word did not shift children's attention away from thematic relations as much as the unfamiliar word did. One possible explanation for this is that children in the Novel Word condition were trying to figure out the meaning of the new word, and were therefore more aware that a word was involved. Consequently, they were more aware than children in the Basic Word condition that they should be searching for categorical relations.

There is one last piece of evidence that something different was going on in the Novel Word and Basic Word conditions. If children in the Novel Word condition were translating into a basic level word, then we might suppose that the basic word should be salient to them and should appear fairly often in their justifications. But the proportion of justifications in which a basic word name for the target appeared was only 28% for the Novel Word condition, compared to 49% for the Basic Word condition, $t(38) = 2.78$, $p < .01$.

In sum, the results for Experiment 3 replicated the findings of Experiment 2, providing even stronger support for the hypothesis. Hearing a new word diminishes children's tendency to look for thematic relationships, and causes them to look for categorical relationships instead. There is at least some evidence that children focus on categorical relationships because of the sheer presence of the word, and not because of any particular knowledge about the meaning of the word.

**Experiment 4**

Post hoc analyses from Experiment 3 were used to argue that translation of the novel word into a basic level word could not account for children's categorical choices. Experiment 4 is designed to provide additional evidence that children use abstract knowledge about words rather than specific known meanings to facilitate taxonomic responding. In this study, pictures of artificial objects were used instead of real objects. Children are not likely to translate unfamiliar names for these pictures into known words, because they do not know real word names for them. If the presence of an unfamiliar word still causes children to shift from thematic to taxonomic responding when the materials are alo unfamiliar, then this would rule out translation as an explanation for the effect.

*Methods*

*Subjects*  Thirty-two children attending nursery schools in Palo Alto, Californa, and surrounding towns participated in the study. The children ranged in age from 4 years 6 months to 5 years 11 months, with a mean age of 5 years 2 months. An additional three children were dropped from the study because of response bias. The children were randomly assigned to two conditions, 16 per condition, with the constraint that the conditions be roughly equated for age and sex.

*Procedure*  The design and procedure for this study are essentially the same as that of Experiment 3. The main difference is that the experimenter first described the taxonomic and thematic relations for the artificial objects before asking children to select the picture that was like the target.

*No Word condition.*  Each child was seen individually for one 20-min session. Subjects were shown eight sets of pictures in random order. Each set included a target picture, and two choice pictures, one thematically related and one taxonomically related to the target. Before children saw the target picture and the two choices, they were shown two training pictures that illustrated how the target picture related to each of the choice pictures. One picture showed the target object and the taxonomic choice, side by side. For these pairs, children were told a common function that the two

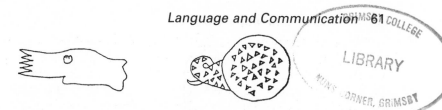

**Figure 5.1** Sample taxonomic training picture in Experiment 4.

objects shared. An example taxonomic training picture is shown in Figure 5.1. For this example, the experimenter said 'This swims in the water' (pointing to the left hand object). 'This swims in the water' (pointing to the right hand object).

A second training picture showed the target and the thematic choice in an interactive relationship. The experimenter told the children how the two objects interacted. The thematic training picture for the set just given is shown in Figure 5.2. For this example, the experimenter said, 'This catches this' (pointing to the objects she was referring to as she said the sentence). Children were asked to repeat the spoken information to make sure that they were paying attention. The first training picture was left on the table as the second training picture was introduced, so that children could see the connection between the target in the first picture and the target in the second picture. The order of presentation of training pictures was randomized so that taxonomic and thematic training pictures were each presented first half of the time.

A second example taxonomic training picture is shown in Figure 5.3. For this example the experimenter said, 'This pokes holes in things' (pointing to the left hand object). 'This pokes holes in things' (pointing to the right hand object). The thematic training picture for the same set is shown in Figure 5.4. For this picture, the spoken information was 'You keep this in here.'

After children saw the two training pictures in a set, the pictures were removed from the table. The rest of the trial was a match to sample task following the same procedure as the No Word condition of Experiment 3. The experimenter said, 'I'm going to show you something. Then I want you to think carefully, and find another one.' The experimenter then placed the target picture face up on the table directly in front of the child and said, 'See this?' She placed the two choice pictures to the left and right of

**Figure 5.2** Sample thematic training picture in Experiment 4.

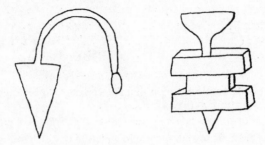

**Figure 5.3**  Sample taxonomic training picture in Experiment 4.

the target and said, 'Can you find another one?' Note that the choices were pictures of the individual objects as in the previous studies, rather than pictures of two objects together. After children made a choice, the experimenter asked them to justify their response: 'How did you know it was this one?' The left-right order of choices was randomized so that taxonomic choices each appeared half the time on the left and half the time on the right.

*Novel Word condition.* The materials and procedure for this condition were identical to those of the No Word condition, except that a novel word was used to label the target picture during the match to sample task. After children saw the training pictures, the experimenter said, 'I'm going to show you a dax. Then I want you to think carefully, and find another dax. See this dax? Can you say dax? Can you find another dax?' A different unfamiliar word was used for each set. Children again were asked to justify their choices.

Because of the unfamiliarity of the materials, children in both conditions found it difficult to justify their responses, so the justifications will not be discussed.

*Results*

The results for the choices were parallel to those found for Experiments 2 and 3. As usual, when children in the No Word condition had to select between

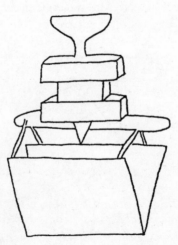

**Figure 5.4**  Sample thematic training picture in Experiment 4.

another member of the same category and a thematically related object, they often chose the thematic relation. They selected the other category member a mean of only 3.00 times out of 8 (37%), $SD = 1.79$. This was significantly less than chance, $t(15) = 2.24, p < .05$. When the target picture was labeled with an unfamiliar word, children were more likely to select categorically. They now chose the other category member a mean of 5.06 times out of 8 (63%), $SD = 2.38$. This was more than chance by a one-tailed $t$ test, $t(15) = 1.78, p < .05$. Children hearing a novel word were significantly more likely to select an object from the same category than children not hearing a label, $t(30) = 2.77, p < .01$.

When the results were analyzed with items as a random factor and conditions as a within groups factor, we again found the predicted difference. Pictures labeled with unfamiliar words elicited significantly more taxonomic responses than the same pictures not labeled, paired $t(7) = 4.07, p < .005$, and the difference held up for every item.

**Discussion**

The hypothesis tested by these studies is that children place an abstract constraint on what single nouns might mean. Children limit words to refer mainly to objects that share some property or function rather than allowing words to refer to objects that are united by thematic relations. This would help explain how children acquire words that refer to categories even though, in many other situations, they seem to find the thematic associations between objects to be more salient. The simple presence of a noun, even an unfamiliar one such as 'dax,' should cause children to search for objects that share perceptual or functional properties. Thus, labeling a picture as 'a dax' and asking children to find 'another dax' should help override their preference for choosing thematically.

*Overview of results*

The results from four studies supported the hypothesis. The main results from all of the studies are summarized in Table 5.3.

As can be seen from the results of Experiment 1, even children as young as 2 and 3 years place constraints on what an unfamiliar word might mean. When presented with two basic level objects – for example, two different kinds of dogs – and a third object that was thematically related, such as dog food, very young children often selected a dog and dog food as being the same kind of thing. If, however, one of the dogs was called by an unfamiliar label, e.g., 'dax,' and children were told to find another dax, they were now much more likely to select the two dogs.

By 4 or 5 years of age, children have set further constraints on what a word might mean, as Experiments 2 and 3 demonstrate. A word induces them to search for categorical relations even among objects that can only be related at the superordinate level of categorization. For example, with no word present, children often selected a dog and dog bone as being the same kind of thing because of the strong thematic association between dog and bone. When one of the dogs was called a 'dax', however, and children were asked to find another dax, they more often selected a dog and a cat as being the same, because they are both in the same superordinate category, animals.

At the superordinate level of categorization, the same pattern of choices was obtained for two different sets of instructions. Even when the No Word instructions emphasized taxonomic relations, as in Experiment 2 ('Find another one that is the same kind of thing as this one.'), we found an increase in taxonomic responding in the Novel Word condition. In Experiment 3 when the No Word instructions were more neutral ('Find another one.'), there was an even bigger shift toward more taxonomic responding in the presence of a new word.

The justification data corroborated the choices. Children who heard a novel word tended to give more justifications that referred to the categorical relations between the objects, whereas children who did not hear a label for the objects referred more to thematic relations (see column 2 of Table 5.3). Even when children chose thematically in the Novel Word condition, they seemed reluctant to justify the thematic choice with a thematic explanation (see column 3 of Table 5.3). For example, when children select a dog and a dog bone as being the same, they ordinarily justify this by saying that the dog eats the bone. However, those children who had heard the dog labeled with an unfamiliar term, yet nevertheless selected the dog bone, now justified their choice by saying that the dog and the bone were both white, for example, or refused to explain their selection. There was no such reluctance to justify thematic choices thematically when no label was given.

The hypothesis is that the presence of an unfamiliar word shifts children's attention to taxonomic relations because of an abstract constraint children place on possible word meanings, and not because they know the meaning of

**Table 5.3**   Main results for experiments 1–4

| | Percent of taxonomic choices | Percent of all choices justified thematically | Percent of thematic choices justified thematically |
|---|---|---|---|
| Experiment 1: Basic level categories in 2–3-year-olds (taxonomically biased instructions) | | | |
| No Word | 59% | – | – |
| Novel Word | 83% | – | – |
| Experiment 2: Superordinate level categories in 4–5-year-olds (taxonomically biased instructions) | | | |
| No Word | 49% | 51% | 84% |
| Novel Word | 69% | 19% | 44% |
| Basic Word | 57% | 38% | 67% |
| Experiment 3: Superordinate level categories in 4-year-olds (neutral instructions) | | | |
| No Word | 25% | 67% | 79% |
| Novel Word | 65% | 25% | 44% |
| Basic Word | 62% | 38% | 70% |
| Experiment 4: Unfamiliar categories in 4–5-year-olds (neutral instructions) | | | |
| No Word | 37% | – | – |
| Novel Word | 63% | – | – |

the word. Thus, we would like to rule out translation into a known word as accounting for the effect. Based on our results and on other research on language acquisition (e.g., Anglin, 1977; Clark, 1973; Mervis and Rosch, 1981), it is extremely unlikely that children would translate the unfamiliar terms into superordinate level terms. Children seeing a dog and hearing the word 'dax,' for example, would be very unlikely to translate 'dax' into 'animal' or 'mammal' or even 'pet.' If they were translating at all, they would think that 'dax' meant 'dog.' Even when children were specifically asked to translate the novel word in the Translation condition of Experiment 2, they rarely translated it into a superordinate level term. Thus translation into a superordinate level word cannot account for the increase in taxonomic responding for children who heard the picture labeled with an unfamiliar word.

Had children been translating into a basic level term, it would have helped them to select taxonomically. When the target picture was labeled with a basic object word, children selected more taxonomically related pictures than children who heard no label (see column 1, Experiments 2 and 3 in Table 5.3). However, the increase in taxonomic responding when children heard a novel word cannot be fully accounted for by translation of the novel word into a basic level word. Children's justifications provide one source of evidence that they were not simply translating the word into a basic level term. When children heard the novel words they seemed reluctant to justify their choices thematically, even in those cases where they had selected a thematically related picture. In contrast, when children heard familiar basic level words, they were happy to justify their choices in terms of thematic relationships (see columns 2 and 3 of Table 5.3). In the Basic Word condition, children heard, for example, the dog called 'dog' and were told to 'find another dog.' When these children selected the dog and dog bone, they showed no reluctance to justify their choice by saying that the dog eats the bone. Perhaps when children heard the basic level term they tried to generalize it to other items. When they failed, the fact that the familiar term was a count noun may not have been salient enough to prevent them from claiming that it referred to a thematic relationship. In contrast, children who heard the novel word tried to figure out what it might mean. This may have heightened their awareness that a word was involved. As a consequence, children in the Novel Word condition may have felt more reluctant than children in the Basic Word condition to describe the word as referring to a thematic relation.

The most compelling evidence that translation into known terms cannot account for the results comes from the fourth study, where unfamiliar objects were used as well as unfamiliar words. Here children were shown three novel objects. They were taught a taxonomic relation for two of the objects and a thematic relation for two. When no label was used children often selected the two objects that were related thematically as being the same. When an unfamiliar word was used to label the target picture, children now selected the two objects that were related taxonomically. Children could not have been translating in this study because they did not know what these unfamiliar objects were and had no familiar labels for them. Nevertheless, the results from this study replicated the results from the studies that used familiar objects. Again, the presence of an unfamiliar meaningless word caused children to shift from selecting objects that are thematically related to selecting objects that are taxonomically related. This suggests that children have placed an abstract constraint on what words can mean that is not mediated by the meaning of known terms.

By constraining the meaning of a term to categorical relations, children are able to rule out a huge number of other potential meanings for any given term. For example, suppose an adult points to a cup and says 'cup.' With no constraints on possible meanings, a child would have to consider that the table might also be a 'cup' because the cup was on the table, or that coffee is also called 'cup' because the cup was filled with coffee, or that mother might be a 'cup' because mother was lifting the cup. All of these relational meanings would be eliminated from consideration by the constraint that nouns refer to object categories. By limiting the number and kind of hypotheses that children need to consider, this constraint tremendously simplifies the problem of language learning.

*Origins of sensitivity to constraints on word meaning*

These findings raise the question of how children come to constrain their hypotheses about what a word can mean. What leads children to assume that a word is likely to refer to objects that are similar in some way rather than to objects that participate in the same event or context? There are at least two possibilities. One is that sensitivity to the constraint is innate – from the start, children assume words will refer to categories of similar objects. Having such implicit knowledge would provide children with an entry into the formidable problem of learning language. Children would at least be able to readily acquire count nouns, and once they had a reasonable vocabulary of category terms, they could then begin to comprehend other linguistic forms. In fact, the huge majority of children's first words are count nouns (Clark, 1983; Nelson, 1973; Hutenlocher, 1974).

Another possibility is that the constraint is induced from early language experience. Having learned many count nouns, almost all of which refer to objects that are taxonomically related, children may come to expect this to be true of subsequent terms they learn. If so, then this induction must take place fairly rapidly at an early point in language acquisition, since we found that even 2-year-olds believe that count nouns are more likely to refer to objects that belong to the same category than to objects that are thematically related.

It is not clear whether or not very young language learners limit the constraint to count nouns. Particularly if children have some innate knowledge of the constraint, they may at first overextend it, indiscriminately believing that any word they hear must refer to a taxonomic category. Only somewhat later might they become sensitive to form class and expect count nouns to be more likely than other classes of words to refer to categorical relations.

*The role of language in aiding concept acquisition*

Children's sensitivity to this constraint raises the possibility that language may help children acquire new categories. In contrast, it is often argued that words must map onto concepts that have already been worked out nonlinguistically (Clark, 1973; Huttenlocher, 1974; Macnamara, 1972; Nelson, 1974; Wittgenstein, 1953, 1958). In this view, language plays little role in concept learning. But this view may underestimate the importance of language. Young children may create concepts to fit new words, guided by abstract constraints on word meaning. This alternative view is a mild form of linguistic determinism (Whorf, 1956), in that language is believed to shape thought. It is quite different, however, from Whorf's conception that each language imposes a particular world view on its speakers and that cognition is determined and limited by the specific language one speaks. First, all languages are likely to share similar constraints on possible meanings for count nouns. Thus the hypothesis is that, regardless of native language, children look for categories of similar objects when they hear new nouns. Second, although nouns help focus children's attention on categorical relations, we are not arguing that children would be incapable of forming categories without exposure to language.

The small amount of research that bears on this milder form of linguistic determinism suggests that children can use abstract knowledge of the semantic correlates of form class to help them discover the concept to which a word refers. Brown (1957) found that 3- to 5-year-old children interpreted an unfamiliar count noun ('a dax') as referring to a new concrete object, whereas they interpreted an unfamiliar mass noun ('some dax') as referring to a novel undifferentiated mass. In a study by Katz, Baker and Macnamara (1974), children as young as $1\frac{1}{2}$ years old interpreted an unfamiliar proper noun ('Dax') as referring to an individual. At the same time, these young children understood an unfamiliar count noun ('a dax') as referring to a category of similar objects.

To return to our findings, hearing a noun caused children to shift their attention from thematic to taxonomic organization. These results lead us to speculate that linguistic input may serve more generally to shape the conceptual structure of the child in the direction of greater taxonomic organization. A word may draw members of a category together for a child, highlighting their common category membership. Language may thus play a direct role in making categorical relations a salient and highly structured mode of organization.

*Possible reasons for taxonomic organization of language*

The question arises as to why language is organized this way. Why don't words refer typically to objects that are thematically related? As we earlier pointed out, thematic relations between objects certainly are important for adults as well as for children. In naturally occurring situations, objects are not found organized by category, but rather are embedded in spatial, temporal, and causal contexts. Such relational structures as events and themes are a common way of organizing information to make sense of what we encounter (cf. Mandler, 1979; Markman, 1981).

Given that these thematic event-like organizations are a natural way of construing the world, why should languages force a taxonomic or categorical structure rather than capturing this thematic bias? Why don't we have single words for a boy and his bike, a baby and its bottle, a spider and its web? One reason may be that if nouns referred exclusively to relations such as a baby and its bottle or a boy and his bike, there would be no easy way to express hierarchical taxonomic relations. Because a taxonomy groups objects into categories nested within broader categories, it allows deductive inferences to be made that go beyond the first-hand knowledge one has about a specific object. If one knows, for example, that a particular object is an animal, one can be fairly sure that it takes in food, moves about, reproduces, and has internal organs. In contrast, knowing that something is a 'dax,' where 'dax' could be a boy or his bike, tells one very little else about it. One reason why nouns tend not to refer to thematically related objects, then, may be because of the advantages of hierarchical organization.

Another more important reason may be that if a language had single nouns referring exclusively to pairs of thematically related objects, it would be at great cost. The enormous expressive power of language would be lost. The expressive power of language derives from its ability to convey new relations through combinations of words. There are a potentially infinite number of thematic relations that one might want to express. The many thematic relations can easily be described through combinations of words – e.g., sentences and phrases. If single words referred only to thematic relations, however, there would be an extraordinary proliferation of words, probably more than humans could learn. One would need separate words for a baby and its bottle, a baby and its crib, a baby and its mother, a baby and its diaper, etc. Thus, the combinatorial power of language would be wasted. This, then, may be the major reason why nouns refer primarily to taxonomic categories rather than to thematically related objects.

**Notes**

1 There are a few exceptions, however. Relational information is contained in the meaning of kinship terms such as 'brother' or 'cousin.' The term 'friends' also refers to people who have a particular kind of thematic relationship with each other.

2 Rosch, Mervis, Gray, Johnson and Boyes-Braem (1976) showed that 3-year-old children are capable of using category membership to sort objects at the basic level of categorization, even though they fail to sort objects taxonomically at the superordinate level. In the Rosch et al. (1976) study, children were presented with two objects related at the basic level, along with an unrelated distractor, and were asked to find the two that are alike. Three-year-olds almost always selected the two category members over the unrelated distractor. Because this study failed to include any competing thematic relations, however, it did not establish the relative salience of thematic and categorical relations. In a preliminary study, we demonstrated that when a competing thematic relation is present

(e.g., a baby and a bottle), 2- and 3-year-olds often select it over the basic level category (e.g., two babies). When an unrelated distractor was used, children selected the categorical associate 94% of the time, as in the Rosch et al. (1976) study. When a thematically related distractor was used, however, children selected the categorical associate only 56% of the time. This finding allows us to address the main question about the role of a word in inducing categorical organization.

## References

Anglin, J. (1977). *Word, object, and conceptual development.* New York: Norton.

Brown, R. (1957). Linguistic determinism and the part of speech. *The Journal of Abnormal and Social Psychology, 55,* 1–5.

Carey, S. (in press). Are children fundamentally different kinds of thinkers and learners than adults? In S. Chipman, J. Segal and R. Glaser (Eds.), *Thinking and learning skills.* Hillside, NJ: Erlbaum, Vol. 2.

Clark, E. V. (1973). What's in a word? On the child's acquisition of semantics in his first language. In T. E. Moore (Ed.), *Cognitive development and the acquisition of language.* New York: Academic Press.

Clark, E.V. (1983). Meanings and concepts. In J. H. Flavell and E. M. Markman (Eds.), *Cognitive development,* Vol. 3 of P. H. Mussen (General Ed.), *Handbook of child psychology.* New York: Wiley.

Denney, N. (1974). Evidence for developmental changes in categorization criteria for children and adults. *Human Development, 17,* 41–53.

Denney, N., and Ziobrowski, M. (1972). Developmental changes in clustering criteria. *Journal of Experimental Child Psychology, 13,* 275–282.

Gelman, R., and Baillargeon, R. (1983). A review of some Piagetian concepts. In J. H. Flavell and E. M. Markman (Eds.), *Cognitive development,* Vol. 3 of P. H. Mussen (General Ed.), *Handbook of child psychology.* New York: Wiley.

Gibson, E. J., and Spelke, E. S. (1983). The development of perception. In J. H. Flavell and E. M. Markman (Eds.), *Cognitive development,* Vol. 3 of P. H. Mussen (General Ed.), *Handbook of child psychology.* New York: Wiley.

Huttenlocher, J. (1974). The origins of language comprehension. In R. L. Solso (Ed.), *Theories in cognitive psychology: The Loyola symposium.* Potomac, MD: Erlbaum.

Inhelder, B., and Piaget, J. (1964). *The early growth of logic in the child.* New York: Norton.

Katz, N., Baker, E., and Macnamara, J. (1974). What's a name? On the child's acquisition of proper and common nouns. *Child Development, 45,* 469–473.

Macnamara, J. (1972). Cognitive basis of language learning in infants. *Psychological Review, 79,* 1–13.

Mandler, J. M. (1979). Categorical and schematic organization in memory. In C. R. Puff (Ed.), *Memory organization and structure.* New York: Academic Press.

Mandler, J. M., Scribner, S., Cole, M., and DeForest, M. (1980). Cross-cultural invariance in story recall. *Child Development, 51,* 19–26.

Markman, E. M. (1981). Two different principles of conceptual organization. In M. E. Lamb and A. L. Brown (Eds.), *Advances in developmental psychology.* Hillside, NJ: Erlbaum, Vol. 1.

Markman, E. M., and Callanan, M. A. (1983). An analysis of hierarchical classification. In R. Sternberg (Ed.), *Advances in the psychology of human intelligence.* Hillside, NJ: Erlbaum, Vol. 2.

Mervis, C. B., and Rosch, E. (1981). Categorization of natural objects. In M. R. Rosenzweig and L. W. Porter (Eds.), *Annual review of psychology.* Palo Alto, CA: Annual Reviews, Vol. 32.

Nelson, K. (1973). Structure and strategy in learning to talk. *Monographs of the Society for Research in Child Development, 38,* (Serial No. 149).

Nelson, K. (1974). Concept, word and sentence: Interrelations in acquisition and development. *Psychological Review, 81,* 267–285.

Nelson, K. (1977). The syntagmatic–paradigmatic shift revisted: A review of research and theory. *Psychological Bulletin, 84,* 93–116.

Quine, W. V. O. (1960). *Word and object.* Cambridge, MA: MIT Press.

Rosch, E. H. (1978). Principles of categorization. In E. H. Rosch and B. B. Lloyd (Eds.), *Cognition and categorization.* Hillsdale, NJ: Erlbaum.

Rosch, E. H., and Mervis, C. B. (1975). Family resemblances: Studies in the internal structure of categories. *Cognitive Psychology, 7,* 573–605.

Rosch, E. H., Mervis, C. B., Gray, W., Johnson, D., and Boyes-Braem, P. (1976). Basic objects in natural categories. *Cognitive Psychology, 3,* 382–439.

Smiley, S. S., and Brown, A. L. (1979). Conceptual preference for thematic or taxonomic relations: A nonmonotonic age trend from preschool to old age. *Journal of Experimental Child Psychology, 28,* 249–257.

Whorf, B. L. (1956). *Language, thought and reality.* Cambridge, MA.: MIT Press.

Wittgenstein, L. (1953). *Philosophical investigations.* New York: Macmillan.

Wittgenstein, L. (1958). *The blue and brown books.* New York: Harper.

**Reference note**

1 Horton, M. S. (1982). *Category familiarity and taxonomic organization in young children.* Unpublished doctoral dissertation, Stanford University.

# 6 Gary F. Marcus
## 'Why Do Children Say "Breaked"?'

Reprinted in full from: *Current Directions in Psychological Science* **5**, 81–85 (1996)

Errors can yield special insights into learning mechanisms. In language development, perhaps the most notorious error is the past-tense overregularization. Most English verbs form their past tense regularly, by adding the suffice -ed (e.g., *walk-walked*). About 180 verbs, though, form their past tense idiosyncratically (e.g., *sing-sang*). Overregularizations result when the regular -ed suffix is applied to an irregular verg (e.g., *singed*).

Because parents almost never overregularize, these errors demonstrate that language learning involves more than mere imitation. Instead, children must possess mechanisms that detect and extend linguistic generalizations.

Although the production of overregularizations has typically been ascribed to the application of a mental rule, the mere fact that the regular pattern has been overextended does not guarantee that overregularization errors are produced by a rule. Instead, as Rumelhart and McClelland showed, a single uniform neural network that contains no explicit rules and makes no explicit distinction between regular and irregular words can produce overregularizations.[1]

In 1988, Pinker and Prince pointed out several limitations to Rumelhart and McClelland's model.[2] Since then, characterizing the mechanisms responsible for overregularization has become a central focus of detailed empirical comparisons between symbolic, rule-based models and connectionist neural network models that explicitly forsake rules in favor of networks of connections between nodes.

## The rule-and-memory model

A model of overregularization that my colleagues and I have proposed depends on the existence of mental rules. According to this model, children's grammars and adults' grammars are structured as similarly as possible. The model has three simple components.

First, speakers have access to a symbolic, default rule that says roughly, 'To form the past tense, add -ed to any word carrying the symbol [verb].' What makes this a rule is that it can apply to any verb, regardless of its resemblance to stored examples. What makes it a default is that it applies any time access to the lexicon fails, that is, to any word that lacks a stored past tense form, including low-frequency words (*snarfed*), unusual sounding words (*ploamphed*), and complex words that are not treated as roots, such as verbs derived from nouns (*The solders ringed the city*). Children readily generalize the -ed inflection to nonsense words like *wug* and to novel verbs derived from nouns (e.g., *ring*, meaning to put a ring on a finger).[3]

Second, past-tense forms of irregular roots are stored in memory. Because all memory is fallible, memory for irregular verbs is imperfect.

Third, a stored irregular form always takes precedence over the rule; hence, *sang* blocks *singed*. The default applies if and only if no irregular inflected form can be found.

When memory for irregular verbs is taxed, even adults may overregularize. For instance, many adults overregularize *strive* as *strived*, because the irregular form *strove* is rare and hence difficult to retrieve. Upon retrieval failure, the default rule steps into the breach, yielding an overregularization.

The rule-and-memory model holds that children's grammars are structured similarly to adults'. But because children have had less exposure than adults to correct forms, their memories for irregular forms are weaker. Whenever access to an irregular past-tense form fails, the child adds *-ed*, producing an overregularization.

To test this model, using data from a publicly available archive of children's spontaneous speech, CHILDES,[4] my colleagues and I conducted a systematic, quantitative analysis of children's overregularizations, extracting and analyzing 11,521 past-tense utterances from the spontaneous speech of 83 children.[5]

Several observations support the rule-and-memory model. First – contrary to popular opinion reported everywhere from *Newsweek* to the primary literature – there is no stage in which children completely replace correct forms with overregularizations. Instead, we discovered that children overregularize in only about 4% of their opportunities, demonstrating a systematic preference for correct irregular forms. Thus, errors appear to be a consequence of performance limitations rather than a qualitatively inaccurate grammar. The representative longitudinal plots of three children in Figure 6.1 show that low rates of overregularization are not artifacts of averaging over time; our data also show that these low rates are consistent across children and hold for most individual verbs.

Second, if overregularizations are the consequence of retrieval failure, verbs that are more difficult to remember should be more likely to be overregularized. To test this hypothesis, we used frequencies of parents' use of irregular verbs as an index of retrievability. As predicted, the more often a parent used a verb, the less likely the child was to overregularize it. The correlation was in the predicted direction for 18 of 19 children, with a mean of $-.34$.[6]

Third, irregular forms that are reinforced by similar-sounding irregular forms should be easier to remember than irregular forms that lack such reinforcement. Thus, *sing*'s past tense *sang* should be easier to remember because of the presence of similar-sounding verbs that follow similar patterns, such as *ring-rang* and *drink-drank*. Indeed, we found that verbs with greater irregular-cluster strength (as measured by the number and frequency of use of similar forms) were less prone to overregularization. The correlation was in the predicted direction for 16 of 19 children's overregularization rates, with a mean of $-.08$. This correlation holds even if we statistically factor out the effects of the verb's frequency.

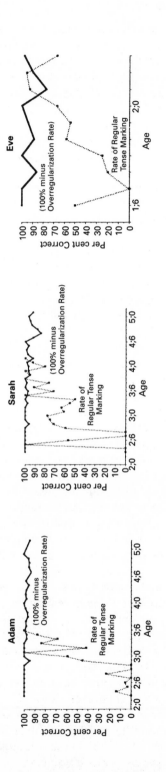

**Figure 6.1.** Overregularization and regular tense marking in three children as a function of age. In each panel, the heavy line plots the percentage of overregularization subtracted from 100%, and the dashed line plots the percentage of regular-past-tense contexts in which the child has successfully supplied the regular past tense.

Fourth, if overregularization errors disappear as a consequence of improving facility at retrieving correct forms, rather than qualitative grammatical change, then they should disappear gradually. Indeed, the sample of preschoolers that we studied overregularized at a rate of 4.2%; rates for first graders and fourth graders were 2.5% and 1%, respectively, and even adults overregularize occasionally, about once in every 25,000 opportunities.

Finally, the 'add -*ed*' rule, because it is English-specific, cannot be innate. Before it is learned, retrieval failures should be left unmarked (e.g., *I sing yesterday*). These errors should be replaced by overregularizations only after the English-specific default -*ed* is acquired. As the rule-and-memory model predicts, before children reliably inflect regular verbs for past tense in contexts that require it (e.g., *I walked yesterday*), they go through an initial period in which irregular verbs are used correctly or left unmarked, but never overregularized. Figure 6.1 shows that the onset of overregularization appears to coincide with the development of reliable regular past-tense marking in contexts that demand past-tense inflection. Rates of regular tense marking are significantly greater during the period of overregularization than before (Adam: 73% vs. 8%; Sarah: 85% vs. 44%; Eve: 66% vs. 11%), suggesting that overregularization is tied to the acquisition of a rule.[5]

**Parallel distributed processing**

Consider now the connectionist alternative. In single uniform networks such as those proposed by Rumelhart and McClelland and by Plunkett and Marchman, words are represented as distributed patterns of activation over a network of nodes and connections. In a simplified version of such a network, *sing* would be represented as a set of units representing the initial consonant, the vowel nucleus, and the final consonant. An external teacher presents a network with pairs of stem and past-tense forms. Learning the mapping from *sing* to *sang* involves strengthening connections that run from the input nodes that represent the sound *ing* to the output nodes that represent the sound *ang*. Similar-sounding words overlap in their representations, yielding an explanation for why adults sometimes inflect the novel word *spling* as *splang*.[7]

Regular inflection is treated identically: Exposure to *walk-walked* strengthens the connections between input nodes representing *alk* and output nodes representing *alked*, generalizing to similar words like *talk-talked*.

Overregularizations are produced when regular patterns exert too strong an attraction on irregular verbs. For instance, *grow* might be overregularized to *growed* because pairs like *glow-glowed* increase the strength of the connection between nodes representing the input *ow* and the output *owed*. As the network is exposed to more such pairs the chance of overregularization increases. Thus, 'the level of generalizations . . . [is] closely related to the total number [and proportion] of regular verbs in the vocabulary.'[8] This relationship might be dubbed the *regular-attraction hypothesis*, and it is central to most connectionist models of inflection.[9]

But although the network's overregularization is driven primarily by attraction to stored pairs in which stems are linked to regular-past-tense forms, four types of evidence suggest that children's overregularizations may not be.

### Longitudinal test

In typical network models, overregularization occurs during sudden shifts in the proportion of vocabulary that is regular.[10] Children's overregularization, however, appears to be independent of changes in the composition of vocabulary. Quantitatively, there is no positive correlation between increases in the number or proportion of regular verbs acquired (whether measured in *types*, the number of different verbs used, or *tokens*, the number of times each word has been used) by a child and the child's rate of overregularization. Instead, as Figure 6.2 shows, the proportion of regular verbs in Adam's and Sarah's vocabulary increases less rapidly during the period of overregularization than before – precisely the opposite of the regular-attraction hypothesis.[11] Thus, the onset of overregularization does not depend on dramatic increases in the proportion of vocabulary that is regular.

### Lexical test

The regular-attraction hypothesis predicts that irregular verbs will be more frequently overregularized if they are similar to regular verbs; thus, *feel* should be drawn to *feeled* by similar neighbors such as *heal-healed* and *peel-peeled*. To test this hypothesis, we calculated a verb-wise measure of regular-cluster strength, based on the number (and frequency of use) of each verb's similar-sounding regular neighbors. There was no correlation between regular-cluster strength and overregularization: Verbs with many regular neighbors were no more likely to be overregularized than verbs with few regular neighbors, suggesting that overregularizations are not the result of an attraction to regular verbs.

### Comparison between noun plurals and verbs

In English, the system for noun plurals contains a greater proportion of regular words (excluding learned Latinate plurals like *bacterium-bacteria*, more than 98% of noun plural types are regular) than does the system for the past tense (only 86% of the 1,000 most frequent types are regular). But like *-ed*, the *-s* plural is generalized whenever no irregular root can be found in the lexicon, including cases of memory failure in which existing roots cannot be accessed, but also including cases in which there is no irregular root, such as regular words (*cat*), plurals derived from names (*We had a fabulous meal at the Childs*), onomatopoeia (*The cartoon climax had seven POWs*), and unusual-sounding words (*kiosks*). Further evidence that regular inflection is generalized independently of type frequency comes from the fact that individual children's rates of overregularizing the plural do not differ significantly from their rates of overregularizing the past tense.[12]

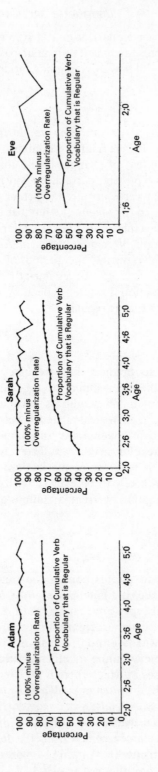

**Figure 6.2** Overregularization and the proportion of verb vocabulary that is regular in three children as a function of age. In each panel, the upper line plots the percentage of overregularization subtracted from 100%, and the lower line plots the proportion of the child's cumulative verb vocabulary that is regular.

*Cross-linguistic test*

If generalization of regular inflection is truly independent of type frequency, speakers should generalize regular inflection even when there are far fewer regular words than in the English systems for noun plurals and past tense. One test case is the German -s plural, which applies to fewer than 10% of German nouns (whether measured by types or tokens) and is just one of five different plural suffixes, [ls1], -e, -er, -(e)n, s. Despite its infrequency, the -s plural behaves as the default. Just as the English plural -s applies when no irregular form is available, as with names, borrowings, and onomatopoeia, so too does the German -s plural apply to names (*Thomas Manns*), borrowings (*Kiosks*), and onomatopoeic words (*Wau-waus*).[9]

German-speaking children often overregularize with -s, more often than might be predicted by a frequency-based approach,[13] and children are more likely to generalize the -s pattern than other patterns to novel words that are unusual sounding or presented as names.[14] These facts strengthen the conclusion that generalization of the default does not require that the regular pattern be highly frequent.

## Conclusions

Overregularization errors do not correspond with increases in the proportion of vocabulary that is regular, are not more common for irregular words that resemble other regular words than for irregular words that do not, are not more common in inflectional systems that have a higher proportion of regular words, and occur even in languages in which the regular pattern is infrequent. Rather than generalizing default inflection by analogy to stored exemplars, children generalize default inflection by a rule that applies whenever access to irregular forms fails.

Default inflection seems to be a natural property of many linguistic systems and to be readily learned by children. Although the input to children varies widely, English- and German-speaking children, for example, rapidly converge on the same sorts of inflectional systems. The English past tense, English noun plural (almost entirely regular), and German noun plural (almost entirely irregular) appear to develop similarly. Because single uniform neural networks tend to be closely tied to the input, they have difficulty explaining why children develop similar linguistic systems despite differing input conditions. Instead, generalization of regular inflection seems to be best explained in terms of a rule.

The key property of a rule appears to be its ability to treat all instances of a class equally, regardless of their degree of resemblance to stored forms. Rules do not generalize in a gradient of similarity, but rather apply in an all-or-none fashion depending on whether or not an item carries the appropriate symbol. For example, the 'add -ed' rule applies equally readily to any novel word carrying the symbol [verb]. This mode of generalization, which is driven not by resemblance but by the presence of a symbol, may be central to other domains of cognition.

For example, this ability to suppress resemblance and treat all tokens of a class equally is crucial for word recognition. A speech segment such as /ba/ can be uttered in many different ways, varying in pitch, amplitude, accent, and other characteristics. But the output of the speech perception system remains the same, regardless of whether a given utterance of /ba/ is more or less similar to previously heard examples.

Similarly, people can identify someone as a grandmother regardless of whether she has gray hair or cooks chicken soup; likewise, they can override perceptual similarity to identify a raccoon as a raccoon, even if it has been surgically transformed to look like a skunk.[15] There is little doubt that the mind can track information about similarity and resemblance (and calculate that Priscilla Presley is not a typical grandmother), but the ability to override information about resemblance and treat all members of a class identically – precisely the work done by rules that manipulate symbols – also appears to be an essential property of cognition.

A simple model that depends on the existence of such symbolic rules explains a wide range of data: Irregular forms are retrieved from memory and block the application of the default regular rule (add -*ed*); if a child fails to retrieve the past tense of an irregular form, the regular rule applies by default, and the child produces an overregularization.

**Acknowledgements.** I thank my collaborators S. Bartke, U. Brinkmann, H. Clahsen, M. Coppola, M. Hollander, J. J. Kim, T. J. Rosen, M. Ullman, R. Wiese, F. Xu, and especially S. Pinker. For helpful comments on an earlier draft, I thank Paul Bloom. The research described in this article was supported by a National Defense Science and Engineering Graduate Fellowship and University of Massachusetts Faculty Research Grant to the author, by Grant No. 18381 from the National Institutes of Health and Grant No. BNS 91–09766 from the National Science Foundation to S. Pinker, and by an American Council of Learned Societies/Deutscher Akademischer Austauschdienst (German Academic Exchange Service) collaborative research grant to H. Clahsen, S. Pinker, and the author.

## Notes

1 Rumelhart, D., and McClelland, J. (1993). On learning the past tenses of English verbs: Implicit rules or parallel distributed processing? in *Parallel Distributed Processing: Explorations in the Microstructure of Cognition*. J. McClelland, D. Rumelhart, and the PDP research group (Eds.), (MIT Press, Cambridge, MA, 1986); for a more recent model, see K. Plunkett and V. Marchman. From rote learning to system building: Acquiring verb morphology in children and connectionist nets. *Cognition, 48*, 21–69.

2 Pinker, S., and Prince, A. (1988). On language and connectionism: Analysis of a Parallel Distributed Processing model of language acquisition. *Cognition, 28*, 73–193.

3 Berko, J. (1991). The child's learning of English morphology, *Word, 14*, 150–177 (1958); J. J. Kim, G. F. Marcus, S. Pinker, M. Hollander and M. Coppola. Sensitivity of children's inflection to grammatical structure *Journal of Child Language 21*, 173–209 (1994). S. Pinker, Rules of language. *Science, 253*, 530–555.

4 MacWhinney, B., and Snow, C. (1985). The Child Language Data Exchange System. *Journal of Child Language, 12*, 271–296.

5 Marcus, G. F., Pinker, S., Ullman, M., Hollander, M., Rosen, T. J., and Xu, F. (1992). Overregularization in language acquisition. *Monographs of the Society for Research in Child Development, 57* (4, Serial No. 228).

6 Lexical correlations could be tested for only 19 children because for the remainder we lacked individual databases or found no overregularizations in our samples.

7 Prasada, S., and Pinker, S. (1993). Similarity-based and rule-based generalizations in inflectional morphology. *Language and Cognitive Processes, 8,* 1–56.

8 Plunkett and Marchman, note 1, p. 55.

9 Marcus, G. F., Brinkmann, U., Clahsen, H., Wiese, R., and Pinker, S. (1995). German inflection: The exception that proves the rule. *Cognitive Psychology, 29* 189–256.

10 The model of Plunkett and Marchman (note 1) displays a similar, abrupt external change, in which the onset of overregularization coincides with a sudden shift in training regime from a slow pace that allows the network to learn each irregular verb individually to a rapid pace that forces the network to generalize. See Marcus, G. F. (1995). The acquisition of inflection in children and multilayered connectionist networks. *Cognition 56*, 271–279.

11 Using novel sampling techniques from biostatistics, my colleagues and I (Marcus et al., note 5, chap. V) have shown that this finding is not an artifact of a cumulative vocabulary measure that necessarily decelerates over time.

12 Marcus, G. F. (1995). Children's overregularization of English plurals: A quantitative analysis. *Journal of Child Language, 22*, 447–459.

13 The only systematic study of how input frequency affects network generalization is a series of simulations conducted by Plunkett and Marchman (note 1). In this study, when the initial proportion of regular vocabulary was less than 50%, their simulation failed to generalize the regular pattern to 'novel indeterminate stems' (i.e., novel words).

14 Bartke, S., Marcus, G. F., and Clahsen, H. (1995). Acquiring German noun plurals, in *Proceedings of the 19th Annual Boston University Conference on Language Development*, D. MacLaughlin and S. McEwen (Eds.), Boston, Cascadilla Press.

15 Keil, F. C. (1989). *Concepts, Kinds, and Cognitive Development*, Cambridge, MA: Bradford Books; G. F. Marcus, Children's overregularization and its implications for cognition, in *Models of Language Acquisition: Inductive and Deductive Approaches*, P. Broeder and J. M. J. Murre (Eds.) (1996). Cambridge, MA: MIT Press.

# 7 Shirley B. Heath
## 'Oral and Literate Traditions Among Black Americans Living in Poverty'

Reprinted in full from: *American Psychologist* **44**, 367–373 (1989)

Within the past decade, scholars from a wide variety of disciplines have given considerable attention to the oral and literate traditions of Black Americans, especially in an attempt to compare their family and community patterns with those of the school and other mainstream institutions. Anthropologists, social historicans, and folklorists have detailed the long-standing rich verbal forms of Afro-American rhymes, stories, music, sermons, and joking and their interdependence with Black-White relations as well as male-female and cross-age interactions within Black communities (Folb, 1980; Hannerz, 1969; Levin, 1977; Smitherman, 1977; Whitten and Szwed, 1970). Yet schools and employers have repeatedly pictured a majority of Black students and workers as victims of language poverty and called for increased emphasis on literacy skills for Black Americans – young and old.

It is important to bring together these divergent views about language abilities, especially as they relate to oral and written language uses, and to compare family and community language socialization, on the one hand, with the expectations and practices of schools and workplaces, on the other. When children learn language, they take in more than forms of grammar: They learn to make sense of the social world in which they live and how to adapt to its dynamic social interactions and role relations. Through the reciprocal processes of family and community life that flow through communication, children develop a system of cognitive structures as interpretive frameworks and come to share to greater or lesser degrees the common value system and sets of behavioral norms of their sociocultural group (Schieffelin and Ochs, 1986). These frameworks and ways of expressing knowledge in a variety of styles and through different symbolic systems will vary in their congruence with those of the school and other mainstream institutions. Similarly, those of the school may differ from those of employers. It is important, therefore, to consider the actual – as opposed to the idealized – degrees of congruence from home and community to school and workplace.

In all these settings, judgments about language use extend to evaluations of character, intelligence, and ways of thinking; thus, negative assessments of language abilities often underlie expressions of sweeping prejudicial charac-terizations of Black Americans, especially those living in poverty. We consider first the primary uses of language in family and community life of poor and Black Americans, rural and urban, and then those of the school and the workplace, taking a comparative view across these varied contexts.

**Family and community language socialization**

Families socialize their children so that they will learn the forms and functions of language that will help them achieve some self-identity as group members and also meet the needs of everyday interactions. American Black families during slavery and subsequently in the often tumultuous and ever-changing circumstances of their daily lives socialized their young to respond to change, to adapt their communicative behaviors, and to define family in terms that extended beyond kin to neighbor, church, and community (Sobel, 1988; Wood, 1974). In response to the perils and pressures of White society, Black communities formed independent organizations – from schools and churches to mutual aid societies – that embodied their sense of being 'a people within a people,' capable of relying on their own resources and responding to the ever-shifting circumstances of their society (Nash, 1988). Children had to learn from an ever-shifting network, continuously adapting through considering when to apply, discard, reform, and supplement facts and skills that others transmitted to them. Standing behind this self-reliance were an array of literate behaviors – interpreting oral and written texts, preparing and practicing oral performances and written summations of them, feeding texts through the tests of individual experience, and remaking texts conceived by other groups in other times and places into confirmations of current group identities and purposes.

In traditional patterns of rural life, especially in the southeastern part of the United States, open spaces and climatic conditions have favored a considerable amount of outdoor public life that, in turn, ensured that youngsters heard and participated in a great variety of oral language performances (Levine, 1977). Children inherited an ethos of group involvement in oral decision making. These public occasions for oral performances helped sustain certain other characteristics such as persistence, assertive problem-solving, and adaptability in role-playing (Spencer, Brookins and Allen, 1985). Family members and trusted community members assumed child-rearing responsibilities and demanded numerous kinds of role-playing from the young apparently in the belief that children learn best that which is not directly taught (Barnes, 1972; Hill, 1972; Stack, 1970; Ward, 1971; Wilson, 1987; Young, 1970). Looking, playing, imitating, listening, and learning when to be silent complemented children's learning of oral language skills for negotiating, interpreting and adapting information. These abilities transferred well into individual and group survival in adult life.

Since the 1960s, numerous demographic and socio-economic changes have affected Black Americans. Many have entered the middle and upper classes; yet many remain in poverty, primarily in the rural Southeast or in the inner cities of many parts of the country where their parents or grandparents migrated in the early decades of the 20th century. Then ghettos consisted primarily of two-family dwellings or small apartment houses; with the 1960s came high-rise, high-density projects, where people took residence not through individual and free choice of neighbor and community, but through bureaucratic placement.

In the late 1980s, nearly half of all Black children live in poverty, and most of these, especially in urban areas, grow up in households headed by a mother under 25 years of age who is a school dropout. Between 1970 and 1980, the proportion of young Black families with fathers fell drastically; the Children's Defense Fund estimates that approximately 210,000 Black men in their 20s are not accounted for in the 1980 census (Edelman, 1987, p. 11). Multiple explanations are offered to account for the 'hidden' Black men and the relatively low Black marital rates for men in their 20s (Wilson, 1987). However, in over half of the states, children – regardless of how low the family's income is – are not eligible for Aid for Families with Dependent Children if an unemployed father resides in the household (Edelman, 1987). Furthermore, housing rules restrict the number of occupants of a single apartment, and assignments of apartments can rarely take into account the needs or expressed desires of members of extended families to live close to each other. Regardless of the theories – economic and social – for these changed family circumstances, the effects on language socialization of the young are undeniable.

Differences in the space and time of social interactions in rural and urban Black communities of poverty greatly influence both the degree of their divergence from earlier patterns of language socialization and the increased extent of disparity between rural and urban child-rearing patterns. The picture that most closely resembles that of earlier years comes from those areas in which either agricultural or mill work remain viable options and a majority of families still live in single or dual-family dwellings.[1] Much of the social life is out-of-doors, and times of employment, especially for men, vary with seasonal and daily shift patterns. Both male and female adults of several ages are often available in the neighborhood to watch over children who play outside and to supplement the parenting role of young mothers.

Older adults do not simplify or mediate the world for children of the community, but they expect the young to adapt to changing contexts, speakers, and caregivers. They say of the young: 'Children have to make their own way in this world' and 'have their own heads.' Speakers neither censor nor simplify their talk around children, and when they want children to hear them, they often do not address children directly, assuming they are active listeners to the multiparty talk that swirls around them in everyday life (Heath, 1983, in press; Ward, 1971; Young, 1970).

Caregivers ask children only 'real' questions – those to which the adults do not know the answers. They accept from children and issue to them direct commands and reprimands. To the grandmother who has just started to iron, the toddler says, 'Stop that now; stop it,' or 'Ma, sit down.' To the toddler who has removed the top from a perfume bottle, the grandmother says 'Put that top back on and come on' as she starts out the door.

Adults tease children, asking them questions and often threatening to take away their possessions, getting them to show their ready wits in front of an audience (Ward, 1971; cf. Miller, 1986). In the following interaction between two-year old Tyrone and his grandmother, his biological mother and an aunt and uncle sit on the porch talking. Several conversations take place at the same time, but all participants are mindful of the drama between younger and older combatants.

| | |
|---|---|
| Grandmother: | 'That your hat? Can I have it?' [she is sitting on the porch in a low chair with a lap full of beans to shell, and Tyrone plays nearby with an old hat] |
| Tyrone: | 'Huh?' |
| Grandmother: | 'Can I have it?' |
| Tyrone: | 'Yea.' |
| Grandmother: | 'Give it here then.' |
| Tyrone: | 'Huh?' |
| Grandmother: | 'Let me have it.' |
| Tyrone: | 'NO!' [in a loud voice] |
| Grandmother: | 'I buy me one.' |
| Tyrone: | 'Huh?' |
| Grandmother: | 'I buy one.' |
| Tyrone: | 'Buy one then.' |
| Grandmother: | 'I buy one this big. I buy one that big.' [stretching out her hands] |
| Tyrone: | 'That more big.' [stretching out his arms] |
| Grandmother: | 'You get one bigger than that?' |
| Tyrone: | 'Yea.' |
| Grandmother: | 'I don't care. I get one bigger than that. I get one this big.' [stretching out her arms] |
| Tyrone: | 'Huh?' |
| Grandmother: | 'I get one this big.' [repeating her arm stretch] |
| Tyrone: | 'I get big.' [standing up and stretching out his arms and one leg] |
| Grandmother: | 'So.' [with an air of resignation to the fact that she can neither stand nor stretch out either leg] |
| Tyrone: | 'Yea.' |
| Grandmother: | 'Yea.' (see footnote 1) |

Tyrone's requests for repetition by which he builds on his grandmother's sentences illustrate just one kind of challenge game that fills long hours of interactions between youngsters and available older family and community members. Children take adult roles, issue commands and counterstatements, and win arguments by negotiating nuances of meaning verbally and nonverbally. Adults goad children into taking several roles and learning to respond quickly to shifts in mood, expectations, and degrees of jest. Adults expect children *to show* what they know rather than *to tell* what they know (Heath, 1983, 1986, in press).

Numerous forms of written language enter these communities through either bureaucratic or commercial transactions, as well as from the school and church. Adults make public the most significant of these written messages, in order to debate their meanings, offer judgments, and negotiate appropriate actions. For those who participate in the many organizations surrounding the church, there are many occasions for both writing long texts (such as public prayers) and reading Biblical and Sunday School materials, as well as legal records of property and church management matters. Through all of these activities based on written materials, oral negotiation in groups makes the writing matter. The spoken word carries behind it personal relations, institutional affiliations, and common goals and ideals (Rosenberg, 1970). The community values access to written sources and acknowledges the need to produce written materials of a variety of types for their own purposes, as well as for successful interactions with mainstream institutions. Yet they do not necessarily value the accumulation of all skills within every individual; instead, different levels and types of talent within the community provide a range of varied resources for the community. Thus, some members become valued as the best story-tellers, others as mediators or peacemakers, others as invaluable sources of underground information, and still others as careful record-keepers and schedulers. For example, within Black churches, members acknowledge some members as appropriate treasurers, others as secretaries, and others as brokers who interpret documents from city and state bureaucracies (Bethel, 1979). Within families, members ideally distribute and alternate among many roles, especially those related to caregiving for children and the elderly or infirm (Slaughter, in press; Slaughter and Epps, 1987).

Within these communities, members maintain interpersonal stability by challenging individuals to try to outwit or outdisplay others, while at the same time members expect, and indeed depend on, having a range of sources of knowledge, degrees of expertise, and access to power within the group. The community regards as accomplished, smart, and literate those who have the ability to change forms of interactions, to gather and use information from a variety of sources outside their personal experience, to adjust knowledge to fit different interpretations, and to act on information in individual ways.

The picture of family and community life given above differs radically from that of blighted urban areas of high-rise housing projects. There, spatial and interpersonal boundaries, as well as time constraints of the dominant 8 a.m. to 5 p. m. time frame of employment, and the prevalence of young single mothers contribute to socialization patterns that contrast sharply with those of rural or small-town residents. Small apartments and public housing rules discourage extended families; high-rise buildings often eliminate the possibility of free play outside by very young children.

Young mothers, isolated in small apartments with their children, and often separated by the expense and trouble of cross-town public transportation from family members, watch television, talk on the phone, or carry out household and caregiving chores with few opportunities to tease or challenge their youngsters verbally. No caring, familiar, and ready audience of young and old is there to appreciate the negotiated performance. Playmates and spectators are scarce, as are toys and scenes for play. The mother's girlfriends, the older children of neighbors, visits to the grocery store, welfare office, and laundromat, and the usually traumatic visits to the health clinic may represent the only breaks in daily life in the apartment.

One mother agreed to tape-record her interactions with her children over a two-year period and to write notes about her activities with them (for a full discussion of these data, see Heath, in press; for an explanation of this participatory data collection technique used with another dropout mother, see Heath and Branscombe, 1984, 1985; Heath and Thomas, 1984). Within approximately 500 hours of tape and over 1,000 lines of notes, she initiated talk to one of her three preschool children (other than to give them a brief directive or query their actions or intentions) in only 18 instances. On 12 occasions, she talked to the children as a result of introducing some written artifact to them. In the 14 exchanges that contained more than four turns between mother and child, 12 took place when someone else was in the room. Written artifacts, as well as friends or family members anxious to listen to talk about the children's antics, stimulated the mother's talk to her preschoolers.

The spatial – and resultant social – isolation of urban project life often forces such young mothers into dyadic rather than multi-party interactions with their children. Even for those mothers who were themselves socialized through multi-party teasing and rich community and church life, their child-hood playful and teasing exchanges drop away when there is no audience of new potential challengers. Cut off from the family and communal activities of rural life, these young mothers find it difficult to arrange tasks on which to collaborate with their children. Thus, little of their talk surrounds either planning or executing actions with or for the young. Few allegiances, such as church life, provide a sustaining ideology of cultural membership, pride in being Black, or guidance in collecting, assessing, and interpreting informa-tion. Instead these young mothers depend in large part on each other, with only infrequent contact with older members of their own families, or they acquiesce to the advice and interpretations of bureaucratic and educational representatives, such as social workers.

## Institutional supports of language learning

The implications of this shift from association with family and community alliances are wide ranging. For example, in a comparative study of Black dropouts and high school graduates in Chicago, those who graduated had found support in school and community associations, as well as church attendance; 72% of the graduates reported regular church attendance whereas only 14% of the dropouts did. Alienation from family and community, and subsequently school, seems to play a more critical role in determining whether a student finishes high school than the socioeconomic markers of family income or education level (Williams, 1987). In a study carried out in inner-city Boston, positive effects on the academic success of children came with the association of their mothers with organizational ties beyond the family (and with friends who had such ties) and with nondenominational religious affilia-tions, as well as with stability in the labor force over a number of years (Blau, 1981).

In many housing developments, the diversity of languages, ethnic groups, and regional and religious backgrounds punctuate young mothers' isolation. These strange and unfamiliar surroundings cut sharply into possibilities of building mutual trust and shared responsibilities for childcare. Poverty and the stretch for more than the wages can meet erode family bonds, as do the ever-accessible alcohol and drugs of inner-city life. Once children are old enough to leave the isolation of their apartments, they join life on the street, where linguistic and cognitive stimulation abound, often inviting role-switching in language and demeanor (Lefkowitz, 1987; Lipsitz, 1977; Rappaport, 1985). However, the potential of older peers to channel the energies and goals of the younger in societally beneficial directions is often overcome by the environmentally harmful conditions that surround youth in the inner city: malnutrition, child abuse, substance-related damage, and criminal activities. Those who manage to transform these street experiences into success in mainstream academic life may suffer considerably from the sociocultural schizophrenia of being both Black and mainstream American (Anson, 1988). They may live (often with devastating outcomes) with the ringing questions that surrounded W. E. DuBois's (1961/1903) analysis of double-consciousness in *The Souls of Black Folk*.

### The school's view of spoken and written language

The school has seemed unable to recognize and take up the potentially positive interactive and adaptive verbal and interpretive habits learned by Black American children (as well as other nonmainstream groups), rural and urban, within their families and on the streets. These uses of language – spoken and written – are wide ranging, and many represent skills that would benefit all youngsters: keen listening and observational skills, quick recognition of nuanced roles, rapid-fire dialogue, hard-driving argumentation, succinct recapitulation of an event, striking metaphors, and comparative analyses based on unexpected analogies (Baugh, 1983).

Many educators tend to deny the fundamental contribution of these verbal abilities to being literate in the broadest sense. Rather, schools tend to deal with literacy skills as mechanistic abilities that separate out and manipulate discrete elements of a written text, such as spelling, vocabulary, grammar, topic sentences, and outlines, apart from the meaning and interpretation of a text as a whole. Being literate often means having a labeling familiarity with the content of specific written texts (Hirsch, 1987).

The insistent focus in school on learning to read and write as the natural forerunner of reading and writing to learn creates innumerable classroom scenes of individuals reading aloud and responding to teacher and test questions about the content of reading materials. After the solo writing of short-phrase answers in the early school years come the short essays and research papers of the secondary school. Teachers usually constrain time and task so that these longer pieces of writing are first drafts only, and they too are solo pieces written without opportunities to shape and test ideas by talking with others. These expectations stand in sharp contrast to those of family and street associates of children from Black and other nonmainstream communities.

The majority of teachers and a major portion of commercial language arts materials stress that children (as well as adults) must learn to read and write as individuals and display their skills and knowledge in the prespecified and limited forms of work-sheets, standardized tests, brief academic essays, and answers to teacher and textbook questions. Inner-city schools and those perennially at the bottom of educational profiles receive the most intense pressure to improve the verbal scores of their students; thus, they tend to rely more on teaching materials of the above sort than other districts.

Thus, for the majority of students that score poorly on standardized tests, the school offers little practice and reward in open-ended, wide-ranging uses of oral and written language (such as giving and reinterpreting directions or creating and debating alternative plans of action). Occasions for extended reading, writing, or talking on a sustained topic are relatively few and far between (Applebee, 1981, 1984; Goodlad, 1984). Yet such occasions lie at the very heart of being literate: sharing knowledge and skills from multiple sources, building collaborative activities from and with written materials, and switching roles and trading expertise and skills in reading, writing, and speaking.

## Language in the workplace: changing needs

Across almost the entire first century of industrialization and urbanization in the United States, the image of the isolated factory worker carrying out directions given from superiors stood behind many school activities: Good students who followed directions and predictably worked on their own made good workers (Graff, 1979, 1987). But during this century of industrial growth, governmental and human service agencies increased their influence over individual lives by generating more and more documents that needed interpretation – generally negotiated orally and with several interchanges with both individuals and groups. To take action on matters ranging from childcare to insurance choices and appliance warranties, all Americans came increasingly to need oral negotiation skills and practice in interpreting written documents.

Yet ironically, schools offered little practice or instruction in those language uses related to negotiation and collaboration in groups. In schools direct and single 'right' answers given by individuals predominate over group interpretations of written texts. The underlying basis of group work – that most 'real' questions have no direct or right answers – is that no single individual is likely to have the range of information or technical skills needed for most of the decisions we must take. In most interactions with bureaucracies and other institutions beyond the family, adults – young and old – depend on distributed cognition or the construction of knowledge that is possible through talk that compares, questions, and assesses a wide range of forms of written and spoken language (Rogoff and Lave, 1984; Wertsch, 1985).

Similarly, in a rapidly growing percentage of current employment settings, employers rely less on individuals acting to follow directions and more on individuals collaborating and negotiating under conditions of almost constant flux. From jobs paying minimum wage to professional and executive positions, workers must be able to draw inferences from a variety of types of information, understand and transmit instructions, develop alternatives, reach conclusions, and express their decisions effectively. For example, in fast-food restaurants, cashiers, cooks, and dishwashers negotiate orally with each other and interpret written directions and numerous highly technical and legal specifications that abound in commercial establishments and public agencies (e.g., health inspections and building codes). In the mid-1980s American manufacturers and service sector employers consistently began to call for workers who were 'well-grounded in fundamental knowledge and who have mastered concepts and skills that create an intellectual framework to which new knowledge can be added' (National Academy of Sciences, 1984, p. 17). Increasingly, even the first jobs of young adults assume collaborative work settings and occasions for sharing orally the group's knowledge about ways to solve problems in the workplace. Earlier single-task factory jobs or apprenticed craft positions demanded very different types of language skills. But in the 1980s, advancement depends increasingly on the ability to compose and read graphic and text information about real-world decisions, consult source materials, handle and explain mathematical concepts, control and take responsibility for complex equipment, and transmit information to those both above and below in the work hierarchy (Carnegie Forum on Education and the Economy, 1986; Gainer, 1988).

Institutions – from governmental bureaucracies to commercial workplaces – acknowledge that information and contexts of work now change constantly. These institutions require collaboration and shared knowledge building, as well as individual responsibility and commitment. Most of their members, as well as the citizens and workers who come in contact with them, operate primarily and most effectively through a wide range of types of oral language uses as well as an awareness of the power and purposes of written documents. The most valued oral language habits include giving directions, asking clarification questions, offering rapid and on-the-spot summaries, laying out short-term as well as long-range plans, and giving effective and nonthreatening assessments or recommendations to fellow workers. Rarely is any single individual entrusted with writing a document of any significance and for a wide audience: Drafts, multiple readers, and several editions intervene before any final written version. Even more rarely is the reading of a document of any importance given over to a single individual; instead several read the document and meet to discuss its meaning and relevance for action (Barbee, 1986; Mikulecky, 1982; Mikulecky and Ehlinger, 1986; Mikulecky and Winchester, 1983).

In the valuation of collaboration and numerous verbal forms of displaying knowledge, as well as taking multiple approaches to interpreting a wide variety of types of texts, formal schooling does not mesh well with either nonmainstream communities or workplaces. Schooling pursues actions and evaluations of students that validate answers instead of questions, fixed knowledge accumulated by individuals reading in isolation, an assumption that learning once acquired need not change in relation to context, and individual performance of one-time-only writing of a very narrow range of genres.

**Reexamining what it means to be literate**

The insistence of the school on individualizing literacy and separating it from its social and oral roots has ignored traditional oral and literate habits of Black Americans. Yet, ironically these traditional habits match the demands and needs of employers in the late 20th century far better than those of most classrooms. The workplace of the late 20th century demands language skills far beyond those identified as important and taught in schools. Classrooms' narrow focus on only certain kinds of literate behaviors typically discourages Black children's positive transfer of adaptability, keen interpretive talents, and group collaboration to either academic life or employment. Too often Black students, worn down by the effects of poverty and/or the realities of inner-city life, lose hope in themselves. Furthermore, current changes in Black family and community structures of inner-city life are rapidly eroding earlier socialization patterns that offered adaptability, persistence, and strong self-identification within a group. In schools, teachers identify the subject matter and skills to be taught and determine as well the path of development along which the learner *should* move to reach certain prespecified goals. Repeated denial, punishment, and truncation of family and community language socialization patterns minimize the chances that students will manage to transfer these profitably to either the classroom or workplace.

In contrast to Black American family and community life, as well as to new demands of the workplace, in school the competitive display of knowledge by individuals breaks apart the communal acceptance of differential levels of talent and expertise. The focus on general and leveled knowledge across all individuals and the movement of learning along a path prespecified by scope and sequence isolate the learner from the learning group and privatizes knowledge and skills. The school generally insists that adults must always be the teachers, that the verbal display of knowledge is central, and that individual demonstration of literacy prowess is both valued and valuable.

The descriptions given in this article have been of how Black Americans in rural and urban poverty have tried to sustain traditional patterns of learning and roles for spoken and written language. Other nonmainstream sociocultural groups also hold expectations of language and learning that differ markedly from the school's majority premises about literacy. Studies of different groups of Native Americans, as well as those from communities of any one of the several different Hispanic groups (e.g., Puerto Rican, Chicano, recent Mexican-origin, Dominican Republican, Cuban), also document the varieties of ways that young children learn to use oral and written language.

Group sharing, down-playing individual achievement, and remaining available as a resource to members of one's family and primary community have supported language uses and have been among the ideals of many nonmainstream cultural groups throughout American history. Most certainly, numerous exceptions to these ideals have come in recent decades. Individual minority members have left their family connections and communities to join the mainstream and operate ostensibly apart from their cultural and linguistic roots. In addition, environmental and economic forces have cut deeply into traditional community-sustaining patterns of oral and written language use. For Afro-Americans and Native Americans – and increasingly for Hispanic groups – many economic and social policy forces have eroded family and community-based efforts to sustain group cohesion, shared goals, and negotiated intentions.

The majority of the American population wants to hang onto their folk theories about literacy and continue their faith in school as the place where individuals learn to read and write in order to get good jobs. A major function of research in the social sciences is to offer evidence that such premises do not apply universally across cultures or periods of history. Moreover, basing norms and practices of formal schooling on such folk theories may diminish the larger society's ability for self-assessment and adaptation. In the late 1980s, multidisciplinary investigations of language in the life of minority communities and workplaces strongly suggest that the public adopt a radically different conception of literacy than that which drives formal schooling. These studies (Schieffelin and Ochs, 1986) find within families and communities a wide variety of ways that oral and written language can sustain the adaptive and innovative strategies of problem solving that American employers and public service proponents see as rich human resource investments. If, as our folk theories maintain, schools are in the business of improving benefits for society, they have much to learn from the oral and literate traditions of Black American family and community life.

### Notes

1 I have detailed (Heath, 1983, 1986) language socialization in the Black working-class community of Trackton in the piedmont Carolinas between 1960 and 1977. I have also (Heath, in press) described the language socialization of Black children in both a small-town neighborhood and in a high-rise, inner-city project and contrasted the patterns of the current generation with those of their parents not quite two decades ago. Data and generalizations that follow in this section come from unpublished transcripts and fieldnotes of language interactions in the homes of four preschoolers who are the children of two young women who were children at the time of the original Trackton study.

### References

Anson, R. S. (1988). *Best intentions.* New York: Random House.

Applebee, A. (1981). *Writing in the secondary school: English and the content areas.* Urbana, IL: National Council of Teachers of English.

Applebee, A. (1984). *Contexts for learning to write: Studies of secondary school instruction.* Norwood, NJ: Ablex.

Barbee, D. E. (1986). *Methods of providing vocational skills to individuals with low literacy levels: The U.S. experience.* Geneva: International Labour Office.

Barnes, E. (1972). The black community as the source of positive self-concept for black children: A theoretical perspective. In R. Jones (Ed.), *Black psychology.* New York: Harper.

Baugh, J. (1983). *Black street speech: Its history, structure, and survival.* Austin: University of Texas Press.

Bethel, E. (1979). *Social and linguistic trends in a black community.* Greenwood, SC: Lander College, Department of Sociology.

Blau, Z. S. (1981). *Black children/white children: Competence, socialization, and social structure.* New York: Free Press.

Carnegie Forum on Education and the Economy (1986). *A nation prepared: Teachers for the 21st century.* New York: Author.

DuBois, W. E. (1961). *The souls of black folk.* New York: Fawcett (Original work published 1903).

Edelman, M. W. (1987). *Families in peril.* Cambridge, MA: Harvard University Press.

Folb, E. A. (1980). *Runnin' down some lines: The language and culture of Black teenagers.* Cambridge. MA: Harvard University Press.

Gainer, L. (1988). *Best practices: What works in training and development.* Alexandria, VA: American Society for Training and Development.

Goodlad, J. I. (1984). *A place called school: Prospects for the future.* New York: McGraw-Hill.

Graff, H. (1979). *The literacy myth: Literacy and social structure in the nineteenth-century city.* New York: Academic Press.

Graff, H. (1987). *The labyrinths of literacy: Reflections on literacy past and present.* London: Falmer Press.

Hannerz, U. (1969). *Soulside: Inquiries into ghetto culture and community.* New York: Columbia University Press.

Heath, S. B. (1983). *Ways with words: Language, life, and work in communities and classrooms.* Cambridge, England: Cambridge University Press.

Heath, S. B. (1986). Separating 'things of the imagination' from life: Learning to read and write. In W. Teale and E. Sulzby (Eds.), *Emergent literacy* (pp. 156–172). Norwood, NJ: Ablex.

Heath, S. B. (in press). The children of Trackton's children: Spoken and written language in social change. In J. Stigler, G. Herdt and R. A. Shweder (Eds.), *Cultural psychology: The Chicago symposia.* New York: Cambridge University Press.

Heath, S. B., and Branscombe, A. (1984). Intelligent writing in an audience community. In S. W. Freedman (Ed.), *The acquisition of written language: Revision and response* (pp. 3–32). Norwood, NJ: Ablex.

Heath, S. B., and Branscombe, A. (1985). The book as narrative prop in language acquisition. In B. Schieffelin and P. Gilmore (Eds.), *The acquisition of literacy: Ethnographic perspectives* (pp. 16–34). Norwood, NJ: Ablex.

Heath, S. B., and Thomas, C. (1984). The achievement of preschool literacy for mother and child. In H. Goelman, A. Obert, and F. Smith (Eds.), *Awakening to literacy* (pp. 51–72). Exeter, NH: Heinemann Educational Books.

Hill, R. (1972). *The strengths of black families.* New York: Emerson-Hall.

Hirsch, E. D. (1987). *Cultural literacy.* Boston: Houghton Mifflin.

Lefkowitz, B. (1987). *Tough change: Growing up on your own in America.* New York: Free Press.

Levine, L. W. (1977). *Black culture and Black consciousness: Afro-American folk thought from slavery to freedom.* New York: Oxford University Press.

Lipsitz, J. (1977). *Growing up forgotten.* Lexington, MA: D. C. Heath.

Mikulecky, L. (1982). Job literacy: The relationship between school preparation and workplace actuality. *Reading Research Quarterly, 17.* 400–419.

Mikulecky, L., and Ehlinger, J. (1986). The influence of metacognitive aspects of literacy on job performance of electronics technicians. *Journal of Reading Behavior, 18,* 41–62.

Mikulecky, L., and Winchester, D. (1983). Job literacy and job performance among nurses at varying employment levels. *Adult Education Quarterly, 34,* 1–15.

Miller, P. (1986). Teasing as language socialization and verbal play in a White working-class community. In Schieffelin, B. and Ochs, E. (Eds.), *Language socialization across cultures* (pp. 199–212). New York: Cambridge University Press.

Nash, G. B. (1988). *Forging freedom: The formation of Philadelphia's black community, 1720–1840.* Cambridge, MA: Harvard University Press.

National Academy of Sciences (1984). *High schools and the changing workplace: The employers' view.* Washington, DC: National Academy Press.

Rappaport, R. N. (1985). *Children, youth, and families: The action-research relationship.* Cambridge, MA: Harvard University Press.

Rogoff, B., and Lave, J. (Eds.), (1984). *Everyday cognition.* Cambridge, MA: Harvard University Press.

Rosenberg, B. A. (1970). *The art of the American folk preacher.* New York: Basic Books.

Schieffelin, B., and Ochs, E. (1986). Language socialization. *Annual Review of Anthropology* (Vol. 15). Palo Alto, CA: Annual Reviews.

Slaughter, D. T. (Ed.), (in press). *Black children and poverty.* San Francisco, CA: Jossey-Bass.

Slaughter, D. T., and Epps, E. G. (1987). The home environment and academic achievement of Black American children and youth: An overview. *Journal of Negro Education, 56*(1), 3–20.

Smitherman, G. (1977). *Talkin' and testifyin': The language of Black America.* Boston: Houghton Mifflin.

Sobel, M. (1988). *The world they made together: Black and white values in eighteenth-century Virginia.* Princeton: Princeton University Press.

Spencer, M., Brookins, G., and Allen, W. (Eds.). (1985). *The social and affective development of Black children.* Hillsdale, NJ: Erlbaum.

Stack, C. B. (1970). *All our kin: Strategies for survival in a Black community.* New York: Harper and Row.

Ward, M. (1971). *Them children: A study in language learning.* New York: Holt, Rinehart and Winston.

Wertsch, J. V. (1985). *Culture, communication, and cognition: Vygotskian perspectives.* Cambridge, England: Cambridge University Press.

Whitten, N. E. Jr., and Szwed, J. F. (1970). *Afro-American anthropology: Contemporary perspectives.* New York: Free Press.

Williams, S. B. (1987). A comparative study of black dropouts and black high school graduates in an urban public school system. *Education and Urban Society, 19,* 311–319.

Wilson, W. (1987). *The truly disadvantaged.* Chicago: University of Chicago Press.

Wood, P. (1974). *Black majority.* New York: W. H. Norton.

Young, V. H. (1970). Family and childhood in a southern negro community. *American Anthropologist, 72,* 169–288.

# 8    D. H. Skuse
## 'Extreme Deprivation in Early Childhood'

Reprinted in full from: *Language Development in Exceptional Circumstances* (Psychology Press, 1993), 29–46

Many writers on the intellectual nature of man have attempted to supply a chapter for which human experience afforded no materials, by conjecturing what would be the condition of a being secluded, from infancy to youth, from all knowledge of the external world and from all intercourse with his species, and, therefore, destitute of the common experience, the appetites, and the acquirements, which result from the circumstances in which a human being is usually placed. The probable character of his feelings and perceptions on viewing the glories of nature which he had never witnessed, and his sensations amidst the business and forms of life of which he had no previous notion, (affords) matter for very interesting speculation.

So begins an account of the life of Caspar Hauser, in the Penny Magazine of the Society for the Diffusion of Useful Knowledge, published in 1834. Caspar Hauser was a mysterious young man, just over 16 years of age, who had been discovered in a street in Nuremberg, in Bavaria, in 1828. He was initially without comprehensible language or social skills, having allegedly spent the greater part of his life in a dark cramped cell with no human company, for reasons that were never discovered. Despite possessing a vocabulary at discovery of not more than six or so words he was able, after 15 months' tutelage under the guidance of a certain Professor Daumer, to comment on the night sky 'That is indeed the most beautiful sight I have ever seen in the world. But who has placed all those numerous beautiful candles there? Who lights them? Who puts them out?'.

Over many centuries man has considered that a careful analysis of the sequelae of extreme deprivation of human contact in early childhood might reveal valuable insights into how normal language develops. To this end children have occasionally been deliberately raised in conditions of extreme isolation. The Egyptian pharaoh, Psammetichos, the Holy Roman Emperor Frederik II and King James IV of Scotland all allegedly attempted such experiments (Curtiss 1981a), in the latter instance the purpose being to discover which was the more ancient language, Latin or Greek. In our times, the development of twin sisters under conditions of minimal perceptual and social stimulated was studied by psychologists (see Dennis 1941) from the first to the fourteenth month of life. There are in addition a number of reports concerning individual children who spent their early years in conditions of exceptional impoverishment and deprivation as the result of deliberate action by nefarious, ignorant or incompetent caretakers (Davis 1940, Mason 1942, Koluchova 1972, Curtiss 1977, Douglas and Sutton 1978, Skuse 1984, Thompson 1986). Before considering those case histories in detail an account will be given of some valuable observations that have been made on children whose environmental deprivation resulted from an upbringing in neglectful and unstimulating institutions.

### Studies of children in institutions

One of the earliest descriptions of the impact of poor institutional care upon children's mental abilities was given by Harold Skeels. In his well-known and celebrated study Skeels (1966) reviewed the outcome of developmentally delayed children who had spent their earliest years in an unstimulating orphanage, back in the 1930s. His follow-up study contrasted the fortunes of 13 who were rehabilitated to an institution for mentally retarded adults (at an average age of 20 months) with a contrast group who remained in the orphanage. Those orphans who were rehabilitated were actively encouraged to make close relationships with one mother figure; later all but two were removed and placed in adoptive homes. The contrast group of 12 children, initially higher in intelligence, were exposed to the relatively unstimulating atmosphere of the orphanage for a prolonged period. Both groups were followed into adulthood, 21 years later. Their outcomes were strikingly different. Those who had been adopted were functioning normally, both in terms of mental and socio-emotional development. Many of the contrast group were still in institutional care and they presented a sorry picture. One important message to remember from this study is that within the 'experimental' group major gains in mental abilities were made *before* adoptive placement, in the relatively brief period (an average 19 months) the children spent with their temporary foster mothers. It should be pointed out that a damning article was published a few years ago by Longstreth (1981) in which the entire Skeels' project was criticized and pronounced worthless. However, it is arguable that Longstreth did not undermine Skeels' main conclusion, that infants from a very poor and deprived background can make a substantial and lasting recovery when removed to stimulating environments.

Other studies along the same lines include Dennis's (1973) report on a terribly impoverished foundling home in Beirut, Lebanon. He discovered a temporary, apparently environmentally induced developmental retardation which began around 3 months of age and reached a maximum by 12 months, when the mean 'behavioural quotient' of the subject infants was said to be 50. If the children were subsequently adopted by the age of 2 years they developed intellectually at a normal rate, but those who were adopted after 2 years did not make a full recovery despite follow-up to 10–14 years of age. Incidentally, the comparable findings from the Skeels' (1966) project (pp. 10, 22) show a correlation between duration of early follow-up (range 38–81 months) and gains in IQ (range 2–58 points) of 0.59.

Hakimi-Manesh and colleagues (1984) also reported on an orphanage, this time in Iran, which provided good physical nurturance but little mental stimulation for the infants in its care. An intervention study demonstrated that with relatively simple environmental manipulation for a brief interval, appreciable progress could be made in the mental and psychomotor functioning of the children and that gains attained persisted over a six month follow-up period.

One general caveat that should be borne in mind when interpreting the results of all these orphanage studies is that those infants or children who were adopted were unlikely to be a random selection. Prospective adoptive parents were likely to choose a more appealing or lively infant within an orphanage. Additionally, the staff would not promote the adoption of children they considered to have physical handicaps or stigmata (such as congenital syphilis) or even 'evident mental retardation' (see Longstreth 1981).

## Theoretical implications

Findings both from the institution-reared children and from the case studies raise important theoretical issues regarding the resilience of potential mental abilities in the face of extreme environmental adversity. For example, language development would seem to be achieved, with varying degrees of success, over a wide range and variety of upbringings.

Shatz (1985) suggested that the processes of language development are controlled by a genetic programme that has evolved to ensure success, in the sense of acquiring the power of communication (an adaptive skill) under a broad but bounded range of environmental circumstances. Evidence in favour of this hypothesis comes from a variety of sources, many of which are discussed in this book (e.g. the acquisition of sign language by deaf children). But some of the most striking corroborative findings have been made by those who have studied formerly extremely deprived and neglected children; such scientifically-minded observers' interest is excited by age old but still unanswered questions. What makes us human? To what extent does heredity determine the development of human personality and intellect? How plastic or perfectable is the human organism?

Certain features are common to both recent victims and their historical counterparts. First, they are initially lacking basic human attributes such as speech or social skills; skills that are ubiquitous except in severely retarded or dysphasic children or those with autistic features. Secondly, removal from the impoverished conditions is often followed by a remarkable and usually relatively rapid recovery of their cognitive and other faculties.

These findings bear on a number of issues that are still exciting the interest of developmental psychologists, but have implications that go far beyond the rarified atmosphere of the psycholinguistic laboratory. Given the complexity of language and its importance to humans, the ability to develop language (gestural and/or spoken) must at some level be robust and resilient in extreme conditions. In general, children in a wide variety of settings achieve that skill, and, except for the most severely congenitally mentally handicapped children, retarded individuals appear to follow patterns of language development similar to those of normal children, although at a slower rate (Morehead and Ingram 1976).

At the earliest stages of development (up to two-word combinations) children seem to acquire language according to a predetermined trajectory; the path they follow may be fairly independent of higher cognitive processes (see Corrigan 1979) and the frequency with which they are exposed to certain aspects of a particular language.

The conundrum, as stated by Shatz (1985), is that since children usually do manage to learn the particular language and dialect to which they are exposed, the system has to be responsive to a variety of environmental influences. Accordingly, the acquisition system must be both sensitive to changing circumstances but also robust, in the sense that ultimately the goal of language competence must be achieved by one means or another.

Reviewing the evidence for relevant early environmental influences upon cognitive development Clarke and Clarke (1976) comment that there is now unequivocal evidence that a poor environment that improves in middle or even late childhood can lead to major gains in language capacity. Kagan et al (1978) concur with their opinion, adding that persistent defects imply a persistence of adverse experiences. It follows that the language acquisition system, whatever its nature, must possess and retain a good deal of adaptive flexibility all the way through to puberty. Yet it must also be sufficiently robust to withstand insult, whether environmental or biological.

The concept of adaptive flexibility is often referred to as *plasticity* (Siple 1985). The term implies that the organism retains the capacity to compensate for adversity in such a way that little functional deficit results from insults to the system, whether these are biological (such as overt brain damage) or environmental (such as a perceptually impoverished upbringing). In both cases the child possesses the *potential* for functional recovery up to certain limiting or boundary conditions. It might be easier to understand the concept of *plasticity* by considering the impact of biological insults to the central nervous system. For example, left hemisphere lesions acquired very early in life do not selectively impair language development, whereas those acquired in adulthood frequently cause aphasia. The concept of a 'critical period', during which unilateral lesions do not lead to persistent aphasic impairment and after which they invariably do so, is now regarded as an oversimplification. Studies of brain-damaged children have enabled provisional delineation of the boundary conditions for biological insults.

It should also be possible to establish boundary conditions by looking at language development in atypical environments; under what circumstances does the organism lose the capacity to 'catch-up' to normal levels of language competence on removal from impoverished to adequately stimulating conditions, given an intact central nervous system? The human organism is equipped with both homeostatic mechanisms (such as those that maintain the body's temperature) and homeorhetic mechanisms (such as those that maintain a trajectory of growth in stature). We can conceive of such mechanisms as being under the control of a genetic programme, guiding their application to attainment of a goal which is, broadly speaking, adaptation to the environment (see Waddington 1977).

No doubt our capacity to acquire language is under genetic control, ensuring success under a broad but bounded range of environmental circumstances. These issues have recently been discussed by Shatz (1985) and

MacDonald (1986). In the remainder of the chapter a detailed presentation of the findings from case reports on language development under conditions of extreme environmental deprivation will serve as the basis for a discussion about what current knowledge allows us to conclude about these important issues.

## Case studies of extreme neglect and deprivation

The findings on groups of children raised in unstimulating institutional care are complemented by a small number of intensive case studies on individuals or sibling groups. All but one report concern children who were brought up in what were nominally home environments rather than institutions. Detailed information is presented about the circumstances both before and after removal from adversity, and about outcome at follow-up. Briefly the facts of each case are as follows:

### Anna (Davis 1940, 1947)

On 6 February 1938 the New York Times reported that a girl of more than 5 years had been found tied to an old chair in a storage room on the second floor of her farm home 17 miles from a small Pennsylvania city. She had apparently been there since babyhood. The child, Anna, was wedged into the chair which was tilted backwards to rest upon a coal bucket, her spindly arms tied above her head. She was unable to talk or move, and was dressed in a dirty shirt and napkin. Her hands, arms and legs were just bones, with skin drawn over them, so frail she could not use them. This state of cachexia was due to the fact that she had never had enough nourishment. Anna never grew normally and the chair on which she lay, half reclining and half sitting, was so small she had to double her legs partly under her. Immediately following her discovery Anna was removed to a children's home, where she was noted to be completely apathetic and lay in a limp supine position, immobile, expression-less and indifferent to everything. She was believed to be deaf, possibly blind.

Anna was placed initially in a county home for the aged and infirm. Nine months later she was transferred to a foster home. Although little progress had been made in the original establishment, where one nurse cared for over 300 inmates, the 'unremitting attention' of her foster mother led to rapid improvement in a wide variety of motor and cognitive skills. After a further nine months she was, for reasons that remain obscure, placed in a private home for retarded children. Few further advances were made at first, although she began to develop speech after two years had passed there. Shortly before her death from jaundice 12 months later, Anna was reported to be repeating single words and able to try and carry on a conversation.

### Isabelle (Mason 1942; Davis 1947)

Born just 1 month later than Anna, another extremely deprived girl (who has been given the pseudonym Isabelle), was discovered in November 1938. At the time she was approximately $6\frac{1}{2}$ years old. She was an illegitimate child and had been kept in seclusion for that reason. Her mother was deaf and mute and it seemed that she and Isabelle had spent most of their time together in a dark room shut away from the family who had rejected them. Lack of sunshine and inadequacy of diet had caused Isabelle to develop rickets and her legs were 'so bowed that as she stood erect the soles of her shoes came nearly flat together', and she got about with a skittering gait. Isabelle's mother eventually escaped with her child after nearly 7 years' seclusion and the girl was brought to the Children's Hospital in Columbus, Ohio on 16 November 1938 for orthopaedic surgery and physiotherapy. Her behaviour towards strangers, especially men, was found to be that of a 'wild animal'. She manifested much fear and hostility and, in lieu of speech, made only a strange croaking sound.

Once in hospital Isabelle seemed miserable and withdrawn, and she was initially entirely mute. However, after just one week she began to attempt vocalization, although she had formerly used only gesture to communicate with her mother. Acquisition of vocal competence was observed to pass through normal developmental stages but at a greatly accelerated pace, so that within two months she was singing nursery rhymes, and within a year she was able to read and write with fair competence. After 18 months she had a vocabulary of 2000 words and could compose imaginative stories.

### Koluchova twins (Koluchova 1972, 1976)

Jarmila Koluchova reported in 1972 the case record of monozygotic male twins, who were born on 4 September 1960. Their mother died shortly after giving birth and for 11 months they lived in a children's home. They then spent 6 months with a maternal aunt but were subsequently taken to live with their father and stepmother. For $5\frac{1}{2}$ years, until their discovery at the age of 7, the twins lived under most abnormal conditions, in a quiet street of family houses in Czechoslovakia. Because of the actions of their stepmother, who had her own children whom she actively preferred, the boys grew up in almost total isolation, never being allowed out of the house but living in a small unheated closet. They were often locked up for long periods in the cellar, sleeping on the floor on a plastic sheet, and they were cruelly chastized. When discovered at the age of 7 they could barely walk and suffered from acute rickets. They showed reactions of surprise and horror to objects and activities normally very familiar to children of that age, such as moving mechanical toys, a TV set or traffic in the street. Their spontaneous speech was very poor, as was their play.

After discovery and removal the boys were placed at first in hospital, where they remained for a few weeks before going to a small children's home. Their mental age was initially around the 3 year level, whereas their chronological age was 7 years 3 months. After approximately 18 months in the children's home they were placed with a foster family with whom they remained until adulthood. Tremendous gains in cognitive attainments were made within a few months of rescue, and a further significant increase in the rate of improvement occurred on transfer to the foster home. The long-term outcome was excellent and the boys developed above average linguistic skills as well as making good socioemotional adjustment to adolescence.

## Genie (Curtiss 1977)

One of the most extraordinary cases of severe deprivation yet reported is that of Genie, who was born in USA in April 1957. She was found at the age of 13 years 7 months, a painfully thin child who appeared 6 or 7 years old. From the age of 20 months she had been confined to a small room under conditions of extreme physical restraint. In this room she received minimal care from a mother who was herself rapidly losing her sight. Genie was physically punished by her father if she made any sound. Most of the time she was kept harnessed into an infant's potty chair but at night she was confined in a homemade sleeping bag fashioned like a strait jacket and lay in an infant's crib covered with wire mesh. She was fed only infant food. Genie's father was convinced that she would die; he was positive that she would not live past the age of 12 and promised that the mother could seek help for the child if she did so. But when the age of 12 had come and gone and she survived, the father reneged on his promise. It was not until Genie was $13\frac{1}{2}$ years old that her mother managed to get away, leaving home and husband to stay with the maternal grandmother. Several weeks later, whilst her mother was seeking welfare benefit, the child's strange demeanour was noticed by a clerk who alerted the authorities. Genie was admitted to hospital immediately. At this time Genie could not stand erect and could walk only with difficulty, shuffling her feet and swaying from side to side. Having been beaten for making any noise she had learned to suppress almost all vocalization save a whimper. She salivated copiously, spitting onto anything at hand, and was incontinent of urine and faeces. Curtiss comments 'Genie was unsocialized, primitive, hardly human'.

Genie was admitted to a children's hospital where she gained rapidly in height and weight, entered puberty and showed considerable cognitive achievements. Within seven months she was passing items on the Vineland and Leiter scales (nonverbal cognitive development tests) at virtually a 4 year level. She subsequently went to live with a foster family where slow progress continued. Genie never acquired true linguistic competence, nor was her social adjustment ever reported as approaching age-appropriate levels.

## Alice and Beth (Douglas and Sutton 1978)

This was another pair of deprived twins. For the first three months of their lives their mother was working to support herself and they had no contact with her at all. She had separated from her husband, an itinerant musician, whilst pregnant. Alice and Beth were initially looked after by friends and then some distant relatives took charge and planned to adopt them, but their own marriage broke up. The twins were then taken into care for a few weeks, after which an aunt and uncle looked after them for the remainder of their first year. During that same year their mother returned to her husband for a time, became pregnant, and left him again after three months. Soon after that she moved with the twins into a council house, but it was damp, infested with mice and due for demolition. She suffered from depression badly enough to require medical treatment. It seems the girls received very little stimulation and, although they learned to walk at the normal time, they were very slow in learning to talk. When nearly 5 and due to move to infants school they still could not talk intelligibly, except to each other in a private language incomprehensible to others.

The parents were very co-operative with the intervention planned by the authors of this account and the children were not removed from home. The twins were separated at school and put in different classes, where they received language training for a period of six months. The greatest acceleration in acquisition of language abilities occurred when specific remedial help was being given. Within one year they had achieved close to normal scores on verbal and nonverbal intelligence test items and could readily cope with mainstream schooling.

*Mary and Louise ( Skuse 1984)*

In the autumn of 1977 a little girl of almost 9 years was referred to the Children's Department at a large postgraduate teaching hospital. Over the previous year Mary had exhibited increasingly disruptive behaviour in the small children's home where she had lived for the previous 6 years with her sister Louise, who was 14 months her elder. When their early history was investigated further it transpired that these children had spent their early lives in a remarkably deprived environment on account of their having a mother (Patricia) who was not only mentally retarded and microcephalic but may additionally have been suffering from a serious psychiatric disorder. When discovered in March 1971 by the Social Services the comment was made that 'Louise and Mary are very strange creatures indeed'. Aged 3 years 6 months and 2 years 4 months respectively, they took no notice of anything or anyone except to scamper up and sniff strangers, grunting and snuffling like animals. They both still sucked dummies and no attempt had been made to toilet train them, so they remained in nappies. Neither child had any constructive play but picked up objects and handled, then smelt and felt them. Mary had no speech whatsoever and made no hearing responses. Her vocalization seemed limited to a few high pitched sounds. Later that year something came to light which had not been noticed by the authorities before but had apparently been going on daily ever since the children became mobile. The health visitor found them tied on leashes to a bed, a measure their mother had taken partly because she insisted on keeping the flat spotlessly clean and partly because she was worried they would fall off the balcony. If they became too noisy or active the children were put onto a mattress and covered with a blanket. They were subsequently removed from her and taken into care.

The sisters were later placed in a small children's home, run as a family unit. Their developmental achievements diverged, with very rapid initial gains being made in verbal and nonverbal abilities by both children but only

Louise went on to achieve normal competence in language skills, and only she received mainstream schooling. Mary persistently displayed a number of autistic behaviours which were thought to be linked to an inherited predisposition, and she received special education throughout her childhood.

### Adam (Thompson 1986)

Adam was abandoned, in 1972, in a small town in Colombia, South America. Nothing is known about his natural parents: he was placed in a girls' reformatory school where he remained until 16 months of age. During the day he lay in a windowless room on a single bed. He suffered repeated infections, including gastroenteritis and intestinal parasites, whooping cough and measles. His diet was limited to watery soup or porridge and he had no toys and no companions. On removal from these dire circumstances he had signs of marasmus (severe protein-energy malnutrition), was anaemic, and infested with parasites. His development was grossly retarded and he was emotionally withdrawn and passive; he cried when he was handled and resented being touched.

Adam was adopted aged 34 months and was followed up until nearly 14 years. By that time he was functioning very well in all aspects of social and scholastic adjustment, and his growth trajectories were age-appropriate.

### Environmental factors in severe neglect: case studies

Table 8.1 illustrates the early environmental stimuli and influences upon these unfortunate children. The table is arranged so that those individuals whose outcome was relatively poor (Anna, Genie, Mary) may be relatively easily contrasted with those who had a good prognosis (Isabelle, Koluchova twins, Alice and Beth, Louise and Adam).

### Malnutrition

The first point to consider is the fact that many of the children had been seriously malnourished. Now, the evidence for a direct link between malnutrition and the development of language is tenuous. When we attempt to relate acute and chronic nutritional deprivation to mental competence we should take account of a number of issues (Stein and Susser 1985): first, the timing and duration of malnutrition upon fetal development; secondly, the severity of malnutrition and the dietary constituents affected; thirdly, the precise cognitive deficits that result – in this case whether language is affected more or less severely than other aspects of mental competence; fourthly, the social context – the nature of the broad environment in which the malnourished child is raised.

With regard to the postnatal phase of mental development, in diverse studies, using different designs and outcome measures, malnutrition alone during this phase has not been shown to produce permanent mental impairment. However, in combination with a lack of intellectual and social stimulation mental

**Table 8.1** Early environmental stimuli and influences

| Name | D.O.B. | Severe malnourishment | Maltreatment[+] | Longest period in normal environment | Consistent social contacts* | Exposure to Language | |
|---|---|---|---|---|---|---|---|
| | | | | | | Spoken | Gesture |
| Anna (Davis) 1940 | 1.3.32 | Yes | NRE | Birth–6 months | MS | Minimal | Minimal |
| Genie (Curtiss) 1977 | ?.4.57 | Yes | NREA | Birth–1.8 | MFS | Minimal | Minimal |
| Mary (Skuse) 1982 | 24.11.68 | No | RE | None | MSF | Limited | Limited |
| Isabelle (Mason) 1942 | ?.4.32 | Yes | E | None | M(Mute) | Minimal | Significant stimulation |
| Koluchova Twins (MZ boys) P.M. and J.M. 1972 | 4.9.60 | Yes | NAE | Birth–1.6 | MFS(4) | Minimal | Minimal |
| Douglas and Sutton Twins (?Z) Alice Beth 1978 | 2.2.69 | No | E | Birth–1.0 | MF (from 4 yr) | Limited | Limited |
| Louise (Skuse) 1982 | 30.9.67 | No | RE | ?Birth–1.2 | MS (from 1.2)F | Limited | Limited |
| Adam (Thompson) 1986 | ?.1.72 | Yes | E | Nil | None | Nil | Nil |

[+]N = Gross neglect
E = Impoverished environment with minimum stimulation
*M = Mother
R = Physical restraint
F = Father (inc. cohabitee)
A = Physical abuse/chastisement
S = Sib(s)

performance *is* likely to be depressed. The question arises, is that depression reversible and if so under what conditions? Of the children reviewed in Table 8.1 five were definitely severely malnourished for varying periods. Despite this, the outcome for the Koluchova twins, Isabelle and Adam was good whereas Anna and Genie exhibited profound handicaps. There is no evidence that Mary and Louise were malnourished. Perhaps we should concur with John Dobbing (1984) when he concludes in a recent commentary on this subject, 'Malnutrition is beguiling in its pseudo-simplicity. Is it not possible that malnutrition may add to ninety nine other environmental disadvantages *when* they are present, . . . its functional ill effects can be compensated for by corresponding advantages when *not* enough of them (are present), even though the malnutrition may have produced irreversible deficits and distortions . . . in the growing brain?'

*Auditory-verbal stimulation*

All the cases reported were brought up in conditions of abnormal auditory stimulation, although we lack exact information about the quality of experience which was available, except in the case of Genie where virtually the only sound she heard for 13 years was from an adjoining bathroom. In the case of Isabelle her sole companion was a deaf mute mother; Mary and Louise had each other for company as did the twins described by Douglas and Sutton. Anna, Isabelle and Mary were all thought to be deaf when first discovered (subsequently disconfirmed in all three cases), although there does not seem to have been that concern about the other children. Anna initially showed a peculiar pattern of hearing responses in that she would, for example, turn her head towards a ticking clock yet neither clapping hands nor speech produced a reaction. This behaviour is reminiscent of Bonnaterre's (1800) account of the wild boy of Aveyron, who would not flinch at a pistol shot yet showed immediate interest in the sound of a cracking nut.

Dennis (1941) commented, in his experimental study of deliberate deprivation of twin girls, 'we carefully refrained from baby talk and from babbling, as we wanted to know whether such vocalizations would occur without example'. Interestingly, it proved impossible for him to maintain the strict scientific objectivity he desired because 'from the 15th week onward they almost invariably greeted us with a smile and a vocalization . . . we decided in week 27 to return their smile of greeting and to speak to them as we approached'.

A great deal of research has been published in the past decade on the importance of 'prelinguistic behaviour' in the context of the infant's earliest environment (e.g. Bruner 1983). Its relationship to the development of initial speech acts is not clear but a prelinguistic period in a stimulating environment may be of great importance if speech acquisition is to occur in the normal way. Psychosocial deprivation has been reported to impair preverbal vocalization and babble (Provence and Lipton 1962), but we do not have any reliable account of these phenomena in the children reviewed here. In Dennis's (1941) study, despite minimal opportunity for verbal interaction with their caretakers, by 12 months of age the twins had expressed a wide range of preverbal vocalizations, including ba-ba, da-da, la-la, by-by. However, neither child came to use any sound which corresponded to a real word within the 61 week period covered by the experiment.

In the series of children under review here only Mary, Isabelle and Adam suffered a persistently linguistically deprived environment from birth. Isabelle was in an exceptional situation because of the stimulation she received by gesture and interaction with her mute mother. This experience prior to discovery was almost certainly of benefit in facilitating her rapid later acquisition of spoken language.

*Opportunities for play*

Language development may be correlated with the development of spontaneous play: in Piaget's (1967a) term both are aspects of the same semiotic ability and as such, play may be considered to be a cognitive activity that contributes to the infant's knowledge of the world about him (Rosenblatt 1977). We may follow, through the development of play, the process by which the child learns that events, objects and ultimately symbols have an existence, function and purpose outside himself. In the strict Piagetian account of the emergence of language, although it is an essential instrument in cognitive constructions at the highest level, language is merely one particular instance of the semiotic or symbolic function. It is this function as a whole (including mental imagery, symbolic play and so on), and not language alone, which causes sensorimotor behaviour to evolve to the level of representation or thought (Piaget 1971). Thus Piaget would say that for a child to use any kinds of words at all requires quite advanced symbolic abilities; recent research has shown this view may be mistaken. The earliest use of words is usually in the context of, and refers to, a social relationship (Gopnik and Meltzoff 1985). This and similar research (Tomasello and Farrar 1984) has shown that children begin by using certain words such as 'there', 'no', 'more' and 'bye-bye' in social contexts, but later use them to refer to their own plans. Finally, in a third stage, they are used to refer to objects and events in the outside world. Accordingly, it is fascinating to learn that Genie's spontaneous productive vocabulary at the age of 13 years 7 months (Curtiss 1977) included only the holophrastic terms 'stopit' and 'nomore'. Of relevance here may be the view held by Vygotsky (1978) regarding the importance of social interaction as the source of the child's knowledge of the world, and his claim that all human abilities are first used in an interactive context and only later used alone. This claim can be seriously tested only by longitudinal data, to see whether activities displayed by an individual child first appear in interaction or in solitary activities. Data of relevance are provided by the findings on the play of these severely environmentally deprived children, who for the most part had little or no opportunity for interactive play during their confinement.

We can categorize play in developmental terms under three broad headings (Rosenblatt 1977). First, functional or sensorimotor play, which consists of no more than the manipulation of objects with reference to their attractive and inherent properties. Secondly, representational play, which includes using toys

**Table 8.2** Characteristics of extremely deprived children at discovery

| Name | D.O.B. | Age at discovery | Physical stigmata at discovery | Motor* retardation (degree) | Speech | | Formal psychometric assessment | Emotional expression & social behaviour |
|---|---|---|---|---|---|---|---|---|
| | | | | | Comprehension | Expression | | |
| Anna (Davis) 1940 | 1.3.32 | 5;11 | Cachexia | +++ | Nil | Nil | SB <2;6 | Profoundly withdrawn. Completely apathetic |
| Genie (Curtiss) 1977 | ?.4.57 | 13;7 | Cachexia Dwarfed | ++ | PPVT 1.6 | Echoes single words | LIPS (wide scatter on subtests) 4;9 VSM 1.05 | Alert and curious. Eager for social contact. Silent tantrums |
| Mary (Skuse) 1982 | 24.11.68 | 2;4 | Microcephaly Syndactyly | + | Nil | Nil | CJ (non-verbal skills) Nil | Withdrawn. Gaze avoidance. Temper tantrums |
| Isabelle (Mason) 1942 | ?.4.32 | 6;6 | Rickets | ++ | Simple gestures only | Simple gestures only | SB 1;7 VSM 2;6 | Withdrawn. Fearful. Hostile towards strangers |
| Koluchova Twins (MZ boys) P.M. & J.M. 1972 | 4.9.60 | 6;11 | Rickets | ++ | (RE) 2 years | (RE) 1;6 | CJ (non-verbal skills) 3;0 | Timid and mistrustful |
| Douglas & Sutton Twins (?Z) Alice & Beth 1978 | 2.2.69 | 4;11 | No | None | RDLS (at 5;4) Alice 3;4 Beth 3;8 | Unintelligible | SB 3;7 | Friendly. Amenable to adults |
| Louise (Skuse) 1982 | 30.9.67 | 3;6 | No | + | CJ 1;0 | CJ <1;0 | CJ (non-verbal skills) <1;6 | Affectionate. Happy. Temper tantrums |

**Table 8.2** continued

| Name | D.O.B. | Age at discovery | Physical stigmata at discovery | Motor* retardation (degree) | Speech | | | Formal psychometric assessment | Emotional expression & social behaviour |
|------|--------|------------------|-------------------------------|----------------------------|--------|-----------|------------|-------------------------------|-----------------------------------------|
| | | | | | | Comprehension | Expression | | |
| Adam (Thompson) 1986 | ?.1.72 | 1;4 | Marasmus | +++ | Nil | Nil | Nil | CJ 0;3 | Passive, withdrawn, resented contact |

CJ   – Contemporaneous clinical judgement
VSM – Vineland social maturity scale
RE   – Retrospective estimation (from written reports)
LIPS – Leiter international performance scale
SB   – Stanford-Binet intelligence scale
PPVT – Peabody picture vocabulary test
RDLS – Reynell developmental language scale
*+   = mild
++   = moderate
+++ = severe

as if they were corresponding real objects, for example, where a miniature teaset is manipulated to stimulate the child's real life experience of a tea party. Thirdly, symbolic play, which implies that the child is using an object in the play seen to stand for something else, its original meaning having been transcended as, for example, when the child uses a ruler as an aeroplane. It should be noted, however, that this simple account of the stages which lead to truly symbolic play has been criticized on the grounds that the play activities of young children should not be interpreted as if the activities displayed served the same symbolic function for children as they would for adults (Zukow 1986).

Truly symbolic play usually begins around the age of 24 months and is well established by 30 months. Mary and Louise showed no play when first seen, although Louise made relatively good progress in her nursery group. Within 18 months she was using functional and occasional representational skills. Mary, on the other hand, was $4\frac{1}{2}$ years old when she began to display even the rudiments of functional play, two years after discovery. It was a further two years before representational play became established. Louise had reached this stage at five years of age, but for both girls the achievement was coincident with their having achieved a language comprehension age-equivalent of $2\frac{1}{2}$ years.

The close relationship between the development of a capacity for using symbolic functions and associations, and the onset of representational play, has been described by several workers (e.g. Rosenblatt 1977). It is also well known that autistic children suffer a severe handicap in both areas (Rutter 1985). Even so, children suffering from specific developmental language disorders may play with some representational features (Egan 1975). In normal children the correlation seems to exist between language comprehension (but not expression) and symbolic play (Largo and Howard 1979).

We have little information about the play of severely deprived children other than Mary and Louise. Anna's freedom of movement and the range of objects available for her tactile exploration were both certainly very limited. This was also true for Genie, whose 'toys' consisted of empty cheese cartons and two plastic raincoats. We do not know what toys were available to Isabelle, but the evidence suggests that they were few if any.

The Koluchova twins had only a handful of building bricks. Koluchova (1972) comments that the twins' spontaneous play was very primitive (functional/sensorimotor), but imitative (non-representational) play soon developed. Anna, just one year after discovery, was said 'hardly to play, when alone'. Isabelle on the other hand enjoyed undressing dolls very shortly after first being brought into hospital. Within a few months she was drawing and colouring with crayons and over the next two years play is said to have become 'highly imaginative'. Genie showed little in the way of play for several years. A little sensorimotor activity with toys or other materials plus an inclination to hoard is all that was observed, until $4\frac{1}{2}$ years after discovery she first engaged in an acting fantasy with Susan Curtiss. Adam was apathetic and withdrawn when rescued at the age of 16 months, but within two weeks was said to be 'smiling and reaching out for toys'. Intriguingly the historical figure Caspar Hauser had allegedly similarly been deprived of opportunities to play in his confinement:

In his hole he had two wooden horses and several ribbons: with these horses he had always amused himself so long as he remained awake; and his only occupation was to make them run by his side, and to fix or tie the ribbons about them in different positions. . . whenever any trifle, a ribbon, a coin, or a little picture was given to him he cried 'Ross! Ross!' (horse) and expressed by his looks and motions a desire to hang all these pretty things upon a horse. This suggested to a police soldier the idea of giving him a wooden horse for a plaything. The possession of this toy seemed to affect a great alteration in Caspar. He lost his insensibility, his indifference, and his dejection, and he conducted himself as if he had found an old and long desired friend . . . He never ate his bread without holding any morsel of it to some one of his horses, – for more was given him, – nor did he ever drink water without first dipping their mouths in it, which he afterwards carefully wiped off . . . as the powers of Caspar's mind opened, he became less interested by the playthings with which he had been at first so entirely absorbed. Even his love for horses was transformed from the wooden representation to the living animal, and in an amazingly short time he became a most accomplished and fearless horseman'.

### Can outcome be predicted?

All the children reviewed had very limited language abilities at discovery but in most cases subsequent progress was very rapid indeed. One important question is, would it have been possible to predict which child would do well after rescue from the depriving environment on the basis of what was found at discovery. The evidence is not clear-cut, but the answer seems to be in the negative. Immediately upon discovery Mary was 2 years 4 months, and Louise 3 years 6 months. Yet in terms of their appearance and behaviour they were remarkably similar, both to each other and to other well-documented cases such as the Koluchova twins. At this early stage each child was said to exhibit 'autistic tendencies'. The subsequent development of these sisters is unusually well documented (Skuse 1984). After just 6 months in a preschool playgroup, which they attended irregularly for 2 hours a day, Louise was clearly making rapid progress in all aspects of her development, whereas Mary did not give the impression of being a normal child.

   Louise's recovery of expressive and receptive language is contrasted with that of Mary in Figures 8.1 and 8.2. Her pattern of accelerated attainment is in keeping with the accounts of Isabelle and the Koluchova twins' own development of language after rescue. Recovery may have been aided by the consistent speech therapy she received. Acquisition of comprehension proceeded more rapidly than the facility to express herself, an observation which accords with the findings in several other accounts (e.g. Genie, Isabelle, the Koluchova twins, Alice and Beth). The course of Mary's development was, in contrast, less successful, but she was probably a child with constitutional anomalies which would have restricted her abilities to acquire certain cognitive skills in any event. She was a microcephalic child, as was her mother, who was herself mentally retarded, with a Stanford-Binet IQ of less than 50. Certain of Mary's nonverbal cognitive skills developed virtually as rapidly as those of her sister, but even the pattern of her achievements in these tasks was very uneven. She performed best on those items which were least verbally loaded. Additionally,

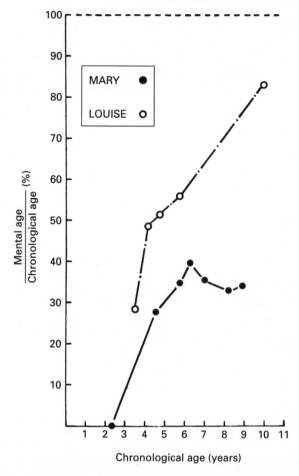

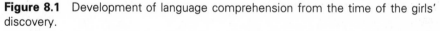

**Figure 8.1** Development of language comprehension from the time of the girls' discovery.

Mary rarely used gesture or mime, never expressed social greetings or people's names, and the form of her language when it did develop was deviant. She exhibited recurrent echolalia and some stereotyped utterances, although no pronominal reversal. Her social relationships were disordered, she showed stereotypies of motor behaviour and in later years it became more obvious that she was expressing an autistic pattern of behaviour. The overall severity was rather less than in Kanner's classical (1943) description (see Ch. 12). She had, incidentally, a half-brother who was definitely autistic and severely developmentally delayed, and who had been fostered soon after birth.

Genie was not brought out of her hopeless social conditions until 13 years and 7 months of age, and she failed to develop any useful conversational speech although she did gain enormously in comprehension over the following five years. Lenneberg (1967) may have been correct when he suggested that language acquisition must occur during the first 12 years if it is to proceed

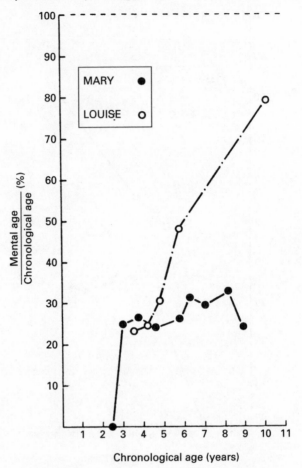

**Figure 8.2** Development of expression of language from the time of the girls' discovery.

normally, and Genie's history is often taken as evidence for his hypothesis (e.g. Rutter 1981, Curtiss 1981b). We do have good evidence that after unilateral brain damage children may switch cerebral dominance for various functions relatively easily, at least until puberty supervenes. In this connection Curtiss (1977) concludes, after a detailed account of her painstaking assessment of Genie's linguistic abilities, that the child is a 'holistic' right hemisphere thinker in respect of both verbal and nonverbal tasks. She believes this may be a direct result of Genie not acquiring language during the so-called 'critical' period. It seems a pity therefore that nowhere does she produce evidence to confirm that the left hemisphere of this unfortunate girl was functioning normally from a neurophysiological point of view.

Latest reports on the children's achievements in terms of language skills are summarized in Table 8.3. This shows that Isabelle, the Koluchova and Douglas and Sutton twins, Louise and Adam, reached virtually age-appro-

**Table 8.3** Latest available reports on the children's developmental level

| Name | D.O.B. | Age at Discovery | Language | | Formal tests of cognition | |
|---|---|---|---|---|---|---|
| | | | Comprehension | Expression | Performance | Verbal |
| Anna (Davis) 1940 | 1.3.32 | 5;11 | (C.A. 10;3) RE 2;6 | (C.A. 10;3) RE 2;6 | (C.A. 8;1) M-P 1;7 | (C.A. 8;1) |
| Genie (Curtiss) 1977 | ?.4.57 | 13;7 | (C.A. 16;10) ITPA Auditory Reception 5;0 | (C.A. 16;10) ITPA Verbal Expression 3;8 | (C.A. 17;9) RCPM 11;0 FGPT 11;0 | (C.A. 18;9) PPVT 5;10 |
| Mary (Skuse) 1982 | 24.11.68 | 2;4 | (C.A. 13;0) RDLS 4;0 | (C.A. 13;0) (RDLS 3;5) | (C.A. 8;11) WISC 94 | |
| Isabelle (Mason) 1942 | ?.4.32 | 6;6 | (C.A. 8;2) Reported as age appropriate | Reported as age appropriate | (C.A. 8;2) | Reported as of normal intelligence |
| Koluchova twins (MZ boys) P.M. | 4.9.60 | 6;11 | (C.A. 10;0) RE 9;0 | (C.A. 10;0) RE 9;0 | (C.A. 10;0) WISC 85 | (C.A. 10;0) WISC 97 |
| J.M. 1972 | 4.9.60 | 6;11 | (C.A. 10;0) RE 9;0 | (C.A. 10;0) RE 9;0 | (C.A. 10;0) WISC 86 | (C.A. 10;0) WISC 94 |
| Douglas and Sutton twins Alice | 2.2.69 | 4;11 | (C.A. 6;4) RDLS <6;0 | (C.A. 6;4) RDLS 6;0 | (C.A. 6;4) WPPSI 108 | (C.A. 6;4) WPPSI 102 |
| Beth 1978 | 2.2.69 | 4;11 | (C.A. 6;4) RDLS 5;1 | (C.A. 6;4) RDLS 5;3 | (C.A. 6;4) WPPSI 92 | (C.A. 6;4) WPPSI 85 |
| Louise (Skuse) 1982 | 30.9.67 | 3;6 | (C.A. 14;5) | (C.A. 14;5) (SR) Age appropriate | (C.A. 10;1) WISC 80 | (C.A. 10;1) WISC 77 |
| Adam (Thompson) 1986 | ?.1.72 | 1;4 | (C.A. 13;10) Reported as age appropriate | (C.A. 13;10) | (C.A. 8;9) WISC 113 full scale | (C.A. 8;9) |

ITPA – Illinois test of psycholinguistic abilities
RCPM – Ravens coloured progressive matrices
M-P – Merrill-Palmer scale of mental abilities
PPVT – Peabody picture vocabulary test
WISC – Wechsler intelligence scale for children
RDLS – Reynell developmental language scale
WPPSI – Wechsler preschool and primary scale of intelligence
RE – Retrospective estimation from written reports
FGPT – Figure ground perception test
SR – School report
C.A. – Chronological age at assessment

priate levels within a few years, despite the variety of ages at which they were removed from their formerly understimulating circumstances.

From the results of these studies one can reach a variety of conclusions about the nature of language development under extremely adverse environmental conditions. First, it seems to be more vulnerable than other cognitive faculties in view of the evidence of profound retardation at discovery in all cases reviewed, even when other features of mental development (such as perceptuomotor skills) have been relatively unaffected (e.g. Alice and Beth). Expressive speech is more seriously retarded at discovery, and develops less rapidly than comprehension after placement in a normal environment. The exact role of environmental influences upon the form and pace of normal language acquisition is still a matter of debate (e.g. Kuczaj 1986), but there can be no disputing the primacy of *interpersonal* interaction as a necessary pre-condition.

In contrast, perceptuomotor skills are reported to be less retarded at discovery, and this could imply that they are relatively resilient to a lack of interpersonal interaction, as is gross motor development. In other words, the propensity perceptually to explore the environment that we see in normal infants is likely to be preserved despite gross deprivation, and the opportunity for practising these potential skills must be relatively more accessible even in the most impoverished and unstimulating settings. Because language develops in the context of *social* interaction, if opportunities for interaction are absent semiotic abilities seem to rest in abeyance.

If we try to predict which children will do well and which poorly on the basis of features at discovery, limited conclusions may be drawn. The complete absence of comprehension and expressive speech at discovery seems ominous, especially where there is a large discrepancy between nonverbal and verbal abilities (e.g. Anna, Genie, Mary). In view of the fact that initial social behaviour was highly variable between cases, correlations with later social adjustment are necessarily weak. Nevertheless, there are indications that the early combination of profound language deficit, and apathy or withdrawal from social contact which lasts more than a week or two, means that the child will have especial difficulties developing a normal range and quality of relationships in later life (see Anna and Mary). It may of course indicate that the child has a constitutional disorder which will limit the speed and quality of recovery.

Following removal from deprivation the evidence suggests that, if recovery of normal language ability is going to occur, rapid progress is the rule with substantial achievements being made within a few months (e.g. Isabelle and Adam). In those cases where it was several years before the children had caught up to age appropriate levels of language ability, improvements had nevertheless been noticeable and significant in the earliest months (e.g. Louise).

If a discrepancy is found between the rate of recovery of visuospatial skills and of speech, as was the case with Mary, this may be additional evidence in favour of the hypothesis that there exist constitutional limitations on achievement. Genie, for example, was subject to highly skilled education by Susan

Curtiss for over four years, but developed few normal or appropriate acts of communication. Perhaps the few children such as Genie, who did not make a full recovery after rescue should be considered exceptions to the general rule. If at least part of the explanation for their poor recovery is that some had suffered from a biological handicap, perhaps they had initially been maltreated because they were in some way abnormal; there is evidence that Genie was eventually found to have many features of childhood autism and that these had been recognized by her family years before discovery (Clarke, personal communication).

One is also reminded of Itard's valiant but ultimately unsuccessful efforts to teach Victor, the wild boy of Aveyron, vocal speech. Despite Lane's (1977) assertions to the contrary, it does not seem likely that his failure was entirely due to inadequate techniques of therapy, and the child was probably abandoned in middle childhood because he was found to have developmental features of childhood autism (Wing 1976a).

A striking contrast is also seen in these cases between those who were initially eager to attract adult attention and understanding at discovery and those who were apathetic and disinterested in social interaction. Perhaps the distinction is most striking in the case of the sisters, Mary and Louise; both girls did receive speech therapy soon after discovery, but when little progress was made with Mary it was abandoned. Her relative lack of social communication and language had become reminiscent of autism by the age of 9 years. However, it should be noted that four years later a remarkable transformation had taken place and she had made tremendous progress in both areas which was coincident with the disappearance of those autistic features. Despite having been placed in a variety of children's homes over that period she did receive some consistent and intensive speech therapy which, reports suggest, was successful in engendering a change in social attitudes. This observation is in itself important because it suggests that further progress may be made with children several years after removal from deprivation, even in cases when the obstacle to success is thought to consist of constitutional anomalies.

Koluchova (1976) comments; 'In spite of the fact that the twins had scarcely spoken at all until the age of 7 (their) development was quickest after the ninth year when they came to their foster family, which provided them with all the prerequisites, both in the development of speech and for the whole personality'. Although they did subsequently attend speech therapy, this seems to have been with the aim of improving pronunciation and articulation rather than in instilling a desire to communicate by vocal language. Similarly, Isabelle received nearly two years of intensive speech therapy from a team of therapists under the direction of Marie Mason, who capitalized on the child's motivation.

We can thus conclude that the general rule seems to be that the children either start to improve rapidly or that they do not recover the normal use of language at all. There is no lag before recovery of speech begins to occur in those cases with the best prognosis. This point is linked to the rapid development of social adjustment, and attachment behaviour, suggestive of the tremendously powerful need for otherwise normal children to form close relationships with their caretakers. Formation of an early focus of attachment onto one special adult seems to have distinguished Mary's from Louise's behaviour in their first nursery group. This urge to make a single loving relationship was commented on by Skeels (1966). He asserts 'This highly stimulating emotional impact was observed to be the unique characteristic and one of the main contributions of the experimental (i.e. first postorphanage) setting' (p. 17).

Thus in the context of a loving relationship recovery of language begins almost immediately, without delay, and proceeds rapidly. The duration of deprivation prior to discovery does not predict how long recovery will take to become complete. Whether the age of the affected child at discovery is a limiting factor is uncertain, for there is contradictory evidence on that matter. The tale of Caspar Hauser presents us with a detailed account of a child who was discovered at the age of 16 years 1 month, and made a full recovery of language. Unfortunately, despite the vast literature about him it has never been clear whether his was a genuine case of deprivation or whether he was in fact an imposter (Curtiss 1981a). Genie, who was rescued at the age of 13 years 7 months may, as has already been discussed, have been an abnormal child in the first place.

### Interaction of genetic and environmental influences on development

Recently, Money and his colleagues at the Johns Hopkins University (1983) reported an important series of children who had been seriously abused in early childhood and who had, as a consequence, excessively short stature and gross impairment of cognitive development. The age of the children at rescue varied between 2 years 4 months and 17 years 5 months, and follow-up was up to a maximum of 12 years 6 months. Tremendous gains in IQ over that period were seen, up to 90 points, and there was virtually linear relationship between the quantitative improvement in IQ and the duration of the post-rescue follow-up period.

The evidence both from the studies of extreme early deprivation followed by rescue and rehabilitation, and from studies of children who were raised in abusive and neglectful situations of lesser severity, goes completely against the notion of IQ constancy. The implication is that, although the polygenic mode of inheritance of intelligence is by now well established (e.g. Teasdale and Owen 1984), genes exert their effects 'indirectly' and those effects depend upon the particular environment in which individuals find themselves. For example, in a recent book, Wilson and Herrnstein (1986) suggest that 60% of the variation of IQ scores is in some way attributable to genetic variation. The correct interpretation of this figure is as follows. Since there is no practical method of separating the physical and social effects of genes, heritability estimates include both. This means that heritability estimates set a lower bound on the explanatory power of the environment, not an upper bound. If genetic variation explains 60% of the variation in IQ scores, environmental variation must explain the remaining 40%. But it may explain as much as

100%. It all depends *how* the genes affect IQ scores, and we are still a long way from knowing the answer to that riddle. In extreme environments, the role of environmental factors in determining the apparent IQ will be of greater importance than in an average environment (see Shields 1980).

### Degree of recovery and remedial strategy

Finally, we need to consider whether degree of recovery is influenced by specific remedial measures after rescue. In general, intensity of intervention does not seem to be of singular value in bringing about recovery. Qualitative rather than quantitative influences are paramount and Koluchova's (1976) conclusions are apposite: 'The most effective and integrative curative factor is (the) foster mother and the whole environment of (the) family' (p. 185).

In conclusion, extreme deprivation in early childhood is a condition of great theoretical and practical importance. Clinically it is essential that such children are recognized and differentiated from cases of global mental retardation, so that appropriate environmental mental manipulation and educational experience may commence as soon as possible. Fortunately, the evidence reviewed suggests that, in the absence of genetic or congenital anomalies or a history of gross malnourishment, victims of such deprivation have an excellent prognosis. Some subtle deficits in social adjustment may persist. Theoretical observations include the implication that most human characteristics, with the possible exception of language, are strongly 'cana-lised' (in Scarr-Salapatek's (1976) conception) and hence virtually resistant to obliteration by even the most dire early environments. On removal to a favourable situation, the remarkable and rapid progress made by those with good potential seems allied to the total experience of living in a stimulating home and forming emotional bonds to a caring adult. We may hypothesize that a caregiver's qualities of emotional availability, sensitive responsivity, encouragement and provision of perceptual stimulation shown to be important for normal infants' development (Moore 1968, Bradley and Caldwell 1976, Clarke-Stewart 1977) are also the salient influences bearing on later learning and maturation in these unfortunate children.

### References

Bonaterre, P. J. (1800). Historical notice on the Sauvage de L'Aveyron. *Translated in The Wild Boy of Aveyron (Lane H.)*. London: George Allen and Unwin.

Bruner, J. (1983). *Child's talk: learning to use language*. New York: Norton.

Clarke, A. M. and Clarke, A. D. B. (1976). *Early experience: Myth and evidence.* London: Open Books.

Corrigan, R. (1979). Cognitive correlates of language: differential criteria yield differential results. *Child Development, 50*, 617–631.

Curtiss, S. (1977). *Genie: A psycholinguistic study of a modern day 'wild child'.* London: Academic Press.

Davis, K. (1940). Extreme social isolation of a child. *American Journal of Sociology, 45*, 554–565.

Davis, K. (1947). Final note on a case of extreme isolation. *American Journal of Sociology*, **52**, 432–437.

Dennis, W. (1941). Infant development under conditions of restricted practice and of minimal social stimulation. *Genetics of Psychology Monographs*, *23*, 143–189.

Dennis, W. (1973). *Children of the crèche*. New York: Appleton-Century-Crofts.

Douglas, J. E. and Sutton, A. (1978). The development of speech and mental processes in a pair of twins: a case study. *Journal of Child Psychology and Psychiatry*, *19*, 49–56.

Gopnik, A. and Meltzoff, A. N. (1985). From people, to plans, to objects. *Journal of Pragmatics*, *9*, 495–512.

Hakimi-Manesh, Y., Mojdehi, H. and Tashakkori, A. (1984). Short communication: effects of environmental enrichment on the mental and psychomotor development of orphanage children. *Journal of Child Psychology and Psychiatry*, *25*, 643–650.

Kagan, J., Kearsley, R. and Zelazo, P. (1978). *Infancy: its place in human development*. Cambridge, Mass: Harvard University Press.

Koluchova, J. (1972). Severe deprivation in twins: a case study. *Journal of Child Psychology and Psychiatry*, *13*, 107–114.

Koluchova, J. (1976). The further development of twins after severe and prolonged deprivation: a second report. *Journal of Child Psychology and Psychiatry*, *17*, 181–188.

McDonald, K. (1986). Developmental models and early experience. *International Journal of Behavioural Development*, *9*, 175–190.

Mason, M. K. (1942). Learning to speak after six and one half years of silence. *Journal of Speech and Hearing Disorders*, *7*, 295–304.

Piaget, J. (1971). *Biology and Knowledge*. Edinburgh: Edinburgh University Press.

Provence, S. and Lipton, R. C. (1962). *Infants in institutions: a comparison of their development with family-reared infants during the first year of life*. New York: International University Press.

Rosenblatt, D. (1977). Developmental trends in infant play. In B. Tizard and D. Harvey (Eds.), *Biology of Play. Clinics in Developmental Medicine No 62*. London: SIMP/Heinemann.

Shatz, M. (1985). An evolutionary perspective on plasticity in language development: a commentary. *Merrill-Palmer Quarterly*, *31*, 211–222.

Siple, P. (1985). Plasticity, robustness and language development: an introduction to research issues relating sign language and spoken language. *Merrill-Palmer Quaterly*, *31*, 117–126.

Skeels, H. M. (1966). Adult status of children with contrasting early life experiences: a follow-up study. *Monographs of the Society for Research in Child Development*, *31*, 3.

Skuse, D. (1984). Extreme deprivation in early childhood I. Diverse outcomes for three siblings from an extraordinary family. *Journal of Child Psychology and Psychiatry*, *25*, 523–541.

Thompson, A. M. (1966). Adam – a severely deprived Colombian orphan: a case report. *Journal of Child Psychology and Psychiatry*, *27*, 689–695.

Tomasello, M. and Farrar, M. (1984). Cognitive bases of lexical development: object permanence and relational words. *Journal of Child Language*, *11*, 477–495.

Vygotsy, L. S. (1978). Play and its role in the mental development of the child. In M. Cole, V. John-Steiner, S. Scribner and E. Souberman (Eds.), *Mind in Society*. Cambridge, Mass: Harvard University Press.

Waddington, C. H. (1977). *Tools for Thought*. London: Jonathan Cape.

# SECTION III
## COGNITION AND REPRESENTATIONS

### Editors' Introduction

Discovering how the cognitive system works is a central goal of psychological research. Research with infants and children can provide information about the basic structure and workings of the cognitive system. Models of cognition focus on two separate but related components – the operations of the system and the internal representations that the cognitive system acts upon or manipulates. The nature of representations is a central part of the equation. A representation is something that stands for something else, so for example a drawing of a house is a representation of an input stimulus. As we know by looking at children's drawings, their pictorial notations change with time (Thomas and Silk, 1990). Development can, in theory, entail changes in either the representational system, the computational elements or both. By corollary cognitive deficits (such as in autism or Down's syndrome) also occur. Such deficits may be related either to the representational system or to the computations that support the representations. Different cognitive models focus on different aspects of the system. Information processing models, for example, are concerned with the encoding and transformation of information that the child encounters.

There is considerable debate about the ways in which people represent knowledge. Studying the mental representations of neonates and infants provides a basis for our understanding of how particular elements in the stimulus are selected for encodings. Piaget argued that infants' capacities for representation were very different from those of the pre-schooler. It is postulated that a major shift in representational abilities occurs when the infant moves from the sensori-motor stage to the preoperational stage (at about 18 months). In contrast, others have argued that the infant is born with an innate ability to represent the world. As the chapter by McShane illustrates much of the debate in this area has focused on the development of the object concept and on babies' early imitative capacities. McShane demonstrates there are important methodological and theoretical concerns in studying babies' abilities. You should read carefully his critique of the evidence for imitation in neonates. Two different lines of argument are developed. The first, methodological, focuses on the tasks used by the experimenters. The second questions the kinds of inferences that can be validly drawn even from the most reliable data.

When you have completed the chapter you should consider at what point in development it becomes meaningful to make claims about the infant's ability to represent events. Later readings will further demonstrate that it is possible to attribute certain innate processes/ structures to the human neonate without denying the crucial role of environment.

The article by Annette Karmiloff-Smith is a précis of her book. Reading the précis does not provide the richness and depth of the book, but does, however capture the major theoretical distinctions she draws. To appreciate the significance of the data it is necessary to read the relevant chapters in the book. The précis covers 12 key problems in the quest to understand development. Underpinning these 12 problems is the central theme of representational change over time. The claim is not the trivial one that children get better, rather she argues there are fundamental changes in development that have profound implications for our understanding of the cognitive system. The central issue is the status of the different representations underlying different capacities and the multiple levels in which knowledge is stored and accessible. She draws an important distinction between domain specificity and the Fodorian view of modularity. Fodor has proposed that we possess specialized modules which can deal with specific aspects of cognition, such as the processing of speech or visual information (Fodor, 1976). He supposes these modules are largely independent of other cognitive operations, they are automatic in the processing of information as no conscious effort is needed (i.e. we do not have to think how to understand most speech we hear) and they do not undergo significant changes with development. A contrast is provided between this viewpoint and 'domain general theories' such as those of Piaget which see development proceeding as a result of a few innate mechanisms which operate across most if not all aspects of intelligent activity. Karmiloff-Smith puts forward a different position which includes ideas from both of these perspectives. She advocates a phase model of development.

It is Karmiloff-Smith's focus on a phase model that is of major significance. Developmental psychologists have usually assumed that children progress from being unable to succeed in a task to being successful [you might like to consider the data on U-shaped development for a different perspective (see Strauss and Stavy, 1982)]. This simple dichotomous view of the acquisition of knowledge is challenged in the précis and in her book. One important feature of her theory of 'representational redescription' is that children (and adults) show a progressive increase in their knowledge from being able to do something without being able to explain how success is achieved, to being able to be successful and explain how this success is achieved. Karmiloff-Smith suggests that at the lowest level children can be successful in a task such as balancing different lengths of wood on a fulcrum, but this success is the result of them treating each problem as a new task and by using proprioceptive feedback about the weight of a beam to balance it. The next level in the model involves the use of a coherent strategy, but in the case of the balancing task this usually involves children attempting to balance things at the geometric centre, irrespective of whether this is the correct balance point. Thus, the children's representations are more advanced, but their overall rate of success declines. At both these levels Karmiloff-Smith supposes that children are not able to gain conscious access to their representations and as a result they are unable to explain why they are successful or unsuccessful. At the next level children have access to their representations, but are not able to translate this into verbal explanations. As a result, the child might be able to pick out which of several pictures shows the correct balance point of a length of wood, but not be able to explain why this is the correct picture. At the most advanced level children are once again able to balance all types of beams and are able to explain their success in terms of weight and distance. An interesting comparison can be made between the work of Karmiloff-Smith's explanations of the child's changing performance in the balance scale problem and that of Siegler (1983). What accounts for the differences between the two views? Karmiloff-Smith's paper is published in *Behavioural and Brain Sciences*, a journal which includes a peer commentary section. If you look at the journal you will find different authors offering critiques of the précis. These critiques will come from a range of different theoretical and empirical stances and thereby offer a comprehensive view of the area.

Studies of atypical development have helped our understanding of the workings of the cognitive system (Hodapp and Burack, 1990). Autism is such a case. It is a rare condition, but the characteristics of autism, which are described in the review paper by Frith and Happé, provoke questions about the causes and mechanisms of the disorder. The idea that children with autism lack a theory of mind has attracted considerable interest. Having a theory of mind refers to the ability to appreciate that someone else may have a different set of ideas from yourself. Several tasks have become widely used demonstrations of children's understanding of mental states. One such task involves a smartie tube. A child is shown a smartie container and asked what is in it. Virtually without exception four year olds will say smarties or sweets. Then the child is shown that the box really contains a pencil. They are then asked what their friend who has not seen inside the box will think is there. It has been found that children below about 4 years of age are unsuccessful with this type of task – they commonly say a pencil. It is argued that the 4 year old does not realize that the knowledge they possess is not necessarily shared by others. However, not everyone accepts that younger children are unable to appreciate and understand the thoughts and beliefs of others. For example, arguments have been put forward that the complexity of infant–adult social interaction would not be possible without some appreciation, on the infant's part, that they were dealing with a being that has similar capacities to themselves. Whatever the resolution of such arguments it seems that there are important changes that occur in the fourth year in the way that children are able to think about other individual's thoughts. Interestingly, Piaget's work captured a related capacity, that of egocentrism, and the decline of egocentrism involved children's capacity to view the world from the perspective of others (see also the paper by Hughes and Donaldson).

Frith and Happé argue that although the majority of children with autism lack a theory of mind, this does not provide a complete explanation for the characteristics of the condition. They briefly discuss the idea of deficits in executive functioning, an idea which is currently the subject of research. Here it is supposed that individuals with autism are unable to inhibit familiar responses, so, for example, they are unable to inhibit an immediate response they would give in theory of mind tasks and as a result they provide the incorrect answer. Frith and Happé discuss in more length their own explanation which involves the idea of central coherence. This is the idea that children with autism are very good at attending to the details of a situation or problem, but have difficulty in forming an overall picture. One of the tasks they have used to assess this capacity involves reading homographs (words which are spelt the same way, but are pronounced differently, e.g. a *tear* in your eye vs the dress has a *tear*). Individuals with autism were found to perform very poorly on such tasks. At present no one theory seems to account for all the characteristics shown by children with autism; as Frith and Happé show, each theory is better at explaining some characteristics than others.

We have already seen that children's representations can be described in a variety of ways. Recently, there has been growing interest in the way that computers can be used to investigate and simulate cognitive development. Moreover, as you will see in the Karmiloff-Smith paper there is interest in the possibility that developmental theories should be testable through simulations. Much of the work in this area involves the use of connectionist modelling (sometimes this work is referred to as involving neural nets or neural networks). The last chapter in this section reviews ways that connectionist models can be used to help understand processes of development. Most connectionist models involve the use of computer programs which are designed to receive information (input) and learn to produce appropriate responses (sometimes termed output). The input is usually in the form of a binary code of some type of information which children receive (this can be visual information, speech, the position of weights on a balance beam, etc.). Usually the connectionist net (i.e. the computer program) generates a response to this information. At the beginning of learning the connectionist net is often only able to produce a random response. If the response is incorrect then the connectionist net is designed to make mathematical corrections to the formula used to generate the output and the corrections are designed to provide a higher probability of producing a correct response on the next occasion. An important feature of connectionist models is that rule like behaviours can be produced, but there is no explicit rule anywhere in the model.

It is rare for claims to be made that connectionist models imitate the way that a child processes information. Instead, as can be seen by the review by Plunkett et al. connectionist modelling can be used to test ideas and theories. For example, connectionist models can show that it is possible for a single mechanism to produce the type of learning of the past tense shown by English children. This is relevant to theoretical debates about the way language acquisition occurs. However, it is important to realize that the successful performance of a connectionist net does not prove that language acquisition occurs in the same way, only that it could occur in this or a similar way. Thus, an important benefit of connectionist models is that they can be used to assess whether certain forms of information are sufficient to allow new cognitive abilities to be acquired, and they can also be used to examine whether mechanisms that involve the general processing of information can mimic the development of cognition. Because connectionist models tend to use similar general processes they have often been used to attack the ideas about modularity (see Elman et al., 1996).

How we represent the world is of central concern to developmentalists. Representations cover many domains and problems. As these readings show, researchers consider the ways in which children represent the world in their own heads in very different ways. There is debate about the range and types of representations that children possess and develop. Yet, the structure of our representations can influence the way we learn and the ways in which we store and manipulate knowledge. Many of our ideas about mental representations are uncertain or controversial but by careful experimental and theoretical work we are gradually clarifying our understanding of the development of representations.

## References

Elman, J., Bates, E. Johnson, M. Karmiloff-Smith, A., Parisi, D., and Plinkett, K. (1996). *Rethinking Innateness: A connectionist perspective on development.* Cambridge Ma.: MIT Press.

Fodor, J. A. (1976). *The Language of Thought.* Harvester.

Hodapp, R. M. and Burack, J. A. (1990). What mental retardation teaches us about typical development: The examples of sequences, rates, and cross-domain relations. *Development and Psychopathology, 2,* 213–226.

Siegler, R. S. (1983). Information processing approaches to development. In P. Mussen (Ed.), *Handbook of Child Psychology, Vol I, History, Theory and Methods.* New York: Wiley.

Strauss, S. and Stavy, R. (1982). *U-Shaped Behavioural Growth.* Academic Press: NY.

Thomas, G. V. and Silk, A. (1990). *An Introduction to the Psychology of Children's Drawings.* London: Harvester Wheatsheaf.

## Further Reading

Goswami, V. (1998). *Cognitive Development.* Psychology Press.

Grove, N. and Dockrell, J. E. (in press). Children with learning disabilities. In D. Messer and S. Millar (Eds.), *Developmental Psychology.* London: Arnold.

McShane, J. (1991). *Cognitive Development: An information processing approach.* Oxford: Blackwell.

Pine, K. (in press). Theories of cognitive development. In D. Messer and S. Millar (Eds.), *Developmental Psychology. London: Arnold.*

Smith, P. (in press). Children's drawing. In D. Messer and S. Millar (Eds.), *Developmental Psychology.* London: Arnold.

# 9    J. McShane
### 'The Origins of Representations'

Reprinted in full from: *Cognitive Development* (Blackwell
Publishers Ltd, 1991), 96–125

## Representations and information processing

Information begins as a stimulus in the environment that is detected by the
organism's perceptual receptors and is then processed by the cognitive system.
During this processing certain features of the stimulus will receive attention
and be retained. Other features will be ignored and discarded. The features
retained may be transformed in various ways. At this point we are not
particularly concerned with the details of how information is selected and
transformed, merely with the fact that it happens. In some cases the final
information encoded and stored by the cognitive system may be quite unlike
the environmental stimulus that acted as input to the cognitive system.
Nevertheless, there is a lawful relation of representation between what is
encoded and the stimulus that initiated the encoding; the information
encoded is a representation of the stimulus input. How information is represented depends very much on the processes that act upon it, because processes
transform the input in various ways. Processes can be thought of as acquired
procedures for manipulating information. The infant will have had little
opportunity to acquire procedures through experience. This means that,
initially, representations are very much a function of innate architectural
mechanisms. As development proceeds, additional learnt procedures for
processing information will come to play a more significant role than they
do initially.

A representation is, essentially, something that stands for something else.
This, as Palmer (1978) points out, implies the existence of two related but
functionally separate worlds; the represented world and the representing
world. The representing world need not model all aspects of the represented
world; in fact the essence of a representation is that it is *not* a faithful picture
of that which is represented but that it accurately denotes some aspect of what
it represents. Figure 9.1(a) shows a map of the type that might be used by one
person giving directions to another. In this case it is likely to represent the
spatial relations accurately but unlikely to do so for distance. The same
information can be represented in other ways also as in (b), while (c) provides
an alternative set of cues to (a). In all cases the represented world is the same
but the representing world presents a selective amount of the information
available in the represented world. A representation is, essentially, a stylized
picture of the represented world.

The key elements of the representational relations depicted in figure 9.1 are
that the representing world is different from the represented world and that,
because of this, the representing world contains a selection of the potential

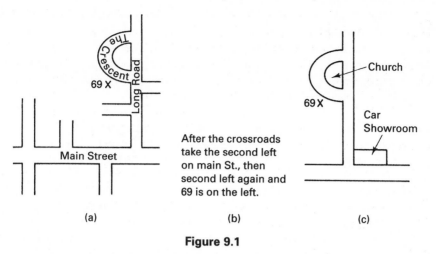

After the crossroads
take the second left
on main St., then
second left again and
69 is on the left.

(a)          (b)          (c)

**Figure 9.1**

information present in the represented world. Obviously, the manner in which this selection is done is of extreme importance, not least because once a particular representation has been constructed, it will contain only certain information.

This chapter will be mainly concerned with the origin of the child's capacity to create internal representations of the environment. In particular, it will address the issue of how representations of the environment arise. As has been remarked, a representation is not an exact copy of the features of the environment but is some stylized economical version of the environment. Mental representations are selective symbolic encodings of the external environment. It must be part of a theory of cognitive development to explain the origins of mental representations. Representations cannot be observed directly; they must be inferred from the behaviour of the child. Thus, the methodology of the investigative procedure and the inferences that the methodology warrants will be issues of critical significance in discussing infant representations. Methodology and scientific inference are always, of course, issues of significance, but they assume particular importance in discussing the origins of representations because the theories that will be discussed differ radically in what they attribute to the infant.

Obviously, representations cannot develop out of nothing; they must be explained with reference to some initial state of the cognitive system that is capable of creating from the environmental input the variety of representational systems the adult possesses. Developmental theorists do not agree on what is the initial state of the cognitive system. In fact, the initial state is an issue of major fundamental disagreement. At one extreme there are those who argue that the infant's initial state is one of a complete lack of mental organization. This has been the dominant view until comparatively recently. It is evident in Locke's *tabula rasa* view of the human mind and in William James's view that the infant's mind is one of 'blooming, buzzing confusion'. At the other extreme are innatist theories of cognition that argue that the infant's initial state is one in which there is already a rich representational structure, predisposed to interpret experience in certain ways. Somewhere between these extremes lies Piaget's theory. Piaget recognized the need for an innate endowment to make adaptive behaviour a possibility. To this extent his thinking is like that of an innatist theorist. However, unlike innatist theorists, he considered that the infant had only a limited repertoire of innate behaviours; the rest had to be acquired through experience. This balance would seem to push Piaget more towards the empiricist than the innatist end of the spectrum. However, here again Piaget had something different to offer. Experience is the stimulus for development in Piaget's theory but what develops is not simply a copy of what is experienced but a set of cognitive structures with which to interpret experience. Out of experience the child constructs a cognitive system, beginning from a few innate reflexes. This view is often called a *constructivist* view of development to set it apart from both empiricism and innatism. One of the most important constructions of the early years of life is a system for mentally representing objects and events.

### Piaget's theory of sensorimotor development

Piaget's view of development is one in which the newborn infant enters the world with a limited repertoire of hereditary behaviour patterns. During the first two years of life the child builds on these hereditary endowments and acquires a variety of more complex behavioural patterns for interacting with and manipulating the immediate environment. These are *schemes*, which are meant to convey the presence of organization but the absence of a mental component in that organization. The label 'sensorimotor' reveals the level at which Piaget believes the organization of behaviour exists. As a practical example of the difference between a scheme and a mental representation consider a 1-year-old infant playing with a ball that rolls out of reach. The infant cannot first think about how the ball might be retrieved but can activate a motor scheme, such as crawling, that may lead to the successful recovery of the ball. The key aspects of a scheme are that it involves motor activity on the part of the infant and that it refers to some basic organizational structure that underlies particular actions – in the example above the organizational structure would be the motor program for crawling. But schemes are limited in that they apply only to objects that are immediately present. They can never be used to imagine or think about objects and situations that are not present. In the example above, if the ball rolls just out of reach, but also out of sight, the infant will not crawl to where the object vanished and search for it. The infant cannot reason about what to do because he or she does not possess any mental symbols with which to represent the absent ball.

Piaget's proposal about the world of the infant is an extremely radical one. He postulates a way of experiencing the world for infant that is very different from the way we normally experience the world. Mandler (1983: pp. 424–5) has captured the flavour well:

According to Piaget, the sensorimotor child before Stage 6 (18 to 24 months) does not have a capacity for representation in the true sense, but only sensorimotor intelligence. Knowledge about the world consists only of perceptions and actions; objects are only understood through the child's own actions and perceptual schemata. It is a most un-Proustian life, not thought, only lived. Sensorimotor schemata (or, in our sense, representation as knowledge) enable a child to walk a straight line but not to think about a line in its absence, to recognize his or her mother but not to think about her when she is gone. It is a world very difficult for us to conceive, accustomed as we are to spend much of our time ruminating about the past and anticipating the future. Nevertheless, this is the state that Piaget posits for the child before $1\frac{1}{2}$, that is, an ability to recognize objects and events but an inability to recall them in their absence. Because of this inability, this lack of concepts of things and symbols to represent them, Piaget does not consider the sensorimotor child's knowledge to be 'mental representation'; to be mental means to be thought and the sensorimotor child cannot think. Note that lack of thought in this view does not merely mean that the child is still missing the ability to reason or make deductive inferences; it means that the child cannot even remember what he or she did a few minutes ago, what his room looks like or what she had for lunch, except accidentally in the course of carrying out actions relevant to these past perceptions and activities. What is missing, according to Piaget, is both a system of concepts and a mobile, flexible symbol system capable of pointing to, or referring to, those concepts.

The missing element of representation identified by Mandler serves both to define the sensorimotor stage by its absence and to mark the beginning of the end of that stage when it first appears. The move out of the sensorimotor stage begins with the development of mental symbols that can represent objects and events in their absence.

Piaget uses the term 'representation' in two different senses that he calls broad and narrow. In the broad sense representation is identical with thought. In the narrow sense representation is the relation between a symbol and its external referent. Piaget (1936a/1952: p. 243) remarks: 'Representation in the narrow sense is the capacity to evoke by a sign or a symbolic image an absent object or an event not yet carried out.'

Before considering Piaget's views on the development of representation in more detail it will be useful to obtain a general overview of the sensorimotor period. Piaget divides the period into six substages and he discussed the development of representation, as manifested particularly in imitation and play, within the framework of these substages. Table 9.1 presents a synopsis of the six substages.

The initial point of departure for Piaget's theory is a small set of innate reflexes, such as sucking and grasping, which are present at birth. Initially these reflexes are the limits of the infant's knowledge of the world and everything with which the infant comes into contact can be 'known' only in so far as it triggers a reflex, otherwise it is not known at all. Thus, Piaget's view of the innate architecture of cognition is that it consists only of reflexes and mechanisms of assimilation and accommodation. The rest is constructed; the child, while learning about the world, constructs the cognitive system with which to interpret the world.

**Table 9.1**  Piaget's substages of sensorimotor development

| Substage | Age (months) | Dominant Scheme | Major Developments |
|---|---|---|---|
| I | 0–1 | Reflex | Sucking, grasping |
| II | 1–4 | Primary circular reactions | Adaptations of reflexes to external environment; systematic protrusion of tongue; sucking of thumb; beginning of eye-hand co-ordination |
| III | 4–8 | Secondary circular reactions | Beginning of intentional means-end behaviour; increased co-ordination of looking and grasping; search for partially hidden objects |
| IV | 8–12 | Co-ordination of secondary schemes | Widespread flexible combination of previously separate schemes; search for hidden objects; emergence of ability to predict one external event from another |
| V | 12–18 | Tertiary circular reactions | Discovery of new means through experimentation with means-end behaviours |
| VI | 18–24 | Mental representations | Symbolic representation of external events; invention of new means through mental combinations |

Reflexes constitute the first six substages of sensorimotor development. However, some reflex behaviours are repeated by the infant because of the desirable or reinforcing consequences of the behaviour itself. This repetition has a fundamentally different origin from the reflex itself: it is not innately triggered but voluntarily engaged in. This behaviour constitutes the second substage of sensorimotor development, the stage of primary circular reactions. Learning, in the conventional sense, first occurs during this substage, and this leads Piaget to conclude that sensorimotor schemes are first established during this substage. A scheme is the first example of the abstract structures that Piaget postulates in order to explain the organizational pattern he perceives in the infant's behaviour. The theoretical move from reflex to scheme is central to the theory and to Piaget's attempt to link biology and psychology; behaviour is established by biological principles but these only serve as the necessary foundation for the further construction of the mind on psychological principles.

As the infant acts, some actions will have consequences on the world. Swiping a hand, for example, may cause a mobile to move, or to make a noise. Actions that are repeated because of the consequences they have on the world define the third substage of sensorimotor development. These actions are called secondary circular reactions. Secondary circular reactions further reflect the drift away from innate behaviours in that they are learnt adaptations to environmental events and they are reinforced by external consequences (as opposed to internal consequences at substage II). Thus, there is now a contingent relation between the infant's behaviour and environmental events. This represents a journey during the first year of life from an organism whose behavioural repertoire consists almost entirely of reflex responses to one that is responsive to the information that can be gained from acting on the environment and observing the consequences of those actions. The infant is still severely constrained in his or her interpretation of the structure of the environment and its relation to behaviour; concepts of causality, space, object permanence and many more still require considerable development during the remainder of the sensorimotor period. Nevertheless, the basic interactive relation between organism and environment is established by substage III. Consequently, substage IV does not consist of the development of new behaviours but of the co-ordination of behaviours already in place.

During substage IV previously acquired schemes are generalized to new situations, and behaviours that have developed independently as secondary circular reactions are co-ordinated to yield more powerful and more adaptive schemes. Where previously each scheme existed in isolation, different schemes can now be combined together in a sequence. One example offered by Piaget (1936a/1952) is the ability to move one object aside (one scheme) in order to grasp an object (another scheme) that it is obstructing. Piaget described the situation as follows:

> I present a box of matches above my hand, but behind it, so that he cannot reach it without setting the obstacle aside. But Laurent after trying to take no notice of it, suddenly tries to hit my hand as though to remove or lower it; I let him do it to me and he grasps the box. I recommence to bar his passage, but using as a screen a sufficiently supple cushion to keep the impress of the child's gestures. Laurent tries to reach the box, and bothered by the obstacle, he at once strikes it, definitely lowering it until the way is clear. (Piaget, 1936a/1952: p. 217)

The behaviour described by Piaget is an example of the infant's increasing sophistication in reasoning about the external world and in co-ordinating schemes to solve problems that arise when a goal cannot be attained directly.

This increasing facility for problem-solving provides the key for substage V, which Piaget describes as the substage of tertiary circular reactions. Primary circular reactions were behaviours repeated for their own intrinsic reinforcement value; secondary circular reactions were behaviours repeated for the environmental effects they produced; tertiary circular reactions are behaviours repeated, *with modifications*, in order to achieve a given goal. They thus constitute a systematic exploration of the relations between means and ends. Piaget describes, as an example, a phenomenon well known to every parent, when the infant discovers the variety of ways in which things can be dropped from a crib, and proceeds to conduct the relevant experiments.

Tertiary circular reactions are the culmination of an intelligence based on schemes. The final substage of the sensorimotor period is the development of a new way of interacting with the environment by mentally representing it. Piaget infers the presence of a mental representation when there is a gap in time between the infant observing something and later repeating what was observed.

Piaget's reasoning is that if a behaviour is observed at some particular time and imitated at some later time, there must be storage of the observed event in the interim and such storage requires a symbolic encoding of events. This ability to represent events by internal symbols brings the sensorimotor period to an end. Once events can be stored symbolically the child has embarked on the long road of learning to process and manipulate stored information. Cognitive development proper has now begun.

## Imitation and representation

### *Piaget's account of the origins of representations*

Piaget (1945/1951) attempts to trace the emergence of symbolic behaviour from its origins in sensorimotor development. His general method is essentially the same as in his other works on sensorimotor development: he presents detailed observational reports on behaviours that might be considered symbolic or proto-symbolic in origin and offers interpretations of these behaviours and their symbolic status. Before discussing Piaget's account in more detail it will be useful to consider the criterion he uses to infer the presence of mental symbols.

Piaget infers the presence of mental symbols that represent the external world on the basis of one criterion: 'the deferred character of the reaction' (p. 98). That is to say, there must be a temporal interval between the behaviour that serves as evidence for a mental symbol and the event in the world to which the behaviour relates. Thus, imitation has a representational basis when it occurs sometime after the event imitated and language has a representational basis when words describe events that occurred some time previously. The criterion of temporal delay is used to infer a symbolic system that mediates between the original stimulus and its later reproduction by the child.

It is easy enough to see that this criterion of temporal delay allows Piaget to infer a representational system with some certainty. However, it is not self-evident that the criterion is necessary. Piaget's criteria, in general, tend to err on the conservative side in the attribution of cognitive structures; the criterion for representational thought is no exception. While the representation may be inferred from 'the deferred character of the reaction', a representation is not defined by a delay between stimulus input and response output. In order to understand the origins of mental representations it is necessary to define, within a theoretical framework, what are to count as representations, and then to propose ways of detecting the presence of representations. It is not adequate, as a methodological practice, to work backwards from a convenient, probably overcautious, measure to the theoretical construct. An objection to this criticism might be that Piaget intends the term 'representation' to stand for that which makes deferred responses possible. Unfortunately, this simply creates a circular relation between the construct and its operational measure. In any case, this is patently not what the term 'representation' is intended to capture. There is a reasonably clear theoretical view of what a mental repre-sentation is: it is a symbolic encoding of some aspect of the external environ-ment. Mental representations can be legitimately attributed to the child once evidence exists for the use of symbolic encoding in the organization of behaviour. The major methodological task that this creates is to show how symbolic encodings can be detected in an unambiguous fashion. We shall return to this issue later. Given Piaget's criterion for inferring cognitive representations, imitation is an obvious behaviour on which to test the account. In order to imitate it is necessary at minimum (1) to observe the behaviour of another, (2) to process and encode that observation, and (3) to use the results of that processing to effect a similar sequence of behaviour in the correct serial order. If there is a time lapse between (1) and (3) then clearly we are observing a behaviour that is controlled by a cognitive representation.

Piaget does not report any examples of imitation during the first of his six substages of sensorimotor development. It will be recalled that this substage consists entirely of reflex behaviours. Since imitation involves reproducing some behaviour of a model, and therefore depends upon experience, it would be odd for it to be observed among the reflexes of substage I. It is not until substage II that some sporadic imitation is observed. Piaget reports instances of both vocal imitation of sounds and visual imitation of head movements. However, there are constraints on what can be imitated; the model that the infant imitates must be assimilated to a circular schema that the infant has already acquired. Thus, imitation will only occur if the model presents behaviours that the infant has already performed spontaneously.

During the third substage of sensorimotor development imitation of sounds occurs for quite long periods and imitation of movements continues provided, still, that the infant can make these movements spontaneously. However, Piaget claims that the infant is not able to imitate new sounds that he or she has not previously produced spontaneously. Imitation of movements will only occur if the infant can observe the movement while he or she is making it. Thus, an infant could imitate hand gestures made in front of the face because these can be observed while they are being made but could not imitate scratching the back of the head because the infant cannot observe his or her own movements in doing this. However, Piaget was too inquisitive an observer and too honest a scientist not to report some success at eliciting imitation of tongue protrusion from his daughter Jacqueline. For example, he reported some observations that did not neatly fit his framework. He accom-modates these observations to his theory by categorizing them as 'pseudo-imitations' on the grounds that the behaviour is not maintained unless its training is prolonged and constantly kept up.

Obs. 17. At 0;5 (2) J put out her tongue several times in succession. I put mine out in front of her, keeping time with her gesture, and she seemed to repeat the action all the better. But it was only a temporary association. A quarter of an hour later, no suggestion on my part could induce her to begin again. There was the same negative reaction the next few days.

Substage IV, it will be recalled, consists of the co-ordination of schemes. Once this co-ordination is achieved the infant begins to imitate movements of the body not directly visible while being carried out. Piaget argues that this development is a result of the infant assimilating the movements of others to those of his or her own body. At this point let us pick up the story of tongue protrusion.

Obs. 20. At 0;8 (9) I put out my tongue in front of J, thus resuming the experiment interrupted at 0;8 (3) which up till then had given only negative results (Obs. 17). At first J watched me without reacting, but at about the eighth attempt she began to bite her lips as before, and at the ninth and tenth she grew bolder, and thereafter reacted each time in the same way. The same evening her reaction was immediate: as soon as I put out my tongue she bit her lips.

Here, the infant responds predictably and consistently to the adult's behaviour but she does not imitate that behaviour; when Piaget puts out his tongue, Jacqueline bites her lip. This continued for nearly a month until biting the lips and tongue protrusion began to co-occur. About a week later tongue protrusion has become the dominant response. Piaget reports:

At 0;9 (11) she finally succeeded in definitely distinguishing between the two schemas. I put out my tongue at her when she had not been doing it just before. Her first reaction was to bite her lips at once, and then after a moment, to put out her tongue several times. I interrupted the experiment, and then again put out my tongue. She watched me attentively, biting her lips, but she put her tongue out more quickly and more distinctly. After a second pause, I put out my tongue, and she then put hers out very definitely without biting her lips, after having watched me very carefully. This must obviously have been conscious imitation.

During substage IV direct imitation of actions that the infant cannot see becomes fully developed. What then of imitation of sounds during this substage? Piaget remarks that when the infant becomes capable of imitating movements he or she has already made but cannot see, attempts are then made to imitate sounds and gestures that are new. It is interesting to note the strong priority given to motor movements in this account. Given that the imitation of movements that cannot be seen and sounds that are new both occur within the same substage, there is no logical reason to see one development as the result of the other.

Substage V is the period of exploring means–end relations. The infant, during this substage, engages in systematic exploration of the various elements that constitute an imitatory scheme.

Obs. 39. At 1;0 (20) J watched me removing and replacing the top of my tobacco jar. It was within her reach and she could have tried to achieve the same result. She merely raised and lowered her hand, however, thus imitating the movement of my hand but not its external effect.

In this example, the infant is obviously capable of isolating the behavioural component of the adult's act from its effect on the environment; the means and the end are clearly differentiated from each other.

According to Piaget, three new elements can be evidenced in imitation during substage VI: immediate imitation of complex new models, deferred imitation, and imitation of material objects resulting in representation. Of these, the latter two are of most theoretical importance. The following two examples are reported by Piaget. The first is of deferred imitation and the second is of imitation of material objects.

Obs. 52. At 1;4(3) J had a visit from a little boy of 1;6, whom she used to see from time to time, and who, in the course of the afternoon got into a terrible temper. He screamed as he tried to get out of a play-pen and pushed it backwards, stamping his feet. J stood watching him in amazement, never having witnessed such a scene before. The next day, she herself screamed in her play-pen and tried to move it, stamping her foot lightly several times in succession. The imitation of the whole scene was most striking. Had it been immediate, it would naturally not have involved representation, but coming as it did after an interval of more than twelve hours, it must have involved some representative or pre-representative element.

Obs. 57. At 1;4 (0) L tried to get a watch chain out of a match-box when the box was not more than an eighth of an inch open. She gazed at the box with great attention, then opened and closed her mouth several times in succession, at first only slightly and then wider and wider. It was clear that the child, in her effort to picture to herself the means of enlarging the opening, was using as 'signifier' her own mouth, with the movements of which she was familiar tactually and kinesthetically as well as by analogy with the visual image of the mouths of others. It is possible that there may also have been an element of 'causality through imitation', L perhaps still trying, in spite of her age, to act on the box through her miming. But the essential thing for her, as the context of the behaviour clearly showed, was to grasp the situation, and to picture it to herself actively in order to do so.

With the development of deferred imitation Piaget is willing to attribute a representational capacity to the child. He remarks: 'representation begins when sensorimotor data are assimilated not to elements that are actually perceptible but to those that are merely evoked' (1945/1951; p. 277). Thus, as a result of the emergence of representation at substage VI, behaviour in which a symbolic system plays an essential role becomes possible for the first time.

Piaget's account of the development of mental representations is best exemplified in his account of the development of imitation. His account contains an astonishing wealth of detailed observation and a consistent attempt to do justice to those observations by interpreting them within a theoretical framework of stage-like development.

## Replication studies

Let us turn now to subsequent studies of imitation and compare their findings with those of Piaget. The studies that will be discussed fall into two broad types. First, there are replication studies that attempt to repeat the observations of Piaget. Second, there are a number of experimental studies of neonatal imitation, some of which challenge Piaget's conclusions.

Uzgiris and Hunt's (1975) studies are the most detailed attempt to replicate Piaget's observations. They were concerned, in general, with attempting to devise a detailed scale of the major content areas of sensorimotor development – namely space, object permanence, circular reactions, imitation and causality – and to address issues such as whether homogeneous substages existed during which behaviour in the various content areas were all at the same level of development. They found little evidence of substage homogeneity across the different behaviours studied. Infants were quite likely to show a spread of development with one type of behaviour being more advanced than average and another type less advanced. In other words, substages do not exist in the sense that there are superordinate organizing constructs determining the developmental level of all behaviours at a given time. However, Uzgiris and Hunt did support the *sequence* of behaviours observed by Piaget in the different content areas. Similar findings for the two content areas of object permanence and space have also been reported by Corman and Escalona (1969).

As far as imitation is concerned Uzgiris and Hunt (1975) report the results of several cross-sectional studies, while Uzgiris (1972) reports a longitudinal study of 12 infants between the ages of 1 month and 2 years. Overall, their findings lend broad support to Piaget's observations. At first infants only reproduce actions that are in their repertoire, such as cooing sounds. This is similar to the observations reported by Piaget at substage II. A more complex form of imitation is reported by Uzgiris and Hunt when infant and experimenter alternate in turntaking in imitation. Contemporaneous with this observation is the observation that infants will now attempt to imitate complex actions (although they may not successfully imitate the whole act). These observations correspond to Piaget's substage III. The next step reported by Uzgiris and Hunt is the successful imitation of actions that cannot be seen by the infant, which corresponds to the observations reported by Piaget for substage IV. Finally, Uzgiris and Hunt report the imitation of unfamiliar sounds and actions, which corresponds to Piaget's substage V.

The studies reported by Uzgiris (1972) and Uzgiris and Hunt (1975) serve to confirm the sequence of imitation reported by Piaget. However, they do not critically test that sequence as do other studies discussed below nor do they address the underlying theory that postulates that representations are absent during the entire period of sensorimotor development.

*Neonatal imitations*

A number of investigators have claimed that the imitation of facial gestures, which, according to Piaget, first occurs during substage IV of sensorimotor development, can actually be observed during the early weeks of life. Gardner and Gardner (1970) reported a single case study of facial imitations at 6 weeks. The first systematic experimental evidence was provided by Meltzoff and Moore (1977). Because this study is controversial and because it helps to illustrate the methodological issues that surround research with infants, we shall discuss it in some detail.

In their first experiment Meltzoff and Moore modelled four different gestures to six infants between 12 and 21 days old and videotaped the infants' responses. The gestures were tongue protrusion, lip protrusion, mouth openings, and sequential finger movements. (The last of these will be ignored in the rest of the discussion.) The gestures were modelled for each infant in a different order. Each gesture was modelled four times in a 15-second modelling period followed by a 20-second response period in which the experimenter faced the infant with a neutral unresponsive face. The infants' responses were recorded on video during this period. The video-tape recordings were then scored by judges who did not know which gesture had preceded the response being coded. For purposes of analysis, facial and manual gestures were coded separately. The six judges who coded facial responses were informed that the infant had been shown one of four gestures: lip protrusion, mouth opening, tongue portrusion, and passive face. They were instructed to order these four gestures by rank from the one they thought it most likely the infant was imitating to the one they thought was least likely. The two highest and the two lowest ranks were then collapsed yielding a 'yes'/'no' judgement as to whether or not the infant imitated the gesture presented. This means that if, for example, lip protrusion had been modelled and a judge scored the likelihood of the gesture being imitated in the order mouth opening, lip protrusion, tongue protrusion and passive face, the infant would be credited with imitating lip protrusion. This is a somewhat unconventional method of scoring observer judgements. A further caveat that could be entered about the method is that it presumes that the infant is imitating; there is no category equivalent to 'did not imitate'.

Meltzoff and Moore reported that in all four cases the judged behaviour of the infant varied significantly as a function of the gestures shown. Meltzoff and Moore concluded that babies can imitate during the second week of life.

In a second experiment Meltzoff and Moore reported data for 12 2-week-old infants. In this case the rates of mouth opening and of tongue protrusion were compared during three 150-second time periods. The first was a baseline period during which the experimenter stared at the infant with an impassive face. One of the two gestures was then demonstrated repeatedly for a 15-second period and a further 150-second observation period ensued during which the experimenter resumed his impassive face. The other gesture was then demonstrated and the final 150-second observation period followed. The infants' faces were videotaped during all three observation periods. An independent coder viewed the recordings and scored the number of tongue protrusions and mouth openings for each infant during each period. It was found that significantly more tongue protrusions occurred following tongue protrusion by the experimenter and significantly more mouth openings following mouth opening. Again, the conclusion is that infants are capable of selective imitation. However, as Kaye (1982: p. 163) has pointed out the data seem less than impressive on close inspection:

The 12 infants opened their mouths a total of eight times (on the average, once every 225 seconds) after the experimenter did so; but they only opened their mouths a total of two times (once every 15 minutes) in each of the other two conditions. Tongue protrusions were a little more frequent, and they too were significantly more frequent after they had been modeled: The 12 tongues were protruded 39 times during the segments following the tongue-protrusion demonstration, 15 times after each of the other conditions. A problem with this study was that Meltzoff and Moore, by reporting the total numbers of occurrences instead of the actual rates or the numbers of babies producing any responses at all, accentuated the (statistically significant) differences between experimental conditions and played down the fact that the rates of responding were extremely low. Very few of the 12 babies produced any imitative responses at all; but a few of them did so, at a sufficient rate to make the total numbers significantly different under each of the conditions.

Since Meltzoff and Moore's original study there have been several attempted replications. Some attempts have failed (Hayes and Watson 1981; Koepke, Hamm and Legerstee, 1983; McKenzie and Over, 1983), while others have succeeded (Field, Woodson, Greenberg and Cohen, 1982; Meltzoff and Moore, 1983). This suggests that the phenomenon is far from robust. Some babies appear to imitate some of the time.

What implications do such findings have for the origins of mental representations? Consider the fact that the infant receives perceptual input and uses motor output to reproduce the form of the input. This might seem to imply that infants are capable of creating some perceptual representation of an adult's behaviour, possibly as an image, and then of using this representation to create a motor output. In order to do this, infants would have to be able to link, in some way, elements of the image with components of the motor behaviour. This would seem to demand rather a lot from an infant's information processing system during the first few weeks of life. Meltzoff and Moore overcame this problem by arguing, following Bower (1974), that the translation from a perceptual representation to a motor output is not necessary because information is initially represented in a form common to all the senses. They state (1977: p. 178):

> The hypothesis we favor is that this imitation is based on the neonate's capacity to represent visually and proprioceptively perceived information in a form common to both modalities. The infant could thus compare the sensory information from his own unseen motor behaviour to a 'supramodal' representation of the visually perceived gesture and construct the match required. In brief, we hypothesize that the imitative responses observed are . . . accomplished through an active matching process and mediated by an abstract representational system . . . The ability to act on the basis of an abstract representation of a perceptually absent stimulus becomes the starting point for psychological development in infancy and not its culmination.

This is a radically different interpretation of the cognitive abilities of infants from that offered by Piaget. It encapsulates something that will recur frequently throughout this book: the extreme contrast between how the cognitive system is viewed by theorists disposed towards interpretations in terms of innate representational abilities and those not so disposed.

A study by Jacobson (1979) is of particular interest in relation to infant imitation. She observed infants at 6, 10, and 14 weeks in a longitudinal study. Two of the gestures modelled by Meltzoff and Moore were studied, namely tongue protrusion and hand movements. In addition three other stimuli were presented, namely a ball, a pen being moved towards the infant's mouth, and a ring being raised and lowered. Jacobson found that tongue protrusion *and* the movement of a ball or pen towards the infants mouth all produced tongue protrusions. Jacobson suggests that the infants' behaviour may not have been genuine imitation but more like the fixed action patterns described by Tinbergen (1951), which are automatically released by certain stimuli. However, by 14 weeks tongue protrusion was primarily elicited by adult tongue protrusion. Thus, even if the behaviour of the infants is initially akin to a fixed action pattern, it is certainly much less stereotyped than the fixed action patterns described by Tinbergen. Meltzoff and Moore (1977) argue against such an interpretation on the grounds that it is unwieldy in view of the fact that infants imitate a variety of different behaviours. The logic of this point is sound but its empirical basis is not. In Meltzoff and Moore's (1977) first experiment the rate of imitative responses was not directly measured. In their second experiment there was a moderate number of tongue protrusions but a very low number of mouth openings. Thus the only behaviour for which there is at present a reasonably clear case to be made for neonatal imitation is tongue protrusion. This conclusion is bolstered by the results of two further studies. Kaitz, Meschulach-Sarfaty, Auerbach and Eidelman (1988) compared the ability of infants to imitate tongue protrusion and facial expressions (for which positive results had been reported by Field et al., (1982)). Kaitz et al. replicated the positive findings for tongue protrusion but failed to replicate the imitation of facial expressions. Abravanel and Sigafoos (1984) modelled five actions three times in succession for infants between the ages of 4 and 21 weeks. The actions were tongue protrusion, mouth opening, and chest tapping. They found no evidence of imitation for any of the actions. However, in a second study they increased the amount of modelling to an unlimited number for the duration of the infants' attention during a 3-minute period. They also decreased the number of actions to three: tongue protrusion, hand opening, and chin tapping. With this procedure there was evidence of imitation of tongue protrusions only for infants in the 4 to 6 week age range. No other comparison was statistically significant at any of the ages sampled. In fact, there was a significant *decline* in the amount of imitation with increase in age.

The issue of infant imitation is currently a hotly-debated topic. It is difficult at this stage to draw definite conclusions because there are too many conflicting results for a clear pattern of empirical data to emerge that call for interpretation. At present, both data and interpretation are at issue. The best that can be done is to consider the current alternatives.

Meltzoff and Moore (1977; 1985) have urged the strongest interpretation. They argue that infants are capable of creating abstract mental representations of the behaviour of others and of using this abstract representation to create a matching response of their own. In order to create a mapping from the visual input to the proprioceptive output they postulate (following Bower, 1974) that infants represent the adult act not as an image or other perceptual representation (which would leave the problem of 'translating' this image to a motor output) but as a 'supramodal' or non-modality-specific representation. Unfortunately, there is no further specification of the nature of this supramodal representation.

The major alternative interpretation is that the infant's imitations derive from innate reflexive behaviours that are elicited by various stimuli in the environment. The strongest version of this argument would have it that tongue protrusions are elicited by a range of different stimuli and that there is little evidence for other types of imitation. It is at this point that the debate about the status of the empirical data is critical but is, unfortunately, unresolved. Kaitz et al. (1988) point out that tongue protrusion in infants is a behaviour with a high base-line relative to other behaviours and thus has a high probability of being involuntarily triggered by a variety of stimuli. Kaitz et al. doubt that the reproduction of tongue protrusions in response to a similar facial gesture of the model is true imitation. True imitation, in their view, requires the voluntary co-ordination of motor output to produce the same behaviour as the adult. They argue also that if the intermodal skills postulated by Meltzoff and Moore (1977) were generally available to the infant, imitation would not have been limited to one of four expressions, as found in their own study. Vinter (1986) draws attention to the role of movement in eliciting neonatal imitation and suggests that the behaviour may be controlled by subcortical rather than cortical mechanisms. This suggestion is consistent with the decline in imitation reported by Abravanel and Sigafoos (1984) and is reminiscent of the findings reported on the development of visual orientation to the source of an auditory stimulus. Many investigators of neurological development have stressed the continuity from prenatal to postnatal neurological control of movement and a subsequent change in the developmental course of neurological and behavioural variables around the end of the second month (Prechtle, 1984). It may be a general rule of development that as control of motor behaviour moves from subcortical to cortical mechanisms, there is a general decline in early reflexive actions (McGraw, 1943; Touwen, 1976). If this is true, then neonatal imitation is a behaviour of a fundamentally different type from later imitation.

*Summary of imitation and representation*

The discussion of imitation began by considering Piaget's account. His account stressed the gradual emergence of more complex forms of imitation throughout the first two years of life. The general pattern he observed has been confirmed by others, notably by Uzgiris (1972). The greatest challenge to Piaget's account has come from the experiments on neonatal imitation. If the interpretation urged by Meltzoff and Moore (1977, 1985) is accepted then the

Piagetian *theory* of imitation is completely erroneous. However, the type of interpretation of neonatal imitation urged by others such as Abravanel and Sigafoos (1984), Kaitz et al. (1988) and Vinter (1986) is much closer to Piaget's general view that early imitations are not indicative of mental representations. While the debate about neonatal imitation has been a lively issue it has had one unfortunate consequence: the fact is that, however one interprets the neonatal evidence, imitation itself undergoes developmental change by mechanisms that are still little understood. The debate on neonatal imitation as an encapsulated phenomenon has taken the emphasis off the need to create a theory of the origins of mental representations that accommodates within its framework the changes in the infant's abilities to imitate.

Imitation provided Piaget with the most direct type of evidence for his claim that mental representations are absent until the end of the sensorimotor period. However, his claim was a general one about the child's thought during the first year and a half or so of life. Accordingly, we can ask to what extent evidence from other areas of sensorimotor development supports Piaget's claim. The area for which the greatest amount of evidence is available is that of object permanence. We shall now consider its development.

## The object concept

Perhaps the most intriguing aspect of Piaget's research on sensorimotor development is that concerned with the concept of object permanence. A series of ingenious explorations of his children's reactions to the disappearance of objects led Piaget to conclude that until the end of sensorimotor development children do not fully understand that an object that is occluded continues to exist. This may seem like a startling conclusion but the reaction of an infant is equally startling in failing to search for an object over which a cloth has been draped in full view of the infant in such a way that the object's outline is clearly visible underneath the cloth. Piaget claims that the infant has to construct a concept that the world consists of permanent enduring objects and not merely of perceptions and sensations. It is worth bearing in mind that at the time Piaget wrote, very little was known about the actual perceptual capacities of infants.

Piaget's investigation of the infant's object concept employs one particular methodology: an object is occluded in full view of the infant and the infant's attempts to retrieve the object are observed. During the early stages of sensorimotor development, infants simply lose interest when an object is hidden – it seems as if out of sight is out of mind. Piaget concludes that the infant believes that an object is re-created each time it appears. Only perceptual appearances exist for the infant; there is no independent world of objects that gives rise to these perceptual appearances as there is for the adult.

By 6–8 months, during substage III of sensorimotor development, the infant has discovered by active exploration that his or her own actions can produce perceptual contact with objects. An infant will now recover a partially occluded object but fail to recover one that is completely occluded. The reason Piaget advances for this failure is central to his theory of sensorimotor development. The sensorimotor period is one in which the external world is known by the actions performed on it. Thus, an object is known by the action schema that the infant performed in interacting with it. An object grasped is known only through the act of grasping. If an object has been grasped previously then it may elicit the same response when encountered again. However, an occluded object cannot elicit this behaviour in virtue of the object being hidden. The fact that the outline shape of the object may be visible under the cloth that occludes it is irrelevant. Infants cannot reason that the shape is related to the object that was visible previously because that object was known only as a graspable phenomenon.

By substage IV infants will recover a completely occluded object. They have now begun, in some sense, to be able to relate the occluded object to the object that disappeared. This appears to be a significant step forward as far as the mental representation of objects is concerned. However, the infant is still, according to Piaget, constrained by the action schemas used to recover objects. Infants will not recover an object occluded in any place; they will only recover an object if it is occluded in a location where it was previously found. This can be illustrated by the following experiment. Two cloths are placed side by side and an object is hidden under one cloth. The infant retrieves the object. This is allowed to occur several times and then the object is hidden under the other cloth. The infant will usually search under the cloth where the object was previously found and not under the cloth where the object has been hidden. The infant frequently looks very puzzled on failing to find the object and may turn the cloth over and over but still fail to search under the other cloth, through which the outline of the object may be clearly visible. This suggests that the improvement that has occurred over substage III is simply one of a more sophisticated action schema: an object can be retrieved if it has successfully been retrieved from that location previously. However, the story is not this simple. The first retrieval at any given location cannot be explained in this way. More importantly, the infant's behaviour, when faced with occluded or hidden objects at substage IV, is more complex than the outline account suggests. We shall return to this below.

By substage V the error of searching where an object was previously found has been eliminated but the infant may still be fooled by more devious hiding. If an object is hidden in the experimenter's hand and the hand then placed under a cloth and withdrawn again, leaving the object behind, the infant will search for the object in the hand, where he or she has seen it hidden, but will fail to search under the cloth. By substage VI the full object concept is acquired and infants will search in all probable places where the object may have been hidden.

Piaget used his findings on the object concept to illustrate his argument that the infant only knows the world through the action schemas used to act on the world. But Piaget also saw the infant as having a more profound difficulty due to egocentrism. Because the infant only knows the world through his or her action schemas, the infant believes that the schemas themselves cause events in the world; the world is not seen as having an existence independently of the action schemas. Thus, the act of searching for an object at a location caused the object to be at that location because search has previously located objects there. From this perspective, searching where an object was previously found rather than where it has just been observed to be hidden is not odd at all; it is a perfectly natural consequence of the infant's egocentrism.

Such is the outline of Piaget's account of the development of object permanence. His observations have given rise to a very large number of experimental studies of this concept. In the main, studies that employ Piaget's criterion of search for a hidden object support the general outline of Piaget's account. As is usual when modern developmental psychologists consider Piaget however, the interpretation of the findings are in dispute. Various interpretations of the infant's failures in object search have been offered, and we shall discuss some of these. However, the more radical challenge comes from a different type of research. Search is not the only behaviour that can be used in investigating how infants respond to the disappearance of objects. Due to refinements in experimental procedures in the last quarter-century, it is now possible to conduct sophisticated experiments on the infant's visual and surprise responses to the disappearances and reappearances of objects. These experiments have the advantage that they can be conducted with young infants who are not capable of searching. Thus, we shall begin with these studies.

*Measures of disappearance and reappearance*

The pioneering experiment in this area was carried out by Bower (1967). He investigated the reactions of 2-month-old (substage I–II) infants to various different types of disappearance. Infants were trained to suck for an auditory reward and a sphere was visible throughout the training period. The sphere was then made to disappear in one of four ways: (1) gradual occlusion by a screen; (2) gradual fading; (3) instantaneous occlusion by a screen; and (4) instantaneous implosion. Bower compared the effect of these four conditions on sucking. He found that sucking was least disrupted by the first condition, which, according to Michotte's (1955) theory, specifies the continued existence of an invisible object, unlike the other three conditions. Bower concluded that the infants believed that the sphere continued to exist behind the screen.

In a series of follow-up studies Bower examined the effect of disappearance and reappearance under the various conditions, this time using spontaneous sucking as the dependent measure. He found that gradual occlusion led to the most suppression but that sucking recovered when the object reappeared so long as the interval between disappearance and reappearance was not longer than five seconds. Bower interpreted these results as showing that the infants suppress sucking while they wait for the occluded object to reappear. Bower interprets this as evidence that the infants possess object permanence. However, it should be noted that the sucking response is different in the two experiments. In one it is maintained, in the other it is suppressed, in response to the same condition. This creates an interpretive problem: it cannot reasonably be maintained that both responses indicate a belief in object permanence. While it certainly seems that gradual occlusion is seen as different from other types of disappearance by young infants, it is not clear that this indicates that young infants possess object permanence. As Brainerd (1978a) has pointed out, it is not possible to separate what may be responses to visual displays from what may be responses to objects in these experiments. Bower and his associates have also conducted a series of experiments with substage III infants. These experiments used the infants' tracking of objects as they moved across the visual field as a dependent measure. In one experiment (Bower, Broughton and Moore, 1971a) a train was made to move along a track containing a tunnel across the infant's line of sight. The issue of interest is what the infant does when the train enters the tunnel. If the infant immediately loses interest then it can be concluded that the infant was simply responding to the perceptual phenomenon and that once the phenomenon has disappeared from sight it has, effectively, ceased to exist for the infant. Out of sight is out of mind. However, the infants did not immediately lose interest. Bower et al. found that, by about 3 months of age, the infants immediately looked to the opposite end of the tunnel as if anticipating the re-emergence of the train. They concluded that this indicated that object permanence had developed by this age. However, further research by Bower and others has suggested that there may be alternative explanations of the infant's behaviour. Bower and Patterson (1973) used a train and tunnel but stopped the train just before it entered the tunnel. Even though the train was in full view the infants continued to track along the trajectory the train would have taken for some distance and then stopped. This result was also obtained when the tunnel was removed altogether and the train simply stopped at some point. This would seem to suggest that what Bower et al. (1971a) had interpreted as anticipation of the train's reappearance was simply the result of perseverative tracking. This interpretation is bolstered by the findings of Nelson (1971) who tested children's tracking of a train around an oval track, with a tunnel on one side. The infants tracked the train when it was visible but when it disappeared and then reappeared there was a delay of one or two seconds before the train was spotted. Clearly, if the infants had anticipated the re-emergence of the train there would have been no such delay. More recently Meicler and Gratch (1980) have replicated this result.

It would seem that there is no clear evidence from these tracking experiments that infants possess object permanence during the early months of life. The experiments do not, of course, show that infants do not possess object permanence. The real problem is that it is extremely difficult to relate how an infant tracks in any simple way to a belief in object permanence. Perseverative tracking, does not, for example, indicate an absence of object permanence because Chromiak and Weisberg (1981) have shown that adults track moving objects that stop suddenly in exactly the same way as infants: their eyes continue along the expected path of movement. This is an extremely important result that tells us a good deal about the relation between infant and adult behaviour. It also suggests that tracking is not a behaviour that has direct or automatic dependency on a belief in object permanence.

A number of studies have used tracking in a different way to investigate object permanence. In these studies an object moves along a track, disappears behind a screen and a different object re-emerges at the other side of the screen along the same track. Will infants exhibit any surprise at such a change? The reasoning here is that if infants of this age possess the concept of object permanence they should clearly expect the same object that disappeared to reappear. If, on the other hand, tracking is a behaviour that occurs independently of a concept of object permanence, infants should not be particularly surprised at the disappearance of one object and the reappearance of another.

Goldberg (1976) found no difference in surprise (as measured by heart rate) or in visual fixation in infants of 5 months between the reappearance of a novel and a familiar object. Two later studies have replicated this result. Muller and Aslin (1978) tested 2-, 4-, and 6-month old infants and altered either the shape or colour of the object to no effect on tracking. Meicler and Gratch (1980) reported similar results with 5- and 9-month olds. However, Moore, Borton and Darby (1978) reported more looking back towards the place of re-emergence when identity was altered than when it was not.

On balance, studies that have replaced one object by another during the disappearance of a tracked object behind a screen have not provided positive evidence that infants possess a concept of object permanence. Again, these findings do not prove that infants do not have a concept of object permanence. The negative results may be due to reasons other than an absence of a belief in object permanence. The infant may, for example, regard the disappearance of one object and the reappearance of another as an interesting game. However, there is no need to indulge in this type of speculation to make the essential methodological point: failure to observe surprise in the infants simply fails to support the hypothesis that infants do possess object permanence without telling us that they do not.

Recently, an experiment by Baillargeon (1986) has tipped the balance of interpretation positively in the infant's favour in a more complex tracking experiment. Infants of 6 and 8 months were first shown a car travelling along a track, disappearing behind a screen, and then reappearing at the other side. After several such presentations the screen was removed so that the complete track was visible and a box was placed either on the track or beside it. The screen was then replaced and the infants saw the car move along the track, disappear behind the screen, and reemerge at the other side. The infants looked longer at the car that emerged when the box had been placed on the track than when it had been placed beside it. This could be taken to suggest that the infants were puzzled as to how the car had managed to move through the box placed on the track, which in turn suggests that the infants were aware that the box continues to exist when it has been occluded by the screen.

There are two points to which it is worth drawing attention in the design of Baillargeon's experiment: The first is that the experiment is designed in such a way that the infant's surprise can be attributed to the presence of the box on the track, which is out of sight at the time that the measurement is made. This contrasts with the design in which one object disappears and a novel object reappears. In these experiments, the object intended to elicit a surprise reaction is present at the time of measurement, which would make the interpretation of positive results somewhat problematic. The second point is that the experiment includes a control condition in which all the elements of the first condition are present, but arranged in such a way that the infant should not be surprised to see the car emerge. This condition reduces the likelihood that any positive results might be due to an artifact of the experiment.

The results of Baillargeon (1986) suggest that 6-month old infants possess a concept of object permanence. Nevertheless infants of 12 months and older make a variety of errors in searching for hidden objects, which led Piaget to conclude that object permanence had not developed at this age.

*Search*

If we now turn to search itself, then the general sequence of development reported by Piaget has been verified in a number of replication studies (Corman and Escalona, 1969; Kramer, Hill and Cohen, 1975; Uzgiris and Hunt, 1975). These studies show that the sequence reported by Piaget constitutes an accurate description but they do not address the interpretation of that sequence.

Studies of the emergence of manual search during substage III show that the infant's failure to search under a cloth is not due to a lack of manual skill. Bower and Wishart (1972) and Gratch (1972) compared a transparent with an opaque cloth and found that infants were more likely to retrieve the object when it was under the transparent cloth. Presumably the same degree of manual skill is required in both situations. However, an object covered by a transparent cloth can itself be seen, and thus may elicit an action to effect its recovery whereas an object under an opaque cloth cannot be seen and must be represented as being hidden before it can be searched for.

The infant's substage IV error in continuing to search where an object has been previously found rather than where it has been hidden has been widely researched. Although the research has added considerable detail to the original picture, it has not quite succeeded in clarifying the cause of the infant's error. To begin with, the error does not always occur; in fact it seems to occur on approximately 50 per cent of trials (Butterworth, 1975; 1977). This is essentially a pattern of random responding rather than a pattern of perseverating where the object has been previously found. A further factor is that the error disappears altogether if the infant is allowed to search immediately (Gratch, Appel, Evans, Le Compte and Wright, 1974; Harris, 1973). Putting these findings together suggests that the difficulties infants have at substage IV is due to limitations on their information processing capacity rather than to their egocentrism as Piaget had suggested. When search is immediate and the ability of the information processing system is, presumably, less strained than when there is delay, the error does not occur. However, when search is delayed by more than a few seconds a pattern of random responding to the cloths occurs. This suggests that the infants no longer have access to the stored information about the object. In this context a longitudinal study by Diamond (1985) of infants between 7 and 12 months is of particular significance. Like previous studies, she found that when an object was hidden at a new location, having been previously hidden repeatedly at another location, the delay between the hiding of the object at the new location and the commencement of search was a crucial determinant of the infants' behaviour. The delay needed to elicit a perseverative error at the old hiding place was three seconds at 8 months but increased continuously over time to 10 seconds at 12 months. Diamond suggests that these data can be interpreted as a product of competing response tendencies generated by information in short-term memory and a conditioned tendency to repeat a previously successful response. Information about the new hiding place is stored in short-term memory. If acted upon more or less immediately, this information will form the basis of the infant's search. However, if not acted upon there is a competing response tendency to repeat previously successful searches.

A number of experimental results suggest that the likelihood of a perseverative error (i.e. a true perseverative error as opposed to searching under the cloths in a random fashion) is reduced if objects are hidden under, in, or behind salient landmarks. Bremner (1978b) and Butterworth, Jarrett and Hicks (1982) showed that when two hiding places were distinct from one another infants tended to search correctly. In these experiments the infants appear to have used the salient landmark cues provided to guide their search. An earlier study by Acredolo (1978) lends further weight to the importance of landmark cues in object search. In this study the presence or absence of useful landmarks was systematically varied and children of different ages were tested. Children of 6 months tended to perseverate irrespective of the presence or absence of a landmark. The 11-month-old infants were more accurate if a landmark was present, whereas the 16-month-old infants were accurate whether or not a landmark was present.

In summary, the perseveration error of substage IV seems to depend crucially on there being a delay before search is allowed and an absence of distinctive landmarks. This suggests that the final answers to the infant's errors are to be found in a detailed understanding of the constraints of the infant's information-processing system and how this system uses environmental information.

By comparison with substage IV, substages V and VI of the development of object permanence have not been heavily researched. Several studies have replicated Piaget's finding that visible displacements are easier than invisible displacements (Kramer, Hill and Cohen, 1975; Uzgiris and Hunt, 1975). However, more recent studies have found that if the object is hidden under one of two distinctive containers, and the containers are then rotated, search is fairly accurate (Bremner, 1978a; Cornell, 1979; Goldfield and Dickerson, 1981). This suggests that landmark cues again play a large role in helping the infant discover the location of an object.

By substage VI Piaget claims that the infant is able for the first time to represent mentally the absent object. An experiment by Ramsay and Campos (1978) attempted to assess Piaget's claim. They used the technique of hiding one toy but surreptitiously substituting another in its place before the infant had searched. Infants who had reached substage VI were more likely to smile if they found the toy they had seen hidden but to persist in searching if they found a different toy. Ramsay and Campos argue that it is only at substage VI that the infants can recall the identity of the object to be found so that its recovery elicits a smile and its absence elicits further search. However, there are several factors confounded in this interpretation. Failure to search for a toy is not definitive proof that its identity cannot be recalled. The child may recall the identity but given the absence of any clue as to where the object might be, simply has no idea of where to search. A further factor to be considered as a general issue in relation to such experiments is whether such odd conditions of environmental manipulation are really the most appropriate way to unlock the cognitive system that the infant uses in dealing with the natural environment.

### The origins of representations

The ability to represent mentally events in the world is the foundation of human cognitive development. In this chapter we have considered two views that are at opposite extremes as far as development is concerned. One view postulates an innate ability to represent the world. The evidence in favour of this view is, at present, somewhat weak. The other view denies that the infant is capable of any representations at all until well into the second year of life. The evidence against this view is accumulating. Where then does the truth lie?

A characteristic of much recent debate on the origins of representations is a lack of critical reflection of what constitutes a representation. As the introduction to this chapter pointed out, it is possible to have multiple representations of any event, with each one serving to highlight and encode a different aspect of the event. Unfortunately, this point has often been pushed to the background in the welter of methodological and empirical controversy over whether or not an example of representation has been demonstrated. This point applies equally to innatist and Piagetian research. The point is probably obvious enough in relation to recent innatist claims to have demonstrated mental representations in the first few weeks of life, not to need further labouring. It may be less obvious in relation to Piagetian research. Piaget, however, relied exclusively on one type of evidence for representation: temporal delay between the environmental stimulus and the infant's response, during which a 'mental copy' of the event was preserved. Kaye (1982) has argued that this is an unnecessarily restrictive view of representations. He comments:

> When schemas accommodate in some lasting way to some class of stimulating events, we can say that a schema *represents* that class of equivalent events in terms of a class of appropriate intentional actions. The 3-month-old has a representation of bottles in the form of the ability to recognize them visually and orient to them correctly with hand and mouth. That is the dawn of representation. (p. 167)

This is not to say that representation begins at 3 months rather than 18 months but to argue that once mental computation of some sort is involved – such as categorizing events into a class whose members will be treated as functionally equivalent – then it is meaningful to make claims about the infant's mental representation of events. The major emphasis of a theory of the development of representation (which we do not yet possess) should be on what types of more complex representations emerge during the course of development and the mechanisms by which they develop from earlier representations. Kaye, for example, goes on to emphasize that the kind of representations possessed by a 3-month old are not the kind that use one thing to stand for another, which is what Piaget wished to reserve the term 'representation' for. That is an unacceptable reservation, if only because of the apparent discontinuity it needlessly introduces.

If we consider the object concept, then it would seem that infants do not so much lack a concept of object as lack a representation system that links objects with the spatial cues in the environment. Why this should be, does, of course, require explanation and, to date, no entirely satisfactory explanation has been proposed. However, to explain the infant's behaviour in these terms does represent a shift in emphasis from Piaget's perspective on the problem.

If representations do not begin in the middle of the second year, they do not end there either. The major issue to which Piaget drew attention in relation to representation was the way in which objects and events could be represented by symbols in the forms of images and words. Some recent research by De Loache (1987) has brought a renewed interest in the development of symbolic representation. In De Loache's experiment children 2.5 and 3 years of age watched an attractive toy hidden within a scale model of a room. The children were then required to find an analogous toy in the real room. In one example, a miniature dog was hidden behind a small couch in the model. The child was then asked to find a larger stuffed dog hidden behind a full-sized couch in a regular-sized room. In order to perform the task correctly the child has to use the model as a representation of the full-size room.

De Loache found that 2.5-year-old children were very poor at finding the toy hidden in the regular-sized room, whereas the 3-year-olds were very good at this task. The 2.5-year-olds made fewer than 20 per cent errorless retrievals in the regular-sized room whereas the 3-year-olds made almost 80 per cent errorless retrievals. The difficulty of the younger group cannot have been due to a failure to remember where the object had been hidden in the model because they were subsequently able to retrieve the object originally hidden at a similar level to the 3-year-olds – approximately 80 per cent errorless retrievals for both groups.

De Loache postulates that the younger children were unable to treat the model of the room as both a model and an object in its own right. Quite why this should be so is, at present, an open question. The data serve to highlight, however, the fact that the development of mental representations is not a phenomenon that occurs at a given point in time, but extends throughout the whole period of development. The issue is not whether representation (in the singular) is absent or present but what types of representations (in the plural) are available to a child at any given point of development and, of course, how these representations come to be available and to change.

## References

Abravanel, E., and Sigafoos, A. O. (1984). Exploring the presence of imitation during early infancy. *Child Development, 55,* 381–92.

Acredelo, L. P. (1978). Development of spatial orientation in infancy. *Developmental Psychology, 141,* 224–34.

Baillargeon, R. (1986). Representing the existence and the location of hidden objects. *Cognition, 23,* 21–41.

Bower, T. G. R. (1967). The development of object-permanence: Some studies of existence constancy. *Perception and Psychophysics, 2,* 411–18.

Bower, T. G. R. (1974). *Development in Infancy.* San Francisco: W. H. Freeman.

Bower, T. G. R., Broughton, J. M., and Moore, M. K. (1971a). Development of the object concept as manifested in the tracking behaviour of infants between 7 and 20 weeks of age. *Journal of Experimental Child Psychology, 11,* 182–93.

Bower, T. G. R., and Patterson, J. G. (1973). The separation of place, movement and object in the world of the infant. *Journal of Experimental Child Psychology, 15,* 161–8.

Bower, T. G. R., and Wishart, J. G. (1972). The effects of motor skill on object permanence. *Cognition, 1,* 165–71.

Brainerd, C. J. (1978a). *Piaget's Theory of Intelligence.* Englewood Cliffs, NJ: Prentice-Hall.

Bremner, J. G. (1978b). Egocentric versus allocentric coding in nine-month-old infants: factors influencing the choice of code. *Developmental Psychology, 14,* 346–55.

Butterworth, G. (1975). Object identity in infancy: The interaction of spatial location codes in determining search errors. *Child Development, 46,* 866–70.

Butterworth, G. (1977). Object disappearance and error in Piaget's stage IV task. *Journal of Experimental Child Psychology, 23,* 391–401.

Butterworth, G., Jarrett, N., and Hicks, L. (1982). Spatio-temporal identity in infancy: perceptual competence or conceptual deficit. *Developmental Psychology, 18,* 435–49.

Chromiak, W., and Weisberg, R. W. (1981). The role of the object concept in visual tracking: Childlike errors in adults. *Journal of Experimental Child Psychology, 32,* 531–43.

Corman, H. H., and Escalona, S. K. (1969). Stages of sensorimotor development: A replication study. *Merill-Palmer Quarterly, 15,* 351–61.

Cornell, E. H. (1979). The effects of cue reliability on infants' manual search. *Journal of Experimental Child Psychology, 28,* 81–91.

De Loache, J. (1987). Rapid change in the symbolic functioning of very young children. *Science, 238,* 1556–7.

Diamond, A. (1985). Development of the ability to use recall to guide action, as indicated by infants' performance on AB. *Child Development, 56,* 868–83.

Field, I. M., Woodson, R., Greenberg, R., and Cohen, D. (1982). Discrimination and imitation of facial expressions by neonates. *Science, 218,* 179–81.

Gardner, J., and Gardner, H. (1970). A note on selective imitation by a 6-week-old infant. *Child Development, 41,* 1209–13.

Goldberg, S. (1976). Visual tracking and existence constancy in five-month-old infants. *Journal of Experimental Child Psychology, 22,* 478–91.

Goldfield, E. C., and Dickerson, D. J. (1981). Keeping track of locations during movements in 8- to 10-month-old infants. *Journal of Experimental Child Psychology, 32,* 48–64.

Gratch, G. (1972). A study of the relative dominance of vision and touch in six-month-old infants. *Child Development, 43,* 615–23.

Gratch, G., Appel, K. L., Evans, W. F., LeCompte, G. K., and Wright, N. A. (1974).

Piaget's stage IV object concept error: Evidence of forgetting or object conception? *Child Development, 45*, 71–7.

Harris, P. L. (1973). Perseverative errors in search by young infants. *Child Development, 44*, 28–33.

Hayes, L. A., and Watson, J. S. (1981). Neonatal imitation: Fact or artifact? *Developmental Psychology, 17*, 655–60.

Jacobson, S. W. (1979). Matching behaviour in the young infant. *Child Development, 50*, 425–30.

Kaitz, M., Meschulach-Sarfaty, O., Auerbach, J., and Eidelman, A. (1988). A re-examination of newborns' ability to imitate facial expressions. *Developmental Psychology, 24*, 3–7.

Kaye, K. (1982). *The Mental and Social Life of Babies*. Chicago: University of Chicago Press.

Koepke, J. E., Hamm, M., and Legerstee, M. (1983). Neonatal imitation: Two failures to replicate. *Infant Behaviour and Development, 6*, 97–102.

Kramer, J., Hill, K., and Cohen, L. (1975). Infant's development of object permanence: A refined methodology and new evidence of Piaget's hypothesized ordinality. *Child Development, 46*, 149–55.

Mandler, J. M. (1983). Representation. In P. H. Mussen (Ed.), *Handbook of Child Psychology*, Vol. III: *Cognitive Development*. New York: Wiley.

McGraw, M. B. (1943). *The Neuromuscular Maturation of the Human Infant*. New York: Columbia University Press.

McKenzie, B. E., and Over, R. (1983). Young infants fail to imitate facial and manual gestures. *Infant Behaviour and Development, 6*, 85–95.

Meicler, M., and Gratch, G. (1980). Do five-month-olds show object conception in Piaget's sense? *Infant Behaviour and Development, 3*, 265–82.

Metlzoff, A. N., and Moore, M. K. (1977). Imitation of facial and manual gestures by human neonates. *Science, 198*, 75–8.

Meltzoff, A. N., and Moore, M. K. (1983). Newborn infants imitate adult facial gestures. *Child Development, 54*, 702–9.

Meltzoff, A. N., and Moore, M. K. (1985). Cognitive foundation and social functions of imitation and intermodel representation in infancy. In J. Mehler and R. Fox (Eds.), *Neonate Cognition: Beyond the Blooming Buzzing Confusion*. Hillsdale, NJ: Erlbaum.

Michotte, A. (1955). Perception and cognition. *Acta Psychologica, 11*, 69–91.

Moore, M. K., Borton, R., and Darby, B. L. (1978). Visual tracking in young infants: Evidence for object identity or object permanence? *Journal of Experimental Child Psychology, 25*, 183–98.

Muller, A. A., and Aslin, R. N. (1978). Visual tracking as an index of the object concept. *Infant Behaviour and Development, 1*, 309–19.

Nelson, K. (1971). Accommodation of visual-tracking patterns in human infants to object movement patterns. *Journal of Experimental Child Psychology, 12*, 182–96.

Palmer, S. E. (1978). Fundamental aspects of cognitive representation. In E. Rosch and B. B. Lloyd (Eds.), *Cognition and Categorization*. Hillsdale, NJ: Erlbaum.

Piaget, J. (1936a). *The Origins of Intelligence in a Child*. (Trans. by M. Cook.) London: Routledge and Kegan Paul. 1952.

Piaget, J. (1945). *Play, Dreams and Imitation in Childhood*. (Trans. by C. Gattegno and F. M. Hodgson.) London: Heinemann, 1951.

Prechtl, H. F. R. (1974). Continuity and change in early neural development. In H. F. R. Prechtl (Ed.), *Continuity of Neural Function from Prenatal to Postnatal Life*. Oxford: Blackwell.

Ramsay, D. S., and Campos, J. J. (1978). The onset of representation and entry into stage VI of object permanence development. *Developmental Psychology, 14*, 79–86.

Tinbergen, N. (1951). *A Study of Instinct*. Oxford: Oxford University Press.

Touwen, B. (1976). *Neurological Development in Infancy*. London: Spastics International and Heinemann.

Uzgiris, I. C. (1972). Patterns of vocal and gestural imitation in infants. In F. Monks, W. Hartup, and J. de Wit (Eds.), *Determinants of Behavioural Development*. New York: Academic Press.

Uzgiris, I., and Hunt, J. McV. (1975). *Assessment in Infancy: Ordinal Scales of Psychological Development*. Urbana: III. University of Illinois Press.

Vinter, A. (1986). The role of movement in eliciting early imitations. *Child Development, 57*, 66–71.

# 10 Annette Karmiloff-Smith

## 'Précis of *Beyond Modularity: A Developmental Perspective on Cognitive Science'*

Reprinted in full from: *Behavioral and Brain Sciences* **17**, 693–745 (1994)

It is less illogical than it first appears to speak of instincts for inventiveness. (Marler 1991, p. 63)

## Taking the developmental perspective seriously

*Beyond modularity: A developmental perspective on cognitive science* (Karmiloff-Smith 1992a) not only aims to reach developmental psychologists, but also strives to persuade cognitive scientists to treat cognitive development as a serious theoretical science contributing to the discussion of *how* the human mind/brain develops and is organized internally, and not merely as a cute empirical database addressing the question of the age at which external behaviour can be observed. Nowadays much of the literature focuses on what cognitive science can offer the study of development. In *Beyond modularity*, I concentrate on what a developmental perspective can offer cognitive science and attempt to pinpoint what is specifically human about human cognition.

As Piaget's conception of the sensorimotor infant is being severely undermined by new paradigms for studying infancy, the battle between nativism and constructivism once again rears its rather unconstructive head. In *Beyond modularity*, I do not choose between these two epistemological stances, one arguing for predominantly built-in, domain-specific knowledge, and the other for a minimum innate underpinning to subsequent domain-general learning. Rather, I suggest that nativism (when redefined within a truly epigenetic perspective of genetic expression rather than genetic unfolding), on the one hand, and Piaget's constructivism, on the other, are complementary in fundamental ways, and that the ultimate theory of human cognition will encompass aspects of both. *Beyond modularity* is intended to excite the reader about the possibilities of a developmental perspective embracing both domain-specific predispositions and constructivism and to demonstrate that one can attribute various innate processes/structures to the human neonate without denying the crucial roles of the physical and sociocultural environments and without jeopardizing the deep-seated conviction that we are special – creative, cognitively flexible, capable of conscious reflection, novel invention, and occasional inordinate stupidity!

Developmental psychologists of the Piagetian school are loath to attribute domain-specific predispositions to the human infant, yet they would not hesitate to do so with respect to the ant, the spider, the bee, or the chimpanzee. Why would Nature have endowed every species except the human with some domain-specific predispositions? Yet, if it turns out that all species have such predispositions, that most can maintain a goal in the face of changing environmental conditions, and that most have the capacity for learning on the basis of interaction with conspecifics and the physical environment, what is special about human cognition? Is it simply that the *content* of knowledge differs between species? Is it language that makes humans special? Or, compared to other species, are there qualitatively different processes at work across many domains of the human mind? Does human cognitive change affect all domains of knowledge more or less simultaneously, or does development occur in a domain-specific fashion? These are some of the questions addressed in *Beyond modularity*.

I argue that domain-specific predispositions give development a small but significant kickstart by focusing the young infant's attention on proprietary inputs. The early period is followed by intricate interaction with environmental input which in turn critically affects brain development as subsequent learning takes place. But development does not stop at efficient learning. A fundamental aspect of human development is the hypothesized process by which information that is *in* a cognitive system becomes progressively explicit knowledge *to* that system. I call this the 'representational redescription' hypothesis (henceforth RR). Support for the theoretical discussions of Chapter 1 is explored in Chapters 2 through 6, calling on empirical findings on the child as a linguist, a physicist, a mathematician, a psychologist, and a notator. Each chapter concentrates first on the initial state of the infant mind/brain and on subsequent domain-specific learning in infancy and early childhood, and then goes on to explore empirical data on older children's problem solving and theory building, with particular focus on evolving cognitive flexibility and metacognition. Throughout, I place particular emphasis on the status of representations underlying different capacities and on the multiple levels at which knowledge is stored and accessible.

In Chapters 7 and 8, I reconsider the reconciliation between nativism and Piaget's constructivism, and I discuss the need for more formal developmental models. Here, I compare aspects of the RR framework with connectionist stimulations of development. The book ends with a final look at the RR framework and conjectures about the status of representations underlying the structure of behavior in nonhumans, who never become redescribers of the implicit knowledge embedded in their behavior, no matter how complex the behavior.

If our focus is on cognitive flexibility and conscious access to knowledge, why not explore the data from adult psychology? Surely adults are far more flexible cognitively than children, so what justifies a developmental perspective? Not, rest assured, the fact that child data are 'cute'! One need only glance at the developmental literature to notice that many researchers are absorbed with the ages at which children reach cognitive milestones. Decades of developmental research were wasted, in my view, because the focus was entirely on lowering the age at which children could perform a task successfully, without concern for *how* they processed the information. I once began an article (Karmiloff-Smith 1981, p. 151) as follows: 'The enticing yet awful fact about child development is that children develop! Awful, because it has provoked a plethora of studies, totally unmotivated theoretically, accepted for publication in certain types of journal because the results are 'significant' – significant *statistically*, since it is indeed easy to obtain differential effects between, say, 5 and 7 year olds, but questionable as to their significance *scientifically*.' Some researchers, however, use the study of development as a theoretical tool for exploring the human mind/brain from a cognitive science perspective. We are not really interested in children per se but in human cognition in general, which we believe can be more fully understood via its development.

A developmental perspective is essential to the analysis of human cognition because understanding the predispositions of the human mind/brain, the constraints on subsequent learning, and *how representations change progressively over time* can provide subtle clues to representational format in the adult mind. The work of Spelke (1991), which I discuss in Chapter 3, has been particularly influential in pointing to the importance of a developmental perspective on cognitive science. For example, the processes for segmenting visual arrays into objects are overlaid, in preschool children and adults, by other processes for recognizing object categories. But by focusing on how very young infants segment visual arrays into objects before they are able to categorize certain object kinds, Spelke is able to generate new hypotheses about how the visual system may actually function beyond infancy and in adults.

Another area in which the developmental perspective can change our view of the adult mind concerns the status of different types of representations. Distinctions such as declarative/procedural, conscious/unconscious, explicit/implicit, and controlled/automatic, which are often used to explain cognitive processing in adults, turn out to involve far more than a dichotomy when explored within a developmental context. But in assuming a developmental perspective we must take the notion 'developmental' seriously. Paradoxically, studies on neonates and infants are often not developmental at all. Like studies on adults, they frequently focus not on change but on real-time processing within steady-state systems. It is of course essential to determine the initial state of the human mind/brain, but the 'developmental' notion goes beyond the specification of initial predispositions. It does not simply mean a focus on learning in children of different ages rather than the adult. When one makes theoretical use of development in cognitive science the specific age at which children can successfully perform a task is, to some extent, irrelevant.

A developmental perspective focuses on behavioral and representational change over time. I often use a later phase in a developmental sequence to understand the status of representations underlying earlier behavior – particularly in the interesting cases where child and adult behaviors are practically identical. This notion of *representational change over time* is the focus throughout *Beyond modularity*. It is for all these reasons that I hold that a developmental perspective is essential to cognitive science's efforts to understand the human mind more fully.

**Is the initial architecture of the infant mind/brain modular?**

Fodor's 1983 book, *The modularity of mind*, made a significant impact on developmental theorizing by suggesting how the nativist thesis and the domain-specificity of cognition are relevant to constraints on the architecture of the human mind/brain. In *Beyond modularity*, I critically discuss Fodor's thesis at some length but, since it has been the subject of a BBS treatment (Fodor 1985) it is unnecessary to reiterate all the details in the present Précis. A brief summary suffices to recall that according to Fodor the mind/brain is made up of genetically specified, independently functioning, special-purpose 'modules' (or input systems). Each functionally distinct module has its own dedicated processes and proprietary inputs. Information from the external environment first passes through a system of sensory transducers, which transform the data into formats that each special-purpose module can process. Each module, in turn, outputs data in a common format suitable for central, domain-general processing. The modules are deemed to be hard-wired (not assembled from more primitive processes), of fixed neural architecture, domain specific, fast, autonomous, mandatory, automatic, stimulus driven, giving rise to shallow outputs; they are informationally encapsulated and insensitive to central cognitive goals. For Fodor, it is the co-occurrence of all the properties that defines a module. Modules, then, are the parts of the human mind that are inflexible and unintelligent. They are the stupidity in the machine – but they are just what a young organism might need to get initial cognition off the ground speedily and efficiently.

Fodor posits a built-in dichotomy between what is computed blindly by the modules and what the organism 'believes'. It is in 'central processing' that computations relevant to the human belief system are processed, by deriving top-down hypotheses about what the world is like from the interface between the outputs of modules and what is already stored in long-term memory. Fodor considers central processing, in contrast to modules, to be influenced by what the system already knows, and therefore to be relatively unencapsulated, slow, nonmandatory, controlled, often conscious, and influenced by global cognitive goals. Central processing receives outputs from each module which are automatically translated into a common representational format, a language of thought (Fodor 1975). Central processing, then, is general-purpose. It is devoted to the fixation of belief, the building up of encyclopedic knowledge, and the planning of intelligent action, in contrast to the special-purpose, domain-specific computations of modules.

Although I endorse the importance of some aspects of Fodor's thesis for understanding the human mind/brain, I do not maintain the notion that modules are prespecified in detail, and I question the strictness of the dichotomy that Fodor draws between modules and central processing. I also challenge his contention that the outputs of modules are automatically encoded into a single common language of thought. I focus on the argument that a crucial aspect of development involves the RR process of going beyond modularity.

### Prespecified modules versus a process of gradual modularization

Fodor's detailed account of the encapsulation of modules focuses predominantly on their role in on-line processing. There is little discussion of ontogenesis. I draw a distinction between the notion of prespecified modules versus that of a process of 'modularization' (which, I speculate, occurs repeatedly as the *product* of development). Here I differ from Fodor's strict nativist conception. I hypothesize that if the human mind/brain ends up with any modular structure, then this is the result of a process of modularization *as development proceeds*. My position takes account of the plasticity of early brain development (Johnson 1990; 1993; Neville 1991), suggesting that a fairly limited number of innately specified, domain-specific predispositions would be sufficient to constrain the classes of inputs that the infant mind computes. These predispositions can operate at many different levels and do not have to be limited to representational content (see Karmiloff-Smith 1992b for more recent discussion). It can thus be hypothesized that, *with time*, brain circuits are progressively selected for different domain-specific computations. In certain cases, relatively encapsulated modules would be formed as a product of development. In other cases, there would be more room for influence from other computations.

Only future research using on-line brain activation studies with neonates and young infants can distinguish between the two hypotheses. If Fodor's thesis of prespecified modules is correct, such studies should show that, from the very outset (or the moment at which the infant shows sensitivity to particular forms of input), specific brain circuits are activated in response to domain-specific inputs. By contrast, if the modularization thesis is correct, activation levels should initially be relatively distributed across the brain, and only with time (and this could be a short or relatively long time during infancy, depending on the domain) would specific circuits be activated in response to domain-specific inputs. The modularization thesis allows us to speculate that, although there are maturationally constrained attention biases and domain-specific predispositions that channel the infant's early development, this endowment involves far more than mere triggering. Rather, it interacts richly with, and is in return affected by, the environmental input.

Research with other species also demonstrates the brain's plasticity. In studies of the rat, for example, Greenough et al. (1987) have shown that the brain's losses and gains of synapses are a function of different types of experience. Thus, when placed merely for exercise in a treadmill, the rat shows an increase in blood capillaries in the cerebellum, but a decrease in synapses (due to pruning of existing neural pathways, because of the lack of stimulation other than physical exercise). However, when the rat is placed in a rich environment that challenges it to learn, substantial increases in dendritic growth and synaptic connectivity are generated.

Despite my reservations regarding Fodor's modularity thesis, I, together with a number of cognitive developmentalists, believe that Fodor's thesis has pointed to where a domain-general view of development such as Piaget's is likely to be wrong. In *Beyond modularity*, however, I argue for a more dynamic view of development that Fodor's modularity of mind and I challenge Fodor's dismissal of the relevance of a developmental perspective on cognitive science. Moreover, I question Fodor's often cited claim that 'the limits of modularity are also likely to be the limits of what we are going to be able to understand about the mind' (1983, p. 126). I argue that cognitive scientists can go beyond modularity to study the more creative aspects of human cognition. But my contention is that such an endeavor is greatly enhanced by a developmental perspective on the problem.

### Development from a domain-general perspective

Fodor's nativist thesis is in sharp contrast with domain-general theories of learning, such as Piaget's constructivist epistemology, once so popular in the developmental literature. According to Piagetian theory neither processing nor storage is domain specific. Of course, implicitly at least, Piagetians acknowledge that there are different sensory transducers for vision, audition, touch, and so forth. They do not accept, however, that the transducers transform data into innately specified domain-specific formats for modular processing. Rather, for Piagetians, all data are processed by the same mechanisms and development involves domain-general changes in representational structures.

By opposing the domain-general view to the domain-specific explanation of development, I suggest that Piaget and behaviorism have much in common. Neither the Piagetian nor the behaviorist grants the infant any innate structures or domain-specific knowledge. Each grants only some domain-general, biologically specified processes: for the Piagetians, a set of sensory reflexes and three functional processes (assimilation, accommodation, and equilibration); for the behaviorists, inherited physiological sensory systems and a complex set of laws of association. These domain-general learning processes are held to apply across all areas of linguistic and nonlinguistic cognition. Piaget and the behaviorists thus concur on a number of conceptions about the initial state of the infant mind/brain. The behaviorists saw the infant as a *tabula rasa* with no built-in knowledge (Skinner 1953). Piaget's view of the young infant as assailed by 'undifferentiated and chaotic' inputs (Piaget 1955) is substantially the same.

Needless to say, there are fundamental differences between these two schools. Piagetians view children as active information constructors; behaviorists view them as passive information storers. Piagetians conceive of development as involving fundamental stagelike changes in logical structure, whereas behaviorists invoke a progressive accumulation of knowledge. However, in the present state of developmental theorizing, Piagetians and behaviorists have much in common in their view of the neonate's 'knowledge-empty' mind and their claims that domain-general learning explains subsequent development across all aspects of language and cognition.

## Development from a domain-specific perspective

The domain-specific thesis projects a very different picture of the young infant. Rather than being assailed by incomprehensible, chaotic data from many competing sources, the neonate is seen as having domain-specific predispositions allowing it to process specific types of inputs. Contrary to the Piagetian or the behaviorist theses, the domain-specific thesis gives the infant a very good start. This does not, of course, mean that nothing changes during infancy and beyond; the infant has much to learn, but subsequent learning is guided by innately specified, domain-specific principles, and these principles determine how subsequent learning takes place (Gelman 1990a; Spelke 1991).

Irrespective of whether they agree with Fodor's strict modularity thesis, many psychologists now consider development to be domain-specific. Indeed, much depends on what one understands by 'domain,' and it is important not to confuse domain with 'module.' From the point of view of the child's mind, a domain is the set of representations sustaining a specific area of knowledge: language, number, physics, and so forth. A module is an information-processing unit that encapsulates that knowledge and the computations on it, thus, considering development to be domain specific does not necessarily imply considering it modular. In other words, the storing and processing of information may be domain specific without being encapsulated, hardwired, mandatory, and so on. Throughout *Beyond modularity,* I argue for the domain specificity of development rather than modularity in the strict Fodorian sense. I retain the term 'domain' to cover language, physics, mathematics, and so forth. I also distinguish 'microdomains' such as gravity within the domain of physics and pronoun acquisition within the domain of language. These microdomains can be thought of as subcomponents within particular domains.

The need for this finer distinction of what constitutes a domain stems from the fact that I put forward a *phase* model of development, rather than a *stage* model. In a stage model, such as Piaget's, overarching changes occur more or less contemporaneously across different domains. One alternative view is that broad changes occur within a domain – for example, that a particular type of change occurs first with respect to language and later with respect to physics. The model discussed in *Beyond modularity* differs from both of these. It invokes *recurrent phase changes* at different times across different micro-domains and repeatedly within each domain.

The domain specificity of cognitive systems is also suggested by developmental neuropsychology, that is the existence of children in whom one or more domains are spared or impaired. For example, high functioning autistic individuals show a serious deficit in communication and reasoning about mental states (theory of mind), [see Gopnik: 'How We Know our Minds' *BBS* 16(1) 1993; Tomasello et al.: 'Cultural Learning' *BBS* 16(3) 1993.] the rest of their cognition being relatively unimpaired (Frith 1989). Individuals with Williams syndrome, by contrast, display a very uneven cognitive profile in which language, face recognition, and theory of mind seem relatively spared, whereas number, spatial cognition, and problem solving are severely retarded (Bellugi et al., 1988; Karmiloff-Smith et al. submitted). Whether autism and Williams syndrome involve domain-specific representational deficits or computational deficits, or both, remains an open question. There are also numerous cases of idiot savants in whom only one domain (such as drawing or calender calculation) functions at a high level, while capacities are extremely restricted over the rest of the cognitive system (Hermelin and O'Connor 1986). Domain-general theorists have difficulty explaining such within-domain and across-domain dissociations.

Adult brain damage also points to domain specificity. It is remarkably difficult to find examples in the neuropsychological literature of an across-the-board, domain-general disorder (Marshall 1984), although a case could be made for an overall deficit in planning in patients with prefrontal damage (Shallice 1988). In many instances, however, disorders of higher cognitive functions, as a consequence of brain damage, are often domain-specific – that is, they affect only face recognition, number, language, or some other facility, leaving the other systems relatively intact.

So if adults manifest domain-specific damage, and if it can be shown that infants come into the world with some domain-specific predispositions, does that not mean that the nativists have won the debate over the developmentalists still ensconced on the theoretical shores of Lake Geneva (Piaget's former bastion of antinativism and antimodularity)? Not necessarily, for two reasons. First, most nativist accounts call on detailed genetic unfolding, simply triggered by environmental stimuli. An epigenetic view is very different (see the excellent discussion in Oyama 1985). Second, it is important to bear in mind that the greater the number of the fixed domain-specific properties of the infant mind/brain, the less creative and flexible the subsequent system would be (Chomsky 1988). Although the fixed constraints provide an initial adaptive advantage, there is a tradeoff between efficiency and automaticity, on the one hand, and relative inflexibility, on the other. This leads me to a crucial point: *The more complex the picture we ultimately build of the innately specified predispositions of the infant mind, the more important it becomes for us to explain the flexibility of subsequent cognitive development.* It is toward such an end – exploring the flexibility and creativity of the human mind beyond the initial state – that my work in language acquisition and cognitive development has been concentrated, in an attempt to determine both the domain-specific and the domain-general contributions to development. It is implausible that development will turn out to be entirely domain specific *or* entirely domain general. And, although I will need to invoke some initial constraints, development clearly involves a more dynamic process of interaction between mind/ brain and environment than the strict nativist stance presupposes.

### Reconciling nativism and Piaget's constructivism

What theory of development could encompass the dynamics of a rich process of interaction between mind/brain and environment? At first blush, a theory with a central focus on epigenesis and constructivism, like Piaget's, would seem the most appropriate. The notion of constructivism in Piaget's theory is the equivalent at the cognitive level of the notion of epigenesis at the level of gene expression. For Piaget, both gene expression and cognitive development are emergent products of a self-organizing system that is directly affected by its interaction with the environment. Fodor (1983, p. 33) uses the term 'constructivism' very differently from Piaget. For Fodor, it is a form of empiricism, whereas Piaget argued that his constructivist genetic epistemology was an alternative to both nativism and empiricism. This general aspect of Piaget's theory, if more formalized, may well turn out to be appropriate for future explorations of the notion of progressive modularization discussed above. Much of the rest of Piaget's theory, however, has come under a great deal of criticism.

A growing number of cognitive developmentalists have become disenchanted with Piaget's account of the infant as a purely sensorimotor organism. For Piaget, the newborn has no domain-specific knowledge, merely sensory reflexes and the three domain-general processes of assimilation, accommodation, and equilibration. By contrast, the infancy research I discuss in the first part of Chapters 2 through 6 of *Beyond modularity* suggests that there is considerably more to the initial state of the mind/brain than Piaget's theory posits. But the exclusive focus of nativists like Fodor and Chomsky on biologically specified modules suggests that they think there is nothing of interest to say about development beyond modularity. Moreover, Fodor's concentration on input systems – he has far less to say about either output systems or central processing – does not help us to explore the ways in which children turn out to be active participants in the construction of their own knowledge.

Although for Chomsky (1988) and Spelke (1991) a nativist/modularity stance precludes constructivism, I argue that nativism and Piaget's epigenetic constructivism are not necessarily incompatible, with certain provisos. First, to Piaget's view one must add some innately specified predispositions that would give the epigenetic process a head start in each domain. This does not imply merely adding a little more domain-general structure than Piaget supposed. Rather, it means adding domain-specific biases to the initial endowment. But the second proviso for the marriage of constructivism and nativism is that the initial endowment involves far less detailed specifications than some nativists presuppose, and a more progressive process of modularization (as opposed to prespecified modules) where the structure of the input plays an essential role in the structure of the resulting module. Fodor does not, for instance, discuss the cases in which the operation of one of his prespecified modules cannot be triggered by its proprietary input (e.g., auditory input in the case of the congenitally deaf). We know that in such cases the brain selectively adapts and reconfigures itself to receive other (e.g., visuomanual) nonauditory inputs (Changeux 1985; Neville 1991; Poizner et al. 1987). Many cases of early brain damage indicate that there is far more plasticity in the brain than Fodor's strict modularity would imply. The brain is not prestructured with ready-made representations which are simply triggered by environmental stimuli; it is channeled to progressively *develop* representations via interaction with both the external environment and its own internal environment. Furthermore, it is important not to equate innateness with presence at birth or with the notion of a static genetic blueprint for maturation. Whatever innate component we invoke, it becomes part of our biological potential only through interaction with the environment; it is latent until it receives input (Johnson 1988; 1993; Marler 1991; Oyama 1985; Thelen 1989) and the input required is either relatively specific or simply in the form of environmental stimuli per se (Greenough et al. 1987; Johnson and Bolhuis 1991). The interaction with the input crucially in turn affects the development of the brain.

Nativists argue that development follows similar paths because all normal children start life with the same innately specified structures. The role of the environment is reduced to that of a mere trigger. [See Lightfoot: 'The Child's Trigger Experience: Degree-0 Learnability' *BBS* 12(2) 1989; Crain: 'Language Acquisition in the Absence of Experience' *BBS* 14(4) 1991.] But the fact that development proceeds in similar ways across normal children does not necessarily mean that development must be innately specified in detail, because it is *also* true that all children evolve in a species-typical environment (Johnson and Morton 1991) and we are discovering that environments are more structured than was originally thought (see Elman 1990; 1993). Thus, it is the *interaction* between similar innate constraints and similar environmental constraints that gives rise to common developmental paths.

The proposed reconciliation of nativism and constructivism will allow us to adhere to Piaget's epigenetic-constructivist view of the developmental process but to drop his insistence on domain generality in favor of a more domain-specific approach. Furthermore, the Piagetian focus on output systems (i.e., on the infant's and the child's *action on* the environment) is an important addition to the nativist's accent on input systems. But Piaget's strong anti-nativism and his arguments for across-the-board major structural stages no longer constitute a viable developmental framework.

The need to invoke domain specificity is apparent throughout *Beyond modularity*. For example, domain-general sensorimotor development alone cannot explain the acquisition of language. Syntax does not derive simply from exploratory problem solving with toys, as some Piagetians claim. [cf. interesting discussion by Greenfield: 'Language, Tools and Brain' *BBS* 14(4) 1991.] Lining up objects does not form the basis for word order. Trying to fit one toy inside another has nothing to do with embedded clauses. General sensorimotor activity alone cannot account for specifically linguistic constraints. If it could, then it would be difficult to see why chimpanzees, who manifest rich sensorimotor and representational abilities, do not acquire anything remotely resembling the complex structure of human language despite very extensive training (Premack 1986).

Despite these criticisms of Piaget's view of early infancy and my rejection of his stage view of development, I hope that *Beyond modularity* will persuade readers that important aspects of Piaget's epistemology should be salvaged, and that there is far more to cognitive development than the unfolding of a genetically specified program simply triggered by environmental stimuli. If we are to understand the human mind, our focus must stretch well beyond any innate specifications and embrace the interaction of both domain-specific constraints and domain-general processes.

## The empirical data

Because of the space limitations of a Précis, I refer the reader to Chapters 2 through 6 in *Beyond modularity* for discussions of the empirical data and the literature referenced therein. New infancy research and the *representational status of infant knowledge* form the detailed focus of the first part of each chapter, showing the linguistic, physical, mathematical, psychological, and notational domain-specific constraints on early development. Future research may lead to reinterpretations of the present infancy data, but I remain convinced that we will have to invoke *some* domain-specific predispositions which initially constrain the infant mind/brain. For each cognitive domain, I go on to consider data suggesting that development involves much more than the domain-specific constraints. My research strategy has always been rather different from that of developmentalists who study a given capacity, from failure to partial success through to complete mastery. By contrast, I focus on an age group in each domain where the particular capacity under study is already proficient. I then attempt to trace subsequent representational change. The most important and subtle data in Chapters 2–6 are, in my view, those pointing to a level of representation in which knowledge is explicitly defined (i.e., represented differently from the information embedded in special-purpose domain-specific procedures of the earlier phase) but not yet available to conscious access and verbal report. Spontaneous repairs to linguistic output, unsuccessful problem solving subsequent to success, redundant behaviors, and so forth (data often ignored in developmental and adult research) are all used as vital clues to this phase of development.

At several points throughout *Beyond modularity*, I allude to abnormal development. Nature, alas, often presents the scientist with experiments of its own, in which different capacities are either spared or impaired. Such cases warrant study in their own right, but they also help us gain a deeper understanding of normal development and domain specificity/modularity. Again, for space reasons I merely allude to them here (for more recent detailed discussion, see Karmiloff-Smith 1992c).

Development involves, then, two complementary processes of progressive modularization and progressive explicitation. In the remainder of this Précis, I will concentrate on the second of these two processes, that is, on my hypothesis that development involves representational redescription, a process that increases the flexibility and manipulability of the knowledge stored in the mind, by turning information that is *in* the mind into progressively more explicit knowledge *to* the mind.

## Beyond domain-specific constraints: How new knowledge gets into the mind

How does information get stored in the child's mind? I argue that there are several different ways. One is via innate specification as the result of evolutionary processes. Predispositions can be either specific or nonspecific (Johnson and Bolhuis 1991). In both cases, environmental input is of course necessary. Should an innate component be specified in detail (if it ever is), then it is likely that the environment acts simply as a trigger for the organism to select one parameter or circuit over others (Changeux 1985; Chomsky 1981; Piatelli-Palmerini 1989). By contrast, when a predisposition is specified merely as a bias or as a skeletal outline, then the environment acts as much more than a trigger, it influences the subsequent structure of the brain via a rich epigenetic interaction between the mind/brain and the physical/sociocultural environment (for discussions, see Johnson and Karmiloff-Smith 1992). The skeletal outline involves attention biases toward particular inputs and a certain number of predispositions constraining the computation of those inputs.

There are several other ways in which new information gets stored in the child's mind. One occurs when the child fails to reach a goal and must take information from the physical environment into account. New knowledge is also acquired when the child has to take into account and to represent information provided by the sociocultural environment, often in the form of a direct linguistic statement. These are both external sources of change from environmental input, but there are also internal sources of change. One is illustrated by the above-mentioned process of modularization when input and output processing become progressively less influenced by other processes in the brain. This causes knowledge to become more encapsulated and less accessible to other systems. Another essential facet of cognitive change goes in the opposite direction, however, with knowledge becoming progressively more accessible.

My claim is that a specifically human way to gain knowledge is for the mind to exploit internally the information that it has already stored, by redescribing its representations or, more precisely, by iteratively rerepresenting in different representational formats what its internal representations represent. This is what I hypothesize is particular to human cognition (see details in section 9 below).

Finally, there is a form of knowledge change that is far more obviously restricted to the human species: explicit theory change, which involves conscious construction and exploration of analogies, thought experiments and real experiments, typical of older children and adults (Carey 1985; Klahr 1992; Kuhn et al. 1988). I argue, however, that this more obvious characteristic of human cognition is possible only on the basis of the more subtle prior representational redescription, which turns *implicit* information embedded in special-purpose procedures into *explicit* knowledge but is not yet available to conscious verbal report.

To give a more tangible feel for the theoretical discussion on which I am about to embark, let's consider the pathway to learning to play the piano. There is a first period during which a sequence of separate notes is laboriously practiced. The beginning pianist pays conscious attention to particular notes. There is a second period during which chunks of several notes are played together as blocks, until finally the whole piece can be played more or less automatically. In other words, the sequence gradually becomes proceduralized (see Anderson 1980). It is something like this that I call 'reaching behavioral mastery.' But the automaticity is constrained by the fact that the learner can neither start in the middle of the piece nor play variations on a theme (Hermelin and O'Connor 1989). The performance is generated, I hypothesize, by procedural representations which are simply run off in their entirety. There is little flexibility. At best, in a third period, the learner is able to play the *whole piece* softer, louder, slower, or faster. The pianist's 'knowledge' is embedded in the procedural representations sustaining the execution. But most learners do not stop there. During a fourth period, the learner can interrupt the piece and start at, say, the third bar without having to go back to the beginning and repeat the entire procedure from the outset.

I hypothesize that this fourth period cannot take place on the basis of the automatized procedural representations. Rather, it involves a process of representational redescription such that the knowledge of the different notes and chords (rather than simply their run-off sequence) becomes available as manipulable data. It is only after a period of behavioral mastery that the pianist can generate variations on a theme, change sequential order of bars, introduce insertions from other pieces, and so forth. This differentiates, for instance, jazz improvisation from strict adherence to sheet music. The end result is representational flexibility and control, which allows for creativity. Also important is the fact that the earlier proceduralized capacity is not lost: for certain goals, pianists can call on the automatic skill; for others, they call on the more explicit representations that allow for flexibility and creativity. (Of course, the playing of some pianists remains simply at the procedural level.)

This movement from implicit information embedded in an efficient problem-solving procedure, to rendering the knowledge progressively more explicit, is a theme that recurs throughout *Beyond modularity*. And this, together with the process of modularization discussed earlier, is precisely what I think development is about. Children are not satisfied with success in learning to talk or to solve problems; they want to understand how they do these things. In seeking such understanding, they become little theorists and to do so they have to change the nature of their internal representations.

Development and learning, then, seem to take two complementary directions. On the one hand, they involve the gradual process of proceduralization and at times modularization (that is, rendering behavior more automatic and less accessible). On the other hand, they involve a process of 'explicitation' and increasing accessibility (that is, explicitly representing information that is implicit in the procedural representations). Both are relevant to cognitive change, but the main focus of *Beyond modularity* is the process by which the representational 'explicitation' which, I posit, occurs in a variety of linguistic and cognitive domains throughout development.

## The process of representational redescription

For a number of years I have been trying to understand how internal representations change in the course of development, even when overt behavior may look identical. In this attempt, I have developed the hypothesis of a reiterative process of *representational redescription* (RR). First, I will make some general points about the hypothesis; then I will provide a summary.

The notion of RR attempts to account for the way in which children's representations become progressively more manipulable and flexible. Ultimately, this leads, in each domain at different times, to the emergence of conscious access to knowledge and children's theory building. RR involves a cyclical process by which information already present in the organism's independently functioning, special-purpose representations is made progressively available, via redescriptive processes, to other parts of the cognitive system, first within a domain and then sometimes across domains.

The RR process is posited to occur spontaneously as part of an internal drive toward the creation of intradomain and interdomain relationships. Although I stress the endogenous nature of representational redescription, clearly the process may at times also be triggered by external influences.

The actual *process* of RR is domain general, but it is crucially affected by the form and level of explicitness of the representations supporting particular domain-specific knowledge at a given time. When I state that RR is domain-general, I do not mean to imply that it involves a simultaneous change across domains. Rather, I mean that, within each domain, the RR process operates in a similar way.

Let us look now at the RR hypothesis in some detail. Development, I argue, involves three *recurrent* phases. During the first phase the child focuses predominantly on information from the external environment. This initial learning is data driven. Phase 1 culminates in consistently successful performance on whatever microdomain has reached that level. This is what I term 'behavioral mastery.' Behavioral mastery does not necessarily imply that the underlying representations are equivalent to the adult's, even though the behavioral output may be the same. The same performance (say, correctly producing a particular linguistic form, or managing to balance blocks on a narrow support) can be generated at various ages by very different representations. Later (phase 3) behavior may appear identical to phase 1 behavior. We thus need to draw a distinction between 'behavioral change' (which sometimes gives rise to a U-shaped developmental curve) and 'representational change' because behavioral mastery is not tantamount to the end point of the developmental progression in a given mocrodomain.

Phase 1 is followed by an internally driven phase during which the child no longer focuses on the external data. Rather, system-internal dynamics take over such that internal representations become the focus of change. In phase 2, the current state of the child's representations of knowledge in a microdomain predominate over information from the incoming data. The temporary disregard for features of the external environment during phase 2 can lead to new errors and inflexibilities. This can, but does not necessarily, give rise to a decrease in successful behavior – a U-shaped developmental curve. This is deterioration at the behavioral level, not at the representational level.

Finally, during phase 3, internal representations and external data are reconciled, and a balance is achieved between the quests for internal and external control. In the case of language, for example, a new mapping is made between input and output representations in order to restore correct usage.

But what about the format of the internal representations that sustain these reiterated phases? The RR framework argues for at least four levels at which knowledge is represented and re-represented. I have termed them Implicit (I), Explicit-1 (E1), Explicit-2 (E2), and Explicit-3 (E3). The RR framework postulates different representational formats at different levels. At level I, representations are in the form of procedures or action patterns for responding to stimuli in the external environment. A number of constraints operate on the representational adjunctions that are formed at this level:

- Information is encoded in procedural form.
- The procedure-like encodings are sequentially specified.
- New representations are independently stored.
- Level-1 representations are bracketed, and hence no intradomain or interdomain representational links can yet be formed.

Information embedded in level-1 representations is therefore not available to other operators in the cognitive system. Thus, if two procedures or action patterns contain identical information, this potential interrepresentational commonality is not yet represented in the child's mind. A procedure *as a whole* is available as data to other operators; however, its *component parts* are not. It takes developmental time and representational redescription (see discussion of level E1 below) for component parts to become available for the marking of potential intradomain and interdomain relationships, a process which ultimately leads to interrepresentational flexibility and creative problem-solving capacities (see discussion of levels E2/E3). At this first level, however, the potential representational links and the information embedded in procedures or action patterns remain implicit. This gives rise to the ability to compute specific inputs in preferential ways and to respond rapidly and effectively to the environment. But the behavior generated from level-1 representations is relatively inflexible.

Level-E1 representations are the result of redescription, into a new format, of the procedurally encoded representations at level-I. The redescriptions are abstractions and, unlike level-I representations, they are not bracketed (that is, the component parts are now open to potential intradomain and interdomain representational links). The E1 representations are reduced descriptions that lose many of the details of the procedurally encoded information. As a nice example of what I have in mind here, consider the details of the grated image delivered to the perceptual system of a person who sees a zebra (Mandler 1992). A redescription of this into 'striped animal' (either linguistic or image-like) has lost much of the perceptual precision. To Mandler's discussion, I would add that the redescription allows the *cognitive* (as opposed to the *perceptual*) system to understand the analogy between an actual zebra and the road sign for a so-called 'zebra crossing' (a European crosswalk with broad, regular, black and yellow stripes), although the zebra and the road sign deliver very different inputs to the *perceptual* system. A species without representational redescriptions would not make the analogy between the zebra and the zebra crossing sign. The redescribed representation is, on the one hand, simpler and less special-purpose but, on the other, more flexible cognitively (because it is transportable to other goals and useable to make other inferences). Unlike perceptual representations, conceptual redescriptions are productive; they make possible the invention of new terms (e.g., 'zebrin,' the antibody which stains certain classes of cells in striped patterns).

Note that the original level-I representations remain intact in the child's mind and can continue to be called for particular cognitive goals which require speed and automaticity. The redescribed representations are used for other goals where explicit knowledge is required.

As representations are redescribed into the E1 format, we witness the beginnings of a flexible cognitive system upon which the child's nascent theories can subsequently be built. Level-E1 representations go beyond the constraints imposed at level 1, where procedure-like representations are simply used in response to external stimuli. Once knowledge previously embedded in procedures is explicitly defined, the potential relationships between procedural components can then be marked and represented internally. Moreover, once redescription has taken place and explicit representations become manipulable, children can introduce violations to their data-driven, veridical descriptions of the world – violations which allow for instance, for pretend play, false belief, and the use of counterfactuals.

It is important to stress that although E1 representations are available as data to the system, they are not available to conscious access and verbal report. Throughout the book I examine examples of the formation of explicit representations which are not yet accessible to conscious reflection and verbal report, but which are clearly beyond the procedural level. In general, developmentalists have not distinguished between implicitly stored knowledge and E1 representations in which knowledge *is* explicitly represented but is not yet consciously accessible. Rather, they have drawn a dichotomy between an undefined notion of something implicit in behavior (as if information were not represented in any form) and consciously accessible knowledge that can be stated in verbal form. According to the RR framework, the human representational system is far more complex than a mere dichotomy. It is particularly via a developmental perspective that one can pinpoint this multiplicity of levels of representational formats.

In the RR framework, conscious access and verbal report are possible only at levels beyond E1. At level E2, it is hypothesized, representations are available to conscious access but not to verbal report (which is possible only at level E3). Although for some theorists consciousness is reduced to verbal reportability, in the RR framework E2 representations are accessible to consciousness but they are in a representational code similar to that of the E1 representations of which they are redescriptions. Thus, for example, E1 spatial representations are recoded into consciously accessible E2 *spatial* representations. (We often draw diagrams of problems we cannot easily verbalize.)

At level E3, knowledge is recoded into a cross-system code. This common format is hypothesized to be close enough to natural language for easy translation into statable, communicable form. It is possible that some knowledge learned directly in linguistic form is immediately stored at level E3. Children learn a lot from verbal interaction with others, but knowledge may be stored in linguistic code and not yet linked to similar knowledge stored in other representational formats. Linguistic knowledge (e.g., a mathematical principle governing subtraction) often fails to constrain nonlinguistic knowledge (e.g., an algorithm used for actually doing subtraction) until both have been redescribed into a similar format, so that interrepresentational constraints can operate (Hennessy 1986).

The empirical examples throughout *Beyond modularity* illustrate levels 1, E3, and particularly the subtleties of level E1. In the book, I do not distinguish between levels E2 and E3, both of which, I believe, involve conscious access, because thus far research has not been directly focused on level E2 (conscious access without verbal report). Most, if not all, metacognitive studies focus on verbal report (i.e., level E3). Thus, E2 remains to be tested empirically. Nevertheless, I do not wish to foreclose the possibility of spatial, kinesthetic, and other *nonlinguistically encoded* representations that are available to conscious access, and it may well be that E2 and E3 redescriptional formats are both made directly on the basis of the E1 format, rather than E3 being a redescription of E2. This is discussed fully in Chapter 1.

The end result of these various redescriptions is the existence in the mind of multiple representations of similar knowledge at different levels of detail and explicitness. This notion of multiple encoding is important; the development of the mind does not seem to be a drive for economy. Indeed, the human mind may turn out to be a very redundant store of knowledge and processes.

Let me stress again the concept of reiterative developmental phases. There is no such thing as a 'phase E2 child.' The child's representations are in different representational formats with respect to particular microdomains.

Although the process of representational redescription can occur on line, I suggest that it also takes place without ongoing analysis of incoming data or production of output. Thus, change can occur outside normal input/output relations, that is, simply as the product of system-internal dynamics, when there are no external pressures. Representational change *within* phases involves adding representations; here, negative feedback (failure, incompletion, inadequacy, mismatch between input and output, etc.) plays an important role, leading progressively to behavioral mastery. But in the transition *between* phases, it is hypothesized that *positive* feedback is essential to the onset of representational redescription. In other words, according to this success-based view of cognitive change, it is representations that have reached a stable state (the child having reached behavioral mastery) that are redescribed. Representational redescription is a process of 'appropriating' stable states to extract the information they contain, which can then be used more flexibly for other purposes. Many of the studies discussed in *Beyond modularity*, and new data from Siegler and Crowley (1991), show that change often follows success, not only failure. In other words, children explore domain-specific environments beyond their successful interaction with them.

This is not to deny the importance of instability, failure, conflict, and competition as generators of other types of change (Bates and MacWhinney 1987; Piaget 1967a; Thelen 1989). It is worth reiterating this point. Competition can occur on line between different processes and can cause behavioral change, but the hypothesis I develop throughout *Beyond modularity* is that competition leading to representational change takes place after each of the potential competitors has been consolidated (i.e., is stable in its own right). In Chapter 3, for example, it is shown how counterexamples are not taken into account (do not have the status of a counterexample) until the child's theory about a particular microdomain has been consolidated. Similar examples are to be found in the history of science and in children's strategies of scientific experimentation (Klahr and Dunbar 1988; Kuhn et al. 1988; Kuhn and Phelps 1982; Schauble 1990), as well as across the various domains of knowledge discussed throughout *Beyond modularity*.

### Are there domain-general processes at work?

Invoking domain-specific constraints on development does not deny the existence of some domain-general mechanisms. The infancy tasks explored in each chapter make it very clear that infants can call on complex inferential processes across different domains. Moreover, young infants go well beyond sensorimotor encodings and make use of domain-general processes such as representational redescription to recode sensorimotor input into accessible formats (see also Mandler 1992). Domain-general processes sustaining inference and representational redescription operate throughout development, but invoking general *processes* that are the same across different domains is not equivalent to invoking domain-general *stages of change*. It is the latter that *Beyond modularity* rejects.

Yet there might turn out to be *some* across-the-board domain-general changes also, perhaps linked to major maturation of particular regions of the brain (e.g. prefrontal cortex). One such change suggested by an abundance of empirical data seems to occur around 18 months of age. This holds for several domains, particularly with respect to holding two representations simultaneously in mind and representing hypothetical events in general (Meltzoff 1990; Perner 1991), rather than theory-of-mind computations in particular (Leslie 1991). Eighteen months is also the age Piaget singled out for a change in representational structure which allowed for the onset of pretend play, language, and mental imagery. The precise way in which Piaget accounted for such a change in terms of the closure of a purely sensorimotor period is likely to be wrong, but the conviction that something fundamental occurs around 18 months may turn out to be well-founded.

The other age at which an across-the-board, domain-general change may occur is somewhere around three and a half to four years. This age does not correspond to a stage change in Piagetian theory, but it seems to be when fundamental changes occur in various domains. Moreover, this is also roughly the age at which the human child differs radically from the chimpanzee. As Premack (1991, p. 164) put it, 'a good rule of thumb has proved to be: if the child of three and a half years cannot do it, neither can the chimpanzee.'

If it turns out that across-the-board, domain-general changes do occur, we may be able to use them as a diagnostic for fundamental neural changes in the brain, and vice versa. This of course remains an open question, but the flourishing new field of developmental cognitive neuroscience may soon provide some relevant answers. Even if some across-the-board changes were to hold, however, it is important to recall that their effects would be manifest somewhat differently across domains, since they would interact with domain-specific constraints. Development will not turn out to be *either* domain-specific *or* domain-general. It is clearly the intricate interaction of *both* – more domain-general than is presupposed by most nativist/modularity views of development, but more domain-specific than Piagetian theory envisages.

So, does Piagetian theory retain any role in developmental theorizing? To me, the answer is affirmative. Theories of cognitive development (and recent connectionist modeling of cognitive development [McClelland and Jenkins 1990; Parisi 1990; Plunkett and Sinha 1992], which I discuss in Chapter 8) continue to draw inspiration from Piaget's *epistemology* – his quest to understand emergent properties and his general stance with regard to epigenesis and the importance of the child's action on the environment. It is the details of his *psychological* description of across-the-board stagelike changes in logicomathematical structure that are no longer viable. I believe that it is possible to retain the essence of Piagetian theory while doing away with stage and structure. The problem with Piaget's theory (and indeed, with the RR framework too), however, is that it is underspecified in comparison with, say, theories expressed as computer models. I now turn briefly to this issue.

## Modeling development

One of the aims of *Beyond modularity* is to persuade cognitive scientists of the value of a developmental perspective for understanding the workings of the human mind. Yet, at the heart of much of the work in cognitive science is the use of computer models to test psychological theories. It is therefore essential to devote some space to a discussion of how the RR framework might be relevant to attempts to express developmental theories in the form of computer simulations.

What type of framework is RR? Throughout *Beyond modularity*, I describe RR in verbal terms. It is, as Klahr (1992) has put it, at the 'soft-core' end of the modeling of cognitive development, the 'hard-core' end being the implementation of theories as computer programs. Klahr's contrast captures an important distinction between a focus on general principles of development and a focus on the specification of precise mechanisms. Klahr argues that the very process of simulating development in the form of computer programs leads to insights about the mechanisms underlying developmental change, whereas verbal descriptions generally underspecify the mechanisms. I agree, but soft-core and hard-core approaches should not be considered mutually exclusive.

In my view, soft-core approaches often lead to a broader intuitive understanding of general principles of change, whereas both the information-processing use of the flow chart and the symbolic approach to computer simulation run the risk of reifying into one or more boxes of single-named operators what is in fact the product of a highly interactive system. Nonetheless, at the hard-core end of modeling there have been a number of interesting attempts to express developmental theories in various information-processing terms – for example, in the form of scripts (Nelson 1986; Schank and Abelson 1977), developmental contingency models (Morton 1986), and self-modifying production systems (Klahr et al. 1987). In Chapter 8, however, I take as my main example some recent connectionist simulations, since they seem to be closest to the spirit of epigenesis and constructivism (for fuller discussions, see Bates and Elman 1993; Clark and Karmiloff-Smith 1993; Elman et al., in press; Karmiloff-Smith 1992b; 1992c; Karmiloff-Smith and Clark 1993; McClelland and Jenkins 1990; Parisi 1990; Plunkett and Sinha 1992). Connectionist simulations also address the problems I raise in *Beyond modularity* with respect to stage theories, in that they show that by incremental learning one can obtain stagelike shifts in overt behavior without the need for qualitatively different structures and mechanisms (McClelland and Jenkins 1990).

Although the connectionist framework has come under severe criticism (Pinker and Mehler 1988), a growing number of cognitive developmentalists see within this framework a considerable theoretical potential for explicating the more general tenets of Piaget's epistemology (e.g., Bates and Elman 1993; Bechtel and Abrahamsen 1991; Elman et al., in press; Karmiloff-Smith 1992b; 1992c; Clark and Karmiloff-Smith 1993; Karmiloff-Smith and Clark 1993; McClelland and Jenkins 1990; Plunkett and Sinha 1992). Moreover, a number of features of the RR framework, developed quite independently in the 1970s and early 1980s, map interestingly onto features of recent connectionist simulations.

Chapter 8 of *Beyond modularity* describes the main features of connectionist models, but since a BBS treatment has dealt extensively with such models (Smolensky 1988), I will not repeat the description in the Précis. Instead, I will go on to explore directly the extent to which connectionist simulations can and cannot capture what I deem to be crucial to a model of developmental change. To the extent that they can, connectionism would offer the RR framework a powerful set of hard-core tools by applying the mathematical theory of complex dynamical systems to cognitive development (van Geehrt 1991). And to the extent that connectionist models fail to model development adequately, the RR framework suggests some crucial modifications.

Many of the details of phase 1 learning, which leads to behavioral mastery and level-I representations, turn out to be captured particularly well in a connectionist model. However, the very aspect of development on which *Beyond modularity* focuses – the process of representational redescription – is precisely what seems to be missing from connectionist simulations of development.

**Connectionism: The starting state, the role of the input, and the process of representational redescription**

Let us now look at some of the specific issues discussed throughout *Beyond modularity* and how they can be informed by, as well as inform, the connectionist framework.

*The starting state*

Most connectionist researchers adopt a non-nativist view as their research strategy. This makes it possible to explore the extent to which developmental phenomena can be simulated from a *tabula rasa* starting state – that is, from random weights and random activation levels, with no domain-specific knowledge. This has led some to interpret the results of connectionist modeling as strong evidence for the antinativist position, but there is nothing about the connectionist framework that precludes the introduction of initial biased weights and connections (i.e., the equivalents of innately specified predispositions as a result of evolution) rather than random weights and connections. Also, specific architectures, learning algorithms, learning rates, and so on which are part of the starting state, clearly affect how an input set is learned.

Various ways of simulating developmental change have been proposed. One is to start a network with a small number of hidden units and, as 'development' proceeds, to recruit more and more units or an extra hidden layer to compress the data even further (Shultz 1991). This is rather like the neo-Piagetians' notion that processing capacity increases with age (Case 1985; Halford 1982). Other researchers (Bechtel and Abrahamsen 1991) have suggested the equivalent of 'maturational' change, such that the network would start by using one learning algorithm (e.g., contrastive Hebbian learning) and, with maturation, come to use a different learning algorithm (e.g., backpropagation). Incremental learning has also been used, such that the network first sees only part of the input at a time, rather than the whole input set in one go (Elman 1990; Plunkett and Marchman 1991). These are all domain-general solutions to developmental change, but we are beginning to witness an increasing tendency on the part of connectionists to explore the ways in which domain-specific constraints might also shape learning. This is in my view, likely to be a future focus for connectionist models of development.

It might seem at present that connectionist models deny, either implicitly or explicitly, the need for domain-specific learning. In favor of domain generality, connectionists stress that their models use the *same* learning algorithms for different categories of input presented to different networks. But, in effect, architectures are fine-tuned to specific types of input. For example, a recurrent architecture is used for sequential input (see Elman 1990) whereas an associative network is used for concept learning (see Plunkett and Sinha 1992). To my knowledge, little work has been done on networks which progressively develop their own architecture as a function of the input they happen to process. Moreover, no single network has been presented with an array of inputs from *different* domains (e.g., language, spatial tasks, tasks involving physical principles). Networks designed to simulate language acquisition (e.g., Elman 1990; 1993) see only linguistic strings. A similar network could be used for physics input, but the very same network could not be used without totally upsetting the language learning that has already taken place unless it also continues to be trained on the original set. In other words, the fact that each network is dedicated to a specific type of input, in a specific learning task, with a specific architecture and learning algorithm, turns out to be equivalent to domain specificity in the human. Infants seem to process proprietary, domain-specific inputs separately, and so do networks. We will probably end up requiring multiple networks with different architectures and different learning algorithms.

A final point with respect to the starting state: networks are not 'modules' in the sense of the distinction I drew between modules and a process of modularization. In fact, networks mimic the process of modularization because, with few or no built-in representational biases, it is only as learning proceeds that they *become* increasingly like special-purpose modules.

*The role of the input*

Although connectionist models have potential for developmental theorizing, they have several shortcomings. One concerns the input presented to networks. First, decisions about input representation are entirely external to the network and often are not motivated theoretically. Second, with some exceptions, connectionists have, until now, not really modeled development; they have modeled *tasks*. This becomes particularly apparent if we look at the example of the balance scale that is so popular in all kinds of computer modeling, including connectionist (Langley et al. 1987; McClelland and Jenkins 1990; Newell 1990; Shultz 1991; Siegler and Robinson 1982). The models have focused on children's performance on the balance-scale tasks, not on how children learn about general physical phenomena in real life (see also Shultz 1991 for discussion). Many children come to a balance scale experiment with no experience of balance scales, but this does not mean that they bring no relevant knowledge to the task. They may focus on weight in tasks using the traditional balance scale because weights are what the experimenter more obviously manipulates. But in other block balancing tasks not presented in the form of a balance scale, many young children ignore weight and focus solely on length. Children come to such tasks having already learned something about how rulers fall from tables, how seesaws work, and so forth. But a seesaw is not a balance scale. It does not have a neat line of equidistant pegs on which children of absolutely equal weight can be placed one on top of another! Development is not simply task-specific learning. It involves deriving knowledge from many sources and using that knowledge in a goal oriented way. Thus, in my view, far richer input vectors and the simulation of goal oriented behaviors are needed if we are to model the ways in which real children learn in real environments.

*Behavioral mastery*

Chapter 3, on the child as a physicist, and Chapter 6, on the child as a notator, give particularly clear examples of how a lengthy period of behavioral mastery precedes representational change. Indeed, throughout *Beyond modularity*, I argue that behavioral mastery is a prerequisite for representational change. An analysis of learning in a connectionist network, however, already reveals in the hidden units the existence of some representation of subsequent change *before* it is observable in the output. This suggests a way in which connectionist modeling might change the RR framework in that full behavioral mastery may not be a prerequisite to change; that is, representational change may start to occur prior to *overt* behavioral mastery.

*Implicit to explicit representational change*

It has often been difficult to convey, particularly to developmental psychologists, precisely what I meant by 'level-I implicit representations.' [See also Shanks and St John: 'Characteristics of Dissociable Human Learning Systems' *BBS* 17(3) 1994.] Researchers have often used the term 'implicit' to explain away efficient behavior that appears 'too early' for the tenets of a particular theory, but no definition of implicit has been offered. The connectionist framework may help to give a more precise definition. Indeed, some recent connectionist simulations of language learning (Elman 1990; 1993), for instance, are particularly illustrative of the status of implicit level-I representations. Elman's model is discussed fully in *Beyond modularity*. It demonstrates how grammatical function (noun/verb, transitive/intransitive verb, singular/plural, etc.) can be progressively inferred from statistical regularities of the input set and can be represented in the hidden units as learning proceeds. The full details of the learning process need not concern us here, rather, we should focus on the *status of the representations* that the network progressively builds. First, Elman shows that, as with most connectionist networks using nonlinear functions, a lengthy initial period is essential to learning. At first, the network's predictions are random. However, with time the network learns to predict, not necessarily the actual next word, but the correct *category* of word (noun vs. verb; if noun, animate vs. inanimate, edible vs. nonedible, etc.), as well as the correct subcategorization frame for the next verb (transitive or intransitive), and the correct number marking on both noun and verb (singular or plural). This cannot be done by mere association between adjacent surface elements. For example, whereas in the case of the simple strings, a network could learn always to predict that strings without an 's' (plural verb) follow strings with an 's' (plural noun), it cannot do so for embedded relative clause strings. Here, a plural verb may follow a singular noun (e.g., 'the boys that chase the *girl see* the dog'). In such cases, the network must make *structure-dependent* predictions. Thus, the network moves progressively from processing mere surface regularities to representing something more abstract, but without this being built in as a prespecified linguistic constraint.

This seemingly impressive grammatical knowledge is only implicit in the system's internal representations. Note, however, that this does not mean that the grammatical knowledge is not represented. As in the case of early learning in the child, I would argue that it is represented in level-I format. But it is we, as external theorists, who use level-E formats to label the trajectories through weight space as nouns, verbs, subjects, objects, intransitives, transitives, plurals, singulars, and so on. The network itself never goes beyond the formation of the equivalent of stable (but unlabeled) level-I representations. In other words, it does not spontaneously go beyond its efficient behavioral mastery. It does not redescribe the representations that are stored in its activation trajectories. Unlike the child, the network does not spontaneously 'appropriate' the knowledge it represents about different linguistic categories. It cannot directly use the higher-level, more abstract knowledge for any other purpose than the one it was designed for, nor can it engage directly in internetwork knowledge transfer because its representations are input/task specific. The notion of, say, nounhood, always remains implicit in the network's system dynamics. The child's *initial* learning is like this, too. But, as several examples throughout *Beyond modularity* show, children go on to redescribe spontaneously their linguistic (and other) knowledge. This pervasive process of representational redescription gives rise to the manipulability and flexibility of the human representational system.

Now, it is not difficult to build a network, inspired by RR, that would redescribe stable states in weight space such that the implicit information represented in trajectories could be used as knowledge by the same or other networks. However, this would suggest a change in the architecture of the network, involving perhaps the creation of special nodes not implicated in other aspects of the on-line processing. Furthermore, the RR framework suggests that what is abstracted during the redescriptive process involves a loss of detail and a gain in accessibility. Thus, one would not want the entire trajectories of the network to be redescribed – only the product of the most important ones. (This would be equivalent to, say, labeling the phase-state portraits of the principal-component analysis.) The RR framework postulates that redescribed knowledge capturing abstract notions such as 'verb' and 'noun' must be in a format different from that of the original level-I representations. In other words, redescriptions would have to be in a representational format usable across networks which had previously processed *different* representations at the input level: hence the need for representational redescription into different (level E) formats. Simple copies of level-I representations would not be usable/transportable from one network to another because they would be too dependent on the specific features of their inputs.

In Chapter 2, I discuss a particularly relevant example of what progressive RR might look like in the human case. When three- to six-year-olds are asked to repeat the last word the experimenter had said before a story was interrupted, some of the youngest subjects (three years old) could not do the task at all, despite lengthy modeling and help from the experimenter. Yet their fluent language and their lack of segmentation errors suggest that they do represent formal word boundaries for the majority of words they use and understand, but that they are not yet ready to go beyond that behavioral mastery. There were other children (four to five years old) who could not do the task immediately but who, with one-off modeling for a few open-class words, were able *immediately* to extend the notion of 'word' to *all* open-class and closed-class categories. Their level-I representations were ready for level-E1 redescription triggered by the experimenter from outside, but slightly older children (five to six years) who had never had a grammar lesson had spontaneously undergone the redescriptive process on their own. These showed immediate success, even on the practice story. Finally, six- to seven-year-olds' representations showed signs of having undergone further redescription into the E3 format; these children were able to access their knowledge consciously and to provide verbal explanations of what counts as a word and why. This process of *multiple* redescription of knowledge that becomes increasingly accessible to different parts of the system is an essential component of human development and one that connectionist modelers need to take into account.

It seems plausible that connectionist models can lend precision to an account of what I have called phase 1 learning – the phase that results in behavioral mastery (i.e., the period of rich interaction with the environment during which level-I representations are built and consolidated). However, there is much more to development than this. I have intimated at various points that connectionist simulations stop short of accounting for certain essential components of human development. Indeed, whereas behavioral mastery is the endpoint of learning in connectionist models, in the RR framework it is the starting point for new flexibility – that is, for generating redescriptions of implicitly defined level-I representations. Until now, connectionist models of development have had little to say about how to move from implicit representations to explicit ones, an essential process called for by RR. How could a network appropriate its own stable states? Clark (1989), Dennett (1993), and McClelland (1991) have argued that all that would have to be added to a connectionist network is another network that uses the equivalent of public language, implying that the only difference between implicit and explicit knowledge is that the latter is linguistically encoded. I have, however, provided numerous examples of children's knowledge that is explicitly represented, but with children unable to articulate it linguistically. The RR framework offers a far more complex view of multiple levels of representational redescription, of which language is but one manifestation. Finally, the fact that most connectionist models blend structure and content makes it difficult for the network to exploit knowledge components. Yet, in several chapters I show that children extract knowledge components from the procedural representations in which they are embedded, re-represent them, and use them in increasingly manipulable ways.

How representational redescription might be modeled in a connectionist network remains an open question. Can it be done simply by adding layers to the architecture of a single network, or by creating, say, a hierarchy of interconnected networks? Should a node, external to the online processing, be fed gradually with information from the developing internal representations when hidden units reach a certain threshold of stability? How can internet relations be introduced while keeping in mind the constraints suggested by RR regarding common transportable representational format? Or will we have to opt for hybrid models containing both parallel distributed processing and more classical sequential manipulation of discrete symbols (see discussions in Clark and Karmiloff-Smith 1993; Karmiloff-Smith 1987; 1992b; 1992c; Karmiloff-Smith and Clark 1993; Schneider 1987)? As connectionist networks become more complex, I think the issue of whether something is truly 'hybrid' will lose relevance. Future developmental modeling must, in my view, simulate *both* the benefits of rapid processing via implicit representations and the benefits gained by further representational redescription – a process that I suggest makes possible human creativity (for a BBS treatment of creativity, see Boden: 'Précis of: *The creative mind*' *BBS* 17(3) 1994).

**Concluding remarks**

I started *Beyond modularity* distinguishing between the representations that sustain complex behavior and the things that a given species can do with that complexity. My argument throughout has been that, far more pervasively even than that of its near cousin the chimpanzee, the human mind exploits its representational complexity by re-representing its implicit knowledge into many levels of explicit form. The knowledge thereby becomes applicable beyond the special-purpose goals for which it is normally used and representational links across different domains can be forged.

This is rarely if ever true of other species. The plover (discussed in Chapter 5), for example, displays a complex set of behaviors to keep competitors at bay – behaviors that, in human terms, would be called deceit. But these behaviors (keeping competitors away from their hatching eggs) are not available for other, even closely related, purposes (keeping competitors away from food). What about the chimpanzee, with whom we share close to 100% of our genetic makeup? Do chimpanzees, likd children, play with *knowledge*, just as they play with physical objects and conspecifics? According to discussions I have had with Premack, there are no obvious indicators of representational redescription in the behavior of the chimpanzee. There are numerous examples of how the chimpanzee goes beyond a specified task; for example, when the task is to assemble the pieces of a puzzle of a chimp face, a chimpanzee might, after succeeding, add extra pieces as decoration to form a hat or a necklace (Premack 1975). But Premack could find no example that revealed that the chimpanzee spontaneously analyzes the components of its successful behavior in the way a child does. It is, of course, not immediately obvious how we would recognize representational redescription in the chimpanzee if it did exist. The higher levels of redescription (into, say, linguistic format) are obviously ruled out. We know, however, that in many instances children develop explicit representations (E1) which lie between the implicit representations and the verbally reportable data. In the child, level E1 representational redescription is frequently manifest after overt behavioral mastery. The chimpanzee, by contrast, seems to be content to repeat its successes continuously;

it does not go beyond behavioral mastery. Yet, throughout *Beyond modularity*, examples are explored of how human children spontaneously seek to understand their own cognition, and of how this leads to the sort of representational manipulability that eventually allows them to become folk linguists, physicists, mathematicians, psychologists, and notators.

My conjecture is that either the process of representational redescription is not available to other species or, if it is (perhaps to the chimpanzee), the higher-level codes into which representations are translated during redescription are very impoverished. It is conceivable that 'language-trained' chimpanzees will show signs of representational redescription, but this would be due, not to the existence of a languagelike code per se, but to the possibility of redescription into any other more explicit code (for fuller discussion, see Karmiloff-Smith 1983).

RR is basically a hypothesis about the specifically human capacity to enrich itself from within, by exploiting knowledge already stored rather than by simply exploiting the human and physical environment. Intradomain and interdomain representational relations are the hallmark of a flexible and creative cognitive system. The pervasiveness of representational redescription is what makes human cognition specifically human. This is, of course, a challenge to ethologists and one I look forward to pursuing in the future. What indices should we be seeking in other species? What machinery would we have to add to the plover, the ant, the spider, the bee, or the chimpanzee to make the process of representational redescription possible?

In the final pages of *Beyond modularity*, I present a caricature drawing of the difference between humans and other species. In the top half of the caricature is drawn a human and an animal in reciprocal interaction with the external environment. In the bottom half, the drawing shows just the human figure with an arrow going around the head from one side to the other. This (rather silly) caricature is intended to illustrate that level-I representations exist as cognitive tools, allowing an organism (human or nonhuman) to act on the environment and to be affected by it in return. The second part of the figure is not meant to suggest that, in the human, knowledge goes in one ear and out the other! Rather, it is a reminder that, in the human, *internal representations* become objects of cognitive manipulation such that the mind extends well beyond its environment and is capable of creativity. Let me go so far as to say that the RR process is, in Marler's (1991) terms, one of the human instincts for inventiveness.

In *Beyond modularity*, and even in this short Précis, I hope to have convinced the reader that the flourishing new domain of cognitive science needs to go beyond the traditional nativist-empiricist dichotomy that permeates much of the field, in favor of an epistemology that embraces both innate predispositions and constructivism. Cognitive science also has much to gain by going beyond modularity and taking developmental change seriously.

A Précis necessarily makes conceptual leaps, misses out on the richness of the empirical data, as well as on numerous references to relevant literature. It also, alas, leaves no room for the humor. Nevertheless, it has given a relatively complete idea of the theoretical issues raised in the book. I began this Précis with a quotation from Marler that I find particularly conducive to my thinking, and that I used as a colophon for one of the book chapters, but I began the actual book with a quotation from Fodor, and ended with the following one: 'Deep down, I'm inclined to doubt that there is such a thing as cognitive development in the sense that developmental cognitive psychologists have in mind' (Fodor 1985, p. 35).

If this Précis has encouraged you to read the book in full, I hope that by the time you reach the end, deep down you will disagree with Fodor's statement and, with me, you will conclude that development goes far beyond the triggered unfolding of a genetic program, that where modularity occurs it is the result of a gradual process of modularization, and that representational redescription allows the human mind to go beyond modularity.

## Acknowledgment

Many people have read and commented on *Beyond modularity* and they are thanked in the preface to the book. Here I would like to express my gratitude to my colleague, Geoff Hall, for having read and provided useful comments on this Précis.

## References

Anderson, J. R. (1980). *Cognitive psychology and its implications*. Freeman.
Bates, E. and Elman, J. L. (1993). Connectionism and the study of change. In: *Brain development and cognition: A reader*, ed. M. H. Johnson. Blackwell.
Bates, E. and MacWhinney, B. (1987). Competition, variation and language learning. In: *Mechanisms of language acquisition*, ed. B. MacWhinney. Erlbaum.
Bechtel, W. and Abrahamsen, A. (1991). *Connectionism and the mind: An introduction to parallel processing in networks*. Blackwell.
Bellugi, U., Marks, S., Bihrle, A. M. and Sabo, H. (1988). Dissociation between language and cognitive functions in Williams syndrome. In: *Language development in exceptional circumstances*, ed. D. Bishop and K. Mogford. Churchill Livingstone.
Braine, M. D. S. (1994). Is nativism sufficient? *Journal of Child Language*, *21*, 9–31.
Carey, S. (1985). *Conceptual change in childhood*. MIT Press.
Case, R. (1985). *Intellectual development: Birth to adulthood*. Academic Press.
Changeux, J. P. (1985). *Neuronal man: The biology of mind*. Pantheon.
Chomsky, N. (1981). *Lectures on government and binding*. Foris.
Chomsky, N. (1988). *Language and problems of knowledge*. MIT Press.
Clark, A. C. (1989). *Microcognition: Philosophy, cognitive science, and parallel distributed processing*. MIT Press.
Clark, A. C. and Karmiloff-Smith, A. (1993). The cognizer's innards: A psychological and philosophical perspective on the development of thought. *Mind and Language*, *8(3)*, 487–568.
Clements, W. and Perner, J. (1994). Implicit understanding of false belief. Presentation at the Tenth Annual Conference of the Cognitive Section of the British Psychological Society. Cambridge, September.
Cromer, R. F. (1991). *Language and thought in normal handicapped children*. Basil Blackwell.

Dennett, D. C. (1993). Learning and labeling. Peer commentary on Clark and Karmil-off-Smith 'The cognizer's innards'. *Mind and Language, 8(3)*, 540–48.

Elman, J. L. (1990). Finding structure in time. *Cognitive Science, 14*, 179–211.

Elman, J. L. (1993). Learning and development in neural networks: The importance of starting small. *Cognition, 48(1)*, 71–99.

Elman, J. L., Bates, E., Johnson, M. H., Karmiloff-Smith, A., Parisi, D. and Plunkett, K. (1996) *Rethinking innateness: Connectionism in a developmental framework*. MIT Press.

Fodor, J. A. (1975). *The language of thought*. Thomas Crowell.

Fodor, J. A. (1983). *The modularity of mind*. MIT Press.

Fodor, J. A. (1985). Précis of *The modularity of mind. Behavioral and Brain Sciences, 8(1)*, 1–46.

Frith, U. (1989). *Autism: Explaining the enigma*. Blackwell.

Gelman, R. (1990a). Structural constraints on cognitive development. *Cognitive Science, 14*, 39.

Gentner, D. (1983). Structure-mapping: A theoretical framework for analogy. *Cognitive Science, 7*, 155–70.

Gottlieb, G. (1981). Roles of early experience in species-specific perceptual development. In: *Development of perception*, vol. 1, ed. R. N. Aslin, J. R. Alberts and M. P. Peterson. Academic Press.

Greenough, W. T., Black, J. E. and Wallace, C. S. (1987). Experience and brain development. *Child Development, 58*, 539–59.

Halford, G. S. (1982). *The development of thought*. Erlbaum.

Harnad, S. (1990). The symbol grounding problem. *Physica D, 42*, 335–46.

Hennessy, S. (1986). The role of conceptual knowledge in the acquisition of arithmetic algorithms, Ph. D. dissertation, University College, London.

Hermelin, B. and O'Connor, N. (1986). Idiot savant calendrical calculators: Rules and regularities. *Psychological Medicine, 16*, 885–93.

Johnson, M. H. (1988). Memories of mother. *New Scientist, 18*, 60–62.

Johnson, M. H. (1990). Cortical maturation and the development of visual attention in early infancy. *Journal of Cognitive Neuroscience, 2*, 81–95.

Johnson, M. H. (1993). Constraints on cortical plasticity. In: *Brain development and cognition: A reader*, ed. M. H. Johnson. Blackwell.

Johnson, M. H. and Bolhuis, J. J. (1991). Imprinting, predispositions and filial preference in the chick. In: *Neural and behavioural plasticity*, ed. R. J. Andrew. Oxford University Press.

Johnson, M. H. and Karmiloff-Smith, A. (1992). Can neural selectionism be applied to cognitive development and its disorders? *New Ideas in Psychology, 10*, 35–46.

Johnson, M. H. and Morton, J. (1991). *Biology and cognitive development: The case of face recognition*. Blackwell.

Johnston, T. D. (1987). The persistence of dichotomies in the study of behavioural development. *Developmental Review, 7*, 149–82.

Karmiloff-Smith, A. (1981). Getting developmental differences or studying child development? *Cognition, 10*, 151–58.

Karmiloff-Smith, A. (1983). A new abstract code or the new possibility of multiple codes? *Behavioral and Brain Sciences, 6(1)*, 149–50.

Karmiloff-Smith, A. (1992a). *Beyond modularity: A developmental perspective on cognitive science*. MIT Press.

Karmiloff-Smith, A. (1992b). Nature, nurture and PDP: Preposterous development postulates? *Connection Science, 4(3/4)*, 253–69.

Karmiloff-Smith, A. (1992c). Abnormal behavioural phenotypes and the challenges they pose to connectionist models of development. Technical Reports in Parallel Distributed Processing and Cognitive Neuroscience. TR.PDP.CNS.92.7, Carnegie Mellon University.

Karmiloff-Smith, A., Klima, E., Bellugi, U., Grant, J. and Baron-Cohen, S. (in press). Is there a social interaction module? Language, face processing and theory of mind in subjects with Williams syndrome. *Journal of Cognitive Neuroscience.*

Karmiloff-Smith, A., and Clark, A (1993). What's special about the human mind/ brain? A reply to Abrahamsen, Bechtel Dennett, Plunkett, Scutt and O'Hara. *Mind and Language, 8(3)*, 569–82.

Klahr, D. (1992). Information-processing approaches to cognitive development. In: *Developmental psychology: An advanced textbook*, 3d ed., ed. M. H. Bornstein and M. E. Lamb. Erlbaum.

Klahr, D. and Dunbar, K. (1988). Dual search space during scientific reasoning. *Cognitive Science, 12*, 148.

Klahr, D., Langley, P. and Neches, R., eds. (1987). *Production system models of learning and development.* MIT Press.

Kuhn, D., Amsel, E. and O'Loughlin, M. (1988). *The development of scientific thinking skills.* Academic Press.

Kuhn, D. and Phelps, E. (1982). *The development of problem-solving strategies.* In: *Advances in child development and behavior*, vol. 17. ed. H. Reese. Academic Press.

Langley, P., Simon, H. A., Bradshaw, C. L. and Zytkow, J. M. (1987). *Scientific discovery: Computational explorations of the creative processes.* MIT Press.

Leslie, A. M. (1992). Pretense, autism and the theory of mind module. *Current Directions in Psychological Science, 1*, 18–21.

Levitt, P. and O'Leary, D., eds. (1993). Mechanisms of cortical specification. *Perspectives on Developmental Neurobiology, 1(2)*, 63–113.

Lewis, C. (1994). *Events, episodes, and narratives in the child's understanding of mind*, ed. C. Lewis and P. Mitchell. Erlbaum.

Mandler, J. M. (1988). How to build a baby: On the development of an accessible representational system. *Cognitive Development, 3*, 113–36.

Mandler, J. M. (1992). How to build a baby II: Conceptual primitives. *Psychological Review, 99(4)*, 587–604.

Marler, P. (1991). The instinct to learn. In: *Epigenesis of the mind: Essays in biology and knowledge*, ed. S. Carey and R. Gelman. Erlbaum.

Marshall, J. C. (1984). Multiple perspectives on modularity. *Cognition, 17*, 209–42.

McClelland, J. L. (1991). Paper given at meeting of the Society for Research in Child Development, Seattle.

McClelland, J. L. (1994). The interaction of nature and nurture in development: A parallel distributed processing perspective. In: *International perspectives on psychological science*, vol. 1. ed. P. Bertelson, P. Eelen *et al.* Hove, England UK: Lawrence Erlbaum Associates.

McClelland, J. L. and Jenkins, E. (1990). Nature, nurture and connectionism: Implications for connectionist models for cognitive development. In: *Architectures for intelligence*, ed. K. van Lehn. Erlbaum.

Meltzoff, A. N. (1990). Towards a developmental cognitive science: The implications of cross-modal matching and imitation for the development of memory in infancy. *Annals of the New York Academy of Sciences, 608*, 1–37.

Morton, J. (1986). Developmental contingency modelling. In: *Theory building in developmental psychology*, ed. P. van Geehrt. Elsevier.

Nelson, K. (1986). *Event knowledge, structure and function in development.* Erlbaum.

Neville, H. J. (1991). Neurobiology of cognitive and language processing: Effects of early experience. In: *Brain maturation and cognitive development: Comparative and cross-cultural perspectives*, ed. K. R. Gibson and A. C. Petersen. Aldine de Gruyter.

Newell, A. (1990). *Unified theories of cognition.* Harvard University Press.

Nijhout, H. F. (1990). Metaphors and the role of genes in development. *BioEssays, 12*, 441–46.

Ohlsson, S. and Rees, E. (1991) The function of conceptual understanding in the learning of arithmetic procedures. *Cognition and Instruction, 8*, 103–79.

Oyama, S. (1985). *The ontogeny of information: Developmental systems and evolution.* Cambridge University Press.

Parisi, D. (1990). Connectionism and Piaget's sensory-motor intelligence. Paper presented at conference on *Evolution and Cognition: The Heritage of Jean Piaget's Epistemology*, Bergamo, Italy.

Perner, J. (1991). *Understanding the representational mind.* MIT Press.

Piaget, J. (1955). *The child's construction of reality.* Routledge & Kegan Paul.

Piaget, J. (1967a). *Biologie et connaissance.* Gallimard.

Piatelli-Palmerini, M. (1989). Evolution, selection, and cognition: From "learning" to parameter setting in biology and the study of language. *Cognition, 31*, 1–44.

Pinker, S. and Mehler, J., eds. (1988). Connectionism and symbol systems: Special edition. *Cognition, 28.*

Plunkett, K. and Marchman, V. (1991). U-shaped learning and frequency effects in a multilayered perception: Implications for child language acquisition. *Cognition, 38*, 43–102.

Plunkett, K. and Sinha, C. (1992). Connectionism and developmental theory. *British Journal of Developmental Psychology, 10*, 209–54.

Poizner, H., Klima, E. S. and Bellugi, U. (1987). *What the hands reveal about the brain.* MIT Press.

Povinelli, D. J. and deBlois, S. (1992). Young children's (Homo sapiens) understanding of knowledge formation in themselves and others. *Journal of Comparative Psychology, 106*, 228–38.

Premack, D. (1975). Putting a face together. *Science, 188*, 228–36.

Premack, D. (1986). *Gavagai! Or the future history of the animal language controversy.* MIT Press.

Premack, D. (1991). "Does the chimpanzee have a theory of mind?" revisited. In: *Machiavellian intelligence*, ed. R. Byrne and A. Whiten. Oxford Science Publications.

Quartz, S. R. (1993). Nativism, neural networks, and the plausiblity of constructivism. *Cognition, 48*, 123–44.

Schank, R. C. and Abelson, R. P. (1977). *Plans, goals and understanding: An inquiry into human knowledge structures.* Erlbaum.

Schauble, L. (1990). Belief revision in children: The role of prior knowledge and strategies for generating evidence. *Journal of Experimental Child Psychology, 1*, 31–57.

Schneider, W. (1987). Connectionism: Is it a paradigm shift for psychology? *Behaviour Research Methods, Instruments and Computers, 19(2)*, 73–83.

Shallice, T. (1988). *From neuropsychology to mental structure.* Cambridge University Press.

Shanks, D. R. and St. John, M. F. (1994). Characteristics of dissociable human learning systems. *Behavioral and Brain Sciences, 17(3)*, 367–447.

Shastri, L. and Ajjanagadde, V. (1993). From simple associations to systematic reasoning: A connectionist representation of rules, variables and dynamic bindings using temporal synchrony. *Behavioral and Brain Sciences, 16*, 417–94.

Shultz, T. R. (1991). Simulating stages of human cognitive development with connectionist models. In: *Machine learning: Proceedings of the eighth international work-
shop.* ed. L. Birnbaum and G. Collins. Morgan Kaufmann.

Siegler, R. S. and Crowley, K. (1991). The microgenetic method: A direct means for
studying cognitive development. *American Psychologist, 46(6)*, 606–20.

Siegler, R. S. and Robinson, M. (1982). The development of numerical understanding.
In: *Advances in child development and behavior*, vol. 16, ed. H. W. Reese and L. P.
Lipsett. Academic Press.

Skinner, B. F. (1953). *Science and human behaviour.* Macmillan.

Smolensky, P. (1988). On the proper treatment of connectionism. *Behavioral and Brain
Sciences, 11*, 1–74.

Spelke, E. S. (1991). Physical knowledge in infancy: Reflections on Piaget's theory. In:
*Epigenesis of the mind: Essays in biology and knowledge*, ed. S. Carey and R. Gelman.
Erlbaum.

Sur, M. (1994). Cortical specification: Microcircuits, perceptual identity and an overall
perspective. *Perspectives on Developmental Neurobiology, 1(2)*, 109–13.

Thelen, E. (1989). Self-organization in developmental processes: Can systems
approaches work? In: *Systems and development. Minnesota symposium in child
psychology*, vol. 22, ed. M. Gunnar and E. Thelen. Erlbaum.

Van Geehrt, P. (1991). A dynamic systems model of cognitive and language growth.
*Psychological Review, 98*, 3–53.

# 11  Uta Frith and Francesca Happé
## 'Autism: Beyond "Theory of Mind"'

Reprinted in full from: *Cognition* **50**, 115–132 (1994)

## The theory of mind account of autism

In 1985 *Cognition* published an article by Baron-Cohen, Leslie, and Frith, entitled: Does the autistic child have a 'theory of mind'? The perceptive reader would have recognized this as a reference to Premack and Woodruff's (1978) question: Does the chimpanzee have a theory of mind? The connection between these two was, however, an indirect one – the immediate precursor of the paper was Wimmer and Perner's (1983) article on the understanding of false beliefs by normally developing pre-school children. Each of these three papers has, in its way, triggered an explosion of research interest; in the social impairments of autism, the mind-reading capacities of non-human primates, and the development of social understanding in normal children. The connections which existed between the three papers have been mirrored in continuing connections between these three fields of research – developmental psychology (Astington, Harris and Olson, 1989; Perner, 1991; Russell, 1992; Wellman, 1990), cognitive ethology (Byrne and Whiten, 1988; Cheney and Seyfarth, 1990), and developmental psychopathology (Cicchetti and Cohen, in press; Rutter, 1987). There can be little doubt that these contacts have enriched work in each area.

Perceptive readers would also have noticed the inverted commas surrounding the phrase 'theory of mind' in the 1985 paper. Baron-Cohen, Leslie, and Frith followed Premack and Woodruff's definition of this 'sexy' but misleading phrase: to have a theory of mind is to be able to attribute independent mental states to self and others in order to explain and predict behaviour. As might befit a 'theory' ascribable to chimpanzees, this was not a conscious theory but an innately given cognitive mechanism allowing a special sort of representation – the representation of mental states. Leslie (1987, 1988) delivered the critical connection between social understanding and understanding of pretence, via this postulated mechanism; metarepresentation is necessary, in Leslie's theory, for representing pretence, belief and other mental states. From this connection between the social world and the world of imaginative play, sprung the link to autistic children, who are markedly deficient in both areas.

The idea that people with autism could be characterized as suffering from a type of 'mind-blindness', or lack of theory of mind, has been useful to the study of child development – not because it was correct (that is still debatable) but because it was a *causal* account which was both *specific* and *falsifiable*. The clearest expression of this causal account is given in Frith, Morton, and Leslie (1991). What is to be explained? Autism is currently defined at the behavioural level, on the basis of impairments in socialization, communication and imagination, with stereotyped repetitive interests taking the place of creative play (DSM-III-R. American Psychological Association, 1987). A causal account must link these behavioural symptoms to the presumed biological origins (Gillberg and Coleman, 1992; Schopler and Mesibov, 1987) of this disorder.

Specificity is particularly important in any causal account of autism because autistic people themselves show a highly specific pattern of deficits and skills. The IQ profile alone serves to demonstrate this: autistic people in general show an unusually 'spiky' profile across Wechsler subtests (Lockyer and Rutter, 1970; Tymchuk, Simmons and Neafsey, 1977), excelling on Block Design (constructing a pattern with cubes), and failing on Picture Arrangement (ordering pictures in a cartoon strip). This puzzling discrepancy of functioning has caused many previous psychological theories of autism to fail. For example, high arousal, lack of motivation, language impairment, or perceptual problems are all too global to allow for both the assets and deficits of autism.

**Fine cuts along a hidden seam**

What are the specific predictions made by the hypothesis that people with autism lack a 'theory of mind'? The hypothesis does not address the question of the spiky IQ profile – it is silent on functioning in non-social areas – but it focuses on the critical triad of impairments (Wing and Gould, 1979). Not only does it make sense of this triad, but it also makes 'fine cuts' *within* the triad of autistic impairments. Social and communicative behaviour is not all of one piece, when viewed from the cognitive level. Some, but not all, such behaviour requires the ability to 'mentalize' (represent mental states). So, for example, social approach need not be built upon an understanding of others' thoughts – indeed Hermelin and O'Connor (1970) demonstrated to many people's initial surprise that autistic children prefer to be with other people, just like non-autistic children of the same mental age. However, sharing attention with someone else does require mentalizing – and is consistently reported by parents to be missing in the development of even able autistic children (Newson, Dawson and Everard, 1984).

The mentalizing-deficit account has allowed a systematic approach to the impaired and unimpaired social and communicative behaviour of people with autism. Table 11.1 shows some of the work exploring predictions from the hypothesis that autistic people lack mentalizing ability. The power of this hypothesis is to make fine cuts in the smooth continuum of behaviours, and in this it has been remarkably useful. It has sparked an enormous amount of research, both supporting and attacking the theory (reviewed by Baron-Cohen, Tager-Flusberg, and Cohen, 1993; Happé, 1994a; Happé and Frith, in press).

The fine cuts method, as used in the laboratory, has also informed research into the pattern of abilities and deficits in real life (Table 11.2), although this enterprise has still some way to go. This technique which aims to pit two behaviours against each other which differ only in the demands they make upon the ability to mentalize, pre-empts many potential criticisms. It is also

**Table 11.1** Autistic assets and deficits as predicted by the 'fine cuts' technique, between tasks which require mentalizing and those which do not

| Assets | Deficits |
| --- | --- |
| Ordering behavioural pictures | Ordering mentalistic pictures (Baron-Cohen et al., 1986) |
| Understanding see | Understanding know (Perner et al., 1989) |
| Protoimperative pointing | Protodeclarative pointing (Baron-Cohen, 1989b) |
| Sabotage | Deception (Sodian and Frith, 1992) |
| False photographs | False beliefs (Leslie and Thaiss, 1992; Leekam and Perner, 1991) |
| Recognizing happiness and sadness | Recognizing surprise (Baron-Cohen et al., 1993) |
| Object occlusion | Information occlusion (Baron-Cohen, 1992) |
| Literal expression | Metaphorical expression (Happé, 1993) |

References refer to Assets and Deficits.

peculiarly suitable for use in brain-imaging studies. By looking at performance across tasks which are equivalent in every other way, except for the critical cognitive component, intellectual energy has been saved for the really interesting theoretical debates.

Another key benefit of the specificity of this approach is the relevance it has for normal development. The fine cuts approach suits the current climate of increased interest in the modular nature of mental capacities (e.g., Cosmides, 1989; Fodor, 1983). It has allowed us to think about social and communicative behaviour in a new way. For this reason, autism has come to be a test case for many theories of normal development (e.g., Happé, 1993; Sperber and Wilson's 1986 Relevance theory).

### Limitations of the theory of mind account

The hijacking of autism by those primarily interested in normal development has added greatly to the intellectual richness of autism research. But just how

**Table 11.2** Autistic assets and deficits observed in real life

| Assets | Deficits |
| --- | --- |
| Elicited structured play | Spontaneous pretend play (Wetherby and Prutting, 1984) |
| Instrumental gestures | Expressive gestures (Attwood, Frith and Hermelin, 1988) |
| Talking about desires and emotions | Talking about beliefs and ideas (Tager-Flusberg, 1993) |
| Using person as tool | Using person as receiver of information (Phillips, 1993) |
| Showing 'active' sociability | Showing 'interactive' sociability (Frith et al., in press) |

References refer to Assets and Deficits.

well does the theory of mind account explain autism? By the stringent standard, that explanatory theories must give a *full* account of a disorder (Morton and Frith, in press), not that well. The mentalizing account has helped us to understand the nature of the autistic child's impairments in play, social interaction and verbal and non-verbal communication. But there is more to autism than the classic triad of impairments.

### Non-triad features

Clinical impressions, originating with Kanner (1943) and Asperger (1944; translated in Frith, 1991), and withstanding the test of time, include the following:

- Restricted repertoire of interests (necessary for diagnosis in DSM-III-R, American Psychological Association, 1987).
- Obsessive desire for sameness (one of two cardinal features for Kanner and Eisenberg, 1956).
- Islets of ability (an essential criterion in Kanner, 1943).
- Idiot savant abilities (striking in 1 in 10 autistic children, Rimland and Hill, 1984).
- Excellent rote memory (emphasized by Kanner, 1943).
- Preoccupation with parts of objects (a diagnostic feature in DSM-IV, forthcoming).

All of these non-triad aspects of autism are vividly documented in the many parental accounts of the development of autistic children (Hart, 1989; McDonnell, 1993; Park, 1967). None of these aspects can be well explained by a lack of mentalizing.

Of course, clinically striking features shown by people with autism need not be specific features of the disorder. However, there is also a substantial body of experimental work, much of it predating the mentalizing theory, which demonstrates non-social abnormalities that are specific to autism. Hermelin and O'Connor were the first to introduce what was in effect a different 'fine cuts' method (summarized in their 1970 monograph) – namely the comparison of closely matched groups of autistic and non-autistic handicapped children of the same mental age. Table 11.3 summarizes some of the relevant findings.

### The talented minority

The mentalizing deficit theory of autism, then, cannot explain all features of autism. It also cannot explain all people with autism. Even in the first test of the hypothesis (reported in the 1985 *Cognition* paper), some 20% of autistic children passed the Sally-Ann task. Most of these successful children also passed another test of mentalizing – ordering picture stories involving mental states (Baron-Cohen, Leslie and Frith, 1986) – suggesting some real underlying competence in representing mental states. Baron-Cohen (1989a) tackled this apparent disconfirmation of the theory, by showing that these talented

**Table 11.3** Experimental findings not accounted for by mind-blindness. Surprising advantages and disadvantages on cognitive tasks, shown by autistic subjects relative to normally expected asymmetries

| Unusual strength | Unusual weakness |
| --- | --- |
| Memory for word strings | Memory for sentences (e.g., Hermelin and O'Connor, 1967) |
| Memory for unrelated items | Memory for related items (e.g., Tager-Flusberg, 1991) |
| Echoing nonsense | Echoing with repair (e.g., Aurnhammer-Frith, 1969) |
| Pattern imposition | Pattern detection (e.g., Frith, 1970 a,b) |
| Jigsaw by shape | Jigsaw by picture (e.g., Frith and Hermelin, 1969) |
| Sorting faces by accessories | Sorting faces by person (e.g., Weeks and Hobson, 1987) |
| Recognizing faces upside-down | Recognizing faces right-way-up (e.g., Langdell, 1978) |

References refer to Unusual strength and Unusual weakness.

children still did not pass a harder (second-order) theory of mind task (Perner and Wimmer, 1985). However, results from other studies focusing on high-functioning autistic subjects (Bowler, 1992; Ozonoff, Rogers and Pennington, 1991) have shown that some autistic people can pass theory of mind tasks consistently, applying these skills across domains (Happé, 1993) and showing evidence of insightful social behaviour in everyday life (Frith, Happé and Siddons, in press). One possible way of explaining the persisting autism of these successful subjects is to postulate an additional and continuing cognitive impairment. What could this impairment be?

The recent interest in *executive function deficits* in autism (Hughes and Russell, 1993; Ozonoff, Pennington and Rogers, 1991) can be seen as springing from some of the limitations of the theory of mind view discussed above. Ozonoff, Rogers and Pennington (1991) found that while not all subjects with autism and/or Asperger's syndrome showed a theory of mind deficit, all were impaired on the Wisconsin Card Sorting Test and Tower of Hanoi (two typical tests of executive function). On the basis of this finding they suggest that executive function impairments are a primary causal factor in autism. However, the specificity, and hence the power of this theory as a causal account, has yet to be established by systematic comparison with other non-autistic groups who show impairments in executive functions (Bishop, 1993). While an additional impairment in executive functions may be able to explain certain (perhaps non-specific) features of autism (e.g., stereotypes, failure to plan, impulsiveness), it is not clear how it could explain the specific deficits and skills summarized in Table 11.3.

**The central coherence theory**

Motivated by the strong belief that both the assets and the deficits of autism spring from a single cause at the cognitive level, Frith (1989) proposed that autism is characterized by a specific imbalance in integration of information at different levels. A characteristic of *normal* information processing appears to be the tendency to draw together diverse information to construct higher-level meaning in context; *'central coherence'* in Frith's words. For example, the gist of a story is easily recalled, while the actual surface form is quickly lost, and is effortful to retain. Bartlett (1932), summarizing his famous series of experiments on remembering images and stories, concluded: 'an individual does not normally take [such] a situation detail by detail . . . In all ordinary instances he has an overmastering tendency simply to get a general impression of the whole; and, on the basis of this, he constructs the probable detail' (p. 206). Another instance of central coherence is the ease with which we recognize the contextually appropriate sense of the many ambiguous words used in everyday speech (son–sun, meet–meat, sew–so, pear–pair). A similar tendency to process information in context for global meaning is also seen with non-verbal material – for example, our everyday tendency to misinterpret details in a jigsaw piece according to the expected position of the whole picture. It is likely that this preference for higher levels of meaning may characterize even mentally handicapped (non-autistic) individuals – who appear to be sensitive to the advantage of recalling organized versus jumbled material (e.g., Hermelin and O'Connor, 1967).

Frith suggested that this universal feature of human information processing was disturbed in autism, and that a lack of central coherence could explain very parsimoniously the assets and deficits shown in Table 11.3. On the basis of this theory, she predicted that autistic subjects would be relatively good at tasks where attention to local information – relatively piece-meal processing – is advantageous, but poor at tasks requiring the recognition of global meaning.

**Empirical evidence: assets**

A first striking signpost towards the theory appeared quite unexpectedly, when Amitta Shah set off to look at autistic children's putative perceptual impairments on the *Embedded Figures Test*. The children were almost better than the experimenter! Twenty autistic subjects with an average age of 13, and non-verbal mental age of 9.6, were compared with 20 learning disabled children of the same age and mental age, and 20 normal 9-year-olds. These children were given the Children's Embedded Figures Test (CEFT; Witkin, Oltman, Raskin and Karp, 1971), with a slightly modified procedure including some pretraining with cut-out shapes. The test involved spotting a hidden figure (triangle or house shape) among a larger meaningful drawing (e.g., a clock). During testing children were allowed to indicate the hidden figure either by pointing or by using a cut-out shape of the hidden figure. Out of a maximum score of 25, autistic children got a mean of 21 items correct, while the two control groups (which did not differ significantly in their scores) achieved 15 or less. Gottschaldt (1926) ascribed the difficulty of finding embedded figures to the overwhelming 'predominance of the whole'. The ease and speed with which autistic subjects picked out the hidden figure in

Shah and Frith's (1983) study was reminiscent of their rapid style of locating tiny objects (e.g. thread on a patterned carpet) and their immediate discovery of minute changes in familiar lay-outs (e.g., arrangement of cleaning materials on bathroom shelf), as often described anecdotally.

The study of embedded figures was introduced into experimental psychology by the Gestalt psychologists, who believed that an effort was needed to resist the tendency to see the forcefully created gestalt, at the expense of the constituent parts (Koffka, 1935). Perhaps this struggle to resist overall gestalt forces does not occur for autistic subjects. If people with autism, due to weak central coherence, have privileged access to the parts and details normally securely embedded in whole figures, then novel predictions could be made about the nature of their islets of ability.

The *Block Design* subtest of the Wechsler Intelligence Scales (Wechsler, 1974, 1981) is consistently found to be a test on which autistic people show superior performance relative to other subtests, and often relative to other people of the same age. This test, first introduced by Kohs (1923), requires the breaking up of line drawings into logical units, so that individual blocks can be used to reconstruct the original design from separate parts. The designs are notable for their strong gestalt qualities, and the difficulty which most people experience with this task appears to relate to problems in breaking up the whole design into the constituent blocks. While many authors have recognized this subtest as an islet of ability in autism, this fact has generally been explained as due to intact or superior general spatial skills (Lockyer and Rutter, 1970; Prior, 1979). Shah and Frith (1993) suggested, on the basis of the central coherence theory, that the advantage shown by autistic subjects is due specifically to their ability to see parts over wholes. They predicted that normal, but not autistic, subjects would benefit from pre-segmentation of the designs.

Twenty autistic, 33 normal and 12 learning disabled subjects took part in an experiment, where 40 different block designs had to be constructed from either whole or pre-segmented drawn models (Figure 11.1). Autistic subjects with normal or near-normal non-verbal IQ were matched with normal children of 16 years. Autistic subjects with non-verbal IQ below 85 (and not lower than 57) were compared with learning disabled children of comparable IQ and chronological age (18 years), and normal children aged 10. The results showed that the autistic subjects' skill on this task resulted from a greater ability to segment the design. Autistic subjects showed superior performance compared to controls in one condition only – when working from whole designs. The great advantage which the control subjects gained from using pre-segmented designs was significantly diminished in the autistic subjects, regardless of their IQ level. On the other hand, other conditions which contrasted presence and absence of obliques, and rotated versus unrotated presentation, affected all groups equally. From these latter findings it can be concluded that general visuo-spatial factors show perfectly normal effects in autistic subjects, and that superior general spatial skill may not account for Block design superiority.

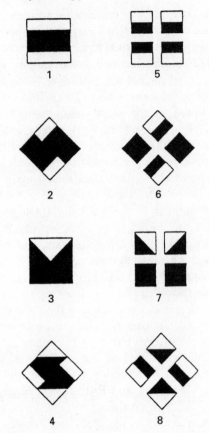

**Figure 11.1** Examples of all types of design: 'whole' versus 'segmented' (1, 2, 3, 4 vs. 5, 6, 7, 8) 'oblique' versus 'non-oblique' (3, 4, 7, 8 vs. 1, 2, 5, 6) 'unrotated' versus 'rotated' (1, 3, 5, 7 vs. 2, 4, 6, 8).

### Empirical evidence: deficits

While weak central coherence confers significant advantages in tasks where preferential processing of parts over wholes is useful, it would be expected to confer marked disadvantages in tasks which involve interpretation of individual stimuli in terms of overall context and meaning. An interesting example is the processing of faces, which seems to involve both featural and configural processing (Tanka and Farah, 1993). Of these two types of information, it appears to be configural processing which is disrupted by the inverted presentation of faces (Bartlett and Searcy, 1993; Rhodes, Brake and Atkinson, 1993). This may explain the previously puzzling finding that autistic subjects show a diminished disadvantage in processing inverted faces (Hobson, Ouston and Lee, 1988; Langdell, 1978).

One case in which the meaning of individual stimuli is changed by their context is in the disambiguation of homographs. In order to choose the correct (context-appropriate) pronunciation in the following sentences, one must process the final word as part of the whole sentence meaning: 'He had a pink *bow*'; 'He made a deep *bow*'. Frith and Snowling (1983) predicted that this sort of contextual disambiguation would be problematic for people with autism. They tested 8 children with autism who had reading ages of 8–10 years, and compared them with 6 dyslexic children and 10 normal children of the same reading age. The number of words read with the contextually appropriate pronunciation ranged from 5 to 7 out of 10 for the autistic children, who tended to give the more frequent pronunciation regardless of sentence context. By contrast, the normal and dyslexic children read between 7 and 9 of the 10 homographs in a contextually determined manner. This finding suggested that autistic children, although excellent at decoding single words, were impaired when contextual cues had to be used. This was also demonstrated in their relative inability to answer comprehension questions and to fill in gaps in a story text. This work fits well with previous findings (Table 11.3) concerning failure to use meaning and redundancy in memory tasks.

### The abnormality of excellence

The hypothesis that people with autism show weak central coherence aims to explain both the glaring impairments and the outstanding skills of autism as resulting from a single characteristic of information processing. One characteristic of this theory is that it claims that the islets of ability and savant skills are achieved through relatively abnormal processing, and predicts that this may be revealed in abnormal error patterns. One example might be the type of error made in the Block Design test. The central coherence theory suggests that, where errors are made at all on Block Design, these will be errors which violate the overall pattern, rather than the details. Kramer, Kaplan, Blusewicz, and Preston (1991) found that in normal adult subjects there was a strong relation between the number of such configuration-breaking errors made on the Block Design test and the number of local (vs. global) choices made in a similarity-judgement task (Kimchi and Palmer, 1982). Preliminary data from subjects with autism (Happé, in preparation) suggest that, in contrast to normal children, errors violating configuration are far more common than errors violating pattern details in autistic Block Design performance.

A second example concerns idiot savant drawing ability. Excellent drawing ability may be characterized by a relatively piece-meal drawing style. Mottron and Belleville (1993) found in a case study of one autistic man with exceptional artistic ability that performance on three different types of tasks suggested an anomaly in the hierarchical organization of the local and global parts of figures. The authors observed that the subject 'began his drawing by a secondary detail and then progressed by adding contiguous elements', and concluded that his drawings showed 'no privileged status of the global form . . . but rather a construction by local progression'. In contrast, a professional draughtsman who acted as a control started by constructing outlines and then proceeded to parts. It remains to be seen whether other savant abilities can be explained in terms of a similarly local and detail-observant processing style.

### Central coherence and mentalizing

Central coherence, then, may be helpful in explaining some of the real-life features that have so far resisted explanation, as well as making sense of a body of experimental work not well accounted for by the mentalizing deficit theory. Can it also shed light on the continuing handicaps of those talented autistic subjects who show consistent evidence of some mentalizing ability? Happé (1991), in a first exploration of the links between central coherence and theory of mind, used Snowling and Frith's (1986) homograph reading task with a group of able autistic subjects. Autistic subjects were tested on a battery of theory of mind tasks at two levels of difficulty (first- and second-order theory of mind), and grouped according to their performance (Happé, 1993). Five subjects who failed all the theory of mind tasks, 5 subjects who passed all and only first-order tasks, and 6 subjects who passed both first- and second-order theory of mind tasks were compared with 14 7–8-year-olds. The autistic subjects were of mean age 18 years, and had a mean IQ of around 80. The three autistic groups and the control group obtained the same score for total number of words correctly read. As predicted, however, the young normal subjects, but not the autistic subjects, were sensitive to the relative position of target homograph and disambiguating context: 'There was a big tear in her eye', versus 'In her dress there was a big tear'. The normal controls showed a significant advantage when sentence context occurred before (rare pronunciation) target words (scoring 5 out of 5, vs. 2 out of 5 where target came first), while the autistic subjects (as in Frith and Snowling, 1983) tended to give the more frequent pronunciation regardless (3 out of 5 appropriate pronunciations in each case). The important point of this study was that this was true of all three autistic groups, irrespective of level of theory of mind performance. Even those subjects who consistently passed all the theory of mind tasks (mean VIQ 90) failed to use sentence context to disambiguate homograph pronunciation. It is possible, therefore, to think of weak central coherence as characteristic of even those autistic subjects who possess some mentalizing ability.

Happé (submitted) explored this idea further by looking at WISC-R and WAIS subtest profiles. Twenty-seven children who failed standard first-order false belief tasks were compared with 21 subjects who passed. In both groups Block Design was a peak of non-verbal performance for the majority of subjects: 18/21 passers, and 23/27 failers. In contrast, performance on the Comprehension subtest (commonly thought of as requiring pragmatic and social skill) was a low point in verbal performance for 13/17 'failers' but only 6/20 'passers'. It seems, then, that while social reasoning difficulties (as shown by Wechsler tests) are striking only in those subjects who fail theory of mind tasks, skill on non-verbal tasks benefiting from weak central coherence is characteristic of both passers and failers.

There is, then, preliminary evidence to suggest that the central coherence hypothesis is a good candidate for explaining the persisting handicaps of the talented minority. So, for example, when theory of mind tasks were embedded in slightly more naturalistic tasks, involving extracting information from a story context, even autistic subjects who passed standard second-order false belief tasks showed characteristic and striking errors of mental state attribution (Happé, 1994b). It may be that a theory of mind mechanism which is not fed by rich and integrated contextual information is of little use in everyday life.

The finding that weak central coherence may characterize autistic people at all levels of theory of mind ability goes against Frith's (1989) original suggestion that a weakness in central coherence could by itself account for theory of mind impairment. At present, all the evidence suggests that we should retain the idea of a modular and specific mentalizing deficit in our causal explanation of the triad of impairments in autism. It is still our belief that nothing captures the essence of autism so precisely as the idea of 'mind-blindness'. Nevertheless, for a full understanding of autism in all its forms, this explanation alone will not suffice. Therefore, our present conception is that there may be two rather different cognitive characteristics that underlie autism. Following Leslie (1987, 1988) we hold that the mentalizing deficit can be usefully conceptualized as the impairment of a single modular system. This system has a neurological basis – which may be damaged, leaving other functions intact (e.g., normal IQ). The ability to mentalize would appear to be of such evolutionary value (Byrne and Whiten, 1988; Whiten, 1991) that only insult to the brain can produce deficits in this area. By contrast, the processing characteristic of weak central coherence, as illustrated above, gives both advantages and disadvantages, as would strong central coherence. It is possible, then, to think of this balance (between preference for parts vs. wholes) as akin to a cognitive style, which may vary in the normal population. No doubt, this style would be subject to environmental influences, but, in addition, it may have a genetic component. It may be interesting, then, to focus on the strengths and weaknesses of autistic children's processing, in terms of weak central coherence, in looking for the extended phenotype of autism. Some initial evidence for this may be found in the report by Landa, Folstein, and Isaacs (1991) that the parents of children with autism tell rather less coherent spontaneous narratives than do controls.

**Central coherence and executive function**

With the speculative link to cognitive style rather than straightforward deficit, the central coherence hypothesis differs radically not only from the theory of mind account, but also from other recent theories of autism. In fact, every other current psychological theory claims that some significant and objectively harmful deficit is primary in autism. Perhaps the most influential of such general theories is the idea that autistic people have executive function deficits, which in turn cause social and non-social abnormalities. The umbrella term 'executive functions' covers a multitude of higher cognitive functions, and so is likely to overlap to some degree with conceptions of both central coherence and theory of mind. However, the hypothesis that autistic people have relatively weak central coherence makes specific and distinct predictions even within the area of executive function. For example, the 'inhibition of pre-potent but incorrect responses' may contain two separable elements: inhibition and recognition of context-appropriate response. One factor which can make a pre-potent response incorrect is a change of context. If a stimulus is treated in the same way regardless of context, this may look like a failure of inhibition. However, autistic people may have no problem in inhibiting action where context is irrelevant. Of course it may be that some people with autism do have an additional impairment in inhibitory control, just as some have peripheral perceptual handicaps or specific language problems.

**Future prospects**

The central coherence account of autism is clearly still tentative and suffers from a certain degree of over-extension. It is not clear where the limits of this theory should be drawn – it is perhaps in danger of trying to take on the whole problem of meaning! One of the areas for future definition will be the *level* at which coherence is weak in autism. While Block Design and Embedded Figures tests appear to tap processing characteristics at a fairly low or perceptual level, work on memory and verbal comprehension suggests higher-level coherence deficits. Coherence can be seen at many levels in normal subjects, from the global precedence effect in perception of hierarchical figures (Navon, 1977) to the synthesis of large amounts of information and extraction of inferences in narrative processing (e.g., Trabasso and Suh, 1993, in a special issue of *Discourse Processes* on inference generation during text comprehension). One interesting way forward may be to contrast local coherence within modular systems, and global coherence across these systems in central processing. So, for example, the calendrical calculating skills of some people with autism clearly show that information within a restricted domain can be integrated and processed together (O'Connor and Hermelin, 1984; Hermelin and O'Connor, 1986), but the failure of many such savants to apply their numerical skills more widely (some cannot multiply two given numbers) suggests a modular system specialized for a very narrow cognitive task. Similarly, Norris (1990) found that building a connectionist model of an 'idiot savant date calculator' only succeeded when forced to take a modular approach.

Level of coherence may be relative. So, for example, within text there is the word-to-word effect of local association, the effect of sentence context, and the larger effect of story structure. These three levels may be dissociable, and it may be that people with autism process the most local of the levels available in open-ended tasks. The importance of testing central coherence with open-ended tasks is suggested by a number of findings. For example, Snowling and Frith (1986) demonstrated that it was possible to train subjects with autism to give the context appropriate (but less frequent) pronunciation of ambiguous homographs. Weeks and Hobson (1987) found that autistic subjects sorted photographs of faces by type of hat when given a free choice, but, when asked again, were able to sort by facial expression. It seems likely, then, that autistic weak central coherence is most clearly shown in (non-conscious) processing preference, which may reflect the relative cost of two types of processing (relatively global and meaningful vs. relatively local and piece-meal).

Just as the idea of a deficit in theory of mind has taken several years and considerable (and continuing) work to be empirically established, so the idea of a weakness in central coherence will require a systematic programme of research. Like the theory of mind account, it is to be hoped that, whether right or wrong, the central coherence theory will form a useful framework for thinking about autism in the future.

## References

American Psychological Association (1987). *Diagnostic and Statistical Manual of Mental Disorders.* 3rd revised edition (DSM-III-R). Washington, DC: American Psychological Association.

Asperger, H. (1944). Die 'autistischen Psychopathen' im Kindesalter. *Archiv für Psychiatrie und Nervenkrankheiten, 117*, 76–136.

Astington, J. W., Harris, P. L., and Olson, D. R. (Eds.) (1989). *Developing theories of mind.* New York: Cambridge University Press.

Attwood, A. H., Frith, U., and Hermelin, B. (1988). The understanding and use of interpersonal gestures by autistic and Down's syndrome children. *Journal of Autism and Developmental Disorders, 18*, 241–257.

Aurnhammer-Frith, U. (1969). Emphasis and meaning in recall in normal and autistic children. *Language and Speech, 12*, 29–38.

Baron-Cohen, S. (1989a). The autistic child's theory of mind: A case of specific developmental delay. *Journal of Child Psychology and Psychiatry, 30*, 285–297.

Baron-Cohen, S. (1989b). Perceptual role taking and protodeclarative pointing in autism. *British Journal of Developmental Psychology, 7*, 113–127.

Baron-Cohen, S. (1992). Out of sight or out of mind? Another look at deception in autism. *Journal of Child Psychology and Psychiatry, 33*, 1141–1155.

Baron-Cohen, S., Leslie, A. M., and Frith, U. (1985). Does the autistic child have a 'theory of mind'? *Cognition, 21*, 37–46.

Baron-Cohen, S., Leslie, A. M., and Frith, U. (1986). Mechanical, behavioural and intentional understanding of picture stories in autistic children. *British Journal of Developmental Psychology, 4*, 113–125.

Baron-Cohen, S., Spitz, A., and Cross, P. (1993). Can children with autism recognise surprise? *Cognition and Emotion, 7*, 507–516.

Baron-Cohen, S., Tager-Flusberg, H., and Cohen, D. J. (Eds.) (1993). *Understanding other minds: Perspectives from autism.* Oxford: Oxford University Press.

Bartlett, F. C. (1932). *Remembering: A study in experimental and social psychology.* Cambridge, UK: Cambridge University Press.

Bartlett, J. C., and Searcy, J. (1993). Inversion and configuration of faces. *Cognitive Psychology, 25*, 281–316.

Bishop, D. V. M. (1993). Annotation. Autism, executive functions and theory of mind: A neuro-psychological perspective. *Journal of Child Psychology and Psychiatry, 34*, 279–293.

Bowler, D. M. (1992). 'Theory of mind' in Asperger's syndrome. *Journal of Child Psychology and Psychiatry, 33*, 877–893.

Byrne, R., and Whiten, A. (Eds.) (1988). *Machiavellian intelligence: Social expertise and the evolution of intellect in monkeys, apes, and humans.* Oxford: Clarendon Press.

Cheney, D. L., and Seyfarth, R. M. (1990). *How monkeys see the world.* Chicago: University of Chicago Press.

Cicchetti, D., and Cohen, D. J. (Eds.) (in press). *Manual of developmental psychopathology* (Vol. 1). New York: Wiley.

Cosmides, L. (1989). The logic of social exchange: Has natural selection shaped how humans reason? Studies with the Wason selection task. *Cognition, 31,* 187–276.

Fodor, J. A. (1983). *Modularity of mind.* Cambridge, MA: MIT Press.

Frith, U. (1970a). Studies in pattern detection in normal and autistic children: I. Immediate recall of auditory sequences. *Journal of Abnormal Psychology, 76,* 413–420.

Frith, U. (1970b). Studies in pattern detection in normal and autistic children: II. Reproduction and production of color sequences. *Journal of Experimental Child Psychology, 10,* 120–135.

Frith, U. (1989). *Autism: Explaining the enigma.* Oxford: Basil Blackwell.

Frith, U. (1991). Translation and annotation of 'Autistic psychopathy' in childhood, by H. Asperger. In U. Frith (Ed.), *Autism and Asperger syndrome.* Cambridge, UK: Cambridge University Press.

Frith, U., Happé, F., and Siddons, F. (in press). Theory of mind and social adaptation in autistic, retarded and young normal children. *Social Development.*

Frith, U., and Hermelin, B. (1969). The role of visual and motor cues for normal, subnormal and autistic children. *Journal of Child Psychology and Psychiatry, 10,* 153–163.

Frith, U., Morton, J., and Leslie, A. M. (1991). The cognitive basis of a biological disorder: Autism. *Trends in Neuroscience, 14,* 433–438.

Frith, U., and Snowling, M. (1983). Reading for meaning and reading for sound in autistic and dyslexic children. *Journal of Developmental Psychology, 1,* 329–342.

Gillberg, C., and Coleman, M. (1992). *The biology of the autistic syndromes.* London: Mac Keith Press.

Gottschaldt, K. (1926). Ueber den Einfluss der Erfahrung auf die Welt der Wahrnehmung von Figuren. *Psychologische Forschung, 8,* 261–317.

Happé, F. G. E. (1991). *Theory of mind and communication in autism.* Unpublished Ph.D. thesis, University of London.

Happé, F. G. E. (1993). Communicative competence and theory of mind in autism: A test of relevance theory. *Cognition, 48,* 101–119.

Happé, F. G. E. (1994a). Annotation: Psychological theories of autism. *Journal of Child Psychology and Psychiatry, 35,* 215–229.

Happé, F. G. E. (1994b). An advanced test of theory of mind: Understanding of story characters' thoughts and feelings by able autistic, mentally handicapped and normal children and adults. *Journal of Autism and Developmental Disorders, 24,* 1–24.

Happé, F. G. E. (submitted). Theory of mind and IQ profiles in autism: A research note.

Happé, F. G. E. (in preparation). Central coherence, block design errors, and global-local similarity judgement in autistic subjects.

Happé, F., and Frith, U. (in press). Theory of mind in autism. In E. Schopler and G. B. Mesibov (Eds.), *Learning and cognition in autism.* New York: Plenum Press.

Hart, C. (1989). *Without reason: A family copes with two generations of autism.* New York: Penguin Books.

Hermelin, B., and O'Connor, N. (1967). Remembering of words by psychotic and subnormal children. *British Journal of Psychology, 58,* 213–218.

Hermelin, B., and O'Connor, N. (1970). *Psychological experiments with autistic children.* Oxford: Pergamon.

Hermelin, B., and O'Connor, N. (1986). Idiot savant calendrical calculators: Rules and regularities. *Psychological Medicine, 16,* 885–893.

Hobson, R. P., Ouston, J., and Lee, T. (1988). What's in a face? The case of autism. *British Journal of Psychology, 79,* 441–453.

Hughes, C. H., and Russell, J. (1993). Autistic children's difficulty with mental disengagement from an object: Its implications for theories of autism. *Developmental Psychology, 29,* 498–510.

Kanner, L. (1943). Autistic disturbances of affective contact. *Nervous Child, 2,* 217–250.

Kanner, L., and Eisenberg, L. (1956). Early infantile autism 1943–1955. *American Journal of Orthopsychiatry, 26,* 55–65.

Kimchi, R., and Palmer, S. E. (1982). Form and texture in hierarchically constructed patterns. *Journal of Experimental Psychology: Human Perception and Performance, 8,* 521–535.

Koffka, K. (1935). *Principles of Gestalt psychology.* New York: Harcourt Brace.

Kohs, S. C. (1923). *Intelligence measurement.* New York: McMillan.

Kramer, J. H., Kaplan, E., Blusewicz, M. J., and Preston, K. A. (1991). Visual hierarchical analysis of block design configural errors. *Journal of Clinical and Experimental Neuropsychology, 13,* 455–465.

Landa, R., Folstein, S.E., and Isaacs, C. (1991). Spontaneous narrative-discourse performance of parents of autistic individuals. *Journal of Speech and Hearing Research, 34,* 1339–1345.

Langdell, T. (1978). Recognition of faces: An approach to the study of autism. *Journal of Child Psychology and Psychiatry, 19,* 255–268.

Leekam, S., and Perner, J. (1991). Does the autistic child have a metarepresentational deficit? *Cognition, 40,* 203–218.

Leslie, A. M. (1987). Pretence and representation: The origins of 'Theory of Mind'. *Psychological Review, 94,* 412–426.

Leslie, A. M. (1988). Some implications of pretence for mechanisms underlying the child's theory of mind. In J. W. Astington, P. L. Harris, and D. R. Olson (Eds.), *Developing theories of mind.* New York: Cambridge University Press.

Leslie, A. M., and Thaiss, L. (1992). Domain specificity in conceptual development: Evidence from autism. *Cognition, 43,* 225–251.

Lockyer, L., and Rutter, M. (1970). A five to fifteen year follow-up study of infantile psychosis: IV. Patterns of cognitive ability. *British Journal of Social and Clinical Psychology, 9,* 152–163.

McDonnell, J. T. (1993). *News from the Border: A mother's memoir of her autistic son.* New York: Ticknor & Fields.

Morton, J., and Frith, U. (in press). Causal modelling: A structural approach to developmental psychopathology. In D. Cicchetti and D. J. Cohen (Eds.), *Manual of Developmental Psychology* (Vol. 1, Ch. 13). New York: Wiley.

Mottron, L., and Belleville, S. (1993). A study of perceptual analysis in a high-level autistic subject with exceptional graphic abilities. *Brain and Cognition, 23,* 279–309.

Navon, D. (1977). Forest before trees: The precedence of global features in visual perception. *Cognitive Psychology, 9,* 353–383.

Newson, E., Dawson, M., and Everard, P. (1984). The natural history of able autistic people: Their management and functioning in social context. Summary of the report to DHSS in four parts. *Communication, 18,* 1–4; *19,* 1–2.

Norris, D. (1990). How to build a connectionist idiot (savant). *Cognition, 35,* 277–291.

O'Connor, N., and Hermelin, B. (1984). Idiot savant calendrical calculators: Maths or memory. *Psychological Medicine, 14*, 801–806.

Ozonoff, S., Pennington, B. F., and Rogers, S. J. (1991). Executive function deficits in high-functioning autistic children: Relationship to theory of mind. *Journal of Child Psychology and Psychiatry, 32*, 1081–1106.

Ozonoff, S., Rogers, S. J., and Pennington, B. F. (1991). Asperger's syndrome: Evidence of an empirical distinction from high-functioning autism. *Journal of Child Psychology and Psychiatry, 32*, 1107–1122.

Park, C. C. (1967). *The siege: The battle for communication with an autistic child.* Harmondsworth, UK: Penguin Books.

Perner, J. (1991). *Understanding the representational mind.* Cambridge, MA: MIT Press.

Perner, J., Frith, U., Leslie, A. M., and Leekam, S. R. (1989). Exploration of the autistic child's theory of mind: Knowledge, belief, and communication. *Child Development, 60*, 689–700.

Perner, J., and Wimmer, H. (1985). 'John *thinks* that Mary thinks that . . . ': Attribution of second-order beliefs by 5–10 year old children. *Journal of Experimental Child Psychology, 39*, 437–471.

Phillips, W. (1993). Understanding intention and desire by children with autism. Unpublished Ph.D. thesis, University of London.

Premack, D., and Woodruff, G. (1978). Does the chimpanzee have a theory of mind? *Behavioural and Brain Sciences, 4*, 515–526.

Prior, M. R. (1979). Cognitive abilities and disabilities in infantile autism: A review. *Journal of Abnormal Child Psychology, 7*, 357–380.

Rhodes, G., Brake, S., and Atkinson, A. P. (1993). What's lost in inverted faces? *Cognition, 47*, 25–57.

Rimland, B., and Hill, A. L. (1984). Idiot savants. In J. Wortis (Ed.), *Mental retardation and developmental disabilities* (vol. 13, pp. 155–169). New York: Plenum Press.

Russell, J. (1992). The theory-theory: So good they named it twice? *Cognitive Development, 7*, 485–519.

Rutter, M. (1987). The role of cognition in child development and disorder. *British Journal of Medical Psychology, 60*, 1–16.

Schopler, E., and Mesibov, G. B. (1987). *Neurobiological issues in autism.* New York: Plenum Press.

Shah, A., and Frith, U. (1983). An islet of ability in autistic children: A research note. *Journal of Child Psychology and Psychiatry, 24*, 613–620.

Shah, A., and Frith, U. (1993). Why do autistic individuals show superior performance on the Block Design task? *Journal of Child Psychology and Psychiatry, 34*, 1351–1364.

Snowling, M., and Frith, U. (1986). Comprehension in 'hyperlexic' readers. *Journal of Experimental Child Psychology, 42*, 392–415.

Sodian, B., and Frith, U. (1992). Deception and sabotage in autistic, retarded and normal children. *Journal of Child Psychology and Psychiatry, 33*, 591–605.

Sperber, D., and Wilson, D. (1986). *Relevance: Communication and cognition.* Oxford: Blackwell.

Tager-Flusberg, H. (1991). Semantic processing in the free recall of autistic children: Further evidence for a cognitive deficit. *British Journal of Developmental Psychology, 9*, 417–430.

Tager-Flusberg, H. (1993). What language reveals about the understanding in minds in children with autism. In S. Baron-Cohen, H. Tager-Flusberg, and D. J. Cohen (Eds.), *Understanding other minds: Perspectives from autism.* Oxford: Oxford University Press.

Tanka, J. W., and Farah, M. J. (1993). Parts and wholes in face recognition. *Quarterly Journal of Experimental Psychology, 46A*, 225–245.

Trabasso, T., and Suh, S. (1993). Understanding text: Achieving explanatory coherence through on-line inferences and mental operations in working memory. *Discourse Processes, 16*, 3–34.

Tymchuk, A. J., Simmons, J. Q., and Neafsey, S. (1977). Intellectual characteristics of adolescent childhood psychotics with high verbal ability. *Journal of Mental Deficiency Research, 21*, 133–138.

Wechsler, D. (1974). *Wechsler Intelligence Scale for Children – Revised.* New York: Psychological Corporation.

Wechsler, D. (1981). *Wechsler Adult Intelligence Scales – Revised.* New York: Psychological Corporation.

Weeks, S. J., and Hobson, R. P. (1987). The salience of facial expression for autistic children. *Journal of Child Psychology and Psychiatry, 28*, 137–152.

Wellman, H. M. (1990). *The child's theory of mind.* Cambridge, MA: MIT Press.

Wetherby, A. M. and Prutting, C. A. (1984). Profiles of communicative and cognitive-social abilities in autistic children. *Journal of Speech and Hearing Research, 27*, 364–377.

Whiten, A. (1991). *Natural theories of mind.* Oxford: Basil Blackwell.

Wimmer, H., and Perner, J. (1983). Beliefs about beliefs: Representation and the constraining function of wrong beliefs in young children's understanding of deception. *Cognition, 13*, 103–128.

Wing, L., and Gould, J. (1979). Severe impairments of social interaction and associated abnormalities in children: Epidemiology and classification. *Journal of Autism and Developmental Disorders, 9*, 11–29.

Witkin, H. A., Oltman, P. K., Raskin, E., and Karp, S. (1971). *A manual for the Embedded Figures Test.* California: Consulting Psychologists Press.

# SECTION IV
# THE DEVELOPMENT OF LITERACY AND NUMERACY

### Editors' Introduction

Over recent years research in developmental psychology has directed more attention to the skills that children acquire in schools and their precursors. Studies investigating typical patterns of acquiring reading and number development have grown, but so have investigations into scientific knowledge, notations systems and oral language skills. The literature investigating typical patterns of development has been enhanced by studying children who have difficulties in acquiring these skills. Many of these skills are fundamental to the child's ability to access the curriculum and succeed in an educational environment. For education to be effective it is essential that developmental psychologists provide a detailed understanding of how children learn and the specific problems that they can face. This entails both an analysis of the necessary prerequisites to school based learning as well as a specification of the challenges of the conventional curriculum.

For most of us reading is an effortless process that provides us with pleasure and allows us to extend our knowledge. Because of this it is sometimes easy to overlook both the complexity of the reading process and the problems that it presents to the novice. Arguably one of the first skills the child must master is the ability to recognize single words. Much research has been carried out to discover how children learn to decode words. We read both by *ear* and by *eye*. When we read by *eye* alone, we recognize words directly. This is sometimes called 'whole word recognition'. This direct lexical access by word recognition does not necessarily require one to have any knowledge of the components (i.e. the letters) that make up a word. When we read by *ear*, we transform the visual input into a phonological representation. We do this when we sound out a word that is unfamiliar to decide whether its pronunciation is familiar and the word recognizable. Some books will describe this as grapheme–phoneme correspondence. This means that individuals match the letters on the page (grapheme) with the sound of the letters (phoneme). This process is extremely important in the development of the ability to decode written text. It is an essential skill for reading unfamiliar words.

The first paper by Bradley and Bryant is regarded by many as a classic study. It is regarded as a seminal piece of research because it was the first study to use both a longitudinal approach and specified interventions in the study of children's reading development. Using this combination of approaches Bradley and Bryant were able to demonstrate the importance of a child's ability to categorize sound on their subsequent reading and spelling skills. The central question is whether a causal relationship exists between sound categorization and success in reading and spelling. Longitudinal studies on their own present data that is correlational. As we know correlation does not mean causation – other unassessed factors, such as intelligence or social background, might explain the correlation. However, if it can be shown that specific interventions change the child's performance then it can be concluded that the particular variable tested influences development. You will recall that we made similar arguments about studies of language acquisition. However, intervention data on their own cannot demonstrate that the same processes are at work in normal development, for this longitudinal data is required. As you read this paper carefully examine the tests that were administered. Could they be assessing anything other than sensitivity to rhyme and alliteration? Why were four different groups used? Consider carefully their argument about phonological training (Group 1) versus conceptual training (Group 3). You should closely examine the data. How justified is their claim about phonological training given that the differences between these two groups is not statistically significant. In a more recent study Bryant and his associates (Bryant et al., 1990) showed that a sensitivity to rhyme was related both to the development of reading skills and to the emergence of an awareness of the phonemic structure of words. This is a line of research which has continued to be very active. Issues related to sound categorization have been extended to include children's spelling skills but also difficulties that occur in the initial stages of language learning. Learning to decode text is only part of learning to read. Children also have to develop skills for understanding the written text.

Gathercole and Baddeley also consider critical features in the acquisition of reading. They, however, change the focus of investigation in a subtle but important way. They locate the basis of children's progress (or lack of it) in their memory capacities. Their focus is on individual differences in children's abilities to store and rehearse phonological material. You should contrast the types of inferences that are being made in this paper to the ones made by Bradley and Bryant. Gathercole and Baddeley's work is an example of careful hypothesis testing and the use of different sorts of evidence to develop their model. As they state, the first indication that differences in phonological working memory might be an important factor in development came from investigations of children with specific language impairments. (If you wish to find out more about specific language impairment you should read Donaldson, 1995.) Here is another example of how work examining atypical development can inform our understanding of typical development. Their second source of evidence came from a longitudinal study of children designed to assess the role of phonological working memory in vocabulary acquisition. Remember that this data is correlational – why is this important? Moreover, the correlations vary quite markedly across the age ranges. Why might this be? Their third piece of evidence considers the relationship between phonological memory and later reading achievement, arguing that phonological memory impacts on one specific aspect of reading – phonological decoding.

The final piece of evidence addresses the link between phonological working memory and phonological awareness. Do phonological awareness and phonological memory have dissociable influences on reading development? Their preliminary conclusion is that the two types of skills are to some extent unique. However it is possible that an apparent development in working memory capacity may reflect other factors such as improved memory in a particular domain and the greater use of efficient memory strategies (Chi, 1978). A similar argument is made by Valian et al. (1996) about early language. To what extent do you consider this to be a valid critique of the work of Gathercole and Baddeley?

Being able to derive meaning from text requires the operation of a large number of processes. Oakhill and Garnham (1988) estimate that up to 10% of children who can read fluently have difficulties comprehending what they have read. The chapter by Oakhill and Yuill addresses these issues. They consider the differences in processing skills of children with poor comprehension but age appropriate decoding skills. Three areas are examined: making inferences from texts; understanding the structure of a text; and monitoring comprehension of a text. In all three cases they demonstrate the difficulties that children with poor comprehension have with these processes. Their explanation of these difficulties is interesting because it considers both within child factors and environmental factors. The focus of their explanations is poor working memory. They argue that the children's poorer working memory is preventing them from efficient text processing and limiting their ability to make inferences. In addition, however, they suggest that these poor comprehenders have actually had less exposure to stories (in terms of actually hearing stories). Thus the difficulties are thought to be a result of an interaction of these two factors. Oakhill and Yuill proceed to consider the results of their studies for intervention. They focus on the remediation of processing strategies. The results of their training studies are impressive, however you should note the caveats they mention at the end of the chapter.

Oakhill and Yuill discuss intervention strategies for children with comprehension problems but like reading skills, reading difficulties can be analysed at two levels: decoding and comprehension. The evidence suggests that the most common cause of decoding difficulties is a problem in mapping between letters and their sounds. These problems are common to children who are sometimes labelled dyslexic and those who are simply regarded as poor readers. Comprehension difficulties are sometimes the result of poor decoding skills. Often children who have had difficulty in learning to decode, process text on a word-by-word basis rather than at the level of phrases and sentences. This leads to poor comprehension. As we have seen comprehension difficulties also occur independently of decoding skills. If you wish to consider specific literacy difficulties further you should read Margaret Snowling's review paper (1991).

Many children find mathematics or 'number work' difficult in their early school years and onwards. Much research has been aimed at finding out how mathematical knowledge develops. Less work has addressed the problems of children with numeracy difficulties (see Dockrell and McShane, 1993). An early view of number development

stressed the accumulation of number facts through practice and reinforcement of associations between a stimulus, e.g. 'two plus three' and
the correct response, 'five'. Thorndike (1922) discussed this approach
and its implications for teaching. In contrast, the constructivist
approach focuses on how individuals think about mathematical
problems they encounter: they try out solutions, make generalizations
and derive rules (the chapter by Marcus in the section on language
acquisition also considers children's use of rules). Gradually the individual builds an understanding of abstract and universal mathematical
concepts. Geary's paper examines the possible factors underlying
difficulties in mathematics. This paper requires careful reading to
follow the detailed argument. The paper starts from the premise that
many of the studies investigating children's mathematical skills are
limited because of a failure to examine performance on a trial by trial
basis thereby resulting in a limited understanding of the children's
computational skills. Geary avoids this methodological problem and
focuses on children's strategies for solving simple arithmetical sums.
You should note the careful choice of stimuli and the counterbalancing
and controls used in the presentation of the material. Why is this
important? Equally important is the careful and systematic analysis
of the data. The combination of clearly articulated hypotheses, carefully designed materials and statistical analysis allow Geary to arrive at
some interesting conclusions. The results demonstrate that the learning disabled group make more counting errors but also make greater
use of the (developmentally less sophisticated) sum strategy. From
this they conclude that the normal and improved groups are qualitatively different from children who still have mathematical difficulties.
Their suggestion is that the learning disabled group have a difference
(rather than a delay) in development and that this is a result of an
underlying cognitive deficit. How valid is this conclusion? Why do you
think that Geary is more definite about the difference model of mathematics than Oakhill and Yuill are about the teaching of comprehension.
What implications might we draw from this paper about assessing
children's early mathematical skills?

The final chapter in this section focuses on the development of
children's early notations. This is a relatively recent area of study for
developmentalists. A number of authors have argued that investigations of children's notations for numbers and words should begin
before children enter formal schooling. Rather, there are certain representational principles underlying early spontaneous notations and
studies of the notations allow us to identify these precursors. As you
will see as you read Tolchinsky-Landsmann's paper the children's marks
are not considered to be idiosyncratic but rather a selection and elaboration of the information provided in the environment. Such work raises
many theoretical and empirical issues. Examinations of the functions of
writing need to be discriminated from the functions of numerical notations. For example, when does a child treat their scribbles for twos
differently from their scribbles for words. Tolchinsky-Landsmann
argues that there is evidence not only for discrimination between
notations for different domains but also within the domain of writing.
Of course such studies raise thorny methodological problems. You
should consider what evidence you would want to collect to substanti-

ate the claims that are made about the Catalan boy and the Israeli girl in Figure 16.2. Moreover, consideration of the notations and what the children say they are going to write challenges our methods for assessing reliability and generalizability. Yet one cannot help but be fascinated by the ways that these early notations may provide clues to how the child's representation meshes with the environmental input, resulting in a creative and flexible system. (Chapter 6 in Karmiloff-Smith (1992) develops these ideas further.)

There have been many developments in educational policy and practice over the last decade. As Nunes (1997) has argued 'effective teaching cannot be accomplished without a good understanding of how children learn'. There is much knowledge which has been accumulated in developmental psychology that can inform these debates. In many cases this knowledge has been acquired by a careful analysis of the component skills that lead to successful performance. Once we have established the component skills it is possible to consider and evaluate intervention and support programmes. Is it important to learn multiplication tables by rote? How should spelling be taught? Developmental psychologists possess data that can address these questions. Literacy and numeracy are areas of the curriculum where theory driven developmental research can lead to sound educational policies.

## References

Bryant, P., MacLean, M., Bradley, L., and Crossland, J. (1990). Rhyme and alliteration, phoneme detection, and learning to read. *Developmental Psychology*, *26*, 429–438.

Chi, M. (1978). Knowledge structures and memory development. In R. S. Siegler (Ed.), *Children's Thinking: What develops?*. Hillsdale, NJ: Erlbaum.

Dockrell, J. E. and McShane, J. (1993). *Children's Learning Difficulties: A cognitive approach*. Oxford: Blackwell.

Donaldson, M. (1995). *Children with Language Impairments: an introduction*. London: Jessica Kinglsey.

Karmiloff-Smith, A. (1992). *Beyond Modularity: a developmental perspective on cognitive science*. London: MIT Press.

Nunes, T. (1997). Do teachers really know how children learn?. *Parliamentary Brief*, *5*. 44–45.

Oakhill, J. V. and Garnham, A. (1988). *Becoming a skilled reader*. Oxford: Blackwell.

Snowling, M. (1991). Developmental reading disorders. *Journal of Child Psychology and Psychiatry*, *32*, 49–78.

Thorndike, E. L. (1922). *The Psychology of Arithmetic*. New York: Macmillan.

Valian, V., Aubry, S., and Hoeffner, J. (1996). Young children's imitation of sentence subjects: Evidence of processing *limitations*. *Developmental Psychology*, *32*, 153–164.

## Further Reading

Nicolson, R. (in press). Reading, learning and dyslexia. In: D. Messer and S. Millar (Eds.), *Developmental Psychology*, London: Arnold.

Wood, D. (1998). *How Children Think and Learn*. Oxford: Blackwell.

# 12 L. Bradley and P. E. Bryant
## 'Categorizing Sounds and Learning to Read – A Causal Connection'

Reprinted in full from: *Nature* 301, 419–421 (1983)

Children who are backward in reading are strikingly insensitive to rhyme and alliteration[1] They are at a disadvantage when categorizing words on the basis of common sounds even in comparison with younger children who read no better than they do. Categorizing words in this way involves attending to their constituent sounds, and so does learning to use the alphabet in reading and spelling. Thus the experiences which a child has with rhyme before he goes to school might have a considerable effect on his success later on in learning to read and to write. We now report the results of a large scale project which support this hypothesis.

Our study combined two different methods. The first was longitudinal. We measured 403 children's skills at sound categorization before they had started to read, and related these to their progress in reading and spelling over the next 4 yr: at the end of this time the size of our group was 368. The second was intensive training in sound categorization or other forms of categorization given to a subsample of our larger group. We used both methods because we reasoned that neither on its own is a sufficient test of a causal hypothesis and that the strengths and weaknesses of the two are complementary. Properly controlled training studies demonstrate cause-effect relationships, but these could be arbitrary; one cannot be sure that such relationships exist in real life. On the other hand longitudinal studies which control for other variables such as intelligence do demonstrate genuine relationships; but it is not certain that these are causal. For example simply to show that children's skills at categorizing sounds predict their success in reading later on would not exclude the possibility that both are determined by some unknown *tertium quid*. Thus the strength of each method makes up for the weakness of the other. Together they can isolate existing relationships and establish whether these are causal.

This combination of methods has not been used in studies of reading or, as far as we can establish, in developmental research in general.

Initially we tested 118 4-yr-olds and 285 5-yr-old children (Table 12.1) on categorizing sounds. None of the children could read (that is, were able to read any word in the Schonell reading test). Our method, as before[1] was to say three or four words per trial, all but one of which shared a common phoneme (Table 12.2): the child had to detect the odd word. There were 30 trials. In such a task the child must remember the words as well as categorize their sounds. To control for this we also gave them 30 memory trials: the child heard the same words and had to recall them straightaway. In addition we tested verbal intelligence (EPVT).

At the end of the project (as well as at other times) we gave the children standardized tests of reading and spelling, and we also tested their IQ (WISC/

**Table 12.1** Details of sample

|  | Children initially tested at age 4 yr | Children initially tested at age 5 yr |
|---|---|---|
| N at end of project | 104 | 264 |
| *Initial tests* |  |  |
| Mean age (months) | 58.62 | 65.52 |
| Mean EPVT | 110.62 | 109.39 |
| *Final tests* |  |  |
| Mean age (months) | 101.85 | 101.42 |
| Mean IQ (WISC) | 113.38 | 106.79 |
| Mean reading age (months) |  |  |
| Schonell | 103.13 | 100.03 |
| Neale | 105.13 | 101.30 |
| Mean spelling age (months) |  |  |
| Schonell | 97.27 | 93.94 |

R) to exclude the effects of intellectual differences. To check that our results were specific to reading and spelling and not to educational achievement in general we also included a standardized mathematical test (MATB-NFER), which we administered to 263 of our total sample of 368.

There were high correlations between the initial sound categorization scores and the children's reading and spelling over 3 yr later (Table 12.3). Stepwise multiple regressions established that these relationships remained strong even when the influence of intellectual level at the time of the initial and the final tests and of differences in memory were removed (Table 12.3). In every case categorizing sound accounted for a significant proportion of the variance in reading and spelling with these other factors controlled.

So a definite relationship does exist between a child's skill in categorizing sounds and his eventual success in reading and spelling. The design of the project, for the reasons just given, included a training study as a check that any such relationship is a causal one. 65 children were selected from our

**Table 12.2** Examples of words used in initial sound categorization tests and mean scores on these tests

| | 4-yr group | | | | 5-yr group | | | |
|---|---|---|---|---|---|---|---|---|
| | Words given to children | | | Mean correct (out of 10) | Words given to children | | | Mean correct (out of 10) |
| *Sounds in common* | | | | | | | | |
| First sound | hill | pig | pin | 5.69 (1.90) | bud | bun | bus | rug | 5.36 (2.29) |
| | bus | bun | rug | | pip | pin | hill | pig | |
| Middle sound | cot | pot | hat | 7.53 (1.96) | lot | cot | hat | pot | 6.89 (2.35) |
| | pin | bun | gun | | fun | pin | bun | gun | |
| End sound | pin | win | sit | 7.42 (2.09) | pin | win | sit | fin | 6.67 (2.33) |
| | doll | hop | top | | doll | hop | top | pop | |

Standard deviations given in parenthesis.

**Table 12.3** Correlations between initial sound categorization and final reading and spelling levels

*Correlations between initial scores and final scores*

| | Initial scores: | | | | | |
| | Sound categorization | | EPVT | | Memory | |
|---|---|---|---|---|---|---|
| Final scores | 4 | 5 | 4 | 5 | 4 | 5 |
| Reading: Schonell | 0.57 | 0.44 | 0.52 | 0.39 | 0.40 | 0.22 |
| Reading: Neale | 0.53 | 0.48 | 0.52 | 0.44 | 0.40 | 0.25 |
| Spelling: Schonell | 0.48 | 0.44 | 0.33 | 0.31 | 0.33 | 0.20 |

*Multiple regressions testing relationship of initial sound categorization to final reading and spelling levels*

| | Schonell reading | | Neale reading | | Schonell spelling | |
| | 4 | 5 | 4 | 5 | 4 | 5 |
|---|---|---|---|---|---|---|
| % Of total variance accounted for by all variables | 47.98 | 29.88 | 47.55 | 34.52 | 33.59 | 24.77 |
| % Of total variance accounted for by sound categorization* | 9.84† | 4.06† | 6.24† | 4.56† | 8.09† | 5.59† |

\* IQ, EPVT, final CA and memory controlled.
† $P < 0.001$.

sample and divided into four groups closely matched for age, verbal intelligence and their original scores on sound categorization. These children were drawn from those with lower scores on sound categorization (at least two standard deviations below the mean); they could not read when the training began. Starting in the second year of the project two of the groups (I and II) received intensive training in categorizing sounds. The training involved 40 individual sessions which were spread over 2 yr. With the help of coloured pictures of familiar objects the children were taught that the same word shared a common beginning (hen, hat), middle (hen, pet) and end (hen, man) sounds with other words and thus could be categorized in different ways. Group I received this training only, but group II in addition was taught, with the help of plastic letters, how each common sound was represented by a letter of the alphabet (see ref. 2 for further details of this method). The other two groups were controls. Group III was also taught over the same period in as many sessions and with the same pictures how to categorize but here the categories were conceptual ones; the children were taught that the same word could be classified in several different ways (for example, hen, bat (animals); hen, pig (farm animals)). Group IV received no training at all.

The training had a considerable effect which was specific to reading and spelling (Table 12.4). At the end of the project group I (trained on sound categorization only) was ahead of group III (trained on conceptual categorization only) by 3–4 months in standardized tests of reading and spelling. This suggests a causal relationship between sound categorization and reading and spelling. Group II (trained with alphabetic letters as well as on sound categorization) succeeded even better than group I (trained on sound

**Table 12.4** Training study: details of groups and mean final reading, spelling and mathematics levels

| | | Mean scores | | | |
| | | Experimental groups | | Control groups | |
| | Groups | I | II | III | IV |
| --- | --- | --- | --- | --- | --- |
| | N | 13 | 13 | 26 | 13 |
| Aptitude tests | | | | | |
| Initial EPVT | | 103.00 | 103.00 | 102.34 | 102.69 |
| Final IQ (WISC/R) | | 97.15 | 101.23 | 102.96 | 100.15 |
| Final educational tests | | | | | |
| Schonell: reading age (months) | | 92.23 | 96.96 | 88.48 | 84.46 |
| Neale: reading age (months) | | 93.47 | 99.77 | 89.09 | 85.70 |
| Schonell: spelling age (months) | | 85.97 | 98.81 | 81.76 | 75.15 |
| | N | 9 | 8 | 20 | 7 |
| Maths MATB (ratio score) | | 91.27 | 91.09 | 87.99 | 84.13 |

Reading, spelling and mathematics mean scores are adjusted for two covariates: age and IQ.

categorization only) in reading and particularly in spelling. This suggests that training in sound categorization is more effective when it also involves an explicit connection with the alphabet. That the relationship is specific to these two skills is shown by the mathematics results where the differences were a great deal smaller.

Analyses of covariance, in which the covariates were the children's final IQ scores and their age at the time of the final reading and spelling tests, established that the group differences were significant in the case of reading (Schonell: $F = 5.23$; d.f.3,58; $P < 0.003$. Neale: $F = 7.80$; d.f.3,58; $P < 0.001$) and of spelling ($F = 12.18$; d.f.3,58; $P < 0.001$)) but not in the case of mathematics ($F = 1.64$; d.f.3,39; $P$, not significant). Post tests (Tukey's HSD) showed that group II was significantly better than both control groups (groups III and IV) in Schonell and in Neale reading ($P < 0.05$) and in Schonell spelling ($P < 0.01$). There was no significant difference between groups I and II (the two groups trained in sound categorization) in the two reading tests but group II did surpass group I in spelling ($P < 0.05$). Although reading and spelling scores in group I were always ahead of those of group III this difference did not reach significance in the post tests. But the consistent 3–4-month superiority of group I over group III does strongly suggest that training in sound categorization affects progress in reading and spelling. Group I was significantly better than group IV (the untrained control group) in the two reading tests and in the spelling test ($P < 0.05$). On the other hand there were no significant differences at all between the two control groups (III and IV).

Put together our longitudinal and training results provide strong support for the hypothesis that the awareness of rhyme and alliteration which children acquire before they go to school, possibly as a result of their experiences at home, has a powerful influence on their eventual success in learning to read and to spell. Although others have suggested a link between phonological awareness and reading[3–5] our study is the first adequate empirical evidence that the link is causal. Our results also show how specific experiences which a child has before he goes to school may affect his progress once he gets there.

We thank Morag Maclean for help with gathering and analysing the data, the Oxford Education Authority and the schools for their cooperation, and the SSRC for supporting our research.

## References

Bradley, L., and Bryant, P. E. (1978). *Nature, 271*, 746–747.

Bradley, L. (1980). *Assessing Reading Difficulties.* Macmillan: London.

Goldstein, D. M. (1976). *Journal of Educational Psychology, 68*, 680–688.

Liberman, I. (1977) *et al.* In A. Reber, and D. Scarborough (Eds.), *Toward a Psychology of Reading.* Hillsdale, NJ: Lawrence Erlbaum Associates, Inc.

Lunderg, I., Olofsson, A., and Walls, S. (1980). *Scandinavian Journal of Psychology, 21*, 159–173.

# 13 Susan E. Gathercole and Alan D. Baddeley
## 'Phonological Working Memory: A Critical Building Block for Reading Development and Vocabulary Acquisition?'

Reprinted in full from: *European Journal of Psychology of Education* **8**, 259–272 (1993)

## Introduction

In this article we take the opportunity to review some of our recent work on the contribution of phonological working memory to the development during the early school years of two language processing skills: *reading* and *vocabulary acquisition*. As measures of these skills are often used by both educationalists and psychologists as convenient indices of a child's intellectual development, the nature of the developmental constraints on vocabulary and reading development is an issue of exceptional theoretical and practical importance. Our work suggests that children's phonological memory skills as they start school represent one such constraint. Convergent findings from longitudinal and cross-sectional studies, and from experimental comparisons of children with specific language-related difficulties, indicate that young children's skills at temporarily storing phonological material may place significant limits on the ease and rate with which they both develop their vocabulary knowledge and learn to read.

We discuss four specific issues concerning the developmental role of phonological memory in language development that have guided our recent research. These issues concern links between phonological memory and developmental language disorders, vocabulary acquisition, reading development and phonological awareness, and each issue is addressed in a separate section below. Before considering in detail our findings and their theoretical and practical implications, however, our theoretical framework for conceptualizing children's phonological memory skills is outlined.

## The development of phonological working memory

According to the working memory model introduced by Baddeley and Hitch (1974) and developed by Baddeley (1986), there is one component of memory that is specialized for the temporary maintenance and processing of verbal material. This component is termed the 'phonological loop'. The phonological loop system consists of two sub-components: the short-term phonological store, and an articulatory rehearsal process. Information is held in phonological form in the short-term store, from which it decays with time unless the material is rehearsed. The effect of rehearsal is to refresh the phonological traces in the short-term store, and so to offset decay. In this way, the short-term store and the rehearsal process are semi-independent processes which function in concert with one another in memory tasks. However, the work discussed in the present article does not attempt to distinguish between the phonological short-term store and rehearsal as sources of individual differences in children's phonological memory skills. We therefore prefer to use the more neutral term phonological working memory to refer to the parts of working memory, such as the phonological loop, that are involved in the temporary storage of verbal material.

Phonological working memory undergoes dramatic development during childhood, with memory span for words increasing almost three-fold between the ages of 4 and 11 years (Nicolson, 1981; Hulme, Thomson, Muir and Lawrence, 1984). Much of this developmental increase appears to be attributable to the increasing rapidity of subvocal articulatory rehearsal as children become more experienced language users. As a consequence of this increase in rehearsal rate, more items can be actively maintained in the phonological store and so the functional capacity of the phonological loop expands.

Although the phonological working memory skills of preschool children are limited in comparison with older children and adults, they show a considerable degree of individual variation. In fact we have recently shown that in children as young as 2 years of age, performance on short-term memory tasks such as digit span (involving the immediate recall of a series of spoken digits) and nonword repetition (in which the task is simply to repeat an unfamiliar phonological form such as 'biffle') are closely associated with one another, indicating systematic differences in phonological memory ability (Gathercole and Adams, 1993). The roots of differences in phonological memory skill in very young children such as these are as yet unknown, although recent evidence reveals a close link with speech production abilities (Adams and Gathercole, in prep.). For the moment, though, the important point is that some preschool children are much better at temporarily storing phonological material than others.

### Developmental language disorders: The consequences of poor phonological working memory skills?

The first indication for us that these individual differences in children's phonological memory skills may directly influence both reading development and vocabulary acquisition arose from working with a group of children with disordered language development (Gathercole and Baddeley, 1990a). Also known as specific language-impaired, children with this developmental disorder have deficits in a wide range of language abilities in the absence of any detectable physical, social or emotional disturbances. A large body of research has documented the multiple language deficits of language disordered children (e.g., Aram and Nation, 1975; Benton, 1978; Leonard, 1982; Stark and Tallal, 1981). Hallmarks of the disorder include poor vocabulary growth, language comprehension difficulties, and impaired literacy acquisition.

Our principal interest was in the phonological working memory skills of language disordered children. Deficits of verbal short-term memory in such populations had already been established (Graham, 1980; Kirchner and Klatzky, 1985; Locke and Scott, 1979; Wiig and Semel, 1976), although previous work had not been guided by a detailed model of short-term memory. We wanted to know what particular aspect of working memory was deficient in children with developmental disorders of language. Accordingly, a group of language disordered children attending a Language Unit for remedial instruction in language skills were selected for the study. The children were aged between 6 and 10 years, and on standardized tests each child performed well below the appropriate level for their age on measures of vocabulary knowledge, reading and language comprehension. This group were individually matched with two control groups: a group matched on nonverbal intelligence of the same age, and a group of children on average aged 2 years younger than the language disordered children but who were matched on vocabulary and reading measures.

A range of standard tests of phonological working memory was given to each group of children. These included nonword repetition, and serial recall of lists of short words, long words and phonologically similar words. On each measure, the language disordered children were significantly impaired compared with both control groups. The poor memory abilities of the disordered group were therefore not simply a consequence of their low level of language development, as this was matched with the younger control children. Interestingly, though, the language disordered children were no less sensitive to variables known to influence the phonological loop such as word length and phonological similarity, despite their lower level of overall recall. It therefore appears that their phonological loop systems were intact, but were of reduced capacity.

The most striking results arose with a test of nonword repetition, in which the child hears an unfamiliar phonological form (such as 'blonterstaping') and has to repeat it immediately. The nonwords ranged in length from one to four syllables, and the accuracy of each repetition was scored. This test appears to be particularly sensitive to phonological memory skills (Gathercole, Willis, Emslie and Baddeley, 1991). The language disordered children were much less accurate at nonword repetition, scoring on average only 52% correct, whereas both control groups correctly repeated on average 84% of the nonwords. Moreover, scores on this test perfectly discriminated the disordered children from the controls. Figure 13.1 summarizes the repetition performance of the three groups as a function of the number of syllables in the nonwords. The language disordered children were as accurate at repeating the one- and two-syllables items as the controls, but their performance declined dramatically for the lengthier stimuli. The phonological loop system is known to be sensitive to the temporal duration of memory items, with recall declining as a function of the number of syllables in memory items in both adults and children (Baddeley, Thomson and Buchanan, 1975; Hulme et al., 1984). The differential sensitivity of the language disordered children to the length of the nonwords is therefore entirely consistent with the view that their phonological loop systems have a reduced capacity.

The nonword repetition test administered to the language disordered children and their control was also given to a large unselected cohort of

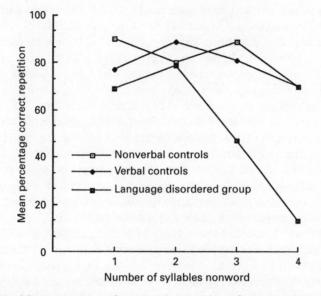

**Figure 13.1**   Mean accuracy of nonword repetition of the language disordered group (LDG) and the two groups of control children (Verbal Controls), as a function of the number of syllables.

children in the Cambridge longitudinal study described in the section below (Gathercole, Willis, Emslie and Baddeley, 1992). We therefore have normative data on this test. Applying these data, the nonword repetition scores of the language disordered children (mean score 21.8, with an average age of eight years in the group) corresponded to those obtained for normal four-year old children (mean score 22.0) from the longitudinal study. In nonword repetition performance, therefore, the language disordered group were developmentally delayed on average by about four years. This finding indicates that the phonological memory deficits of the disordered group were even greater in magnitude than their developmental language problems: on standardized tests of vocabulary, reading and comprehension, the mean delays of the group ranged between 18 and 24 months.

Nonword repetition deficits of similar magnitude in samples of language disordered children have also been reported by Bird (1991) and Taylor, Lean, and Schwartz (1989). In our sample, there was no indication that the disordered group had either phonological discrimination problems or slow articulatory output rates. It therefore appears that a deficit in phonological storage, rather than perceptual or articulatory output skills, formed the basis of the repetition deficits of these children (see, also, Taylor et al., 1989).

One possible explanation for the profile of deficits of the language disordered children is that their poor phonological memory skills are instrumental to their failure to develop language normally. We were interested specifically in whether the memory impairments had contributed to these children's difficulties in vocabulary acquisition and in learning to read. In order to explore these hypotheses directly, we conducted a longitudinal study over a 4-year period which allowed us to evaluate developmental associations between phonological memory skills and both vocabulary and reading development.

### Phonological working memory as a longitudinal predictor of vocabulary acquisition

We have now completed a longitudinal study of 118 children who were tested initially at the age of 4, within two months of joining infant school in the Cambridge area of England. Subsequently, the children were tested at ages 5 and 6 years, and then finally at age 8. At each age, measures of phonological memory skill, nonverbal intelligence, receptive vocabulary and reading were taken. The principal measure of phonological memory skill was a test of nonword repetition (Gathercole and Baddeley, 1990a; Gathercole et al., 1991). Complete data from each of the four waves of the study is available for 80 children (see Gathercole and Baddeley, 1989, and Gathercole, Willis, Emslie and Baddeley, 1992, for further details).

It seemed very likely to us that the children's skills at temporarily maintaining phonological material, assessed by the nonword repetition test, might act as a significant constraint on their abilities to construct a long-term representation of the phonological form of a new word. Quite simply, if a child cannot retain an item sufficiently well to be able to repeat it immediately, he or she will stand little chance of being able to retrieve that item from long-term memory some time later. And certainly, the findings that language disordered children have impaired phonological memory skills and poor vocabulary growth is entirely consistent with this view. So too was the finding that a neuropsychological patient with a highly selective deficit of the phonological loop was unable to learn novel phonological forms such as the vocabulary of a foreign language (Baddeley, Papagno and Vallar, 1988).

Correlations between the nonword repetition and vocabulary tests were significant at each of the 4 waves of the longitudinal study: the correlation coefficients were .559 at age 4, .524 at age 5, .562 at age 6 and .284 at age 8. These associations were consistent with the hypothesis that phonological memory ability constrains vocabulary learning, although it is noteworthy that the association between repetition and vocabulary scores is significantly reduced at age 8 relative to the three earlier waves. Correlations cannot, however, establish the direction of causality between two abilities. In order to assess whether there was a causal association between phonological memory skills and vocabulary acquisition, we turned to the technique of cross-lagged correlations (Crano and Mellon, 1978). Across each one-year time interval within the four years of the project, the forward partial correlations between nonword repetition and vocabulary scores, and between vocabulary and nonword repetition scores (adjusted for age, nonverbal intelligence and scores on the later measure at the earlier point in time, in each case), were compared. For example, the partial correlation between nonword repetition at 4 and vocabulary at age 5 was compared with the partial correlation between vocabulary at age 4 and repetition at age 5. According to the logic

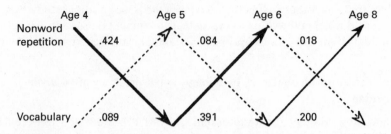

**Figure 13.2** Cross-lagged partial correlations (with age, nonverbal intelligence scores on the outcome variable one year earlier controlled) between nonword repetition and vocabulary scores (Gathercole et al., 1992). Lines shown in bold denote partial correlations that are significantly greater than the cross-lagged.

of cross-lagged correlations), causal developmental relationships will be reflected in a stronger forward than backward association in time between the causal factor and its consequent (see Figure 13.2).

The patterns of associations across the time panels are summarized in Figure 13.2. The causal underpinning of the developmental association between nonword repetition and vocabulary appears to shift dramatically at age 5. Between 4 and 5 years, the pacemaker in the developmental relationship is clearly the phonological memory measure. Whereas the partial correlation between repetition scores at 4 and the vocabulary measure at 5 is highly significant, the converse association between vocabulary at 4 and repetition at 5 is nonsignificant. Between 5 and 6, however, it is the partial correlation between vocabulary and later repetition which is significant, while the converse association between nonword repetition at 5 and vocabulary at 6 is near zero. The same pattern of a forward association between vocabulary and later nonword repetition scores and a nonsignificant converse relationship is reflected between the ages of 6 and 8. Note too that one other measure of phonological memory skill was taken at each wave, and that these data showed the same shift in the causal relationship with vocabulary during the course of the longitudinal study (Gathercole et al., 1992).

The results from the first two waves of the study are entirely consistent with the notion that phonological working memory plays a critical role in establishing long-term memory representations of the phonological forms of new words. They also fit well with experimental findings that normal 5-year old children with good phonological memory skills learn new names of toy animals more rapidly than children of low memory skills but comparable nonverbal intelligence (Gathercole and Baddeley, 1990b). Recent findings by Service (1992) that the nonword repetition abilities of Finnish children predicted their achievement in second language learning over two years later similarly point to phonological memory skills representing an important developmental constraint on word learning. Although the nature of normal individual variation in these skills is not yet entirely clear, it does appear that the discriminability and persistence of the phonological traces in memory will directly influence whether those traces will be held in more stable long-term storage and so link semantically with stored representations of the new word's conceptual attributes.

Beyond the age of 5, though, vocabulary knowledge appears to become the driving force, becoming a very good predictor of subsequent repetition ability. There are a number of reasons why this developmental change may occur. It may be that children learn to use their existing vocabulary knowledge to mediate the repetition of nonwords, perhaps by accessing words which share some of the phonological segments of the nonword to alleviate the burden on temporary phonological storage (Gathercole et al., 1991). This may explain the emergence of a causal link between vocabulary knowledge and subsequent nonword repetition performance. Why, though, does the phonological memory measure not maintain its strong positive association with future vocabulary scores? Perhaps other constraints on vocabulary development become more important during middle childhood. Children's phonological memory skills develop very rapidly during the first years at school, so that for most children temporary storage factors may no longer limit their word learning. Also, it seems likely that as children mature, the words that they learn become more abstract in nature, showing less direct correspondence to tangible physical events. The child's abilities to understand the conceptual attributes of novel words may therefore become a more critical word learning constraint. A further emerging factor may be the child's experience of reading. Recent work by Cunningham and Stanovich (1991) suggests that vocabulary acquisition in late childhood is influenced by the extent of the child's exposure to print. There is indirect evidence for this factor in our longitudinal study, too: reading ability at age 6 correlated highly ($r = .681$) with vocabulary scores two years later.

So, phonological memory constraints appear to be important in natural vocabulary learning in the early school years, although they become less critical during middle childhood as memory skills improve and other factors come into play. This does not, however, mean that phonological working memory has no role to play in word learning in late childhood and adults. Work with both older children and adults has shown that phonological memory is important in situations where the long-term learning of the novel phonological form cannot be readily mediated by more semantically-based strategies, for example in foreign vocabulary learning where the foreign word is very distinctive in sound structure from words within the first language (Papagno, Valentine and Baddeley, 1991; Service, 1992).

**Phonological working memory as a longitudinal predictor of reading development**

Links between reading ability and phonological working memory skills during the primary school years are already well-established (see Jorm, 1983; and Wagner and Torgesen, 1987, for reviews). Most of the evidence, though, is based on cross-sectional correlational associations between reading and memory measures; in a typical experiment, lower scores of a test of serial recall of verbal material are found in 8-year old children of poor rather than good reading ability (e.g., Shankweiler, Liberman, Mark, Fowler and Fischer, 1979). Such studies are of value in establishing the deficits associated with poor reading achievement, but cannot distinguish between alternative causal hypotheses. For example, it could either be that phonological memory problems retard normal reading development, or that reading achievement itself stimulates phonological memory development.

In order to distinguish between these alternative theoretical accounts of the positive link between phonological memory skills and reading development, we have investigated whether phonological memory skill before children started learning to read can be used as a predictor of later reading achievement, by studying the children from the Cambridge longitudinal study who could not read when they were first tested. Although there have been a small number of longitudinal studies which have looked at the developmental associations between phonological memory and reading, there are methodological problems with each. In one case the majority of children at initial test had started to read (Ellis and Large, 1988) and in another, no reading test was reported to have been administered at selection making it impossible to determine which children had not yet started to read (Mann and Liberman, 1984). Wagner and Torgesen (1987) point out that unless the children are prereaders at initial test, the possibility that a significant link between phonological memory skill and later reading achievement is mediated by an early causal contribution of reading success to memory development cannot be rejected. Therefore in our study, data are only reported for children who failed to correctly identify any of the words in the reading test administered in the first wave (Gathercole, Willis, Emslie and Baddeley, in prep.) (see Table 13.1).

The children were tested at regular intervals until the age of 8, when they were given the range of reading tests illustrated in Table 13.1. Other measures taken from the cohort included a test of arithmetic ability and a language comprehension test. Our primary interest was in whether the measure of phonological memory skill taken before the children started to read, which was scored on the nonword repetition test, was a significant predictor of reading achievements at age 8. This was estimated using a fixed-order multiple regression procedure which allowed us to control for differences in age and nonverbal intelligence at age 4. Further regression analyses were also performed in which differences in prereading vocabulary scores were also controlled. This second set of analyses was performed in order to maintain

**Table 13.1** Partial correlations between nonword repetition scores at age 4 and outcome measures at age 8 (additional $r^2$ shown)

| Test | Example of a line from the test |
| --- | --- |
| British Abilities Scales[1] | said water bird wood running |
| Neale Test[2] | The bird hopped up to my window |
| Primary Reading Test[3] | He opened his _____ to shout (asleep chest mouth ears pocket) |

Note: [1] Elliot (1983); [2] Neale (1989); [3] France (1981).

comparability of statistical procedure with an earlier influential longitudinal study reported by Bradley and Bryant (1983) which showed that awareness of rhyme in prereading children was significantly associated with reading ability at age 8. However, as discussed in the previous section, phonological memory skill appears to play an important role in vocabulary development in the early school years (Gathercole, Willis, Emslie and Baddeley, 1992). Partialling out the variance in later reading scores associated with the early vocabulary measure will therefore lead to significant underestimation in the strength of the developmental relationship between prereading phonological memory skill and reading achievement.

The results are summarized in Table 13.2. When obvious confounding factors were taken into account, the nonword repetition measure at age 4 was a significant predictor of only one measure of age 8 reading ability, the Primary Reading test. Performance on the other reading measures, and on the tests of arithmetic and language comprehension abilities, showed no indication of a separable positive link with earlier scores on this phonological memory test. The predictive relationship between nonword repetition and reading development therefore shows a surprising degree of specificity. Not only was the forward association restricted to reading performance, ruling out the possibility that the repetition measure is an intellectual facilitator of a more general nature, but its influence was restricted to one particular measure of reading.

The important question is, of course, why there is this high degree of specificity to the developmental relationship between prereading phonological memory skills and later reading achievement. In attempting to answer this question, it is necessary to consider in detail the nature of the three reading tests, illustrated in Table 13.1. The factor that we consider most clearly distinguishes the Primary Reading test from the other measures is the extent to which a strategy of phonological recoding unfamiliar words is likely to be successful for the child. Consider first the single-word reading test, taken from the British Abilities Scales. No linguistic context is provided for the words the child has to read, so the test probably provides a relatively pure measure of the

**Table 13.2** Examples of items from the Reading Tests used in the longitudinal study

| Measure | With age and nonverbal intelligence controlled | With age, nonverbal intelligence and vocabulary controlled |
|---|---|---|
| *Reading measures* | | |
| BAS | .014 | .001 |
| Neale accuracy | .015 | .001 |
| Neale comprehension | .017 | .000 |
| Primary reading | .088** | .049* |
| *Other measures* | | |
| Arithmetic[1] | .000 | .001 |
| Comprehension[2] | .010 | .005 |

Note: [1] Weschler (1974); [2] Bishop (1982); * $p < .05$; ** $p < .01$.

child's word decoding skills. Moreover, many of the words in the test involve irregular or inconsistent spelling patterns; by our calculations, at least 50% of the first 30 words. A strategy of phonological recoding from print into sound will therefore not be very successful in this test. And even for the regular words, the child would need to successfully recode all of the letters in order to generate the correct pronunciation in the absence of any contextual cues. The partial recoding strategy which many young children adopt, focussing on the initial one or two letters of a word only, is not very likely to yield the right word in this test. Performance on this reading measure therefore seems likely to largely reflect the child's sight vocabulary; that is, the words whose visual configurations the child had already learned prior to the test.

The Neale test is rather different. It involves the child reading aloud short stories which are illustrated in pictures. This test therefore allows context to be used to guide the recognition of unfamiliar words. However, as many of the words in the sentences are not highly predictable from the preceding context, a sophisticated guessing strategy in which the child matches a partial phonological code with plausible candidates for the word may not be particularly effective unless either the word is regular or the child uses the strategy very efficiently. Performance on this test therefore seems likely to reflect both the child's sight vocabulary and use of context, and to a lesser extent phonological recoding skills.

In contrast, the design of the Primary Reading test is highly compatible with the use of a phonological recoding strategy. The phonological form of the target word is provided either by the accompanying picture in the early test items, or by the rest of the sentence in the later items. The child's task is to choose which of the five alternative words corresponds to the target word. For half of the items in the test, none of the foils share the same initial letter (or phoneme) of the target words. The degree of letter overlap between the target and foils in the remaining items is variable, but in no cases would the child have to accurately graphemically recode more than the first three phonemes of the target (or, phonologically recode more than the first three letters in the five words) in order to make the correct selection. Thus a partial recoding strategy for unfamiliar words is likely to be very successful in this test.

We therefore consider it likely that a strategy of partial phonological recoding of unfamiliar words will be much more successful in the Primary Reading test than the BAS test, a view that fits well with the relatively low correlations between the tests. This analysis raises the interesting possibility that phonological memory skills constrain the development of a phonological recoding strategy. We have considered a number of ways in which this developmental constraint may operate. Phonological memory may be used to temporarily store the phonological segments generated when a child maps successive graphemes onto their phonological equivalents, prior to output of the blended phonological sequence (Baddeley, 1978). So, children with small phonological memory capacities may be relatively less successful at developing this recoding strategy. Alternatively, the ease of long-term learning of correspondences between letters and sounds may depend on the child being able to retain adequate temporary representation of the sound segments, in the same way that short-term phonological memory appears to limit the long-term learning of novel words (Baddeley and Gathercole, 1992; Gathercole and Baddeley, 1993). In this way, poor phonological memory skills may retard the acquisition of the rule-based knowledge needed to exploit the regularities between the spoken and written forms of language.

## Phonological working memory and phonological awareness

These results suggest that children's phonological memory skills as they start school have an important influence both on their vocabulary acquisition in the near future and possibly on the development of a phonological recoding strategy for reading some years later. An important issue that we have not considered so far concerns the relationship between phonological working memory and another skill known to be closely related to reading success: phonological awareness. This term refers to the ability to respond to the explicit sound structure of spoken language, and is reflected in a wide range of measures which include asking the child to tap out the number of component sounds in words (Liberman, Shankweiler, Fischer and Carter, 1974), to add or delete sounds at the beginning or end of words (Morais, Cary, Alegria and Bertelson, 1979) and to judge which words in a list do not share a common sound sequence (Bradley and Bryant, 1978).

Bradley and Bryant (1983) found that awareness of rhyme in prereading children, assessed by asking the child to identify which of three words does not share the same sequence of sound (e.g., 'peg, mat, cat'), is a significant predictor of later success in reading and spelling (see, too, Bryant, Maclean, Bradley and Crossland, 1990). Scores on the rhyme task before the children started to read accounted for between 4 and 10% of unique variance in reading and spelling performance when the children were aged 8, and so were of a similar predictive strength to the nonword repetition measure used in the Cambridge longitudinal study over the same interval of time. On the basis of these findings, it has been suggested that children need to have awareness of the componential structure of spoken language in order to capitalize upon the regularity of spelling-sound relationships.

A pressing question which is not yet fully answered is whether the two types of measure, of phonological awareness and phonological working memory, have the same or dissociable influences on reading development. It certainly appears likely that good phonological memory skills are necessary if a 4-year old child is to succeed on Bradley and Bryant's (1983) rhyme awareness task, in which the child chooses which word of three does not rhyme with either of the other two. The phonological structures of each word need to be held while the child makes at least two pairwise comparisons. As the memory span for the average 4-year old child is somewhere between two and three words (Hulme et al., 1984), it follows that at least some of the children will be unable to perform the task reliably because their phonological memory capacity will be exceeded.

This analysis certainly fits well with the positive correlations between measures of phonological awareness and phonological working memory skill in children during the early years of school. In a cross-sectional study (Gathercole, Willis, and Baddeley, 1991), we found that rhyme awareness scores in four-year old children were positively associated with nonword repetition but not with digit span scores ($r = .274$, $p < .05$, and $r = .228$, n.s., respectively). Most of these children failed to read any words on the single-word reading test of the British Abilities Scales (Elliot, 1983). For the five-year old children, the links between rhyme awareness and phonological memory measures were much stronger: $r = .597$, $p < .001$, with repetition and $r = .519$, $p < .001$, with digit span. The majority of this older subject group (34 of a total of 51) were able to read one or more words in the single-word reading test. However, despite the associations between the awareness and memory scores in the five-year olds, the measures of rhyme awareness and phonological memory (nonword repetition and digit span) had dissociable links with reading and vocabulary ability. In particular, whereas scores on the phonological memory tasks accounted for significant unique portions of variance in vocabulary knowledge, awareness of rhyme did not. Also, whereas the rhyme awareness measure was closely linked with reading scores in both age groups, the association between phonological memory skill and reading emerged only for the older, five-year old, children. Similarly, Ellis and Large (1988) found differential time courses to the developmental associations between reading and the two types of phonological processing ability.

On present evidence, it looks as though phonological awareness and phonological working memory abilities do share a common phonological processing component, perhaps because phonological memory is needed in tasks designed to assess awareness of the sound structure of language. With respect to reading and vocabulary development, however, it looks as though the contributions of the two types of skills are, to some degree, unique (see Gathercole and Baddeley, 1993). One possibility is that phonological awareness is a prerequisite for distinguishing the component sounds in spoken words, whereas phonological working memory is used both in learning the associations between these phonemes and the letters, and in storing sound segments generated by the child when attempting to phonologically recode an unfamiliar printed word. In other words, awareness and working memory may make different contributions and place differentiable constraints upon the component processes involved in phonological recoding. This view is consistent in principle at least with recent analyses which have identified several critical stages in the development of an efficient phonological recoding strategy in reading (e.g., Byrne and Fielding-Barnsley, 1989).

Proper resolution of the debate over whether phonological working memory and phonological awareness make common or differentiable contributions to reading development, though, can probably only be achieved by a direct empirical evaluation of the longitudinal contribution of the two phonological processing skills to literacy acquisition. To this end, a project currently in progress in our laboratory is tracing the development of rhyme awareness, phonological working memory, and many other verbal and nonverbal skills during the preschool and early school years. We hope that the results of this study will answer at least some of the remaining questions about the nature of the developmental contributions of phonological awareness and memory to literacy acquisition.

## Practical implications

Evidence from both normal and language disordered children suggests that phonological memory skills are directly related to the child's abilities to learn new words, and to develop an important reading strategy. A child whose ability to temporarily retain phonological material is inadequate therefore seems likely to be at risk of poor vocabulary growth and developmental reading difficulties. The practical implications seem straight forward: promoting phonological memory skills in children with below-average abilities in this domain should yield important benefits and may even offer immunity from serious disorders of language development. The approach could be used either remedially, to improve the language abilities of children with developmental language problems that have already been identified, or preventatively, in younger children of low phonological working memory ability.

The idea of training phonological memory in children as a way of boosting their language development has not so far received much attention, and as yet little is known about the nature of suitable training techniques. Traditional methods of promoting verbal short-term memory skills have involved recruiting resources from other parts of memory, and using them to avoid reliance upon the limited phonological memory system (e.g., Paivio, 1971; Ericsson and Chase, 1982). These techniques are therefore not designed to directly enhance phonological working memory.

One possibility is that phonological working memory may be boosted by enriching the linguistic environment of the child. Mann (1984) suggested that methods such as providing practice in naming letters and objects, in remembering spoken sequences and nursery rhymes, and at listening to stories, may all be useful for children at risk of developing reading problems. Indeed, they may directly enhance the efficiency of phonological encoding, and hence of retaining phonological material in working memory. Another way of promoting phonological memory skills may be to provide children with practice in repeating unfamiliar phonological forms, which may encourage them both to perceive the essentially combinatorial basis of the phonetic structure of language (Lindblom, 1989), and to develop articulatory gestural skills which may themselves mediate speech perception (Liberman and Mattingley, 1985).

## Summary

Our longitudinal study of phonological working memory skills and their associations with important aspects of language development such as vocabulary and reading acquisition has yielded a rich database. There do appear to be close links between working memory and both vocabulary learning and reading development, but the nature of the relationships is more dynamic than we expected (in the case of vocabulary growth) and also more specific (in the case of reading). This, we suspect, is one of the most powerful features of the longitudinal study: the opportunities for discovering hitherto unsuspected developmental relationships, and hence for provoking theoretical development, appear to be notably greater than in cross-sectional studies.

## References

Adams, A.-M., and Gathercole, S. E. (in prep). *Developmental associations between speech production and phonological working memory.*

Aram, D. M., and Nation, J. E. (1975). Patterns of language behaviour in children with developmental language disorders. *Journal of Speech & Hearing Research, 18,* 229–241.

Baddeley, A. D. (1978). Working memory and reading. In P. A. Kolers, M. E. Wrolstad, and H. Bouma (Eds.), *Processing of Visible Language, Vol. 1,* (pp. 355–370). New York: Plenum Press.

Baddeley, A. D. (1986). *Working Memory.* Oxford: Oxford University Press.

Baddeley, A. D., and Gathercole, S. E. (1992). Learning to read: The role of the phonological loop. In J. Alegria, D. Holander, J. J. de Morais, and M. Radeau (Eds.), *Analytic Approaches to Human Cognition,* (pp. 153–168). Elsevier.

Baddeley, A. D., and Hitch, G. J. (1974). Working memory. In G. Bower (Ed.), *The Psychology of Learning and Motivation, Vol. 8,* 47–90.

Baddeley, A. D., Papagno, C., and Vallar, G. (1988). When long-term learning depends on short-term storage. *Journal of Memory & Language, 27,* 586–596.

Baddeley, A. D., Thomson, N., and Buchanan, M. (1975). Word length and the structure of short-term memory. *Journal of Verbal Learning & Verbal Behavior, 14,* 575–589.

Benton, A. (1978). The cognitive functioning of children with developmental aphasia. In M. Wyke (Ed.), *Developmental Dysphasia.* New York: Academic Press.

Bishop, D. (1982). *Test for the Reception of Grammar.* Available from the author at MRC Applied Psychology Unit, Cambridge, UK.

Bird, J. (1981). *The auditory perception, phonemic awareness and literacy skills of phonologically disordered children.* Unpublished PhD thesis from the University of Manchester.

Bradley, L., and Bryant, P. E. (1978). Difficulties in auditory organization as a possible cause of reading backwardness. *Nature, 271,* 746–747.

Bradley, L., and Bryant, P. E. (1983). Categorizing sounds and learning to read – a causal connection. *Nature, 301,* 419–420.

Bryant, P. E., Maclean, M., Bradley, L., and Crossland, J. (1990). Rhyme and alliteration, phoneme detection, and learning to read. *Developmental Psychology, 26,* 429–438.

Byrne, B., and Fielding-Barnsley, R. (1989). Phonemic awareness and letter knowledge in the child's acquisition of the alphabetic principle. *Journal of Educational Psychology, 81,* 313–321.

Crano, W. D., and Mellon, P. M. (1978). Causal influence of teachers' expectations on children's academic performance: A cross-lagged panel analysis. *Journal of Educational Psychology, 70,* 39–49.

Cunningham, A. E., and Stanovich, K. E. (1991). Tracking the unique effects of print exposure in children: Associations with vocabulary, general knowledge and spelling. *Journal of Educational Psychology, 83,* 264–274.

Elliott, C. D. (1983). *British Abilities Scales*. Windsor: NFER-Nelson Publishing Company Ltd.

Ellis, N., and Large, B. (1988). The early stages of reading: A longitudinal study. *Applied Cognitive Psychology, 2*, 47–76.

Ericsson, K. A., and Chase, W. G. (1982). Exceptional memory. *American Scientist, 70*, 607–615.

France, N. (1981). *Primary Reading Test (Revised Edition)*. NFER-Nelson Publishing Company Ltd: Windsor.

Gathercole, S. E., and Adams, A.-M. (1993). Phonological working memory in very young children. *Developmental Psychology, 29*.

Gathercole, S. E., and Baddeley, A. D. (1989). Evaluation of the role of phonological STM in the development of vocabulary in children: A longitudinal study. *Journal of Memory & Language, 28*, 200–213.

Gathercole, S. E., and Baddeley, A. D. (1990a). Phonological memory deficits in language disordered children: Is there a causal connection? *Journal of Memory & Language, 29*, 336–360.

Gathercole, S. E., and Baddeley, A. D. (1990b). The role of phonological memory in vocabulary acquisition: A study of young children learning arbitrary names of toys. *British Journal of Psychology, 81*, 439–454.

Gathercole, S. E., and Baddeley, A. D. (1993). *Working Memory and Language Processing*. Hove: Lawrence Erlbaum Associates.

Gathercole, S. E., Willis, C. S., and Baddeley, A. D. (1991). Differentiating phonological memory and awareness of rhyme; Reading and vocabulary development in children. *British Journal of Psychology, 82*, 387–406.

Gathercole, S. E., Willis, C., Emslie, H., and Baddeley, A. (1991). The influences of number of syllables and word-likeness on children's repetition of nonwords. *Applied Psycholinguistics, 12*, 349–367.

Gathercole, S. E., Willis, C., Emslie, H., and Baddeley, A. (1992). Phonological memory and vocabulary development during the early school years: A longitudinal study. *Developmental Psychology, 28*, 887–898.

Gathercole, S. E., Willis, C. S., Emslie, H., and Baddeley, A. D. (in prep.). *Phonological memory skill in prereading children as a predictor of later reading achievement.*

Graham, N. C. (1980). Memory constraints in language deficiency. In F. Margaret Jones (Ed.), *Language Disability in Children*, (pp. 69–94). Baltimore: University Park Press.

Hulme, C., Thomson, N., Muir, C., and Lawrence, A. (1984). Speech rate and the development of short-term memory span. *Journal of Experimental Child Psychology, 38*, 241–253.

Jorm, A. (1983). Specific reading retardation and working memory: A review. *British Journal of Psychology, 74*, 311–342.

Kirchner, D., and Klatzky, R. L. (1985). Verbal rehearsal and memory in language-disordered children. *Journal of Speech & Hearing Research, 28*, 556–565.

Leonard, L. B. (1982). Phonological deficits in children with developmental language impairment. *Brain & Language, 16*, 73–86.

Liberman, A. M., and Mattingley, I. G. (1985). The motor theory of speech perception revisited. *Cognition, 21*, 1–36.

Liberman, I. Y., Shankweiler, D., Fischer, F. W., and Carter, B. (1974). Explicit syllable and phoneme segmentation in the young child. *Journal of Experimental Child Psychology, 18*, 201–212.

Lindblom, B. (1989). Some remarks on the origin of the phonetic code. In A. von Euler, I. Lundberg and G. Lennerstrand (Eds.), *Brain and Reading*, (pp. 27–44). Stockton Press.

Locke, J. L., and Scott, K. K. (1979). Phonetically mediated recall in the phonetically disordered child. *Journal of Communication Disorders, 12*, 125–131.

Mann, V. A. (1984). Longitudinal prediction and prevention of early reading difficulty. *Annals of Dyslexia, 34*, 117–136.

Mann, V. A., and Liberman, I. Y. (1984). Phonological awareness and verbal short-term memory. *Journal of Learning Disabilities, 17*, 592–599.

Morais, J., Cary, L., Alegria, J., and Bertelson, P. (1979). Does awareness of speech as a sequence of phones arise spontaneously? *Cognition, 7*, 323–331.

Neale, M. (1989). *Neale Analysis of Reading Abilities (Revised British Edition)*. Windsor: NFER Nelson.

Nicolson, R. (1981). The relationship between memory span and processing speed. In M. Friedman, J. P. Das, and N. O'Connor (Eds.), *Intelligence and Learning*, (pp. 179–184). Plenum Press.

Paivio, A. (1971). *Imagery and Verbal Processes*. New York: Holt, Rinehart and Winston.

Papagno, C., Valentine, T., and Baddeley, A. (1991). Phonological short-term memory and foreign-language vocabulary learning. *Journal of Memory & Language, 30*, 331–347.

Service, E. (1992). Phonology, working memory and foreign-language learning. *Quarterly Journal of Experimental Psychology, 45A*, 21–50.

Shankweiler, D., Liberman, I. Y., Mark, L. S., Fowler, C. A., and Fischer, F. W. (1979). The speech code and learning to read. *Journal of Experimental Psychology: Human Learning & Memory, 5*, 531–545.

Stark, R., and Tallal, P. (1981). Selection of children with specific language deficits. *Journal of Speech and Hearing Disorders, 46*, 114–122.

Taylor, H. G., Lean, D., and Schwartz, S. (1989). Pseudoword repetition ability in learning-disabled children. *Applied Psycholinguistics, 10*, 203–219.

Wagner, R. K., and Torgesen, J. K. (1987). The nature of phonological processing and its causal role in the acquisition of reading skills. *Psychological Bulletin, 101*, 192–212.

Wechsler, D. (1974). *Manual for the Wechsler Intelligence Scale for Children – Revised*. New York: Psychological Corporation.

Wiig, E., and Semel, E. M. (1976). *Language Disabilities in Children and Adolescents*. Columbus, OH: Charles E. Merrill.

# 14  J. Oakhill and N. Yuill
### 'Learning to Read: Psychology in the Classroom'

Reprinted in full from: *Learning to Read: Psychology in the Classroom* (Blackwell Publishers Ltd, 1995)

## Introduction

In this chapter, we will be considering the problems of children who have good word recognition, can understand sentences and can read aloud apparently fluently, but who have only a rudimentary understanding of what they have just read. There are many skills needed to understand a text adequately. The meanings of the individual sentences and paragraphs must be integrated, and the main ideas of the text identified. On-going comprehension also needs to be monitored, so that any failures can be corrected. We are going to concentrate on three main areas of comprehension skill, and illustrate the problems of less-skilled comprehenders with some of our own work in each of the areas.

The first area is *Inference skills*. In many cases, inferences will be needed to go beyond what is explicitly stated in a text. Authors, of necessity, leave some of the links in a text implicit, and the reader will need to assess, at some level, which inferences need to be made. Second, readers need to *understand the structure* of the text they are reading. In the case of stories, this might include identifying the main character(s) and their motives, following the plot of the story, identifying the main theme. The third area, *comprehension monitoring*, requires the readers to assess their understanding as they are reading. Not only should they be able to identify any comprehension problems, they should know what to do about them, if they do find them. We shall present some of our own research on children with specific comprehension difficulties and, in particular, work that relates to the three areas outlined above.

Our studies have compared groups of skilled and less-skilled comprehenders. Typical groups of subjects are shown in Table 14.1.

The groups were selected using the Neale Analysis of Reading Ability and the Gates–MacGinitie Vocabulary Test. The Neale Analysis provides measures both of reading accuracy (word recognition) and comprehension (assessed by ability to answer a series of questions about each passage). The Gates–MacGinitie test requires the child to select one of four words to go with a picture. Thus, it acts as a measure of silent word recognition, and provides an index of the child's vocabulary. In all our studies, the groups of

**Table 14.1** Characteristics of groups of skilled and less-skilled comprehenders

|  | Chronological age (years) | Accuracy age (years) | Comprehension age (years) | Gates–MacGinitie (score/48) |
|---|---|---|---|---|
| Less skilled | 7.9 | 8.4 | 7.3 | 38.0 |
| Skilled | 7.9 | 8.4 | 9.1 | 38.3 |

skilled and less-skilled comprehenders were matched for word recognition ability (Neale accuracy and Gates–MacGinitie) and chronological age, but differed in Neale comprehension scores. In general, all children were above average at word recognition. One group were also very good comprehenders; the other group were poor comprehenders, particularly with respect to their ability to recognize words.

Some theories of poor comprehension, for example that of Perfetti,[1] have proposed that comprehension problems are really an extension of word recognition problems. Such theorists argue that accuracy of word recognition is not sufficient for good comprehension: recognition must also be fast and automatic so that, in a limited-capacity system, the lower-level (word recognition) processes do not use up the resources needed for higher-level (comprehension) processes. However, we have found no differences between groups as selected above in decoding speed or automaticity (see Yuill and Oakhill[2]) so, although we do not deny that such factors are likely to lead to comprehension problems in some children, we argue that poor comprehenders exist who do not have difficulties at the word level. Another possibility is that poor comprehenders have difficulties at the level of sentences, failing to understand certain syntactic constructions. However, when we tested the children on Dorothy Bishop's *Test for Reception of Grammar*[3] we found no differences between the groups. Let us turn now to the areas in which we have found differences.

**Making inferences**

One persistent finding in our work is that less-skilled comprehenders have difficulties in making inferences from text. Here, we will outline just one experiment to illustrate the sorts of difficulties that they have. In this experiment, Oakhill[4] explored the children's ability to make inferences about things that were only implicit in texts. The experiment also looked at how the groups responded to the memory demands needed for answering questions about texts. Most measures of comprehension, including the Neale Analysis, require children to answer questions from memory without referring to the text, so one simple, and not very theoretically interesting, explanation of poor comprehenders' problems is that they have a general memory deficit.

To test this possibility, the children were required to answer questions in two conditions: either without referring to the text, or when the text was freely available for them to refer to. They read the passages aloud (and were given help with words as needed) and were then asked two sorts of questions about the text: ones that could be answered from information immediately available in the text (literal), and ones that required an inference. An example text, with questions, is shown below.

*Example story: 'John's Big Test'*

John had got up early to learn his spellings. He was very tired and decided to take a break. When he opened his eyes again the first thing he noticed was the clock on the chair. It was an hour later and nearly time for school. He picked up his two books and put them in a bag. He started pedalling to school as fast as he could. However, John ran over some broken bottles and had to walk the rest of the way. By the time he had crossed the bridge and arrived at class, the test was over.

LITERAL QUESTIONS (examples)
1 What was John trying to learn?
2 How many books did John pick up?

INFERENCE QUESTIONS
1 How did John travel to school?
2 What did John do when he decided to take a break?

The child first attempted to answer the questions from memory, and then the experimenter re-presented the questions and asked the child to check the answers to the questions in the text. In this second condition, the child was free to re-read the text to find the answers to the questions. The children's responses to the questions indicated that, as expected, it was easier to answer them with, than without, the text and good comprehenders performed better overall. What was of particular interest, however, were the different patterns of performance between the good and poor comprehenders with and without the passage. The performance of the two groups in the different conditions is shown in Table 14.2. When they could not see the passage, the good comprehenders were reasonably good, and better than the less-skilled comprehenders, on both types of question. When the passage was present, the poor comprehenders improved their performance on the literal questions to the same level as that of the good comprehenders in that condition (i.e. near perfect); however, they still made many errors on the questions requiring an inference: over 35 per cent in this condition (the good comprehenders' error rate was 10 per cent). This strikingly high error rate shows that the poor comprehenders' difficulties cannot be attributed to a straightforward memory problem – they have great difficulty in making inferences even with the story available to refer to.

Why might poor comprehenders have such problems? One possibility is that they simply lack the knowledge required to make some of the inferences. We did not test for this possibility explicitly, though it seems likely that 7 year olds would have available such knowledge as that pedalling implies riding a bicycle. Moreover, some recent (unpublished) work by Kate Cain at Sussex has shown that even poor comprehenders do have such knowledge available to them when they are questioned about it directly. A second possibility is that less-skilled

**Table 14.2** Percentages of errors on literal and inferential questions

|  | Unseen | | Seen | |
|  | Literal | Inferential | Literal | Inferential |
|---|---|---|---|---|
| Less skilled | 29.2 | 45.8 | 3.6 | 35.4 |
| Skilled | 10.9 | 15.6 | 1.0 | 9.9 |

comprehenders may not realize the relevance of inferences to understanding a text – they may be concentrating on 'getting the words right', and may process the text at a superficial level. A third possibility is that the children may know about the importance of inferences for text understanding but may be unable to elicit the relevant knowledge and integrate it with the information in the text itself because of processing limitations. We shall argue later that both the second and the third possibilities apply to some extent.

In our book,[2] we review more work showing that less-skilled comprehenders have difficulties with other types of inference. They are less likely to make inferences to connect up ideas from different parts of a text (even when all the information needed for the inferences is explicitly stated in the text), and they are less likely to make inferences about the particular meanings of words from the contexts in which they occur.

### Understanding text structure

Our research in this area serves to illustrate the generality of the less-skilled comprehenders' problem, as well as their difficulties in understanding a story's structure. Our main work on children's understanding of story structure comes from tasks where the children were asked to *tell* stories, rather than to read them. Their story-telling was prompted by picture sequences which told a simple story. These experiments showed that less-skilled comprehenders did not seem to have an integrated idea of the stories as a whole – they tended to give picture-by-picture accounts rather than connecting together the events in each picture to create a cohesive whole.

One index of story cohesion is the use of connective words, including temporal ones (e.g. *then*), contrastive ones (e.g. *but*) and the most sophisticated ones, causal connectives (e.g. *because*). We told children in the two skill groups a very simple story, with pictures (shown in Figure 14.1) containing only temporal connectives (*and, then, when*). Twelve of the sixteen skilled comprehenders, when they retold the story, added new connective terms of all three types, whereas only four of the less-skilled group did so, and none of these additions were causal. The different flavour of the resulting stories is best shown by examples, the first from Anne, a poor comprehender, and the second from Hayley, a good one. The connectives that were not in the original story are in italics.

(ANNE) Sally was getting up for school. Her mum done her lunchbox. She went to school. She's singing a song. She put her lunchbox down. She's doing her lessons. She's doing her lessons again. She goes and gets the wrong lunchbox. She eats the wrong lunch. Another girl came with hers and they had their lunch together.

(HAYLEY) One day there was a little girl and she got off . . . out of bed *because* she . . . she forgot school. [Here the child seemed to mean that the girl was rushing because she had forgotten it was time for school.] Her mum has got . . . has got her breakfast ready. *And then* she took her lunchbox and said goodbye to her mum.

**Figure 14.1** The pictures used in the story retelling experiment.

Then she went to school with her lunchbox la'ing to herself. Then she put her lunchbox on the table and then she did her lessons. *After that*, she . . . it was lunchtime, she went to get her lunchbox. *But* she got the wrong lunchbox. *So* they went into the room with different lunchboxes. And then she sat down and she said, 'I've got the wrong sandwiches'. Then she went . . . and another girl came along and said, 'You've got my lunchbox'. *So* they had lunch together. Yum!

Notice that Hayley's story is full of false starts and speech repairs, but shows an obvious attempt to add cohesion to a simple story. Anne's story, on the other hand, is list-like. This impression of a list is created by several features of the story in addition to the lack of connectives. First, Anne uses the present continuous tense (*was getting up, is doing*), which gives a 'running commentary' style, while Hayley uses the past. Anne also repeatedly mentions the same event, and this does not contribute to the story line (*she's doing her lessons again*). This phrase also suggests that she is not recounting a story, but describing in turn the contents of each picture as a separate entity. Hayley's production integrates narrative and descriptive information (*she went to school . . . la'ing to herself*), uses various connectives (e.g. *but*, *so*), and includes phrases conventionally used in stories (*one day there was . . .* ).

This evidence, however, is somewhat impressionistic. We therefore looked more systematically at children's narrative productions by asking them to tell their own stories from a series of pictures, and we scored their stories for various features that we found to differentiate between the two stories above. First we looked at the tenses of the verbs used. There was a striking difference between the two groups: only 19 per cent of the poor comprehenders' stories used the past tense, compared with 57 per cent of the skilled childrens' stories. We are not claiming that past tense is 'better': many talented writers use the present tense to great effect. But poor comprehenders tended to use just this tense, contributing to the list-like quality of their stories, while good comprehenders were more likely to vary the tense used to fit the demands of the story: predominantly past tense but with occasional uses of the present, perhaps for dramatic effect and immediacy.

We also looked at the way children referred to characters in the story: whether the references were appropriately varied and unambiguous (e.g. *the man saw the table . . . he went into the shop*) or whether they were either repetitious (e.g. *the man saw the table . . . the man went into the shop*) or ambiguous (e.g. *he saw the table . . . he went into the shop*, where the referent of 'he' has not been introduced). There was a tendency for skilled children to use the first pattern, which was smoother and clearer, more frequently than the less skilled children did. However, more interesting than this was the way that the children in the two groups were influenced by the conditions under which they told the story. For some of the stories, we presented the pictures one at a time, and the children did not know what would happen next. This makes it quite difficult to plan any coherent strategy for the use of referring expressions, because you do not know who is the main character or who will appear in the next picture. There was little difference between the two groups here: both used the repetitious or ambiguous style about half of the time. In a second condition, we showed the children all the pictures before they told the story. This gave them the opportunity to plan the best way of referring to the characters, for example using pronouns more often for the main character. This mode of presentation gave no advantage to the poor comprehenders: they carried on using the same style they had used in the other condition. But the good comprehenders could derive benefit from this condition: they used the more varied and appropriate pattern of reference for 83 per cent of the stories. The differences between the narratives of the two groups can be seen in these examples, from a poor comprehender, Tina, and a good one, Lucy, respectively:

> (TINA) A man and a lady is walking along and the doggie is behind them and there's some chicken hanging out of their bag and the dog bites it and they have a picnic and all the food is gone.

(LUCY) Once there was a man and a lady and a dog and they went for a walk to have a picnic and they took two legs with them. When they came near the spot they were gonna have their picnic, the dog was trying to get their food because he thought the food was for him so he ate the food, and when they got to their picnic spot they looked in and everything was gone and they were so surprised they went home and got their dinner at home.

Lucy seems to have some general plan in mind, as she mentions the couple's intention to have a picnic, and their approach to the picnic spot, which only appears in the final picture of the sequence. This planning requires her to look ahead, and to modify the description of the current picture with respect to what will be said about subsequent ones. Tina merely describes one or two aspects of each picture, and seems to focus on each picture in isolation, to provide an external place-marker of where she is in the story. Also, notice that the central point of the story is not clear in Tina's story. There is no indication that the couple are surprised at the disappearance of the chicken, and it is not even clear why 'all the food has gone': without seeing the pictures, a listener might assume that the couple ate the food themselves.

These stories bring out a more general issue about how to tell a good story: you need to have an idea of the 'point' of the narrative, otherwise the story has no interest or purpose. We investigated children's understanding of story points in another story-narration study with 8–9-year-old children. After they had told a story from picture sequences, children were asked to choose, from four statements: 'What was the most important thing about the story, the point of it?' So, for example, in a story where a cowboy goes into a cowboy accessories shop, he pretends he wants to examine a lasso, and uses it to tie up the shopkeeper, and robs the till. We asked the children to choose one of the following four statements (adults were unanimous in choosing statement 1):

1  A cowboy tricks and robs the shopkeeper.
2  A cowboy buys a lasso.
3  A cowboy is in the shop.
4  A kind shopkeeper gives the cowboy some money.

Overall the skilled comprehenders picked the main point of the stories 79 per cent of the time, compared with only 46 per cent for the less-skilled comprehenders. It is clear that the good comprehenders are much better at understanding the main point of a story, and it is interesting that they are better at understanding the point of even picture sequences.

Some other work that is related to this issue has been done recently by Kate Cain at Sussex. She assessed how good and poor comprehenders understood the role of a title. The children were asked what a title could tell the reader about a story. If they seemed unsure, or did not respond, they were asked what a specific title might tell them about a story, e.g. 'Jack and the Beanstalk'. The children's responses were scored as correct if they said things like the title 'tells you what it's about', or gave an example such as: 'The Princess and the Pea – well, you can tell it's going to be about a princess and a pea'. Other responses, such as 'the words that are in the story' or 'whether it's good or not' were not allowed as correct. Overall, far more skilled than less-skilled comprehenders were able to produce an acceptable answer.

These findings indicate that less-skilled comprehenders have less clear ideas than skilled ones about how stories are typically structured – they tend to produce 'stories' that are less integrated and coherent than those of skilled comprehenders, and do not appreciate the main point of stories, even when the stories are presented as a series of pictures.

### Comprehension monitoring

The third skill area we mentioned was that of comprehension monitoring. Some recent work in this area has shown that less-skilled comprehenders have difficulty in detecting problems of various kinds in short texts. Previous developmental studies, for instance by Ellen Markman,[5] have shown that young children generally have difficulty in saying explicitly what is wrong with a text so, in the experiments we report here, we used slightly older good and poor comprehenders (9–10 year olds).

In the first experiment (an undergraduate project, conducted by Deborah Samols), we explored both 'spontaneous' and 'directed' comprehension monitoring whilst the children were reading short passages which contained misspelt words and jumbled sentences. An example passage is shown below:

*Comprehension monitoring: example passage*
*Fortune tellers*

> We all know about events in the past because we can remember them, but we do not know about the future in the same kind of way. The future is uncertain. It is for us to be sure impossible about what will happen.
>
> There are people who say that they know what will take place in the future. Some of these people are called 'fortune tellers'. If you go to see them, they will tell you what they think will happen to you. For example, you might be told that you will be going on a long trep. You might be told that someone who seems to be a friend is really an enemy.
>
> The fortune teller may perp into a crystal ball, where she says she can see pictures of the future. She may tell you that the pictures are incomplete or imperfect, so she can only give you clues. In this a better chance way she has of being right. The more detail she gives, the more likely she is to get it wrong.

To assess spontaneous monitoring, the children were simply asked to read aloud the passages, without any indication that anything was wrong. Their ability to detect the errors was assessed by monitoring their hesitations, repetitions and self-corrections as they read aloud. The children were also asked if they had noticed anything that did not make sense in the texts. We found no differences between the groups on the measures of spontaneous monitoring. However, 67 per cent of the good comprehenders reported noticing that parts of the passages did not make sense when asked if they had noticed anything unusual, whereas only 17 per cent of the less-skilled group reported doing so – a highly significant difference. Disappointingly, however, only one of the good comprehenders could identify the problematic lines in the texts. There were clear differences between the groups when they were told that some parts of the story might not make sense, and they were specifically requested to underline any words or sentences that they did not understand (directed monitoring). The numbers of problematic words and phrases as a proportion of the total numbers of words or phrases underlined was calculated. Surprisingly, even the good comprehenders were not very good at this task: only 51 per cent of their word underlinings and 56 per cent of their phrase underlinings were correct. However, these figures were markedly better than those for the less-skilled comprehenders: 17 per cent and 25 per cent respectively. Thus, there were large differences between the good and poor comprehenders in their ability to detect both problematic words and phrases. The children were also asked questions about the passages, after both the spontaneous and the directed conditions. Overall, the skilled comprehenders were better than the less-skilled comprehenders at answering questions. However, the directed condition did not lead to better performance on the comprehension questions in either group.

In a further study, comprehension monitoring was assessed using an inconsistency detection paradigm (similar to that used by Markman[5] for example). In this study, the children have to detect inconsistencies that depended on the integration of information between two sentences in the text. For example, they might read that 'Moles cannot see very well, but their hearing and sense of smell are good' and, later in the same passage, that 'Moles are easily able to find food for their young because their eyesight is so good'. The passage from which this example is taken is shown below.

*Inconsistency detection: example passage*
*Moles*

Moles are small brown animals and they live underground using networks of tunnels.
*Moles cannot see very well, but their hearing and sense of smell are good.*
They sleep in underground nests lined with grass, leaves and twigs.
Moles use their front feet for digging and their short fur allows them to move along their tunnels either forwards or backwards.
They mainly eat worms but they also eat insects and snails.
Moles are easily able to find food for their young because their eyesight is so good.

— This passage makes sense, it does not need to be changed.
— This passage does not make sense, it needs to be changed.

In this experiment, there was a further variable: the inconsistencies were either in adjacent sentences, or were separated by several sentences. Thus, for some children, the italicized sentence (which was not, of course, italicized in the texts shown to the children) appeared immediately prior to the final sentence of the passage. In this way, the memory load intrinsic to the task was manipulated. There were also a number of control passages, which did not contain inconsistencies, to ensure that the children were not trying to find problems where none existed. Once again, 9–10-year-old subjects were used in this experiment.

The children were asked to read the passages out loud, and to identify anything that 'didn't make sense'. They were given an example of a blatant inconsistency of the sort that they should be looking for. They were asked to read at their own pace, to underline any problems they found in the passage, and then to tick an overall assessment of the passage at the bottom of the page (as shown above). The children were also asked to explain any problems that they identified. If they did not identify a problem on the first reading, testing did not stop immediately. They were told that there was a problem in the passage, and they were asked to re-read the passage and try to identify it. If the child still failed to identify the inconsistency on the second reading, the experimenter underlined the two inconsistent sentences and asked if they made sense together. If a child was still unable to identify the problem at this stage, the experimenter turned to the next passage. The child was allocated a score of 0–3 for each passage, depending on whether or not they identified the inconsistency, and how much prompting they required before they could do so. Thus a maximum score was obtained if they marked the correct option at the end of the passage and were able to explain the inconsistency.

The results showed that the skilled comprehenders were better at detecting the inconsistencies overall (mean score 5.1 out of 6) than the less-skilled group (mean score 3.7). There was also an effect of the distance between the two inconsistent sentences: when the two sentences were adjacent, the task was much easier. However, the difference was much greater for the poor than for the good comprehenders – good comprehenders' performance was barely affected by whether the sentences were adjacent in the text, or were separated by several other sentences. The performance on the control passages (which did not contain any inconsistencies) was uniformly high in both groups. The performance on the inconsistent passages suggests that the integration of information across sentences in a passage is much more difficult for less-skilled than for skilled comprehenders. We (Yuill, Oakhill and Parkin[6]) found similar results with younger children in a task that required the detection of apparent anomalies in text. The less-skilled comprehenders could readily resolve anomalies in passages (e.g. a boy is *praised* by his mother for not sharing his sweets with his little brother) only if the apparent anomaly and the information that resolved it (in this case, that the little brother was on a diet) were in adjacent sentences. If the two items of information were separated by a few sentences, the less-skilled comprehenders could not seem to integrate them, and performed very poorly. These findings indicate that the performance of children on these tasks may be related to their ability to integrate information in working memory, and we will discuss this issue in the next section.

**Working memory and text comprehension**

Work with adults, by Meredyth Daneman and Patricia Carpenter,[7] has shown that a variety of comprehension skills are related to performance on a verbal working memory test in adults. These findings led us to assess working memory in our groups of good and poor comprehenders. The children who participated in the anomaly-detection study outlined above also had their working memory assessed using a non-linguistic working memory test. In this test, the children were required to read out loud sets of three digits, and recall the final digits in each of the sets without looking back at them. So, for example, they might read the sets.

$$9 - 4 - 1$$
$$5 - 3 - 6$$
$$2 - 7 - 8$$

and have to recall the final digits, 1, 6, 8, in order. The difficulty of the test was increased by increasing the number of sets of digits to be processed and thus the number of final digits to be recalled: the children had to recall either two, three or four digits. We found that the skilled and less-skilled comprehenders performed very similarly on the easiest version of the task, but that the less-skilled comprehenders were worse than the skilled ones on the two harder versions of the task. We have not replicated this pattern of findings many times.

Thus, one plausible reason for the problems of the less-skilled comprehenders might be that their poorer working memories are preventing them from efficient text processing, and limiting their ability to make inferences, integrate information and understand the overall structure of a text. However, other work of ours indicates that deficient working memory cannot provide a complete explanation for the less-skilled comprehenders' problems. For instance, some recent work by Kate Cain at Sussex has been looking into children's reading habits. She has been asking both children and their parents questions about the amount of reading they do at home, the numbers of books owned, and library membership and use. (This study differs from the recent work brought together by Keith Topping and Sheila Wolfendale,[8] which primarily addresses the effects of parents listening to their children read, or actively coaching them in reading, rather than literacy activities more broadly.) Although the numbers of participants in Cain's study are fairly small at the moment, some interesting findings are emerging. For instance, skilled comprehenders are *read to* significantly more frequently than less-skilled comprehenders. Similarly, more of the skilled than less-skilled comprehenders said they had visited a library, and more of their parents said they were members of a library, though the latter differences did not reach statistical significance. These findings may mean that the poorer comprehenders have not had the same level of exposure to stories and story structures from a very early age that skilled comprehenders might have had. Thus, they might have missed out on hundreds or even thousands of hours of story reading and book sharing from a very early age, and this experience, if it proves to be crucial to later reading comprehension skill, would be exceedingly difficult to compensate for (even if such compensation were found to be effective at a later age). Of course, it could be that poorer comprehenders are read to less *because* they are poor comprehenders, and perhaps do not enjoy being read to, or are not rewarding to read to. We end this chapter on a more optimistic note, because we have found that even relatively short-term training studies can be very effective in improving comprehension.

### Remediation studies

There are three main ways in which comprehension of and learning from text might be improved, only one of which we consider in any detail here. First, additions and changes to the text could be made, to improve its comprehensibility and memorability. Additions might include pictures, subheadings and summaries; other changes might be to improve the organization or coherence of the text. These sorts of changes are ones that are made *for* readers, and do not require any effort on their part. Second, readers can be encouraged to engage in various activities either while they are reading or after reading a text, for example note-taking, underlining or summary-writing (such activities are often called 'study aids'). Research discussed by Oakhill and Garnham[9] has also shown that they can be used to improve comprehension. Third, children can be taught to apply processing strategies as they are reading: ways of thinking about the text, whether it relates to what they know, and whether their understanding is adequate. Such strategies differ from the first two types in that they rely on what is going on *in the reader's head*, rather than on external aids to comprehension. Most remediation studies have attempted to train children in such strategies on the assumption that it is most useful to develop procedures that can be applied to any text.

The aim of the studies we describe in this section was to see if less-skilled readers' comprehension could be improved. The rationale was that, if less-skilled children can be trained in the skills they are supposed to lack, then their comprehension should improve. If the poor comprehenders' understanding is deficient *because* they lack the skills in which they are being trained, then we would expect that the less-skilled comprehenders might improve to the same level as the skilled ones following training, but the skilled ones would not benefit from training (since they already have the skills being trained).

The general idea of the first study (Yuill and Oakhill[10]) we will describe here was to try to make children more aware of, and get them more involved in, their own comprehension: to encourage inferencing and comprehension monitoring. As well as the group who received training (which we will come to in a moment), there were two 'control' groups, who spent the same amount of time with the experimenter but doing activities which we did not expect to improve their comprehension. All three groups spent a total of seven sessions of about thirty minutes each with the experimenter. One of the control groups simply spent their time answering questions about a series of short passages. The other group had training in rapid word decoding. As we mentioned earlier, one theory of poor comprehension suggests that *accurate* word recognition is not sufficient for efficient comprehension, but that words must also be recognized quickly and automatically. If they are not, then the resources devoted to word recognition will not be available for comprehension processes, which will suffer. This group read the same texts as the other group, and practised decoding lists of words from them. Thus, the improvement of the trained group could be compared with that of the control groups.

Like the control groups, the groups who received training were seen in seven separate sessions of about thirty minutes each. There were three components to the training. First, practice in *lexical inferences* was included in all seven sessions. Here, the children were encouraged to say what they could work out about a sentence or story from the individual words. For instance, in the sentence 'Sleepy Tom was late for school again', we can infer from 'sleepy' in that context that Tom has probably only just got up, and perhaps that he went to bed late, or habitually goes to bed late. The name 'Tom' suggests that Tom is a pupil, rather than a teacher, at the school because he is referred to by his first name, rather than being called 'Mr', and so on. The children were given practice in applying this technique, first with sentences, and then with short abstract stories of the sort shown below. Second, in four of the sessions, the children engaged in *question generation*. They were invited to generate questions such as 'Who was crying?' and 'Where was Billy?' for the passage shown (the questions listed were *not* presented in this training condition). The children took turns to generate questions. Third, in one session, they were encouraged to engage in *prediction*. In this session, part of the text was covered and the children were encouraged to guess at what was missing. After they had done so, the text was revealed and the appropriateness of their guesses was discussed with them.

The control group who did comprehension exercises were first told about the importance of accurate comprehension. The children in the group shared the reading of the text, and took turns at attempting to answer the set question on it. A sample text with questions is shown below.

*Inference training: example text*

Billy was crying. His whole day was spoilt. All his work had been broken by the wave. His mother came to stop him crying. But she accidentally stepped on the only tower that was left. Billy cried even more. 'Never mind,' said his mother, 'We can always build another one tomorrow.' Billy stopped crying and went home for his tea.

EXAMPLE QUESTIONS (exercise group only)

Where was Billy?
Why was Billy crying?
What had the wave broken?
Why did his mother go to him?
Why did Billy cry even more?

The children were given little feedback on their answers by the experimenter, except that obvious errors were corrected. However, the children often discussed the answers amongst themselves which, as we shall see later, may have influenced the results. The children in the other control group, who were given training in rapid decoding, practised reading words, including the most difficult words, from the same texts as quickly as possible.

After a period of about two months, during which the training took place, the children were re-tested on a different form of the Neale Analysis. The improvement scores for the six groups are shown in Table 14.3. As can be seen, the very smallest increase in improvements was six months. However, the absolute differences in improvement mean very little because the different forms of the Neale Analysis may not be exactly parallel, or because the children just happen to make rapid progress in reading at the time of year the testing was done. What is remarkable, though, are the *relative* differences in improvement in the various groups. The less-skilled comprehenders bene-fited from inference training more than the skilled comprehenders, and the less-skilled group who received inference training improved more than those given decoding practice. However, the surprising aspect of these results, from our point of view, was that comprehension exercises also improved compre-hension. Indeed, the improvement of the inference groups was not signifi-cantly different from those given comprehension exercises. Training did not differentially affect reading speed or accuracy of word decoding – there were no differences between the groups on these measures. The gains in compre-hension scores after this relatively short period of training were impressive. However, it was surprising that the group given inference training did not improve more than those given comprehension exercises. One possible expla-nation for this result is that children in the latter group discussed their answers, and often argued with one another about what was the correct answer. These discussions may have had the effect of increasing their aware-ness of their comprehension. In addition, as can be seen from the example text, the texts used were rather abstract and obscure (to provide suitable material for the group given inference training) and this in itself may have encouraged more inferential processing and reflection than would have occurred with more traditional stories.

We have also explored, in collaboration with Sima Patel at Sussex, the effects of training in generating mental images of the events in a text on comprehension. Michael Pressley's work, for example,[11] has shown that imagery can be successful as a way of improving children's comprehension of stories, but it is not until about 8 that children can learn to use self-generated images. We explored whether less-skilled comprehenders might benefit from imagery training, and also addressed the issue of whether imagery might be particularly suitable for aiding memory for particular sorts

**Table 14.3**   Inference training study: average improvement (months)

|  | Rapid decoding | Comprehension exercises | Inference training |
|---|---|---|---|
| Less-skilled | 6.00 | 13.71 | 17.38 |
| Skilled | 10.33 | 5.43 | 5.92 |

of information (Oakhill and Patel[12]). We did this by asking the children three different sorts of question. The first type, 'factual' questions, tapped memory for facts that were explicit in the texts. The second type, 'inferential', asked about information that could only be inferred from the story, and the third, 'descriptive', asked about details that might be particularly likely to come to the reader's attention if an image had been formed. An example text, with the three types of question, is shown below.

*Imagery training study: example story and questions*

The step ladder was put away safely behind the door which was just to the right of the cooker. The three shelves were up at last and, even with a sore thumb, Terry Butcher was happy. The hammer that had caused the pain was put away in the tool box with the other tools.

Linda, Terry's wife, came into the room with a box of crockery. 'The shelves are for my little model aeroplanes,' said Terry, in a stern voice. 'We'll see,' was the reply from Linda.

A little while later, when Terry was putting away the tool box, he heard a loud scream and the sound of breaking glass and china. Terry walked back into the room and was angry. 'I warned you about those shelves,' he said to Linda.

EXAMPLE QUESTIONS

How many shelves had been put up? (factual)
Why did Terry have a sore thumb? (inferential)
Describe the scene in the room when Linda screamed (descriptive)

We selected good and poor comprehenders with a mean age of 9.7. Each group was divided into two subgroups, one of which was given training in imagery. The imagery training took place in small groups (four or five children) over three sessions, on different days. The children were told that they would be learning to 'think in pictures' as they read stories, to help them to answer questions about them. Nine stories were used altogether: four for training, and five in the test session. In the first training session the children read one of the stories, and the experimenter then produced two drawings: one was a cartoon-like sequence of four pictures, which represented the main sequence of events in the story. The other was a single picture, which represented the main event in the story. The children were shown how each of the pictures related to the story, and were encouraged to use these 'pictures in their minds' to help them to answer questions about the stories. For a second story in this session, the children were not shown pictures but were encouraged to formulate their own mental images. They discussed their pictures and received feedback and suggestions from the experimenter. In a second session, a similar procedure was followed. In the final training session, the children were not shown any drawings. The imagery procedure was reiterated, and the children read and answered questions about a new story and a discussion of their 'mental pictures' took place, as in the first two sessions.

The children who did not receive imagery training saw the same stories, also spread over three sessions. They read the stories and answered the questions, and their answers were then discussed with them. The children in these groups spent as long with the experimenter as those in the imagery training groups. In the test phase, the groups who had received the imagery training were reminded of this strategy before they read the test stories, and were reminded to use their mental pictures to help them to answer the questions. The children in the control condition were told to read the stories very carefully and to answer the questions in as much detail as possible.

The results showed that, overall, the good comprehenders answered more questions correctly than poor ones, and that the children given imagery training performed better than the control group. As predicted, the poor comprehenders given imagery training showed a marked improvement in memory for the passages: they performed significantly better on the test questions than did the control group of poor comprehenders. There was no such difference between the groups of good comprehenders. Imagery training did not have a differential effect for the different types of questions: where there was improvement, it was general, and not related to particular question types. These results show that imagery training was especially beneficial for those children who do not possess adequate comprehension skills. Poor comprehenders may show a particular benefit from imagery training because it enables them, or forces them, to integrate information in the text in a way that they would not normally do. Of course, the finding that the comprehension of the good group did not improve with imagery does not necessarily mean that they already use imagery. It may be that they have some equally efficient strategy for remembering information from text, and that training in imagery gives them no additional advantage. Imagery may help poor comprehenders by giving them a strategy to help them to overcome some of the limitations on their comprehension skills. For instance, the ability to use imagery strategies may give poor comprehenders a way to help circumvent their memory limitations by enabling them to use a different, and perhaps more economical, means of representing information in the text.

In conclusion, we have shown that two very different types of training can have substantial effects on the comprehension scores of less-skilled comprehenders, at least in the short term. However, further work is needed to establish the long term effects of such training. Although these findings give us cause for optimism, we conclude this section with two notes of caution. First, most methods of improving comprehension assume that poor comprehenders will benefit from being taught the skills that good readers use. However, the picture might not be so simple: the fact that poor readers lack some skills might indicate that, at least in some cases, they are unable to use them. Second, some forms of instruction might need to wait until after the beginning stages of learning to read, until decoding skills are fairly well established. A related point is that young readers may find learning to use skills such as imagery and comprehension monitoring very difficult – it is not until about 9, for instance, that children are typically able to understand and use imagery. Of course, these reservations about specific training in comprehension skills should not be taken to mean that reading for meaning should not be encouraged from the very beginning, but just that deliberate training of comprehension skills may need to be delayed.


## Conclusions

The general picture that emerges of less-skilled comprehenders is of children who are poor at making inferences and connecting up ideas in a text. Their problem seems not to be restricted to understanding the written word: in general they also have difficulties with listening comprehension and in understanding picture sequences. Working memory may play a part in such skills: our work has shown that less-skilled comprehenders perform poorly on a test of working memory. Such a deficit could readily explain the less-skilled comprehenders' problems in making inferences, understanding story structure and monitoring their comprehension. However, patterns of causality have yet to be established. In any case, this seems very unlikely to be a complete explanation of the less-skilled children's problem, since inference skills can be trained, and one would not expect working memory to be susceptible to training. One possibility that reconciles these two sets of findings is that less-skilled comprehenders do have a basic deficit in working memory which affects their comprehension, but that they can be taught strategies that help them to circumvent their memory limitations. In addition, some findings are emerging to show that extensive experience of being read to may be important. It may be that being read to from an early age turns out to be a crucial factor in the development of comprehension skills.


## Notes

1 Perfetti, C. A. (1985). *Reading Ability.* Oxford: Oxford University Press.
2 Yuill, N. M., and Oakhill, J. V. (1991). *Children's Problems in Text Comprehension: An Experimental Investigation.* Cambridge: Cambridge University Press.
3 Bishop, D. (1983). *Test for Reception of Grammar.* Manchester: Department of Psychology, University of Manchester.
4 Oakhill, J. V. (1984). 'Inferential and memory skills in children's comprehension of stories'. *British Journal of Educational Psychology, 54,* 31–9.
5 Markman, E. (1977). 'Realizing that you don't understand: a preliminary investigation'. *Child Development, 48,* 986–92.
6 Yuill, N. M., Oakhill, J. V., and Parkin, A. J. (1989). 'Working memory, comprehension ability and the resolution of text anomaly'. *British Journal of Psychology, 80,* 351–61.
7 Daneman, M., and Carpenter, P. (1980). 'Individual differences in working memory and reading'. *Journal of Verbal Learning and Verbal Behavior, 19,* 450–66.
8 Topping, K., and Wolfendale, S. (Eds.) (1985). *Parental Involvement in Children's Reading.* London: Croom Helm.
9 Oakhill, J. V., and Garnham, A. (1988). *Becoming a Skilled Reader.* Oxford: Blackwell.
10 Yuill, N. M., and Oakhill, J. V. (1988). 'Effects of inference awareness training on poor reading comprehension'. *Applied Cognitive Psychology, 2,* 33–45.

11 Pressley, G. M. (1976). 'Mental imagery helps eight-year-olds remember what they read'. *Journal of Educational Psychology, 68*, 355–9.
12 Oakhill, J. V., and Patel, S. (1991). 'Can imagery training help children who have comprehension problems?'. *Journal of Research in Reading, 14*, 106–15.

# 15 David C. Geary
'A Componential Analysis of an Early Learning Deficit in Mathematics'

Reprinted in full from: *Journal of Experimental Child Psychology* **49**, 363–383 (1990)

A learning disability in mathematics achievement is characterized by the failure to acquire grade appropriate knowledge and problem-solving skills (Schoenfeld, 1987a). While traditional achievement measures allow for the identification of learning disabled (LD) students, they do not provide detailed information on the factors underlying the academic deficit. The information-processing approach to the study of human abilities provides a methodology which should enable a more accurate representation of the factors which contribute to a learning disability. Indeed, several studies of mathematically disabled children have followed the information-processing approach and have identified a number of potential underlying deficits (Fleischner, Garnett, and Shepherd, 1982; Garnett and Fleischner, 1983; Geary, Widaman, Little, and Cormier 1987; Goldman, Pellegrino, and Mertz, 1988; Svenson and Broquist, 1975).

These studies have focused on addition and suggest that the performance characteristics of young mathematically disabled students, relative to their academically normal peers, include the frequent use of inefficient problem-solving strategies, rather long solution times, and frequent computational and memory-related errors (Geary et al., 1987; Goldman et al., 1988). Moreover, this pattern of deficits which characterizes poor achievement in arithmetic in young children appears to parallel the deficits associated with the lack of mastery of more abstract domains, such as calculus (Schoenfeld, 1987b). Nevertheless, the just cited studies have been limited by the lack of a clearly defined theoretical orientation and an important methodological confound.

With regard to the methodological confound, not one of the above cited studies directly recorded problem-solving strategies on a trial-by-trial basis. Rather, it was assumed with these studies that each individual subject employed the same strategy (e.g., counting) to solve each individual problem (Fleischner et al., 1982; Garnett and Fleischner, 1983; Geary et al., 1987), or a general distribution of strategies (e.g., 50% counting and 50% memory retrieval) was inferred based upon patterns of performance on reaction time (RT) measures (Goldman et al., 1988). However, young children clearly use a variety of strategies to solve any given set of arithmetic problems and may in fact use a different strategy to solve the same problem on two different occasions (Carpenter and Moser, 1984; Geary and Burlingham-Dubree, 1989; Siegler, 1986, 1987; Siegler and Shrager, 1984). Thus, the above described performance characteristics of LD children may be inaccurate due to the fact that the methodologies employed in previous studies did not allow for the precise measurement of either problem-solving strategies or of the duration of the problem-solving process (see Siegler, 1987).

The present study was designed to address both of the above mentioned limitations. First, the assessment of the potential deficits of young mathematically disabled children for solving addition problems was based upon a well-articulated theoretical model; that is, the distributions of associations model of strategy choices (Siegler and Shrager, 1984; Siegler, 1986, 1989). Second, strategies, and their associated RTs, were recorded on a trial-by-trial basis and classified in accordance with the strategy choice model. In this way, a more precise measurement of the problem-solving strategies and solution times of LD children, as compared to their academically normal peers, was obtained. Finally, the strategy choice model, described below, served as the theoretical framework for the interpretation of performance differences comparing normal and LD children (cf. Siegler, 1988a), and these performance characteristics were, in turn, used to test specific predictions of the strategy choice model.

*Strategy choice model*

Within the strategy choice model, four basic strategies for solving addition problems have been identified (Siegler, 1986; Siegler and Robinson, 1982; Siegler and Shrager, 1984). Of these four strategies, three are visible or audible, overt strategies, and are termed (a) counting fingers – children use their fingers to physically represent the problem integers and then count their fingers to reach a sum; (b) fingers – children use their fingers to represent the integers but do not visibly count them before giving an answer; and (c) verbal counting – children count audibly or move their lips as if counting implicitly. The fourth strategy was termed no visible strategy, because children provide an answer without the use of their fingers or by visibly counting. This fourth strategy is thought to reflect the retrieval of an addition answer from long-term memory (Siegler and Shrager, 1984).

The strategy chosen for problem solving is governed by the distribution of associations between a problem and all potential answers to that problem. More precisely, the strategy selected for problem solving is a function of the associative strength between the problem and its correct answer, which is indexed by the probability of correctly retrieving that answer, combined with a confidence criterion. The confidence criterion represents an internal standard against which the child gauges confidence in the correctness of the retrieved answer.

The problem-solving process begins with the child first setting two parameters: (a) the confidence criterion and (b) a search length time which indicates the maximum number of retrieval attempts a child will make before choosing an alternative strategy. Retrieval is then attempted and continues as long as the value of the confidence criterion exceeds the associative strength of each retrieved answer, and as long as the number of searches does not exceed the value of the search length parameter. If no answer exceeds the value of the confidence criterion and the value of the search length parameter is exceeded, then the child will resort to the use of a backup strategy. Here, the child will typically use either the counting fingers strategy or the verbal counting strategy to complete problem solving; although some children will occasionally use the fingers strategy (Baroody, 1987; Geary and Burlingham-Dubree, 1989; Siegler, 1987).

*Counting algorithms.* With the use of either the counting fingers strategy or the verbal counting strategy, the child can execute one of several alternative counting procedures (Carpenter and Moser, 1984; Fuson, 1988; Groen and Parkman, 1972). According to Groen and Parkman, all counting algorithms involve the manipulation of an internal incrementing device, which in fact likely involves implicit counting (Ashcraft, Fierman and Bartolotta, 1984; Kaye, Post, Hall and Dineen, 1986). With one such often used procedure, counting begins with the cardinal value of the larger integer and involves incrementing in a unit-by-unit fashion a number of times equal to the value of the smaller or minimum (min) integer until a sum is obtained. Another common computational strategy involves counting, from zero, in a unit-by-unit fashion a number of times equal to the cardinal value of both the augend and the addend. When problem solving requires counting, the majority of problems will be solved with the use of either the former min (or counting-on) procedure or the latter sum (or counting-all) procedure (e.g., Carpenter and Moser, 1984; Siegler, 1987).

## Method

### Subjects

The subjects were selected from a single elementary school which served a rural working-class population. The sample included a total of 52 first or second grade academically normal or LD students. The normal group consisted of 13 male and 10 female first-grade children with a mean age of 86.9 months ($SD = 5.7$). The LD group consisted of 11 male and 18 female first- or second-grade students with a mean age of 88.6 months ($SD = 7.9$). The difference in mean age comparing the normal and LD groups did not differ significantly ($p > .05$). Subjects included in the LD group were, at the time of the study, receiving Chapter 1 remedial education services in mathematics. Chapter 1 services involved 20 min per day, 5 days per week, of specialized instruction in number concepts and mathematical procedures – e.g., they were instructed in the use of the min counting strategy for solving addition problems. All of the LD subjects attended general education courses for most of their school day, although many of these children also received remedial services in reading. Descriptive information for performance on the Science Research Associates Survey of basic skills, from the previous academic year and obtained from school files, is presented in Table 15.1. Here, it can be seen that the normal group showed a significantly higher mean percentile ranking than did the LD group on both the mathematics and the reading achievement measures ($ps < .001$).

The initial classification of subjects into the normal and LD groups was based upon whether the child was or was not receiving Chapter 1 services. However, based on the current year's achievement test scores, the LD subjects were placed into two subgroups: LD-improved and LD-no-change. The LD-improved group included 13

**Table 15.1** Descriptive information for subjects by grade and academic status

|  | Grade 1 | | Grade 2 |
|---|---|---|---|
|  | Normal | Learning disabled | Learning disabled |
| Mathematics | 64.8(19.4) | 24.6(14.9) | 40.4(16.7) |
| Reading | 77.1(15.5) | 40.6(20.5) | 44.8(25.8) |
| N | 23(15) | 22(14) | 7(5) |

Note: Tabled values refer to mean national percentile ranking for the associated section of the Science Research Associates survey of basic skills; associated standard deviations are in parentheses. N = total number of subjects for each group, and the adjacent numbers, in parentheses, indicate the number of subjects for which achievement scores were available.

subjects who had tested out of the remedial education program in mathematics, and the LD-no-change group included 16 subjects whose test scores (below the 46th percentile on the mathematics achievement measure) indicated the continued need for remedial education in mathematics. The more recent achievement scores for the normal subjects were also examined and revealed one of these subjects scored below the 46th percentile on the mathematics test and scores were missing for one additional subject. Thus, data from these two subjects were not used in any subsequently described analyses.

Descriptive information for the more recent achievement test scores is presented in Table 15.2. Dependent $t$ tests comparing the first time of measurement with the second time of measurement revealed one significant change; the LD-improved group showed a higher mean percentile ranking for the second time of measurement on the mathematics test, $t = 4.81$, $p < .01$. Finally, Bonferroni $t$ tests indicated that for the second time of measurement the mean standing for the normal and LD-improved groups on the mathematics achievement test did not differ significantly ($p > .05$), but the LD-improved group now scored significantly higher on the mathematics test than did the LD-no-change group ($p < .05$). All remaining mean differences comparing the normal group with both groups of LD subjects differed significantly ($ps < .05$).

## Experimental task

*Stimuli.* The experimental stimuli consisted of 40 pairs of vertically placed single-digit integers. Stimuli were constructed from the 56 possible nontie (a tie problem is, e.g., 2 + 2, 4 + 4) pairwise combinations of the integers 2 to 9. The frequency and placement of all integers were counterbalanced. That is, each integer (2 to 9) appeared five times as the augend and five times as the addend, and the smaller value integer appeared 20 times as the augend and 20 times as the addend. No repetition of either the augend or the addend was allowed across consecutive problems.

*Apparatus.* The addition problems were presented at the center of a 30-cm × 30-cm video screen controlled by an IBM PC-XT microcomputer. A Cognitive Testing Station clocking mechanism ensured the collection of RTs with ± 1-ms accuracy. The timing mechanism was initiated with the presentation of the problem on the video screen and was terminated via a Gerbrands G1341T voice operated relay. The voice operated relay was triggered when the subject spoke the answer into a microphone connected to the relay.

For each problem, a READY prompt appeared at the center of the video screen for a 1000-ms duration, followed by a 1000-ms period during which the screen was blank.

**Table 15.2** Descriptive information for subject performance following 1 year of remedial education in mathematics

| | Normal | | Learning disabled | | | |
| | | | Improved | | No change | |
| | Time 1 | Time 2 | Time 1 | Time 2 | Time 1 | Time 2 |
|---|---|---|---|---|---|---|
| Mathematics | 64.8(19.4) | 79.9(14.4) | 29.5(13.2) | 63.6(13.2) | 28.2(19.2) | 28.9(12.4) |
| Reading | 77.1(15.5) | 80.0(15.6) | 44.3(19.1) | 44.1(28.4) | 39.8(23.6) | 29.1(19.1) |
| N | 21 | | 13 | | 16 | |

Note: Tabled values refer to mean national percentile ranking for the associated section of the Science Research Associates survey of basic skills; associated standard deviations are in parentheses. Improved refers to the group of learning disabled subjects who scored greater than the 45th percentile on the mathematics achievement test for the second time of measurement. No change refers to the group of learning disabled subjects who scored less than the 46th percentile on the mathematics achievement test for the second time of measurement.

Then, an addition problem appeared on the screen and remained until the subject responded. The experimenter initiated each problem presentation sequence via a control key.

*Procedure*

Each subject was tested individually and in a quiet room. The subjects were told that they would solve 40 addition problems, preceded by eight practice problems, presented one at a time on the video screen and were encouraged to use whatever strategy made it easiest for them to obtain the answer. Equal emphasis was placed on speed and accuracy. The experimental session was conducted 1 to 4 weeks after the second administration of the achievement measures.

During the experimental session, the strategy used to solve each problem was recorded by the experimenter and each was classified as one of the four strategies described by Siegler and Robinson (1982): (a) counting fingers, (b) fingers, (c) verbal counting, or (d) no visible strategy (memory retrieval). The counting fingers and verbal counting trials were further classified in accordance with the specific algorithm used for problem solving. Here, the trials were classified as min, based on counting the smaller value integer, or sum/max, based on counting both integers or counting the larger value integer, respectively (nearly all of these trials involved the use of the sum rather than the max procedure). Finally, after each trial subjects were asked to describe how they got the answer. Comparisons of the child's description and the experimenter's initial classification indicated agreement between the experimenter and the subject was obtained on 98% of the trials. For those trials on which the experimenter and the subject disagreed the strategy was classified based on the child's description.

**Results**

For clarity of presentation the results with brief discussion will be presented in two major sections, followed by a more general discussion of the results and their implications. In the first section, analyses of group differences in the distribution and characteristics of strategy choices will be presented. The second section presents a componental analysis, of the RT data, designed to assess potential group differences in the rate of executing the various arithmetical processes, e.g., rate of implicit counting.

## Strategy choices

Group differences in the overall distribution of strategy choices and the basic characteristics of these strategies were initially assessed by means of Multivariate Analysis of Variance procedures. A significant result was, in turn, followed by a univariate Analysis of Variance for each of the four strategies. Finally, comparisons of individual group means were based on the Bonferroni $t$ procedure.

Table 15.3 presents the group-level characteristics of addition strategies. Inspection of Table 15.3 reveals that verbal counting and memory retrieval were the primary strategy choices for each of the three groups (Siegler, 1987). Indeed, initial analyses indicated no significant group differences in the overall distribution of strategy choices, $F(8, 88) = 0.75$, $p > .50$, but overall differences in error rates were significant, $F(8, 88) = 2.96$, $p < .01$. Univariate $F$ tests revealed error rates differed significantly only for the verbal counting strategy, $F(2, 47) = 11.13$, $p < .01$. Here, the normal and LD-improved groups did not differ significantly ($p > .05$), but both of these groups made significantly fewer counting errors than did the LD-no-change group ($ps < .05$).

Further analyses revealed significant group differences in the frequency of verbal counting errors when both the min procedure, $F(2, 47) = 9.15$, $p < .001$, and the sum procedure, $F(2, 47) = 7.89$, $p < .01$, were used for problem solving. Again, Bonferroni $t$ tests revealed the LD-no-change group made significantly more verbal counting errors than did either of the two remaining groups when both the min algorithm and the sum algorithm were executed ($ps < .05$); differences comparing the normal group and the LD-improved group were not significant ($ps > .05$).

A final Multivariate Analysis of Variance assessed group differences in the overall (across the counting fingers and verbal counting strategies) frequency with which the sum strategy was used for problem solving, and again a significant result was obtained, $F(4, 92) = 5.37$, $p < .001$. Univariate $F$ tests indicated significant differences across groups only with the use of the verbal counting strategy, $F(2, 47) = 8.96$, $p < .001$. Here, the normal and LD-improved groups did not differ significantly ($p > .05$), but both of these groups employed the sum strategy less frequently than did the LD-no-change group ($ps < .05$).

In summary, the distribution of strategy choices and the basic characteristics of these strategies did not differ significantly comparing the normal and LD-improved groups. The LD-no-change group differed from the remaining two groups in terms of (a) a greater frequency of verbal counting errors, and (b) the relatively frequent use of the sum counting procedure on verbal counting trials; although, for this group the sum procedure was used for only 14% of these trials.

*Sum counting trials.* The next set of analyses sought to determine what factors might have contributed to the relatively frequent use of the sum

**Table 15.3** Characteristics of addition strategies

| Strategy | Trials on which strategy used (%) | | | Mean RT(sec)[a] | | | Percentage of errors | | | Trials on which min strategy used % | | | Error % min strategy | | |
|---|---|---|---|---|---|---|---|---|---|---|---|---|---|---|---|
| | Normal | Improved | No change | Normal | Improved | No change | Normal | Improved | No change | Normal | Improved | No change | Normal | Improved | No change |
| Counting fingers | 5 | 3 | 6 | 6.3 | 5.8 | 6.4 | 21 | 8 | 50 | 100 | 100 | 69 | 21 | 8 | 27 |
| Fingers | 0 | 0 | 3 | – | – | 5.2 | – | – | 54 | – | – | – | – | – | – |
| Verbal counting | 60 | 48 | 64 | 4.6 | 3.8 | 4.7 | 7 | 10 | 31 | 100 | 90 | 86 | 7 | 11 | 29 |
| Retrieval | 35 | 49 | 26 | 2.8 | 2.6 | 2.1 | 5 | 7 | 22 | – | – | – | – | – | – |

Note: Columnar totals may not sum to 100 due to rounding. Improved refers to the group of learning disabled subjects who scored greater than the 45th percentile on the mathematics achievement test for the second time of measurement; No change refers to the group of learning disabled subjects who scored less than the 46th percentile on the mathematics achievement test for the second time of measurement.

[a] Mean RT excluded errors and spoiled trials and are based on min counting trials for the counting strategies.

procedure by the LD-no-change group. Here, correlations among variables which represented the frequency with which the sum algorithm was employed by this group, the associated error rates, and variables which indexed problem characteristics were computed. These results indicated that the sum procedure was most likely to be employed when the value of difference comparing the augend and the addend was small, $r = -.60$, $p < .0001$. That is, the sum procedure appeared to be used when the smaller value integer was not easily identified (Goldman et al., 1988; Svenson and Broquist, 1975). The frequency of errors produced using the sum procedure was significantly correlated with both the size of the smaller value integer (i.e. min), $r = .55$, $p < .001$, and with the value of the correct sum, $r = .38$, $p < .02$. Both of these correlations indicate that the frequency of counting errors increased as the number of required incrementations increased (Siegler and Shrager, 1984).

*Distribution of errors.* To test a specific prediction of the strategy choice model, the pattern of verbal counting errors was compared to the pattern of retrieval errors. The model predicts that the pattern of retrieval errors should mirror the pattern of counting errors because, theoretically, a miscount would increase the associative strength between this wrong answer and the presented problem (but see Baroody, 1988, 1989). Thus, for subsequent retrieval attempts the probability of retrieving this incorrect answer is increased.

Overall, the most common counting error involved under-counting by 1 and represented 56% and 82% of the counting errors for the normal and LD-improved groups, respectively. Consistent with the prediction of the strategy choice model, the most common retrieval error involved stating an answer 1 less than the correct sum for both the normal (55% of errors) and LD-improved (41% of errors) groups. For the LD-no-change group, 45% and 62% of the counting errors involved under-counting by 1 for the min and sum trials, respectively; 14% of the counting errors involved over-counting by 1. Finally, the most common retrieval error for the LD-no-change group involved stating an answer 1 greater than the correct sum (35% of errors) followed by an answer 1 less than the correct sum (32% of errors). Unlike the normal and LD-improved groups, the pattern of counting errors as compared to the pattern of retrieval errors for the LD-no-change group was not consistent with the just noted prediction of the strategy choice model.

*Adaptive strategy choices.* A second prediction of the strategy choice model is that there should be an inverse relationship between the probability of correct retrieval and the probability of visible strategy use; that is, as the probability of correct retrieval increases the probability of visible strategy use should decrease. To test this prediction, within each group and across the 40 experimental stimuli, the frequency of correct retrieval trials was correlated with the frequency of visible strategy trials. The predicted relationship was supported by the resulting coefficients of $-.93$, $-.91$, $-.45$ for the normal, LD-improved, and the LD-no-change groups, respectively ($ps < .01$). The strength of the relationship, however, was significantly weaker for the LD-no-change group relative to the two remaining groups ($ps < .05$).

The just described analyses indicated that as the frequency of correct retrieval trials increased, the frequency of visible strategy trials decreased.

For those analyses, the individual addition problem served as the unit of measure. The subsequently described analyses were also designed to determine the relationship between retrieval trials and the use of the backup strategies (e.g., verbal counting), but here the unit of measure was the individual subject. In this way, an indicator of individual differences in the adaptive use of the various strategies can be obtained and the validity of this indicator can be assessed by the strength of its relationship to external achievement and ability measures (see Geary and Burlingham-Dubree, 1989).

In all, both the above described analyses and the current procedure provided an indicator of the adaptive use of alternative problem-solving strategies. An adaptive strategy choice is likely a function of two variables: (a) the probability of alternative strategies producing the correct answer combined with (b) the relative duration of these alternative strategies. To illustrate, memory retrieval will nearly always produce the shortest solution time, relative to the backup strategies, but retrieval is an adaptive strategy choice only if the obtained answer is likely to be correct (Geary and Burlingham-Dubree, 1989; Siegler 1988a, 1988b). Otherwise, an adaptive strategy choice would require the execution of a more time consuming but more accurate process, such as counting on fingers (Siegler, 1986).

To determine whether subjects comprising each of the three groups varied in the adaptive use of alternative problem-solving strategies, an equation presented by Geary and Burlingham-Dubree (1989) was slightly modified for use in the present study. Here, a theoretically justifiable index (Keating and MacLean, 1987), which was the composite of two variables, was derived. The first of these variables represented the adaptive use of the retrieval strategy and was coded as follows: (number of correct no visible strategy trials/number of total no visible strategy trials). A high score on this variable would indicate that when the retrieval process was used for problem solving it produced the correct answer. The second variable, which was termed backup, was coded so as to represent strategy choices and the accuracy of the associated strategy when facts were not correctly retrieved from long-term memory. If the frequency of counting trials, both the correct and incorrect verbal counting and counting fingers trials, was greater than the frequency of incorrect no visible strategy trials (i.e., retrieval errors) then backup was coded, [number of correct min counting trials + (.5) (number of correct sum counting trials)] − (number of incorrect counting trials); otherwise, backup was coded, 0 − (number of incorrect no visible strategy trials). The min trials were given a higher weight than the sum trials because the sum procedure represents a developmentally less mature strategy (Goldman et al., 1988; Groen and Resnick, 1977).

In all, a high backup variable score would indicate the accurate use of the most efficient (i.e., min) counting algorithm when no number met the confidence criterion, whereas a low score would represent frequent guessing. The backup variable was significantly correlated with the first variable, $r = .50$, $p < .001$, which indicated that subjects who effectively used the retrieval process to solve some problems tended to accurately employ a counting procedure to solve more difficult problems. Scores for both variables were transformed to $Z$ scores and summed to create the composite strategy choice variable. Four subjects never used the retrieval strategy and their score on the first variable was therefore undefined. Thus, the following analyses excluded the data from these four subjects. Finally, scores for the composite variable were significantly correlated with scores on the mathematics achievement measure for the second time of measurement, $r = .42$, $p < .01$. This result suggests that the composite variable provides a meaningful indicator of early mathematical ability (Geary and Burlingham-Dubree, 1989).

Initially, a Multivariate Analysis of Variance was employed, using the two strategy choice variables as dependent measures, to assess group differences in the adaptive use of alternative problem-solving strategies. This analysis indicated significant group differences, $F(4, 84) = 3.36, p < .05$. Univariate $F$ tests also revealed significant group differences for the retrieval variable, $F(2, 43) = 4.52, p < .05$, the backup variable, $F(2, 43) = 4.64, p < .05$, and the composite variable, $F(2, 43) = 5.98, p < .01$. For each of these three variables, the mean standing for the LD-no-change group was significantly lower than the mean standing for the normal group ($ps < .05$). No other group differences were significant ($ps > .05$). In all, both the analyses which used the problem as the unit of measure and the analyses which used the subject as the unit of measure suggest that the LD-no-change subjects made rather poor strategy choices. That is, these subjects did not adaptively use the alternative problem-solving strategies.

### Componential analysis

The componential analyses were designed to determine whether the rate of executing the various problem-solving processes, such as implicit counting, differed across groups. All of these analyses were based on correct RT trials, but excluded trials on which the voice operated relay was triggered early or late (i.e., the initial response was inaudible).[1] Process models for addition were fit to average RT data using regression techniques for each of the three groups. Here, RTs were analyzed separately for verbal counting trials (when the min procedure was used) and retrieval trials.

First, for each group, verbal counting (min) and retrieval trial RTs were correlated with alternative search/compute structural variables, representing the five counting-based models proposed by Groen and Parkman (1972), the square of the correct sum (Ashcraft and Battaglia, 1978), the problem's product (Geary, Widaman and Little, 1986; Miller, Perlmutter, and Keating, 1984), and with various indexes which may be used to represent the associative strength in long-term memory between any given simple addition problem and its correct answer. Specifically, average RTs were correlated with the probability of correctly retrieving an answer (Siegler, 1986), a variable which represented the ranked difficulty of the problems (Hamann and Ashcraft, 1985; Wheeler, 1939), the percentage of children who mastered each problem on a learning task (Wheeler, 1939), and variables which reflected the frequency with which simple addition problems were presented in kindergarten and first-grade mathematics textbooks (Hamann and Ashcraft, 1986).

*Verbal counting strategy.* The min variable showed the strongest zero-order correlation with verbal counting strategy RTs for each of the three groups. The resulting regression equations are presented in the top portion of Table 15.4. Here, the intercept terms (e.g., 2653 for the LD-no-change group) theoretically represent a combined estimate for rate of encoding digits, and for the rate of the strategy selection and the answer production processes (e.g., Campbell and Clark, 1988; McCloskey, Caramazza, and Basili, 1985). The regression weight for the min variable provides an estimate of the counting rate per incrementation. A noteworthy aspect of the results presented in the top portion of Table 15.4 is that the level-of-fit for the LD-no-change group (represented by $r = .736$) is significantly lower than the level-of-fit for both the normal and LD-improved groups ($ps < .01$). This result is reflected in the relatively large MSe (814-ms) for the LD-no-change group, and suggests that these subjects were very variable in the rate with which they executed the min counting strategy.

The next series of analyses were designed to determine if the rate of implicit counting and the rate of executing the processes subsumed by the intercept term differed across groups. Here, the statistical procedures described by Geary et al. (1986) were followed and revealed that the estimates for the rate of implicit counting (raw regression weights for the min variable) did not differ significantly across groups ($ps > .05$). The value of the intercept term, however, was significantly higher for the LD-no-change group than for both the academically normal group, $F(1, 76) = 3.77$, $p = .056$, and the LD-improved group, $F(1, 76) = 17.24$, $p < .0001$. Finally, the intercept term for the LD-improved group was significantly lower than the intercept term for the normal group, $F(1, 76) = 9.66$, $p < .01$.

Briefly, these results indicate that counting rates, per incrementation, did not differ significantly across groups; although, the LD-no-change subjects appeared to be rather variable in the rate with which they executed this process. The rate with which the strategy selection and/or number production

**Table 15.4** Statistical summaries of regression analyses

| Equation | R | F | df | MSe |
|---|---|---|---|---|
| Verbal counting strategy LD-no-change RT = 2,653 + 513(min) | .736 | 44.90 | 1,38 | 814 |
| LD-improved RT = 1,079 + 682(min) | .927 | 231.01 | 1,38 | 476 |
| Academically normal RT = 1,919 + 653(min) | .922 | 214.27 | 1,38 | 474 |
| Retrieval strategy LD-improved RT = 1,561 + 36.3(prod) | .484 | 11.00 | 1,36 | 1,093 |
| Academically normal RT = 2,175 + 20.9(prod) | .494 | 12.29 | 1,38 | 617 |

Note: All models are significant at the $p < .01$ level. Min = the cardinal value of the smaller integer; Prod = augend × addend.

processes were executed did however appear to vary across groups. Further studies are needed to determine whether these differences are related to the duration of the strategy selection or number production processes.

*Memory retrieval strategy.* For each of the three groups, no single variable clearly provided the best representation of retrieval trial RTs. So, to make these analyses comparable to those of a previous study (Geary et al., 1987), the product (prod) variable was used to represent average retrieval trial RTs for the normal and LD-improved groups. The resulting regression equations are presented in the bottom portion of Table 15.4. No equation is presented for the LD-no-change group because average RTs for correct retrieval trials were not significantly correlated with any of the previously described variables. In short, the solution times for correct retrieval trials for this group, unlike those of the two remaining groups, were unsystematic. This finding indicates that the variable (prod) which was used to represent the long-term memory representation of addition facts (see Geary et al., 1986), and the associated retrieval process, for the normal and LD-improved groups did not provide an adequate representation of the long-term memory network, or of the retrieval process, for the LD-no-change group.

Based on the just described finding, post hoc analyses of the retrieval trials were conducted. These analyses indicated that the proportion of retrieval errors was significantly higher for the LD-no-change group as compared to both the normal, $z = 4.66$, $p < .001$, and LD-improved, $z = 3.77$, $p < .003$, groups. Thus, although the absolute frequency of retrieval errors did not differ significantly across groups, $F(2, 47) = 1.21$, $p > .25$, when the LD-no-change subjects did use the retrieval strategy they were much more likely to make an error than were the subjects comprising either of the two remaining groups.

Inspection of the bottom portion of Table 15.4 indicates the product variable was only modestly correlated with correct retrieval trial RTs for both the normal and LD-improved groups. (In fact, for these two groups retrieval trial RTs showed only modest correlations with each of the previously described variables.) This result stands in contrast to the strong relationship between solution times for comparable addition problem sets and the prod variable found for adults (Geary et al., 1986; Miller et al., 1984; Widaman, Geary, Cormier, and Little, 1989). Moreover, the parameter estimates for the prod variable for both groups indicate a retrieval rate of more than double the rate estimated for adults (Geary et al., 1986; Widaman et al., 1989). The pattern of results described thus far suggests an immature memory representation of addition facts for the normal and LD-improved groups (Ashcraft, 1982; Brown, 1975; Hamann and Ashcraft, 1985) and perhaps an anomalous representation for the LD-no-change group.

Finally, the use of procedures identical to those described for the verbal counting strategy indicated the value of the intercept term and the regression weight for the prod variable did not differ significantly comparing the normal and LD-improved groups ($ps > .05$). These findings indicate that the duration of the encoding, strategy selection, and answer production processes for retrieval trials and the retrieval rate did not differ significantly for the subjects comprising the normal and LD-improved groups.

**Discussion**

The purpose of the present study was to provide a detailed comparison of young mathematically disabled and academically normal children in terms of the distribution of strategies, and the associated solution times, used to solve simple addition problems. To achieve this end, problem-solving strategies, and the associated RTs, were recorded on a trial-by-trial basis and each was classified in accordance with the distributions of associations model of strategy choices (Siegler and Shrager, 1984; Siegler, 1986). The strategy choice model thus serves as the theoretical framework within which the performance characteristics of the normal, LD-improved, and LD-no-change groups can be interpreted and, in turn, these performance character-istics provide empirical data from which basic predictions of the strategy choice model can be tested.

The performance characteristics of the normal and LD-improved groups were essentially the same and consistent with several predictions of the strategy choice model. First, as predicted by the model, a strong inverse relationship between the frequency of correct retrieval trials and the fre-quency of visible strategy trials was found. Moreover, the pattern of retrieval errors generally mirrored the pattern of counting errors. The first of these results supports the argument that strategy choices are influenced by the probability of retrieving the correct answer, and the second finding suggests that the distribution of associations between a problem and all potential answers to that problem develops based upon the execution of more basic numerical operations, such as counting (Siegler and Robinson, 1982; Siegler and Shrager, 1984; Siegler, 1986).

The finding of highly similar performance characteristics for the normal and LD-improved groups for solving addition problems stands in contrast to the initial mathematics achievement test scores of the LD-improved subjects, but this finding is consistent with the achievement test scores for the second time of measurement. Thus, the initial poor achievement scores of the LD-improved group were likely due to inadequate preacademic skills (Tramontana, Hooper, and Selzer, 1988) and/or the initial misclassification of some of these subjects (i.e., false positives), and not due to an underlying cognitive or metacognitive deficit (Butterfield and Ferretti, 1987). In all, the children included in the LD-improved group could be described as showing a developmental delay in the acquisition of mathematics skills and not a developmental difference (Goldman et al., 1988). A different picture emerges, however, when the performance of the LD-no-change children is considered.

In brief, the performance characteristics of the LD-no-change group, relative to the two remaining groups, included: (a) frequent verbal counting errors; (b) the relatively frequent use of the sum counting strategy; (c) poor strategy choices; (d) a rather variable rate of executing the verbal counting strategy; (e) a higher proportion of retrieval errors; and (f) solution times for retrieval trials which appeared to be random or unsystematic. Several, but not all, of the just listed performance deficits can be easily accommodated by the strategy choice model.

First, the higher proportion of retrieval errors for the LD-no-change group is similar to a result reported by Siegler (1988a) for 'not-so-good' students, as compared to 'good' students and 'perfectionists.' For both the LD-no-change group and the group of 'not-so-good' students the relatively high proportion of retrieval errors can be interpreted as being due to 'two underlying dimensions: stringency of confidence criteria and peakedness of distributions of associations' (Siegler, 1988a, p. 847). In short, the subjects included in these two groups appeared to have a lenient confidence criterion combined with a relatively low probability of retrieving the correct answer and therefore tended to state retrieved answers even if those answers were likely to be incorrect. This view is also consistent with the poor strategy choices and the unsystematic retrieval trial solution times for the LD-no-change group. For these subjects, a more adaptive approach to strategy choices could have been achieved by raising the criterion for stating retrieved answers and thereby decreasing the probability of retrieval errors.

The unsystematic solution times for retrieval trials suggest that the representation of addition facts in long-term memory, or the basic pattern of the distribution of associations between a problem and all potential answers to that problem, differs comparing the LD-no-change group with the two remaining groups (Lindgren, Richman, and Eliason, 1986; Richman, 1983). If so, the relatively high proportion of retrieval errors for these children could, in addition to a lenient confidence criterion, be related to an anomalous long-term memory representation of addition facts. Moreover, the finding that the LD-no-change subjects made counting errors similar (i.e., under-counting by 1) to the subjects comprising the two remaining groups combined with the finding of a different pattern of retrieval errors provide further evidence that for the LD-no-change subjects the manner in which information is represented in long-term memory may be abnormal.

The remaining performance deficits of the LD-no-change group might be explained in terms of poor self-monitoring of the problem-solving process (Geary et al., 1987; Goldman et al., 1988) or in terms of a deficit in the attentional allocation aspect of working memory capacity (Woltz, 1988). Poor self-monitoring of problem solving could result in under- or over-counting and therefore frequent verbal counting errors.

Individual differences in working memory capacity have been found to be related to *variability* in the rate of information processing (cf. Larson and Saccuzzo, 1989); the poorer the working memory capacity the greater the variability in speed of processing. Thus, the variable rate of implicit counting for the LD-no-change group could have been due to a relatively small working memory capacity or to difficulties in allocating attention within working memory. A working memory capacity deficit might also underlie the relatively frequent use of the sum counting procedure, by the LD-no-change subjects, when the value of difference between the augend and addend was small. In such cases, the determination of which is the smaller value integer, particularly when verbal counting is the chosen strategy, requires the representation and comparison of the cardinal value of both integers in working memory. As the difference between the value of the two integers decreases the difficulty of this comparison and the associated demands on working memory capacity likely increase. Thus, the LD-no-change subjects might have relied on the sum strategy when the difference between the augend and addend was small because for these problems determining which was the smaller number might have been a relatively difficult task. In all, the performance of the LD-no-change subjects could be characterized as a developmental difference rather than a developmental delay (Goldman et al., 1988).

For the final interpretation of the results of this study consider Siegler's (1988b) recent argument that adaptive strategy choices are 'part and parcel of the system's basic retrieval mechanism' (p. 272). An implication of Siegler's argument is that the use of backup strategies might not require conscious 'mindful' self-regulation or metacognition. Rather, a backup strategy would be automatically executed if memory retrieval failed to produce an acceptable answer. In other words, the processes that enable mathematical problem solving might comprise a 'functional system' or schemata for processing complex information. A functional system would be consistent with neuropsychological theory and data (e.g., Allen, 1983; Campbell and Clark, 1988; Luria, 1980; McCloskey et al., 1985) and in fact is compatible with the strategy choice model, with the exception that memory retrieval would be subsumed by a more general mechanism rather than being the primary determinant of strategy choices and therefore ability development.

In this view, the development of basic numerical abilities would require the (a) maturation and development of the neural structures underlying basic processes, such as the representation and retrieval of facts and procedures from long-term memory, and (b) development of a more general mechanism involved in the integration and coordination of these basic processes into a functional system. The coordination of fundamental processes might initially require 'mindful' metacognitive processes; that is, systems of interrelated processes could be compiled by the child to meet frequent task demands (Keating and MacLean, 1988). As the *system* becomes automatized, however, 'mindful' self-regulation might not be necessary.

Within this model, the performance of the normal and LD-improved groups would reflect the age appropriate development of the structure and processes defining fundamental numerical operations (e.g., memory representation and retrieval), as well as the development of the system for processing numerical information. With regard to the LD-no-change group, each of the earlier described deficits is consistent with the failure to develop such a functional system and with a rather more specific cognitive deficit; that is, an abnormal long-term memory representation of addition facts.

Finally and more practically (Keating and MacLean, 1988), the results of this study provide several implications for remedial education in mathematics. First, for some LD children, such as those included in the LD-no-change group, frequent drilling and rote memorization of basic facts might not be an appropriate teaching approach, given that a subset of these children might not be able to remember many of these facts. On the other hand, drilling and frequent practice of basic skills might be a very reasonable approach to teaching children such as those represented by the LD-improved group. Here, given no underlying cognitive deficit, extra practice should enable such children to quickly 'catch-up' to their peers. Second, for some LD children the use of strategies which reduce demands on working memory resources, such as counting on fingers, should be encouraged rather than suppressed. Finally, neither of these recommendations should be put into practice until more sensitive assessment measures are developed, because the measures currently available would fail to differentiate the type of learning disability underlying the initial poor performance of the LD-improved and LD-no-change groups.

## Notes

1 With the use of the verbal counting strategy, some children audibly counted. During this count, if the voice-operated relay was triggered before the child stated the final answer, then the solution time was 'spoiled' and not used in any of the RT analyses.

## References

Allen, M. (1983). Models of hemispheric specialization. *Psychological Bulletin, 93*, 73–104.

Ashcraft, M. H. (1982). The development of mental arithmetic: A chronometric approach. *Developmental Review, 2*, 213–236.

Ashcraft, M. H., and Battaglia, J. (1978). Cognitive arithmetic: Evidence for retrieval and decision processes in mental addition. *Journal of Experimental Psychology: Human Learning and Memory, 4*, 527–538.

Ashcraft, M. H., Fierman, B. A., and Bartolotta, R. (1984). The production and verification tasks in mental addition: An empirical comparison. *Developmental Review, 4*, 157–170.

Baroody, A. J. (1987). The development of counting strategies for single-digit addition. *Journal for Research in Mathematics Education, 18*, 141–157.

Baroody, A. J. (1988). Mental-addition development of children classified as mentally handicapped. *Educational Studies in Mathematics, 19*, 369–388.

Baroody, A. J. (1989). Kindergartners' mental addition with single digit combinations. *Journal for Research in Mathematics Education, 20*, 159–172.

Brown, A. L. (1975). The development of memory: Knowing, knowing about knowing, and knowing how to know. In H. W. Reese (Ed.), *Advances in child development and behavior* (Vol. 10, pp. 103–152). New York: Academic Press.

Butterfield, E. C., and Ferretti, R. P. (1987). Toward a theoretical integration of cognitive hypotheses about intellectual differences among children. In J. G. Borkowski and J. D. Day (Eds.), *Cognition in special children: Comparative approaches to retardation, learning disabilities, and giftedness* (pp. 195–233). Norwood, NJ: Ablex.

Campbell, J. I. D., and Clark, J. M. (1988). An encoding-complex view of cognitive number processing: Comment on McCloskey, Sokol, and Goodman (1986). *Journal of Experimental Psychology: General, 117*, 204–214.

Carpenter, T. P., and Moser, J. M. (1984). The acquisition of addition and subtraction concepts in grades one through three. *Journal for Research in Mathematics Education, 15,* 179–202.

Fleischner, J. E., Garnett, K., and Shepherd, M. J. (1982). Proficiency in arithmetic basic fact computation of learning disabled and nondisabled children. *Focus on Learning Problems in Mathematics, 4,* 47–56.

Fuson, K. C. (1988). *Children's counting and concepts of number.* New York: Springer-Verlag.

Garnett, K., and Fleischner, J. E. (1983). Automatization and basic fact performance of normal and learning disabled children. *Learning Disability Quarterly, 6,* 223–230.

Geary, D. C., and Burlingham-Dubree, M. (1989). External validation of the strategy choice model for addition. *Journal of Experimental Child Psychology, 47,* 175–192.

Geary, D. C., Widaman, K. F., and Little, T. D. (1986). Cognitive addition and multiplication: Evidence for a single memory network. *Memory & Cognition, 14,* 478–487.

Geary, D. C., Widaman, K. F., Little, T. D., and Cormier, P. (1987). Cognitive addition: Comparison of learning disabled and academically normal elementary school children. *Cognitive Development, 2,* 249–269.

Goldman, S. R., Pellegrino, J. W., and Mertz, D. L. (1988). Extended practice of basic addition facts: Strategy changes in learning disabled students. *Cognition and Instruction, 5,* 223–265.

Groen, G. J., and Parkman, J. M. (1972). A chronometric analysis of simple addition. *Psychological Review, 79,* 329–343.

Groen, G., and Resnick, L. B. (1977). Can preschool children invent addition algorithms? *Journal of Educational Psychology, 69,* 645–652.

Hamann, M. S., and Ashcraft, M. H. (1985). Simple and complex mental addition across development. *Journal of Experimental Child Psychology, 40,* 49–72.

Hamann, M. S., and Ashcraft, M. H. (1986). Textbook presentations of the basic addition facts. *Cognition and Instruction, 3,* 173–192.

Kaye, D. B., Post, T. A., Hall, V. C., and Dineen, J. T. (1986). Emergence of information-retrieval strategies in numerical cognition: A developmental study. *Cognition and Instruction, 3,* 127–150.

Keating, D. P., and MacLean, D. J. (1987). Cognitive processing, cognitive ability, and development: A reconsideration. In P. A. Vernon (Ed.), *Speed of information processing and intelligence* (pp. 239–270). Norwood, NJ: Ablex.

Keating, D. P., and MacLean, D. J. (1988). Reconstruction in cognitive development: A post-structuralist agenda. In P. B. Baltes, D. L. Featherman, and R. M. Lerner (Eds.), *Life-span development and behavior* (Vol. 8, pp. 283–317). Hillsdale, NJ: Erlbaum.

Larson, G. E., and Saccuzzo, D. P. (1989). Cognitive correlates of general intelligence: Toward a process theory of g. *Intelligence, 13,* 5–31.

Lindgren, S. D., Richman, L. C., and Eliason, M. J. (1986). Memory processes in reading disability subtypes. *Developmental Neuropsychology, 2,* 173–181.

Luria, A. R. (1980). *Higher cortical functions in man* (2nd ed.). New York: Basic Books.

McCloskey, M., Caramazza, A., and Basili, A. (1985). Cognitive mechanisms in number processing and calculation: Evidence from dyscalculia. *Brain and Cognition, 4,* 171–196.

Miller, K., Perlmutter, M., and Keating D. (1984). Cognitive arithmetic: Comparison of operations. *Journal of Experimental Psychology: Learning, Memory, and Cognition, 10,* 46–60.

Richman, L. C. (1983). Language-learning disability: Issues, research, and future directions. In M. Wolraich and D. K. Routh (Eds.), *Advances in developmental and behavioral pediatrics* (Vol. 4, pp. 87–107). Greenwich, CT: JAI Press.

Schoenfeld, A. H. (1987a). *Cognitive science and mathematics education.* Hillsdale, NJ: Erlbaum.

Schoenfeld, A. H. (1987b). What's all the fuss about metacognition. In A. H. Schoenfeld (Ed.), *Cognitive science and mathematics education* (pp. 189–215). Hillsdale, NJ: Erlbaum.

Siegler, R. S. (1986). Unities across domains in children's strategy choices. In M. Perlmutter (Ed.), *Perspectives for intellectual development: Minnesota symposia on child psychology* (Vol. 19, pp. 1–48). Hillsdale, NJ: Erlbaum.

Siegler, R. S. (1987). The perils of averaging data over strategies: An example from children's addition. *Journal of Experimental Psychology: General, 116,* 250–264.

Siegler, R. S. (1988a). Individual differences in strategy choices: Good students, not-so-good students, and perfectionists. *Child Development, 59,* 833–851.

Siegler, R. S. (1988b). Strategy choice procedures and the development of multiplication skill. *Journal of Experimental Psychology: General, 117,* 258–275.

Siegler, R. S. (1989). Mechanisms of cognitive development. *Annual Review of Psychology, 40,* 353–379.

Siegler, R. S., and Robinson, M. (1982). The development of numerical understandings. In H. W. Reese and L. P. Lipsitt (Eds.), *Advances in child development and behavior* (Vol. 16, pp. 241–312). New York: Academic Press.

Siegler, R. S., and Shrager, J. (1984). Strategy choice in addition and subtraction: How do children know what to do? In C. Sophian (Ed.), *Origins of cognitive skills* (pp. 229–293). Hillsdale, NJ: Erlbaum.

Svenson, O., and Broquist, S. (1975). Strategies for solving simple addition problems: A comparison of normal and subnormal children. *Scandinavian Journal of Psychology, 16,* 143–151.

Tramontana, M. G., Hooper, S. R., and Selzer, S. C. (1988). Research on the preschool prediction of later academic achievement: A review. *Developmental Review, 8,* 89–146.

Wheeler, L. R. (1939). A comparative study of the difficulty of the 100 addition combinations. *Journal of Genetic Psychology, 54,* 295–312.

Widaman, K. F., Geary, D. C., Cormier, P., and Little, T. D. (1989). A componential model for mental addition. *Journal of Experimental Psychology: Learning, Memory, and Cognition, 15,* 898–919.

Woltz, D. J. (1988). An investigation of the role of working memory in procedural skill acquisition. *Journal of Experimental Psychology: General, 117,* 319–331.

# 16  Liliana Tolchinsky Landsmann
### 'Early Literacy Development: Evidence from Different Orthographic Systems'

Reprinted in full from: *Literacy Acquisition* (Ablex Publishing, 1990), 223–239

## Introduction

This chapter is about spontaneous writing development. I use 'spontaneous' in the sense Piaget used it for describing, for instance, the physical knowledge that develops by subject–environment interaction. Piaget never considered specifically the case of written language. Nevertheless, since Piaget believed that every symbolic expression stems from a unique function, he would have included writing among the expressions of the 'semiotic function'. According to him, symbolic expressions depend on cognitive development, in both senses of dependence: being determined or conditioned by, and occupying a lower status. This statement could have called for empirical verification in the field of writing like in spoken language (cf. Sinclair, 1967), investigating the developmental relationships between cognitive development and writing. This was not the case. The conception that writing and reading are school subjects rather than developmental domains was so strong that psychologists did not conceive for any 'spontaneous' development in need to be tapped. Instead of analyzing how do non-conservers read or write, success in conservation tasks, was considered a sort of cognitive pre-requisite for learning how to read.[1] The Piagetian statement was understood as an invitation to postpone any systematic interaction with writing. If symbolic expressions depend on cognition, it is useless to start teaching writing until children are cognitively mature to start. Some researchers sustained that it is 'even deleterious' (Auzias, Casati, Cellier, Delaye, and Verleure, 1977, 40).

These researchers neglected the main Piagetian message, i.e., that subjects are active constructors of their knowledge and have a tendency to constant 'cognitive growth'. As such they have the capability to select and to attend to relevant features of their environment. And writing is indeed part of children's environment. Children growing in an alphabetized society are surrounded by written artifacts, e.g., text, labels, and inscriptions and by people interacting with them and through them. Moreover, writing is also a 'point of view' always mediating our perceptions, our speech and our social relationship. 'By their own symbolism getting under a culture's skin and changing social perception in terms of the written word' (Illich and Sanders, 1988). Therefore, if children have proved to have their own ideas in other domains, e.g., number, space, or time, why should they remain indifferent to writing? This was the point of departure of the constructivist approach to literacy (Ferreiro and Teberosky, 1979). Within this approach, writing is considered as an object of knowledge like physical, or mathematical objects are. In line with this approach, I investigated the systems of representations children construct about writing from its very beginning. I think that this developmental information can become an adequate heuristics of children's performance in reading and writing and a pedagogical tool to build reading and writing programs that are appropriate to children's conceptions. This approach regains literacy as an object of inquiry both for psychologists and for kindergartners.[2]

## Early literate knowledge

In the following lines I present empirical evidence of the kind of knowledge children construct before school. Further I dwell on a particular conception that emerges during early literacy development, the conception that there must be some congruence between certain semantic distinctions, the formal characteristics of writing and the writing-act. Finally, I discuss how writing evolves an articulated linguistic notation. Most of the data was gathered in a series of studies conducted in Hebrew, but it will be constantly compared with findings from different orthographic systems. The experimental paradigm used in the majority of the studies is very simple. Very young children, from three to seven years of age, were asked to write words, sentences, or full texts and to read what they have written or what has been written by others. The tasks set before the children usually exceed their acknowledged expertise. This turns the experimental setting into a problem-solving situation and allows the experimenter to follow up the onset of a new kind of knowledge.

## Writing is a particular kind of object

The first paradigm through which writing is defined, is *by the activities it yields*. This paradigm turns the cultural object called writing into a psychic object. By means of these activities a particular object of knowledge is created; an object that is neither physical, although it has physical features, nor biological: a text. Like any other object, the initial activities texts yield are to suck, to eat, or to squeeze. Neither the physical support of the text nor the graphic inscriptions on it have a unique definition. This way of understanding texts, however, has a relative short life.

After a series of studies looking at mother–infant dyads while dedicated to picture book reading, Snow and Ninio (1986, 119) concluded that from 8 to 18 months of age 'the child had progressed from an attempt to eat the page to being able to participate fully in the verbal dialogue' while looking at the books. Initially, this dialogue is produced on the pictures rather than on the text. At the age of two children think that when reading, one reads the pictures but within a few months children start to make distinctions between text and picture (Ferreiro, 1986). They call each one differently they affirm that when reading one reads the printed text of the books, not the pictures 'because there are letters'. Some researchers attribute to bed-time stories or to story book reading a determinant role in this demarcation process and in the selection of activities. Having mothers 'looking at' and saying, particularly saying objects-names may influence the generality of this behavior. Apart from the possible influence of this experience on an individual level, it is indubitable that the mother's decision to turn a book into an object of common experience is an instantiation of literacy as a cultural representation.

In a series of studies carried out with American children from a variety of racial and ethnic backgrounds as well as range of economic levels Goodman (1986) showed that at least 60% of all the three-year-old subjects can 'read' environmental print. Some researchers place importance on environmental reading because it is not based on letter-sound correspondence but rather on contextual or figurative cues. It is not crucial for my argument whether children's interpretation is guided by figurative cues or even if what children say coincides with what is written. The point is that in front of a text children produce an utterance. On this skeleton builds further development.[3]

**Texts are constrained**

The second paradigm through which writing is internally defined is through its formal features. Through this paradigm texts are defined not in terms of the activities they yield but in terms of their formal constraints. We know from the work of Susan Carey (1985) that, in children's minds, giving birth is a distinctive feature of biological objects. And from the work of Rochelle Gelman (Macario, Gelman, and Shipley, in progress) that color is a distinctive feature of food. By the same token there are certain conditions a graphic display has to fulfil in order to be defined as a text. I think that the graphic features of writing, its perceptual configuration, play a very important role in the demarcation of writing as a particular object.

Ferreiro (1985, 1986) distinguishes between figurative aspects and constructive aspects of writing. The figurative aspects include: quality of trace, predominant orientation (from left to right or inversely), orientation of individual characters, the use of writing instrument, speed, tendency to make discrete symbols, constriction in space, letters correctly formed, spelling. Constructive aspects are related 'with what do we want to represent and the means that are utilized to create difference between representations' (1986, 16). The opposition between figurative and constructive preserves one of the classical oppositions in Piagetian accounts and is equivalent to other related oppositions: state vs. transformation, significant vs. signified. According to Piaget (1966) intelligent activities imply two poles, the figurative and the operative. The figurative pole in contrast to the operative, grasps states but not transformations, acts as signifier but not as signified.

Figurative aspects express the primacy of accommodation over assimilation (Piaget, 1948, 1960; Piaget and Inhelder, 1966). Ferreiro's claim is that in studying the development of writing she was 'obliged to put these aspects on the back shelf in order to let the constructive aspects emerge to light' (1986, 15–16). From Ferreiro's description the reader gets the message that figurative aspects are the less important. My contention is that neither children nor adult writers put the various aspects Ferreiro considers figurative, on the 'back shelf'. I think that this distinction is misleading when it comes to analyze this conventionalized notational system because it underestimates some of the intrinsic features of writing. Being a graphic notational system imposes certain conditions that are central and not peripheral to writing.

Language can be analyzed without taking into account that speech occurs over time. Nevertheless, time-organization plays a central role in speech production and interpretation. Likewise for writing. The graphic features can be underrated when analyzing orthographic systems. Nevertheless, characteristics like two dimensionality, discreteness, speed, the writing instrument compel the process of production and interpretation of writing. Differences in speed between speaking and writing motivate some of the distinctive discursive features in these modalities (Chafe, 1982); changing the writing instrument, e.g., from pencil to computer, brings about decisive changes in the writing process and in the quality of the written outcome (Turkle, 1984). I can understand the reasons that led Ferreiro to the distinction. At a time when writing was solely viewed as graphics or as a motor skill, it was necessary to highlight the representational principles underlying the quality of trace or the precise shape of the letters. Moreover, from an educational point of view it was fundamental for teachers to distinguish between letter drawing and writing so that they could appreciate the underlying logic and the content of children's written productions. Once this task has been done, at least in the literature, I think one has to reset the role of the so called figurative aspects. If the first paradigm, i.e., by activities, is essentially nourished by the social and cultural uses of texts, this second paradigm is nourished by the formal characteristics of the writing system. The first conditions children impose on graphics in order to determine that it is writing, are linearity and relative size. A graphic display is classified as 'good for reading' or 'good for writing' if their elements are organized along a linear axis and of a relative small size (Ferreiro and Teberosky, 1979). Those are the features Gibson and Levin called superordinate (Gibson and Levin, 1970) because they are common to any writing system. This graphic distinction is also evident in children's productions. When asked to draw and to write, very few three-year-olds produced writing and drawing that are graphically indistinguishable. By the age of four, children's writing appears as a linearly arranged string of distinct units separated by regular blanks and by the age of five, children used conventional letters almost exclusively (Tolchinsky Landsmann and Levin, 1985). The fact that children differentiate so early between writing and drawing and the progression from superordinate to ordinate (i.e., orthography-specific) features, are supported by many studies carried out with English-speaking children. This development seems to be independent of race, socioeconomic status, or microcultural milieu (Bissex, 1980, 1985; Clay, 1982; Harste, Woodward and Burke, 1984). The demarcation phase is not completed, however, until children determine the prototypical writing. From a child's point of view, the best exemplar of the class of written objects is qualified by two principles: the 'minimum quantity' principle and the principle of 'inter-relational differentiation'. Accordingly, pieces of writing containing around three of not repeated elements are preferred over

**Figure 16.1** Examples of writing produced by two 4-year-olds. On the upper part a Catalan girl and below an Israeli boy.

single letters. This prototypical writing seems to be general across orthographies and age dependent.

Figure 16.1 presents writings produced by two four-year-olds.

Those in the upper part of the figure were produced by a Catalan child exposed to Spanish and Catalan; those on the lower part were produced by an Israeli child exposed to Hebrew. Nevertheless they look very similar. The more general distinctive feature of texts in graphic terms is their appearance as a discontinuous series of characters of even size linearly organized. As possible to see in the figure, that is how children's written productions look before being constrained by the two principles of 'minimum quantity' principle and 'interrelational differentiation'. The girl was asked to write different words and sentences and each time she was required to read what she had written she repeated verbatim what the experimenter asked her to write.[4] The boy was asked to write a word and a sentence and like the girl did, he simply repeated the stimuli when reading back his own writing.

On the basis of the graphic imitation of the general features of a text, starts a process of internal differentiation of graphic units that leads to the constitution of a generally constrained graphic string.

Figure 16.2 presents writings produced by five-year-olds. In these examples it is already possible to distinguish between the writing produced by the Catalan child and the one produced by the Israeli child, due to the influence of the respective alphabets. The Catalan boy was asked to write three words that differ in number of syllables while the Israeli child was asked to write her name, a bisyllabic word and a short sentence. In spite of it, they used an almost fixed number of non-repeated characters for writing every utterance.

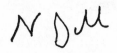

Figure 16.2   Examples of writing produced by a 5-year-old Catalan boy and an Israeli 5-year-old girl.

The principles underlying their writing in both cases, are similar. These two children have selected features from the writing system they are exposed to but have applied on these features their own constraints.

While writing was unconstrained, children accepted that different utterances can be read on similar strings and conversely different strings can be produced for similar utterances. When strings start to be constrained two operations become possible: similarities and differences become manageable and mapping utterances onto graphic units start to be under control. It is understandable, then, that at this point children start striving about what perceived differences have to be noted. Should they describe sound differences or differences in meaning, should they describe them by changing the number of written units or their variety? (Levin and Tolchinsky Landsmann, in press.)

**The semantic congruence hypothesis**

During this period, some children play with the idea that there must be a sort of congruence between difference in meaning and the way it is reflected in writing, they tend to look for the signified relationships in the signifiers' relations. For instance, when asked to write a plural noun they tend to use more letters than for its singular counterpart but they may use the same number of letters for writing a bisyllabic versus a trisyllabic word. The representation of the differences in the first case is facilitated by the fact that the phonological lengthening coincides with the referential increment involved and both correspond to the way the written system notes the modification, i.e., the increment of letters (Tolchinsky Landsmann and Levin, 1987).

In order to prove the generality of this phenomenon to other than referential differences we conducted a study in which different semantic relationships were tested. Five- to six-year-old preschoolers, native Hebrew speakers dealt with ten pairs of sentences. One written on a card (WS), the other, orally delivered (OS). The written sentence was always read first by the experimenter, then together with the child. Then the OS was presented, with the written model still in front of him. This experiment differs from all we have mentioned so far in that the child was presented with a written model he can use or disregard for writing the required sentence. Using the same technique the child was confronted with ten pairs of sentences. In one pair the OS was an exact reiteration of the WS. There was an *Identity* relationship between the sentences. In another pair, the OS was totally different from the WS, there was a *Total Difference* relationship between the sentences. In the eight restant pairs the OS was a partial modification of the WS. Three syntactic modifications were manipulated: addition of one word (e.g., WS: The boy eats chocolate and OS: The boy eats sweet chocolate), deletion of one word and change in word order. The same syntactic modification, however, produced different effects in the semantic relationship between the sentences. In one of the pairs the addition of a word to the WS produced an *Inconsistency* relationship between the WS and the OS. Both sentences can not be true in the same context (Lyons, 1977). In the other pair the same syntactic modification, addition of one word to the WS, produced an *Entailment* relationship (Lyons, 1977) between the WS and the OS. The OS represented a specification of the WS. In a third pair, the same syntactic modification, addition of one word, touched mainly the superficial form of the constituents. The addition of a pronoun to the OS produced an alternative habitual form having the same meaning as the WS. There was a *Redundancy* relationship (Lyons, 1977) between the two sentences. Similarly, by deleting one word, the same three different semantic relationships were produced in the other three pairs. The third syntactic manipulation could be used to produce only two semantic relationships: *Inconsistency* and *Redundancy* since no *Entailment* relationships can be produced in Hebrew by a change in word order. Table 16.1 presents the list of sentences, translated into English, by the syntactic modification produced and the resulting semantic relationship. The sentences that were presented on the cards appear in the table in italics. In order to represent the relationship between the WS and the OS in the case of Identity (pair 1), the required writing procedure is to copy the written model entirely. In order to represent the Total Difference relationship (pair 10), the required writing procedure is to produce a totally different message. For the pairs 2, 3, and 4 the required writing procedure is to copy the entire WS and add an additional word; for pairs 5, 6, and 7 the required writing procedure is to copy partially the entire written model except for one word. In the pairs 8 and 9 what children had to do was to copy the entire WS but changing the order of the words. The purpose was to test the effect of semantic relations on children's writing procedure. If what counts, from the child's point of view, is the addition,

**Table 16.1** List of sentences according to the syntactic modifications produced and the resulting semantic relationships

| Syntactic modifications | Semantic relationships | | | | |
|---|---|---|---|---|---|
| | Inconsistency | Entailment | Redundancy | Identity | Total difference |
| Verbatim reiteration | | | | The sun shines The sun shines (1) | |
| Deletion of one word | The boy doesn't want to sleep The boy wants to sleep (2) | The cat drinks white milk The cat drinks milk (3) | We went for a walk (0) went for a walk (4) | | |
| Addition of one word | The boy eats an apple The boy doesn't eat an apple (5) | The boy eats chocolate The boy eats sweet chocolate (6) | (0) put on a shirt We put on shirt (7) | | |
| Change in word order | The cat runs after the dog The dog runs after the cat (8) | | (We) ran all day all day (we) ran (9) | | |
| Total change | | | | | The boy reads a book A chicken squawks (10) |

**Table 16.2** Number of children who produced a required writing procedure by sentence (*n* = 55)

| Syntactic modifications | Semantic relationships | | | | |
|---|---|---|---|---|---|
| | Inconsistency | Entailment | Redundancy | Identity | Total Difference |
| Verbatim reiteration | | | | 41 | |
| Deletion of one word | 1 | 12 | 8 | | |
| Addition of one word | 3 | 12 | 6 | | |
| Change in word order | 10 | | 6 | | |
| Total change | | | | | 36 |

deletion, or change in word order, i.e., the syntactic modification, the number of children producing the required writing procedures should not differ greatly from the sentences that undergo the same syntactic modification. Table 16.2 presents the number of children that produced the required writing procedure by pair of sentences. (See Tolchinsky Landsmann, 1988 for detailed scoring procedures.)

Very few children had difficulties in copying the written model when the OS was identical to the WS; or writing a different message when the OS was totally different from the WS. I think that this was so for two reasons. First, because those sentences required the child to centralize either in similarities or in differences and second, because the required writing behavior was consistent with the semantic relationship. They had to copy the entire WS of Identity and to produce a different message for Total Difference. The problems start for the pairs in which the OS was a partial modification of the WS. Here the difficulty lies in that children had to coordinate similarities and differences. They had to copy part of the WS, and delete, change or add another part. However, not all the pairs that required to coordinate similarities and differences, that is undergo the same syntactic modification, were equally difficult. The most difficult were the two pairs in which an *Inconsistency* relationship was created by negation. The created *Inconsistency* made it very difficult for the children to copy (and delete or add some part) a WS that was negated by an OS and vice versa. That seems to be the reason why the third pair in which *Inconsistency* was created by changing the actor–patient relationship could be represented by changing word order. Apparently, children viewed change in word order as an acceptable way to represent changes in the semantic relations. The same search for congruence between the required writing behavior and the semantic relationship may explain why the easiest pairs were those in which an *Entailment* relationship was created. Partial addition or partial copy seem to be viewed as a valid way to represent *Entailment*. This phenomenon is a clear instance of children searching for a certain agreement between the signifiers organization, the writing act, and the differences in meaning. Writing would have been a very rational system of notation if this were the case. This solution will be substituted with age. As children get older they increasingly rely on the sound pattern of the words as a guideline for the organization of the signifiers.

### Writing as an articulated linguistic notation

From the initial behaviors at seeing a written display, from the verbal expressions they produce in front of a written production it is evident that children know that writing has to do with language. It has been shown, however, that it takes some time for the children to discover the particular relationship between language and writing, to realize what level of language writing describes and which is the unit of description. My contention is that the interplay between the two paradigms by which writing is defined facilitates the move from conceiving writing as a particular object formally constrained to conceive it as an articulated linguistic notation.

When the activities that yield a written display are applied on formally constrained strings, the process of mapping becomes manageable. First mapping is global, but leaded by the discrete graphic units of the written string children start to segment their emissions and to look for units of correspondence. Previous research with Spanish speaking children indicates that when children start to look for letter-sound correspondences they resort to the syllabic hypothesis, the hypothesis that each letter corresponds to a syllable. Only later, after a series of 'cognitive conflicts' they discover the alphabetic principle, i.e., the principle by which letters represent consonantal and vocalic segments. It is understandable why children look for syllabic correspondences before phonemic ones. Syllables are units of behavior, they have phonic substance, phonemes are linguistic constructs. Nevertheless, the emergence of the syllabic hypothesis may depend on the specific language syllabic structure. Some languages have very uniform syllabic structure, e.g., only CV sequences, others tolerate great variations. French speakers listening to French words resort to syllabification while no trace of syllabification was found in English speakers listening to English words (Cutler, Mehler, and Segui, 1986). This may explain why there is no mention of a syllabic period in early literacy research that was carried on with English speaking children (Bissex, 1980; Goodman, 1982). Similarly regarding the alphabetic hypothesis. Hebrew speaking children do not arrive at an exhaustive alphabetic hypothesis. They may produce some syllabic-alphabetic representation but only for those cases for which the orthographic system provides orthographic representation. What I am suggesting here is that at this point – the point of establishment of the phonographic rules – writing development turns language specific. Throughout this chapter I have focussed on the development of writing as a notational system. I made no references to the content or to the syntactic and discursive features that children consider appropriate to be written. The process of becoming literate involves not only the appropriation of the phonographic rules of the correspondent orthography but also of basic cultural distinctions regarding register and functions of writing. The prevailing view is that children younger than seven either do not know how to write or are so occupied with the technical aspects of writing that they can hardly cope with other demands (Bereiter, 1980; Scardamalia, 1981). I believe that children under seven grasp the differential intentionality underlying diverse communicative circumstances and are able to find the linguistic means to express it. My main contention is that even before having a full command of the conventions of writing children have ideas about 'the language to be written' (Blance Benveniste, 1982). A few studies in emergent literacy have already provided empirical evidence for this contention. Children from age three recognized the diverse functions of writing (Haussler, 1985), preschoolers have definite expectations as to the kind of discourse that corresponds to newspapers, story-books, and letters (Ferreiro and Teberosky, 1979). Moreover, first graders are capable of creating surface texts including lingustic and graphic patterns which mark their genre. When six- to nine-year-olds were required to write news, 'like journalists do' they produced forms that characterize the journalist style and are seldom met in conversation. All the text children produced presented lexical forms in the subject proceeded by pronominal forms and many of them contained apposition in the subject. Moreover children organized the information provided in the text in the typical pyramidal style of journalism, putting fundamental information at the top of the text, followed by less relevant information (Teberosky; in press). Likewise when five- to seven-year-olds are required to write a known fairy tale and to describe one of its significative elements they are able to find distinctive linguistic features. To mention some of them, the verbal constructions preferred for narratives included mostly event verbs while those used in descriptions included almost exclusively stative verbs. Narrative texts progressed usually through a syntagmatic increment, by inclusion of complements, direct, and reported speech. Descriptive texts in contrast, progress by addition of a list of lexical items occupying the same syntagmatic position.

Again at this level the interplay between the two paradigms, the functional and the formal is evident. Children reproduce the discursive forms that were available to them as the register socially associated to the written modality. Furthermore, they are sensitive to the graphic confliguration that these registers usually assume in print. The format used in writing narratives is clearly distinguishable from the format used in descriptions and titles appear always on the top and centered.

It is important to note that in order to see these linguistic features we have to consider as a text not only the written marks left on the paper but also what children say they are going to write and they said they have written. I think that by considering these text levels it is possible to reach children's literate competence (Tolchinsky Landsmann, in progress).

## Conclusion

It is evident from the reviewed studies that children demonstrate for writing as for cognitive domains, a definite 'pedagogic disposition'. Premack (1984) defined as 'pedagogic disposition' the uniquely human quality to well seize the chance to demonstrate or to correct performance in a way no other earthly species does. Children come equipped with a propensity to extend knowledge by systematically monitoring naturally occurring variation and the results of their own active experimentation (Gelman and Brown, 1985). Successive interactions with an object of knowledge bring about cognitive change and since the interaction with writing is almost unavoidable it was reasonable to find children's ideas changing with age. As in other domains, literate knowledge progresses by transformations and correspondences (Sinclair, 1988). Children's ideas are not idiosyncratic inventions – although they may appear as such – but rather, selection and elaboration of the information provided by the environment. This elaboration brought about some transformations in the rules of the written system, e.g., when they established the minimum quantity principle or when they looked for semantic congruence, but they are constantly confronted with the features of the writing system, with the social uses of writing, and with the knowledge that significant others have about writing.

## Notes

1 The educational implications of this posture during the seventies were dramatic. Piagetian based curricula separate between 'thinking activities' and 'basic academic abilities such as reading, writing, and arithmetic' (Furth and Wach, 1974) as though thinking is not involved in reading or writing. Moreover, for the basic abilities almost no didactic change was introduced, they continued to be taught as traditionally as always.
2 Kindergarten and primary school curricula based on this conception are currently being applied in Barcelona, Spain under the direction of Ana Teberosky.
3 In his autobiographical memories, Jean Paul Sartre relates the way he learned to read. He was a devoted listener of stories that were usually read to him by his mother. One day, since his mother was absent and his baby-sitter sleepy, he decided to try by himself. He took the book and started 'saying' the story he already knew by heart, while looking at the pages. 'Au debut d'un instant j'avais compris: c'était le livre qui parlait' (1964, 34). I thank Ana Teberosky who provided me this reference.
4 This example was provided by Rosa Belles and was gathered during an individual interview.

## Acknowledgement

This paper was written while the author was a visiting scholar at the ICE University of Barcelona and enjoyed a Spencer Fellowship from the National Academy of Education U.S.A.

# References

Auzias, M., Casati, I., Cellier, C., Delaye, R., and Verleure, F. (1977). *Ecrire à cinq ans?* Paris: P.U.F.

Bereiter, C. (1980). Development in writing. In L. W. Gregg and E. R. Steinberg (Eds.), *Cognitive processes in writing.* Hillsdale, NJ: Lawrence Erlbaum Associates.

Bissex, G. (1980). *Gyns at work. A child learns to write and to read.* Cambridge, Mass.: Harvard University Press.

Bissex, G. (1985). Watching young writers. In A. Jagger and M. Trika Smith-Burke (Eds.), *Observing the language learner.* Newark, Del. I.R.A.

Blance Benveniste, C. (1982). In E. Ferreiro and M. Gomez Palacio (Eds.), *Nuevos aportes sobre los procesos de lectura y escritura.* Mexico: S XXI.

Carey, S. (1985). *Conceptual change in childhood.* Cambridge, Mass.: MIT Press.

Chafe, W. L. (1982). Integration and involvement in speaking, writing, and oral literature. In D. Tannen (Ed.), *Spoken and written language. Exploring orality and literacy.* Norwood, NJ: Ablex.

Clay, M. (1982). *What did I write? Beginning writing behaviour.* NH: Heinemann Educational Books.

Cutler, A., Mehler, J., and Segui, J. (1986). The syllable's differing role in the segmentation of French and English. In *Journal of Memory and Language, 25,* 385–400.

Ferreiro, E. (1985). *La presentacion del lenguaje y los procesos de alfabetizacion.* Cadernos de Pedagogia.

Ferreiro, E. (1986). In W. Taele and E. Sulzby (Eds.), *Emergent literacy: Writing and reading.* Norwood, NJ: Ablex.

Ferreiro, E., and Teberosky, A. (1979). *Los sistemas de escritura en el desarrollo del niño.* Mexico: S XXI.

Furth, H., and Wach, H. (1974). *Thinking goes to school: Piaget's theory in practice.* New York: Oxford University Press.

Gelman, R., and Brown, A. (1985). *Early foundations of cognitive development.* The 1985 Annual Report of the Center for Advance Study in Behavioral Sciences. Stanford, California.

Gibson, E., and Levin, I. (1970). *Psychology of reading.* Cambridge, Mass.: MIT Press.

Goodman, Y. (1982) El desarrollo de la escritura en niños muy pequeños. In: E. Ferreiro and M. Gomez Palacio (Eds.), *Nuevos aportes sobre los procesos de lectura y escritura.* Mexico: S XXI.

Goodman, Y. (1986). In W. Teale and E. Sulzby (Eds.), *Emergent literacy: Writing and reading.* Norwood, NJ: Ablex.

Harste, J. C., Woodward, V. A., and Burke, C. L. (1984). *Language stories and literacy lessons.* Portsmouth, NH: Heinemann Educational Books.

Haussler, M. A. (1985). Young child's developing concepts of print. In A. Jaggar and M. Trika Smith-Burke (Eds.), *Observing the language learner.* Newark, Del. I.R.A.

Illich, I., and Saunders, B. (1988). *The alphabetization of the popular mind.* San Francisco: North Point Press.

Levin, I., and Tolchinsky-Landsmann, L. (in press). Becoming literate: Referential and phonetic strategies in early reading and writing. In *European Journal of Behavioral Development.*

Lyons, J. (1977). *Semantics.* Cambridge: Cambridge University Press.

Macario, Gelman, and Shipley (in progress). *Using color when it matters: Preschool understanding of foods and canonicaly colored objects.*

Piaget, J. (1948). *La representation de l'espace chez l'enfant.* Paris: P.U.F.

Piaget, J. (1966). *Les mechanismes perceptifs.* Paris: P.U.F.

Piaget, J. (1960). *Les problèmes de psychologie génétique.* Denoël-Gonthier.

Piaget, J., and Inhelder, B. (1966). *L'image mentale chez l'enfant.* Paris: P.U.F.

Premack, D. (1984). Pedagogy and aesthetics as sources of culture. In M. Gazzaniga (Ed.), *Handbook of cognitive neuroscience.* Plenum.

Sartre, J. P. (1964). *Les mots.* Paris: Gallimard.

Scardamalia, M. (1981). How children cope with the cognitive demands of writing. In C. H. Frederiksen, M. F. Whiteman, and J. F. Dominic (Eds.), *Writing: The nature, development and teaching of written communication.* Hillsdale, NJ: Lawrence Erlbaum Associates.

Sinclair, H. (1967). *Acquisition du langage et development de la pensée.* Paris: Dunod.

Sinclair, H. (1988). *Constructivism and the psychology of mathematics.*

Snow, C., and Ninio, A. (1986). The contracts of literacy: What children learn from learning to read books. In W. Teale and E. Sulzby (Eds.), *Emergent literacy: Writing and Reading.* Norwood, NJ: Ablex.

Teberosky, A. (in press). Informative texts in children from 6 to 9. In C. Pontecorvo (Ed.), *La costruzione dei primi testi nei bambino.* Roma: Nova Italia.

Tolchinsky Landsmann, L. (1988). Form and meaning in the development of written representation. In *European Journal of Psychology, 3.*

Tolchinsky Landsmann, L., and Levin, I. (1985). Writing in preschoolers: An age related analysis. In *Journal of Applied Psycholinguistics, 6,* 319–339.

Tolchinsky Landsmann, L., and Levin, I. (1987). Writing in four to six year olds. Representation of phonetic similarities and differences. In *Journal of Child Language, 14,* 127–144.

Tolchinsky Landsmann, L. (in progress). *Text production and text differentiation in early childhood.*

Turkle, S. (1984). *The second self: computers and the human spirit.* New York: Simon and Schuster.

# SECTION V
## *OTHERS AND THEIR INFLUENCE: BEYOND THE SELF*

### Editors' Introduction

Piaget has had an enormous influence on psychology. His work author-itatively described the process of cognitive development from birth to adolescence. At the time when he formulated his ideas there were few competing perspectives which were able to describe development in such a thorough manner. Piaget's impact has been to focus attention on the way that children's understanding of the world increases as they learn from their own actions and in the later years as they learn from the arguments and discussions with others. There has been a reaction against his ideas and his very authority made him a target of attack. The first paper in this section illustrates one general criticism of Piaget's method – the tendency in his work to present children with tasks that were not particularly engaging or comprehensible to them (see also Donaldson, 1978). When tasks are made more understand-able then children, at younger ages than predicted by Piaget's stages, are able to achieve success. Such studies have highlighted the impor-tance of being sensitive to the needs of children and the difficulties children face when they encounter an unfamiliar task. These studies have also shown that the context in which information is presented can be very important in determining whether children are successful. Such studies indicate that children are not acting as isolated proces-sors of information, but are sensitive to non-verbal context and to their interpretation of the motivation and intentions present in the people who interact with them and in the activities they have to perform (see also the Introduction).

Originally when planning this reader we had decided to include a paper by Wood, Bruner and Ross (1976) which has been widely quoted because it identified the way that adults scaffold children's behaviour. The idea of scaffolding is often employed to help explain the process whereby a child is helped by an adult or a more competent child to acquire new skills or knowledge and to achieve success. Scaffolding focusses on the processes which enable the tutor to assist a child's development, such as limiting the opportunities to those which will result in success. Thus, with a jigsaw puzzle, adults may pick out those bits that go together, but leave the child successfully to fit together the individual pieces. One reason why the idea of scaffolding has attracted attention is that it fits in with Vygotsky's view of development. Vygotsky has often been portrayed as providing a very different perspective from Piaget because of his interest in the role of social processes in relation to development (see Smith, Dockrell and Tomlinson, 1997). Thus, scaffolding could be seen as one form of social interaction which assists children's learning and development. One of the original authors of the paper on scaffolding has recently published a review of this classic study together with a consideration of other similar perspectives. In the review David and Heather Wood consider the process of scaffolding and the way this is related to other models of learning and tuition, an issue which is the focus of their current research into computer aided learning. In their article they compare the effectiveness of humans and computers in providing a tutorial for a child. Wood and Wood then go on to discuss the theory and research of J. A. Anderson who they argue employs similar ideas to scaffolding, from an information processing perspective, when designing computer tutoring. This discussion raises issues about the usefulness of scaffolding as an educational tool.

There has been considerable interest in the process of peer interaction among young children. This interest can be attributed to several influences. One comes from Piaget's belief that peers would be more effective than adults in changing children's ideas and beliefs. This was based on the assumption that because adults are authority figures children would accept their ideas but not really understand them. In contrast, having to argue with someone of your own age is more likely to produce real cognitive change, rather than passive acceptance because the child attempts to understand the other person's perspective rather than passively accepting the conclusions. Another source of this interest was in the educational benefits of group discussion, particularly around computer based tasks. As resources have not allowed most children individual access to their own computer in schools, research has examined the benefits of group work on computers. The majority of studies have found that working in groups is as effective as working by oneself, and that in many circumstances working in a small group can be more effective than a child working on their own. The next paper in this section examines the way that some of the effects of group interaction might be due to children performing better, merely because they are in the presence of other individuals. This has been termed social facilitation in research on adults (Zajonc, 1965).

The articles considered so far have highlighted both the way in which the presentation of problems by experimenters and others can influence a child's success and learning, and the ways in which people structure information can assist a child's learning and success. The next two papers in this section provide a different view about the influence of other people, by examining the way that family relationships influence development, and by examining the way that the wider context of culture needs to be taken into account when studying child development (see the models of development identified in the introduction).

The role of siblings on each other largely has been neglected by developmental psychologists. Part of the reason for this is that it is difficult enough studying children as individuals without having to take into account the added complexity of the relationships they have with siblings. A notable exception to this tendency has been the work of Judy Dunn. In her review article she considers issues and findings from research which has investigated the way that siblings are treated differently within the same family, and the way that sibling relationships influence children's development of social understanding. We have already mentioned that a considerable amount of research has been concerned with the idea that children do not develop a 'theory of mind' (an understanding that other people can have different ideas from their own) until around 4 years of age. However, as Dunn points out much younger children appear able to engage in complex social processes which seem to involve some understanding of the other person's mind. As we have already mentioned there is a claim that even newborns have some understanding that other people are beings which are like themselves. Thus, it is of interest that Dunn has found that children who experience certain forms of social interaction perform better when they are older on formal tests of their theory of mind ability. All this work emphasizes the importance of viewing children, not just in terms of themselves but also in terms of their family. The work also raises questions about whether children may be able to give more sophisticated responses when the situation and task is familiar to them, than a more artificial task with unfamiliar people.

Barbara Rogoff and Gilda Morelli take this argument further by discussing the cultural context of children's development. Although it is often difficult to stand back and view children and ourselves without the assumptions that have been created by our own culture, such views are needed if we wish fully to understand child development. Adopting a cross-cultural perspective has also led a number of psychologists to become dissatisfied with experimental methods because they lack ecological validity, and they fail to examine children's thinking as it occurs as an everyday activity (Crook, in press). Rogoff and Morelli point out cross-cultural research has provided a variety of lessons about the developmental process, ranging from the way cultural patterns influence sleeping to the failure to find Piagetian stages that he hypothesized as universal. They also comment on the way that Vykotsky's theory has or can provide a framework for much of this research because of his focus on the role of social and cultural processes in cognitive development. Their third argument is that there has been a welcome move away from the study of minority groups in terms of 'deficits' in child development, to an increasing recognition partly as a result of cross-cultural perspectives, that a deficit view is partly a product of the value we place on certain outcomes (see also the chapter by Heath in Section II). Furthermore, cross-cultural research also has suggested that different patterns of childrearing from that usually practised in the West may provide certain advantages to children in their own culture.

This section has highlighted the way that children's thinking and development needs to be placed in a wider context. Children are not solitary thinkers. They are influenced by the way information is presented to them and by the way adults and peers interact with them. Both Piaget and Vygotsky have discussed the way social interaction can facilitate cognitive development, although each has his own perspective on the matter. There is also increasing awareness of the way that we need to position children's thinking within the broader context of family and cultural influences if we are to understand fully the process of development (see Smith, Dockrell and Tomlinson, in press).

## References

Crook, C. (in press). The uses and significance of electronic media during development. In D. Messer and S. Millar (Eds.). *Developmental Psychology*. London: Arnold.

Donaldson, M. (1978). *Children's Minds*. London: Fontana.

Smith, L., Dockrell, J., and Tomlinson, P. (1997). *Piaget and Vigotsky*. London: Routledge.

Wood, D., Bruner, J., and Ross, G. (1976). The role of tutoring in problem solving, *Journal of Child Psychology and Psychiatry, 17*, 89–100.

Zajonc, R. B. (1965). Social facilitation. *Science, 149*, 269–274.

## Further Reading

Crook, C. (in press). Media, technology and learning with others. In D. Messer and S. Millar (Eds.), *Developmental Psychology*. London: Arnold.

Durkin, K. (1995). *Social Development*. Oxford: Blackwell.

Terwogt, M. M. and Steege, H. (in press). Emotional development and cognitive growth. In D. Messer and S. Millar (Eds.), *Developmental Psychology*. London: Arnold.

Woollett, A. (in press). Families and their influence on children's development. In D. Messer and S. Millar (Eds.), *Developmental Psychology*. London: Arnold.

# 17 Martin Hughes and Margaret Donaldson
## 'The Use of Hiding Games for Studying the Coordination of Viewpoints'

Reprinted in full from: *Educational Review* 31, 133–140 (1979)

One of Piaget's best known claims is that children below the age of six or seven years are highly egocentric, and cannot take account of another person's point of view (e.g. Piaget, 1926; Piaget and Inhelder, 1969). Piaget has devised several tasks for demonstrating the egocentrism of young children, one of which is the classic mountain task (Piaget and Inhelder, 1956, chapter 8).

The mountain task was designed to test whether young children could take another person's point of view in the literal sense of being able to calculate what that person could *see*. In a typical version of the task the child is seated before a model of three mountains, each of which is a different colour, and a doll is placed so that it is looking at the mountains from a different point of view. The child is shown a set of pictures of the mountains taken from different angles and is asked to choose the picture which shows what the doll sees. Piaget and Inhelder found that children below about eight years were unable to do this; indeed there was a powerful tendency among children below the age of six or seven to choose the picture showing their *own* point of view. This finding is extremely reliable, and has been replicated several times (e.g. Aebli, 1967; Dodwell, 1963; Garner and Plant, 1972).

Piaget and Inhelder concluded from their findings that the children's egocentrism was preventing them from working out what the doll could see: 'the children . . . all really imagine that the doll's perspective is the same as their own, they all think the little man sees the mountains in the way they appear from where they themselves sit' (Piaget and Inhelder, 1956, p. 220). According to Piaget and Inhelder, the young child is unable to *decentre*: that is, he is unable to see his own viewpoint as one of a set of possible viewpoints, and to coordinate these different points of view into a single coherent system.

The child's performance on the mountain task would indeed seem to justify the conclusions of Piaget and Inhelder. However the mountain task is not the only way to test children's ability to recognise and coordinate different points of view. In the present paper we outline a different way of investigating these abilities.

In the studies described below the task is presented to the child as a hiding game. The child is asked to hide a small boy doll from one or more toy policemen who are 'looking for the boy'. In the first study the child has to do this by placing a small model wall between one of the policemen and the boy; in the other studies he has to hide the boy within various configurations of walls. Thus the child is not asked directly to calculate what the policemen can see. Nevertheless, this demand is implicit in the task: he cannot succeed without taking account of what the various policemen can see.

In choosing a task that in many ways resembles a game we were implicitly following the example of Peel (1967), who devised a game to investigate children's understanding of logical terms such as 'if . . . then . . .'. In Peel's game the experimenter and child took turns to put coloured beads or counters into a box, according to rules such as: 'If and whenever I draw a red bead you are not to draw a red counter'. Peel argued that games such as this are particularly useful for studying children's thinking skills, in that a formally complex task can be presented to children in a way that retains their interest and enjoyment. This belief also underlies the studies presented here.

### Study one

The task used in our first study was the most straightforward of the three. The child was seated at a low table, in the middle of which were placed a policeman, the boy, and a wall. The policeman and boy were about 6 cm high, and the wall was 7 cm high by 4 cm wide. The experimenter told the child that the policeman was looking for the boy, and that the boy wanted to hide from the policeman. The policeman and boy were then placed facing each other near the edge of the table, at P and b respectively (see Figure 17.1(a)), and the child was asked to '*put the wall so that the policeman cannot see the boy*'. The child had thus to place the wall so that it blocked the line PB.

The task was repeated for two more positions of the policeman and boy: first, with the line PB perpendicular to the edge of the table (Figure 17.1(b)), and secondly, with the line PB across the corner of the table (Figure 17.1(c)). We included this last position because of the claim by Piaget and Inhelder that young children find it particularly difficult to imagine a straight line across the corner of a table (Piaget and Inhelder, 1956, chapter 6). In each case the policeman and boy always faced each other and the child could always see the policeman's face.

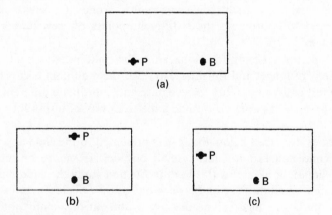

**Figure 17.1**   Positions of policeman (P) and boy (B) in Study One.

These three versions of the task were given to a group of 10 three-year-olds (range 3:3 to 3:11, mean 3:8) and 10 four-year-olds (range 4:2 to 4:9, mean 4:6). Somewhat surprisingly, the children's performance was virtually error-less, with nine out of ten children in each age group placing the wall correctly in all versions of the task. There were no differences between the various versions of the task: all children, three- and four-year-olds alike, succeeded on the 'across the corner' version.

These results already make it clear that three- and four-year-old children can perform in a non-egocentric fashion in certain situations. None of the children showed any signs of confusing their own view of the boy with the policeman's view (for example, by placing the wall between *themselves* and the boy). All the children were clearly aware that placing the wall on the line PB prevented the policeman from seeing the boy, and the fact that the boy was still clearly visible to *them* did not seem to influence their judgements. Accordingly, we decided to use the same basic idea to see if young children could coordinate two different points of view at once.

**Study two**

In the second study we used three small dolls – two policemen and a boy – and a cross-shaped configuration of walls (see Figure 17.2). The children were asked to hide the boy from *both* the policemen, and thus had to keep in mind two different points of view at once.

Each child was introduced to the task very carefully to give him every chance of fully understanding the situation. The experimenter placed the boy, the walls, and a single policeman on the table and told the child, as in the first study, that the policeman was looking for the boy and that the boy wanted to hide from the policeman. The experimenter then arranged the walls and the policeman as shown in Figure 17.2(a), so that the policeman could see into the sections marked B and C, but not into sections A and D. The boy doll was then placed in section A, and the child was asked '*can the policeman see the boy?*' This was repeated for sections B, C, and D in turn. The experimenter

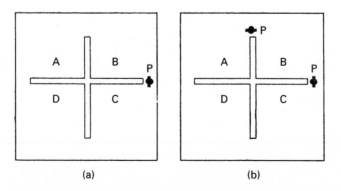

(a)  (b)

**Figure 17.2**  Positions of policemen (P) in Study Two.

then moved the policeman to the opposite side, so that he could see into sections A and D, but not sections B and C. This time the child was asked to '*hide the boy so that the policeman can't see him*'. If the child made any mistakes at these preliminary stages, his error was pointed out to him and the question repeated until the correct answer was given. But in fact very few mistakes were made (only 8% overall).

When it was clear that the child fully understood the situation, the experimenter brought out the other policeman, saying '*Here's another policeman. He is also looking for the boy. The boy must hide from BOTH policemen*'. The two policemen were then positioned as shown in Figure 17.2(b), leaving only section D unobserved. The child was asked to '*hide the boy so that BOTH the policemen can't see him*'. This was repeated three times, each time leaving a different section as the only hiding place.

The task was given to 30 children aged between 3:6 and 4:11, with a mean age of 4:3. The overall success rate was again surprisingly high, with 22 children correct on all four trials, and five children correct on three out of four trials. The younger children were no less successful than the older ones, and it was clear that virtually all the children tested were able to take account of and coordinate two different points of view.

**Study three**

In view of the ease with which the children had performed in Study Two, we decided to make the task even harder in the next study. We used two versions of the task. In the first, the wall arrangement had five sections, and the two policemen were positioned so that only one section was left unobserved (see Figure 17.3(a)). The child's task was again to '*hide the boy so that BOTH the policemen can't see him*'. In the second version of the task, the wall arrangement had six sections, and this time there were *three* policemen looking for the boy (see Figure 17.3(b)). The child was asked to '*hide the boy so that NONE of the policemen can see him*'. Each task consisted of four trials, corresponding to four different positions of the policeman. As in the previous study, both tasks

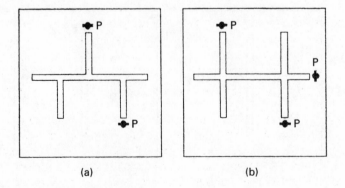

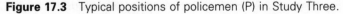

**Figure 17.3** Typical positions of policemen (P) in Study Three.

were introduced to the children carefully and gradually, to give them every chance of understanding the situation.

The subjects in this study were 20 three-year-olds (range 3:1 to 3:11, mean 3:6) and 20 four-year-olds (range 4:0 to 4:9, mean 4:5). None of these children had been subjects in either of the two previous studies. The children were divided into two groups, matched as far as possible for age and sex. One group performed the first version of the task, while the other group performed the second version.

Despite the increased complexity of the task, the four-year-olds still had little trouble with either version. Nine out of 10 four-year-olds made no errors at all on the five-section, two-policemen task, and eight out of 10 made no errors in the six-section, three-policemen task. The three-year-olds had more difficulty with the tasks, although their performance was still fairly high: six out of 10 made one or no errors in the first task and seven out of 10 made one or no errors on the second task. The difference between three- and four-year-olds was significant at the 0.05 level for the first task only ($U = 23$, Mann-Whitney $U$ test, two-tailed). As can be seen, there were no major differences between the two versions of the task. This finding was somewhat surprising as we had predicted that the three-policemen task would be harder than the two-policemen task.

Very few of the errors produced by the three-year-olds could in any sense be termed egocentric. No child confused his own view with the policemen's by consistently hiding the boy so that the boy was out of sight from the child. Indeed, two of the children who failed on the task consistently placed the boy doll in the sections *nearest* to them, so that the doll was fully visible to them as well as to the policemen. Two children chose to play a different game from the one which the experimenter had in mind; one consistently hid the boy under the table, and the other hid him in her hand! These responses – which were perfectly adequate in their own way – were somewhat reluctantly scored as incorrect. The remaining errors were mainly the occasional mistakes made in calculation by children who otherwise performed well on the task.

**Discussion**

The level of performance found in these three studies is remarkably high. Very few of the children – three-year-olds or four-year-olds – had any difficulty either with the one-policeman task used in Study One, or with the simpler two-policemen task used in Study Two. It was only when the task was made more complex still, in Study Three, that the three-year-olds started to make an appreciable number of errors, and even then the majority of children still performed extremely well.

These findings clearly have important implications for the notion of early childhood egocentrism, and we will return to these implications shortly. First, however, it is worth pausing to look at the children's performance on the tasks in more detail, and to consider the kinds of thinking skills they might be using.

When one watches the children perform these tasks, it often seems as though they are playing an enjoyable little game with the experimenter, somewhat like a simple form of chess. The experimenter places the policemen in position, and asks the child to hide the boy: the child responds by putting the boy within one of the sections of the walls. The experimenter then moves one of the policemen to another position, so that the boy is now visible: the child in turn replies by moving the boy to a new safe position. The experimenter moves the policemen again, the child replies again and so it goes on: move and counter-move, threat and reply. These games are obviously very enjoyable to the children and they seem to have no difficulty in understanding what to do. Indeed, the child will often respond before any instructions are given, as if he understands the rules of the game well enough and does not need reminding of what he has to do. This, as we shall see later, is an important point.

The analogy with chess is reinforced by the habit of some children who pick up the boy, move him to a section of the walls and, *without letting go of him*, look around to see if he is visible to any of the policemen. If he is, they move him to another section and try again. This is very similar to what often happens when a beginner starts to play chess: he will pick up a piece, move it to a square on the board, and without letting go, will look around to see if the piece can be captured, or if the move is otherwise unsafe. This practice soon disappears as the beginner learns to internalize the whole process instead. By analogy, it is tempting to suppose that the children who succeed on the policemen task without moving the boy from one section to another have likewise managed to internalize the process of trying each section to see which is safe.

If this is so, then it raises interesting questions about the thought processes which might be involved. Do they involve imagery – in that the child imagines the boy in a particular section and then works out if he is visible or not – or is it rather a primitive case of inference, with the child thinking along the lines:

'If I move him to section A, then he will be visible. I don't want this, so I won't move him to section A.'

'If I move him to section B, . . . etc.'?

The process could, of course, involve both imagery and inference. Indeed, it is likely that for advanced chess players, who can 'see' many moves ahead, both imagery and inferences are involved. This kind of thinking has been little studied, however, either in adults or in children, and at present we can only speculate on what might be involved.

While it remains unclear precisely what thought processes are required to succeed on our tasks, there can be little doubt that they reveal the presence of well-coordinated, 'decentred' thinking in three- and four-year-old children. In successfully coordinating the viewpoints of three different policemen at once, the children show themselves to be virtually unhampered by the constraints of egocentrism. These findings thus add further support to a growing body of evidence which shows that young children can – in certain circumstances – calculate what another person can see (see review by Flavell, 1974; also Borke,

1975). In addition, there are findings from two further studies which support those presented here. In one study, Light (1974) gave two tasks involving hide and seek situations to a group of children around their fourth birthdays, and one of the tasks was similar to that used in Study Two. Light found that performance was high on both tasks, with well over half the children giving predominantly correct responses. In the other study, Flavell, Shipstead, and Croft (1978) gave various versions of a hiding task, similar to that used in Study One, to children aged between $2\frac{1}{2}$ and $3\frac{1}{2}$ years. They found that almost all the children could hide an object from a toy dog by moving the object behind a screen, but that it was significantly harder to hide the object by moving the screen. All the same, most of the 3- and $3\frac{1}{2}$ year-olds were able to do this latter version of the task.

There is thus substantial evidence to show that three- and four-year-olds are by no means as egocentric as Piaget has claimed. But why, in that case, do they fail on the mountain task? Why do so many children pick their own view of the mountains when asked to select the doll's view? One factor which undoubtedly influences the children's performance is the complexity of the array. The mountain task is particularly difficult in that it requires the child to perform both front/back and left/right reversals in order to work out the doll's view, and there is indeed evidence that performance improves as the array is simplified (Fishbein, Lewis, and Keffer, 1972; Flavell *et al.*, 1968). However it seems that another factor may also be involved. It could well be that in the mountain task the child has considerable difficulty in *understanding what he is supposed to do*.

Support for this idea comes from a study one of us carried out with a simplified version of the mountain task (Hughes, 1978). Instead of mountains, Hughes used three dolls of different colours each facing outwards from the corner of a triangular base. The array was positioned between the child and the experimenter, so that the child saw the face of the doll nearest him (say, a red doll) and the experimenter saw the face of a different doll, the one nearest him (say, a blue doll). Hughes found that when three- and four-year-olds were asked, in the standard manner, to select a picture showing the experimenter's view, very few could do this. However, the great majority of them could succeed when this question was preceded by questions referring to particular features of the array ('which doll's face do I see?/do you see?', etc.) and to the same features of the pictures ('which doll's face do you see in this picture?', etc.). By drawing the child's attention to these features, the preliminary questions helped him understand what was involved in the task.

In contrast, the tasks used in the present studies were extremely clear to the children, and they immediately grasped what they were supposed to do. We were careful to introduce the tasks in ways which would help the child understand the situation, but in fact these precautions were largely unnecessary. The children understood the rules of the game at once and, as we have already seen, they often responded to each trial without any reminders from the experimenter as to what the game was about.

Why do children find these tasks so easy to grasp, compared with problems like the mountain task? We believe it is because the policemen tasks make *human sense* in a way that the mountain task does not. The motives and intentions of the characters (hiding and seeking) are entirely comprehensible, even to a child of three, and he is being asked to identify with – and indeed do something about – the plight of a boy in an entirely comprehensible situation. This ability to understand and identify with another's feelings and intentions is in many ways the exact opposite of egocentrism, and yet it now appears to be well developed in three-year-olds. Indeed, as one of us has argued at greater length (Donaldson, 1978), it seems likely that it constitutes a very fundamental human skill, the origins of which may be present even in the first few months of life.

## References

Aebli, H. (1967). Egocentrism (Piaget) not a phase of mental development but a substitute solution for an insoluble task. *Pedagogica Europaea, 3*, pp. 97–103.

Borke, H. (1975). Piaget's mountains revisited: changes in the egocentric landscape. *Developmental Psychology, 11*, pp. 240–243.

Dodwell, P. C. (1963). Children's understanding of spatial concepts. *Canadian Journal of Psychology, 17*, pp. 141–161.

Donaldson, M. (1978). *Children's Minds*. London: Fontana/Croom Helm.

Fishbein, H. D., Lewis, S., and Keiffer, K. (1972). Children's understanding of spatial relations: co-ordination of perspectives. *Developmental Psychology, 7*, pp. 21–33.

Flavell, J. H. (1974). The developmental of inferences about others. In: T. Mischel (Ed.), *Understanding Other Persons*. Oxford: Blackwell.

Flavell, J. H., Botkin, P. T., Fry, C. L., Wright, J. W., and Jarvis, P. E. (1968). *The Development of Role-taking and Communication Skills in Children*. New York: J. Wiley.

Flavell, J. H., Shipstead, S. G., and Croft, K. (1978). Young children's knowledge about visual perception: hiding objects from others (unpublished manuscript).

Garner, J., and Plant, E. (1972). On the measurement of egocentrism: a replication and extension of Aebli's findings. *British Journal of Educational Psychology, 42*, pp. 79–83.

Hughes, M. (1978). Selecting pictures of another person's view. *British Journal of Educational Psychology, 48*, pp. 210–219.

Light, P. (1974). The role-taking skills of four-year-old children. Unpublished *Ph.D. thesis*. University of Cambridge.

Peel, E. A. (1967). A method for investigating children's understanding of certain logical connectives used in binary propositional thinking. *British Journal of Mathematical and Statistical Psychology, 20*, pp. 81–92.

Piaget, J. (1926). *The Language and Thought of the Child*. London: Routledge and Kegan Paul.

Piaget, J., and Inhelder, B. (1956). *The Child's Conception of Space*. London: Routledge and Kegan Paul.

Piaget, J., and Inhelder, B. (1969). *The Psychology of the Child*. London: Routledge and Kegan Paul.

# 18 David Wood and Heather Wood
## 'Vygotsky, Tutoring and Learning'

Reprinted in full from: *Oxford Review of Education* **22**, 5–16 (1996)

### Scaffolding and the zone of proximal development

Almost 20 years ago, Wood, Bruner, and Ross (Wood *et al.*, 1976) introduced the metaphor of 'scaffolding' in the context of tutorial interactions between an adult and individual children. The formulation of this notion was designed to explore the nature of the support that an adult provides in helping a child to learn how to perform a task that, alone, the child could not master. Parallels between the notion of scaffolding and Vygotsky's more general theoretical concept of the *Zone of Proximal Development* or ZPD (Vygotsky, 1978) were soon drawn (Rogoff and Wertsch, 1984).

Vygotsky's ZPD is probably so widely known as to need no definition. However, in case it remains unfamiliar to some, it refers to the gap between what a given child can achieve alone, their 'potential development as determined by independent problem solving', and what they can achieve 'through problem solving under adult guidance or in collaboration with more capable peers'.

Vygotsky's definition of the ZPD leaves open to us the task of identifying the *nature* of the guidance and collaboration that promotes development and a need to specify what gets learned during the course of a given history of tutor/learner interaction. These two key issues provide the main agenda for this paper.

Scaffolding can be seen as one attempt to address the first of these questions; what is the nature of help or guidance? The suggestion was that the adult could serve several key tutoring functions. These included recruitment of the child's interest in the task, establishing and maintaining an orientation towards task-relevant goals, highlighting critical features of the task that the child might overlook, demonstrating how to achieve goals and helping to control frustration. This latter role was achieved by ensuring that the child was neither left to struggle alone with too much complexity, nor, conversely, given too little scope for involvement and initiative in task activity.

Since its formulation, the scaffolding idea has been developed, extended and criticized in several different ways. For example, it was argued that the concept ignored the nature of the relationship between adult and child, was limited to a single, isolated task and said too little about the nature of the communicative mechanisms involved. Several attempts have been made to try to remedy these shortcomings, though the nature of what gets learned or internalized during the course of interaction still remains unclear and controversial.

It is not our intention to try to review here the history of scaffolding nor the formulation of related concepts such as 'cognitive apprenticeship' (Collins *et al.*, 1989), 'guided participation' (Rogoff, 1990), and 'reciprocal teaching' (Brown and Campione, 1990). Extensive, evaluative reviews of these notions have already been undertaken (Rogoff, 1986, 1990) and we have only space here to summarize some of the generalizations that have emerged.

Reviewing the literature on both adult and peer tutoring, Rogoff suggests that laboratory investigation and naturalistic observation have identified several general features of effective collaboration. These are summarized below:

1  Tutors serve to provide a bridge between a learner's existing knowledge and skills and the demands of the new task. Left alone, a novice might not appreciate the relations between what the task demands and what they already know or can do that is relevant.
2  By providing instructions and help in the context of the learner's activity, tutors provide a structure to support the learner's problem solving. For example, while focused on their immediate actions, learners, left alone, might lose sight of the overall goal of the activity.
3  Although the learner is involved in what is initially, for them, 'out of reach' problem solving, guided participation ensures that they play an active role in learning and that they contribute to the successful solution of problems.
4  Effective guidance involves the transfer of responsibility from tutor to learner.
5  Not all guided participation involves deliberate or explicit attempts to teach and learn. Often, interactions with the four characteristics just listed occur when children set out to 'help' their parents, as they participate in everyday activities, or in playful encounters.

These features of everyday interactions involving children as learners are hardly surprising and seemingly self-evident. However, on a socio-historical account of development, like Vygotsky's, it is their very familiarity which indicates their power. If they were not familiar and mundane they could not serve the functions that are claimed for them. They help to explain why, over years of childhood, small-scale 'micro-genetic' changes brought about in such social encounters serve to transmit culture from one generation to the next.

**Contingent instruction**

In our own work, we have focused on the issue of task responsibility and control, seeking to identify aspects of tutorial activity which lead to the progressive acquisition of task competence by the child and to the 'hand over' of task responsibility from tutor to learner. Briefly, we suggested that effective helping involved two ingredients:

1  The first concerns circumstances in which a child gets into difficulty. Here, the tutor immediately offers more specific instruction or help than was

offered previously. For instance, if the tutor had suggested a specific action or goal to the child, but the child did not understand what s/he meant by what s/he said, then the tutor steps in to point out or show the child what to work with next. By fleshing out the meaning of the (initially non-understood) utterances by showing what they entail in action, the tutor eventually negotiates the task-specific meaning of the language used and draws the child into the tutor's conceptualization of the situation.

2 The second ingredient of effective instruction is 'fading'; providing the child with the minimal help needed to ensure joint success. For instance, if, initially, a child needs to be shown what to do in order to succeed, the contingent tutor will attempt to replace showing by telling. As the child comes to understand verbal hints, then the tutor attempts to remain silent (no easy task when teaching) ensuring that, if the child gets into no more difficulty, s/he proceeds to complete the task alone.

Patterns of instruction which are marked by these two principles – give more help when the learner gets into difficulty, and offer less help as they gain in proficiency – we have termed 'contingent' teaching. Others have found that similar principles govern the effectiveness of face-to-face instruction in other task contexts involving parents with infant learners (Heckhausen, 1987), school-aged children learning mathematics (Pratt *et al.*, 1989) and in teaching planning skills (Rogoff, 1990).

The 'rules' for contingent instruction may seem self-evident and simple. In practice, however, contingency is hard to sustain. Empirically, we have observed that many face-to-face teaching interactions involving both parents and professional teachers are almost never maximally contingent. Even an adult trained to teach contingently could not sustain 100% adherence to the rules (Wood *et al.*, 1978). One clear implication is that less than contingent instructional performance is adequate to ensure learning in most cases.

The complexity of the task of achieving contingent instruction is also highlighted by our recent attempts to apply the same principles to the design of computer-based tutoring systems.

**Planning and teaching**

Imagine a situation in which a would-be tutor has made a suggestion to their learner about what they might try to do next. The learner does not follow the instruction but does something else. What they do, however, represents a perfectly sensible way of proceeding; another means for achieving taskrelevant ends. What does the would-be contingent tutor do? If would seem inappropriate (and objectively incorrect) to act in any way that might imply to the learner that what they are attempting to do is wrong. The contingent tutor should suspend their own initial teaching intent and offer any subsequent help in relation to what the learner is inferred to be trying to do. We have termed this aspect of effective helping 'domain contingency'. It involves decisions about *what* to teach next in response to local circumstances.

Achieving such flexibility in computer-based tutoring is difficult. However well the system designer understands the learning domain and how it might be learned, there is always a possibility that the learner will invent a novel means to master it. Unless computer-based systems can be made sufficiently flexible and adaptive to be able to evaluate unexpected activities, they will not achieve maximal contingency. More generally, the ability to integrate behaviour based on a plan with the capacity to depart from that plan as and when the situation demands is a difficult problem for Artificial Intelligence, and current AI systems are not competent at meeting such demands in real time. The implication of this for the current generation of computer-based tutoring systems is that they run the risk of classifying learner innovation as error. Of course, human tutors may also fail to appreciate learner innovation. But they do possess the potential to learn. To the best of our knowledge, no such computer-based systems yet exist.

Having decided what is to be the focus of any help to be offered, the next tutorial task is to determine how specific that help should be, as discussed earlier. Achieving this is relatively easy with a computer-based system. The system is programmed to record any level of help given to an individual learner. When the learner gets into difficulty increasingly specific help is given, up to the point where either the learner follows an instruction successfully or the system provides maximum help by doing the next part of the task itself. The system is thus 'driven' to provide increasingly specific help as a learner struggles but it is programmed always to attempt to fade the level of help offered after success. Although easy for a computer, the demands that these requirements put on human powers of observation, attention, and memory are considerable, which helps to explain why contingent tutoring is easily described but hard to practice.

A third requirement concerns the timing of instruction or 'temporal contingency'. Imagine a situation in which a learner is pondering over their next move. Then think of an episode in which they are so bemused that they have not a clue what to do next. Attention to the posture, facial expression, or other non-verbal features of learner behaviour would probably enable a human tutor to decide what their lack of task activity betokened. Acting contingently, they would decide to leave the learner alone in the first situation but offer help in the second. A computer-based tutoring system has no means whatsoever to make such decisions. All they can be programmed to respond to are the key-presses, mouse movements or whatever by which the learner interacts with the system. Anything that relies on more subtle aspects of non-verbal communication can play no role in human-computer interaction. In designing their systems, then, programmers must either impose some arbitrary time criterion, after which help will be given in such circumstances (wanted or not), or they must leave the learner with the task of requesting help. In either case, the system cannot guarantee temporal contingency.

### From a different direction – J. A. Anderson and learning theory

The research that we have just outlined rests on attempts to describe tutoring activity in a way that relates to learning outcomes. On the basis of such analyses, it has sought to formulate principles, like instructional contingency, which are implicated in effective face-to-face tutoring. Anderson's approach is quite different; he comes from another direction. Over several years, he has developed a theory of learning that is couched in information processing terms and implemented as a computer 'architecture'. On the grounds of the not unreasonable assumption that principles of instruction should be compatible with what one takes to be an adequate theory of learning, he has sought to make a contribution to education by drawing principles of instruction from the theory and testing these out in the design of Intelligent Tutoring Systems (ITSs) which have been evaluated in classrooms.

### Anderson and act theory

We first encountered Anderson's work on ITSs through a 1987 paper which, written with colleagues, offered an overview of their previous work. A principal motivation for the ITS research was to provide a context for an empirical evaluation of the ACT theory of skill learning (ACT standing for the Adaptive Character of Thought).

Citing bloom's (Bloom, 1984) comparative analysis of the relative effectiveness of conventional class teaching versus one-to-one (human) tutoring, Anderson and colleagues suggested that some of the benefits reported by Bloom might be obtained by means of computer systems designed to individualize instruction. Bloom concluded that face-to-face instruction leads to an improvement of two Standard Deviations over conventional class teaching (i.e., about 98% of individually taught learners score above the average for group taught). If computer-based systems could be designed to capture even part of this benefit, then the educational rewards of the research could be highly significant.

What we found striking was the resemblance between the design principles that Anderson and his colleagues had drawn from their theory of learning and the notions of scaffolding and contingent instruction. Since Anderson's group was not only advocating similar tutoring principles, but also justifying these in terms of their theory, then it seemed possible that they could provide an answer to the question being asked by many working with Vygotskian theory; what gets internalized during the course of interactions within the ZPD?

### An information processing approach to tutoring

One of the central features of ITSs, like face-to-face tutoring, is that they can provide instruction contingently in the context of the learner's real-time activity. In Anderson's terms, they honour the principle: (1) *provide instruction in the problem-solving context*. In group situations, where a learner might, say, be talked through a mathematics problem or see a demonstration proof worked out, the teacher might offer advice and guidance about how to solve problems before asking the learners to work at some for themselves. The learner, then, has not only to remember and recall such advice, but also recognize the actual problem contexts to which it relates. In face-to-face teaching, the location and timing of any help can be offered by the tutor at relevant junctures, i.e., contingently. Further, the learner can be prevented from wasting time and losing motivation by spending large amounts of time in confused and fruitless activity. To avoid such confusion, the theory advocates: (2) *immediate response to learner errors.* Within the theory, nothing is learned from errors, they only waste time. Thus, intelligent tutors should provide immediate feedback on error.

Initially, with a learner who understands little of the lesson at hand, the tutor may have to step in frequently to repair error and to show the learner what to do. However, the aim is: (3) to *support successive approximations to competent performance.* The tutor should be programmed not to interfere with successful learner activity. Thus, as the learner learns, the system fades and becomes silent.

Since learners have limited 'working memory capacity' they may overlook important features of the task at hand or lose sight of what they are trying to achieve. The system can support learning: (4) by *providing reminders of the learning goal.* They can also provide reminders by, for instance, showing, on screen, a trace of what the learner has already achieved on a given task. The learner's attention can be directed to this if and when they lose track of what they are doing.

There is much more by way of detail that the ACT theory has to say about these issues. However, the aim here is simply to draw attention to some of the resemblances between ACT theory and the findings from developmental research outlined earlier. We now need to explore the theory which justifies these instructional design principles.

**Theory and practice**

In designing a computer tutor, Anderson identifies three main tasks. The system must:

1 include an ideal student model (i.e. a specification of what needs to be learned);
2 include a model of where an individual learner 'is at' relative to the ideal student; and
3 include the generation of a tutoring strategy adapted to the needs of each learner.

The ideal student model is essentially a statement of the curriculum to be learned. In one sense, this model stands 'outside' the theory in that it is a specification of the 'what' rather than the 'how' of learning. However, and here comes a strong theoretical claim, that curriculum must be subjected to a cognitive task analysis to identify the *rules* that it embodies. According to the ACT theory, these rules must be of a specific nature, i.e. production rules. For those for whom this is a novel concept, an example of production rules for simple arithmetic problems might help to give an impression of their nature:

| IF | the goal is to solve a problem |
| | and C1 is the rightmost column without an answer digit |
| THEN | set a subgoal to write an answer in C1. |
| IF | the goal is to write out an answer in C1 |
| | and d1 and d2 are the digits in that column |
| | let d3 be the sum of d1 and d1 |
| THEN | set a subgoal to write d3 in C1. |

The claim is that human knowledge includes such rules. This does not mean, of course, that when one thinks one is conscious of figuring out 'if–then' propositions. Indeed, according to the theory, procedural knowledge, i.e. what production rules model, is not consciously inspectable. It is a form of 'mentalese' which, though roughly describable in linguistic terms, is not speech *per se*.

In addition to production rules, knowing also involves declarative knowledge. This is knowledge that can be verbally stated or communicated in some other way such as through figures and diagrams. Such communicable or demonstrable knowledge is of itself 'inert'. Thus, a learner might be able, say, to read and even remember a verbal instruction, but until this is connected to procedural knowledge in the service of some goal, it lacks utility. Learning how to act in response to declarative knowledge, i.e. how to proceduralize that knowledge to achieve goals, is at the heart of skill learning in ACT.

The (dynamic) model of each individual learner is built up in the same language of production rules. As the tutoring system presents examples or problems for the learner to solve, it compares their performance with that of the ideal student model (hence the term 'model-based tutoring'). This analysis then provides the tutorial goals of the system. Where a learner demonstrates knowledge of a production rule and its relation to declarative knowledge, the system offers no intervention. However, an individual student may not evidence knowledge of such connections. They may also make an error which signals a lack of sensitivity to the crucial elements of a situation or perform an action which does not take activity closer to the solution being sought. In such circumstances, problems are selected to provide instruction and practice with the rules that have yet to be learned. The system monitors the effects of practice (in terms of the learning theory) to specify when the learner can be moved on to encounter novel productions. The amount of novelty is also theoretically constrained by the theory.

Another central feature of the latest version of the theory (Anderson, 1993) concerns the nature of mechanisms for the generalization of knowledge. Anderson argues that analogy is the key to generalization. In a problematic situation, the learner may seek to draw analogies between their current difficulties and previous experiences with related problems. Worked examples are thus a crucial factor in learning. If and when a learner succeeds in solving a problem by analogy to a previously worked example (which, initially, may be supported by a tutor), then the example is elaborated or 'reified' to start the formation of a 'schema' or meta-procedure. To the extent that this schema supports future learning, it becomes increasingly linked (procedurally) to the class of problems that it serves. Thus, the identification of productive worked examples is central to pedagogical decision making.

### Evaluation

Judged by their own objectives, Anderson and his colleagues can claim a fair degree of success with their tutors. Classroom evaluations of systems designed to support learning in geometry and LISP programming showed evidence of benefits over conventional teaching. Improvements of about one standard deviation in performance levels were obtained (equivalent to a grade level in the US accreditation system) and learning time for computer-based students was around one-third of that taken for group teaching.

The problem with evaluating educational research, of course, is that evidence must be measured against values. Divides over assumptions about what is worth knowing and how knowledge is gained run deep throughout the history of education. Consequently, as one might expect, reactions to Anderson's findings amongst educationalists range from enthusiasm to rejection. Kaput (1992), for instance, argues that procedural learning of the type supported by Anderson's tutors is of limited relevance and value to current educational needs. However, as Anderson points out, critics seldom enter the debate armed with evidence favouring other pedagogical approaches. We will not try to adjudicate such issues here. Instead, we will explore some of the limits to the ACT theory in the next section.

Attempts have also been made to exploit ACT tutors in support of collaborative learning involving pairs of students. The benefits found for individualized tutoring were not replicated with pairs (Anderson, *op cit.*). This result contrasts with several lines of evidence which suggest that computer-based activity can be used to support effective collaboration in learning contexts. It seems, however, that the design of environments for this purpose will need to be based on different principles to those derived from Anderson's theory.

We believe that the evidence showing that ACT tutors do not do well with more than one learner actually offers support for the theory. Since the tutorial actions of the system are derived from a detailed analysis of individual knowledge, it is not surprising that it cannot analyse and support the activities of two or more learners working in collaboration. If the system optimizes to individuals, then any response designed to support one learner will clearly not be guaranteed to fit the instructional needs of another. Tutorial contingency will break down under such circumstances. This observation, we contend, generalizes; it implies that any theory designed to explain how and why individualized instruction works cannot be extended without further theoretical development to a theory of scaffolding of collaborative or group learning.

### Tutoring and self-regulation

Anderson's tutoring systems confront the learner with problems that are well structured and which are set by the system. They are not expected to devise their own problems, nor are they required to find out how to transform 'messy' problematical situations into a form which may enable them to be solved. The problems set by the tutor are expressed in a symbol system or language that is known to support their solution. Learners are given no experience in selecting and experimenting with different ways of representing problems for themselves. Although learners are left to their own devices so long as they are succeeding with a problem, the responsibility for regulating performance when they get into difficulties is external; it rests with the tutor. Thus, learners gain no experience in deciding for themselves when they may be going wrong, nor are they given opportunities to detect and repair their own performance. In situations where tasks are not well structured, a learner may need to decide or negotiate criteria against which their own performance can be assessed. Experience with such demands is not an integral part of the tutoring systems and no analyses or representations of these abilities are offered in the ideal student model, i.e. they are not candidates for instruction.

Such proposed limits on ACT-inspired tutoring underpin the objections that several educationalists and cognitive scientists have levelled against both the theory and the tutoring regimes that it generates.

These, of course, are extremely complex issues that cannot be given due consideration here. It is worth noting, however, that we cannot assume that such competencies are typically engendered through schooling either. In relation to mathematics learning, for example, there is evidence showing that the vast majority of children do not develop the envisaged skills in transforming 'messy' situations into soluble problems. Nor are skills in self-regulation and recovery from error guaranteed. Whether these findings are telling us either: (a) that learning is so situated that such proposed competencies are a myth; (b) that it takes too much time and experience to achieve the necessary knowledge and expertise for us to expect such accomplishments in the normal course of schooling; and/or (c) that we have yet to perfect curricula and teaching methods which would promote such learning, it is not possible to say.

However, returning to our theme of computer-based tutoring, there is a little evidence which suggests that the acquisition of some skills in self-regulation can be supported by one-to-one teaching. To illustrate research which leads us to such an optimistic position, we will outline work by Shute, Glaser, and their colleagues. This group has been studying, among other things, the development of skills in investigation, design, and decision making in both adults and children.

Computer simulated micro-worlds provide the learning environments employed. These include 'Smithtown' (Shute and Glaser, 1990) which models the economic life of a small community, and 'Daytona' (Schauble and Glaser, 1990) an environment in which adults and children were asked to design and test their own simulated racing cars. The educational objective of Smithtown is to develop the learner's understanding of basic principles of micro-economics. Daytona was created to provide detailed analyses of the learner's strategies for investigation, hypothesis testing, and design. The goal is to discover how to design the fastest car possible. In both environments, the (individual) learner sets their own problems, formulates hypotheses and evaluates these by 'driving' the simulations.

The analyses of learner activity have identified features of problem solving activities, in both children and adults, which inhibit discovery and limit the effectiveness of the design processes.

### Confirmation bias

As many previous investigations of human decision making have shown, both children and adults displayed a natural tendency to confirm their own prior beliefs. Thus, experiments or designs which might have generated evidence which could serve to test (and potentially falsify) a belief, or which might lend credence to a hypothesis that was not favoured, were seldom undertaken.

This bias restricted the range of problems set and investigated, thus limiting the extent of the space of possibilities that were searched and evaluated. In consequence, optimal solutions or designs are rarely obtained. For example, in designing racing cars, many learners start out with the assumption that the size of a car's muffler (i.e. exhaust), which influences a car's sound, also constrains its top speed. Attempts to disconfirm this (false) belief were rare.

### Impulsivity

Learners often formulate hypotheses and set out to test them without first examining relevant factors or evidence (available from the system if sought) which could be used to assess the quality or potential decisiveness of the test in question. Thus, adults working with the Smithtown simulation might decide that they were going to establish a new coffee selling business without examining the demographic composition of the area in which they had elected to trade when such factors relate to consumption. The desire to 'get on with it', potentially ignoring crucially relevant information before acting, is another common failing in human exploratory activity.

### Confounding variables and ignoring interactions

Another common cognitive disposition was illustrated by the finding that people conduct experiments or create designs which cannot provide decisive information because two or more potentially interacting factors are confounded. For instance, if one has designed and tested a car with, say, five main attributes, and one wants to decide if two or more are crucially important, then creating a new design in which both are changed (and leaving it at that) will not create a crucial test.

Where two factors or variables interact, most designers/explorers failed to come up with an hypothesis which led to relevant tests. For instance, in the Daytona micro-world, placing a tail fin on a low-powered car will simply add to its weight, increase drag, and lower its top speed. Adding the same fin to a suitably powerful car (where it increases stability at high speeds) will enable the car to travel faster without going out of control. Few designers, adults or children, came up with this idea.

### Implicit (unwarranted) belief in the power of memory

Although the simulation environments provided the means to record the results of tests and designs, it was common for the learner not to exploit such facilities (to the detriment of performance). Their apparent belief in an ability to remember and reason about a complex space of possibilities without using external tools to 'amplify' their cognition further reduced the extent and quality of their search of the space of possibilities.

### Replicating success: pragmatic problem-solving versus scientific discovery

If one manages to bake the most superb of cakes, it seems natural that, in future culinary activities, one will strive to re-duplicate success. However ritualistic or superstitious one becomes in striving to maintain excellence, if the end result is always a superb cake, then one is likely to be satisfied. However, if the goal is to discover the minimum set of necessary and sufficient conditions which lead to a successful outcome, it may well be necessary, along the way, to bake some less than perfect cakes, i.e. one might even need to make 'errors' in order to determine whether one's current hypothesis about the ingredients of success are tenable.

Such pragmatically satisfying attempts to duplicate success were found in the investigations of Shute and Glaser. The incidence and frequency of such activities help to illustrate fundamental differences in the 'stance' that one needs to adopt in scientific investigation as opposed to everyday problem solving.

### Coaching and self-regulation

The list just presented illustrates categories that can be used to record and assess learner activity. In Smithtown, the system was programmed to monitor and log key actions by a learner in the simulation environment. For example, the system recorded whether or not a given learner requested relevant information from the system before starting up some economic venture in the simulation. It also recorded and inspected sequences of activity to see if, say, the learner was attempting some economic experiment which involved confounded variables. When some criterion was reached (e.g. the learner failed to seek relevant information two or three times) the system was programmed to deliver a message to the learner pointing out, for example, information that needed to be evaluated prior to further action.

In general, then, a profile of key features of a learner's strategies for formulating goals, undertaking experiments, recording data, and testing hypotheses was built up. The coach used such information to provide a critique of a learner's performance and took tutorial actions based on specific aspects of the individual profile.

Shute and Glaser (1990) report a large-scale evaluation of the Smithtown coaching system. This involved comparing the examination performances of psychology undergraduates who worked with the system for a few hours with that of economics students who had taken a semester course which was designed to teach similar economic ideas. The authors report that the Smithtown taught students fared as well as those conventionally taught. They also found that, although the Smithtown coach only commented on strategic aspects of behaviour and did not explicate the economic laws or principles upon which the simulation activities were designed, students were often able to infer and state these principles. It seems that they were able to induce or abduct explicit rules from patterns discovered in their problem solving.

Although we would require more extensive and detailed evaluations before accepting the conclusion that skills in self-regulation can be taught, including ways of thinking and acting which override well entrenched biases in decision making, the findings cited by Smithtown's creators offer some hope that this may turn out to be the case.

**Conclusions**

We have argued that principles for the design of effective one-to-one tutoring systems have been identified in research arising out of different theoretical traditions. We have also explored, albeit briefly, a theory of learning which explains how and why such principles work. Though couched in terms which are not commonly heard in discussions of Vygotskian theory, we suggest that ACT needs to be taken seriously by those working in the Vygotskian tradition and that something like the process of rule-learning that it defines is a good candidate for a model of procedural skill learning. According to the theory, what is internalized during instruction is not simply speech, but rules of action, in the service of goals, which become activated by symbol systems such as language and diagrams. Whilst such rules can be described as proposition-like structures, they are not available to conscious inspection. However, they are, we suggest, plausible candidates for the 'inner speech' that Vygotsky argued arises out of social interaction to form higher mental processes.

We have also identified what we take to be important limitations on the scope of the principles of instruction as currently formulated. More specifically, where tutoring supports the development of skills in self-regulation, rather than task performance *per se*, we have argued that a more elaborated analysis of the learning process, one based on different aspects of the learner's knowledge and activity, needs to be taken into account. Whether or not procedural learning theory can be extended to explain the development of self-regulation remains to be seen.

The models that we have been considering are also limited in other, fundamental ways. Central to effective tutoring is a model of the learning domain, what some call the 'ideal student model'. The specification of this model lies outside the scope of the theories considered. Thus, learning theory does not bypass long-standing issues to do with curriculum analysis. For instance, recent research into mathematics learning has provided much enriched accounts of the nature of what needs to be learned (Greer, 1992). Such research, which represents a combination of mathematical and psychological analysis, can provide tutors (human or machine) with new models of what it is that has to be learned. We have also stressed the fact that there is always the possibility of learner innovation which, far from being predictable on the basis of contemporary learning theory, cannot even be recognized by those theories. This, we suspect, indicates a fundamental aspect of human development. We may seek to reconstruct knowledge with children, but they may sometimes find their own means to achieve the goals that we set.

## Acknowledgements

The preparation of this paper and our own research was supported by the Economic and Social Research Council.

## References

Anderson, J. A. (1993). *Rules of the Mind.* Hillsdale, NJ: Erlbaum.

Bloom, B. S. (1984). The 2-sigma problem: the search for methods of group instruction as effective as one-to-one tutoring. *Educational Researcher, 13*, pp. 4–16.

Brown, A. L., and Campione, J. C. (1990). Communities of learning and thinking, or a context by any other name. In D. Kuhn (Ed.), *Developmental Perspectives on Teaching and Learning Thinking Skills.* Contributions to Human Development Series (pp. 108–126). Basle: Karger.

Collins, A., Brown, J. S., and Newman, S. (1989). Cognitive apprenticeship: teaching the crafts of reading, writing and mathematics. In L. B. Resnick (Ed.), *Knowing, Learning and Instruction: Essays in Honor of Robert Glaser* (pp. 453–494). Hillsdale, NJ: Erlbaum.

Greer, B. (1992). Multiplication and division as models of situations. In D. Grouws (Ed.), *Handbook of Research on Learning and Teaching Mathematics.* NCTM/ Macmillan.

Heckhausen, J. (1987). How do mothers know? Infants' chronological age or infants' performance as determinants of adaptation in maternal instruction? *Journal of Experimental Child Psychology,* pp. 212–226.

Kaput, J. J. (1992). Linking representations in the symbol systems of algebra. In D. A. Grouws (Ed.), *Handbook of Research on Mathematics Teaching and Learning,* pp. 167–294. New York: Macmillan.

Pratt, H., Michalewski, H. J., Barrett, G., and Starr, A. (1989). Brain potentials in a memory-scanning task. I. Modality and task effects on potentials to the probes, *Electroencephalography and Clinical Neurophysiology, 72*, pp. 407–421.

Rogoff, B. (1986). Adult assistance of children's learning. In T. E. Raphael (Ed.), *The Contexts of School-Based Literacy.* New York: Random House.

Rogoff, B. (1990). *Apprenticeship in Thinking – Cognitive Development in Social Context.* New York: Oxford University Press.

Rogoff, B., and Wertsch, J. V. (1984). *Children's Learning in the 'Zone of Proximal Development'.* San Francisco: Jossey-Bass.

Schauble, L., and Glaser, R. (1990). Scientific thinking in children and adults. In D. Kuhn (Ed.), *Developmental Perspectives on Teaching and Learning Thinking Skills*, pp. 9–27. New York: Karger.

Shute, V. J., and Glaser, R. (1990). A large-scale evaluation of an intelligent discovery world: Smithtown. *Interactive Learning Environments*, pp. 51–77.

Vygotsky, L. S (1978). *Mind in Society: The Development of Higher Psychological Processes*. In M. Cole, V. John-Steirner, S. Scribner, and E. Souberman (Eds.), Trans. Cambridge MA: Harvard University Press.

Wood, D., Bruner, J. S., and Ross, G. (1976). The role of tutoring in problem solving. *Journal of Child Psychology and Psychiatry, 17*, pp. 2, pp. 89–100.

Wood, D. J., Wood, H. A., and Middleton, D. J. (1978). An experimental evaluation of four face-to-face teaching strategies. *International Journal of Behavioral Development*, pp. 131–147.

# 19 Richard Joiner, David Messer, Paul Light and Karen Littleton
'Peer Interaction and Peer Presence in Computer-Based Problem Solving: A Research Note'

Reprinted in full from: *Cognition and Instruction* **13**, 583–584 (1995)

There has been considerable interest concerning the benefits of peer interaction for cognitive development and learning. Usually this research stems from either a Piagetian (e.g., Doise and Mugny, 1984) or a Vygotskian perspective (e.g., Rogoff, 1990). These two perspectives have a number of differences, but they have in common the fact that they interpret the facilitative effect in terms of certain aspects of the interaction. This assumption has been made very widely in developmental research in this area, even by those who question both of the preceding perspectives (Light and Perret-Clermont, 1989).

This brief article provides a preliminary report of a series of studies that together suggests that the benefits of collaboration may be not only the result of peer interaction but also due to peer presence. In the first study (Blaye, Light, Joiner and Sheldon, 1991), we compared pairs versus individuals on a complex computer-based planning task and found that pairs performed significantly better than individuals and that this effect carried over to an individual posttest. In a subsequent study (Littleton, Light, Joiner, Messer and Barnes, 1992), we once again compared individuals with pairs but found only a rather marginal peer facilitation effect that failed to carry over to a posttest. One possible reason for this failure lay in a procedural difference between the two experiments. In the first experiment, the children in the individual condition worked on their own, with no other children present, whereas in the second experiment, the children in the individual condition worked in groups of four, with each child working silently on separate machines.

A third study was conducted to investigate the possibility that peer presence may be a factor underlying the facilitative effect of pairing. Thirty-two children, aged between 10 and 11 years, were randomly allocated (controlling for sex) to either a peer presence condition or an individual condition. Using the same task, as in the previous studies, we compared 16 children who worked individually with an additional 16 children who worked independently but in the presence of three of their classmates. The results of the study were remarkable. We found that children in the individual condition performed significantly better than children in the peer presence condition. This result suggests that the superior performance we found in the paired condition of the first study may be partly the result of peer presence and not solely attributable to peer interaction.

This finding has important implications for the literature on the peer facilitation of learning, because it shows that, along with any effects of peer interaction, there are also effects of peer presence. Peer presence effects have long been established in social psychology but have rarely been invoked to explain the benefits of child–child interaction (one notable exception being Jackson, Fletcher and Messer, 1992). Researchers, including ourselves, have arguably focused too heavily on interaction in seeking to explain beneficial effects of working with a peer. Researchers need to pay more attention to the emotional and motivational aspects of learning situations and to understand how these can affect learning outcome. A better integration of such social and affective approaches with cognitive approaches may be necessary if we are to gain an adequate picture of peer facilitation of learning.

## References

Blaye, A., Light, P. H., Joiner, R., and Sheldon, S. (1991). Collaboration as a facilitator of planning and problem solving on a computer based task. *British Journal of Developmental Psychology, 9*, 471–483.

Doise, W., and Mugny, G. (1984). *The social development of the intellect.* Oxford, England: Pergamon.

Jackson, A., Fletcher, B., and Messer, D. (1992). When talking does not help: An investigation of microcomputer based problem solving. *Learning and Instruction, 2*, 185–197.

Light, P. H., and Perret-Clermont, A.-N. (1989). Social context effects in learning and testing. In A. Gellatly, D. Rogers, and J. A. Sloboda (Eds.), *Cognition and social worlds* (pp. 99–112). Oxford, England: Clarendon.

Littleton, K., Light, P. H., Joiner, R., Messer, D., and Barnes, P. (1992). *European Journal of Educational Psychology, 7*, 309–323.

Rogoff, B. (1990). *Apprenticeship in thinking: Cognitive development in social context.* Oxford, England: Oxford University Press.

# 20    Judy Dunn
### 'Siblings and Development'

Reprinted in full from: *Current Directions in Psychological Science* **1**, 6–9 (1992)

The great majority of children – around 80% in the United States and Europe – grow up with siblings. Yet the developmental impact of the experience of growing up in close – often uncomfortably close – contact with another child within the family has until recently been little studied. The attention of investigators concerned with early developmental influences has been focused instead chiefly on parents (usually mothers) or family, often characterized in terms of structure (e.g., single-parent versus two-parent) or background variables (e.g., socioeconomic status), or in broad descriptive terms, such as 'enmeshed' or 'disorganized.'

In the last few years, however, studies of siblings within their families have greatly increased in number,[1] and have challenged our assumptions concerning two quite different issues in developmental science. First, such studies have raised serious questions about how families influence individual development – and suggested some intriguing answers. Second, they have also shed light on the development of social understanding in young children. Here, research on siblings observed at home shows that formal assessments of very young children's abilities in experimental settings may have seriously underestimated the nature of young children's social understanding.

As an introduction to the new perspectives on these two developmental issues, consider the following incident, drawn from an observation of a 30-month-old child with his mother and his 14-month-old sister. Andy was a rather timid and sensitive child, cautious, unconfident, and compliant. His younger sister, Susie, was a striking contrast – assertive, determined, and a handful for her mother, who was nevertheless delighted by her boisterous daughter. In the course of an observation of Andy and his sister, Susie persistently attempted to grab a forbidden object on a high kitchen counter, despite her mother's repeated prohibitions. Finally, she succeeded, and Andy overheard his mother make a warm, affectionate comment on Susie's action: 'Susie, you *are* a determined little devil!'

Andy, sadly, commented to his mother, '*I'm* not a determined little devil!' His mother replied, laughing, 'No! What are you? A poor old boy!'

### A new perspective on the development of individual differences

This brief incident serves to illustrate some of the key issues emerging from a series of systematic studies of siblings and parents in the United States and Britain,[2] which highlight why we need to study within-family processes to explain the development of individual differences. Three features of these processes, evident in the exchange between Andy and his mother, are important here: the difference between siblings in personality, the difference in their relationships with their parents, and their responses to exchanges between their siblings and parents.

### Differences between siblings

The striking differences between siblings growing up within the same family – differences in personality, adjustment, and psychopathology – have now been documented in a very wide range of studies,[3, 4] and these differences present a major challenge to investigators studying family influence. Why should two children who share 50% of their segregating genes and the same family background turn out to be so different? After all, the family factors assumed to be key in development (e.g., parental mental health, marital quality, social class background) are apparently shared by siblings.

This question of why siblings are so different is not just a matter of interest to fond parents puzzled by their children's differences. It turns out to be key to understanding the development of individual differences more generally. Extensive studies by behavior geneticists have now shown that the sources of environmental influence that make individuals different from one another work *within* rather than *between* families.[3] To understand the salient environmental influences on individual development, we have to be able to explain what makes two children within the same family different from one another. The message from this research is not that family influence is unimportant, but that we need to document those experiences that are specific to each child within a family, and therefore we need to study more than one child per family, with a new perspective on what are the salient influences within the family.

What could the significant processes within the family be – differences in parent–child relationships, differences within the sibling relationship itself, differences in peer relationships outside the family, or chance experiences that affect one sibling and not another? In a series of studies, the relation of each of these to children's developmental outcomes is being explored. A number of different samples have been studied in the United States and in England, including nationally representative samples, and major longitudinal studies have included adoptive and biological samples (enabling us to explore where genetic similarities and differences enter the picture). A wide variety of methods has been employed, including naturalistic observations of the families and interviews with all family members. The results of this body of research are discussed in a recent book;[2] here some illustrative points will be summarized briefly.

### Differences between siblings' relationships with their parents

It is clear that there are major differences in the affection, attention, and discipline that many siblings experience with their parents – whether the information on these differences comes from parents, children, or observers. The differences in warmth and pride that were evident in the behavior of

Andy's mother toward her two children are very common. The extent of such differences and the domains in which they are most marked have now been documented in a range of differing samples of families, as have the variables related to the degree of parental differentiation (e.g., the developmental stages of the children and the mother's personality, educational background, and IQ). An important lesson from both the observational work and the experimental studies is that children are extremely sensitive to such differences.

### Sensitivity of children to their siblings' interaction with their parents

From a remarkably early age, children monitor and react to their parents' interaction with their siblings. The example of Andy and Susie is typical: Andy monitors and responds to his mother's exchange with his sister, promptly, and with a self-comparison. A recent study showed that 20% of the conversational turns by secondborn children in one sample were attempts to join the conversation between other people.[5] The salient verbal environment for children is not solely the speech addressed to them, but includes conversations between parents and sibling.

Two lines of evidence from recent developmental work confirm the salience for young children of emotional exchanges between other people: laboratory studies of children witnessing exchanges between others and naturalistic studies of children in their families. A wealth of studies have now documented that children from the end of their first year are interested in the behavior of other family members, and especially in their emotional exchanges. In a series of studies, Zahn-Waxler and her colleagues have documented the development of children's responses to emotional displays between others, and the effects of witnessing such exchanges on play and aggressive behavior.[6,7] Naturalistic observations of siblings at home have shown that children rarely ignore disputes between others, but act promptly to support or punish one of the antagonists, and that the behavior of both firstborn and secondborn children is profoundly affected by their mothers' interactions with the other sibling.[8]

How important are these experiences of differential treatment, developmentally? The first investigations show differential experiences are linked to a range of outcome measures: In terms of adjustment, for example, children who receive less maternal affection and attention than their siblings are likely to be more worried, anxious, or depressed than other children in general. And there is now an accumulation of evidence that differential parental behavior is linked to the quality of the relationship between siblings, with more hostility and conflict found in families with greater differential parental treatment, an association found for preschool children, for siblings in middle childhood, for children with disabled siblings, and for children following divorce.[1]

### Other sources of differential experience

Among the other possible sources of differential experience, there is growing evidence that differences in children's experiences within the sibling relationship itself can also be related to adjustment. If instead of focusing on siblings as a dyad, we ask how similarly or differently the two siblings behave toward each other, we find there can be marked differences between the two in the affection or control they show. Whether the information comes from maternal interview, children's own accounts, or observations, the emerging picture is that in only one third of sibling pairs do the two children show very similar degrees of affection toward one another. For hostile behavior there is more reciprocity, but within a pair, the relative differences in negative behavior are correlated with later perceived self-competence, and with conduct problems and anxious or depressed behavior. For example, one study found that the more negative a younger sibling is toward the older, relative to the older's negative behavior, the higher the self-esteem of the younger 3 years later.[2] Of course, these initial findings must be treated with caution until they are replicated, and no causal inferences can be made from such correlational data.

In summary, the focus on siblings and their differential experiences within the family has changed and clarified our picture of what are the salient family influences on individual development. In an important sense children are, it appears, *family members* from early in their second year; they are interested in, responsive to, and influenced by the relationships between their siblings and parents – and this insight brings us to the second developmental arena in which sibling studies have provided illumination, the development of social understanding.

### A new perspective on the development of social understanding

Recall the comments made by Andy in the incident with his sister and mother. Andy, in the emotional circumstances of the family exchange, made a self-evaluative comment following his mother's warm remark praising his sister. *Yet he was only two and a half.* This is startlingly early for a child to be evaluating himself. At this age, according to the received view of the development of self-reflective powers, based on experimental studies, he should not be able to evaluate himself in this way, or be sensitive to social comparison. Could we be misrepresenting children's sociocognitive abilities by studying them only outside the family? Here, observational studies of siblings at home have proved most illuminating.[8]

A focus on children's disputes, jokes, and cooperative play with their siblings has shown that from 18 months on children understand how to hurt, comfort, and exacerbate their siblings' pain; they understand what is allowed or disapproved in their family world; they differentiate between transgressions of different sorts, and anticipate the response of adults to their own and to other people's misdeeds; they comment on and ask about the causes of others' actions and feelings. Analyses of this growing understanding of emotions, of others' goals, and of social rules have shown that the foundations for the moral virtues of caring, consideration, and kindness are well laid by 3 years, but so too children have by this age a sophisticated grasp of how to use social rules for their own ends. The drive to understand others and the social world is, I have argued,[8] closely linked to the nature of a child's relationships within the family over this period: the emotional power of attachment to parents, of rivalry between siblings, and of the conflict between growing independence and socialization pressure. For a young child whose own goals and interests are often at odds with – and frustrated by – others in the family, it is clearly adaptive to begin to understand those other family members and the social rules of the shared family world. The study of siblings has highlighted why it is important that social understanding should be high on the developmental agenda.

The subtlety of social understanding that children show in the family context – in contrast to their limited capabilities when faced with more abstract or formal tasks – has considerably changed our view of children's abilities, and why they change. And in addition to delineating the pattern of normative growth of social understanding, sibling studies are beginning to clarify in detail the causes of individual differences in social understanding. These differences are striking: Children vary greatly in their ability to understand the causes and consequences of emotions and to understand what other people are thinking and how this influences their behavior. In the recent burst of productive experimental research on children's understanding of 'other minds,' there has been little consideration of individual differences: How far such differences are related to verbal intelligence, to the quality of children's relationships, or to other family experiences has not been examined empirically. The study of children with their siblings has enabled us to test predictions concerning the significance of family relationships, parental expressiveness, and children's cognitive ability in accounting for differences in social understanding.[9]

The results highlight the importance – and the independent contribution to the variance – of a number of factors. For example, differences in family discourse about the social world are important: Children who grew up in families in which feelings and causality were discussed performed better than other children on assessments of social understanding 14 months later. But the quality of children's relationships with their siblings is also key: Children who had experienced frequent cooperative exchanges with their siblings, for example, were more successful than other children on tasks assessing their grasp of the connections between another person's belief and subsequent behavior. Also – most notably – differences in children's social understanding are related to the quality of the relationships between their siblings and their mothers. Children who grew up in families in which they witnessed their mothers being highly attentive, responsive, or controlling to their siblings scored particularly high on social cognition assessments 1 year later.

Thus, the work on social understanding links with the first theme – the processes involved in family influence on individual differences. Examining within-family differential experiences of siblings will enlarge our understanding of the salient processes of family influences on personality and adjustment. Similarly, it is clear that studying children in the complex network of sibling and parental relationships within the family can greatly enhance our knowledge about their understanding of the social world. It is within the daily drama of family life that children's social intelligence is revealed and fostered, and siblings play a central role in that drama.

**Notes**

1 Boer, F., and Dunn, J. (1992). *Sibling Relationships: Developmental and Clinical Issues.* Hillsdale, NJ: Erlbaum.
2 Dunn, J., and Plomin, R. (1990). *Separate Lives: Why Siblings Are so Different.* New York: Basic Books.
3 Plomin, R., and Daniels, D. (1987). Why are children in the same family so different from each other? *The Behavioral and Brain Sciences, 10,* 1–16.
4 Scarr, S., and Grajek, S. (1982). Similarities and differences among siblings, in *Sibling Relationships: Their Nature and Significance Across the Lifespan.* M. E. Lamb and B. Sutton-Smith, (Eds.), Erlbaum, Hillsdale, NJ: pp. 357–386.
5 Dunn, J., and Shatz, M. (1989). Becoming a conversationalist despite (or because of) having an older sibling. *Child Development, 60,* 399–410.
6 Zahn-Waxler, C., and Radke-Yarrow, M. (1982). The development of altruism: Alternative research strategies, in *The Development of Prosocial Behavior.* N. Eisenberg-Berg, (Ed.), New York: Academic Press, pp. 109–137.
7 Cummings, E. M. (1987). Coping with background anger. *Child Development, 58,* 976–984.
8 Dunn, J. (1988). *The Beginnings of Social Understanding.* Cambridge, MA: Harvard University Press.
9 Dunn, J., Brown, J., Slomkowski, C., Tesla, C., and Youngblade, L. (1991). Young children's understanding of other people's feelings and beliefs: Individual differences and their antecedents. *Child Development, 62,* 1352–1366.

# 21 Barbara Rogoff and Gilda Morelli
## 'Perspectives on Children's Development from Cultural Psychology'

Reprinted in full from: *American Psychologist* **44**, 343–348 (1989)

*This article summarizes how cultural research can inform mainstream psychology. It focuses on an organizing theme that has been explored in research in non-Western groups: the role of specific cultural practices in organizing human endeavors. This perspective has influenced the direction of mainstream research, encouraging the advancement of our ideas of the domain-specific nature of psychological processes, and their relation to sociocultural practices. The article provides a brief description of Vygotsky's theoretical approach, a perspective comfortable for many working within this tradition. Finally, a discussion of research on children in cultural groups in the United States suggests that the cultural perspective can be useful in advancing research on issues involving American children with different cultural backgrounds.*

Attention to the cultural context of child development has yielded important insights into the opportunities and constraints provided by the society in which children mature. Research with children of different cultures provides a broader perspective on human development than is available when considering human behavior in a single cultural group.

The purpose of this article is to indicate how cultural research can inform mainstream psychology. We discuss one organizing theme that has been explored in research in non-Western groups, the role of specific cultural practices in organizing all human endeavors. This perspective has influenced the direction of mainstream research, encouraging the advancement of our ideas of the domain-specific nature of psychological processes, and their relation to socio-cultural practices. We provide a brief description of Vygotsky's theoretical approach, a perspective comfortable for many working within this tradition. Finally, we suggest that the cultural perspective can be useful in advancing research on issues involving American children varying in cultural background.

## Lessons learned from cross-cultural studies of development

Investigations of the role of culture in development have taken advantage of the impressive variations in the human condition, which occur around the world, to advance understanding of human adaptation. Reviews and discussion of cross-cultural developmental research appear in Bornstein (1980); Dasen (1977); Field, Sostek, Vietze, and Leiderman (1981); Laboratory of Comparative Human Cognition (1979, 1983); Leiderman, Tulkin, and

Rosenfeld (1977); LeVine (in press); Munroe and Munroe (1975); Munroe, Munroe, and Whiting (1981); Rogoff, Gauvain, and Ellis (1984); Rogoff and Mistry (1985); Schieffelin and Ochs (1986); Serpell (1976); Super and Harkness (1980); Triandis and Heron (1981); Wagner and Stevenson (1982); Werner (1979); and Whiting and Edwards (1988).

Cross-cultural studies have focused especially on children in nontechnological (non-Western) societies because these children contrast in important ways with children from the United States and other Western nations. This first section thus describes lessons learned from cross-cultural studies involving children around the world; psychological research on minorities in the United States has followed a somewhat different course, described later.

*Perspectives offered by cross-cultural research*

An important function of cross-cultural research has been to allow investigators to look closely at the impact of their own belief systems (folk psychology) on scientific theories and research paradigms. When subjects and researchers are from the same population, interpretations of development may be constrained by implicit cultural assumptions. With subjects sharing researchers' belief systems, psychologists are less aware of their own assumptions regarding the world of childhood, the involvement of others in child development, and the physical and institutional circumstances in which development is embedded. Working with people from a quite different background can make one aware of aspects of human activity that are not noticeable until they are missing or differently arranged, as with the fish who reputedly is unaware of water until removed from it. Viewing the contrasts in life's arrangements in different cultures has enabled psychologists to examine very basic assumptions regarding developmental goals, the skills that are learned, and the contexts of development.

Cross-cultural research also allows psychologists to use cultural variation as a natural laboratory to attempt to disentangle variables that are difficult to tease apart in the United States and to study conditions that are rare in the United States. For example, one can examine how gender differences manifest themselves in differing cultural circumstances (Whiting and Edwards, 1988). Cross-cultural studies have examined the extent to which advances in intellectual skills are related to schooling versus children's age, a comparison that cannot be made in a country with compulsory schooling (Laboratory of Comparative Human Cognition, 1979; Rogoff, 1981). Other research examines conditions that are seen as normal in other cultures but carry connotations of being problematic in the United States. For example, studies have been made of gender roles in polygynous societies in which fathers are absent from the household because they have several wives (Munroe and Munroe, 1975), and of child care and infant psychological development in societies in which nonmaternal care (care by other adults or by child nurses) is valued and expected (Fox, 1977; Tronick, Morelli and Winn, 1987; Zaslow, 1980).

Another function of cross-cultural studies is to examine the generality of theories of development that have been based on Western children. Examples include investigations of the universality of the stages of development proposed by Piaget, the family role relations emphasized by Freud, and patterns of mother-infant interaction taken to index security of attachment (Bretherton and Waters, 1985; Dasen, 1977; Dasen and Heron, 1981; Greenfield, 1976; Malinowski, 1927; Price-Williams, 1980). In such research, modifications to the assumptions of generality have often been suggested by cross-cultural findings. For example, findings that the highest stage of Piaget's theory, formal operations, seldom can be seen in non-Western cultures prompted Piaget to modify his theory in 1972 to suggest that the formal operational stage may not be universal but rather a product of an individual's expertise in a specific domain.

Research in a variety of cultures has also provided evidence of impressive regularities across cultures in developmental phenomena. For instance, there is marked similarity across cultures in the sequence and timing of sensorimotor milestones in infant development, smiling, and separation distress (Gewirtz, 1965; Goldberg, 1972; Konner, 1972; Super, 1981; Werner, 1988) and in the order of stages in language acquisition (Bowerman, 1981; Slobin, 1973).

*An emphasis on understanding the context of development*

An important contribution resulting from cultural challenges to researchers' assumptions is the conceptual restructuring emphasizing that human functioning cannot be separated from the contexts of their activities. Although there are other sources of contextual theorizing in the field of psychology, an important impetus has been the consistent findings that behavior and development vary according to cultural context.

Developmental researchers who have worked in other cultures have become convinced that human functioning cannot be separated from the cultural and more immediate context in which children develop. They observed that skills and behavior that did not appear in laboratory situations appeared in the same individuals in everyday situations. A subject whose logical reasoning or memory in a laboratory task seemed rudimentary could skillfully persuade the researcher or remind the researcher of promises outside the laboratory, or might be very skilled in a complex everyday task such as navigation or weaving (Cole, 1975; Cole, Hood and McDermott, 1978; Gladwin, 1970; Laboratory of Comparative Human Cognition, 1979; Rogoff, 1981; Scribner, 1976). Such informal observations called into question the widespread assumption that individuals' skills and behaviors have a generality extending across contexts.

Systematic studies noted the close relation between the skills or behavior exhibited by an individual and the contexts of elicitation and practice (Lave, 1977; Saxe, 1988). Children's nurturance and aggression varied as a function of the age and gender of the people with whom they interacted (Wenger, 1983; Whiting and Whiting, 1975). Perceptual modeling skills of Zambian and

English children varied as a function of the cultural familiarity of the specific modeling activity (Serpell, 1979). Literacy provides practice with specific cognitive activities, leading to advances in particular skills rather than conferring general cognitive ability (Scribner and Cole, 1981). Such results point to the importance of considering the contexts in which people practice skills and behaviors, as well as those in which we as researchers observe them.

Many of the cognitive activities examined in developmental research, such as memory, perception, logical reasoning, and classification, have been found in cross-cultural studies to relate to children's experience of schooling (Lave, 1977; Rogoff, 1981; Sharp, Cole and Lave, 1979). The extensive studies of the relation between school and cognitive skills call attention to a context of learning that is easily overlooked as an influence on cognitive development in the United States, where school is ubiquitous in the lives of children.

Remembering or classifying lists of unrelated objects may be unusual activities outside of literate or school-related activities (Goody, 1977; Rogoff and Waddell, 1982). The taxonomic categories seen as most appropriate in literate situations may not be valued in other circumstances, as is illustrated by Glick's (1975) report of Kpelle subjects' treatment of a classification problem. They sorted the 20 objects into functional groups (e.g., knife with orange, potato with hoe) rather than into categorical groups that the researcher considered more appropriate. When questioned, they often volunteered that that was the way a wise man would do things. 'When an exasperated experimenter asked finally, "How would a fool do it," he was given back sorts of the type that were initially expected – four neat piles with food in one, tools in another, and so on' (p. 636).

People who have more schooling, such as older children and Western peoples, may excel on many kinds of cognitive tests because not only the skills but also the social situations of testing resemble the activities specifically practiced in school. In contrast with everyday life, where people classify and remember things in order to accomplish a functional goal, in schools and tests they perform in order to satisfy an adult's request to do so (Skeen, Rogoff and Ellis, 1983; Super, Harkness and Baldwin, 1977). Individuals with experience in school are likely to have more experience carrying out cognitive processes at the request of an adult without having a clear practical goal (Cazden and John, 1971; Rogoff and Mistry, in press).

Similar emphasis on contexts of development has come from other domains of cross-cultural research. In the area of infant sensorimotor development, Super (1981) and Kilbride (1980) have argued that the controversy over precocious development in African infants is best resolved by considering the practices of the cultural system in which the babies develop. African infants routinely surpass American infants in their rate of learning to sit and to walk, but not in learning to crawl or to climb stairs. African parents provide experiences for their babies that are apparently intended to teach sitting and walking – propping young infants in a sitting position supported by rolled blankets in a hole in the ground, exercising the newborn's walking reflex, and bouncing babies on their feet. But crawling is discouraged, and stair-climbing skills may be limited by the absence of access to stairs. Infant sensorimotor tests assess an aggregate of skills varying in rate of development according to the opportunity or encouragement to practice them.

Even infant sleep patterns vary as a function of culturally determined sleeping arrangements (Super, 1981). In the United States, the common developmental milestone of sleeping for eight uninterrupted hours by age four to five months is regarded as a sign of neurological maturity. In many other cultures, however, the infant sleeps with the mother and is allowed to nurse on demand with minimal disturbance of adult sleep. In such an arrangement, there is less parental motivation to enforce 'sleeping through the night,' and Super reported that babies continue to wake about every four hours during the night to feed, which is about the frequency of feeding during the day. Thus, it appears that this developmental milestone, in addition to its biological basis, is a function of the context in which it develops.

Cross-cultural studies demonstrating that individuals' behavior and skills are closely tied to specific activities have contributed to examination of important questions regarding the generality of the development of skills and behaviors, the structure of the ecology of development, and how to conceptualize the sociocultural context of practice of skills and behavior. These issues have recently pervaded the study of developmental psychology, with some large measure of influence from research on culture.

*Conceptualizing the sociocultural context*

Many researchers in the field of culture and development have found themselves comfortable with Vygotsky's theory, which focuses on the sociocultural context of development. Vygotsky's theory, developed in the 1930s in the Soviet Union, has gradually become more accessible to English-speaking researchers, with a rapid upsurge of interest following the publication of *Mind in Society* in 1978 (see also Laboratory of Comparative Human Cognition, 1983; Rogoff, 1982; Scribner and Cole, 1981; Wertsch, 1985a, 1985b). Although Vygotsky's theory focuses on cognitive development, it is gaining interest with researchers in emotional and social development as well, perhaps due to its integration of cognitive and social processes, as well as its emphasis on socialization (see, for example, Newson and Newson, 1975).

Vygotsky's theory offers a picture of human development that stresses how development is inseparable from human social and cultural activities. This contrasts with the image of the solitary little scientist provided by Piaget's theory. Vygotsky focused on how the development of higher mental processes such as voluntary memory and attention, classification, and reasoning involve learning to use inventions of society (such as language, mathematical systems, and memory devices) and how children are aided in development by guidance provided by people who are already skilled in these tools. Central to Vygotsky's theory is a stress on both the institutional and the interpersonal levels of social context.

*The institutional level* Cultural history provides organizations and tools useful to cognitive activity (through institutions such as school and inventions such as the calculator or literacy) along with practices that facilitate socially appropriate solutions to problems (e.g., norms for the arrangement of grocery shelves to aid shoppers in locating or remembering what they need; common mnemonic devices). Particular forms of activity are practiced in societal institutions such as schools and political systems.

For example, Kohlberg's hierarchy of moral development can be tied to the political system of a society, with the bureaucratic systems' perspective (Stage Four) appropriate for people whose political frame of reference is a large industrialized society, but inappropriate for people in small traditional tribal societies: 'The two types of social systems are very different (though of course both are valid working types of systems), and thus everyday social life in them calls forth different modes of moral problem solving whose adequacy must be judged relative to their particular contexts' (Edwards, 1981, p. 274). The political institutions of a society may channel individual moral reasoning by providing standards for the resolution of moral problems.

The cultural institution of Western schooling provides norms and strategies for performance that are considered advanced in cognitive tests. Goodnow (1976) has suggested that differences between cultural groups may be ascribed largely to the interpretation of what problem is being solved in the task and to different values regarding 'proper' methods of solution (e.g., speed, reaching a solution with a minimum of moves or redundancy, physically handling materials versus mental shuffling). The cultural tools and techniques used in school involve specific conventions and genres, such as conventions for representing depth in two-dimensional pictures and story problem genres (similar to logical syllogisms) in which one must rely only on information given in the problem to reach the answer. Cross-cultural studies indicate that nonschooled subjects are unfamiliar with such conventions and genres. For example, they are uncomfortable having to answer questions for which they cannot verify the premises (Cole, Gay, Glick and Sharp, 1971; Scribner, 1977).

*The interpersonal level* In Vygotsky's theory (1978), children develop skills in higher mental processes through the immediate social interactional context of activity, as social interaction helps structure individual activity. Information regarding tools and practices is transmitted through children's interaction with more experienced members of society during development, and patterns of interpersonal relations are organized by institutional conventions and the availability of cultural tools. For example, social aspects of experimental and observational situations relate to cultural practices. The relation between experimenter and subject may be rapidly grasped by Western children familiar with testing in school, but it may be highly discrepant from familiar adult–child interactions for non-Western children and young Western children. In some cultural settings, it is unusual for an adult who already knows an answer to request information from a child who may only partially know the subject matter, and it may be inappropriate for children to show off knowledge (Cazden and John, 1971; Irvine, 1978; Rogoff, Gauvain and Ellis, 1984).

Similarly, in observational situations such as mother–child interaction, culturally varying agendas for public behavior may influence what people do in the presence of an observer (Zaslow and Rogoff, 1981). 'It seems likely that one influence of the observer on parents is to produce a heightened frequency of behavior that the participants judge to be more socially desirable and inhibit behavior considered socially undesirable' (Pedersen, 1980, p. 181). Graves and Glick (1978) found that exchanges between middle-class mothers and their toddlers varied as a function of whether mothers thought that they were being videotaped. Mothers spoke more, used indirect directives more often, and spent more time in joint interactive focus with their children when they thought they were being observed. Clearly, peoples' interpretation of the goals of a task and cultural rules guiding social behavior influence the display of public behavior. Values regarding interpersonal relations may be inseparable from the activities observed for research purposes.

In addition to the cultural structuring of social interaction that has importance for research into human development, social interaction provides an essential context for development itself. Vygotsky stressed that interpersonal situations are important for guiding children in their development of the skills and behaviors considered important in their culture. Working within the 'zone of proximal development,' adults guide children in carrying out activities that are beyond the children's individual skills, and this joint problem solving provides children with information appropriate to stretch their individual skills. Cole (1981) argues that the zone of proximal development is 'where culture and cognition create each other.' Thus Vygotsky's conceptualization of how individual efforts are embedded in the interpersonal and institutional contexts of culture is proving useful for understanding the relation between culture and the individual.

### Research on culture involving minorities in the United States

Historically, research on minorities in the United States has followed a different course than the cross-cultural investigations discussed earlier. For many years, researchers were intent on comparing the behavior and skills of minority children with mainstream children without taking into consideration the cultural contexts in which minority and mainstream children develop. This approach involved 'deficit model' assumptions that mainstream skills and upbringing are normal and that variations observed with minorities are aberrations that produce deficits; intervention programs were designed to provide minority children with experiences to make up for their assumed deficits (Cole and Bruner, 1971; Hilliard and Vaughn-Scott, 1982; Howard and Scott, 1981; Ogbu, 1982).

The deficit model previously used in research on minority children contrasts sharply with the assumptions of the cross-cultural approach, which attempts to avoid ethnocentric evaluation of one group's practices and beliefs as being superior without considering their origins and functions from the perspective of the reality of that cultural group. With research in their own country, however, researchers have had more difficulty avoiding the assumption that the majority practices are proper (Ogbu, 1982). Variations have been assumed to account for the generally lower social status of the minority group members. It is only recently, and largely through the efforts of researchers with minority backgrounds, that deficit assumptions have been questioned in research on minority children.

The working model that appears to predominate in current minority research is one in which the positive features of cultural variation are emphasized. Although this is a valuable shift, we feel that research on minorities must move beyond reiterating the value of cultural diversity and begin more seriously to examine the source and functioning of the diversity represented in the United States to increase our understanding of the processes underlying development in cultural context.

Not only is the diversity of cultural backgrounds in our nation a resource for the creativity and future of the nation, it is also a resource for scholars studying how children develop. To make good use of this information, cultural research with minorities needs to focus on examining the processes and functioning of the cultural context of development. This requires 'unpackaging' culture or minority status (Whiting, 1976) so as to disentangle the workings of the social context of development. This has become a central effort of cross-cultural research on non-Western populations.

Pioneering researchers of minorities are also beginning to look at the contexts in which children from different cultures develop, and these efforts provide a basis for a greater understanding of how culture channels development. (Examples include Brown and Reeve, 1985; Cazden, John and Hymes, 1975; Chisholm, 1983; Erickson and Mohatt, 1982; Laboratory of Comparative Human Cognition, 1986; Ogbu, 1982). It is notable that some of the most interesting efforts involve combining approaches from anthropology and education with those of psychology (see also recent issues of *Anthropology and Education Quarterly*).

The potential from research on cultural groups around the world as well as down the street lies in its challenge to our systems of assumptions and in the creative efforts of scholars to synthesize knowledge from observations of differing contexts of human development. Such a challenge and synthesis is fruitful in the efforts to achieve a deeper and broader understanding of human nature and nurture.

## References

Bornstein, M. H. (1980). Cross-cultural developmental psychology. In M. H. Bornstein (Ed.), *Comparative methods in psychology* (pp. 231–281). Hillsdale, NJ: Erlbaum.

Bowerman, M. (1981). Language development. In H. C. Triandis and A. Heron (Eds.), *Handbook of cross-cultural psychology* (Vol. 4, pp. 93–185). Boston: Allyn and Bacon.

Bretherton, I., and Waters, E. (Eds.), (1985). Growing points of attachment theory and research. *Monographs of the Society for Research in Child Development, 50* (1–2, Serial No. 209).

Brown, A. L., and Reeve, R. A. (1985). *Bandwidths of competence: The role of supportive contexts in learning and development* (Tech. Rep. No. 336). Champaign: University of Illinois at Urbana-Champaign, Center for the Study of Reading.

Cazden, C. B., John, V. P., and Hymes, D. (Eds.), (1975). *Functions of language in the classroom*. New York: Teachers College Press.

Cazden, C. B., and John, V. P. (1971). Learning in American Indian children. In M. L. Wax, S. Diamond, and F. O. Gearing (Eds.), *Anthropological perspectives in education* (pp. 252–272). New York: Basic Books.

Chisholm, J. S. (1983). *Navajo infancy: An ethological study of child development*. Hawthorne, NY: Aldine.

Cole, M. (1975). An ethnographic psychology of cognition. In R. W. Brislin, S. Bochner, and W. J. Lonner (Eds.), *Cross-cultural perspectives on learning* (pp. 157–175). New York: Wiley.

Cole, M. (1981, September). *The zone of proximal development: Where culture and cognition create each other* (Report No. 106). San Diego: University of California, Center for Human Information Processing.

Cole, M., and Bruner, J. S. (1971). Cultural differences and inferences about psychological processes. *American Psychologist, 26*, 867–876.

Cole, M., Gay, J., Glick, J. A., and Sharp, D. W. (1971). *The cultural context of learning and thinking*. New York: Basic Books.

Cole, M., Hood, L., and McDermott, R. P. (1978). Concepts of ecological validity: Their differing implications for comparative cognitive research. *The Quarterly Newsletter of the Institute for Comparative Human Development, 2*, 34–37.

Dasen, P. R. (1977). *Piagetian psychology: Cross-cultural contributions*. New York, Gardner Press.

Dasen, P. R., and Heron, A. (1981). Cross-cultural tests of Piaget's theory. In H. C. Triandis and A. Heron (Eds.), *Handbook of cross-cultural psychology* (Vol. 4, pp. 295–341). Boston: Allyn and Bacon.

Edwards, C. P. (1981). The comparative study of the development of moral judgment and reasoning. In R. H. Munroe, R. L. Munroe, and B. B. Whiting (Eds.), *Handbook of cross-cultural human development* (pp. 501–528). New York: Garland.

Erickson, F., and Mohatt, G. (1982). Cultural organization of participation structures in two classrooms of Indian students. In G. Spindler (Ed.), *Doing the ethnography of schooling* (pp. 132–174). New York: Holt, Rinehart and Winston.

Field, T. M., Sostek, A. M., Vietze, P., and Leiderman, P. H. (1981). *Culture and early interactions*. Hillsdale, NJ: Erlbaum.

Fox, N. A. (1977). Attachment of kibbutz infants to mother and metapelet. *Child Development, 48*, 1228–1239.

Gewirtz, J. L. (1965). The course of infant smiling in four child-rearing environments in Israel. In B. M. Foss (Ed.), *Determinants of infant behavior* (Vol. 3, pp. 205–248). London, England: Methuen.

Gladwin, T. (1970). *East is a big bird*. Cambridge, MA: Belknap Press.

Glick, J. (1975). Cognitive development in cross-cultural perspective. In F. Horowitz (Ed.), *Review of child development research* (Vol. 4, pp. 595–654). Chicago: University of Chicago Press.

Goldberg, S. (1972). Infant care and growth in urban Zambia. *Human Development, 15*, 77–89.

Goodnow, J. J. (1976). The nature of intelligent behavior. Questions raised by cross-cultural studies. In L. B. Resnick (Ed.), *The nature of intelligence* (pp. 169–188). Hillsdale, NJ: Erlbaum.

Goody, J. (1977). *The domestication of the savage mind.* Cambridge, England: Cambridge University Press.

Graves, Z. R., and Glick, J. (1978). The effect of context on mother–child interaction. *The Quarterly Newsletter of the Institute for Comparative Human Development, 2,* 41–46.

Greenfield, P. M. (1976). Cross-cultural research and Piagetian theory: Paradox and progress. In K. R. Riegel and J. A. Meacham (Eds.), *The developing individual in a changing world* (Vol. 1, pp. 322–345). Chicago: Aldine.

Hilliard, A G., III and Vaughn-Scott, M. (1982). The quest for the 'minority' child. In S. G. Moore and C. R. Cooper (Eds.), *The young child: Reviews of research* (Vol. 3, pp. 175–189). Washington, DC: National Association for the Education of Young Children.

Howard, A., and Scott, R. A. (1981). The study of minority groups in complex societies. In R. H. Munroe, R. L. Munroe, and B. B. Whiting (Eds.), *Handbook of cross-cultural human development* (pp. 113–152). New York: Garland.

Irvine, J. T. (1978). Wolof 'magical thinking': Culture and conservation revisited. *Journal of Cross-Cultural Psychology, 9,* 300–310.

Kilbride, P. L. (1980). Sensorimotor behavior of Baganda and Samia infants. *Journal of Cross-Cultural Psychology, 11,* 131–152.

Konner, M. (1972). Aspects of the developmental ethology of a foraging people. In N. Blurton-Jones (Ed.), *Ethological studies of child behavior* (pp. 285–328). Cambridge, England: Cambridge University Press.

Laboratory of Comparative Human Cognition. (1979). Cross-cultural psychology's challenges to our ideas of children and development. *American Psychologist, 34,* 827–833.

Laboratory of Comparative Human Cognition. (1983). Culture and cognitive development. In W. Kessen (Ed.), *Handbook of Child Psychology: Vol. 1. History, theory, and methods* (pp. 294–356). New York: Wiley.

Laboratory of Comparative Human Cognition. (1986). Contributions of cross-cultural research to educational practice. *American Psychologist, 41,* 1049–1058.

Lave, J. (1977). Tailor-made experiments and evaluating the intellectual consequences of apprenticeship training. *The Quarterly Newsletter of the Institute for Comparative Human Development, 1,* 1–3.

Leiderman, P. H., Tulkin, S. R., and Rosenfeld, A. (Eds.), (1977). *Culture and infancy.* New York: Academic Press.

LeVine, R. A. (in press). Environments in child development: An anthropological perspective. In W. Damon (Ed.), *Child development today and tomorrow.* San Francisco: Jossey-Bass.

Malinowski, B. (1927). *The father in primitive psychology.* New York: Norton.

Munroe, R. L., and Munroe, R. H. (1975). *Cross-cultural human development.* Monterey, CA: Brooks/Cole.

Munroe, R. H., Munroe, R. L., and Whiting, B. B. (Eds.), (1981). *Handbook of cross-cultural human development.* New York: Garland.

Newson, J., and Newson, E. (1975). Intersubjectivity and the transmission of culture: On the social origins of symbolic functioning. *Bulletin of the British Psychological Society, 28,* 437–446.

Ogbu, J. U. (1982). Socialization: A cultural ecological approach. In K. M. Borman (Ed.), *The social life of children in a changing society* (pp. 253–267). Hillsdale, NJ: Erlbaum.

Pedersen, R. A. (1980). *The father–infant relationship: Observational studies in the family setting.* New York: Praeger.

Piaget, J. (1972). Intellectual evolution from adolescence to adulthood. *Human Development*, *15*, 1–12.

Price-Williams, D. R. (1980). Anthropological approaches to cognition and their relevance to psychology. In H. C. Triandis and W. Lonner (Eds.), *Handbook of cross-cultural psychology* (Vol. 3, pp. 155–184). Boston: Allyn and Bacon.

Rogoff, B. (1981). Schooling and the development of cognitive skills. In H. C. Triandis and A. Heron (Eds.), *Handbook of cross-cultural psychology* (Vol. 4, pp. 233–294). Boston: Allyn and Bacon.

Rogoff, B. (1982). Integrating context and cognitive development. In M. E. Lamb and A. L. Brown (Eds.), *Advances in developmental psychology* (Vol. 2, pp. 125–170). Hillsdale, NJ: Erlbaum.

Rogoff, B., Gauvain, M., and Ellis, S. (1984). Development viewed in its cultural context. In M. H. Bornstein and M. E. Lamb (Eds.), *Developmental Psychology* (pp. 533–571). Hillsdale, NJ: Erlbaum.

Rogoff, B., and Mistry, J. J. (1985). Memory development in cultural context. In M. Pressley and C. Brainerd (Eds.), *Progress in cognitive development* (pp. 117–142). New York: Springer-Verlag.

Rogoff, B., and Mistry, J. J. (in press). The social and motivational context of children's memory skills. In R. Fivish and J. Hudson (Eds.), *What young children remember and why*. Cambridge, England: Cambridge University Press.

Rogoff, B., and Waddell, K. J. (1982). Memory for information organized in a scene by children from two cultures. *Child Development*, *53*, 1224–1228.

Saxe, G. B. (1988). *Mathematics in and out of school*. Unpublished manuscript, University of California at Los Angeles.

Schieffelin, B. B., and Ochs, E. (Eds.), (1986). *Language socialization across cultures*. Cambridge, England: Cambridge University Press.

Scribner, S. (1976). Situating the experiment in cross-cultural research. In K. F. Riegel and J. A. Meacham (Eds.), *The developing individual in a changing world* (Vol. 1, pp. 310–321). Chicago: Aldine.

Scribner, S. (1977). Modes of thinking and ways of speaking: Culture and logic reconsidered. In P. N. Johnson-Laird and P. C. Watson (Eds.), *Thinking* (pp. 483–500). Cambridge, England: Cambridge University Press.

Scribner, S., and Cole, M. (1981). *The psychology of literacy*. Cambridge, MA: Harvard University Press.

Serpell, R. (1976). *Culture's influence on behavior*. London, England: Methuen.

Serpell, R. (1979). How specific are perceptual skills? A cross-cultural study of pattern reproduction. *British Journal of Psychology*, *70*, 365–380.

Sharp, D., Cole, M, and Lave, C. (1979). Education and cognitive development: The evidence from experimental research. *Monographs of the Society for Research in Child Development*, *44* (1–2, Serial No. 178).

Skeen, J., Rogoff, B., and Ellis, S. (1983). Categorization by children and adults in communication contexts. *International Journal of Behavioral Development*, *6*, 213–220.

Slobin, D. I. (1973). Cognitive prerequisites for the development of grammar. In C. A. Ferguson and D. I. Slobin (Eds.), *Studies of child language development* (pp. 175–200). New York: Holt, Rinehart and Winston.

Super, C. M. (1981). Behavioral development in infancy. In R. H. Munroe, R. L. Munroe, and B. B. Whiting (Eds.), *Handbook of cross-cultural human development* (pp. 181–270). New York: Garland.

Super, C. M., and Harkness, S. (Eds.) (1980). *Anthropological perspectives on child development*. San Francisco: Jossey-Bass.

Super, C. M., Harkness, S., and Baldwin, L. M. (1977). Category behavior in natural ecologies and in cognitive tests. *The Quarterly Newsletter of the Institute for Comparative Human Development, 1*, 4–7.

Triandis, H. C., and Heron, A. (Eds.) (1981). *Handbook of cross-cultural psychology* (Vol. 4). Boston: Allyn and Bacon.

Tronick, E. Z., Morelli, G. A., and Winn, S. (1987). Multiple caretaking of Efe (pygmy) infants. *American Anthropologist, 89* (1), 96–106.

Vygotsky, L. S. (1978). *Mind in society.* Cambridge, MA: Harvard University Press.

Wagner, D. A., and Stevenson, H. W. (Eds.) (1982). *Cultural perspectives on child development.* San Francisco: Freeman.

Wenger, M. (1983). *Gender role socialization in East Africa: Social interactions between 2-to-3 year olds and older children, a social ecological perspective.* Unpublished doctoral dissertation, Harvard University, Cambridge, MA.

Werner, E. E. (1979). *Cross-cultural child development.* Monterey, CA: Brooks/Cole.

Werner, E. E. (1988). A cross-cultural perspective on infancy. *Journal of Cross-Cultural Psychology, 19*(1), 96–113.

Wertsch, J. V. (Ed.) (1985a). *Culture, communication, and cognition: Vygotskian perspectives.* Cambridge, England: Cambridge University Press.

Wertsch, J. V. (1985b). *Vygotsky and the social formation of mind.* Cambridge, MA: Harvard University Press.

Whiting, B. B. (1976). The problem of the packaged variable. In K. F. Riegel and J. A. Meacham (Eds.), *The developing individual in a changing world.* Chicago: Aldine.

Whiting, B. B., and Edwards, C. P. (1988). *Children of different worlds.* Cambridge, MA: Harvard University Press.

Whiting, B. B., and Whiting, J. W. M. (1975). *Children of six cultures: A psycho-cultural analysis.* Cambridge, MA: Harvard University Press.

Zaslow, M. (1980). Relationships among peers in kibbutz toddler groups. *Child Psychiatry and Human Development, 10*, 178–189.

Zaslow, M., and Rogoff, B. (1981). The cross-cultural study of early interaction: Implications from research in culture and cognition. In T. Field, A. Sostek, P. Vietze, and H. Leiderman (Eds.), *Culture and early interactions* (pp. 237–256). Hillsdale, NJ: Erlbaum.

# SECTION VI
## *TOWARDS ADULTHOOD*

### Editors' Introduction

Adolescence is a time when there are increasing social and educational pressures, a time when many individuals have to make decisions about their future life path, and a time of role change which is often accompanied by the lessening of ties with the family. Adolescence is usually regarded as the time between childhood and adulthood. However, such a broad definition conceals many possible ways of identifying the start and the end of adolescence (e.g. the biological changes associated with the start of puberty, being in the teen years, social and legal recognition of sexuality, being able to vote, living independently of the family, and there are cultural markers of such transitions such as bar mitzvahs). Definitions can be further complicated by the lack of clear beginning and end points for some of these markers, for example, puberty is accompanied by a variety of physical changes. Although the range of definitions needs to be noted, this is not a serious problem when conducting most research with this age group providing the investigators are clear about the range in age or other capacities which they are studying.

The adolescence period has tended to be neglected by developmental psychologists. There are a number of reasons for this. One is that the techniques used to study children can be inappropriate for the study of adolescence. Often there is not a need or a desire for precise behavioural descriptions of the process of social interaction – instead questionnaires can be used. Another reason for the difference in methodology is that the focus of studies of adolescents is often different from that of younger children. Instead of interest in the processes of learning and education, there is more interest in topics which involve decision making such as delinquency or drug use. Thus, research questions often concern why adolescents make certain decisions or what they think about certain matters. A further reason for the neglect of adolescence is it falls between childhood and adulthood, so that it has not been central to the concerns of psychologists who study children nor to psychologists who study adults.

The first paper in this section is unusual in that it concerns individuals between 6 and 40 years of age, and as such it spans childhood, adolescence and adulthood. The study is about moral judgment, a topic which has attracted interest because it provides an insight into the ability to reason at different ages, and it is an issue which has a relevance to our understanding of an important aspect of all of our lives. Piaget's observations provided a powerful stimulus for interest in this topic. He compared children's reactions to two stories: in one a child accidentally knocked over a tray with the result that a number of plates were broken; in the other story a child, while being naughty, broke a plate. Children of about 6 years, who are at what Piaget termed the stage of moral realism, usually said that the child who broke the large number of plates was naughtier. Older children at the stage of moral reciprocity would reply in terms of the intentions of the child. From work such as this Piaget suggested that the sophistication of moral reasoning could be related to his stages of cognitive development. However, subsequent work has suggested that young children can give more sophisticated replies if the stories are presented in ways that are easier for them to understand (see Chapter 17).

Lawrence Kohlberg proposed a related and influential theory about moral development which was initially based on interviews with 10–16-year-old boys. However, his ideas have been criticised because they do not pay sufficient attention to the moral reasoning of females, and tend to regard their moral reasoning as less advanced. The study by Walker was designed to address these and other problems in the research on moral reasoning. The findings did not provide support for the idea that Kohlberg's stages discriminated against females, and supported the idea that individuals progress through the stages of moral reasoning proposed by Kohlberg (see also Durkin, 1995; Eckensberger, 1995).

The next four papers provide brief reviews of important topics in research into adolescence. The first of these addresses the issue of biological changes which are often thought to mark the beginning of adolescence. Martha McClintock and Gilbert Herdt argue that in the past the biological maturation of the testes in males and ovaries in females (this is termed gonarche) marks the attainment of adult sexual status. This maturation is of course associated with other biological changes and marks an individual as being capable of sexual reproduction. McClintock and Herdt review a number of findings concerning the beginning of sexual attraction and related behaviours at age 10 which is also the age when the adrenal glands mature (this is termed adrenarche). These glands are an important source of sex steroids. McClintock and Herdt argue that the evidence they present challenges the idea of gonarche being the first and only influence on sexual behaviour. However, they are cautious about making the claim that adrenarche is the cause of changes in sexual attraction. Why is this? (pages xii–xiv of the introduction provide clues about the reason for the caution).

The paper by Farrington summarizes a longitudinal study, taking place over 24 years, which has examined antisocial behaviour and delinquency. The research illustrates the strengths of conducting longitudinal research, but it is important to recognize that studies on this scale are comparatively rare. The findings from this investigation contain a number of important messages. One is that delinquency should not be seen simply as a product of adolescent processes – a number of pre-adolescent characteristics predict adolescent antisocial behaviour. These factors include economic deprivation, poor parenting, family problems, school problems, hyperactivity, and antisocial behaviour. A logistic regression was conducted to find out which of these variables were the best predictors of teenage antisocial behaviour. This can be thought of as similar to conducting a number of correlations to find out which of a set of independent variables is most highly related to antisocial behaviour. Odds ratios are used to identify the extent that the presence of a characteristic increases the probability of children having antisocial behaviour at 18 years – in other words whether there is an association between two behaviours greater than would be expected by chance. The variables were also entered into a logistic regression. In most cases the variables identified by the logistic regression have a high odds ratio. The advantage of the logistic regression is that it takes account of inter-relations between variables and in this way provides a more comprehensive analysis than the odds ratio. Farrington puts forward an explanation for the pattern of findings he has identified in terms of a constellation of factors which result in antisocial behaviour. How convinced are you by his explanation? If you disagree, why is this? Another important question is whether we would expect to find similar processes in females, and if not why not?

Recklessness is a characteristic often associated with adolescence. As we have just seen it is a variable identified by Farrington (e.g. high daring, high impulsivity) to predict antisocial behaviour. Jeffrey Arnett, in his review of this topic, argues that recklessness can be explained on an individual level by sensation seeking, egocentrism, and biologically based aggressiveness. However, he also argues that the expression of recklessness will be influenced by the overall characteristics of the cultural environment of the adolescent. Arnett describes some cultures as permitting recklessness while others constrain it; he cites examples of the different ways in which these influences operate. Thus, he supposes that the overall rates of reckless behaviour will be influenced by cultural patterns. The final part of the review presents an interesting argument about the benefits and costs associated with the way a culture constrains adolescent behaviour. Do you agree with this conclusion? It is also interesting to compare the way Farrington explains antisocial behaviour and the way Arnett conceptualizes cultural influences. Are these explanations mutually exclusive or can they both be used to help us understand behaviour?

The last chapter in this section considers adolescent processes in a more positive light – the benefits of friendships. There are markedly different views about the effect of friendships. One view is that friendships are a positive feature because they facilitate the acquisition of social skills and assist in coping with stress. Another view is that friendships involve negative processes because peer pressure can lead to antisocial and delinquent behaviour. Berndt argues that there is some truth in both these positions. Positive relations with friends do seem to enhance self esteem and result in better adjustment, however, Berndt cautions that these are not powerful effects, some of this can be due to better adjusted individuals forming closer friendships. He also cautions about the assumption that peers will necessarily be a negative influence. Research indicates that friendships persist when there are similarities between the friends, if there are differences then the two individuals will no longer be friends. Thus, we see that the role of friendship in adolescent development is more complex than often supposed, and that there are reciprocal influences between an individual and features of an individual's environment. The paper gives a number of examples of the methods used to investigate adolescence. It would be useful to make a list of these techniques and consider whether they are the best way to answer the research questions that have been asked. Also think about the advantages and disadvantages of reporting findings for whole groups of individuals: do you think this could hide important differences between people?

Adolescents are at the threshold of adulthood. Many of the research questions about this period of life concern the origins and causes of behaviours which have significant impact on adolescent and adult lives. The chapters in this section show that there are a variety of levels and forms of explanation. Some research traces causes back to pre-adolescent ages, some to individual characteristics, some to general biological changes associated with maturation, others to family influences, and still others to cultural factors. All these explanations are likely to have some validity, the problem is in discovering which explanations have the most powerful effects, and if we wish to change processes in adolescence, which variables are most amenable to change. As with other areas of developmental psychology, research findings need to be put in the context of what society wishes to achieve and whether there is a preparedness to fund interventions which might facilitate changes. Research by developmental psychologists has always had practical implications, but there is a growing awareness among researchers that the justification for the funding of research is not just in terms of theoretical advances, but also in terms of the way that the findings can be used for practical gains.

## References

Durkin, K. (1995). *Social Development*, Oxford: Blackwell.

## Further Reading

Eckensburger, L. H. (in press). Social and moral development. In D. Messer and S. Millar (Eds.), *Developmental Psychology*. London: Arnold.

Hendry, L. and Kloep, M. (in press). Adolescence in Europe – an important life phase? In D. Messer and S. Millar (Eds.), *Developmental Psychology*. London: Arnold.

Hendry, L. and Kloep, M. (in press). Challenges, risks and coping in adolescence. In D. Messer and S. Millar (Eds.), *Developmental Psychology*. London: Arnold.

# 22 Lawrence J. Walker
## 'A Longitudinal Study of Moral Reasoning'

Reprinted in full from: *Child Development* **60**, 157–166 (1989)

This article reports the longitudinal data of a project designed to investigate both Kohlberg's (1984) and Gilligan's (1982) models of moral reasoning. Several issues were addressed by data from the initial phase of the project (Walker, de Vries and Trevethan, 1987). Others are better addressed by analyses of longitudinal data; these issues represent the focus here.

The essential contribution of Kohlberg's theory has been the postulation of stages of moral reasoning. These stages are claimed to be acquired in an invariant order; that is, development should be irreversibly progressive, one stage at a time. Testing this claim requires repeated measures of moral reasoning with reports of intraindividual change. Some early studies indicated a relatively high number of violations of the sequence, but such findings are now of questionable relevance given the substantial revisions to stage descriptions and scoring procedures (Colby and Kohlberg, 1987). However, several longitudinal studies have used the current scoring system (Colby, Kohlberg, Gibbs and Lieberman, 1983; Erickson, 1980; Lei, 1984; Murphy and Gilligan, 1980; Nisan and Kohlberg, 1982; Page, 1981; Snarey, Reimer and Kohlberg, 1985), and while these studies indicate that the number of violations typically is small, each is limited in some respect: for example, four studies involved single-sex samples; in two studies, subjects studied Kohlberg's theory; all seven studies were conducted with subjects who initially were adolescents or young adults (thus restricting range); and samples have been small ($N$'s = 17–64). The present study overcomes many of these problems: it is a 2-year longitudinal study with a large sample ($N = 233$) of both sexes and of a wide portion of the life span (initial ages were 5–63 years).

Kohlberg's theory has been controversial, not only because of the strong claims made regarding the moral stage model, but also because some critics (Baumrind, 1986; Gilligan, 1982) have argued that his approach does not adequately represent the moral thinking of females. Although the evidence indicates a nonsignificant pattern of sex differences in level of moral development (Walker, 1984, 1986b), it is possible that the sexes differ in some aspects of moral reasoning. For example, Gilligan (1982) argued that the sexes differ fundamentally in their 'orientation' to the moral domain: males typically having a *justice/rights orientation* and females a *care/response orientation*. Her proposal includes these empirically testable notions: (*a*) There is intraindividual consistency in orientation usage. (*b*) Orientations are sex-related, and (*c*) evident across the life span. (*d*) Hypothetical dilemmas, because of their abstracted nature, will tend to elicit rights considerations, whereas real-life dilemmas, because of their contextualized nature, will elicit response considerations.

These issues informed the design of this project. In an initial interview, participants responded to hypothetical dilemmas and discussed a personally generated real-life dilemma, which were scored for both moral stage and moral orientation. Those data (see Walker et al., 1987) indicated that consistency in orientation usage was low – most people used both orientations to a significant degree. The relation between sex and orientation was inconsistent. Also, responses to real-life and hypothetical dilemmas were similar, and response reasoning increased with age.

To date, no longitudinal data on moral orientations have been reported. The present study involved an initial moral interview (as described above) and a retest interview 2 years later. Several issues regarding Gilligan's model were of interest: Is there intraindividual consistency in orientations over time? Given the cross-sectional age differences in orientation use on the initial interview, is change evident over time? Do the retest data clarify the weak and conflicting evidence regarding sex differences previously found?

Although Gilligan's model has attracted considerable attention, Kohlberg (1976) previously delineated four orientations (in addition to the better-known moral stages), and it has been possible to distinguish these orientations in individuals' reasoning with the current scoring system: The *normative orientation* emphasizes duty and rightness defined by adherence to prescribed rules and roles. The *fairness orientation* emphasizes liberty, equity and equality, and reciprocity and contract. The *utilitarianism orientation* emphasizes welfare or happiness consequences of moral actions for oneself or for others. The *perfectionism orientation* emphasizes attainment of dignity and autonomy, good conscience and motives, and harmony with self and others.

Based on Gilligan's arguments and Kohlberg's descriptions, it seems reasonable to suggest that there might be sex differences in these orientations as well and, indeed, some congruence between Gilligan's and Kohlberg's models. That is, males should have a normative or fairness orientation because of their presumed focus on rights, duties, and justice, whereas females should have a utilitarianism or perfectionism orientation because of their focus on relationships, welfare, and caring. For example, Colby and Kohlberg (1987) argued that a care/response mode of moral reasoning is reflected in the utilitarianism and perfectionism orientations. Of course, Kohlberg's orientations are not synonymous with Gilligan's, but there are many parallel distinctions and themes. Both Pratt, Golding, and Hunter (1984) and Walker (1986a) have examined sex differences in Kohlberg's orientations but failed to find much support for the predicted pattern.

Other researchers have examined the relation between these orientations and social experiences (Nisan and Kohlberg, 1982; Tietjen and Walker, 1985) and between orientations and attitudes (de Vries and Walker, 1986). However, no one has yet examined age trends or the use of these orientations in real-life dilemmas. de Vries and Walker's finding that many people used different orientations when arguing opposing positions on the capital punishment issue suggests that different types of dilemmas may elicit different moral considerations. Thus, the present study examined age trends (both cross-sectional and longitudinal), sex differences, and dilemma-type differences in

Kohlberg's orientations. Also examined was the relation between Gilligan's and Kohlberg's models of moral orientations, and between moral orientations and moral stage.

## Method

### Participants

The initial sample was composed of 80 family triads (mother, father, and child; total $N$ = 240) with the children drawn from grades 1, 4, 7, and 10 (see Walker et al., 1987). The children's ages represented the widest range feasible given that preschoolers would find the interview too demanding and that children older than grade 10 at the time of the initial interview would have completed high school (and possibly left home) by the time of retest. At retest, then, children were in grades 3, 6, 9, and 12. Each family was offered $25 for participation. Only seven individuals did not participate in the retest interview (i.e., 2.9% attrition): a grade 12 boy because of scheduling difficulties, a grade 9 boy and his parents because of family breakup, a grade 3 girl and her parents because of their move out of the country. Thus, the analyses reported here are based on the data of the 233 participants who were interviewed twice. At the time of the initial interview, the participants' ages were as follows: grade 1 children ($M$ = 6.8 years, SD = .48), grade 4 ($M$ = 9.8, SD = .52), grade 7 ($M$ = 12.4, SD = .49), grade 10 $M$ = 15.7, SD = .35), mothers ($M$ = 39.7, SD = 4.3), and fathers ($M$ = 41.3, SD = 5.8).

### Procedure

The procedure was the same at both interviews, which were separated by an interval of approximately 2 years. Families came to the university, at a time convenient for them, to participate. After providing consent, each participant was taken to a small office for an individual interview. These interviews took about 45–90 min and were tape-recorded for later transcription and scoring.

The interview had two parts: three hypothetical dilemmas and the real-life dilemma. Since there are three forms of Kohlberg's Moral Judgment Interview (MJI), the form used with each family was randomly chosen for the initial interview. The same form was used at retest since different forms have been found to elicit slightly different levels of moral reasoning (Colby and Kohlberg, 1987). After responding to the MJI, participants were asked to recall a recent real-life moral dilemma from their own experience. The interviewer probed regarding participants' construction, resolution, and evaluation of this dilemma (following Lyons, 1982).

### Scoring

*Content analysis of real-life dilemmas.* A content analysis of each real-life dilemma was conducted in terms of the nature of the relationship that it entailed – either personal or impersonal. A 'personal' moral conflict was interpreted as one involving a specific person or group of people with whom the subject has a significant relationship, defined generally as one of a continuing nature, whereas an 'impersonal' moral conflict was interpreted as one involving a person or group of people whom the subject does not know well or is not specified or is generalized, or as one involving institutions, or involving an issue primarily intrinsic to self. Interrater reliability was determined with a second rater who independently classified all dilemmas. There was 93.9% agreement.

*Moral development.* The hypothetical dilemmas were scored for moral reasoning development according to Colby and Kohlberg's (1987) manual. This was done blindly and by each dilemma separately across subjects. The scoring of the real-life dilemmas required a slight adaptation of the usual procedure. Since the manual is keyed to particular dilemmas and issues, the scorer relied more on the general stage structure definitions for each criterion judgment than on particular (dilemma-specific) critical indicators. Thus, scores were assigned for every moral judgment that matched a stage structure definition for any criterion judgment in the manual.

Level of moral development was calculated both for the MJI and the real-life dilemma. The *weighted average score* (WAS) includes information regarding usage at all stages and is given by the sum of the products of the percent usage at each stage multiplied by the stage number (range = 100–500). A more qualitative measure is the *global stage score* (GSS), which can be expressed in terms of either a 5- or 9-point scale. The 5-point GSS is simply the modal stage. The 9-point GSS consists of pure and mixed stages (1, 1/2, 2, . . ., 5) and is given by the modal stage or by the two most frequent stages (if two stages have 25% or more of the scores).

Interrater reliability was determined with a second rater who independently scored 32 randomly selected interviews. For the MJI, there was 84.4% exact agreement in GSSs (9-point scale), and $r = .92$ for WASs. For the real-life dilemmas, there was 75.0% agreement in GSSs, and $r = .89$ for WASs.

*Moral orientations (Kohlberg's typology).* In scoring moral judgments according to Colby and Kohlberg's manual, each was classified according to 'stage' (as described above) and 'element.' Moral orientation scores for the four orientations were derived from these scored elements. Each score was expressed as a percentage of all moral judgments attributable to the elements reflecting that orientation. Moral orientation scores were calculated for both the MJI and the real-life dilemma.

Interrater reliability was determined with a second rater who independently scored 32 randomly selected interviews. Reliability for the MJI was .80 and for the real-life dilemmas was .82.

*Moral orientations (Gilligan's typology).* The dilemmas were scored for Gilligan's moral orientations according to Lyons's (1982) manual. This was done blindly and by each dilemma separately. Each 'consideration' presented by the participant was categorized as reflecting either the response or rights orientation. The relative number of considerations determined the *modal orientation* ('response,' 'rights,' or 'split' if there was an equal number). A more quantitative score, the *percent response score*, was also calculated as the percentage of all considerations that reflected the response orientation. (A percent rights score would complement the percent response score and analyses would be redundant.) Scores were determined both for the MJI and the real-life dilemma.

Interrater reliability for scoring rights and response considerations was determined with a second rater who independently scored 32 randomly selected interviews. Reliability for the MJI was .77, and for the real-life dilemmas, .76.

## Results

### Stage sequence

Since the sequence claim is framed in terms of modal stages (development must be to the next higher stage), violations were assessed with modal GSSs, not with more differentiated scores. Of the 233 participants, 14 (6.0%) evidenced regressions and none, stage-skipping. Most of these regressions were not substantial: 13 were to the next lower level in terms of 9-point GSSs (e.g., a reversal of major and minor stages). There was no sex difference in violations of the sequence (eight males and six females). Of course, few regressions are not very convincing if, in general, there is little change; thus it is relevant to examine the ratio of progressive changes to regressions. In terms of modal GSSs, this ratio is substantial given the relatively short 2-year interval, 3.7: 1.

In order to examine age and sex differences in moral development as assessed by the MJI, a 5 (age: grade 1/3, 4/6, 7/9, 10/12, and adults) × 2 (sex) × 2 (time: initial interview, retest) analysis of variance (ANOVA) was conducted with repeated measures on the last factor, using the WAS as the dependent variable. (An ANOVA with unequal $n$'s, as is the case here, is not robust if there is heterogeneity of variance. However, a Box's $M$ test confirmed the homogeneity assumption.) The main effect of sex and all interactions with sex were not significant. The ANOVA revealed highly significant effects for age, $F(4,223) = 135.52$; time, $F(1,223) = 150.03$; and an interaction between them, $F(4,223) = 6.65$, all $p$'s < .001. Subsequent analyses of the effect of time for each age group separately indicated significant increases in moral development level for all groups, all $p$'s < .002. However, the gains for children were substantial (range = 32–47 WAS points), whereas the gain for adults was slight (7 WAS points). In terms of 9-point GSSs, 87 of the subjects (or 37.3%) showed progressive changes: that is, 62.3% of the children but only 25% of the adults.

*Gilligan's moral orientations*

Gilligan claims that individuals focus on one orientation. We (Walker et al., 1987) previously reported, however, that few subjects were consistent in the use of a single orientation across, and even within, dilemmas. The longitudinal data allow an examination of this consistency over time. Stability coefficients for percent response scores were calculated and found to be low: .13 for the hypothetical dilemmas and .35 for the real-life dilemma (cf. the corresponding coefficients for WASs, .89 and .73). An alternate approach is to determine the percentage of subjects who evidenced the same modal orientation for the two interviews. On the real-life dilemma, about half of the participants (49.8%) evidenced a different orientation on the retest than the initial interview.

To examine developmental trends, sex differences, and dilemma-type differences in Gilligan's orientations, a 5 (age) × 2 (sex) × 2 (type of dilemma: hypothetical, real-life) × 2 (time) ANOVA was conducted, with repeated measures on the last two factors and using percent response scores as the dependent variable. (A Box's $M$ test supported the assumption of homogeneity of variance.) This ANOVA yielded a complex pattern of findings: There was a significant effect of age, $F(4,223) = 10.39$; an effect for type of dilemma, $F(1,223) = 11.73$; and an interaction between them, $F(4,223) = 7.37$, all $p$'s < .001. Subsequent analyses of the effect of type of dilemma for each age group

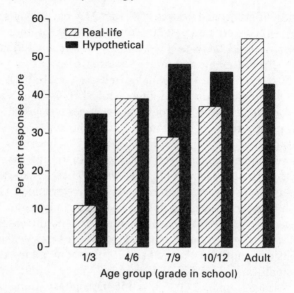

**Figure 22.1** Mean percent response scores across age groups for both dilemma types.

separately revealed that two groups of children (grade 1/3 and 7/9) used more response reasoning on hypothetical dilemmas than the real-life one, whereas adults evidenced the opposite pattern (see Figure 22.1). There were no significant differences for the other groups.

This pattern was qualified by two relatively weak three-way interactions: age × sex × type of dilemma, $F(4,223) = 2.57$; and age × type of dilemma × time, $F(4,223) = 3.20$, $p$'s < .05. Beyond what has already been discussed (and shown in Figure 22.1), subsequent analyses of the age × sex × type of dilemma interaction indicated that there were no sex differences on the hypothetical dilemmas, and none among children on the real-life dilemma. Among adults on the real-life dilemma, however, women had higher response scores than men (59.6% vs. 50.2%). (Incidentally, if modal moral orientations, rather than response scores, are examined for the real-life dilemma, then among children there is no significant sex-related pattern for either interview, whereas among adults, there is on the initial interview but not on the retest.) Analyses of the age × type of dilemma × time interaction indicated that grade 7/9 children's greater use of response reasoning on the hypothetical dilemmas than the real-life one was significant only on the retest and not the initial interview.

In summary, this analysis indicated age-group differences but no change in response reasoning over the 2-year interval. Sex differences were not found with standard dilemmas, nor among children with real-life dilemmas. The pattern of response reasoning across types of dilemmas was conflicting, with two groups of children using more such reasoning with hypothetical dilemmas and with adults using more with real-life ones.

We previously argued (Walker et al., 1987) that a sex-related pattern in moral orientations might be related to the kinds of dilemmas that subjects recall. The absence of sex differences with standard dilemmas, noted above, is consistent with that view. It is important, then, to examine the content of the real-life dilemmas to determine if there is a relation between dilemma content and orientation and if there are sex differences in orientation within types of dilemma content. To accomplish this, a content analysis of the real-life dilemmas was conducted in terms of the nature of the relationship that each entailed (either personal or impersonal). Then, a 2 (sex) $\times$ 2 (dilemma content) ANOVA was conducted for both interviews, using the percent response score as the dependent variable. Both analyses indicated no effect of, nor interaction with, sex; that is, there were no sex differences in orientation use when dilemma content is held constant. However, a strong effect of dilemma content was found, with higher scores on personal- than impersonal-relationship dilemmas for both the initial (52.3% vs. 40.0%) and retest (56.9% vs. 33.7%) interview, $F$'s(1,229) = 6.48 and 27.42, $p$'s < .02 and .001, respectively. Since the only sex difference in orientations that has been found is for adults on the real-life dilemma, these ANOVAs were also conducted for them alone. There was no effect of, nor interaction with, sex; but effects of dilemma content were found, mirroring the pattern just presented. Thus, the nature of the dilemma better predicts moral orientation than does individuals' sex.

### Kohlberg's moral orientations

Age trends (cross-sectional and longitudinal), sex differences, and dilemma-type differences in Kohlberg's alternate typology of moral orientations were examined by a parallel set of ANOVAs (age $\times$ sex $\times$ type of dilemma $\times$ time) for the four orientations (normative, fairness, utilitarianism, and perfectionism), using the orientation scores as the dependent variable. (Box's $M$ tests supported the assumption of homogeneity of variance.) One finding, consistent across all analyses, was that there were no effects of, nor interactions with, sex – failing to support the notion that males have a normative or fairness orientation and females a utilitarianism or perfectionism orientation. Also, there were no effects of, nor interactions with, time – that is, unlike the developmental changes evidenced in moral stages, orientations seem stable. (The stability coefficient for the hypothetical dilemmas was .76 and for the real-life dilemmas, .46. The lower level of stability for the real-life dilemmas can perhaps be attributed to their varying content, whereas the hypothetical dilemmas were constant.) The analyses, however, revealed significant age trends. The normative and utilitarianism orientations, common in childhood, decrease with age, $F$'s(4,223) = 3.23 and 63.30, $p$'s < .02 and .001, respectively, whereas the fairness and perfectionism orientations increase, $F$'s(4,223) = 9.97 and 29.56, $p$'s < .001 (see Figure 22.2).

The analyses also revealed main effects for type of dilemma. Hypothetical dilemmas elicited more of the normative and fairness orientations, $F$'s(1,223) = 39.69, $p$ < .001, and 3.67, $p$ = .06, respectively, whereas real-life dilemmas elicited more of the utilitarianism and perfectionism orientations, $F$'s(1,223) =

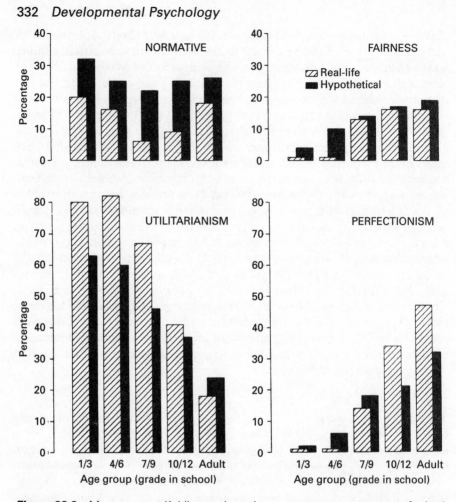

**Figure 22.2** Mean percent Kohlberg orientation scores across age groups for both dilemma types.

29.67, $p < .001$, and 2.59, $p = .10$, respectively. (Note that the effects for the fairness and perfectionism orientations are of marginal significance.) An interaction between age and type of dilemma was also found for both utilitarianism and perfectionism, $F$'s$(4,223) = 6.11$ and 3.62, $p$'s $< .01$, respectively. Subsequent analyses of these interactions revealed that, for the utilitarianism orientation, the effect of type of dilemma was significant only for the three youngest groups, whereas for the perfectionism orientation, it was significant only for the two oldest groups (see Figure 22.2). Thus, hypothetical dilemmas apparently pull *rights*-like orientations (normative and fairness), whereas real-life dilemmas pull *response*-like orientations (utilitarianism and perfectionism).

Another approach in assessing this issue of variability in orientation use as a function of type of dilemma (hypothetical vs. real-life) would be to calculate correlations in orientation scores. For the normative orientation, $r = .10$, N.S., and .19, $p < .01$, for the initial and retest interviews, respectively. For the fairness orientation, $r = .08$, N.S., and .22, $p < .001$. For the utilitarianism orientation, $r = .45$ and .48, $p$'s $< .001$. For the perfectionism orientation, $r = .33$ and .40, $p$'s $< .001$. Thus, although there is some intrapersonal consistency in orientation use (the correlations all are positive and most are significant), the moderate level of consistency overall suggests that different types of dilemmas elicit different moral orientations, as was also indicated by the previous analyses.

Clear cross-sectional age differences have been found both for Kohlberg's moral orientations and for moral stages. These age trends suggest a possible confound between moral stage and moral orientation within Kohlberg's approach. The available data are inconsistent on this issue: some studies indicating a relation (Nisan and Kohlberg, 1982; Pratt et al., 1984; Tietjen and Walker, 1985), others not (de Vries and Walker, 1986; Walker, 1986a). Correlations between the four moral orientations and moral stage (as given by WASs) for the present data are presented in Table 22.1. Moderately strong relations are evident overall, with use of the normative and utilitarianism orientations decreasing at higher stages and with the fairness and perfectionism orientations increasing. These intercorrelations are attenuated somewhat with age partialed out. Thus, there seems to be a relation between moral stage and orientation: Lower-stage reasoning is more likely to entail normative and utilitarian concerns, whereas higher-stage reasoning orients to a greater extent on fairness and perfectionism.

## Relation between the two typologies

The previous sections examined Gilligan's and Kohlberg's models of moral orientations and indicated that, although the relation between orientations

**Table 22.1** Correlations between Kohlberg's moral orientations and moral stage

| Interview | Kohlberg's orientations | | | |
| | Normative | Fairness | Utilitarianism | Perfectionism |
| --- | --- | --- | --- | --- |
| Hypothetical dilemmas: | | | | |
| Initial . . . . . . .. | $-.23^{***}$ | $.57^{***}$ | $-.76^{***}$ | $.72^{***}$ |
| | $(-.28^{***})$ | $(.37^{***})$ | $(-.43^{***})$ | $(.45^{***})$ |
| Retest . . . . . . .. | $-.13^{*}$ | $.53^{***}$ | $-.74^{***}$ | $.68^{***}$ |
| | $(-.16^{**})$ | $(.39^{***})$ | $(-.50^{***})$ | $(.45^{***})$ |
| Real-life dilemmas: | | | | |
| Initial . . . . . . .. | $-.07$ | $.24^{***}$ | $-.55^{***}$ | $.45^{***}$ |
| | $(-.13^{*})$ | $(.19^{***})$ | $(-.26^{***})$ | $(.20^{***})$ |
| Retest . . . . . . .. | $-.05$ | $.23^{***}$ | $-.59^{***}$ | $.53^{***}$ |
| | $(-.19^{**})$ | $(.08)$ | $(-.30^{***})$ | $(.40^{***})$ |

Note: – Partial correlations, controlling for age, are indicated in parentheses.
\* $p < .05$.
\*\* $p < .01$.
\*\*\* $p < .001$.

and type of dilemma differed for the two typologies, there were several similar effects: (*a*) cross-sectional trends, (*b*) the absence of sex differences, and (*c*) no developmental changes over time. Given the somewhat similar findings, it seems appropriate to examine their interrelation more directly. Table 22.2 presents correlations between Gilligan's percent response scores and scores on the four Kohlberg orientations for both dilemma types and interview times. Based on previously presented arguments, one would predict a negative relation between response scores and the normative and fairness (rights-style) orientations and a positive relation between response scores and the utilitarianism and perfectionism (response-style) orientations. Although most of the correlations (69%) are in the predicted directions, they are not strong – only 38% are significant, which is not impressive given the large sample. No consistent relation was found between response scores and either fairness and utilitarianism orientation scores. The clearest trends were found between response scores and the normative orientation (i.e., the expected negative relation) and between response scores and perfectionism (i.e., the expected positive relation). Since cross-sectional age trends were found for both Gilligan's and Kohlberg's models of moral orientations, it is interesting to examine the intercorrelations with age partialed out (see Table 22.2). The overall pattern remains very similar: 88% of the correlations are in the predicted direction, with only 44% reaching significance.

It is also of some theoretical interest to examine the relation between moral stage development and Gilligan's moral orientations. Gilligan argued that Kohlberg's approach undervalues the response orientation, and thus individuals with that orientation should evidence lower levels of moral reasoning than those with a rights orientation, which she believes is favored by Kohlberg's theory. This predicts a negative relation between response scores

**Table 22.2** Correlations between Gilligan's response scores and Kohlberg's moral orientations and stage

| Interview | Kohlberg's orientations | | | | |
|---|---|---|---|---|---|
| | Normative | Fairness | Utilitarianism | Perfectionism | Moral stage |
| Hypothetical dilemmas: | | | | | |
| Initial . . . . . . . . | −.10 | .03 | −.09 | .16** | .15* |
| | (−.09) | (−.04) | (.00) | (.11*) | (.08) |
| Retest . . . . . . . . | −.19** | −.03 | .05 | .10 | .03 |
| | (−.19**) | (−.03) | (.05) | (.14*) | (.06) |
| Real-life dilemmas: | | | | | |
| Initial . . . . . . . . | −.12* | .01 | −.10 | .19** | .27*** |
| | (−.13*) | (−.03) | (.06) | (.08) | (.11*) |
| Retest . . . . . . . . | −.07 | −.02 | −.28*** | .38*** | .40*** |
| | (.12*) | (−.13*) | (−.07) | (.26***) | (.15**) |

Note: – Partial correlations, controlling for age, are indicated in parentheses.
* $p < .05$.
** $p < .01$.
*** $p < .001$.

and moral stage. The right-hand column of Table 22.2 displays the correlations between response scores and WASs. They are modest, but positive – contrary to Gilligan's predictions.

## Discussion

Kohlberg's (1984) model of moral reasoning development posits, among other claims, that moral stages are acquired in an invariant sequence. The data of this study – which are more comprehensive than others currently available because of the large sample size that included a wide age range and both sexes – revealed few instances of violations of the stage sequence, well within the level of expected measurement error. Significant increases in level of moral reasoning were evidenced by all age groups. But, although development was marked among children, relative stability was more characteristic of adults (as might be expected over a relatively brief 2-year interval).

Theories of moral reasoning have also attracted interest because of the issue of sex differences. Gilligan proposed that the sexes typically have different orientations to morality. This study examined several notions concerning the validity of the proposal. First, the data indicated that few individuals evidence a reasonable level of consistency in orientation use across dilemmas or over time (a finding also reported by Rothbart, Hanley, and Albert, 1986). Second, the data regarding developmental trends indicated that, although there were age differences, there was no evidence of development over time (unlike moral stages). Third, data regarding the claim that hypothetical dilemmas elicit rights reasoning and real-life dilemmas elicit response reasoning were equivocal. Fourth, the claim that these orientations are sex-related could not be supported. There were no sex differences among children and adolescents, and none on the standard dilemmas. The only sex difference found was among adults on the real-life dilemma. Furthermore, analyses of real-life dilemma content revealed that, regardless of individuals' sex, personal-relationship dilemmas elicited higher levels of response reasoning than did impersonal-relationship dilemmas. Thus, type of dilemma clearly relates to moral orientation.

It is impossible to determine from these data, however, whether this relation indicates that the nature of a dilemma influences the moral orientation voiced or that one's moral orientation influences the construal of a dilemma. This failure to support Gilligan's proposal could be attributed either to an inadequate conceptualization or to an inadequate operationalization (or both). Problems with Lyons's (1982) coding system were noted earlier (Walker et al., 1987), and admittedly there is, to date, scant evidence to support its reliability or face and criterion validity.

Gilligan's theorizing about moral orientations was actually predated by Kohlberg's (1976) model of four orientations, which has many similar themes and distinctions. Although Kohlberg's typology is less central to his theory than his sequence of stages, and certainly is less well elaborated, it represents a useful extension of the theory. Orientations seem more closely related to the content, rather than the structure, of reasoning and thus may be more readily influenced by situational factors. It was hypothesized that males would evidence a normative and fairness orientation because of the focus on rights, duties, and justice, and that females would evidence a utilitarianism and perfectionism orientation because of the focus on relationships, welfare, caring, and interpersonal harmony. However, no sex differences were found. Cross-sectional age differences were found for Kohlberg's orientations, although longitudinal changes were not evident.

These trends suggest a possible relation between moral stage and moral orientation within Kohlberg's approach. Other analyses revealed that normative and utilitarian orientations are more typical at lower stages, whereas concerns about fairness and perfectionism are more frequently expressed at higher stages. Nevertheless, the present data also indicate that an analysis of orientations provides nonredundant information. For example, there was a strong developmental progression in moral stage over time, whereas orientations were stable. Also, consistency in stage level between hypothetical and real-life dilemmas was found (Walter et al., 1987), whereas the two dilemma types elicited differing orientations. Hypothetical dilemmas elicited rights-type (normative and fairness) orientations, whereas real-life dilemmas elicited response-type (utilitarianism and perfectionism) orientations. Although this is Gilligan's prediction, it is supported only by the Kohlberg typology. The influence of dilemma type on Kohlberg's orientations illustrates their contextual nature (and difference from moral stage) and suggests a fruitful line of research which examines orientation usage across differing moral issues.

The similar themes of Gilligan's and Kohlberg's typologies and the similar pattern of findings (e.g., cross-sectional age trends but no changes over time, absence of sex differences) suggest some interrelation between them. Correlational analyses, however, revealed relatively weak relations, indicating that these typologies seem to be tapping somewhat different aspects of moral reasoning. Finally, the relation between Gilligan's orientations and Kohlberg's moral stages is of considerable interest. Gilligan believes that Kohlberg's approach undervalues the response orientation; thus individuals with that orientation should score at a lower stage level. The correlations between response scores and moral stages were positive, however, albeit not strong. That is, individuals who evidenced a greater usage of the response orientation were more likely to be scored at higher stages of moral reasoning. There is no evidence of bias by Kohlberg's theory against a response/care orientation to moral decision making.

### References

Baumrind, D. (1986). Sex differences in moral reasoning: Response to Walker's (1984) conclusion that there are none. *Child Development, 57*, 511–521.

Colby, A., and Kohlberg, L. (1987). *The measurement of moral judgment* (Vols. *1–2*). New York: Cambridge University Press.

Colby, A., Kohlberg, L., Gibbs, J., and Lieberman, M. (1983). A longitudinal study of moral judgment. *Monographs of the Society for Research in Child Development, 48* (1–2, Serial No. 200).

de Vries, B., and Walker, L. J. (1986). Moral reasoning and attitudes toward capital punishment. *Developmental Psychology*, 22, 509–513.

Erickson, V. L. (1980). The case study method in the evaluation of developmental programs. In L. Kuhmerker, M. Mentkowski, and V. L. Erickson (Eds.), *Evaluating moral development* (pp. 151–176). Schenectady, NY: Character Research Press.

Gilligan, C. (1982). *In a different voice: Psychological theory and women's development.* Cambridge, MA: Harvard University Press.

Kohlberg, L. (1976). Moral stages and moralization: The cognitive-developmental approach. In T. Lickona (Ed.), *Moral development and behavior: Theory, research, and social issues* (pp. 31–53). New York: Holt, Rinehart and Winston.

Kohlberg, L. (1984). *Essays on moral development: Vol. 2. The psychology of moral development.* San Francisco: Harper and Row.

Lei, T. (1984, July). *A longitudinal study of moral judgment development in Taiwan: An interim report.* Paper presented at the Sixth International Symposium on Asian Studies, Hong Kong.

Lyons, N. P. (1982). *Conceptions of self and morality and modes of moral choice: Identifying justice and care in judgments of actual moral dilemmas.* Unpublished doctoral dissertation, Harvard University, Cambridge, MA.

Murphy, J. M., and Gilligan, C. (1980). Moral development in late adolescence and adulthood: A critique and reconstruction of Kohlberg's theory. *Human Development*, 23, 77–104.

Nisan, M., and Kohlberg, L. (1982). Universality and variation in moral judgment: A longitudinal and cross-sectional study in Turkey. *Child Development*, 53, 865–876.

Page, R. A. (1981). Longitudinal evidence for the sequentiality of Kohlberg's stages of moral judgment in adolescent males. *Journal of Genetic Psychology*, 139, 3–9.

Pratt, M. W., Golding, G., and Hunter, W. J. (1984). Does morality have a gender? Sex, sex role, and moral judgment relationships across the adult lifespan. *Merrill-Palmer Quarterly*, 30, 321–340.

Rothbart, M. K., Hanley, D., and Albert, M. (1986). Gender differences in moral reasoning. *Sex Roles*, 15, 645–653.

Snarey, J. R., Reimer, J., and Kohlberg, L. (1985). Development of social-moral reasoning among kibbutz adolescents. A longitudinal cross-cultural study. *Developmental Psychology*, 21, 3–17.

Tietjen, A. M., and Walter, L. J. (1985). Moral reasoning and leadership among men in a Papua New Guinea society. *Developmental Psychology*, 21, 982–992.

Walker, L. J. (1984). Sex differences in the development of moral reasoning: A critical review. *Child Development*, 55, 677–691.

Walker, L. J. (1986a). Experiential and cognitive sources of moral development in adulthood. *Human Development*, 29, 113–124.

Walker, L. J. (1986b). Sex differences in the development of moral reasoning: A rejoinder to Baumrind. *Child Development*, 57, 522–526.

Walker, L. J., de Vries, B., and Trevethan, S. D. (1987). Moral stages and moral orientations in real-life and hypothetical dilemmas. *Child Development*, 58, 842–858.

# 23 Martha K. McClintock and Gilbert Herdt
## 'Rethinking Puberty: The Development of Sexual Attraction'

Reprinted in full from: *Current Directions in Psychological Science* 5, 178–183 (1996)

A youth remembers a time when he was sitting in the family room with his parents watching the original 'Star Trek' television series. He reports that he was 10 years old and had not yet developed any of the obvious signs of puberty. When 'Captain Kirk' suddenly peeled off his shirt, the boy was titillated. At 10 years of age, this was his first experience of sexual attraction, and he knew intuitively that, according to the norms of his parents and society, he should not be feeling this same-gender attraction. The youth relating his memory is a self-identified gay 18-year-old in Chicago. He also reports that at age 5 he had an absence of sexual attractions of any kind, and that even by age 8 he had not experienced overt awareness of sexual attraction. By age 10, however, a profound transformation had begun, and it was already completed by the time he entered puberty; sexual attraction to the same gender was so familiar to him (Herdt and Boxer, 1993) that it defined his selfhood.

Recent findings from three distinct and significant studies have pointed to the age of 10 as the mean age of first sexual attraction – well before puberty, which is typically defined as the age when the capacity to procreate is attained (Timiras, 1972). These findings are at odds with previous developmental and social science models of behavioral sexual development in Western countries, which suggested that *gonadarche* (final maturation of the testes or ovaries) is the biological basis for the child's budding interest in sexual matters. Earlier studies postulated that the profound maturational changes during puberty instigate the transition from preadolescent to adult forms of sexuality that involve sexual attraction, fantasy, and behavior (Money and Ehrhardt, 1972). Thus, adult forms of sexuality were thought to develop only after gonadarche, typically around ages 12 for girls and 14 for boys, with early and late bloomers being regarded as 'off time' in development (Boxer, Levinson and Petersen, 1989). But the new findings, which locate the development of sexual attraction before these ages, are forcing researchers to rethink the role of gonadarche in the development of sexual attraction as well as the conceptualization of puberty as simply the product of complete gonadal maturation.

Many researchers have conflated puberty and gonadarche, thinking that the two are synonymous in development. The new research on sexual orientation has provided data that invalidate the old model of gonadarche as the sole biological cause of adult forms of sexuality. To the extent that sexual attraction is affected by hormones, the new data indicate that there should be another significant hormonal event around age 10. Indeed, there is: the maturation of the adrenal glands during middle childhood, termed *adrenarche*. (The adrenal glands[1] are the biggest nongonadal source of sex steroids.) This biological process, distinctively different from gonadarche, may underlie the development not only of sexual attraction, but of cognition, emotions, motivations, and social behavior as well. This observation, in turn, leads to a redefinition of prepubertal and pubertal development.

## Gonadarche is not a sufficient explanation

Previous biopsychological models of sexual development have attributed changes in adolescent behavior to changes in hormone levels accompanied by gonadarche (Boxer et al., 1989), presumably because of a focus on the most dramatic features of gonadal development in each gender: menarche in girls and spermarche in boys. If gonadarche were responsible for first sexual attractions, then the mean age of the development of sexual attractions should be around the age of gonadarche. Moreover, one would expect a sex difference in the age of first attraction, corresponding to the sex difference in age of gonadarche: 12 for girls and 14 for boys. Neither of these predictions however, has been borne out by recent data.

In three studies attempting to illuminate the sources of sexual orientation, adolescents have been asked to recall their earliest sexual thoughts; their answers are surprising. One study (Herdt and Boxer, 1993) investigated the development of sexual identity and social relations in a group of self-identified gay and lesbian teenagers (ages 14–20, with a mean age of 18) from Chicago. The mean age for first same-sex attraction was around age 10 for both males and females. Moreover, sexual attraction marked the first event in a developmental sequence: same-sex attraction, same-sex fantasy, and finally same-sex behavior (see Table 23.1).

This evidence provides a key for understanding sexuality as a process of development, rather than thinking of it as a discrete event, which emerges suddenly at a single moment in time. Virtually all models of adolescent sexual development, from Anna Freud and Erik Erikson up to the present, have been based on the gonadarche model (Boxer et al., 1989). It conceptualizes the development of sexuality as a precipitous, singular, psychological event, fueled by intrinsic changes in hormone levels. Gonadarche is seen as a 'switch,' turning on desire and attraction, and hence triggering the developmental sequelae of adult sexuality.

Instead, the new data suggest a longer series of intertwined erotic and gender formations that differentiate beginning in middle childhood. Indeed,

**Table 23.1** Ages (years) at which males and females recall having their first same-sex attraction, fantasy, and activity (from Herdt and Boxer, 1993)

| Developmental event | Males | | | Females | | |
|---|---|---|---|---|---|---|
| | M | SD | n | M | SD | n |
| First same-sex attraction | 9.6 | 3.6 | 146 | 10.1 | 3.7 | 55 |
| First same-sex fantasy | 11.2 | 3.5 | 144 | 11.9 | 2.9 | 54 |
| First same-sex activity | 13.1 | 4.3 | 136 | 15.2 | 3.1 | 49 |

the psychological sequence of attraction, fantasy, and behavior may parallel the well-known Tanner stages, which are routinely used by clinicians to quantify the process of physical development during puberty (Timiras, 1972). For example, in girls, onset of sexual attraction may co-occur with Tanner Stage II (development of breast buds); sexual fantasy may co-occur with Tanner Stage III (enlargement of mammary glands); and sexual behavior may co-occur with Tanner Stage IV (full breast development), with each psychosexual stage reflecting a different stage of hormonal development. If so, then we may begin to look for a biological mechanism for psychosexual development in the physiological basis for these early Tanner stages that occur prior to the final gonadal maturation that enables procreation.

The generality of these psychological findings is substantiated by two other recent studies that also reported the age of first sexual attraction to be around 10 (see Figure 23.1). Pattatucci and Hamer (1995) and Hamer, Hu, Magnuson, Hu, and Pattatucci (1993) asked similar retrospective questions of two

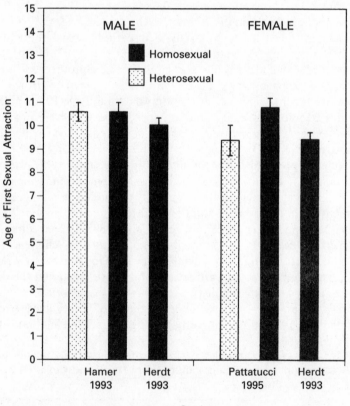

**Figure 23.1** Mean age (± *SEM*) of first sexual attraction reported by males and females, both homosexual and heterosexual. The data are reported in three studies: Herdt and Boxer (1993), Pattatucci and Hamer (1995), and Hamer, Hu, Magnuson, Hu, and Pattatucci (1993).

distinctive samples of gay- and lesbian-identified adults in the United States. Unlike the Chicago study (Herdt and Boxer, 1993), these studies gathered information from subjects throughout the United States and interviewed adults who were mostly in their mid-30s (range from 18 to 55). They also used different surveys and interview methodologies. Nevertheless, all three studies pinpointed 10 to 10.5 as the mean age of first sexual attraction. Admittedly, none of the studies was ideal for assessing early development of sexuality; the age of first recalled sexual attraction may not be the actual age. Nonetheless, this work is an essential part of the systematic investigation of same-gender attractions in children.

The question then arises whether there is a similar developmental pattern among heterosexuals. We know of no reason to assume that heterosexuals and homosexuals would have different mechanisms for the activation of sexual attraction and desire. Fortunately, we could test this hypothesis because both Pattatucci's and Hamer's samples had comparison groups of heterosexuals. Indeed, the reported age of first attraction was the same for heterosexually as for homosexually identified adults (only the attraction was toward the opposite sex). Thus, regardless of sexual orientation or gender, the age of initial sexual attraction hovered just over age 10. In sum, the switch mechanism responsible for 'turning on' sexual attraction seems to be operating at the same time both for boys and for girls, and regardless of whether their sexual orientation is toward the same or opposite gender.

Thus, we surmise that the maturation of the gonads cannot explain the data found independently by these three studies in different samples and geographic areas. There is no known mechanism that would enable the gonads to supply sufficient levels of hormones at that age to cause sexual attraction, because they are not fully developed. The mean age of sexual attraction is the same in both genders and in both structural forms of sexual orientation; therefore, the biological counterpart in both genders and in both structural forms of sexual orientation of sexual attraction is probably the same. These constraints effectively eliminate gonadarche as a candidate to explain the observed findings.

**Adrenarche in middle childhood**

In the pediatric literature, it is well recognized that children between the ages of 6 and 11 are experiencing a rise in sex steroids. These hormones come from the maturing adrenal glands. Adrenarche is clinically recognized primarily by the onset of pubic hair, but it also includes a growth spurt, increased oil on the skin, changes in the external genitalia, and the development of body odor (New, Levine and Pang, 1981; Parker, 1991). Nonetheless, both the psychological literature and the institutions of our culture regard this period of middle childhood as hormonally quiescent. Freud's (1905/1965) classic notion of a 'latency' period between ages 4 to 6 and puberty perhaps best distills the cultural prejudices. In contrast, we have hypothesized that the rise in adrenal steroid production is critical for understanding interpersonal and intrapsychic development in middle childhood.

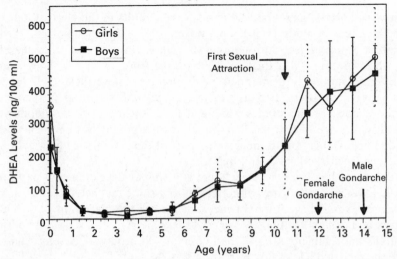

**Figure 23.2** Mean levels (± *SEM*) of the primary adrenal androgen dehydroepian-drosterone (DHEA) from birth through gonadarche in boys (solid error bars) and girls (dashed error bars). (Data redrawn from De Peretti and Forest, 1976).

Both male and female infants have adult levels of sex steroids during the first days of life, and their adrenal androgens also approach the adult range (see Figure 23.2). After a few months, the sex hormone levels begin to fall to a very low level and then remain low until the maturation of the adrenal glands and gonads. When children are between 6 and 8 years of age, their adrenal glands begin to mature. Specifically, the adrenal cortex begins to secrete low levels of androgens, primarily dehydroepiandrosterone (DHEA; see Figure 23.2) (Parker, 1991). The metabolism of DHEA leads to both testosterone and estradiol, the primary sex steroids in men and women.

It is noteworthy that both girls and boys experience a rise in androgens, although androgens are typically misidentified as male hormones. Moreover, there is no sex difference in the age at which these androgens begin to rise or the rate at which they do so. After adrenarche, an individual's level of androgens plateaus until around 12 years of age in girls and 14 years of age in boys, whereupon gonadarche triggers a second hormonal rise into the adult range (Parker, 1991).

In adults, the androgens that are produced by the adrenal cortex and their metabolites are known to have psychological effects in a variety of developmental areas relating to aggression, cognition, perception, attention, emotions, and sexuality. Although adult levels of DHEA are not reached until after gonadarche, levels of this hormone do increase significantly around age 10 (see Figure 23.2; De Peretti and Forest, 1976), when they become 10 times the levels experienced by children between 1 and 4 years of age. It is plausible that this marked increase in androgen levels alters the brain, and thus behavior, either by modifying neural function or by permanently altering cellular structure.

**What is special about the fourth grade?**

We considered the hypothesis that the age of first sexual attraction is similar for boys and girls, both homosexual and heterosexual, because there is some marked change in environmental stimuli, socialization, or cognitive abilities around the age of 10. If so, then the 10-fold rise in DHEA would be only correlated with the emergence of sexuality and should not be considered its direct cause.

A major weakness of the idea that environmental stimuli lead to the emergence of sexual attraction at age 10 is the fact that, in the United States, there is no marked cultural prompt for sexuality in a 10-year-old. Children this age are typically in fourth grade. To our knowledge, there is no overt change in social expectations between Grades 3 and 4, or between Grades 4 and 5, that might account for the developmental emergence of sexual attraction at age 10. In U.S. culture, the typical ages for the so-called rites of passage are 12 to 13, when the adolescent becomes a 'teenager,' or around 15 to 16, when the driver's license is issued. Perhaps between Grades 5 and 6 (or, depending on the school system, between Grades 6 and 7), we might identify a critical change during the transition from elementary to middle school. Yet all of these culturally more prominent transitions occur later than age 10. Other subtle changes, such as girls wearing ornate earrings or boys forming preteenage groups, may occur around age 10, but these social factors seem too weak to adequately explain the sudden emergence of sexual attraction before anatomical changes are noteworthy in the child.

We also considered the possibility that although the social environment does not change at age 10, sexual attraction arises at this age because of an increase in the child's cognitive capability to perceive and understand the sexual and social environment. When the child becomes cognitively capable of understanding sexual interactions among adults, the child is capable also of imitating and putting into action the behaviors he or she has observed. This may be a plausible explanation for development of an awareness of sexual attraction in heterosexuals, and no doubt plays a role in the development of sexuality (after all, people typically do not develop sexuality in a vacuum). But does the explanation hold for children who are sexually attracted to the same gender?

The simple social-learning hypothesis predicts that as soon as children become aware of a strong cultural taboo on the expression of homosexual feelings, they should inhibit or even extinguish these desires in subsequent sexual development. We would therefore expect to find that homosexuals would reveal same-sex attraction significantly later than the age when heterosexuals reveal opposite-sex attraction. But this is not the case.

If 10-year-old children are simply mimicking the sexual behavior most commonly seen in adults (and the biological ability to actually carry out the behavior will arise only with gonadarche), then, given the predominant culture, all 10-year-old boys should demonstrate sexual attraction toward females, and all 10-year-old girls should show sexual attraction toward males. However, this also is not the case.

Other criticisms of simple learning theory hypotheses regarding sexual development are well known and need not be repeated here (Abramson and Pinkerton, 1995). However, the Sambia of Papua New Guinea (Herdt, 1981) provide particularly compelling counterevidence to a simple learning theory model. The Sambia provide powerful reinforcement for same-gender relations by institutionalizing the practice of men inseminating boys over a period of many years, beginning at age 7 to 10. The goal of the men is to masculinize and 'grow' the youths into competent reproductive adult men. This intensive training and reinforcement of sexual relationships between males does not result in exclusive homosexuality in adulthood. Instead, adult Sambia men reveal marked bifurcation of their sexual interest; they generally stop all same-gender relations after marriage and enjoy sexual relations with women.

### The relationship between adrenarche and sexuality: cause or correlation?

Does the inability of the hypotheses of gonadarche and social learning to explain the data imply that adrenarche is the key to the emergence of sexual attraction at age 10? That question cannot yet be answered conclusively. It is entirely possible that the sequential changes in attraction, fantasy, and behavior result from major structural changes in the brain that have their etiology in sources other than sex steroids. However, there has been no documented evidence for such neural structures as of yet. Moreover, if structural changes in the brain do prove to be the cause of the emergence of sexual attraction, modification of all current sexual developmental models and theories will still be needed because they assume that adult desires and behaviors develop from gonadarche.

A change in the nervous system that results from hormones released at adrenarche does look like the most likely developmental mechanism for several reasons. First, girls and boys experience their first sexual attraction, but not gonadarche, at the same age. Second, DHEA, the primary androgen released by the adrenal, is intimately linked with testosterone and estradiol, the major adult sex hormones. Their dynamic relationship is based on the fact that they share many of the fundamental features of steroid function: metabolic pathways that produce the steroids, binding proteins in the blood that carry them to their target tissue, and receptors that enable the cells in the target tissue, including the brain, to change their function in response to the hormonal information. Third, these androgens are known to affect the sexual fantasies and behavior of adolescents and adults, and it is plausible that the same hormones would have similar effects at an earlier age.

### Rethinking puberty: implications for many domains

Given the strong possibility that the currently popular model of puberty is limited, if not incorrect, researchers need to rethink puberty and test the new models in a wide range of psychological disciplines. Adrenarche clearly raises androgens to significant levels, and if these hormones are responsible for the effects seen in sexual attraction, then they are likely to affect a wide range of other behaviors: aggression, cognition, perception, attention, arousal, emotions, and, of course, sexual identity, fantasy, and behavior.

Even if it turns out that hormones released from the adrenal glands are not responsible for the onset of sexual attraction, the behavioral data themselves demonstrate that the concept of puberty must be greatly elaborated and its various stages unpacked. Indeed, Freud's idea of a latency period is seriously flawed. The current behavioral work reinforces the well-established clinical understanding that puberty is composed of at least two separate maturational processes: adrenarche and gonadarche. Any psychosocial research that uses puberty as a stage in development needs to break down the relevant developmental and social behaviors into these two different stages. Researchers need to take into account the hormonal fact that the start of puberty in normal individuals is around ages 6 to 8 and the end of puberty is not until around ages 15 to 17.

The idea of sexuality developing in stages is nothing new to social scientists. But the idea that sexuality is a continuous process that begins from the inside, well before gonadarche, and extends into adulthood is a conceptual advance. These new data from sexual orientation research force a reevaluation of the social and health models of sexual development. No longer can the brain at puberty be treated as a black box, which is suddenly able to process sexual stimuli *de novo* at the time of gonadal change.

Although adrenarche may not be the answer to all the riddles of sexual development, the new data from the developmental and social study of sexual identity have triggered a major conceptual advance in the understanding of both puberty and sexual development as psychobiological phenomena.

### Acknowledgements

We extend our profound thanks to Colin Davis, who coordinated the data and helped substantially with manuscript preparation; to Ruvance Pietrz, who edited text and figures; and to Amanda Woodward for her insightful and constructive comments. This work was supported by National Institute of Mental Health MERIT Award R37 MH41788 to Martha K. McClintock.

### Note

1 The adrenal glands are small, pyramidal glands located above the kidneys. They produce hormones that affect metabolism, salt regulation, response to stress, and reproductive function, in part by binding in the brain and altering neural function.

### Recommended reading

Becker, J. B., Breedlove, S. M., and Crews, D. (Eds.), (1992). *Behavioral endocrinology.* London: MIT Press.
Boxer, A., and Cohler, B. (1989). The life-course of gay and lesbian youth: An immodest proposal for the study of lives. In G. Herdt (Ed.), *Gay and lesbian youth* (pp. 315–335). New York, Harrington Park Press.

Korth-Schütz, S. S. (1989). Precocious adrenarche. In F. G. Maguelone (Ed.), *Paediatric and adolescent endocrinology* (pp. 226–235). New York: Karger.

Rosenfield, R. L. (1994). Normal and almost normal precocious variations in pubertal development: Premature pubarche and premature thelarche revisited. *Hormone Research, 41* (Suppl. 2), 7–13.

# References

Abramson, P., and Pinkerton, S. (Eds.), (1995). *Sexual nature, sexual culture.* Chicago: University of Chicago Press.

Boxer, A., Levinson, R. A., and Petersen, A. C. (1989). Adolescent sexuality. In J. Worell and F. Danner (Eds.), *The adolescent as decision-maker* (pp. 209–244). San Diego: Academic Press.

De Peretti, E., and Forest, M. G. (1976). Unconjugated dehydroepiandrosterone plasma levels in normal subjects from birth to adolescence in humans: The use of a sensitive radioimmunoassay. *Journal of Clinical Endocrinology and Metabolism, 43,* 982–991.

Freud, S. (1965). *Three essays on the theory of sexuality.* New York: Basic Books. (Original work published 1905).

Hamer, D. H., Hu, S., Magnuson, V. L., Hu, N., and Pattatucci, A. M. L. (1993). A linkage between DNA markers on the X chromosome and male sexual orientation. *Science, 261,* 321–327.

Herdt, G. (1981). *Guardians of the flutes.* New York: McGraw-Hill.

Herdt, G., and Boxer, A. (1993). *Children of horizons.* New York: Beacon Press.

Money, J., and Ehrhardt, A. (1972). *Man, woman, boy, girl.* Baltimore: Johns Hopkins University Press.

New, M. I., Levine, L. S., and Pang, S. (1981). Adrenal androgens and growth. In M. Ritzen (Ed.), *The biology of normal human growth: Transactions of the First Karolinska Institute Nobel Conference* (pp. 285–295). New York: Raven Press.

Parker, L. N. (1991). Adrenarche. *Endocrinology and Metabolism Clinics of North America, 20*(1), 71–83.

Pattatucci, A. M. L., and Hamer, D. H. (1995). Development and familiality of sexual orientation in females. *Behavior Genetics, 25,* 407–420.

Timiras, P. S. (1972). *Developmental physiology and aging.* New York: Macmillan.

# 24 D. P. Farrington

**'Childhood Origins of Teenage Antisocial Behaviour and Adult Social Dysfunction'**

Reprinted in full from: *Journal of the Royal Society of Medicine* **86**, 13–17 (1993)

## Summary

The main aim of this research was to investigate the childhood predictors (age 8–10 years) of teenage antisocial behaviour (age 18 years) and adult social dysfunction (age 32 years). A sample of 411 London males was followed up from age 8 years to age 32 years. The most important childhood predictors of both outcomes (and of convictions) were measures of economic deprivation, poor parenting, an antisocial family and hyperactivity-impulsivity-attention deficit. However, childhood nervousness and social isolation were negatively related to teenage antisocial behaviour but positively related to adult social dysfunction. It was concluded that the development of adult social dysfunction depended not only on established causes of antisocial behaviour such as economic deprivation and poor parenting but also on causes of internalizing disorders such as childhood nervousness and social isolation.

## Introduction

In their prospective longitudinal study of 411 London males from age 8 years to age 18 years, West and Farrington[1] concluded that offending was only one element of a larger syndrome of antisocial behaviour. They documented how childhood antisocial behaviour and a constellation of childhood background adversities (including poverty, large families, ineffective child-rearing methods, convicted parents, parental disharmony and separation) tended to lead to a constellation of teenage problems (including offences of dishonesty and violence, heavy drinking, drug abuse, reckless driving, sexual promiscuity and an unstable job record). Farrington[2] extended this follow-up study to age 32 years, and demonstrated the persistence of the syndrome of antisocial behaviour from childhood (age 8–10 years) to the teenage years (age 18 years) and into adulthood (age 32 years). The main aim of the present paper is to study the link between childhood background adversities at age 8–10 years and a variety of indicators of adult social dysfunction at age 32 years.

## Methods

### The study

The present research is part of the Cambridge Study in Delinquent Development, which is a prospective longitudinal survey of 411 males. At the time they were first contacted in 1961/62, they were all living in a working-class area of London. The sample was chosen by taking all the boys who were then aged 8 years and on the registers of six state primary schools within a one-mile radius of our research office. The boys were overwhelmingly white, working class, and of British origin. The major results of this survey can be found in four books[1-5] and in more than 60 papers listed by Farrington and West[6].

The original aim of the survey was to describe the development of delinquent and criminal behaviour in inner-city males, to investigate how far it could be predicted in advance, and to explain why juvenile delinquency began, why it did or did not continue into adult crime, and why adult crime usually ended as men reached their twenties and thirties. The survey was not designed to test one particular theory about crime but to test many different hypotheses about the causes and correlates of offending. Numerous different types of variables were measured, since it was hoped that this survey would yield information of use not only to criminologists but also to those interested in alcohol and drug abuse, educational problems, poverty and poor housing, unemployment, sexual behaviour, aggression, and other social problems.

The study males were interviewed and tested in their schools when they were aged about 8, 10 and 14 years, by male or female psychologists. They were also interviewed in our research office at about 16, 18, and 21 years, and in their homes at about 25 and 32 years, by young male social science graduates. The tests in schools measured individual characteristics such as intelligence, attainment, personality, and psychomotor impulsivity, while information was collected in the interviews about such topics as living circumstances, employment histories, relationships with females, and leisure activities such as drinking, fighting, drug taking, and other kinds of offending. On all occasions except at ages 21 and 25 years, the aim was to interview the whole sample, and it was always possible to trace and interview a high proportion. For example, 389 of the 410 males still alive at 18 years (95%) were interviewed, and 378 of the 403 males still alive at 32 years (94%).

In addition to the interviews and tests with the boys, interviews with their parents were carried out by female social workers who visited their homes. These took place about once a year from when the boy was 8 years until when he was aged 14–15 years and was in his last year of compulsory education. The primary informant was the mother, although many fathers were also seen. The parents provided details about such matters as family income, family size, their employment histories, their child-rearing practices (including attitudes, discipline, and parental agreement), their degree of supervision of the boy, and his temporary or permanent separations from them.

The boys' teachers also completed questionnaires, when the boys were aged about 8, 10, 12 and 14 years. These provided information about the boys' troublesome and aggressive school behaviour, their attention difficulties, their school attainments and their truancy. Ratings were also obtained from the boys' peers when they were in their primary schools, about such topics as their daring, dishonesty, troublesomeness, and popularity.

In addition, repeated searches have been carried out in the central Criminal Record Office in London to try to locate findings of guilt sustained by the boys, by their parents, by their brothers and sisters, and (in recent years) by their wives and cohabitees. Convictions were only counted if they were for offences normally recorded in this Office, thereby excluding minor crimes such as common assault, traffic infractions and drunkenness. The most common offences included were thefts, burglaries, and unauthorized takings of motor vehicles. However, we did not rely on official records for our information about offending, because we also obtained self-reports of offending from the males themselves at every age from 14 years onwards.

The Cambridge Study has a unique combination of features: (1) eight face-to-face interviews with the males have been completed over a period of 24 years, from age 8 to 32 years; (2) the main focus of interest is on crime and delinquency; (3) the sample size of about 400 is large enough for many statistical analyses but small enough to permit detailed case histories of the boys and their families; (4) the attrition rate is unusually low for such a long-term survey; (5) information has been obtained from multiple sources: the males, their parents, teachers, peers and official records: and (6) information has been obtained about a wide variety of theoretical constructs at different ages, including biological (eg heart rate), psychological (eg intelligence), family (eg parental discipline) and social (eg socioeconomic status) factors.

*Measures*

For the present analyses, each variable was dichotomized, as far as possible, into the 'worst' quarter of boys (eg the quarter with the lowest income or lowest intelligence) versus the remainder. This was done in order to compare the importance of different variables and also to permit a 'risk factor' approach. Because most variables were originally classified into a small number of categories, and because fine distinctions between categories could not be made very accurately, this dichotomizing did not usually involve a great loss of information. The one-quarter/three-quarters split was chosen to match the prior expectation that about one-quarter of the sample would be convicted as juveniles. Variables were not included in the analysis if less than 90% of the sample were known on them.

At the age of 18, the convicted males were significantly more antisocial than the unconvicted ones in many different respects. West and Farrington[1] developed a composite measure of antisocial behaviour at age 18 years based on the following components; (1) an unstable job record, reflecting frequent short-term jobs, being sacked, and periods of unemployment; (2) high sexual activity, reflecting a large number of sexual partners, a high frequency of sexual intercourse, and an early age of onset of sex; (3) heavy gambling, reflecting a large amount of money staked each week; (4) heavy smoking, reflecting a high daily consumption and an early age of onset; (5) driving after drinking at least 10 units of alcohol (where 1 unit = 1 half-pint of beer or cider, 1 glass of wine or sherry, or 1 single measure of spirits); (6) drug use, principally marijuana, amphetamines and LSD; (7) spending leisure time hanging about on the street; (8) involvement in antisocial group activities; (9) high violence, reflecting frequent fighting and carrying and using weapons; (10) anti-establishment attitudes (negative to police, school, rich people, civil servants and hard work); and (11) tattooed.

Of the 389 males interviewed at age 18 years, 110 were identified as the most antisocial, because they scored 4 or more points out of 11 on this scale. The components of antisocial behaviour deliberately did not include the kinds of property offences that predominated among convictions. Nevertheless, 70% of the 110 antisocial males were convicted up to age 20 years, in comparison with only 16% of the remaining 279 interviewed at age 18 years, a highly significant difference ($_x{}^2$=102.0, 1 df, $P$<.0001, one-tailed test used in the light of the clear directional prediction; all significance tests in this paper are of this type). This shows again the fact that crimes of dishonesty are essentially one element of a larger syndrome of antisocial behaviour.

By age 32 years, over one-third of the males (153, or 37%) had been convicted of criminal offences. As before, convicted males at age 32 years differed significantly from unconvicted ones in most aspects of their lives. For example, convicted males scored higher than unconvicted ones on the General Health Questionnaire (GHQ), which measures psychiatric disorder.[7] Nearly half (47%) of the 90 males scoring 5 or more on the GHQ (indicating a psychiatric case) were convicted, in comparison with one third (34%) of the remaining 288 interviewed ($_x^2$=4.43, P<0.02).

Farrington *et al.*[8] developed a general measure of social dysfunction at age 32 years, based on the following components: (1) poor accommodation, reflecting renting rather than home ownership, poor home conditions, and frequent moves in the past 5 years; (2) poor cohabitation history, reflecting divorce or separation, no wife or cohabitee, or conflict with a wife or cohabitee; (3) difficulties with children, reflecting separation from children, inconsistent handling, and child problems such as lying, stealing, temper tantrums and restlessness; (4) poor employment history, reflecting low take-home pay, low socio-economic status jobs, and frequent unemployment in the past 5 years; (5) high substance abuse, including alcohol, marijuana and other drugs; (6) involvement in fights in the past 5 years; (7) committing property offences such as burglary, taking vehicles and shop-lifting in the past 5 years; (8) convicted in the past 5 years; and (9) psychiatric disorder, as indicated by a GHQ score of 5 or more.

All the dichotomized components of the dysfunction score were significantly inter-correlated, with only two exceptions: psychiatric disorder was not significantly related to involvement in fights or convictions in the past 5 years. Each man was scored according to the percentage of these nine components on which he was considered to be dysfunctioning. (Where a man was not known on one component, for example if he had no children, the percentage score was based on 8 components.) Other work on this survey[8] showed that men with a dysfunction score greater than 33%, failing on more than three of the nine criteria, were also, independently, rated by the interviewers as leading relatively unsuccessful lives. Although the dysfunction score is somewhat arbitrary in its derivation, it reflects real differences between the men in life success.

The percentage of males who were convicted by age 32 years increased with the dysfunction score. About a quarter of the males had a dysfunction score over 33%, and these 93 males were considered to be relative social failures. Two-thirds of them (67%) were convicted. In comparison, 21% of 90 men scoring 0, 23% of 96 scoring 1–17%, and 36% of 99 scoring 18–33%, were convicted. Teenage antisocial behaviour significantly predicted adult social dysfunction; 41% of the antisocial males became adult failures, versus 19% of the remainder ($_x^2$= 17.9, P <0.0001).

## Results

Table 24.1 shows the childhood (age 8–10) precursors of teenage antisocial behaviour at age 18 years and adult dysfunction at age 32 years. For comparison, the predictors of convictions up to age 32 years are also shown. The strength of each relationship is summarized by the odds ratio (OR). For example, 93 of the males (23%) came from low income families. Of these, 48 (52%) were convicted, compared with 105 of the remaining 318 males (33%). The OR here is the odds of conviction for low income males (48/45) divided by the odds of conviction for the remainder (105/213), and this comes to 2.2. The OR shows the increase in risk associated with each childhood precursor, so low income more than doubled the risk of conviction. The significance of the OR was tested by the value of $\chi^2$ (corrected for continuity) from the 2×2 table. Negative values of the OR indicate negative relationships; for example, boys with few or no friends at age 8 years tended not to be convicted.

**Table 24.1** Childhood precursors of antisocial behaviour, conviction and social dysfunction

| Childhood precursor | Antisocial behaviour | Odds ratio conviction | Social dysfunction |
|---|---|---|---|
| (A) Low family income (23%) | 2.9** | 2.2** | 2.8** |
| (A) Large family size (24%) | 3.1** | 3.1** | 2.3** |
| (A) Poor housing (37%) | 2.1* | 2.6** | 1.5* |
| (A) Low social class (19%) | 2.0* | 1.5 | 1.4 |
| (B) Poor child-rearing (24%) | 1.7* | 1.9* | 1.3 |
| (B) Poor supervision (19%) | 2.4* | 2.6** | 1.8* |
| (B) Separated (22%) | 2.0* | 2.6** | 2.4** |
| (B) Nervous mother (32%) | 2.0* | 1.6* | 1.3 |
| (C) Convicted parent (25%) | 4.0** | 3.3** | 2.4** |
| (C) Delinquent sibling (11%) | 3.1** | 2.7* | 1.4 |
| (C) Behaviour problem sibling (38%) | 2.1* | 2.2** | 2.1* |
| (D) High delinquency school (21%) | 1.8* | 2.6** | 2.2* |
| (D) Low non-verbal intelligence (25%) | 2.3** | 2.5** | 1.3 |
| (D) Low verbal intelligence (25%) | 1.8* | 1.9* | 1.6 |
| (D) Low attainment (23%) | 2.1* | 3.1** | 2.0* |
| (E) High daring (30%) | 3.2** | 3.2** | 1.6* |
| (E) Poor concentration/restless (20%) | 2.0* | 2.0* | 2.2* |
| (E) High impulsivity (25%) | 1.5 | 2.0* | 1.9* |
| (F) High troublesomeness (22%) | 3.6** | 3.8** | 1.9* |
| (F) High dishonesty (25%) | 1.9* | 2.4** | 2.6** |
| (G) Small (18%) | 1.6* | 1.6* | 2.1* |
| (G) Light (18%) | 1.7* | 1.2 | 1.9* |
| (H) Few friends (12%) | −2.4* | −2.6** | 1.1 |
| (H) Nervous-withdrawn (24%) | −1.6 | −1.4 | 1.7* |

*$P< 05$, **$P< 0.001$ (one-tailed)

Following previous research on this study[9,10], the childhood precursors have been grouped into six major conceptual categories, indicated by the letters A–F in Table 24.1: (A) economic deprivation (low family income, large family size, poor housing, low socio-economic status); (B) poor parenting (poor child-rearing, including harsh or erratic discipline and marital disharmony, poor supervision, separation from a parent, and a nervous mother); (C) antisocial family (a convicted parent, siblings with behaviour problems or delinquent); (D) school problems (low intelligence and attainment, high delinquency rate school); (E) hyper-activity-impulsivity-attention deficit (high daring, poor concentration or restlessness, high psychomotor impulsivity); and (F) antisocial child behaviour (troublesomeness or dishonesty). The variables included in each category were significantly interrelated. In addition, a seventh category (G) of physical measures (height and weight) and an eighth category (H) reflecting nervousness and social isolation of the boy are included in Table 24.1.

Logistic regression analyses were carried out to investigate which were the most important independent predictors of teenage antisocial behaviour, convictions, and adult social dysfunction. Troublesomeness and dishonesty were excluded from these analyses, because the aim was to investigate variables that were possibly causal. The link between troublesomeness at age 8–10 years and antisocial behaviour at age 18 years probably reflects the continuity of anti-social personality rather than any causal effect.

Table 24.2 shows the results of the logistic regression analyses. The most important independent childhood predictors of teenage antisocial behaviour were: a convicted parent, high daring (according to peers and parents), large family size (four or more siblings) having few or no friends (negatively related), a nervous mother (based on ratings by psychiatric social workers, psychiatric treatment and high neuroticism scores on a health questionnaire), and low non-verbal intelligence (on the Progressive Matrices test). In order to obtain a measure of the efficiency of the combined predictor, the boys who actually become antisocial (about a quarter of the sample) were compared with an equal number of males with the highest predicted probabilities of becoming antisocial. Just over half (55%) of those predicted to be antisocial actually became antisocial, whereas 18% of those not predicted to be antisocial actually became antisocial, giving quite a high OR for this prediction of 5.7.

**Table 24.2**  Results of logistic regression analyses

|  | LRCS change | P (one-tailed) |
|---|---|---|
| **Antisocial behaviour at 18 years** | | |
| (C) Convicted parent 10 | 28.31 | 0.0001 |
| (E) High daring 8–10 | 23.66 | 0.0001 |
| (A) Large family size 10 | 10.87 | 0.0005 |
| (H) Few friends 8 (-) | 4.12 | 0.02 |
| (B) Nervous mother 10 | 2.82 | 0.05 |
| (D) Low non-verbal intelligence 8–10 | 2.36 | 0.06 |
| **Conviction up to 32 years** | | |
| (A) Large family size 10 | 27.99 | 0.0001 |
| (C) Convicted parent 10 | 16.80 | 0.0001 |
| (E) High daring 8–10 | 14.13 | 0.0001 |
| (A) Poor housing 8–10 | 8.48 | 0.002 |
| (H) Few friends 8 (-) | 10.04 | 0.0008 |
| (B) Separated 10 | 6.74 | 0.005 |
| (D) Low attainment 10 | 6.69 | 0.005 |
| **Social dysfunction at 32 years (vs 8–10)** | | |
| (A) Low family income 8 | 12.82 | 0.0002 |
| (B) Separated 10 | 6.06 | 0.007 |
| (E) Poor concentration/restless 8–10 | 5.10 | 0.01 |
| (H) Nervous-withdrawn 8 | 3.11 | 0.04 |
| (C) Convicted parent 10 | 2.07 | 0.07 |
| **Social dysfunction at 32 years (vs 8–18)** | | |
| Poor relation with parents 18 | 18.53 | 0.0001 |
| Unskilled manual job 18 | 15.99 | 0.0001 |
| No exams taken 18 | 6.53 | 0.005 |
| Nervous withdrawn 8 | 5.91 | 0.008 |
| Small 14 | 3.91 | 0.02 |
| Hospitalized for illness 18 | 3.67 | 0.03 |
| Poor concentration/restless 12–14 | 3.21 | 0.04 |
| High neuroticism 14 | 2.77 | 0.05 |

LRCS=Likelihood Ratio Chi-squared

The most important childhood predictors of convictions were quite similar to the most important predictors of teenage antisocial behaviour: large family size, a convicted parent, high daring, poor housing, few friends (negative), separation from a parent (for reasons other than death or hospitalization) and low junior school attainment. Nearly three-quarters of those predicted were convicted (71%), whereas 22% of those not predicted were convicted, giving a very high OR of 9.0. Hence, convictions could be predicted quite well from childhood factors.

The most important childhood predictors of adult social dysfunction at age 32 years were: low family income, separation from a parent, poor concentration or restlessness, nervous-withdrawn, and a convicted parent. Less than half of those who were predicted (42%) actually showed adult dysfunction, compared with 19% of those not predicted (OR=3.0). Hence, adult social dysfunction was predicted less well than teenage antisocial behaviour, but this is not surprising in light of the much greater time interval between the predictors and the outcome (22 years as opposed to 8 years).

Many variables were measured in this survey after childhood, during the teenage years. In order to investigate how far social dysfunction at age 32 years could be predicted later, at age 18 years, possibly explanatory variables measured up to age 18 years were added to those measured at age 8–10 years in a logistic regression analysis. Unfortunately, it was difficult to decide which variables were possibly explanatory. Variables measuring some type of antisocial behaviour were excluded. However, variables which do not obviously measure antisocial behaviour, such as a poor relationship with the parents, not taking any examinations and an unskilled manual job might conceivably be consequences of an antisocial personality rather than causal. Nevertheless, these kinds of variables were included in the analysis as possible predictors of adult social dysfunction.

Table 24.2 shows that the most important independent predictors of adult social dysfunction at age 32 years were: a poor relationship with the parents at age 18 years, an unskilled manual job at age 18 years, no examinations taken by age 18 years, nervous-withdrawn at age 8 years, relatively small at age 14 years, hospitalized for illness between ages 16 and 18 years, poor concentration or restlessness at age 12–14 years and high neuroticism at age 14 years (on the New Junior Maudsley Inventory). About half of those predicted (52%) showed dysfunction, compared with 15% of those not predicted (OR=6.1). This is a considerable improvement on the predictive efficiency based only on factors measured at age 8–10 years.

## Discussion

It is clear that childhood factors predicted teenage antisocial behaviour, adult dysfunction and offending. The most important predictors were measures of economic deprivation, poor parenting, an antisocial family and hyperactivity-impulsivity-attention deficit.

Farrington[11] proposed a theory to explain why these factors predicted offending by males. He suggested that the most important motives energizing offending were desires for material goods, excitement and status with peers. Boys from poorer families were less able to achieve these goals by legitimate means, and so they tended to commit offences. Boys exposed to effective child-rearing methods (consistent, firm but kindly discipline and close supervision) tended to build up internal inhibitions against offending in a social learning process, whereas those raised in antisocial families tended to develop antisocial attitudes and beliefs in a modelling process. Whether a boy with some degree of antisocial personality offended in any situation depended on his perception of the costs and benefits of offending and non-offending alternatives, and more impulsive boys were more likely to offend because they were less likely to consider future possible consequences (as opposed to immediate benefits).

This theory could be extended to explain the development of adult social dysfunction, which might also depend on similar underlying motives, inhibitions, attitudes and decisions. However, the major difference between teenage antisocial behaviour and adult social dysfunction was that being nervous-withdrawn and having few friends were negatively related to teenage antisocial behaviour but positively related to adult social dysfunction. Childhood social isolation was a protective influence against offending[12], but it was also noted[8] that non-offending males characterized by social isolation tended to be leading rather unsuccessful lives at age 32 years on various criteria.

Adult social dysfunction depends on both 'externalizing'[13] behaviour (eg convictions, violence) and 'internalizing' behaviour (eg psychiatric disorder, substance abuse). Adult psychiatric disorder was specifically predicted by childhood nervousness. Hence, the development of adult social dysfunction should be explained not only by reference to established causes of externalizing (antisocial) behaviour such as economic deprivation, poor parenting and impulsivity but also by reference to causes of internalizing behaviour such as childhood nervousness and social isolation.

## Notes

1 West, D. J., and Farrington, D. P. (1977). *The delinquent way of life*. London: Heinemann.
2 Farrington, D. P. (1991). Antisocial personality from childhood to adulthood. *Psychologist 4*, 389–94.
3 West, D. J. (1969). *Present conduct and future delinquency*. London: Heinemann.
4 West, D. J., and Farrington, D. P. (1973). *Who becomes delinquent?* London: Heinemann.
5 West, D. J. (1982). *Delinquency: its roots, careers, and prospects*. London: Heinemann.
6 Farrington, D. P., and West D. J. (1990). The Cambridge study in delinquent development: a long term follow-up of 411 London males. In H. J. Kerner and G. Kaiser (Eds.), *Criminality: personality, behaviour and life history*. Berlin: Springer-Verlag, 115–38.
7 Goldberg, D. (1978). *Manual of the General Health Questionnaire*. Windsor, Berks: NFER-Nelson.
8 Farrington, D. P., Gallagher, B., Morley, L., St Ledger, R., and West, D. J. (1988). A 24-year follow-up of men from vulnerable backgrounds. In R. L. Jenkins and W.

K. Brown (Eds.), *The abandonment of delinquent behaviour.* New York: Praeger, 155–73.

9 Farrington, D. P. (1990). Implications of criminal career research for the prevention of offending. *J Adolescence, 13*, 93–113.

10 Farrington, D. P. (1992). Explaining the beginning, progress and ending of anti-social behaviour from birth to adulthood. In J. McCord (Ed.), *Facts, frameworks and forecasts.* New Brunswick, NJ: Transaction, 253–86.

11 Farrington, D. P. (1986). Stepping stones to adult criminal careers. In D. Olweus, J. Block, and M. R. Yarrow (Eds.), *Development of antisocial and prosocial behaviour.* New York: Academic Press, 359–84.

12 Farrington, D. P., Gallagher, B., Morley, L., St. Ledger, R. and West, D. J. (1988). Are there any successful men from criminogenic backgrounds? *Psychiatry 51,* 116–30.

13 Achenbach, T. M., and Edelbrock, C. S. (1984). Psychopathology of childhood. *Ann Rev Psychol 35,* 227–56.

# 25    Jeffrey Arnett
## 'The Young and the Reckless: Adolescent Reckless Behavior'

Reprinted in full from: *Current Directions in Psychological Science* **4**, 67–71 (1995)

In Rio de Janeiro in Brazil, they 'surf' on the tops of trains, standing with arms outstretched as the trains rush along. The surfers – adolescents, girls as well as boys – are undeterred by the death of 150 fellow surfers per year and the injury of 400 more, from falling off trains or from hitting the 3,000-volt electric cable that runs above. On Truk Island in the South Pacific, drunkenness, fighting, and sexual experiences with a variety of lovers are all part of typical development for young men in their late teens and early 20s. They also go spearfishing where large sharks are common, and seek out other 'daredevil risks with life and limb.'[1] In urban New Jersey in the United States, adolescent boys steal automobiles, then drive them wildy for a few hours before crashing or abandoning them.

Why do many adolescents seek out experiences that involve physical, psychological, or legal risks? What blend of developmental and socialization factors leads to reckless behavior among adolescents? Researchers and theorists have offered a number of explanations, focusing on such behavior as driving an automobile at high speeds or while intoxicated, having sex without contraception or with someone not known well, using illegal drugs, and committing crimes. Richard Jessor, for example, has suggested that the developmental motivation for such behavior is the desire of adolescents to achieve adult status.[2] His theory also includes personality characteristics (such as self-esteem and value placed on achievement), family environment, and religiosity. Charles Irwin, Jr., presents a model that emphasizes pubertal timing and its effects on risk perception and peer-group association.[3] My own focus is on three developmental predispositions for reckless behavior in adolescence – sensation seeking, egocentrism, and aggressiveness – and their interaction with the cultural socialization environment.

## The developmental basis

### Sensation seeking

One characteristic of adolescent development that contributes to reckless behavior is a heightened level of sensation seeking.[4] Sensation seeking is a propensity for seeking out novel and intense experiences, and many types of reckless behavior are experiences of this kind. Driving a car at high speeds is attractive to many adolescents by virtue of the intensity of the experience. Sexual activity involves sensations that are intense and, for adolescents, novel as well. Trying illegal drugs results in novel forms of consciousness, and 'to see what it was like' is a common response given by adolescents who are asked why they have used illegal drugs. Pervasive forms of adolescent criminal behavior, such as minor theft and vandalism, carry the danger of being apprehended, but many adolescents describe this sense of danger as thrilling, intoxicating. Studies have found measures of sensation seeking to be related to a wide variety of reckless behaviors, and have found sensation seeking to be higher in adolescence than in adulthood.

*Egocentrism*

One of the advances in cognitive development that accompany adolescence is an advance in imaginative capacities. As Jean Piaget explained, adolescents are capable of thinking in terms of hypothetical situations in a way young children are not. Adolescents are able to imagine their own lives in a magnified and grandiose way, and may see themselves as having a specially ordained existence. This 'personal fable' (to use David Elkind's term) may exclude the possibility that their course to the future might be derailed by injury, unintended pregnancy, legal prosecution, drug addiction, or even death as a consequence of reckless behavior. These outcomes are all things adolescents may see as happening to other people, not to themselves. The sense of invulnerability conferred by the personal fable may increase some adolescents' propensity to take part in reckless behavior.

Evidence supporting this theoretical idea comes chiefly from studies indicating that adolescents have a tendency to estimate that the probability of a negative outcome resulting from engaging in reckless behavior is lower for themselves than for other people.[4] For example, adolescent drivers have a stronger tendency than older drivers to rate themselves as less likely than their peers to be involved in an accident. Criminal behavior is inversely related to the perceived risk that negative consequences would result, and the perceived risk is lower in adolescence than in adulthood. Similarly, adolescent girls who have had sex without contraception estimate the probability that pregnancy would result from such behavior as lower than do girls who have not had sex without contraception.

To some extent, these studies are simply indicative of the 'optimistic bias' that investigators of decision making have found to be true of people of all ages; that is, there is a tendency for individuals to believe that unpleasant events are less likely to happen to themselves than to other people. However, as noted, studies of automobile driving and criminal behavior suggest that this tendency is stronger in adolescence than in adulthood.

*Aggressiveness*

Because of the way the levels of hormones related to aggression rise when puberty arrives, aggressiveness seems like an obvious place to look for an explanation of why adolescents are more reckless than children or adults. In particular, levels of testosterone, which has been repeatedly found to be related to aggression, becomes 18 times higher by the end of puberty than at the beginning, for boys, and twice as high for girls; testosterone levels then decline after the mid-20s. These facts help explain not only why adolescents are more reckless than children or adults, but also why boys tend to be more reckless than girls for some types of reckless behavior.

Two types of reckless behavior for which aggressiveness may be particularly important are risky automobile driving and criminal behavior. Some adolescents use automobiles as a way of expressing aggressiveness. Some adults do, too, but adolescents may be more likely to do so than adults, both because testosterone levels are higher in adolescence and because adolescents may have less impulse control than adults and less social pressure to exercise it. Studies indicate that aggressiveness is related to high-speed and risky driving among adolescents and young adults. Aggressiveness also has an obvious relation to certain kinds of criminal behavior. Adolescents (especially males) have the highest rates of automobile accidents and of a wide variety of criminal activities.

### Socialization

Although the developmental predispositions I have described may incline adolescents toward reckless behavior, the socialization environment determines whether those predispositions will be expressed, and to what extent, and in what forms. Although the biological and physical developments of puberty are similar across cultures, the extent and forms of adolescent recklessness vary greatly among cultures because of differences in socialization practices.

In comparing cultures, I make a general distinction between *broad* and *narrow* socialization.[4,5] In cultures characterized by broad socialization, there is an emphasis on promoting individuality and autonomy, with the goal of restraining individuals as little as possible to allow the fullest measure of self-expression. Under narrow socialization, in contrast, obedience and conformity are the highest values, and deviation from the expected standard of behavior is punished physically or socially. In this theory, socialization has sources that include family, peers and friends, school, neighborhood and community, the legal system, the media, and the cultural belief system.

Narrow socialization is narrow in the sense that predispositions for characteristics such as sensation seeking, egocentrism, aggressiveness, and (by extension) reckless behavior are pressed into a narrower range of expression than would be the case if the expression of these characteristics were unimpeded. In cultures characterized by broad socialization, however, a broad range of inherent dispositions in these same characteristics is likely to be expressed, because the standards for behavior are less strict and violations of the standards are less likely to be punished harshly. Not all adolescents in such a socialization environment will be reckless, but those with a relatively strong predisposition for the characteristics that promote reckless behavior will find that the expression of these predispositions is not thwarted.

Evidence for the role of socialization in adolescent reckless behavior can be found in each source of socialization.

*Family*

Broad socialization in the family means that parents allow their adolescents a great deal of unsupervised time and encourage them to be independent and self-sufficient. Narrow socialization in the family means that parents (and perhaps other adults in the extended family) keep a close eye on their adolescents and demand obedience and deference. The importance of family socialization in adolescents' participation in reckless behavior has been supported in studies in several countries, including the United States, Canada, and Finland. These studies indicate that parental restrictions and monitoring are related to lower rates of adolescent recklessness in areas such as sexual behavior, vandalism, and substance use.

Of course, in parents' socialization of their adolescents, not only control matters, but also love. Numerous studies indicate that control without love is ineffective in discouraging antisocial behavior among adolescents. In Japan and India, for example, parents obtain a high degree of obedience from their children and adolescents while using very little overt control.[6] The relationships between parents and adolescents typically are so close emotionally that the threat of guilt and shame before their parents is enough to deter most adolescents from participating in reckless behavior.

*Peers and friends*

Socialization by peers tends to be narrow, in the sense that adolescent friendship groups, or cliques, tend to demand conformity from their members. However, this demand for conformity among peers can be either for or against the standards of desirable behavior promoted by adults in the culture; in particular, it can be either for or against participation in reckless behavior. In some adolescent cliques, members are pressured to drive fast, have sex, try drugs, and otherwise break social norms; in others, the pressure is in the opposite direction, towards avoiding participation in reckless behavior.

Cultures differ in the extent to which they allow adolescents to form peer groups that encourage behavior that defies adult standards. The flexibility and freedoms of broad socialization make it possible for adolescents to form their own 'youth culture' that encourages and rewards behavior (including reckless behavior) that adults would prefer to discourage. With narrow socialization, however, adults control and monitor the activities of adolescent peer groups to ensure that they promote conformity to the same standards of behavior that adults endorse. Among the Mbuti described by Colin Turnbull,[7] for example, arguing and fighting are socially unacceptable. When someone is guilty of these offenses, the adolescent boys of the village have the responsibility of appearing at the offender's hut early the next morning, shouting and yelling, beating on the roof and tearing off leaves and sticks. In this way, the adolescents reinforce the cultural standards of behavior in the offender as well as in each other, while also having an opportunity to express aggressiveness in a socially constructive way.

*School*

Schools characterized by broad socialization have a minimum of rules for dress, attendance, and conduct, and place a high emphasis on respecting and encouraging the individuality of each child. Schools characterized by narrow socialization have strict rules and firm punishments for violating them; often, such schools are founded on a narrow socialization belief system, for example, Catholicism, Judaism, or Islam. In general, school characteristics that imply narrow socialization are associated with lower levels of various types of reckless behavior, both within school and outside of it, even when academic aptitudes are taken into account. The school characteristics consistently found to be of importance are firm discipline, high expectations for perfor- mance, and a foundation in a belief system that provides moral guidance.[8]

*Neighborhood and community*

Sociologists have studied for many decades the role of neighborhood and community characteristics in crime and delinquency. In general, these studies show that some types of reckless behavior are higher where there is high residential mobility and where communities are large. It may be that sociali- zation is broader in larger communities than in smaller communities, in the sense that in larger communities there are fewer adults whom adolescents know and who may monitor and exercise authority over them.

However, this sociological research has taken place mostly in Western countries, and even communities with relatively narrow socialization within Western countries are less narrow in their socialization than communities in many non-Western, preindustrial cultures. In those cultures, socialization in the community is so narrow that adolescents rarely spend time away from the eyes of adults who know them and have authority over them, so adolescents rarely have the opportunity to participate in reckless behavior. Ethnographics such as Gilbert Herdt's on the Sambia in New Guinea demonstrate vividly the socialization practices of a community characterized by narrow socialization. The accounts of these anthropologists show how strongly obedience and conformity may be enforced by an entire community, and how little room such communities leave for antisocial recklessness,[9] in contrast to the rela- tively broad socialization of communities in the West.

*Legal system*

The legal system is not often mentioned in discussions of socialization, but as adolescents in many cultures grow into adolescence and spend an increasing amount of their time away from their families, the legal system is one of the forces that may monitor, restrict, and punish their behavior. Where socializa- tion is broad on the legal dimension, there is a minimum of legal regulation of behavior, and the punishments for taking part in prohibited behavior (includ- ing many types of reckless behavior) tend to be lenient. In contrast, where legal socialization is narrow, the punishments are sure, swift, and harsh, and the legal system includes within its scope certain kinds of behavior that would not be subject to legal regulation under broad socialization. For example, consensual premarital sex is a crime that may be punished under the legal system in some Islamic countries.

In the West, perhaps the most vivid example of socialization by the legal system is in the area of automobile driving. A colleague and I studied adolescents in Denmark and found that they were much less likely to drive an automobile while intoxicated or at high speeds than are adolescents in the United States.[10] Danish adolescents often 'drove' while intoxicated, but the vehicle typically used was a bicycle, not an automobile. The explanation for this difference lies not in cultural differences in family restrictions or peer pressure, but in the simple fact that the legal age for automobile driving is 18 in Denmark, but 16 in most U.S. states. Danish adolescents presumably have no less a developmental tendency for sensation seeking, egocentrism, and aggressiveness than American adolescents do, but because of restrictions set by the legal system, these tendencies are expressed (in part) through bicycles, not automobiles. Consequently, adolescents in Denmark (and in other Western European countries with a legal driving age of 18) have an automobile fatality rate that is markedly lower than in the United States.

*Media*

Many adolescents in the United States are immersed in media for much of their daily lives. The typical American adolescent listens to music for 4 hr a day and watches television for 2 more hr a day, and to this must be added time spent on videos, movies, and magazines, among other media forms. These media are generally an influence toward broad socialization, in that they encourage self-expression and immediate gratification, and discourage impulse control and self-restraint. They could be hypothesized to contribute to reckless behavior because reckless behavior is pleasurable, and adolescents imbibe from the media daily the message that what is pleasurable should be pursued without restraint, regardless of the consequences.

However, the influence of the media on adolescent reckless behavior is difficult to study precisely or directly, and the idea that the media incite reckless behavior among adolescents is still mostly theoretical and anecdotal. It should also be noted that the media can sometimes be an influence toward narrow socialization. For example, it could be argued that the decline in adolescent drug use that took place in the United States from the mid 1970s to the late 1980s was due at least partly to the extensive antidrug media campaign that also took place during that time.

*Cultural belief system*

The cultural belief system is the ultimate source of socialization, because what parents, peers, schools, community members, and members of the legal system do as socializing agents is due at least in part to the beliefs they have learned from their culture. These are not necessarily religious beliefs, but any set of shared beliefs about what is good and bad, right and wrong, or healthy and unhealthy, including beliefs about the proper and most desirable goals of socialization. The belief system underlying narrow socialization is often religious – among the Amish, for example, or the Orthodox Jews – but the political ideology of communism has also served as a narrow-socialization belief system in countries such as China, Cuba, and North Korea, promoting obedience and conformity in the other sources of socialization. The belief system underlying broad socialization is one of expressive individualism: People should be allowed, even encouraged, to do whatever they wish as long as they do not cause direct harm to anyone else.

The cultural belief system not only provides the basis for socialization from the other sources, but also contributes directly to socialization. The nature of these beliefs is crucial to adolescents' understanding of the meaning and value of reckless behavior. If impulse control is highly valued in the culture, and obedience and conformity are considered high virtues – in short, if the cultural belief system is one of narrow socialization – most adolescents will refrain from reckless behavior and associate even the idea of such deviance with a level of shame and guilt strong enough to deter them from taking part in it, regardless of their inherent predispositions for sensation seeking, egocentrism, and aggressiveness. In contrast, if it is not impulse control but impulse gratification that is highly prized, if obedience and conformity are considered not virtues but weaknesses, if adolescents learn that reckless behavior is not shameful but condoned and even tacitly admired – in short, if the cultural belief system is one of broad socialization – adolescents will be more likely to express their tendencies toward sensation seeking, egocentrism, and aggressiveness as reckless behavior.

### Summary and conclusion

Adolescent reckless behavior results from the interaction between certain developmental characteristics that are heightened in adolescence – particularly sensation seeking, egocentrism, and aggressiveness – and the cultural socialization environment. Cultural socialization should be understood to include not just family and peers but also school, neighborhood and community, the legal system, the media, and the cultural belief system. All of these sources contribute to socialization and influence the rates and types of adolescent reckless behavior within a given culture.

Why would any culture allow adolescent behavior that disrupts the lives of other people and undermines social order, as reckless behavior often does? The reason is that cultures must accept some kind of trade-off in socialization between promoting individualism and self-expression, on the one hand, and promoting social order, on the other. Cultures characterized by broad socialization promote individualism and self-expression in an effort to produce autonomous, creative children and adolescents who express the full range of their potentialities. One price of promoting these goals is higher rates of adolescent reckless behavior; adolescent potentialities include sensation seeking, egocentrism, and aggressiveness, and if the expression of these tendencies is not tightly controlled by socialization, the result is likely to be high rates of reckless behavior. Cultures characterized by narrow socialization face a similar trade-off. They wish to promote obedience, conformity, respect for authority, and social order, and in doing so they achieve lower rates of disruptive and antisocial adolescent reckless behavior, and a safer, more orderly society. However, in promoting these goals, they run the risk of extinguishing what is brightest, liveliest, and most original in their adolescent children.

## Notes

1 Gilmore, D. (1990). *Manhood in the Making: Cultural Concepts of Masculinity.* New Haven, CT: Yale University Press, p. 62.
2 Jessor, R. (1987). Problem behavior theory, psychosocial development, and adolescent problem drinking. *British Journal of Addiction, 82,* 331-342.
3 Irwin, C., Jr. (1993). Adolescence and risk taking: How are they related? in *Adolescent Risk Taking,* N. J. Bell and R. Bell (Eds.), Newbury Park, CA: Sage.
4 Arnett, J. (1992). Reckless behavior in adolescence: A developmental perspective. *Developmental Review, 12,* 339–373.
5 Arnett, J. (1992). Socialization and adolescent reckless behavior: A reply to Jessor. *Developmental Review, 12,* 391–409.
6 Roland, A. (1988). *In Search of Self in India and Japan: Toward a Cross-Cultural Psychology.* Princeton, NJ: Princeton University Press.
7 Turnbull, C. (1962). *The Forest People.* Garden City, NJ: Doubleday.
8 Coleman, J. S., Hoffer, T., and Kilgore, S. (1982). *High School Achievement: Public, Catholic, and Private Schools Compared.* New York: Basic Books.
9 Herdt, G. (1987). *The Sambia: Ritual and Gender in New Guinea.* New York: Holt, Rinehart, and Winston.
10 Arnett, J., and Balle-Jensen, L. (1993). The cultural bases of risk behavior: Danish adolescents, *Child Development, 64,* 1842–1855.

## Further reading

Donovan, D. M., Marlatt, G. A., and Salzberg, P. M. (1983). Drinking behavior, personality factors, and high-risk driving. *Journal of Studies on Alcohol, 44,* 395–428.
Morrison, D. M. (1985). Adolescent contraceptive behavior: A review. *Psychological Bulletin, 98,* 538–568.
Shedler, J., and Block, J. (1990). Adolescent drug use and psychological health: A longitudinal inquiry. *American Psychologist, 45,* 612–630.
Wilson, J. Q., and Herrnstein, R. J. (1985). *Crime and Human Nature.* New York: Simon and Schuster.

# 26 Thomas J. Berndt
## 'Friendship and Friends' Influence in Adolescence'

Reprinted in full from: *Current Directions in Psychological Science* **1**, 156–159 (1992)

Friendships have an important influence on adolescents' attitudes, behavior, and development. Theorists do not agree, however, on whether this influence is generally positive or generally negative. One theoretical perspective emphasizes the positive effects of close friendships on the psychological adjustment and social development of adolescents. Theorists who adopt this perspective argue that interactions with friends improve adolescents' social skills and ability to cope with stressful events.[1] A second theoretical perspective emphasizes the negative influence of friends on adolescents' behavior. Theorists who adopt this perspective argue that friends' influence often leads to antisocial or delinquent behavior.[2]

The two perspectives differ not only in their assumptions about the effects of friends' influence, but also in their assumptions about processes or pathways of influence. In the first perspective, the influence of friendships depends on the features of these relationships. For example, friendships that are highly intimate are assumed to enhance adolescents' self-esteem and understanding of other people. In the second perspective, friends' influence depends on the attitudes and behaviors of friends. For example, adolescents whose friends drink beer at parties are assumed to be likely to start drinking beer themselves. Thus, the first pathway of influence focuses on features of friendship and the second focuses on friends' characteristics.

Each perspective contains a kernel of truth, but each provides a one-sided view of the effects of friendships. Theorists who emphasize the positive features of friendship seldom acknowledge that friendships can have negative features, too. Adolescents often have conflicts with friends, and these conflicts can negatively affect adolescents' behavior toward other people. Theorists who emphasize the negative influence of friends' characteristics seldom acknowledge that many adolescents have friends with positive characteristics. These friends are likely to influence behavior positively.

In sum, friends can have positive or negative effects on adolescents via either of the two pathways of influence. In this review, I present evidence for these assertions and argue for more comprehensive and balanced theories of friendship in adolescence.

### Friendship features

'How can you tell that someone is your best friend?' Open-ended questions like this one were used by several researchers to assess the age changes in conceptions of friendships. The responses of children and adolescents confirmed that they regard several features of friendship as important. They said that friendships involve mutual liking, prosocial behavior (e.g., 'we trade tapes with each other'), companionship (e.g., 'we go places together'), and a relative lack of conflicts (e.g., 'we don't fight with each other'). Many adolescents, but few elementary school children, also referred to intimacy in friendships. Adolescents said, for example, that they 'talk about their problems with best friends' and that 'a best friend really understands you.' These findings are consistent with hypotheses that intimate friendships emerge in adolescence.[1]

Gradually, researchers shifted from studies of conceptions of friendships to studies of the actual features of friendships. Researchers also devised structured rating scales for assessing the features identified in earlier studies. The new measures made it possible to examine several questions about the nature and effects of friendships.[3]

Recent research has confirmed that intimacy becomes a central feature of friendship in early adolescence. Adolescents usually rate their own friendships as more intimate than do elementary school children. The increase in intimacy may be due partly to adolescents' growing understanding of the thoughts, feelings, and traits of self and others. It may also be due to the fact that adolescents spend more time with their friends than younger children do. Friendships are more significant relationships in adolescence than earlier.

Girls describe their friendships as more intimate than do boys. Some writers have suggested that the sex difference is merely a matter of style: Girls express their intimacy with friends by talking about personal matters, and boys express their intimacy in nonverbal ways. However, scattered evidence suggests that boys' friendships are less intimate because boys trust their friends less than girls do.[4] More boys than girls say that friends might tease them if they talk about something clumsy or foolish that they did. More girls than boys say that they share intimate information with friends because their friends listen and understand them.

This sex difference does not simply reflect a developmental delay for boys. In adulthood, women also tend to have more intimate friendships than men.[5] Still, the difference should not be exaggerated, because significant differences have not been found on all measures in all studies. Yet when differences are found, females' friendships usually appear more intimate than males' friendships.

Intimacy is closely related to other features of friendship. Adolescents' ratings of the intimacy of their friendships are correlated with their ratings of the friends' loyalty, generosity, and helpfulness. In short, friendships that are highly intimate tend to have many other positive features. Such friendships are comparable to the supportive social relationships that help adults cope with stressful life events.[6]

We might ask, then, if intimate and supportive friendships have equally positive effects on adolescents' adjustment and coping. In several studies, adolescents with more supportive friendships had higher self-esteem, less often suffered from depression or other emotional disorders, and were better adjusted to school than subjects with less supportive friendships.[7] These data are consistent with theories about the benefits of friendship, but come from correlational studies and so are open to alternative interpretations. Most important is the possibility that self-esteem and other indicators of adjustment contribute to the formation of supportive friendships rather than vice versa.

Longitudinal studies help to answer questions about causal direction, but longitudinal studies of adolescents' friendships are rare. The available data suggest that supportive friendships have significant but modest effects on some aspects of behavior and adjustment. Supportive friendships are not a panacea: They do not appear to have as powerful or as general an influence on adolescents as some theorists have suggested. Additional research is needed to identify the specific aspects of behavior and development that are most strongly affected by variations in positive features of friendship.

Equally important for future research is greater attention to the negative features of friendship. Adolescents interviewed about their conceptions of friendship commented on conflicts with friends, but many researchers ignored these comments. Many measures of friendship focus exclusively on positive or supportive features. This is a serious omission, because recent studies suggest that conflicts with friends can contribute to negative interactions with other peers and with adults.[8] With friends, adolescents may develop an aggressive interaction style that they then display with other interaction partners. Theories that emphasize the positive effects of supportive friendships need to be expanded to account for the negative effects of troubled friendships. Researchers need to measure both the positive and the negative features of friendships. New research with both types of measures should provide a more complete picture of friendship effects via the first pathway of influence.

## Friends' characteristics

You and your friends found a sheet of paper that your teacher must have lost. On the paper are the questions and answers for a test that you are going to have tomorrow. Your friends all plan to study from it, and they want you to go along with them. You don't think you should, but they tell you to do it anyway. What would you really do: study from the paper or not study from it?

Many researchers have used hypothetical dilemmas like this one to measure friends' influence on adolescents. In this dilemma, friends supposedly put pressure on an adolescent to engage in antisocial behavior, cheating on a test. Adolescents' responses to similar dilemmas are assumed to show the degree of adolescents' antisocial conformity to friends. Research with these dilemmas has provided the most direct support for theories of friends' negative influence.[2]

However, research with other methods has shown that the hypothetical dilemmas are based on faulty assumptions about the processes and outcomes of friends' influence in adolescence.[7] Some researchers observed friends' interactions in schools, summer camps, and other settings. Other researchers recorded friends' discussions, in experimental settings, as they tried to reach a consensus on various decisions. Both types of research suggest that the studies of conformity dilemmas – and popular writings about peer pressure – seriously distort reality.

In natural settings, influence among friends is a mutual process. Adolescents influence their friends as well as being influenced by them. Mutual influence is most obvious during interactions between a pair of friends. When two friends talk together, each has chances to influence the other. Even when friends interact in a group, decisions are usually made by consensus after group discussion. Groups rarely divide into a majority that favors one decision and one person who favors another. Therefore, models of group decision making describe friends' influence better than do models of individuals conforming to a majority.

In natural settings, influence seldom results from coercive pressure by friends. Friends' influence often depends on positive reinforcement. For example, friends express their approval of certain opinions and not others. Adolescents who are engaged in a discussion also listen to the reasons that friends give for their opinions. The influence of reasoning, or informational influence, may be as important in adolescents' groups as it is in adults' groups.[9] In addition, friends' influence does not always result from explicit attempts to influence. Adolescents admire and respect their friends, so they may agree with friends simply because they trust the friends' judgment.

Of course, friends sometimes do try to put pressure on adolescents. Adolescents also know that they risk disapproval or ridicule if they advocate opinions different from the opinions of most of their friends. In extremely cohesive groups, like some urban gangs, adolescents may even be threatened with physical harm if they do not go along with important group decisions, such as to attack another gang. But such situations and such groups are uncommon. Few friendship groups are as highly organized as an urban gang. Most adolescents simply choose new friends if they constantly disagree with the decisions of their old friends. The freedom of adolescents to end friendships limits their friends' use of coercive pressure as an influence technique.

Research on adolescents' responses to antisocial dilemmas is also misleading because it implies that friends usually pressure adolescents to engage in antisocial behavior. Experimental studies of friends' discussions suggest a different conclusion. So do longitudinal studies in which friends' influence is judged from changes over time in the attitudes or behavior of adolescents and their friends.[7] These studies show that the direction of friends' influence depends on the friends' characteristics. For example, if an adolescent's friends do not care about doing well in school, the adolescent's motivation to achieve in school may decrease over time. By contrast, if an adolescent's friends have good grades in school, the adolescents' grades may improve.

Viewed from a different perspective, the usual outcome of the mutual influence among friends is an increase over time in the friends' similarity. Often, the increased similarity reflects a true compromise: Friends who differ in their attitudes or behaviors adopt a position intermediate between their initial positions. Some adolescents however, are more influential than their friends. Other adolescents are more susceptible to influence than their friends. The sources of these individual differences need further exploration.

Finally, longitudinal studies suggest that the power of friends' influence is often overestimated.[10] In one study, friends' influence on adolescents' educational aspirations was nonsignificant. In another study, friends' influence on adolescents' alcohol use was nonsignificant. These findings are unusual, but even the statistically significant effects that are found are often small.

The conclusion that friends have only a small influence on adolescents is so contrary to the conventional wisdom that its validity might be questioned. Many studies seem to support the assertion of popular writers that friends have a strong influence on adolescents, but these studies often have serious flaws.[7] Researchers have frequently used adolescents' reports on their friends' behavior as measures of the friends' actual behavior. Then the researchers have estimated the friends' influence from correlations for the similarity between adolescents' self-reports and their reports on friends. Yet recent studies have shown that adolescents' reports on their friends involve considerable projection: Adolescents assume their friends' behavior is more like their own than it actually is.

Another flaw in many studies is the estimation of friends' influence from correlations for friends' similarity at a single time. However, influence is not the only contributor to friends' similarity. Adolescents also select friends who are already similar to themselves. On some characteristics (e.g., ethnicity), friends' similarity is due entirely to selection rather than to influence. To distinguish between selection and influence as sources of friends' similarity, longitudinal studies are needed. Recent longitudinal studies suggest that friends' influence on adolescents is relatively weak.

However, weak effects should not be interpreted as null effects. Underestimating the influence of friends would be as serious a mistake as overestimating it. At all ages, human beings are influenced by individuals with whom they have formed close relationships. Adolescents have close relationships with friends and, therefore, are influenced by friends. Friends influence adolescents' attitudes toward school and the broader social world. Friends influence adolescents' behavior in school and out of school. This influence is not a social problem unique to adolescence, but one instance of a universal phenomenon. To understand friends' influence better, theorists need to abandon the simplistic hypothesis of peer pressure toward antisocial behavior and consider the multiple processes of friends' influence and the varied effects of these processes.

**Conclusion**

Current thinking about adolescents' friendships is dominated by two theoretical perspectives that are incomplete and one-sided. One perspective emphasizes the benefits of friendships with certain positive features, such as intimacy. Intimacy is a more central feature of friendships in adolescence than in childhood. Intimate friendships have positive effects on adolescents, but these friendships seem to affect only some aspects of psychological adjustment. Moreover, some adolescents have friendships with many negative features, such as a high rate of conflicts. These conflicts often spill over and negatively affect other relationships. Adults concerned about adolescents' friendships should not only try to enhance the positive features of close friendships, but also try to reduce their negative features.

The second theoretical perspective emphasizes the negative influence of friends whose attitudes and behaviors are undesirable. Adolescents are influenced by their friends' attitudes and behaviors, but adolescents also influence their friends. Over time, this mutual influence increases the similarity between adolescents and their friends. Friends' influence does not generally lead to shifts either toward more desirable or toward less desirable attitudes and behaviors. These findings imply that adults concerned about negative influences of friends should try not to reduce friends' influence but to channel that influence in a positive direction.

## Acknowledgements

The author's research was supported by grants from the Spencer Foundation, the National Science Foundation, and the National Institute of Mental Health.

## Notes

1 Berndt, T. J. (1989). Obtaining support from friends in childhood and adolescence. In *Children's Social Networks and Social Supports*, D. Belle, (Ed.), New York: Wiley. R. L. Selman and L. H. Schultz, (1990). *Making a Friend in Youth: Developmental Theory and Pair Therapy.* Chicago: University of Chicago Press. J. Youniss and J. Smollar (1985). *Adolescent Relations With Mothers, Fathers, and Friends.* Chicago: University of Chicago Press.

2 Bronfenbrenner, U. (1970). *Two Worlds of Childhood.* New York: Russell Sage Foundation. L. Steinberg and S. B. Silverberg (1986). The vicissitudes of autonomy in early adolescence. *Child Development*, 57, 841–851.

3 Berndt, T. J. (1986). Children's comments about their friendships. In *Minnesota Symposium on Child Psychology: Vol. 18. Cognitive Perspectives on Children's Social Behavioral Development*, M. Perlmutter, (Ed.), Hillsdale, NJ: Erlbaum. R. C. Savin-Williams and T. J. Berndt (1990). Friendships and peer relations during adolescence. In *At the Threshold: The Developing Adolescent*, S. S. Feldman and G. Elliott, (Eds.), Cambridge, MA: Cambridge University Press.

4 Berndt, T. J. (in press). Intimacy and competition in the friendships of adolescent boys and girls. In *Gender Roles Through the Life Span*, M. R. Stevenson, (Ed.), Madison: University of Wisconsin Press.

5 Rawlins, W. K. (1992). *Friendship Matters: Communication, Dialectics, and the Life Course.* Hawthorne, NY: Aldine de Gruyter. M. S. Clark and H. T. Reis (1988). Interpersonal processes in close relationships. *Annual Review of Psychology*, 39, 609–672.

6 Cohen, S., and Wills, T. A. (1985). Stress, social support, and the buffering hypothesis. *Psychological Bulletin*, 98, 310–357. H. O. F. Veiel and U. Baumann. (1992). *The Meaning and Measurement of Social Support.* New York: Hemisphere.

7 Berndt, T. J., and Savin-Williams, R. C. (in press). Variations in friendships and

peer-group relationships in adolescence. In *Handbook of Clinical Research and Practice With Adolescents*, P. Tolan and B. Cohler, (Eds.), New York: Wiley.

8  Berndt, T. J., and Keefe, K. (1991, April). *How friends influence adolescents' adjustment to school.* Paper presented at the biennial meeting of the Society for Research in Child Development. Seattle. See also W. W. Hartup (in press). Conflict and friendship relations. In *Conflict in Child and Adolescent Development*, C. U. Shantz and W. W. Hartup (Eds.), Cambridge, England: Cambridge University Press.

9  Berndt, T. J., Laychak, A. E., and Park, K. (1990). Friends influence on adolescents' academic achievement motivation: An experimental study. *Journal of Educational Psychology, 82*, 664–670.

10  Cohen, J. M. (1977). Sources of peer group homogeneity. *Sociology of Education, 50*, 227–241. D. B. Kandel and K. Andrews. (1987). Processes of adolescent socialization by parents and peers. *International Journal of the Addictions, 22*, 319–342.

# SUBJECT INDEX

# NAME INDEX

Abelson, 168
Aber, J. S., 21, 23
Abrahamsen, 168, 169
Abramson, P., 344
Abravanel, E., 135, 136, 137
Achenbach, T. M., 351
Acredolo, L. P., 143
Adams, A.-M., 210
Adamson, L., 34
Aebli, H., 279
Ainsworth, M., 2, 19
Albert, M., 335
Alegria, J., 219
Allen, M., 257
Allen, W., 81
Altmann, S., 24
Anderson, J. A., 161, 292, 293, 294
Anglin, J., 65
Anson, R. S., 86
Appel, K. L., 142
Applebee, A., 87
Aram, D. M., 210
Arnett, J., 356, 363
Ashcraft, M. H., 245, 252, 254
Aslin, R. N., 141
Asperger, H., 180
Astington, J. W., 181
Atkison, I. P., 188
Attwood, A. H., 183
Aubry, S., 31, 183
Auerbach, J., 135, 136, 137
Auzias, M., 261

Baddeley, A., 209, 210, 211, 212, 213,
    214, 215, 216, 217, 218, 219, 220
Baillargeon, R., 49, 141, 142
Bakeman, R., 34
Baker, A. J. L., 21, 23
Baldwin, L. M., 312
Balle-Jensen, L., 363

Banks, M., 10
Barbee, D. E., 88
Barnes, E., 81
Barnett, D., 20
Barnes, P., 301
Barrett, G., 289
Baroody, A. J., 245, 250
Baron-Cohen, S., 177, 178, 179, 180
Barrett, M., 29
Bartke, S., 79
Bartlett, F. C., 182, 184
Basili, A., 257
Bates, E., 1, 32, 37, 45, 121, 166, 168
Batolotta, R., 245
Baugh, J., 86
Baumrind, D., 325
Bechtel, 168, 169
Bell, R. Q., 278
Belleville, S., 189
Belsky, J., 21
Benedict, A., 34
Benton, A., 210
Berko, J., 78
Berreiter, C., 271
Bertelson, P., 219
Berndt, T. J., 369
Bethel, E., 84
Bird, J., 213
Biringen, Z., 25
Bishop, D., 32, 185, 217, 226
Bissex, G., 264, 270
Blance-Benveniste, C., 270
Blau, Z. S., 85
Blaye, A., 301
Blehar, M. S., 19
Block, J., 22
Block, J. H., 22
Bloom, B. S., 291
Blusewicz, M. J., 189
Boer, F., 308